Biblical Theology

In *Biblical Theology*, Ben Witherington examines the theology of the Old and New Testaments as a totality. Going beyond an account of carefully crafted Old and New Testament theologies, he demonstrates the ideas that make the Bible a sacred book with a unified theology. Witherington brings a distinctive methodology to this study. Taking a constructive approach, he first examines the foundations of the writers' symbolic universe – what they thought and presupposed about God – and how they revealed those thoughts through the narratives of the Old and New Testaments. He also shows how the historical contexts and intellectual worlds of the Old and New Testaments conditioned their narratives, and, in the process, created a large coherent biblical world view, one that progressively reveals the character and action of God. Thus, the Yahweh of the Old Testament, the Son in the Gospels, and the Father, Son, and Spirit in the New Testament writings are viewed as persons who are part of the singular divine identity.

Sensitive to do a more than merely thematic reading of the Bible which strips texts out of their original context, Witherington's progressive revelation approach allows each part of the canon to be read in its original context and with its original meaning. The result is a biblical theology that allows Jews and Christians to dialogue about and appreciate the sacred scriptures in both testaments.

The capstone work of an internationally known theologian, *Biblical Theology* also offers new insights on key theological issues, including the character of God, grace, covenants, salvation, election, and eschatology as they relate to the doctrine of God.

Ben Witherington III is Amos Professor of the New Testament for Doctoral Studies at Asbury Theological Seminary and Emeritus doctoral faculty at St. Andrews University, Scotland. A prolific author, he has written more than 40 books and six commentaries, most recently, with Amy-Jo Levine, *Luke*.

Biblical Theology

The Convergence of the Canon

BEN WITHERINGTON III

Asbury Theological Seminary, Kentucky

CAMBRIDGE
UNIVERSITY PRESS

CAMBRIDGE
UNIVERSITY PRESS

University Printing House, Cambridge CB2 8BS, United Kingdom

One Liberty Plaza, 20th Floor, New York, NY 10006, USA

477 Williamstown Road, Port Melbourne, VIC 3207, Australia

314–321, 3rd Floor, Plot 3, Splendor Forum, Jasola District Centre, New Delhi – 110025, India

79 Anson Road, #06-04/06, Singapore 079906

Cambridge University Press is part of the University of Cambridge.

It furthers the University's mission by disseminating knowledge in the pursuit of education, learning, and research at the highest international levels of excellence.

www.cambridge.org
Information on this title: www.cambridge.org/9781108498784
DOI: 10.1017/9781108682299

© Cambridge University Press 2019

First published 2019

Printed and bound in Great Britain by Clays Ltd, Elcograf S.p.A.

A catalogue record for this publication is available from the British Library.

Library of Congress Cataloging-in-Publication Data
Names: Witherington, Ben, III, 1951– author.
Title: Biblical theology : the convergence of the canon / Witherington III, Asbury Theological Seminary, Kentucky.
Description: New York: Cambridge University Press, 2019. |
Includes bibliographical references and index.
Identifiers: LCCN 2019000710 | ISBN 9781108498784 (hardback) |
ISBN 9781108712682 (paperback)
Subjects: LCSH: Bible – Theology.
Classification: LCC BS543.W578 2019 | DDC 230/.041–dc23
LC record available at https://lccn.loc.gov/2019000710

ISBN 978-1-108-49878-4 Hardback
ISBN 978-1-108-71268-2 Paperback

We are only beginning to learn that in order to understand a great teacher's message we must take pains to get his point of view. You cannot possibly understand Browning apart from his point of view. "In Memoriam" only yields its full message to those who know Tennyson's grief at the loss of his friend, Arthur Hallam. *Pilgrim's Progress* becomes a new book when, in thought, you sit by Bunyan's side in Bedford jail. I am not particularly concerned with that as a principle in general educational methods, but as it applies to our understanding of religious truths.

How much more vital and valuable the Bible becomes if we put ourselves in the places of those who first uttered its truths. It saves us from fantastic interpretations. Stand by some grief-stricken father who has come from his days of toil to find his home in ruins, his children slain, and his wife carried off, and you will understand why in the collection there are "vindictive psalms." Sit with the captive Jews on the banks of the river Chebar and the Lamentations of Jeremiah and the rebukes of Ezekiel will take on a new meaning. Gather with a few humble Eastern saints in an upper room at Corinth or Philippi and you will understand Paul's Epistles as never before. Still more does the truth apply to our endeavor to teach Christianity.

Fred Barrett, in his sermon "Put Yourself in His Place" on Ezekiel 3.15,
Luminescence, vol. 3: *The Sermons of Charles Kingsley and
Fred Barrett* (Eugene, OR: Cascade, 2018), 158.

Although these premodern Christians knew that biblical texts had human authors, they read the texts not for what some author "behind" the text might have "meant" but for what the words of the text "said" ... the *main voice* of the text was the text itself. The text was its own agent and had its own voice. People considered that the text was what was speaking, not a historically "reconstructed" author *behind* the text.

Dale B. Martin, *Biblical Truths: The Meaning of Scripture
in the Twenty-First Century* (New Haven, CT: Yale
University Press, 2017), 1–2.

The notion of the readerly creation of meaning is incompatible with the role of a particular set of texts as Christian Scripture. This role requires the communication of determinate meaning to readers. Although the elaboration of that meaning will always be shaped by the context of its reception, it remains possible to argue that texts have a "literal sense" dependent on "authorial intention" and that their ambiguities may be contained (if not eliminated) by a set of "objective," non-context-dependent interpretative procedures ... A determinate communicative intention is embedded in the text; it is not to be found "behind the text" in an authorial psychology or in an "original" historical context.

Francis Watson, *Texts and Truth: Redefining Biblical Theology*
(Grand Rapids, MI: Eerdmans, 1997), 11.

A text without a context is just a pretext for whatever you want it to mean. The biblical text itself is not an autonomous voice or "its own agent with its own voice." It is rather the voice of God speaking through the voices of a myriad of his people down through the ages of the biblical era. To ignore, dismiss, or belittle the need for studying the historical context of God's Word is to deny the *incarnational* nature of that Word, and to give free rein to a postmodern reader to anachronistically read all sorts of current notions, ideals, and shibboleths into the biblical text which the original authors would have rejected. This is not exegesis but rather eisegesis. The Bible is God's living Word not because it is *contextless*, but because there is a living God still using it to speak to us in and through its original contextual meanings.

Ben Witherington (see e.g. *The Living Word of God: Rethinking the Theology of the Bible* [Waco, TX: Baylor University Press, 2007]).

Contents

Contents

Acknowledgments

To all my wonderful editors at all my publishers who have rescued me from numerous mistakes and typos and have given good guidance. I owe you all a great debt. Many of my editors have retired and some have gone on to their eternal reward. Without you all I could never have done all this, but even more than that, divine help was required.

And for all the Durham *Neutestamentler* old and new, in particular Lightfoot, Westcott, Moule, Plummer, Turner, Cranfield, Wright, Watson, and most especially Barrett and Barclay: I am proud to share that heritage with you all.

A special thanks to Dr. David Schreiner, who carefully went over this manuscript and saved me from many typos and formatting mistakes and some OT errors, and who also produced the indices.

Soli Deo gloria

Note on the Text

This work is a capstone project, based on my previous exegetical, theological, and intertextual works, and would not have been possible without the kind permission of several of my publishers to reuse some of my previous work but reorient and reapply it to a different subject which I have not written about previously – biblical theology.

Some material from *The Indelible Image* originally published by InterVarsity Press. Copyright © 2009, 2010, and 2016 by Ben Witherington III. Used by permission of InterVarsity Press, PO Box 1400, Downers Grove, IL 60515. www.ivpress.com.

Some material from *Letters and Homilies for Hellenized Christians* originally published by InterVarsity Press. Copyright © 2006 by Ben Witherington III. Used by permission of InterVarsity Press, PO Box 1400, Downers Grove, IL 60515. www.ivpress.com.

Some material from *Shadows of the Almighty* and the *Gospel of Mark* originally published by Wm. B. Eerdmans Publishing Co., 2140 Oak Industrial Drive NE, Grand Rapids, MI 49505 and used by permission.

Some material from *Torah Old and New, Psalms Old and New, Isaiah Old New*, and *Jesus the Sage* originally published by Fortress Press (2008–17) and used by their kind permission.

In a couple of passages, I have used the NETS Septuagint translation (2007) with the kind permission of Oxford University Press, all rights reserved.

Finally, a special thanks to Stan Gundry for the use of a small bit of the old NIV once again, though most of the translations in this study are my own.

Introduction

We all are theologians – every Christian! "Theology" means God's Word; theologian means one who speaks God's words. Each and every Christian should be such a person.

Martin Luther[1]

It has long been recognized that the term "Biblical Theology" is ambiguous. It can either denote a theology contained within the Bible, or a theology which accords with the Bible ... The first definition understands the task of Biblical Theology to be a descriptive, historical one which seeks to determine what was the theology of the biblical authors themselves. The second understands the task of Biblical Theology to be a constructive theological one which attempts to formulate a modern theology compatible in some sense with the Bible.

Brevard Childs[2]

There is a temptation, which has to be resisted, to throw up one's hands in this age of over-specialization and ask with St. Paul, "Who is sufficient for these things?" Who knows the scope of the Bible and its various writings and its detailed exegesis, and its theologies well enough to write a biblical theology that does anything like justice to this vast subject? The painful truth is that no one can master the whole of the Bible, not even with many decades of close study and hard work. But sufficiency is one thing, mastery is another. I do not claim to have mastered the subject matter of the Bible, but I do think that at this juncture, having written exegetical commentaries on all the books of the NT, and various portions of the OT, and having plumbed a fair bit of the depths of intertextuality that binds the Bible together,[3] and having taught both the OT and the NT and biblical theology itself for some 35 years or so, if I am ever going to be competent and ready to undertake the task, the time is now.

---

[1] Martin Luther, "Sermon Psalm 5," in *Martin Luthers Werke: Kritische Gesamtausgabe* (Schriften) (Weimar: Böhlau, 1883–), 9–11.

[2] B. S Childs, *Biblical Theology of the Old and New Testaments: Theological Reflection on the Christian Bible* (Minneapolis, MN: Fortress Press, 1992), 3.

[3] See e.g. Ben Witherington III, *Isaiah Old and New: Exegesis, Intertextuality, and Hermeneutics* (Minneapolis, MN: Fortress Press, 2017); Ben Witherington III, *Psalms Old and New: Exegesis, Intertextuality, and Hermeneutics* (Minneapolis, MN: Fortress Press, 2017); Ben Witherington III, *Torah Old and New: Exegesis, Intertextuality, and Hermeneutics* (Minneapolis, MN: Fortress Press, 2018).

From the outset, it has been clear to me that biblical theology is a horse of a different color from OT theology or NT theology (on the latter of which I have written various monographs).[4] By this I mean that biblical theology in a Christian context refers to something bigger and more comprehensive than is attempted either in volumes of OT theology or NT theology. Nor is it merely a matter of combining OT and NT theology and calling the task done. When I wrote *The Indelible Image* over a decade ago, I said that it was appropriate to start the conversation about NT theology and ethics with Jesus, for so many reasons, not least that this is where the NT writers mainly seem to start such discussions, precisely because he changed the discussion of theology and ethics, both in his teaching and by his life and its sequel. Biblical theology, however, if it is to be worth its name, cannot start with Jesus precisely because the first 39 books of what we call the Bible do not do so. As I stressed in my three books on intertextuality, to do justice to the biblical texts from a perspective of the whole Christian canon they must be read both forward and backwards. This study will build on that insight and methodology, particularly when it comes to reflecting on both the symbolic universe of the Bible and its narrative thought worlds.

Biblical theology involves more than just combining OT and NT theology. One has to think more globally, more comprehensively, and this means thinking along with both the OT and the NT writers and contributors in terms of how they think about theology. We may thank Brevard Childs for pushing us to think more critically about this subject, but at the end of the day, I am not merely interested in doing what came to be called "canonical" theology, if by that is meant doing Christian readings of the OT which either ignore or do not allow the OT text to have its own say in its own original context, as well as in the contexts in which it is later used after the Christ event. The mistake here, I think, is assuming that when the NT writers use the OT text *homiletically* to make their own Christian points, they are actually attempting to do contextual exegesis of the OT, when in fact, *most of the time they are not attempting that task.*[5] Theirs is, in the main, a hermeneutical rather than an exegetical enterprise of "relecture," re-audiencing, reapplying some of the "old, old, story."

I take it as a basic matter of fairness that we should allow the OT to have its own say, since, after all, it is just as much God's Word as any portion of the NT. Otherwise, what happens is that the OT is turned into a Christian theology textbook, which it is not. The OT, for example, does not much address some of the bedrock theological concerns of the NT – for instance the crucifixion *and resurrection* of the Jewish messiah, or the nature of the Trinity, or the second coming of Christ, or the existence of a divine person called the Holy Spirit and so on. But it teaches us much about the nature of the God we call Father, and his relationship with his chosen people. The OT from Abraham to Malachi is all about that subject and that story in various ways. And it teaches us much about the very nature of our God, who is not merely almighty, but almighty to save, who is both just and merciful, both righteous and loving, both gracious and yet holding his people accountable for their beliefs and behaviors. The OT is largely about God the Father, with some allusions,

---

[4] See e.g. Ben Witherington III, *The Indelible Image: The Theological and Ethical Thought World of the New Testament* (2 vols.; Downers Grove, IL: InterVarsity Press, 2009–10).

[5] See on this very point James Barr, *Old and New in Interpretation: A Study of the Two Testaments* (London: SCM Press, 1966), esp. 65–148.

foreshadowings, and previews of coming attractions about the Son and the Spirit, and the afterlife, to mention but a few subjects. To be clear, this study will be focusing on the doctrine of God, properly speaking, and dealing with other subjects that are necessarily entailed by such a focus. For example, since apart from a few passages in exilic and post-exilic prophetic material the OT has little to tell us about the afterlife or eschatology *per se*, this study will not make such subjects a major focus, because while the NT has much to say about those things, a biblical theology must focus on what the *whole* canon tells us about God and his saving work, not just on what we may learn from some NT passages.[6]

But I have also been concerned all along with operating with the right hermeneutical principles, the chief of which is the notion of progressive revelation. A flat reading of the whole Bible, for instance a topical reading that largely ignores contexts and *developments* and mainly slots material from both the OT and the NT into some abstract grid of "themes" (see e.g. C. H. H. Scobie) does not do justice to the clues in the NT itself that we must read the canon *progressively*. For one thing, Jesus told us so. He says, for example, in Mk. 10 and Mt. 19 that some of the Mosaic instructions were given by God because of the fallen condition of its OT recipients, *due to the hardness of their hearts*. That sort of instruction is no longer directly applicable in the New Covenant, and with the eschatological saving reign of God breaking into human history.

As it turns out, the *lex talionis* of "an eye for eye, and a tooth for a tooth, and a life for a life" was an attempt to *limit*, not *license* the violence of God's fallen people. But already in God's direct "word" to Moses, he was letting us know that his perfect will for us is "no killing," "do no harm to others," which is emphatically made clear in the call to not only love God wholeheartedly, but to love our neighbor as ourselves, and as Jesus was to add, even love our enemies, forgive them, pray for those who persecute us. On further review, the ethic of the Kingdom, the ethic of Jesus, progresses beyond the ethics of some crucial bits of the Mosaic code in a way that suggests that Christians at least are called to a higher ethic by the Lord and Giver of Life. But you could not have fully foreseen this development simply by a close reading of any or all of the OT.

God, as it turns out, speaks his word into specific contexts, in specific ways. And as the author of Hebrews says (in Heb. 1) the revelation given in the past was partial and piecemeal, and the whole of the revelation must be evaluated in light of the fullest revelation of God that comes to us in Christ himself. This applies to the character of God, the nature of salvation, how we should read salvation history, the difference between election and soteriology, what we should think about the end times, and so much more. There is a historical before and after to God's Word in the Bible, and we must keep ever in mind that the OT *was not written by, or in the first instance for Christians* – it was written for the Hebrews, later called Jews.

The fact that a Jewish follower of Jesus could later, and with the benefit of hindsight, say to his largely Jewish Christian audience "it was revealed to them [i.e. the OT prophets] that they were not serving themselves but you, when they spoke of the things that have now been told you by those who preached the Gospel to you" (1 Pet. 1.12) does not negate this fact. Peter is referring to the fact that the prophecies were pointing forward to the

---

[6] For a detailed treatment of eschatology especially in the NT see Ben Witherington III, *Jesus, Paul, and the End of the World: A Comparative Study in New Testament Eschatology* (Downers Grove, IL: InterVarsity Press, 1992).

eschatological age in which the messiah would come and the Spirit would be poured out, and the Good News would be preached. What he is not saying is that the OT was written chiefly for the benefit of Gentile followers of Jesus who had the good fortune of being born after the time of Jesus. Peter's audience is largely Hellenized Jews, for he was an apostle to the "circumcision" (Gal. 2.10).[7]

Instinctively, and necessarily, Christians realized from the outset that the coming of Christ and his saving activity was an eschatological game changer. New occasions taught new theology and new ethics that, while grounded in the OT, went well beyond it in various ways, sometimes leaving some of it behind as obsolescent. They read the story *progressively* from creation to fall to various acts of redemption first in the OT, and then climactically in the Christ event (both the present and future one). This sort of reading of the Bible's theological content seemed to dovetail nicely with a "salvation history" approach to the stories in the Bible (see e.g. O. Cullmann), but the limitation of this approach was that it meant reading the theologizing from front to back, but *not the other way around*. And what about the large quantities of material in the OT that do not seem to be about "salvation history" at all, for instance the Wisdom literature (see e.g. Ecclesiastes or Job)? Something other than redemption, rescue, salvation is the subject matter of a good deal of the OT.[8]

Yes, the NT writers read the story *retrospectively* as well, because the full significance of the OT revelation would not come to light before the coming of Christ. But this retrospective reading found in the OT types and foreshadowings, and occasional foretastes of what was to come, *without* trying to find Jesus under every rock in the OT. The text, in other words, was still assumed to have a historical *givenness* and there was a before and after to the story which was not collapsed into some sort of abstract systematic theologizing, much less an urgency to produce the sort of synthesis that denied the various historical contexts of the various different parts of the canon.

Yes, when the theology of the Son's pre-existence dawned on some NT writers, they did indeed find a place for the Son in the OT story as God's Wisdom who guided God's people all along, but *not* as a historical figure or even an angelic figure in the OT story. Jesus was not Melchizedek in disguise but rather a latter-day priest after the order of Melchizedek. Jesus was not the angel of the Lord, whom many OT figures ran into from time to time. Indeed, the author of Hebrews went to considerable lengths to make clear that the Son in no way fit into the category of a mere angel, even the most exalted one. To the contrary, the writers of the NT felt it fitting to apply language to the Son that had previously been reserved only for the Father.

In other words, there were limits to the Christological and eschatological reading of the OT by the NT writers, which is why the language of fulfillment, *rather than* the language of *identity*, of "this is that," comes up again and again in the NT. And that raises another point which comes up a lot in discussions with Catholic scholars – namely is Protestant biblical theology too Christomonistic? Shouldn't it in fact be Trinitarian in shape?

My answer to those questions is yes, and yes. Protestants are indeed products of the Reformation, which focused very singularly on Christ, to restore the proper biblical

---

[7] On which see Ben Witherington III, *Letters and Homilies for Hellenized Christians*, vol. 2: *A Socio-Rhetorical Commentary on 1–2 Peter* (Downers Grove, IL: InterVarsity Press, 2010).

[8] See the discussion in Childs, *Biblical Theology*, 17–18.

balance on the nature and source of our salvation. It was not to be found in the saints, not even in Mary, but in her Son – Jesus. Nor was our salvation a self-help program, where through penance and infused grace we could be contributors (even partners with God) to our own justification in the sight of God. The cry *sola fide, sola gratia* was quite rightly a negation of all that. Salvation was by grace and through faith in Jesus and his finished work on the cross and in the resurrection. So, necessarily, the Christian discussion of soteriology must focus rather singularly on the NT and what it says about these matters. "Saved" in the OT doesn't mean "believe on the Lord Jesus Christ and his atoning work."

But the Bible is a much larger book than just the NT, and salvation is not its only topic. A proper biblical theology ought to be Trinitarian in nature. It ought to tell us much about the Father, the Son, and the Holy Spirit, and about their roles in the OT and NT. For this reason, after the methodological chapter we will focus at some length on each of the members of the Trinity, a chapter being devoted to each. Even to the beginning reader of the Bible, it becomes obvious that the OT is largely about the one Christians call the Father, the Gospels are largely about Jesus, and the rest of the NT is about the work of the Spirit in conjunction with the Father and the Son. That is, the Bible has a progressively more Trinitarian character the further we read from Genesis to Revelation. Any biblical theology worth its salt ought to do justice to these facts. This approach will distinguish this volume from most other recent "biblical theologies" and I will draw on some four or five of the recent ones. First, we must attend to matters methodological, and the best way to do that is by having an extended interaction with the best introductory textbook on biblical theology – James K. Mead's *Biblical Theology: Issues, Methods, and Themes*.[9]

Perhaps, as we draw this Introduction to a close, one may be wondering why the word "convergence" is in the subtitle of this book. The noun is often used in science to talk about the phenomenon of how parallel lines appear to converge on the horizon. It is also used of what happens when ocean currents from differing sources come together, producing some remarkable effects. I am using the term to refer to the effort to show how the various theologies of the Bible converge and can be said to produce *a single and singular biblical theology*. Like parallel lines, the closer you get to the end of the biblical stories, the end of the canon, and even the foreseen end of human history, the more the trajectories of discussion about Father, Son, and Spirit and their work to save, sanctify, and glorify their creatures and creation converge. In short, the further you go in the Bible, the more Trinitarian things become. I have to believe that this is because the Bible is a book of progressive revelation of the character and work of God, so that the fullest and clearest revelation of God's character and God's salvific plan and work comes not only in Christ, and in the NT in general, but more specifically in the *interpretation* of the Christ event recorded in the Gospels that we find especially from Romans to Revelation. Thanks be to God for the whole canonical witness. We need it all to understand our Triune Creator and Redeemer.

---

[9] James K. Mead, *Biblical Theology: Issues, Methods, and Themes* (Louisville, KY: Westminster John Knox, 2007).

I

A Method to the Madness

There are two kinds of water that are difficult to see through: muddy water and deep water. Biblical theology is deep water.

James K. Mead[1]

Until J. P. Gabler published his essay on the distinction between biblical and dogmatic theology [in 1787], nobody thought of writing "biblical" theology. They wrote theology and the shape of theology was dictated by the traditional doctrines of the creeds.

G. B. Caird and L. D. Hurst[2]

Prolegomena

That biblical theology is a complicated matter is shown by the fact that J. K. Mead's textbook was the first attempt in some 30 years to try and define and refine the category in meaningful ways. At the outset, one has first to decide what counts as "the Bible." For persons of Jewish faith, a perfectly good "biblical theology" can be done simply by studying and analyzing what Christians call "the Old Testament," though ironically when asked about the Christian enterprise called biblical theology, some Jewish scholars say they are simply not interested in the subject.[3] But this would never be sufficient for a Christian study of "biblical theology." Unfortunately, Christians themselves don't agree as to what counts as Scripture, at least in the broad sense.

For the vast majority of Protestants, the Bible is composed of 39 OT books and 27 NT books, *plus nothing*. For those of the Catholic or Orthodox faith there are "deutero-canonical" books that should be included in a study of "biblical theology," books written during the intertestamental period like the Wisdom of Solomon, or like Sirach. It is simply undeniable that various of the early church fathers took various of these books as "Scripture" and theologized on their substance. Indeed, if one examines the early great codices, for instance Codex Sinaiticus, one discovers that bound together with what

---

[1] Mead, *Biblical Theology*, 12.

[2] G. B. Caird and L. D. Hurst, *New Testament Theology* (Oxford: Clarendon Press, 1994), 5.

[3] See J. Levenson, "Why Jews are not Interested in Biblical Theology," in *Judaic Perspectives on Ancient Israel* (ed. J. Neusner, Baruch A. Levine, and Ernest S. Frerichs; Philadelphia: Fortress Press, 1987), 281–307.

Protestants call "the Bible" are books like Tobit, Judith, 1 and 4 Maccabees, Wisdom of Solomon, and Sirach, but also early Christian books like the Epistle of Barnabas and the Shepherd of Hermas. Or consider Codex Vaticanus. It also includes Wisdom of Solomon, Sirach, Judith, and Tobit. It is not clear whether some scribes who composed these great codices (perhaps in at least one case originally at the behest of Constantine) thought all these books were *canonical*, or merely that they all were worthy of Christian reflection and study. Clearly later Orthodox and Catholic thinking on these matters came to consider such books as at least of secondary canonical status, if not full canonical status.

That, however, is far from the only problem. The question also has to be raised about "which OT" we will do biblical theology with. The Greek OT is the OT of choice for the Orthodox traditions and churches. Protestants and most Catholics tend to start with the Hebrew OT. The important point about this is that the LXX and the Hebrew OT often *differ*, not only in their readings of passages in the 39 books of the OT, but they differ in what books they include. The LXX includes Tobit, Judith, 1–3 Maccabees, Esther with additions, the Prayer of Manasseh, Wisdom of Solomon, Sirach, and the Psalms of Solomon (which, while originally in the LXX, is not included in the Orthodox canon). The Hebrew Bible does not include these additional books. In that respect, Jews and Protestants are in some agreement about what counts as the OT. In any case, biblical theology looks different depending on what one counts as included in one's source text – "the Bible."

As Jaroslav Pelikan makes perfectly clear, there was never a time when the Christian community combined the Hebrew OT with the Greek NT to make a single book. Rather, once it had agreed upon the shape of its New Testament it adopted a version of the OT *in Greek* to serve as its OT. This is suggested by an examination of the early codices like Codex Sinaiticus.

Christian biblical theology (as it was originally done when there was a book of two testaments) involved *an all-Greek canon*, which of course is not at all the canonical basis of Protestant and Catholic biblical theology today, which uses the Hebrew Scriptures along with the Greek NT.[4] The term biblical theology today would not mean the same thing that it did when there first was a "complete" Bible, and in any case that sort of approach to Christian theology, including NT theology, threatens to undo, muffle, or produce a false harmony or blending of the discrete witness of the Hebrew Scriptures which has its own Jewish voice, and the equally discrete NT Scriptures which have a largely Jewish Christian voice.

We cannot start with biblical theology and then try to fit NT theology into that Procrustean bed. Nor can we start with the theology in the Hebrew Scriptures and see the NT books as simply a renewal or extension of that theology or those covenants mentioned in the OT, though the Lord knows both of these hermeneutical moves have been tried by scholars. What strikes me is that, historically, this is not how the NT writers viewed things, nor, I think, should we. We must start with the discrete testimonies of the individual testaments and take *some* of our cues from the NT writers as to how Christians should approach the Torah. This is a historical approach which sees biblical theology and biblical ethics as something which must be done *after*, and on the basis of the detailed study of the theologies and ethics of the OT and NT.

---

[4] J. Pelikan, *Whose Bible is It? A History of the Scriptures through the Ages* (New York: Viking, 2005), 101–2.

To be clear from the outset, this exercise in biblical theology will limit itself to the Protestant canon, and with good reason. I take my clues from the writers of the NT, who do not ever cite *as Scripture any of the deutero-canonical books already mentioned.* They cite texts as Scripture only from the 39 books found in the Protestant OT.[5] This is not to say that the NT authors did not use some of these intertestamental books. Indeed, they did. The Gospels, Paul's letters, and James reflect a knowledge of and a use of Wisdom of Solomon and of Sirach. But the material is never *quoted as Scripture*, it is simply drawn on for its ideas, images, concepts. We are thus defining the source material for a biblical theology as involving a Bible of 66 books, though there will be places where we need to point out the influence of extra-canonical sources such as the Wisdom of Solomon.

One of the other limitations I am imposing on myself in writing this book, is that I am going to try and do my best to let the biblical text speak for itself, without the additional assistance of later Protestant, Catholic, or Orthodox theologies. As Childs points out, biblical theology is for the most part a post-Reformation project, for the very good reason that the Bible "functioned within a dogmatic ecclesiastical framework in a subservient role in order to support various traditional theological systems. The Reformation signaled a change in emphasis by its appeal to the Bible as the sole authority in matters of faith."[6] J. P. Gabler was responding to that basic assumption when he wrote his famous discourse in 1787 on "the proper distinction between biblical and dogmatic theology and the correct delimitation of their boundaries."[7]

In my study *The Problem with Evangelical Theology*, I pointed out at length that whenever a theological tradition has tried to say something distinctive (e.g. speaking in tongues is the litmus test of whether you are a Spirit-filled Christian or not, it being the initial evidence that the Spirit is in your life) it is not accidental that those points are the exegetically weakest points in that theological system, whether we are talking about Calvinistic, Arminian, Pentecostal, or Dispensational approaches to the Bible.[8] One could say the same thing, for example, about Catholic theology in regard to various aspects of its Marian doctrine (e.g. the perpetual virginity of Mary, or her bodily assumption into heaven), or Orthodox theology and some of its approach to icons and male-only priests, and so on.

If a theology is going to be worthy of the name "biblical theology" then it needs to be based solidly in the Bible, avoiding as much anachronism as possible. By anachronism I mean the reading back into the biblical text of later theologies of whatever sort. This latter practice is one of the major things that has caused so many divisions within the body of Christ. Biblical theology is neither merely historical theology, nor Reformed theology, nor Arminian theology, nor Catholic theology, nor Orthodox theology, nor any sort of systematic theology. It is *grounded* quite strictly in the exegesis of the biblical texts and their *clearest* implications. *The writers of the OT and the NT were not participants in nor*

---

[5] To be sure, there is a citation from 1 Enoch in Jude, but note that the author doesn't say he is citing "Scripture" but rather quoting "the prophet Enoch," which is not the same thing as citing Scripture. Paul, for example, quotes a Cretan writer about Cretans in the Pastoral Epistles but this hardly means he thinks that writer wrote Scripture. It just means he thought he said something true. And in any case, no Christian group later included 1 Enoch in their canons or canon lists.

[6] Childs, *Biblical Theology*, 4.

[7] *Ibid.*

[8] Ben Witherington III, *The Problem with Evangelical Theology: Testing the Exegetical Foundations of Calvinism, Dispensationalism, Wesleyanism, and Pentecostalism* (2nd edn., Waco, TX: Baylor University Press, 2015).

advocates of any of these later schools of theological thought. They were Jews, almost all of them, with the possible exception of the author of Luke-Acts and 2 Peter.

As Jews, their theology was, not surprisingly, profoundly Jewish in character and it did not involve, for instance, later debates about the inner workings of the Trinity, or the two natures of Christ. Those were debates fueled to a significant degree by later Greek philosophical thinking, which the writers of the NT show little knowledge of, interest in, or inclination to draw upon, with rare exceptions.

What I have discovered in this study is that the more one reads the NT as the Jewish book it is, the less difficulty there is in seeing how the theologies of the OT and the NT are compatible, with the latter to some extent a development of or from the former. Biblical theology becomes a less formidable and daunting task when one does not take a Marcionite approach to the OT and see it as somehow revealing a very different God than one finds in the NT.

James Mead offers a basic definition of biblical theology as follows: "Biblical Theology seeks to identify and understand the Bible's theological message and themes, that is what the Bible says about God, and God's relationship to all creation, especially to humankind."[9] This definition is good as far as it goes, but it is inadequate. The Bible is not in fact about "all of humankind." It is rather a tale told about God's people, his chosen people. Even in the very earliest portions of the Bible in the stories in Genesis 1–3 this becomes clear. Cain and Abel have wives from other people groups which the biblical author is not at all focusing on. All the way back to Adam and Eve, the Bible is the story about the origins of God's people in particular, and other peoples are mentioned tangentially only as they impinge on or enter the story of God's people. Other people only enter the story positively when God's people undertake their given task of being a light to the nations, and when Jesus of Nazareth takes over this role of being that light and sharing that light with the world through his disciples, so that both Jew and Gentile might be united in one people of God in due course.

Despite some protests to the contrary, this story about sharing the light of God with the world in the OT *presupposes human fallenness,* human beings *not* having a proper relationship with the living God.[10] The light that is being shared is not just any kind of light, but a light that redeems, transforms, saves, because humankind needs such redemption. The concept of the Fall does not originate with St. Paul or other Christian theologians but with the stories in Gen. 1–3, as was even recognized by early Jewish writers that were not followers of Jesus. For example, consider 4 Ez. 3.21–22: "For the first Adam, burdened with an evil heart, transgressed and was overcome, as were also all who were descended from him. Thus, the disease became permanent, the law was in the people's heart along

---

[9] Mead, *Biblical Theology,* 1.

[10] Here the Christian approach to various OT texts which are taken to deal with human fallenness often differs dramatically with a dominant Jewish view of such texts in various ways. For example, many Jews do not think Adam's sin affected the whole human race. Rather, they see an inclination toward the good and an inclination toward the evil as resident within each person, and they have a choice about what direction they go. Yes, people sin, but no it is not inevitable. The Christian notion of the bondage of the human will is not part of their calculus. In other words, they are not Augustinians nor Lutherans or Calvinists in their approach to issues such as human fallenness, divine election, free will and the like. Such a view of human nature runs into trouble not just in Gen. 2, but in texts like Ps. 51, or 4 Ezra which speaks about Adamic sin and its consequence for humankind. See Childs, *Biblical Theology,* 26.

with the evil root but what was good departed, and what remained was evil." Or consider 4 Ez. 7.48: "O Adam what have you done? For though it was you who sinned, the fall was not yours alone, but ours also who are your descendants." This does not lead the author to suggest that human beings are not responsible for their sin. To the contrary, they have the freedom to resist it, but they also have the *yetzer hara* – the evil inclination.

Biblical theology must, then, deal with a God that is both a Creator God and a Redeemer God, who chooses a particular people, and later a particular person, through whom to make known his special revelations and possibilities of redemption for all humankind. Even in his final revision of his definition of biblical theology, Mead only speaks about the divine–human encounter, and about God's relationship with creation and all humankind, and the implication of that for relationships between human beings. Nowhere in his definition does the word salvation or redemption show up, nor does human fallenness.[11]

Over half a century ago, my NT professor at Harvard, Krister Stendahl, wrote a seminal article for *The Interpreter's Dictionary of the Bible*, paradoxically entitled "Biblical Theology: Contemporary."[12] Stendahl stressed, quite rightly in my view, that biblical theology must begin with the descriptive task, which involves studying the ancient texts and determining what they meant in their original contexts. Just so. Then, he says, we may ask the second-order question about what it means and how it is to be applied today.

But even if one limits oneself to the descriptive task there is a *presupposition* that is in play that needs to be stated plainly. If you use the phrase *biblical theology*, not biblical theologies, you are assuming that there is some sort of *theological unity* to and in the canon of the Bible. And behind that assumption is normally the further assumption that there is a divine mind behind and expressed through all these various texts written by a plethora of different human beings over the course of more than a millennium. These texts do not line up in a linear progression, if by that one means the later writers of texts know *all the earlier texts* and they are developments based on the earlier ones. In various cases this is simply not so. The Book of Job, for instance, is not a development of really anything that may have been written before it by the author's Jewish forebears. The detailed study of intertextuality of course shows clear evidence that some later writers are dependent on some earlier writers in various ways, but again the themes and ideas develop in different places at different times, involving different persons who have their own judgments, and yet *there is a unity to biblical theology*. It is from this fact that we find a partial basis for the concept of divine inspiration of the Bible. We don't, for example, have advocates of the god Baal writing a book which makes it into the Hebrew Scriptures. The biblical writers are all writing about the same God of the Bible, and saying diverse, but compatible, things about that God and his will and relationship with both creation and his people.

Nevertheless, biblical theology, as we have it in this study, is of course an *ex post facto* thing which I am assembling from the various pieces of evidence in the biblical texts and the way one assembles the data reflects one's own values and understanding. The author of Isa. 40–55, for example, is not playing with the same full deck I am when I lay my cards on the table and say "this is biblical theology." At best, the theologies of the individual writers in the Bible are a subset of what can be called "biblical theology."

---

[11] See Mead, *Biblical Theology*, 242.
[12] Krister Stendahl, "Biblical Theology: Contemporary," *IDB* 1:418–32.

I would draw an analogy with a choir. The choir is all singing the same oratorio, let us say, for the sake of discussion, Handel's *Messiah*. There are many different parts, and no one part constitutes the whole oratorio and its themes. Further, one needs all the parts to get the full effect the composer intends. The sopranos, altos, tenors, and basses are all contributors, but the unity and harmony of the various parts comes from the way the composer composed and ordered the piece. There are places where there is dissonance between some of the parts, which must be resolved into harmony or unity. And there is a before and after to the composition. It is progressive in character, and has a telos, a goal, an end game. Until one reaches the end and sees what the composer was driving at all along, and where the piece was going, one cannot fully assess either the composition or the composer's intentions and indeed the skill and nature of the composer himself. Such is the Bible and biblical theology.

Having said all this, on any reading of the Bible, it should be plain that the Bible is not *just* about theology, or even just about theology and ethics. This being the case, a biblical theology textbook is not about *everything* in the Bible. Some will say it is about the theological interpretation or theological exegesis of the Bible. The problem with that statement is it assumes that the method is where the theologizing lies, rather than in the text itself. It is better to say that biblical theology involves "the reading of Biblical texts with a view toward their theological content and how they function as Scripture for people of faith"[13] I am not entirely happy with the last half of that statement because even non-believers can read the Bible for its theological content, and offer some good analysis of what it means. The latter half of the statement has to do with the hermeneutics of applying that theological content to people of faith. That is not discerning or even doing biblical theology but rather applying biblical theology to some specific audience. Both of those tasks are valuable and necessary for believers, but they are not one and the same task.

A Very Brief History of Biblical Theologizing

Despite the quotation from Caird and Hurst that forms an epigraph for this chapter, it is simply not true that there was no biblical theologizing using various parts of the Bible before the eighteenth century. While one can say that there was no "discipline" of biblical theology before then, in fact the *practice* was already going on during the canonical period, indeed during the OT period.

Mead, for example, rightly points to a text like Exod. 34.6–7 which proclaims God's own words. These very words are picked up again in Num. 14.18, and then are quoted again much later in Neh. 9.17. It is further echoed in Pss. 8.15 and 103.8 and then the prophet Joel uses the text (2.13) as a call to repentance. Jonah confesses that it was precisely the qualities spoken of in the self-revelation of Exod. 34.6–7 that caused him to flee to Tarshish (Jonah 4.2).

It is precisely an example like this that I was alluding to when I suggested that biblical theologizing, a serious reflection and drawing upon the theological content of Scripture, was already going on before the NT was even written. In many ways, the Pentateuch, and especially Deuteronomy, is foundational for much of what follows it in the OT and on

---

[13] Mead, *Biblical Theology*, 11.

into the NT. The theological lens for interpreting the whole history from Joshua through Kings is found in Deuteronomy, which sets up a specific way of reading the successes and failures of the leaders that follow Moses, and especially the kings who follow him. This is why those narratives have been called Deuteronomistic history. But this is not all.

A close reading of the prophets shows that they are prosecutors of the covenantal lawsuit, indicting Israel and Judah alike on the basis of the demands of the Mosaic Law and covenant. These prophets explain why judgment has come on God's people, again and again. But undergirding all of this, and in some cases overriding the judgment, are the promises made to the patriarchs in particular, as well as to Moses, promises which are reiterated generation after generation, promises which connect what God said to Abraham with the redemption of the Hebrews from Egypt, because of the covenant with the patriarchs.[14] This may not be what Christians normally think of when they think of biblical theology, but clearly it is a sort of biblical theologizing already going on in OT times quite apart from the later coming of the Messiah in the person of Jesus.

And lest we think that the NT is *simply and entirely* something new, a detailed study of the use of the OT in the NT will disabuse us of that notion quite quickly.[15] The writers of the NT are dependent upon the previous revelation, and are drawing on, amplifying, and re-audiencing various theological ideas and themes and trajectories in their own work, while viewing all of the OT in light of the Christ event. There is something old and something new going on in NT theology, not just one or the other. In part, this was possible because the OT was for all intents and purposes basically a closed collection by the time the NT writers started writing in the mid first century AD.[16] But the NT writers had some precedents for handling the OT *as a collection of sacred texts*, because we see this already in practice at Qumran and also in early Jewish writers like Jesus ben Sira and Philo, as well as the author of Wisdom of Solomon. In the latter case, the author reinterprets the whole of OT salvation history in light of how Wisdom had guided God's people all along through many trials and tribulations (see especially Wis. Sol. 17–18). Biblical theologizing was not a notion cooked up by the early followers of Jesus, and what we call NT theology could never be, and was never seen by the writers of the NT as, the whole of biblical theology. This is hardly a surprise when one considers they were almost all Jews, many of them raised in Judaism and in the synagogue before becoming followers of Jesus.

But what happens when the church becomes overwhelmingly and almost exclusive Gentile in composition, which is what happened in the second to the fourth century AD? What happened was that honest interpreters of the OT realized that the "plain sense" of Scripture did not refer directly to the post-apostolic church and its post-NT era existence and problems. So, what to do? William Yarchin rightly observes, "Much of the history of biblical interpretation concerns the question of referentiality in the Bible: to what extent are the texts of Scripture to be read for what they *plainly* state, and to what extent as *figures* of something other than their plain reference?"[17]

---

[14] Rightly, Mead, *Biblical Theology*, 16.

[15] Witherington, *Isaiah Old and New*; *Psalms Old and New*; *Torah Old and New*.

[16] I have dealt with this issue of canon at length in Ben Witherington III, *The Living Word of God: Rethinking the Theology of the Bible* (Waco, TX: Baylor University Press, 2007). The NT canon of course was not closed until the late fourth century AD but all the books that were included were books written in the first century AD by apostles, their co-workers, and the next generation of disciples still in touch with the apostolic tradition.

[17] William Yarchin, *History of Biblical Interpretation: A Reader* (Peabody, MA: Hendrickson, 2011), xii.

As students of patristics will tell us, this problem led to two rather different approaches to Scripture by Christian exegetes – a more literal approach sometimes associated with Antioch and exegetes like John Chrysostom, and a more allegorical and figurative approach associated with scholars like Origen and Clement of Alexandria. In both cases, it was assumed that the Bible was God's Word and had some kind of message for the church, and more importantly that there was some theological consistency to the revelation. The God of the OT was the same God revealed in the NT. I have chronicled elsewhere in great detail how that played out with two particular crucial and go-to books of the OT, which are more often quoted than any other OT Text – namely Isaiah and the Psalms.[18]

What is interesting is that the inclination of exegetes of both sorts of interpretive approaches tended to see the *whole* of the OT as in some sense "prophetic" in character – whether it was law, prophets, narrative, wisdom literature, songs, or whatever. By making that hermeneutical move they implicitly recognized that the text involves a before and an after, which is to say while it was spoken to and in one era in the past, it nonetheless was multivalent in character (in the case of Isaiah and the Psalms partly because of its poetical and metaphorical nature) and so one could talk not only about layers of meaning, but about latter-day fulfillment of some of those meanings. But when you talk about fulfillment, you are implicitly recognizing that the original meaning has not been replaced, but rather has come to fruition at a later time and for a later group of people.

This *modus operandi* became crucial to the Christian interpretation of the OT, but when you start talking about literal and figurative meanings in a text there can certainly be confusion in interpretation. For example, when interpretation involves an allegorizing of an otherwise non-allegorical text, not least when the text itself is figurative and poetic in character, as is the prophecy of Isa. 40–55 and the songs in Psalms, all sorts of confusion can ensue. Aquinas was clearly uneasy with all these multiple meanings being found in the OT, some of which seemed like pulling rabbits out of an originally empty hat, and so he stressed "many different senses in one text produce confusion and deception and destroy all force of argument" and so one needs to recognize that "in Holy Writ no confusion results, for all of the senses are founded on one – the literal – from which alone any argument can be drawn."[19]

What this quotation shows, is that well before Luther and Calvin, there was an uneasiness with overly figurative readings of most anything in the OT, and so the Reformation exegetes had some partial precedents for returning to an emphasis on the "literal" sense of Scripture as its "plain meaning" as opposed not only to figurative approaches, but later dogmatic and systematic ways of reading the text in light of later theological systems. Hans Frei has called this early Reformation approach a "realistic" reading of the Bible, which emphasized the historicity of its narratives, the unity of its larger story, and how that story in fact speaks to the experiences of each generation of believers.[20]

---

[18] Witherington, *Isaiah Old and New*, 387–445; *Psalms Old and New*.

[19] Thomas Aquinas, *Summa Theologica*, Part 1, Question 1, Article 10. Cited in Yarchin, *History of Biblical Interpretation*, 95.

[20] H. Frei, *The Eclipse of Biblical Narrative: A Study in Eighteenth and Nineteenth Century Hermeneutics* (New Haven, CT: Yale University Press, 1974), 1–3. See also Ben Witherington III, "Sola Scriptura and the Reformation: But Which Scripture and What Translation?" *JETS* 60.4 (2017): 817–28.

Mead, in his careful study, suggests that among the various effects of the Reformation on biblical interpretation, and partly because the Bible was available to and could now be studied by any literate person quite apart from dogmatic formulae, creeds, confessions and the like, was an attempt to get at the historical basis behind the literal biblical story, which is to say to establish the historicity of the events the stories spoke of, in the light of rising skepticism since the Enlightenment about that historical basis.

This led to the rise of archaeological work, and other sorts of historical enterprises, not least original language study and textual criticism in the attempt to go *ad fontes* to the historical truth of and in those biblical stories. But this same process led to a realization that one needed to do just that sort of study as well to get at the "theological" substance of the Bible, which was profoundly theological in character throughout, but not *solely theological*. There were other sorts of content in the Bible as well – namely history, ethics, and more. This meant that dealing with the theological content of the Bible and so with "biblical theology" could become an enterprise in itself, an enterprise that did not always distinguish between a "theologizing" of the biblical text (and so "theological interpretation"), and a description of the theology inherent in the text.

As Mead goes on to show,[21] the earliest attempts at doing "biblical theology" involved the assembling and lining up of proof texts, centering on certain theological themes. This approach to biblical theology we still see in play in the twenty-first century (e.g. Scobie).[22] But that was not all: "the 1600s reveal some of the earliest examples of written works called 'biblical theologies' that presented overarching systems of Scripture, *often around the theme of covenant.*"[23]

In terms of the modern practice of biblical theology, G. T. Zachariae (1729–77) has been sometimes recognized as the "father" of the discipline, not just because he got beyond the proof-texting method, but because he charted a *via media* between the task of exegesis and the discipline of systematic theology. The way he went about it was to distinguish between what was incidental and historically conditioned in Scripture and the abiding and more universal principles to be found in the text. "He categorized these universal principles in three areas: those related to God, to human sin and divine response to it, and to changes to the human condition and Christian conduct."[24]

Most scholars have recognized J. P. Gabler, who drew on Zachariae and viewed his work favorably, as the real founder of the modern discipline, not least because of his groundbreaking lecture on March 30, 1787, a lecture entitled "An Oration on the Proper Distinction between Biblical and Dogmatic Theology and the Specific Objectives of Each." Gabler insisted that biblical theology was a historical enterprise conveying what the biblical writers thought about matters divine. He thought that there was a three-stage process to doing biblical theology:

(1) the collecting and classifying the key ideas of each biblical writer
(2) a comparing of these various writers' distinct ideas (without stripping them of their particular contexts) in order to arrive at

---

[21] Mead, *Biblical Theology*, 20–25.
[22] C. H. H. Scobie, *The Ways of our God: An Approach to Biblical Theology* (Grand Rapids, MI: William B. Eerdmans, 2003).
[23] Mead, *Biblical Theology*, 22, emphasis added.
[24] *Ibid.*, 25.

(3) those universal ideas that surface when one finds the point of agreement between the biblical writers.

There was, however, a problem. While the NT was written by those who believed in Christ as the Lord, the OT was not. Further, there was a great difference in historical and communal settings of the material written in OT times and the material written in a relatively short period of time by a small minority community of followers of Christ, mostly living in Gentile-majority settings, and often participating in religious communities where Gentiles were dominant in the congregation. Because of these recognized differences, scholars tended to separate the task of doing OT theology from that of NT theology, and those who sought to hold the two together tended to pick *a major theme* they thought bound the corpus together – a theme such as the Kingdom of God, or covenantal theology, or the developing story of salvation history, or the notion of "the living God" and the like.

These sorts of approaches are still being tried with varying degrees of success (e.g. S. Richter's *The Epic of Eden*, or Feldmeier and Spieckermann's *God of the Living*).[25] What characterized all of these works was an implicit recognition not merely that detailed engagement with the biblical text itself in its various contexts was needed, but that there was a considerable difference between a *religionsgeschichtliche* or history of religions approach to the Bible and a biblical theology approach. The former would focus on the religious praxis and also beliefs of the people in the Bible, the latter would focus on the theological content of their thought as they testified to their beliefs about the words and deeds of their God.[26]

Ironically enough, it was a scholar in the early twentieth century who quite rightly became famous for his *Dogmatics*, Karl Barth, who helped turn the twentieth century into a golden age of the writing of biblical theologies, through his landmark commentary on Paul's Letter to the Romans, especially its second edition in 1921. It is not an accident that it was after that, that we got the great OT theologies by W. Eichrodt in the 1930s and G. von Rad in the 1950s, as well as R. Bultmann's controversial but influential NT theology which emerged in the 1950s. Barth's *Dogmatics* showed how theological interpretation of the Bible, in great depth and at great length, could produce some good fruit, and it sparked various efforts thereafter. Mead notes that there was even talk of a biblical theology movement of sorts that emphasized the theological unity of the Bible, God's revelation of his redemptive acts within history, and, to some degree, the distinctiveness of biblical ideas over against the contexts in which the ideas arose. Historical events were the medium in which the message was delivered. Indeed, because God was acting in history, history itself was in some measure "theological history," not merely "theologized history."[27] I remember vividly riding on the train in the late 1970s from Durham to Cambridge with George Carey, then the vicar of the Anglican church in the marketplace in Durham, and later archbishop, and having a conversation about the biblical theology movement and its importance. Alas, the movement seems to have fizzled out before it really got going.

---

[25] R. Feldmeier and H. Spieckermann, *God of the Living: A Biblical Theology* (Waco, TX: Baylor University Press, 2011); Sandra L. Richter, *The Epic of Eden: A Christian Entry into the Old Testament* (Downers Grove, IL: InterVarsity Press, 2008).

[26] Mead, *Biblical Theology*, 34–35.

[27] Ibid., 47.

The sequel to the landmark works of Von Rad and Eichrodt and Bultmann was not merely many different attempts at doing biblical theology in some form, but also some serious reflection on methodology, particularly by Brevard Childs.[28] While sometimes perceived to be a push back against historical critical exegesis of the Bible, Childs actually was suggesting a different methodology without denying the value of historical critical interpretation. His "canonical" approach meant that Christian biblical theology at least would limit itself to the material within the canon and would definitely read the OT in light of the NT, as well as vice versa, to some degree. The history of religions folk took exception to this, especially the reading of the OT through later Christian glasses and concepts, seeing this as a return to allegorizing of the OT, which is to say, denying its historical pre-Christian givenness.

And there has also been push back from Catholic NT scholars like L. T. Johnson, who has said this: "If Scripture is ever again to be a living source for theology, those who practice theology must become less preoccupied with the world that produced Scripture and learn again how to live in the world Scripture produces." He in fact attacks the enterprise of biblical theology, insisting "it suggests the possibility of a theology that is not Biblical, and a study of the Bible that is not theological."[29] In part, what Johnson is objecting to is the notion that one could actually interpret biblical texts without paying attention to the theologizing going on in the text itself, as well as against abstract forms of theologizing that largely ignore the Bible itself, whether engaging more in philosophical reflection (see e.g. Paul Tillich on "the ground of being") or some other sort of approach to the Bible. When I use the phrase *biblical theology*, I do not refer to the theologizing that is behind the text, or in front of the text and done on the basis of the text, but rather the theological reflection *in the text, otherwise it is not biblical theology, but rather some sort of theology that uses the Bible as a jumping-off point or a clue to precursors.*

If we were to isolate one problem area that comes up again and again in the recent discussions of biblical theology, it is that of the relationship of the two testaments when it comes to Christian efforts at biblical theology. There are few that protest the doing of discrete volumes on either OT theology or NT theology, but when one goes beyond that, then there is pushback. In a sense, it is a kind of turf war, with OT scholars not liking NT scholars to encroach on their theological province and becoming even more irritated when anyone tries to do "Christological" readings, for example of the OT, which they would say are "over-readings" of the OT which run roughshod over what those texts originally said and meant. In some cases, these objections are justified, but in some cases there is a failure to recognize that what, for instance, the NT writers are doing with and to the OT is making a homiletical use of the OT for new communities and new settings. *Often they are not doing contextual exegesis.*

There has been an allergic reaction to a variety of "Christian" theological readings of the OT even by scholars within the Evangelical world, for instance by John Goldingay. He wants OT exegesis and OT theology to be allowed to have its own voice without being shouted down by NT voices. So, for example, he says about OT theology that it consists of "what we might believe about God and us if we simply use the Old Testament or if we

---

[28] Particularly, Childs, *Biblical Theology.*

[29] Luke Timothy Johnson, "Imagining the World that Scripture Imagines," *Modern Theology* 14 (1998): 165, 169–71.

let it provide the lenses through which we look at Jesus."[30] Yet, that has not stopped him from writing a "biblical theology."[31] We will interact with this latter volume along the way in this study.

Some scholars, following to some extent the lead of Karl Barth, have seen Christ as the canon within the canon. James Dunn for instance has said, "Whatever the theory of canonicity, the reality is that *all Christians have operated with a canon within the canon*" and when he pauses to say what that is, he suggests "a common faith in Jesus-the-man-now-exalted" [as] "the unifying centre ... the canon within the canon."[32] I think this is too narrow. To say that Christ is the canon within the canon for Christians relegates the OT to a second-class citizenship, and yet orthodox Christians have regularly insisted that the *whole* Bible is God's inspired Word.

I'm inclined to agree with G. Hasel that the real center and unifying force in the Bible is not this theme or that theme, this event or that event, this trajectory of thought or that trajectory of thought, but rather a person – namely the living God.[33] James Barr, in his helpful critical assessment of biblical theology points out that at the end of the day categories such as God, or humankind, or sin are not uniquely Christian categories imposed on the reading of the OT, and so they are perfectly appropriate for the discussion of biblical theology writ large.[34] This is why in the following three chapters we will explore at length "the God of the Burning Bush," "the God of Golgotha," and "the God of the Burning Heart." Theology proper should start with *the discussion about God and the divine character*. One must freely admit as well from the outset the belief that God's character and actions in the Bible are revealed to be consistent from start to finish.

When the author of Hebrews speaks of Christ as "the same yesterday, today, and forever" (Heb. 13.8), he could just as well have been speaking of Yahweh, or the Spirit. God's character is progressively revealed in Scripture as consistent and coherent. The unity of Scripture is based on God's "unity" and consistency from Genesis to Revelation and his consistent revelation from the beginning to the end of Scripture. His character does not change, his actions reflect this consistent character, and so he can be relied upon. The God who redeemed the Hebrews from Egypt and set up a covenantal relationship with that people, is also the God who dealt with the sin problem on the cross of Jesus Christ, and the God who inspired, empowered, enlightened his people about all of this at Pentecost. Not merely the divine plan or divine ideas, or divine actions but the divine person provides a coherency and consistency to Scripture

When one reads the entire Bible from Genesis to Revelation one of the first impressions one should have gotten is that the leading character in the OT is Yahweh, the God of Adam and Noah, of Abraham and Sarah, of Isaac and Jacob of Joseph and Moses, of Miriam and Joshua, of Samuel and Saul, of David and Solomon, of Elijah and Elisha, of

---

[30] John Goldingay, *Old Testament Theology*, vol. 1: *Israel's Gospel* (Downers Grove, IL: InterVarsity Press, 2003), 20.

[31] John Goldingay, *Biblical Theology: The God of the Christian Scriptures* (Downers Grove, IL: InterVarsity Press, 2016).

[32] James D. G. Dunn, *Unity and Diversity in the New Testament* (Philadelphia: Westminster, 1977), 374; 376.

[33] See G. Hasel, *Old Testament Theology* (Grand Rapids, MI: William B. Eerdmans, 1991), 168–71. He is speaking about the OT, and says Yahweh is the unifying center or factor.

[34] James Barr, *The Concept of Biblical Theology: An Old Testament Perspective* (Minneapolis, MN: Fortress Press, 1999), 40–41.

Ruth and Esther, of Ezra and Nehemiah of Isaiah and Jeremiah, of Hosea and Amos, and the list could go on much longer. He is the God of Israel. More than that, he is the Creator God of the universe who made human beings in his image, and he is the God who took as his mission to redeem fallen humanity through choosing a group of human beings to be his witnesses, beginning with Abraham.

When, however, one turns the page to Matthew, one discovers the Son of Man who is at the same time the Son of God, and on almost every page of the Gospels the focus is on Christ, his person and work. When one turns to Acts, one is immediately confronted with the Holy Spirit, who sets the Jesus movement in motion, inspires the apostles and prophets to speak the Good News, enlightens the readers and writers as to how to understand the OT, gives gifts and fruit to all believers, and guides and guards, and goads the followers of Jesus so they will *face* the future and *faith* the future as well. How, and in what ways, does God progressively reveal the divine character in the Bible? He does so by revealing the Almighty God, the Almighty Savior, and the Almighty Spirit. These three are all the living God, all part of the divine identity but that identity is progressively revealed through time and through the corpus of biblical literature from start to finish, from Genesis to Revelation.[35]

If we use the taxonomy I have used before of symbolic universe, narrative thought world, and theologizing into specific situations, then of course God is one of the fixed stars in the symbolic universe of all the biblical writers. Indeed, it is *the* crucial and central one that is presupposed rather than argued for, assumed rather than proved. God is the foundation of the writers' world views, a foundation on which they stand and from which they speak. The stories they tell involve God at every turn, in one way or another – behind the scenes, in the scenes, going with and beside and before the human characters in the drama. And as the stories unfold, it proves necessary for all of them to theologize into specific situations on the basis of what they believe and know about God.

After we discuss God then we can better focus on the narrative thought world of the Bible, and the seminal stories that shape theology, on the plan and purpose and people of God as he seeks to redeem the world, and on the final future for humankind and the new creation among other things. This in turn must be followed by a discussion of the theologizing we find in the Bible, and of necessity this will have to be selective, taking representative samples of that theologizing, old and new. The task of talking about such things in a clear and coherent way is daunting. There are many difficulties to overcome along the way. But we must turn to the task in earnest, praying for the aid of the One about whom we speak.

---

[35] I agree with Richard Bauckham in his discussions of "divine identity" as a better way of talking about the relationship between God, Jesus, and the Spirit. They are all part of the one divine identity. Richard Bauckham, *Jesus and the God of Israel* (Grand Rapids, MI: William B. Eerdmans, 2008), 1–59.

2

The God of the Burning Bush

I do not see the Old Testament as "witness to Christ" in the way he [Brevard Childs] does; it is about God, not about Christ.

John Goldingay[1]

That the issue of "monotheism" is a central issue for Biblical Theology hardly needs arguing … [but] the term "monotheism" itself has become problematic and potentially misleading, if we do not take the trouble to be clear precisely how we are using it.

Richard Bauckham[2]

John Goldingay's statement above, I think, is mostly correct, but not entirely so. The OT is largely about Yahweh, and his relationship to creation and to God's people, as well as some more tangential remarks about his relationship to everyone else who is not a Hebrew. It is not the book that E. W. Hengstenberg (1802–69) thought it was when he wrote his famous and massive four-volume tome entitled *Christology of the Old Testament*, a work still being reprinted, excerpted, and summarized today.[3]

Where I would disagree with Goldingay is in the following. First, the OT does have things to say about personified Wisdom (Prov. 3, 8–9), with hints elsewhere. It's a theme carried forward into the Wisdom of Solomon, Sirach, and then in various places in the NT, where it is insisted on in no uncertain terms that Jesus of Nazareth is not only God's Wisdom come in the flesh, but he was previously involved in Israel's history because he existed as part of the divine identity from before the foundations of the universe (see e.g. 1 Cor. 10 on the involvement in Israel's history and compare Wis. Sol. 17–18, and see Col. 1 on pre-existing and taking part in the work of creation). Christ is distinguished in Hebrews, and elsewhere in the NT, *from all angelic beings*, including "the angel of the Lord" as being in a different category from them. Second, there are some rather clear foreshadowings of Christ in various prophetic texts in the OT, chiefly Isa. 7.9,11 and 52–55, where it seems very clear that it is not just Israel that is "my servant" but also in Isa. 52–55, where a particular Israelite is the referent. Granted this is a matter of foreshadowing,

---

[1] Goldingay, *Biblical Theology*, 16 n. 7.
[2] Bauckham, *Jesus and the God of Israel*, 60–61.
[3] Ernst Wilhelm Hengstenberg, *Christology of the Old Testament* (Grand Rapids, MI: Kregel Publications, 1956).

and the assumption there is such foreshadowing in the OT leads the NT writers to draw heavily on Isaiah in talking about Christ and the Christ event. There was a stimulus as well from Jesus himself to read the Psalms as foreshadowing him in various ways and images (see the discussions of Ps. 110 in Mk. 12.35–37 and par.), a stimulus which seems to have prompted some typological readings of even Pentateuchal narratives and institutions on the part of the author of Hebrews, and others as well. Christ is a priest after the order of Melchizedek.

In all these cases, foreshadowings do not become foretastes. There is no incarnation of the Son of God before the incarnation referred to in the birth narratives and John 1. The Son is a shadowy figure behind the scenes, involved in creation and in guiding God's people even during their wilderness wanderings, and he becomes an object of messianic hope in the later prophetic materials in the OT. But he does not step on the stage of OT history as a character *in* the narrative. The term *Yahweh*, or more broadly Elohim or Adonai in the OT refers to the person Christians came to call God the Father, the Father of the Son of God.

Jesus, in short, cannot be found under every rock in the OT, indeed he is missing in action in the on-stage action of the OT. He is not Melchizedek in disguise, he is not the angel of the Lord, indeed he is not any human or angelic figure spoken of in the OT, not least because he is of a different order of being than these creatures. In this regard, Goldingay is absolutely correct and to say otherwise is to violate the historical givenness of the OT texts. The Christological use of the OT by the writers of the NT is largely a *homiletical* use of the material, not an attempt at the exegesis of the OT. But this is not all that can be said. Since there is only one genuine God (on which see below) and since the Son is part of the divine identity, much can be learned about the character of the Son who is "one" with the Father by studying the character descriptions of Yahweh in the OT. And that is what we must turn to, shortly.

But first we must reflect a bit on the issue of divine self-disclosure, otherwise known as *revelation*. All too often, it has been assumed that theology is nothing but a collection of human thoughts about God, a bottom up enterprise. But what if there really is such a thing as divine revelation, God making known his character to human beings? Here we are helped by recent discussions by Bill Arnold.[4]

Arnold laments that too often, discussions of the issue and nature of revelation have focused not on the earliest biblical period, the period of the patriarchs, but on the revelation God gave on Sinai, often beginning with a discussion of Exod. 19–24 and Deut. 4.[5]

Arnold begins[6] by noticing how different the approach is to divine self-disclosure visually in ANE literature and in the patriarchal narratives. Gods are quite freely imaged as humans or animals, sometimes hybrid animals with the head of one sort of creature and the legs and tail of one or more other creatures (see e.g. Marduk). The representation of

---

[4] Bill T. Arnold, "Divine Revelation in the Pentateuch," *Asbury Journal* 73.2 (2018), 85–103. Arnold is Paul Amos Professor of Old Testament Interpretation at Asbury Seminary, and my colleague for some 25 years at two different seminaries.

[5] He notes how both W. Eichrodt (*Theology of the Old Testament* [Philadelphia: Westminster, 1961], 1:37–38) and G. von Rad (*Old Testament Theology* [New York: Harper & Row, 1962], 1:8) notice these phenomena but don't really see its significance.

[6] All of this comes from an essay, given as a lecture on October 13, 2017 at ATS, entitled "Divine Revelation in the Pentateuch"; used by permission.

the gods is sometimes anthropomorphic, theriomorphic, mixed, and sometimes imaged as inanimate objects such as the sun disk. In other words, it was widely assumed that the gods could be represented physically, as powerful physical beings. Arnold then points out how it was believed that words themselves had a sort of magical or numinous quality, an inherent power, such that spoken curses actually cursed someone or something, and blessings worked similarly, if the speaker was someone powerful, and especially if the speaker was thought to be divine.

Turning to the first revelation of God to Abram at Shechem in Gen. 12.1–6, Arnold notes the remarkable use of the verb for seeing in the *Niphal* which in effect means "Yahweh *allowed himself to be seen* by Abram, saying 'To your seed I will give this land'." What is remarkable here is that the focus is not on what Abram was allowed to *see*, but on what Yahweh *said*. No specifics of how God "looked" or what Abram "saw" are given. Arnold goes on to note that the second appearance of Yahweh to Abram is described in the same terms, using again the *waw*-consecutive Niphal form of the verb to see in Gen. 17.1. "Yahweh appeared to Abram, saying, 'I am El Shaddai, walk before me and be blameless'." Again, there is no description of what Abram saw, the text is not interested in the sensory input, it wants to focus on the content of the divine speech. Herein we see a regular pattern in these patriarchal narratives – what the patriarch sees is not of concern, rather what he hears is crucial. Through the name "El Shaddai" (meaning something like "mighty God," more literally God of the mountains) the character of God is unveiled, and notice in 17.1 the call to a certain ethical lifestyle, just as in Gen. 12 there was a promise from God about his future plans for Abram and his descendants. So already, and before there ever was a Moses, we find that:

Yahweh *appears* to the ancestors at critical junctures in their individual faith journeys in moments for learning more about Yahweh and for making critical life-altering decisions. The emphasis is never on the physical appearance of that which is seen but on the content of the truth revealed or communicated about God and about the patriarch … Divine self-revealing to the ancestors is not given in order to satisfy human curiosity about God, but rather to deepen the relationship in a way that inspires the patriarch to press forward in obedience.[7]

In fact, rather than depicting God as having human features, one could actually talk about the reverse – humans are created in God's image and have some quasi-divine features, attributes, or abilities. This was enough for Abram, for he built an altar and worshipped God having received such a word.

Five points are crucial about all this: (1) the focus is on the word of divine revelation or self-disclosure, not on what Abram saw; (2) the same verb of seeing in the *waw*-consecutive Niphal form will be used to describe the theophany in Exod. 3 which we will be discussing next in some detail. The point is, the revelation to Moses is not really different – the burning bush is not God, it is meant to get Moses' attention so he will hear God's word for him and commission; (3) the narratives are quite clear that the initiative for these encounters is taken by God, not the human recipient of the encounter; (4) at no point are the narratives about human ruminations about God, they are about divine revelation of God's will and character; (5) because the focus is on the verbal communication, it can be conveyed succinctly, and repeated verbatim. As one can see in a text like Ezek. 1 where

---

7 Arnold, "Divine Revelation," 90.

there is a theophany which focuses on what *is seen*, the seen requires description in human language, but what is seen is so overwhelming and bigger than mere human descriptive powers, that the prophet must resort to the word "like" dozens of times (e.g. "he appeared like ..."). In other words, no literal picture could be rendered of the living God, and indeed the biblical religion would be anti-iconic from the start because no such image could ever adequately capture the divine character. God's word, revealing God's nature and will, rather than God's image or talisman or totem, would be the focus of divine revelation. And divine revelation, from the start, is the basis of biblical theology, which is not merely our thoughts about God, but God's self-disclosure. This view of revelation continues like a red thread right through the Bible and is even used to describe the oral preaching of the Gospel by someone like Paul.

For instance, in 1 Thess. 2.13 we hear the Apostle to the Gentiles say, "When you received the Word of God which you heard from us, you accepted it not as a human word, but as what it really is – God's Word which is at work in you believers." This could very well describe what we should deduce happened to Abram at Shechem at that all-important first theophany in Gen. 12. In short, the concept of divine self-disclosure doesn't arise in the first instance at Sinai and with Moses, nor with the forming of the covenant mediated by Moses to God's people. It already exists in the patriarchal stories about Father Abraham.

The Character of the Biblical God

Exod. 3

[13] Moses said to God, "Suppose I go to the Israelites and say to them, 'The God of your fathers has sent me to you,' and they ask me, 'What is his name?' Then what shall I tell them?"

[14] God said to Moses, "I AM WHO I AM. This is what you are to say to the Israelites: 'I AM has sent me to you.'"

[15] God also said to Moses, "Say to the Israelites, 'The LORD, the God of your fathers – the God of Abraham, the God of Isaac and the God of Jacob – has sent me to you.'

"This is my name forever,
the name you shall call me
from generation to generation."

Here is the first place God reveals his preferred "name" to one of his people, and so in a sense, we are in a new phase of the existence of God's people.[8] As Walter Moberly has rightly stressed, the patriarchs worship the *same God* as Moses, but they do not know his name. The fact that the compilers of Genesis use Yahweh language in various ways and places indicate that they saw the God of the patriarchs as one and the same as Yahweh, even if they are adding the name here and there redactionally, but this is not just a matter of mere diction. The relationship changes after the burning bush. With Abraham, it is about a relationship with a person and his family. With Moses, it becomes about a relationship with a people, a chosen people, that are supposed to be distinct from the other

---

[8] A portion of the following appears in another form in some of my previous work: *Torah Old and New*; *Isaiah Old and New*; *Psalms Old and New*. Used by permission of Fortress Press.

nations in their belief, behavior, and worship, hence the strong emphasis on holiness beginning in Exodus (see below).

Moberly articulates the differences this way:

The one whom Israel now knows as YHWH made Himself known otherwise to the patriarchs (and of course the fact that a good number of names in Gen. 12–50 are compounded with "El" and none with "Yah" is one of the clear supports for this). But it's not "just" a matter of the proper name, as the pattern of religious assumptions and practices also changes. My larger thesis, of course, was that the sense of continuity yet difference between the patriarchs and Moses – the one God yet known differently – is strongly analogous to the relationship between God as known in the OT and God as known through Jesus in the NT – the one God, yet now known differently by Christians.

This brought to my mind what Jesus said to the Samaritan woman in John 4, namely that while she is worshipping the biblical God, she worships One whom she does not really know by name.

So, in an email correspondence, I asked Moberly a question. Do Jews and Christians worship "the same God?" His answer was as follows.

Despite the numerous people who would simply answer "yes," I think the question needs to be reframed to be answered properly. That is, Jews and Christians alike worship the one God [of the Bible], but they *know* the one God differently. And I think this bears on how one should depict the continuity yet difference between Genesis and Exodus, and the Old Testament and the New Testament.[9]

What I would want to stress about this is that it rightly presupposes not only the idea of historical development in theological thinking, but progressive revelation by God of who God is.

There are numerous call narratives in the OT, perhaps the most familiar of which are those in Isa. 6 and Ezek. 1. It is the nature of this call narrative, found in Exod. 3.1–4.17, that it sets Moses off from the patriarchs mentioned in Genesis and sets him in the line of the prophets. Moses, unlike the patriarchs, is not merely called to go and to do, to bless and be a blessing, to receive and believe in the promise and its fulfillment. He is also called upon to proclaim God's word even to an inhospitable audience, to perform miraculous deeds and wonders, and to lead his people home, to set them free. As a prophet, Moses is much like his descendants, Isaiah, Jeremiah, and Ezekiel, but he is also unlike them in that he is a liberator, perhaps even a royal liberator, not just a proclaimer, nor just a claimer of God's promises. T. B. Dozeman notes that the two sections of Exod. 3.1–15 and 3.18–4.18, while they focus on the motif of divine commission, are bound together by Moses' repeated resistance to the divine commission.[10] Notice how the identity and mission of Moses is bound up with the identity and purposes of Yahweh.

Moses is out in the Sinai peninsula tending sheep and appears to be "looking for better pasture" when he comes to Mt. Horeb. Horeb appears to be just another name for Sinai, and already here it is called the mountain of God. It is surely no accident that the very mountain where God will reveal his will and presence to his people *later* is where he

---

[9] Both quotations are from email correspondence of September 6, 2017. A far more detailed articulation of his points can be found in R. W. Moberly, *The Old Testament of the Old Testament: Patriarchal Narratives and Mosaic Yahwism* (Minneapolis, MN: Fortress Press, 1992).

[10] Thomas B. Dozeman, *Exodus* (Grand Rapids, MI: William B. Eerdmans, 2009), 119.

reveals his will and presence to Moses *now*. Moses is simply minding his father-in-law's business, having escaped from Egypt and settled into a situation of comfortable domesticity. He is not seeking any close encounters of the third kind with a deity.

The *malak Yahweh* appears to Moses. Several commentators suggest that this messenger of God is God himself, i.e., it is not merely God's angelic representative. The *malak Yahweh* or angel/messenger of Yahweh appears in the older parts of the historical books of the OT directly (Judg. 2.1, 4, 5.23, 6.11ff.). The peculiarity of seeing a bush burn without being consumed intrigues Moses and so he draws closer. God's presence as a flame would seem to imply his holiness (see v. 5) and purifying force, but perhaps also his miraculous power. Any being who can set a bush on fire and not destroy it is a unique being. This event does not seem to be depicted as a supernatural vision (unlike Ezek. 1), but rather a miraculous natural occurrence happening outside of Moses' psyche. Notice the probable wordplay between the word bush *seneh* and the word Sinai, employing the same Hebrew consonants.[11]

God calls Moses by name twice, indicating a certain urgency, and Moses responds immediately, "Here I am." Throughout this discussion, while Moses complains about his inability to be a public speaker, he shows himself more than capable of carrying on a dialogue with God at length, and we have to bear in mind that the previous stories about Moses in Egypt in these earlier chapters also do not suggest he had any problems with speaking. Verse 5 should be translated "don't draw near (as you are doing)." God does not want Moses to experience a premature ministerial burnout, so to speak! The point is that Moses is not ready yet to come into God's presence; he must be prepared and know with whom he is dealing. This he finds out in v. 6.[12]

The place is called a holy place because God is there, not because it is inherently sacred or hallowed ground. This is in fact the first occurrence of the word "holy" in the entire Bible and notice that it is linked with God's presence. This *holiness* characterizes the story of God and his people in Exodus in a way that is not true of Genesis. God is holy, and he requires a holiness and strictness in his people's behavior in a way that is at least not made explicit before the Mosaic era. The taking-off of sandals may be because they were dirty, or it may simply be Middle Eastern practice in God's presence to be without various articles of clothing. Exod. 3.6 refers to "the God of your father" and the point is that Moses will not be called upon to reveal to the Hebrews some new God that Amram worshipped. Rather he is to speak to them in the name of a God they already know from their own ancestry and religion.

Beginning with 3.7, God explains that he has not ignored the cries of his people. Rather, he has both heard them and has come down to do something about their suffering. The story makes clear that it is God, not Moses, who is the prime rescuer of his own people. "I have come down to rescue them ... and bring them up out of that land." He also plans to provide a homeland for them, a land presently inhabited by various other peoples and groups. Further, it is not just any land, but a good and broad land, "flowing with milk and honey." Actually, as various commentators point out, "oozing with milk and honey"

---

[11] *Ibid.*, 124.
[12] Exod. 3.6 and 15 with the phrase "the God of Abraham, Isaac, and Jacob" is one of the most cited verses in the NT (Mt. 22.32; Mk. 12.26; Lk. 20.37; Acts 3.13; 7.32 [closest to the exact words of Exod. 3.6]; Heb. 11.16, "God is called their God."

would be a better translation here. The image is of a verdant land that enables bees to produce lots of honey, and cows lots of milk.[13]

Moses' initial response is understandable. He is overwhelmed. He intimates it is too great a task for one who is only a simple shepherd, and, in any case, he is unworthy of such a job. "Who am I that I should go to Pharaoh?" Moses is not yet making excuses but simply sees himself as inadequate to the task. But has Moses forgotten his previous history altogether? Probably not. In any case, it is not the adequacy of Moses or his worthiness that is at issue, since God, who is fully adequate and worthy, will be with him. Moses' own shortcomings will not prevent God from using him.

The first part of God's answer is simply "I will be with you." This is perhaps a play on God's name, *Yahweh* from the Hebrew root היה (vv. 14–15). The second part of God's twofold answer to Moses in vv. 13–15 is one of the greatest storm centers of controversy in all of OT studies. What is God's name? What does it mean? What sort of question is Moses asking? The matter is extremely complex, but the evidence leads us to the following conclusions.

First, in v. 12, God had said to Moses, "I will be with you" (אֶהְיֶה). Second, in v. 14, we have the same form of the verb (אֶהְיֶה אֲשֶׁר אֶהְיֶה). The paranomastic use of this verb in v. 14 suggests that we are being told something about God's *activity* or self-revelation in his activity, but commentators often render v. 14 as "I am that I am" and interpret it to mean God is a self-existent, self-contained being. But in v. 14 not only do we have the same form of the verb היה as in v. 12, we do not have the personal pronoun. Third, normally when God was going to act or had just revealed himself, he is given a new title or name (Gen. 16.13). Notice that Moses does *not* say, "Who are you?" or even "Who shall I say you are?"

Rather he expects to be asked "What is his name?" (מַה-שְּׁמוֹ) by which is likely meant, "What new revelation have you received from God?" Or "Under what new title has he appeared to you?"[14] Fourth, Moses' question is not posed as a merely hypothetical one, but as the natural and expected reaction of the oppressed Israelites. The authenticity of Moses' mission is linked to a revelation of the divine name, confirming that God is going to do something. Verses 14b–15 do need to be taken to be a refusal of God to reveal himself. It cannot be a suggestion that אֶהְיֶה אֲשֶׁר אֶהְיֶה is a totally enigmatic response. Further, vv. 14b–15 should be seen as parallel explanations or responses, and v. 15 is clear enough. It is the God of their forefathers who is speaking to them and promising this. Fifth, it is probable that the tetragrammaton YHWH (the four consonants in God's name) is a shortening of the whole phrase *ehyeh asher ehyeh* into a personal name, which Dozeman argues should be translated "I will be who/what I will be."[15]

God's character will be revealed to his people in his actions in Egypt. If this rendering is correct, then God would be saying "tell them to wait and *see*" as God's character is unveiled in his redemption of his people. Nevertheless, the imperfect form of the verb היה suggests a *kind* of action, not primarily a *time* of action or an ontological statement. It is an action that could have begun in the past or will begin in the future, but as of the time

---

[13] According to David Schreiner, at Tel Rehov, admittedly dated to the Iron Age II, they have found one of the oldest, if not the oldest, industrial apiaries. So, it adds a real-life anchor point to this statement.

[14] R. A. Cole, *Exodus* (Downers Grove, IL: InterVarsity Press, 2008), 69–70.

[15] Dozeman, *Exodus*, 132–34.

of speaking, it is incomplete and in progress. God then would be suggesting to Moses that he will show his people who he is when this redemption comes to fruition. God is known in his self-revelation through his deeds. There is still some mystery about who he is in his essence. God shall be known as the one who brought Israel out of Egypt (Exod. 20.2).

What this self-revelation of God tells us is that God is deeply involved in human history, and deeply committed to the redemption of his people. He is not the God of the later Deists, who was believed to have created and wound up the universe like a clock and then left it to wind down on its own, leaving it to its own devices. The naming of God is a call for Moses and his people to have faith in a God whom they already partially knew. The God who "will be" is the same God as the God who "has been" the God of the patriarchs. Israel is not called to blind faith in Yahweh, because this God has a track record with their ancestors, and they are called to remember what he did for them.

While the story begins with the indication that the deity in question is the God of the patriarchs, the eventual upshot of the discussion here is that he is also the God of the future – "I will be ..." There is the further rather clear implication that he is a holy and powerful God, and also that he communicates with members of his people directly, personally, and in some detail, though there is also some mystery involved. The revelation is partial, but it is enough to set Moses in motion toward Egypt with an answer to the question "Who sent you?" The God of their fathers, whom they already know in part, is speaking to them, and will act on their behalf. It is God, not Moses, who is their actual redeemer from bondage.

Despite all this, there is however, another way to interpret *ehyeh asher ehyeh* that we need to consider, namely that it should be rendered "I am who I am." In favor of this rendering is: (1) the LXX renders it ἐγώ εἰμι ὁ ὤν, "I am the one being" (the latter is verbal); (2) the "I am" sayings without a qualifier (e.g. "before Abraham was, I am," Jn. 8.58) seem to presuppose the present-tense meaning of the phrase.[16] The imperfect form of the Hebrew verb could be read as either a present or future tense. If it is to be rendered with a present tense it would seem to refer to God's self-existence. God simply is. God exists, having life in himself. He is in no sense a being derived from another being. It could imply not only self-existence but eternality as well. God always is. He always has and always will exist. Indeed, he existed before the creation of the space-time continuum, so talking about God in terms of time (such as "he always was and will be") is problematic.

There is good reason to doubt, however, that the writer of this Exodus passage was engaging in modern philosophical reflections about the existence and nature of God. God has already answered that he is the God of the patriarchs, and this answer has to do with "the name" of the God Moses is to tell his listeners has sent him. While we cannot be certain, it would appear that Yahweh is the abbreviated form of this very Hebrew phrase. The verb היה means "to be" or "to live," so it is possible that the meaning is "tell them I am the living one, the living God, or YHWH for short."[17] This would comport well with the polemic found elsewhere in the OT, including in the Pentateuch, about the other so-called gods being non-gods, or non-entities. As was later said of Jesus, what may be meant here

---

[16] Feldmeier and Spieckermann, *God of the Living*, 29–30.

[17] As Schreiner has pointed out to me, there is a look-alike verb which one would render "to live," but this depends on the *het* being stretched to accommodate the rendering "to live."

is "in him was life." This would then place Exod. 3 into a clearer relationship with other statements about the character of God we are discussing by examining several key passages, as well as with the character as revealed in numerous other places in the OT not currently under discussion. All other things being equal, the explanation of Exod. 3 that has the best potential to explain and relate to other character statements about God is probably the right explanation, which is to say the earlier of these two options mentioned is likely the correct one. The LXX translators, after all, frequently render the Hebrew in ways suitable to their own audiences.

Exod. 34.6–7

And he passed in front of Moses, proclaiming, "The LORD, the LORD, the compassionate and gracious God, slow to anger, abounding in love and faithfulness, 7 maintaining love to thousands, and forgiving wickedness, rebellion and sin. Yet he does not leave the guilty unpunished; he punishes the children and their children for the sin of the parents to the third and fourth generation."

This is one of those passages where in fact we need to dig deep into the Hebrew text and its Greek translation in the LXX so it will be well if we present the relevant portion of both texts here.

וַיַּעֲבֹר יְהוָה עַל־פָּנָיו וַיִּקְרָא יְהוָה יְהוָה אֵל רַחוּם וְחַנּוּן אֶרֶךְ אַפַּיִם וְרַב־חֶסֶד
וֶאֱמֶת נֹצֵר חֶסֶד לָאֲלָפִים נֹשֵׂא עָוֹן וָפֶשַׁע וְחַטָּאָה וְנַקֵּה לֹא יְנַקֶּה פֹּקֵד עֲוֹן אָבוֹת
אַל־בָּנִים וְעַל־בְּנֵי בָנִים אַל־שִׁלֵּשִׁים וְעַל־רִבֵּעִים

Κύριος ὁ Θεὸς οἰκτίρμων καὶ ἐλεήμων, μακρόθυμος καὶ πολυέλεος καὶ ἀληθινός, 7 καὶ δικαιοσύνην διατηρῶν καὶ ἔλεος εἰς χιλιάδας, ἀφαιρῶν ἀνομίας καὶ ἀδικίας καὶ ἁμαρτίας, καὶ οὐ καθαριεῖ τὸν ἔνοχον, ἐπάγων ἀνομίας πατέρων ἐπὶ τέκνα καὶ ἐπὶ τέκνα τέκνων, ἐπὶ τρίτην καὶ τετάρτην γενεάν.

These formulaic sentences actually come up in various contexts in the OT, this one simply being the first of its kind. It recurs on Moses' own lips in Num. 14.18, and in Israel's prayers (see e.g. Neh. 9.17; Pss. 86.15; 103.8; 145.8; Joel 2.13, and ironically Jon. 4.2, though Jonah is not best pleased about the fact that God might be merciful to the Ninevites; emphasizing the end of the saying on the negative side is Nah. 1.2–3). Many things have been said or suggested about the key term *ḥesed* (חֶסֶד) which we find here and in numerous other places in the OT, and unfortunately some of things taken for granted or asserted about this term are likely untrue.

Further, a lot of things have been said about חֶסֶד that are certainly not true. First, we note that the word is regularly and normally translated "mercy" or in this case in the LXX of Exod. 34 "full of mercy" (πολυέλεος), *not* "love." Secondly, the Hebrew term is not always predicated of God's relationship with his covenant people. Here is a brief survey of the meaning of this key term starting with how it is used in Pss. 42–43 and elsewhere in the Psalms. It has sometimes been translated loving kindness or steadfast love, and some have even suggested it means "covenant love," God's love for his chosen people, a love he has promised to give to a specific group of people. But in Pss. 42–43 the word seems to mean no more than a reliable and constant compassion, which is characteristic of the biblical God.

On the one hand, it is clear enough that this word can be used of persons other than God, for example, Jacob asks Joseph to promise to deal with him with compassion or mercy (Gen. 47.29). An even better example is in the exchange between Rahab and the Hebrew spies in Josh. 2.12–14, where she asks them to swear they will deal with her family with חֶסֶד. Rahab is hardly a covenant member or covenant keeper, and the term cannot mean "covenant love" here, but it *does* refer to mercy or compassion, and again we have a context where promising or swearing to act kindly is involved.

If one looks at the paradigmatic example in Exod. 20.6 (cf. Exod. 34.7) we are told that God shows "mercy/compassion to the thousands of those who love me and keep my commandments." Clearly this word is not about some *unilateral* or purely divine love. It is about a quality that is supposed to characterize a good relationship, and one gets the sense that the term emphasizes what we would call mercy or compassion, or less probably kindness. The formulaic use of the term in, say, Num. 14.18, where it is paired with on the one hand God's being slow to anger, and on the other hand with forgiveness of sin, again suggests a reliable, ongoing, constant mercy or compassion. God is merciful in both being slow to anger and offering forgiveness of sins. In Deut. 5.10 again we have the formulaic saying, which indicates that God's mercy is responsive and relational, he shows his steadfast compassion to those who love him and keep his commandments. In Judg. 8.35 we hear about faithless Israelites who failed to show "mercy" or one might even translate it "compassion" to the household of Gideon.

We cannot tarry here to deal with the more than 60 examples where this term shows up in the OT, of which some 14 are found in the Psalter (Pss. 18.50; 25.10; 32.10; 33.5; 52.1; 61.7; 85.10; 86.5; 86.15; 89.2; 89.14; 101.1; 103.4; 141.5),[18] but Ruth 1.8 deserves close scrutiny. Here Naomi commends Ruth, a Moabitess, for dealing "kindly" with her and her now dead sons and says "may the Lord be with you." Clearly enough, God was under no obligation to do so as he had no covenant with Ruth. For that matter, it would be stretching things to say Ruth had some sort of covenant obligation to Naomi and her lost loved ones. After all, Ruth's marriage was at an end and she certainly had no covenant with Naomi herself.

This is why the translation "kindness" or "kindly" or even "mercy" or "compassion" is in order in such a text. In short, while there are contexts where this term refers to a sort of kindness and loyalty that God has promised to give (or expects of his people), even then it is not seen as unilateral, but rather reciprocal and responsive to those who love God, and the term can be used in non-covenantal contexts as well to simply refer to kindness, something unexpected and compassionate, or merciful. *It is the context, not the content of the word that decides such matters, and humans as well as God can and do exhibit this quality.*

In other words, the term does not *mean* "covenant love" as the examples cited above of Rahab and Ruth show, though it can certainly be *used* to characterize how God relates to his people, perhaps especially when they are in need of compassion. It most often seems to mean exactly what the LXX suggested – compassion or mercy, which are qualities needed by those who have failed, sinned, or are in dire circumstances and need help. It is worth pointing out as well that Jesus said "blessed are the merciful, for they shall obtain mercy." Frequently, mercy is brought up in the context of a relationship, not surprisingly. This is

---

[18] Nathan MacDonald, *Deuteronomy and the Meaning of "Monotheism"* (FAT 2; Tübingen: Mohr Siebeck, 2003).

not far from the discussion about forgiveness received and forgiveness given to others in the Lord's Prayer.

Sometimes Exod. 34 has been seen as something of a head-scratcher, because on the one hand it says God is merciful and compassionate and forgiving, and on the other hand it says God is punishing the guilty, even unto succeeding generations. Some have asked, "How are these two sets of attributes compatible?" This is forgetting that the Bible consistently says that God is both just and merciful, both righteous and compassionate, both holy and gracious, always affirming both sides of the equation. It is not an either/or proposition. This is true even for God's people, and indeed perhaps especially for God's people because "to whom more is given, more is required." Furthermore, since "judgment begins with the household of God" as the prophets told us, there is a required accountability for sin. Because of the character of God, he cannot pass over sin forever, as Paul reminds us (Rom. 3.25–26). At some point a righteous God has to judge sin and wickedness, or else he would cease to be righteous. But *how* he deals with it is another matter. Will he deal with it in a merciful way? Exod. 34 says so, but there is still accountability. Notice that Paul as well says there is accountability for misdeeds even for believers (2 Cor. 5.10), even for ministers (1 Cor. 3).

Deut. 4.32–40

Ask now about the former days, long before your time, from the day God created human beings on the earth; ask from one end of the heavens to the other. Has anything so great as this ever happened, or has anything like it ever been heard of? 33 Has any other people heard the voice of God speaking out of fire, as you have, and lived? 34 Has any god ever tried to take for himself one nation out of another nation, by testings, by signs and wonders, by war, by a mighty hand and an outstretched arm, or by great and awesome deeds, like all the things the LORD your God did for you in Egypt before your very eyes?

35 You were shown these things so that you might know that the LORD is God; besides him there is no other. 36 From heaven he made you hear his voice to discipline you. On earth he showed you his great fire, and you heard his words from out of the fire. 37 Because he loved your ancestors and chose their descendants after them, he brought you out of Egypt by his Presence and his great strength, 38 to drive out before you nations greater and stronger than you and to bring you into their land to give it to you for your inheritance, as it is today.

39 Acknowledge and take to heart this day that the LORD is God in heaven above and on the earth below. There is no other. 40 Keep his decrees and commands, which I am giving you today, so that it may go well with you and your children after you and that you may live long in the land the LORD your God gives you for all time.

This great, and exceedingly important, text refers back to the revelation at the burning bush, but adds something new and different, and as we shall see the phrase "and there is no other" becomes crucial, though of course, there has been no end of debate about that phrase, and its possible correlation with what the Shema ("the Lord our God is One") says. The recent discussion among biblical scholars has been stimulated by the important study by MacDonald, entitled *Deuteronomy and the Meaning of "Monotheism."*[19] In essence, MacDonald argued that the very idea of monotheism is an invention of the Enlightenment, and is an inappropriate term and category for what the OT says about the God of the Bible.

---

[19] MacDonald, *Deuteronomy and the Meaning of "Monotheism."*

MacDonald argues the following case: (1) Deuteronomy does not deny the existence of other gods besides Yahweh. The Shema (on which see below) is about monolatry – the worship by God's people of only one God, not about monotheism *per se*; (2) Deuteronomy does not teach that Yahweh is the only God. The phrase "Yahweh is *ha Elohim*" he takes to mean Yahweh is unique, he is the only god who is God (with a capital G), and the only god for Israel; (3) the constant exhortation to Israel to worship and serve only Yahweh implies there are other gods they might and were tempted to serve; (4) whereas modern post-Enlightenment persons assumes there is only one God at all and for all, and so such talk in the Bible is assumed to be universalistic in scope, in Deuteronomy it is merely asserted that Yahweh is the only God for Israel.

There have been a variety of critiques of this view, ranging from mild to stringent, and we will focus on two, that by B. T. Arnold, and that by R. Bauckham. Arnold frames the discussion this way:

> We start with a definition of philosophical monotheism, which is essentially a negative definition or denial about the existence of other gods. In this sense, the OT is not strictly speaking uniformly monotheistic. So far, Nathan is right. But the OT is a monotheizing document. In other words, it moves in that direction and occasionally even arrives at the denial of the existence of other gods (Deut 4.35,39; 32.39; 1 Kgs 8.60; Neh 9.6; Pss 83.10; 96.4–5; and perhaps 82.6–7; Jer 16.19–20; Isa 43.11; 44.6,8; 45.5–7,18,21–22; Joel 2.27). Examples of "implicit monotheism," that is, the incomparability of God, are found in Pss. 18.31; 35.9–10 89.5–8; and 113.5–6. So, while Nathan gets right the OT's failure to drive the point home, he minimizes these references that clearly show… that the OT was moving in that direction. Early Judaism, and later, early Christianity, got all the way there. However, they fixated on the Shema as monotheistic, which technically it isn't. Nathan is right about the Shema; it's not about monotheism, but about the nature and quality of YHWH, without denying the existence of other gods. The opening of the Decalogue (Exod 20.2–3 // Deut 5.6–7) makes the same point; the focus is on the incomparable and exceptional quality and nature of YHWH, not the non-existence of other gods.[20] This last point shows that the OT, as I like to say, is not less than monotheistic, but MORE THAN monotheistic. The definition of monotheism is essentially a philosophical denial, a negative statement about something that does NOT exist. But the OT is laser-focused on positive statements about YHWH, and about devotion and loyalty to YHWH alone. That's the point of the Shema and the Decalogue, even if Judaism and Christianity summarized it as an abstract thought or belief about denial the existence of other gods. The OT itself is focused only on love and devotion to YHWH alone because: (1) He alone is worthy of loyal devotion (*hesed*), and (2) He alone is capable of the kind of salvation and life-giving relationship illustrated in the Exodus and Sinai covenant.[21]

Bauckham, however, goes further than this. He stresses that: (1) Yahweh's uniqueness cannot be limited to the uniqueness of his relationship to Israel; (2) while Israel only recognizes God's uniqueness in the context of its special relationship with God, this does not mean that "this uniqueness cannot include what YHWH objectively is, even independently of Israel"[22]; (3) Deut. 4.35 and 39 need a better interpretation than MacDonald offers. Both these verses emphasize God's supreme power, and it is because of this exercise of power that Israel recognizes God as *ha elohim*; (4) the reference to God being in heaven

---

[20] On this, I do not think Arnold is quite right.

[21] A summary of a personal correspondence (September 2017). It is in essence what Arnold argues in his *Introduction to the Old Testament* (New York: Cambridge University Press, 2014), 6–15; 142–43.

[22] Richard Bauckham, *Jesus and the God of Israel: "God Crucified" and Other Studies on the New Testament's Christology of Divine Identity* (Milton Keynes/Grand Rapids, MI: Paternoster/William B. Eerdmans, 2008/2009), 68.

and earth implies not just his presence but his power throughout those realms, as the parallel in Josh. 2.11 suggests. What makes YHWH "the God" compared to other beings is his unrivalled power, which is to say, this is not just about how he relates to Israel, but what is true about him in relationship to other so-called gods; (5) a careful examination of the phrase *en od milebado* "there is no other beside him" (cf. Isa. 45.6) when compared to how it is used for instance in 1 Kgs. 8.60; Isa. 45.5,6,14,18,22, indicates "there are no other actual gods" – YHWH is incomparable, when other beings, sometimes called gods, are taken into consideration; (6) Bauckham concludes "What Israel is able to recognize about YHWH, from his acts for Israel, that distinguishes YHWH from the gods of the nations is that he is 'the God' or 'the god of gods'. This means primarily that he has unrivalled power throughout the cosmos. The earth, the heavens, and the heaven of heavens belong to him (10.14). By contrast, the gods of the nations are impotent nonentities, who cannot protect and deliver even their own peoples ... [each one of them is a] 'non-god' (32.17 ... 32.21)"[23]; (7) "once we do attend to the ontological implications that MacDonald admits Deuteronomy's 'doctrine of God' must have, this theology is driving an ontological division through the midst of the old category 'gods', such that YHWH appears in a class of his own";[24] (8) "The conclusion that exclusive Yahwism did not exist until the late monarchial period results mainly from treating the biblical texts not just with historical skepticism but with historical skepticism based on very considerable ideological skepticism of the texts."[25]

I would add that it is a skepticism very much like post-Enlightenment Deism's skepticism about a God who intervenes in human history, early, middle, and late in the history of Israel, and as such reflects an anti-supernatural bias as a presupposition of doing "critical historical work on the OT." But there is another point. There is evidence in many layers of the OT, including some of its oldest layers, that Yahweh is the Creator God, the one who made it all. He is not merely almighty over all creation, he is the Creator, and there is no other (see e.g. Ps. 8.3–4 and Neh. 9.6, reflecting on earlier themes). To put the point negatively, H. Niehr says: "No other divinity is the subject of the processes of creation or the taming of the chaos in the [Hebrew Bible]. YHWH alone is the creator and he alone fights chaos. The [Hebrew Bible] texts show that he is a universal god having power over everything in heaven and earth and that he is the supreme god fulfilling deeds other gods cannot fulfill."[26] James A. Sanders rightly puts it this way, that there is "a struggle within and against polytheistic contexts to affirm God's oneness."[27]

In other words, even when we find references to "other gods" in various OT texts, they reflect the *monotheizing tendencies* of the biblical writers, struggling against the dominant religious ethos. It is well to remember that in the ANE, Israel's religion was a small and minority religion clearly swimming against the polytheistic tide. *This point cannot be emphasized strongly enough.* Speaking of Yahweh's "transcendent uniqueness" that puts him in a whole different category from other supernatural beings referred to in the OT,

---

[23] Compare the emphatic statements in 2 Sam. 7.22 and Isa. 45.5, 14, 21: "there is no other god other than Yahweh."

[24] Bauckham, *Jesus and the God of Israel*, 70–71.

[25] *Ibid.*, 73.

[26] H. Niehr, "The Rise of YHWH in Judahite and Israelite Religion. Methodological and Historical Aspects," in *The Triumph of Elohim: From Yahwisms to Judaisms* (ed. D. V. Edelman; Kampen: Kok Pharos, 1995), 67.

[27] J. A. Sanders, *Canon and Community. A Guide to Canonical Criticism* (Philadelphia: Fortress Press, 1984).

Bauckham adds, "Exclusive Yahwism in the Biblical tradition is not an easily made intellectual proposition, but a demand for radical and complete devotion to YHWH."[28]

I agree with Bauckham as well that it is really not possible to trace an evolutionary spiral from polytheism to monolatry to monotheizing to monotheism in the texts of the OT, because it requires specific information about the chronology of tradition history that we *simply do not have*.[29] That being the case, it requires speculation without sound checks and balances and firm mooring in external evidence, including extra-biblical texts. What one can say with rather clear certainty is there is no *advocacy* of polytheism in the OT, even in texts where its existence is acknowledged and commented on. *The OT is univocal in applying monotheizing language to Yahweh.*

The Shema and the Love Command: Deut. 6.4–5

This familiar passage is in fact the beginning of the direct teaching of God's people by Moses, having already passed along the direct revelation of the "Ten Words" (i.e. the Ten Commandments). In a sense this is the bridge between the Ten Words, and the later statutes and ordinances which begin in Deut. 12. As P. Miller notes, the reason Jesus (Mt. 22.40) can say all the commandments hang on these words here is because quite literally the later statutes are spinning out the implications of the Ten Words and the love command as given here.[30] In turn, these words here can be seen as a summary of the Ten Words. Put another way, Deut. 6.4–5 summarizes the essence of the Ten Words and provides the basis for the spinning out of the implications of this great commandment in statutes and ordinances which follow this passage. The Shema begins by dealing with the same issue as the first two of the Ten Commandments, and continues by dealing with the rest of them in the command to love one's neighbor. Notice how often we find the language of the Shema juxtaposed with the prologue and first two commandments language in Deut. 6.12–15; 7.8–10,16b,19b; 8.11,15,19; 9.1; 10.12–13; 11.1,13,16,18–22,28b; 13.2–5,6,10,13; 18.9; 26.16–17; 29.26; 30.2b,6,8,10,16–17.[31] The Shema itself begins as a sort of confession that makes a claim on the confessor, and then leads to a command.

Notably, the phrase that introduces this material is the same as the one that introduces the Decalogue, namely "Listen up Israel," the introduction to the text that came to be

---

[28] Bauckham, *Jesus and the God of Israel*, 92.

[29] Contrast this with the confidence that such a chronology of developing God talk can be had in Feldmeier and Spieckermann, *God of the Living*, 95, where we hear about "early Judaism's increasingly clear delineation of exclusive monotheism evident from Deuteronomy 4.35,39 and Isaiah 45.21." Neither of these texts was likely generated as late as the beginnings of "early Judaism" but rather they reflect a belief that existed in a considerably earlier era, indeed before the exile! Furthermore, texts about monolatry that reflect a knowledge of the existence of other supernatural beings that are worshipped by non-Hebrews, should not be seen as a recognition that these beings deserve to be called "gods" in the sense that Yahweh is God. Even less convincing are the arguments suggested by Feldmeier and Spieckermann that there was a quiet acceptance among some ancient Israelites of Yahweh having a consort, say Asherah. I can find no such "quiet acceptance" of such a practice in the OT. I do find polemics against such practices of polytheism. It is not enough to admit "Most Old Testament texts focus less on the singular or plural nature of divinity than on the significance of YHWH for his people" (95). This is true about many OT texts but as a close examination of Deut. 4 shows, it is not the whole truth.

[30] P. Miller, *Deuteronomy* (Louisville, KY: Westminster John Knox, 1990), 97.

[31] *Ibid.*, 98.

called the "Shema" because of the initial verb. It is as though the writer wishes to make clear how very important these two pieces of tradition are.

MT
Hear, O Israel: The LORD our God, the LORD is one. ⁵ Love the LORD your God with all your heart and with all your soul and with all your strength. ⁶ These commandments that I give you today are to be on your hearts.

LXX
καὶ ταῦτα τὰ δικαιώματα καὶ τὰ κρίματα ὅσα ἐνετείλατο κύριος τοῖς υἱοῖς Ισραηλ ἐν τῇ ἐρήμῳ ἐξελθόντων αὐτῶν ἐκ γῆς Αἰγύπτου ἄκουε Ισραηλ κύριος ὁ θεὸς ἡμῶν

κύριος εἷς ἐστινκαὶ ἀγαπήσεις κύριον τὸν θεόν σου ἐξ ὅλης τῆς καρδίας σου καὶ ἐξ ὅλης τῆς ψυχῆς σου καὶ ἐξ ὅλης τῆς δυνάμεώς σου

LXX in Translation
And these are the statutes and the judgments, which the Lord commanded to the sons of Israel in the wilderness as they were coming out from the land of Egypt. Hear, O Israel: The Lord our God is one Lord. ⁵ And you shall love the Lord your God with the whole of your mind and with the whole of your soul and with the whole of your power. ⁶ And these words that I command you today shall be in your heart and in your soul.

Verse 4 is the call to attention, and the reminder about the unique nature of Israel's God. There has been enormous debate about how exactly to translate the Hebrew of this verse, and whether or not the LXX is a good rendering of it. I have printed the Greek text above so one can see immediately that the word κύριος comes up twice at the end of v. 4, so the question becomes do we translate this "the Lord our God is one Lord" or "the Lord our God is (the only) Lord" or "the Lord our God is a unique Lord." What is the significance of the word "one"? Does it stress unity or uniqueness, or both? And why would the "unity" of Yahweh even be an issue? Is there a stress on this God being solitary, numerically One? The words themselves יְהוָה אֶחָד, as opposed to say יְהוָה לְבַד, have led some to suggest that since אֶחָד normally has to do with unity whilst לְבַד has more to do with uniqueness, this might point the discussion in a particular semantic direction, but the larger context and historical situation has to be taken into account as well.[32]

The polytheistic environment in which this pronouncement emerged would favor the conclusion that it was asserting that Yahweh is the only God, and as such it would not be a statement about the "unity" or nature of God *per se*, nor a statement about his ontological makeup, but rather a statement that Yahweh is the only living or true God.[33] The older rendering "Yahweh is our God, Yahweh is One" is on the right track, and does not settle the issue of what "one" might mean here.[34] D. Christensen, along with others, suggests the rendering of the Hebrew as "Yahweh (is) our God, Yahweh alone."[35] This rendering of course would not rule out that other peoples might have other deities, but for Israel it

---

[32] *Ibid.*, 99.

[33] Bauckham, *Jesus and the God of Israel, passim.*

[34] P. Craigie, *The Book of Deuteronomy* (NICOT; Grand Rapids, MI: William B. Eerdmans, 1976), 168.

[35] Duane L. Christensen, *Deuteronomy 1:1–21:9* (2nd edn.; Nashville TN: Thomas Nelson, 2001). Also, R. D. Nelson, *Deuteronomy* (Louisville, KY: Westminster, 2004), 86.

would be solely Yahweh.[36] Miller suggests: "to confess, therefore, that the Lord is 'one' is to claim that the One who receives ultimate allegiance and is the ground of being and value is faithful, consistent, not divided within mind, heart, or self in any way. The reality of God in one time and place is wholly conformable with all other movements and experiences ... In purpose and in being God is one and the same."[37]

Whichever way one renders it, it is clear that this is as close as one gets to fundamental doctrine or dogma for ancient Israel. The relationship between God and his people is exclusive, and Yahweh is a unique deity, who will brook no rivals. When one compares this passage to the Decalogue itself there is considerable overlap in the whole exclusivity indicated when it comes to the way God's people are to view, relate to, and worship the one true living God. And so not surprisingly, when we turn to v. 5, what God requires of his people is exclusive and wholehearted allegiance, love, loyalty, faithfulness to this unique deity who stands alone in a world thought to be populated by many gods.[38]

The point is not merely that God is the "most High" or top-dog deity in a henotheistic pyramid, but rather that Yahweh is the only *genuine* deity, and there are no other real contenders, only pretenders. This did not prevent either OT or NT writers from suggesting that there were other supernatural beings out there, angels and demons, as they came to be called. Indeed, Paul in 1 Cor. 10 will be quite explicit that monotheism doesn't evacuate the heavens of all other supernatural entities. Paul even calls the pagan deities "demons" (10.21). The point is, they are not nothings, they are spiritually dangerous and so idolatry must be avoided for some very good reasons.

The love command itself in v. 5 is in effect a command to love the true God with one's whole being (cf. 4.9,29; 10.12). Total commitment is what is implied by the combined phrases. This requires not just emotional attachment but real commitment of the whole person, affecting their thoughts, words, deeds, relationships, work habits, worship, and much else besides. It is worth stressing that the word חֶסֶד, does not show up in this verse. Rather we have אָהַבְתָּ. This, in turn, is translated differently in the LXX than חֶסֶד.[39] It is translated with ἀγαπήσεις. Again, we have no reason to think חֶסֶד is some technical term for "covenant love and loyalty."

It has been said that this whole Book of Deuteronomy is in a sense a commentary on this verse, showing Israel what shape this love should take, and the shape is law-shaped, it involves keeping the Law (cf. 10.12–13; 11.1,3; 19.9; 30.16,20, in short "if you love me you will keep my commands").[40] It should also be stressed that the language about loving

---

[36] Duane L. Christensen, *Deuteronomy 1–11* (Word Biblical Commentary; Waco, TX: Word, 1991), 142.

[37] Miller, *Deuteronomy*, 101.

[38] Nelson, *Deuteronomy*, 89, is right in saying that there is no general agreement among scholars as to how to translate v. 4 on two grounds: (1) syntax, and (2) the meaning of "one." Zech. 14.9 would support the understanding that "one" means something like "unique," that is the only God for God's people. It would not then be a comment at all on God's interior or ontological nature. It is also possible to conclude that 2 Sam. 7.23 provides the clue, the meaning being God is unrivaled and unparalleled "Yahweh is the one, the only Yahweh" (i.e. true God). Is this a claim that Yahweh has a unique relationship with his people, or that the other supernatural beings are not genuine gods, or both? Either way, it would not be a comment on Yahweh's constitutional makeup. The idea, however, entails the notion that the one real God, Yahweh, has given his exclusive allegiance to his people, and they should reciprocate.

[39] See the discussion above.

[40] Craigie, *Deuteronomy*, 169.

God was not characteristic of ANE treaty documents or covenants.[41] This is something that is distinctive of the nature of the relationship between Yahweh and his people. The injunction to love is based on the prior demonstration of love by God both in creating and in redeeming a people out of bondage. "Heart" here refers to the center of thought and intention, whereas נֶפֶשׁ refers to the inner self with its emotions, its deepest commitments.[42] The uniqueness of Yahweh as the real God, calls for a unique and unconditional commitment to the real God by his people, hence all the warnings about idolatry, hence all the judgments for infidelity. One of the more interesting differences between the Synoptic treatments of the love command is that whereas in Mt. 22.24–40 and Mk. 12.28–34 the two great love commands (loving God, loving neighbor) are juxtaposed by Jesus himself, by contrast in Lk. 10.25–28 it is the lawyer who combines Deut. 6.5 with Lev. 19.18, though Jesus clearly endorses his answer unequivocally.[43] But there are other oddities about the use of this material in the NT.

For instance, in Mk. 12.29–33 after Jesus cites the text, the scribe he is talking with then repeats Jesus' answer, *but in a different form.* "Beginning with an affirmation ('You are right Teacher; you have truly said that') and an oddly familiar reference to God ('he is one'), he adds 'and besides him there is no other', possibly taken from Deut. 4.35. He then abbreviates the four faculties to three by omitting 'soul' and substituting 'understanding' for 'mind', deducing that this is much more important than all the whole burnt offerings and sacrifices (absent from Matthew and Luke), which Mark regards as a wise answer (12.34)."[44] I would suggest that the reason for the variance between Jesus' citation and what the scribe says is that the scribe is demonstrating his independence from Jesus' wisdom, without being adversarial. In other words, he does not come off as simply a disciple of Jesus, parroting back the Master's words. It has to be remembered that scribes were teachers, theologians, and ethicists in fact, and as such they might speak in their own manner.[45]

On the whole, this crucial passage certainly affirms the uniqueness of Yahweh. He is Israel's sole deity. And probably as well, it is implied that Yahweh is the only real or authentic or legitimate God. Other beings do not deserve the title "God." The love command which follows the Shema requires absolute loyalty and allegiance to this unique

---

[41] Yes, W. L. Moran, "The Ancient Near Eastern Background of the Love of God in Deuteronomy," *CBQ* 25 (1963), 77–87, has shown that the language of love is in some respects reminiscent of treaty language, but when one gets down to cases the language about loving God, exclusively, is not drawn directly from the treaty terminology. See R. E. Clements, *God's Chosen People. A Theological Interpretation of the Book of Deuteronomy* (Valley Forge, PA: Judson Press, 1969), 83.

[42] Nelson, *Deuteronomy,* 91.

[43] R. B. Hays, *Echoes of Scripture in the Gospels* (Waco, TX: Baylor University Press, 2015), 209, suggests that this difference means that Luke is portraying Jesus as bringing no new revelation, but is simply reinforcing what the teachers of Israel say. Yes and no. Luke portrays Jesus as offering an ethic in Lk. 6 that does bring new revelation, but he also reaffirms some of the standing interpretation of Torah of others. There was in any case partial precedent for combining the love commands, cf. Test. Iss. 5.2, "love the Lord and your neighbor," and T. Dan. 5.3, "love the Lord and one another with a true heart." The form of the double commandment is clearly different in these other sources.

[44] S. Moyise, "Deuteronomy in Mark's Gospel," in *Deuteronomy in the New Testament: The New Testament and the Scriptures of Israel* (ed. S. Moyise and Maarten J. J. Menken; London: T&T Clark, 2007), 34–35.

[45] Notice that only Lk. 10.27 also has "strength" like Mark, but this is surely just a variant of the Deuteronomic use of "might."

God, not least because he has given himself in a unique way to Israel as "their God" especially, though he rules over all the nations.

The Holy One of Israel: Isa. 6.1–8

In the year that King Uzziah died, I saw the Lord, high and exalted, seated on a throne; and the train of his robe filled the temple. [2] Above him were seraphim, each with six wings: With two wings they covered their faces, with two they covered their feet, and with two they were flying. [3] And they were calling to one another:

"Holy, holy, holy is the LORD Almighty; the whole earth is full of his glory."

[4] At the sound of their voices the doorposts and thresholds shook and the temple
was filled with smoke.

[5] "Woe to me!" I cried. "I am ruined! For I am a man of unclean lips, and I live among a people of unclean lips, and my eyes have seen the King, the LORD Almighty."

[6] Then one of the seraphim flew to me with a live coal in his hand, which he had taken with tongs from the altar. [7] With it he touched my mouth and said, "See, this has touched your lips; your guilt is taken away and your sin atoned for."

[8] Then I heard the voice of the Lord saying, "Whom shall I send? And who will go for us?"
And I said, "Here am I. Send me!"[46]

As has been widely discussed, God being called *qedosh Yisrael*, the Holy One of Israel, is characteristic of the whole Book of Isaiah, whether one divides it up into two or three parts, or not (cf. Isa. 1.4; 5.19,24; 10.20; 12.6; 17.7; 29.19; 30.11,15; 31.1; 37.23 = 2 Kgs. 19.22, 41.14,16,20; 43.3,14; 45.11; 47.4; 48.17; 49.7; 54.5; 55.5; 57.15; 60.9,14; cf. Jer. 50.29; 51.5). But what actually is the meaning and what are the implications of this predication of God? The context of the theophany text in Isa. 6 suggests strongly that holiness, God's glory, and human uncleanness have something to do with one another. Clearly it has something to do with what came to be called the "perfections" of God, in this case, purity.

God is pure, but humanity is not, not even in the case of God's prophet, Isaiah, and therefore the latter needs to be purified if he is to be a useful and holy vessel, conveying God's holy word. God does not need to be consecrated or purified or sanctified, but human beings do, particularly if they have sinned in word or deed. I would submit that this does not have to do "purely" with ritual purity. What would it mean to say God is "ritually pure"? God does not need a *mikveh*! He is the Holy One of Israel, and because he is, he is "set apart" from sinful human beings, and yet he desires that the whole of his creation be full of his cleansing presence, his *qadosh*. Among other things, passages like Isa. 6 make clear that human fallenness, even in the case of God's servants the prophets, is a reality, and therefore cleansing and sanctifying needs to happen to God's creatures, and Paul will later say, in Rom. 8, it needs to happen to God's whole creation, which is struggling with disease, decay, death, and the futility that comes with fallenness.

Furthermore, God is not satisfied with simply being "holy" and pure, he wants a holy and pure people, which on the one hand requires that he cleanse and sanctify such a people, and on the other hand it also requires that they respond with moral rectitude, by keeping God's commandments. The Holiness Code of Lev. 17–26 makes this clear over

---

[46] For a detailed discussion of this text and its importance in Isaiah, see Witherington, *Isaiah Old and New*, 54–61.

and over again, for example besides the command "be holy as I am holy" we hear in Lev. 22.31–33: "You shall keep my commandments and do them. I am Yahweh. Do not profane my holy name [i.e. by misdeeds or inappropriate speech]. I shall show myself to be holy in the midst of the Israelites. I am Yahweh who sanctifies you, by bring you from the land of Egypt in order to be your God. I am Yahweh."[47] To honor or keep holy God's name doesn't merely mean to avoid misusing it. It also means to obey God's commandments, of various sorts. Holiness of heart and life is what a Holy God expects of his people.

Yahweh is the proper name of God, and it is fair to say it dominates all other names for God in the OT. Feldmeier and Spieckermann suggest "the interplay between the distance that preserves autonomy and attention that bestows participation reflects a peculiarity of God that is closely bound to the proper name YHWH. One would not err to assume that the proper name YHWH, dominates in the Old Testament in precisely this dual determination such that any other divine name acquires its place and justification only in relation to this proper name. *This phenomenon, apparently singular in the history of religions, deserves closer attention.*"[48]

Generally speaking, God can and does use his personal name, but his people avoid it, lest they profane the name, and so instead use circumlocutions or alternate titles like *Adonai.* In other words, God's people do not relate to God on anything close to a parity basis. "The extensive avoidance of the proper name YHWH, applies to both the Hebrew- and the Greek-speaking branches of Judaism. For the most part, the Septuagint renders the Tetragrammaton with κύριος, 'Lord', reflecting that Hellenistic Judaism also hesitated to pronounce the proper name."[49]

Showing just how off-base an anthropological approach to the OT would be is the fact that Yahweh is the most frequently attested theological word in the whole OT, with more than 6,800 occurrences. Compare that to the only 2,600 occurrences of *Elohim*, making it the eighteenth most used word in the OT. *Adonai* is used 439 times, *El* 238 times, *Eloah* 60 times (46 of which are in Job), and often these other terms occur in tandem with Yahweh. Every OT book attests the name Yahweh except Ecclesiastes, Esther, and Song of Songs (although the abbreviated form of the name "Yah" does occur in Song 8.6).[50]

God as Shepherd: Ps. 23

Yahweh is my shepherd, I lack nothing.

[2] He makes me lie down in green pastures, he leads me beside quiet waters,

[3] he refreshes my soul.
He guides me along the right paths for his name's sake.

[4] Even though I walk through the darkest valley, I will fear no evil, for you are with me; your rod and your staff, they comfort me.

[5] You prepare a table before me in the presence of my enemies. You anoint my head with oil; my cup overflows.

[6] Surely your goodness and love will follow me all the days of my life, and I will dwell in the house of the LORD forever.

---

[47] See the helpful discussion in Feldmeier and Spieckermann, *God of the Living*, 19–21.
[48] Feldmeier and Spieckermann, *God of the Living*, 21, emphasis added.
[49] *Ibid.*, 22.
[50] *Ibid.*, 23.

As H. Nouwen reminds us, when one is most personal one is most universal.[51] This certainly applies to Ps. 23. There is general agreement among scholars that this should be seen as a song of trust. We have the difficulty of deciphering what *le Dawid* means here – by, for, or about David, or for use by a Davidic king. The character of the psalm makes it believable that it could go back to David himself, who was indeed a shepherd.

Verses 1–4 focus on the Lord as shepherd, and vv. 5–6 on the Lord as host. Some questions may be raised as to whether we should see these as two distinct images, or whether vv. 5–6 are speaking about a shepherd hosting someone in his tent, in which case there is a natural development of a single metaphor here.

This song does not appear to have any royal focus, and it seems likely that it was originally a personal song of trust and confidence in Yahweh, not a song for worship. The two major themes are that Yahweh protects and Yahweh provides. The psalm begins with a clear statement of faith – Yahweh is my shepherd. The psalmist is on very personal terms with Yahweh, for he uses not only God's personal name but also the possessive – "my shepherd." This implies both a special sense of belonging and a unique relationship. It was not unique to call a god in the ANE a shepherd (cf. *ANET*, 387), but here what stands out is that the psalmist is making a claim not for corporate Israel (cf. Pss. 80.2; 77.21; 95.7) but for himself.

The psalm starts on a serene note – because Yahweh is my shepherd I suffer no lack or want. The psalmist is not saying that God protected him from ever having any hard times. Rather, the point is if you have the Lord as your shepherd. you have all you need to endure and prevail, whether in good times or bad. As B. Anderson says, we who live in a materialistic world have a hard time relating to the claim that God is all one needs.[52] It is, however, true that God is the only absolute necessity in life, for with God come all other blessings according to God's plan and provision.

As Calvin reminds us, it is the sign of a true believer that he/she recognizes and glorifies God whether in good times or bad.[53] One should not forget God in the good times, nor call upon God only in the bad times. In short, the true believer's faith is not dependent on his/her circumstances. Calvin speaks of the believer using God's benefits as ladders to climb up closer to God, not as means to lead one to think one can do without God and be self-sufficient. Our psalmist is supremely confident, not in himself but in God. He is also not naïve, for he has walked through the valley of deep darkness; he has had his brush with death or great evil.

In v. 2 note that God is the subject of the action, as is true throughout the psalm, except for the last verse, where the psalmist reappears. What we are talking about here is the consequences of God's gracious action. The believer not only trusts in God and God's providence, but also sees clearly that he could not make it without God. He sees himself as a sheep that needs to be told when to rest and when to run, that needs to be led and fed, that needs to be guided and guarded, and that needs on occasion to be rescued and disciplined. Even a person with only a minimum of knowledge about animal husbandry knows that sheep are not terribly bright. They need constant supervision or unbreakable

---

[51] See e.g. H. Nouwen, *The Wounded Healer* (New York: Doubleday/Image, 1979).
[52] B. Anderson, *Out of the Depths. The Psalms Speak for Us Today* (3rd edn.; Louisville, KY: Westminster John Knox, 2000).
[53] J. Calvin, *Commentary on the Psalms* (Carlisle, PA: Banner of Truth, 2009).

fences. This must be kept in mind as the psalm progresses. This shepherd cares enough to make the sheep lie down in green pastures where it will have plenty to eat. He also places the sheep beside placid waters. This might mean gently flowing waters, for if a sheep gets too near swift waters it may lose its footing and quickly drown. In short, the image is of both provision and protection. What could be in view is the nomadic shepherd who has led his flock to an oasis and naturally camps there so both he and his flock can rest and refresh themselves. Out of the resting and refreshment place one comes restored – one's life energy returns.

Hence, v. 3 means "he restores my life" (*nephesh*, here as elsewhere means life, not soul). In the desert there are many paths, and it is easy to get lost, but God leads his sheep not only in the right paths but also in the paths of righteousness. Notice, though, he does not do it simply for the sheep's good, but also for God's name's sake. What is at stake here is not just human dreams and wishes, but God's character and reputation and will for his human creatures. His glory will either be poorly or well reflected on earth, depending on the paths the sheep follow here. Because God wishes for his people to reflect and reveal his will for humanity so that all nations may give him the credit the true God is due, he wants to make sure his people do not make him look bad. His people are his witnesses. Here there may be an allusion to God's deliverance of Israel in the Exodus events for his own name's sake.

Verse 4 should be translated "lo, though I walk through the valley of deep darkness." The word *shalmavet* can mean very deep shadow, or possibly even total darkness. The use of this same word should be compared in Amos 5.8, Isa. 9.2, and Ps. 44.19, which suggest that the translation "valley of the shadow of death" is going a bit far. Danger, however, does seem to be connoted here. One commentator suggests seeing the deep valleys of Israel where one's enemy could stand on the rim of a hill and fire arrows at those below. Job 10.21–22 suggests that the threat of death is involved here, though the words simply mean "deep darkness." Notice that the psalmist fears no evil, not because there are no dangerous people or animals out there, but because the Lord is with him, giving him confidence. He believes that greater is God who is with him than any other force that exists in the world. Verse 4b speaks of the comfort of rod and staff. The shepherd carried a crook and club (or rod), the former to pull sheep out of holes and to guide and control them, the latter to ward off attacking wild beasts. Here the image seems to be of fending off the enemy in the darkness of the valley, and the rescuing of the sheep should it fall into a hole. In this sense, these tools of the shepherd are a real comfort to the sheep.

In vv. 5–6 the imagery changes dramatically. Now the creature whom the psalmist envisions is not a sheep but a human being whom God has prepared a feast for in his tent, but even in the presence of his enemies. Understanding of the customs of a nomad helps us here. Once a person came into a nomad's tent that person was safe, guaranteed immunity from harm while under the protection of the host. One may think of the story of Lot in Sodom in Gen. 19. It is not completely clear whether we are meant to think of the psalmist's enemies surrounding the tent where he eats, or whether God has actually planned for him to eat with the enemy, in which case the Shepherd is trying to bring peace and reconciliation between the parties.

Much depends on whether one sees vv. 5–6 as being set in a nomad's tent, as I have suggested, or in the temple, the house of the Lord. We must not overlook the fact that the word temple is not used here, only *bayith* (house), which could equally well refer to the tent of the nomad or possibly the tabernacle of God in the period of Israel's history before the temple. If one sees the temple in view here then perhaps the psalmist would be talking about a post-sacrificial sacral meal meant for reconciliation and fellowship between those who had been enemies. But if this is an early psalm which goes back to David, then one must remember there was no temple in David's day.

It was customary to anoint the head of a guest with oil, when he/she came in off the road, having experienced the hot baking sun that dried out one's scalp. This was a basic act of hospitality referred to on various occasions in the Gospels (see Lk. 7.46). Also, the filling of the cup to overflowing was seen as a part of good hospitality in one's tent and makes sense here at a festive meal. The LXX has "and your cup cheers me like the best wine." The psalmist has seen Yahweh bring about reconciliation even between old foes; thus he is able to exclaim with confidence, "surely goodness and mercy [*HESED!*] will follow me all the days of my life." In short, the psalmist is looking toward a future based on his experience of what God has done for him in the past and present. The very last clause of the psalm indicates the psalmist's personal response to all God's effort on his behalf. He will repeatedly return to the tent of Yahweh and become a sojourner there in order to show his faithfulness and loyalty in response to God's unmerited favor. The psalmist will give God his due, for the God he worships is due repeated and heartfelt responses of loyalty and love, so gracious has Yahweh been through all life's vicissitudes. Thus, the psalmist concludes by saying that as long as he lives he will keep going to the tent to meet and have fellowship with his Shepherd. As P. Craigie points out, it is no accident that Jesus calls himself the Good Shepherd in Jn. 10.11.[54] This can be seen as implying his oneness with Yahweh, who is always Israel's shepherd; and possibly his royalty as well since Israel's leaders were also called shepherds; indeed, the implication in Jn. 10 may be a claim to Jesus' being part of the divine identity.

The Omni-God: Ps. 139

You have searched me, LORD, and you know me.

[2] You know when I sit and when I rise; you perceive my thoughts from afar.

[3] You discern my going out and my lying down; you are familiar with all my ways.

[4] Before a word is on my tongue you, LORD, know it completely.

[5] You hem me in behind and before, and you lay your hand upon me.

[6] Such knowledge is too wonderful for me, too lofty for me to attain.

[7] Where can I go from your Spirit? Where can I flee from your presence?

[8] If I go up to the heavens, you are there;
if I make my bed in the depths, you are there.

[9] If I rise on the wings of the dawn, if I settle on the far side of the sea,

[10] even there your hand will guide me, your right hand will hold me fast.

[11] If I say, "Surely the darkness will hide me and the light become night around me,"

[12] even the darkness will not be dark to you; the night will shine like the day, for darkness is as light to you.

---

[54] P. Craigie, *Psalms 1–50* (2nd edn.; Grand Rapids, MI: Zondervan, 2016), *ad loc.*

¹³ For you created my inmost being;
you knit me together in my mother's womb.

¹⁴ I praise you because I am fearfully and wonderfully made; your works are wonderful, I know that full well.

¹⁵ My frame was not hidden from you when I was made in the secret place, when I was woven together in the depths of the earth.

¹⁶ Your eyes saw my unformed body;
all the days ordained for me were written in your book before one of them came to be.

¹⁷ How precious to me are your thoughts, God! How vast is the sum of them!

¹⁸ Were I to count them, they would outnumber the grains of sand – when I awake, I am still with you.

¹⁹ If only you, God, would slay the wicked! Away from me, you who are bloodthirsty!

²⁰ They speak of you with evil intent; your adversaries misuse your name.

²¹ Do I not hate those who hate you, LORD,
and abhor those who are in rebellion against you?

²² I have nothing but hatred for them; I count them my enemies.

²³ Search me, God, and know my heart; test me and know my anxious thoughts.

²⁴ See if there is any offensive way in me, and lead me in the way everlasting.

Psalm 139 is certainly one of the richest, and theologically most profound of all the Psalms, yet surprisingly it is *never* quoted or alluded to in the NT. In many regards, it creates the same sort of problems for the Christian reader as does Ps. 133, for in the midst of some of the most sublime poetry in the OT we also hear at v. 19 "I wish you would kill the wicked, God," and then at v. 21, "do I not I hate those who hate you ..." It is no wonder that Anderson says that for many, the magnificent things in Ps. 139 are ruined by vv. 19–22.[55] It may help some to point out that the psalmist's hatred and death wish is not for personal enemies but for the enemies of God, but frankly I cannot go along with Augustine when he avers that this psalmist really means he hated their iniquities (i.e. he hated what was wicked in them). Of such nice theological subtleties as hating the sin but loving the sinner the psalmist knows nothing. He simply says he hates them indeed, hates them utterly, and wishes them dead. Here is where I point out, however, that the Psalms reveal the heart of the psalmist, and as such are a true reflection of the psalmist's thoughts and feelings. Those thoughts and feelings do not always correspond well with God's thoughts.[56]

It may be worth noting also the various names used for God in this psalm. God is called Yahweh in vv. 1 and 4, and 21, *El* in vv. 17 and 23, and *Eloh* in v. 19. It may well be one of the oldest psalms in the Psalter, and in any case, it has no heading to orient us. As far as the structure of the psalm, it may be divided up into three or four strophes, four seeming the most natural: (1) vv. 1–6 are about God's omniscience; (2) vv. 7–12 about his omnipresence; (3) vv. 13–18 on his omnipotence and inscrutability; (4) vv. 19–24 are personal petitions, which fall into two sub-sections, petitions about God's foes, followed by petitions about self.

---

55 Anderson, *Out of the Depths, passim.*
56 On this whole matter of the orientation of the Psalms and what they reveal, see Witherington, *Psalms Old and New, passim.*

It has been noted that actually v. 1 reads: "Thou hast searched me and known," there is no personal pronominal suffix after the verb *yada*. The point would be that God knows all, having examined the psalmist.[57] It is also interesting that the Hebrew word translated "search" or "examine" has as its basic meaning to dig, and at Job 28.3 refers to digging for precious metals. It suggests a thorough examination, a getting to the root or heart of the matter.

Verses 2–6 will expand upon what the psalmist means when he says God knows and examines him. God knows when the psalmist sits down, when he rises up, when he walks (travels), and when he lies down to rest. In short, Yahweh knows all of his activities; his ways (*derekim*) or behaviors are thoroughly known to God. Then we will hear that God knows all his thoughts before even he speaks them (*rei* – thoughts, mental activity). The verb used at the beginning of v. 3, *zerah*, actually means to sift or to winnow. The point here is that one's activities have been thoroughly sifted and weighed, analyzed and judged. Verse 4 could mean either that God knows what the psalmist will say before he does, or that the psalmist doesn't need to say anything for God to know what he is thinking. Either way, God knows one internally and externally: there are no secrets from God, nor, as we shall hear, is there any place to hide.

Verse 5 speaks of God besetting the psalmist. Indeed, *tsor* can mean besiege in a hostile sense, but it also can mean protect in a positive context. Likewise, the noun used of God (*keph*) can be used to speak of God's hand or literally palm of protection or punishment. Is the point here that the psalmist cannot escape God? That is what the following verses seem to suggest, in which case we should interpret v. 5 to mean that God encompasses and surrounds the psalmist; he is being pursued by the "hound of heaven." God gives him no quarter, or perhaps he restricts his freedom. The point seems to be that even if the psalmist wished to escape God, he could not. Everywhere he turned he found God, and everything he thought, said, or did was known by God. Such complete knowledge of God is incomprehensible to the psalmist; it is awesome and too amazing to take in (v. 6).

Verse 7 begins the second strophe with a question: where could the psalmist go to get away from God's spirit? This is of course a rhetorical question, to which the implied answer is *nowhere*. The reference to God's spirit is not to the Holy Spirit, but to God's presence in general. Both his spirit and his face express the immanence of God and his presence. There may be some sense, though, in distinguishing between constant encounter and automatic immanence (part of the process). Some have seen here merely the assertion that God is ever present with the believer, as Ps. 23.6 asserts. This may be so.

Verses 8–9 are going to tell us that no height and no depth, no distance in the far east or west, is beyond the parameters of God's presence (this suggests a broader concept of omnipresence than just explained). *Sheol*, here as elsewhere in the OT, refers to the grave or the underworld, not hell in the Christian sense of that term. It may be significant that the psalmist tells us God is in both places, for in pagan mythology one might escape one deity who was of the sea by going to the mountains, or another deity who was a sky god by hiding in the earth. But the God the psalmist worships is the only one, and he is everywhere. Verse 9 seems to refer to the idea of traveling as fast as (or by) the wings of the dawn. F. Delitzsch wanted to render it, "If I should lift up wings such as the morning

---

[57] As Schreiner has pointed out to me, "While the suffix is not there, it's possible that it's supposed to be inferred. The first two clauses (if I counted right) are both 10 syllables. Thus, the presence of the sf would disrupt this. Hebrew poetry has a nasty habit of doing this stuff."

dawn," alluding to the swiftness with which light travels across the whole sky once the sun has risen.[58] The psalmist envisions going to live at the other end of the Mediterranean.

But even there, God's hand would be present to guide him, indeed grab him if necessary. Verse 11 expresses the pointlessness of asking night to come and cover one, for to God light and dark are all one. God can still see and know, no matter what the conditions. Verse 13 is especially interesting. It begins with the Hebrew word *ki*, here probably emphatic, meaning "indeed," rather than causal meaning "nor." God created (*QNH*) the psalmist. He made his kidneys (thought to be the center of conscience). He wove together or knit together his sinews and bones. *Seter* is the word for womb here. God is directly involved in the creative process in the womb. Verse 14 is a reverie on human creation: it actually reads, "I am awesomely wonderful." This is not an ode to egotism, for the psalmist goes on to add that this is so because "wonderful are the things you have made. You know me through and through."

The psalmist returns to his anatomy lesson in v. 15 and says that even though he was formed in a hidden or secret place (the womb), nonetheless his bone structure was not concealed from God's all-seeing eye. Then he speaks of being made deep down in the earth. This seems to be an allusion to the original creation story of Adam formed from the dust of the earth (cf. Job 10.9). Notice Job 1.21, where womb and earth are equated. It is not clear whether we are to see earth here in this psalm as simply a metaphor for womb, or whether what is meant is that each individual was individually formed by God, like Adam from the dust of the earth. Verse 13 would favor such an interpretation.

Verse 16 speaks of God seeing the psalmist's *golem* (from *galem*), which means "wind up" and is used in the Talmud of every kind of unshapen stuff or raw material, such as the wood or metal which would be used to form a vessel. Here what is meant is probably the embryo. It seems since the psalmist clearly sees a continuity between his present self and this *golem* that he sees the *golem* as human life, but it is as yet unshaped, unsculpted, until God takes his hands and does his work. This metaphor may indicate some medical knowledge of how the fetus gradually forms. Verse 16b indicates that in the book of life all the days of one's life are written down, planned in advance, before any of them come to pass. This of course does not say that the plan does not take into consideration what God knows we will or would do in various circumstances, but it is definitely talking about a sort of pre-planning, at least in outline. Notice v. 4 in this psalm indicates that the psalmist's personal choice to speak or not is not annulled by this fact.

God's sovereignty and human freedom are both affirmed in the Bible but the emphasis is on the former here. What is clearly in view here is the determination of the length of life (cf. Exod. 32.32–33). Literally it speaks of days being fashioned for us. The book of life (cf. Pss. 56.8; 69.28) in the OT is a book about earthly life and its extent, not, as in the NT, about who makes it into the "Lamb's book of life." It is not surprising in view of v. 17 that the psalmist says he finds God's thoughts difficult: *yequer* could mean "precious," but in Aramaic it is "difficult"; here it is parallel with *pela*, which means "wonderful, difficult." Unlike the days of a human life, God's thoughts are so vast and so many that they are literally as innumerable as grains of sand on a beach. Verse 18b read literally says, "if I awoke I would be with you still." Some have seen here an allusion to resurrection, but more likely,

---

[58] F. Delitzsch, *Biblical Commentary on the Psalms*, vol. 2 (n.p.: Forgotten Books, 2012).

as Delitzsch argued, what is meant is that even if the psalmist falls asleep counting God's thoughts, when he awakes, he would still be with God, and still be involved in counting.

Then suddenly at v. 19 the tone shifts dramatically. It is not too difficult to imagine the semantic shift here. The psalmist has been thinking about an omni-everything sovereign God. If there is such a God who is good, then why is there evil and wickedness in this world at all? The psalmist cannot answer that question, but he does think that if God is *that* sovereign he could at least eliminate the wicked, wherever they may have come from. He asks God to kill the wicked, to make the "men of blood" (probably meaning blood-thirsty men) leave him alone. These men mention God (i.e. pronounce his name is what *amar* seems to mean here) maliciously, perhaps in a curse. They speak falsely; they even oppose or possibly attack (so a few manuscripts read) God. The psalmist is trying to show his utmost loyalty to God here. He hates those who hate God. God's enemies are his. But in view of v. 19 one wonders if he is not in fact saying "may my enemies be yours, God." Yet though he classifies his enemies as wicked, he does not see himself as beyond scrutiny.

Verses 23–24 should be seen as a protest of innocence at least in this matter. "Examine me God, probe me, and see my anxiety. See if I walk in the way of pain" (*ersev* – pain, torment). What he is talking about is the way of sin which leads to internal and external punishment or torment. Rather, he wishes to be guided in the *derek olam*, the everlasting way (i.e. perhaps the way that leads to everlasting life). The "two ways" language is of course familiar to us from Deut. 30–32 and the covenant. The point is that the psalmist indicates his loyalty to the covenant: he has not been going down a road that leads to pain and torment. Thus, the psalmist asks to be vindicated, not as a perfect person, but as one in right relationship with his sovereign God. Notice of course that he leaves his enemies to God's disposal. He does not take matters into his own hands. L. C. Allen concludes about the themes of this psalm that they are about: "Not omniscience but constant exposure to divine scrutiny ... not so much omnipresence as confrontation with an unseen person at every turn, not omnipotence but divine control of a creature's life – these are the heart-searching themes of the psalm."[59] God is very real to this psalmist, indeed inescapable, and yet also, ironically here he is called upon to be the psalmist's means of escape from the wicked. Such are the imponderables when one truly believes in the God of the Bible. An omni-present God can give one a feeling of complete security if one is in positive relation-ship with him, or of complete helplessness if one is trying to run and hide.

The question this text raises is not whether God has predestined everyone to one or another form of eternity, since this psalm is not about the afterlife, unless one counts Sheol. This psalm is about God knowing all things, and having a plan for a person's life, including its length, in this world. What this text does not say or suggest is a predetermi-nation of all human actions. Notice that the psalmist is concerned about his future well-being, because, quite apart from, and even against, God's will, he from time to time has done something wrong, including in this psalm saying he hates some people who he thinks despises Yahweh.

The question then becomes twofold: (1) how does God exercise his sovereignty, and (2) how is there room in the human economy for an omni-God and at the same time human freedom and responsibility for one's actions? Or even more pointedly, how could

---

[59] L. C. Allen, *Psalms 101–150* (WBC; rev. edn.; Nashville, TN: Thomas Nelson, 2002), 263.

there even be evil or sin if God is all-powerful and also all-good, which the psalmist certainly believes? The problem of theodicy or dis-teleology, of the ultimate origin of evil, really only arises in a monotheistic context, because of course the ancient polytheists could always say that evil came from some deity whom they didn't much like or want a relationship with. For monotheists who believed in a singular good God, this answer was not an option. It is a sign of at least *implicit* monotheism, that the psalmists and many other OT writers keep wondering why bad things keep happening to God's people.

The answer that comes from reading psalms like this and related psalms, including even Ps. 23, is that God exercises his power in a way that leaves room for other sentient beings (humans and *elohim*, angels and "demons") to be moral agents and to have a modicum of choice about which moral direction along the "two ways" they will follow. These choices are not predetermined, but they are guided, and it is also promised that God's people are directed and protected along the way (see Ps. 23).

The Day of Yahweh: The Day of Reckoning: Amos 5.2–27

Hear this word, Israel, this lament I take up concerning you:

[2] "Fallen is Virgin Israel, never to rise again, deserted in her own land, with no one to lift her up."

[3] This is what the Sovereign LORD says to Israel:

"Your city that marches out a thousand strong will have only a hundred left; your town that marches out a hundred strong will have only ten left."

[4] This is what the LORD says to Israel: "Seek me and live;

[5] do not seek Bethel, do not go to Gilgal, do not journey to Beersheba.

For Gilgal will surely go into exile, and Bethel will be reduced to nothing."

[6] Seek the LORD and live,
or he will sweep through the tribes of Joseph like a fire; it will devour them, and Bethel will have no one to quench it.

[7] There are those who turn justice into bitterness and cast righteousness to the ground.

[8] He who made the Pleiades and Orion, who turns midnight into dawn and darkens day into night, who calls for the waters of the sea
and pours them out over the face of the land – the LORD is his name.

[9] With a blinding flash he destroys the stronghold and brings the fortified city to ruin.

[10] There are those who hate the one who upholds justice in court and detest the one who tells the truth.

[11] You levy a straw tax on the poor and impose a tax on their grain. Therefore, though you have built stone mansions, you will not live in them; though you have planted lush vineyards, you will not drink their wine.

[12] For I know how many are your offenses and how great your sins.

There are those who oppress the innocent and
take bribes and deprive the poor of justice in the courts.

[13] Therefore the prudent keep quiet in such times, for the times are evil.

[14] Seek good, not evil, that you may live.

Then the LORD God Almighty will be with you, just as you say he is.

[15] Hate evil, love good; maintain justice in the courts.

Perhaps the LORD God Almighty will have mercy on the remnant of Joseph.

[16] Therefore this is what the Lord, the LORD God Almighty, says: "There will be wailing in all the streets
and cries of anguish in every public square.
The farmers will be summoned to weep and the mourners to wail.
[17] There will be wailing in all the vineyards, for I will pass through your midst," says the LORD.
[18] Woe to you who
long for the day of the LORD!
Why do you long for the day of the LORD? That day will be darkness, not light.
[19] It will be as though a man fled from a lion only to meet a bear,
as though he entered his house and rested his hand on the wall only to have a snake bite him.
[20] Will not the day of the LORD be darkness, not light – pitch-dark, without a ray of brightness?
[21] "I hate, I despise your religious festivals; your assemblies are a stench to me.
[22] Even though you bring me burnt offerings and grain offerings, I will not accept them.
Though you bring choice fellowship offerings, I will have no regard for them.
[23] Away with the noise of your songs!
I will not listen to the music of your harps.
[24] But let justice roll on like a river, righteousness like a never-failing stream!
[25] "Did you bring me sacrifices and offerings forty years in the wilderness, people of Israel?
[26] You have lifted up the shrine
of your king, the pedestal of your idols, the star of your god –
which you made for yourselves.
[27] Therefore I will send you into exile beyond Damascus," says the LORD, whose name is God Almighty.

It is the widely held view of most scholars of all theological stripes that Amos is the first of the classical prophets. Amos was not a professional or court prophet. On the contrary, he was a sheep herder or rancher of sorts, and apparently on the side he dressed fig trees. He did not prophesy for money but because an encounter or several encounters with Yahweh impelled him to. When specifically did Amos prophesy? There are two clues on this score in the text itself.

Firstly, we are told in the superscript to the book that he prophesied two years before the earthquake. Since we have archaeological evidence from Hazor for an earthquake of considerable size somewhere in the period 758–750 BC, this suggests that Amos prophesied shortly before then. Secondly, the prescript says he prophesied during the reign of Uzziah in the south, and Jeroboam in the north. This also locates his prophesy somewhere around 760 or a little later. He was then a contemporary of Isaiah. We learn that Amos was from Tekoa, a small town, not from the north but in Judah, near Bethlehem. This comes as some surprise since his major oracles seem to be primarily directed to and about the north, and we hear in chapter 7 about his prophesying at Bethel in the north. Furthermore, he seems to know the conditions not only of Israel but also of her northern neighbors precisely as well. For this reason, some scholars have conjectured that the Tekoa in question might be a town by that name in the north, but such a town is only attested in post-biblical times. Also, the concluding oracle of hope would make sense as an utterance of Amos if indeed he was a southerner who still had hopes for Judah, though he was ready to write off Israel, it appears.

A few points about the social situation need to be highlighted. Despite the apparent outward prosperity and peace both north and south were experiencing in Amos' day, there was inward and spiritual pollution and corruption. This would not be immediately apparent since the temples seem to have been packed with people and the worship times appear to have been lavish. The problems were, however: (1) a growing two-class system, where the rich who were few were exploiting the poor who were many, and the rich were getting richer; (2) religious syncretism, not only in pagan shrines in Israel but also even in Yahweh's temples, apparently; (3) the officials or even the people who thought that if they maintained the official cult of Yahweh religiously it would guarantee them peace and prosperity for the future. Amos comes to them to deny this bad theology and to link theology with ethics. The vertical relationship with God cannot be properly maintained in a vacuum which ignores horizontal relationships with one's fellows. Some seem to have assumed religion is a purely private matter between the individual and his God. This, according to Amos, is not so at all. Amos will talk to his people about the coming day of Yahweh, as not a day of victory but a day of judgment for those who think in this fashion.

Amos was perhaps a local official in Tekoa or leader in the city gate, disturbed by the lack of justice in the new social structure. It may then come as some surprise that Amos' critique of formal religion as well as the style of living and politics of the day is that the leaders of society were doing too much, not too little in various regards. They were doing too much for Yahweh and the state and receiving too little from him in the way of guidance. There is no doubt that Amos did indeed come and speak to the north about how things ought to be and about Israel's future. But his oracle about Israel is one of unrelenting judgment, with little or no hope mixed in. It was a prophecy of exile that was to come true in a short span for Israel, in 722 BC to be exact. One of the striking features of this book is that Amos starts out in a fashion that would have pleased northern listeners, even rulers, speaking of the doom of their neighbors. But then the surprise comes when he speaks of the judgment of God on his own people as well, which is the climax of the first set of oracles.

Notice, however, that Judah is also not exempt, which indicates that Amos is not entirely on a two-track philosophy about the fates of the sister kingdoms. The divine plan for both is equally demanding in regard to justice and righteousness. It seems right to stress that the final oracle in Amos 9 is of an eschatological nature (i.e. something which transpires after the destruction and deportation oracles are fulfilled, and thus it is probably not seen as imminent). If so, then there is no contradiction between this material and the rest of the book.

We will focus on the theological substance of the crucial oracle in Amos 5. Apparently, we hear of the final fate of Israel, fallen never to rise again. Here we have a formal lament, a funeral dirge. It shows Amos' versatility that he could craft a formal poetic structure used at funerals to lament in advance the inevitable fate of Israel. Strikingly the ones addressed are the corpses to be, and Amos addresses them *as if they were already dead.*

That Israel is called a virgin here suggested she is cut off in the bloom of her youth, prematurely, and thus this is an especially tragic situation. God has deserted her and so she is struck down with no one to help her rise. That she is called a virgin may also be seen as ironic, in view of her idolatry and immoral conduct. Notice at v. 5 that Israel is exhorted to seek Yahweh, and not by means of the temple in Bethel or Gilgal. This is a striking paradox. Israel had assumed that the proper way to seek God was through proper worship and dutiful attention to it. Seek here, *darash*, a cultic term, means not search after but rather to turn to Yahweh. Israel had assumed that proper worship was precisely the means of placating the deity and ensuring their own prosperity and safety. Yahweh is primarily concerned with the content of their character, not so much with the correctness of their religious practices. We cannot and should not read into Amos 5 an anti-sacramental attitude *per se*, but rather Amos is concerned that this particular practice of cultic correctness, coupled with improper conduct, is an affront to God, a mockery. Worship without righteousness and justice in everyday life is not true worship at all. In short Israel had adopted the same attitude about what pleased Yahweh as pagans had about what pleased their deities – namely plentiful and proper sacrifices.

At Amos 5.7 we hear that the Israelites are guilty of turning *mishpat* into wormwood (which was very bitter), and casting *ṣaddiqa* to the ground. The focus of this complaint has to do with what went on in the city gates, in the local judicial assemblies there. In such places, v. 12 says, bribes were being taken, and the poor deprived of justice in the very courts that were intended to uphold the *mishpat*. *Mishpat*, we are told by Amos, is the fruit of *saddiqa* (righteousness), but what do these things mean? *Mishpat* means the judicial process of establishing what is right and implementing that judgment. Thus, it is often translated as justice. Justice is done when the court successfully upholds the rights of the one in the right – the just or innocent one (the *saddiq* person). Unlike our court system, in Israel the system was intended to be a special friend and helper for the poor, widows, and disenfranchised. In short it had an obligation not merely to be fair to all, but to bend over backwards to help the helpless, even to the point of correcting wrongdoing. "Righteousness" is the quality of relationship that should exist between Israelites.

The courts were meant to mend the social fabric of society and repair oversights, or sew up loose ends and holes or gaps. Not just protection of the social order, much less the defending of the law, but also the helping of the just party is the job of the court. Amos' complaint, then, is at the crucial point in time, the country was not living a life of integrity, honesty, and good will. In such times the prudent keep quiet and injustice is done (v. 13).

At Amos 5.18 we hear about the Day of Yahweh. Once again, Amos takes a common, and popular, theological notion of the day and turns it to his own purpose. In popular expectation, the Day of Yahweh (*yom Yahweh*) would be when Yahweh finally came and trampled on Israel's foes once and for all. Amos says woe to those who long for that day, because instead of it being a bright day for Israel, it will mean her judgment, not her redemption. It will be as if they had fled one adversary (another local nation perhaps) only to run into a more fearsome one – Yahweh. This day will strike them unexpectedly, like a snake that slips through a hole in a household wall and bites you. It is interesting that the phrase Day of Yahweh appears almost exclusively in prophetic texts (cf. Isa. 2.12; Jer. 46.10; Ezek. 7.19; Joel 1.15; Obad. 15; Zephan. 1.7,14–18; Zech. 14.1; Mal. 4.5). It is clearly an eschatological concept – an idea about what will happen at the end of history. Probably G. von Rad was right that the idea grew out of the holy war tradition which taught that Yahweh would come as a warrior to fight for his people.[60]

---

[60] G. von Rad, *Old Testament Theology* (one-vol. edn.; Peabody, MA: Prince Press, 2005).

In vv. 21ff. the various elements of Israelite worship – festivals, sacrifice, songs – are taken up one by one and all condemned. The various types of offerings are also mentioned here, so the condemnation is comprehensive. The songs they play sounds like the noise of battle to Yahweh (the word *hamon* usually describes the din of battle). The use of harps suggests elaborate worship, not just average worship. Verse 24 must *not* be seen as an indicative statement about Yahweh making justice flow down. Rather Israel is supposed to do this. Justice is supposed to be so plentiful that it flows down like the streams after the winter rains. Righteousness is to be an ever-flowing stream, not one that dries up depending on circumstances, nor one that only flows intermittently. These are the things that God demands of us to do without ceasing, not in place of worship, but rather in fact as a style of life that makes true worship possible and not a mockery.

What we find in this oracle is that God desires that his own righteous and just character be replicated in his people and in their behavior. Notice that "righteous" character involves mercy on the vulnerable, the poor, the needy, the widow, just as justice and mercy, righteousness and compassion go together in the character of God, as we have noted earlier.

The Parenthood of God: Hos. 11.1–11

When Israel was a child, I loved him,

and out of Egypt I called my son.

² But the more they were called, the more they went away from me.

They sacrificed to the Baals

and they burned incense to images.

³ It was I who taught Ephraim to walk, taking them by the arms; but they did not realize

it was I who healed them.

⁴ I led them with cords of human kindness, with ties of love. To them I was like one who lifts a little child to the cheek, and I bent down to feed them.

⁵ Will they not return to Egypt

and will not Assyria rule over them because they refuse to repent?

⁶ A sword will flash in their cities; it will devour their false prophets and put an

end to their plans.

⁷ My people are determined to turn from me. Even though they call me God Most High, I will by no means exalt them.

⁸ How can I give you up, Ephraim? How can I hand you over, Israel? How can I treat you like Admah?

How can I make you like Zeboyim?

My heart is changed within me; all my compassion is aroused.

⁹ I will not carry out my fierce anger, nor will I devastate Ephraim again.

For I am God, and not a man – the Holy One among you. I will not come against their cities.

¹⁰ They will follow the LORD; he will roar like a lion.

When he roars,

his children will come trembling from the west.

¹¹ They will come from Egypt, trembling like sparrows,

from Assyria, fluttering like doves.

I will settle them in their homes, declares the LORD.

In the passage above, we see God portrayed as a parent, a father or a mother. The imagery as a whole suggests a father. Israel is here collectively called a son. We are however reminded in this passage that God is not, and is not like, a human being. He is not fickle, he will not change his behavior and his love for his child, just because the child has become wayward, even committing idolatry. There is, as Abraham Joshua Heschel said long ago, much *pathos* in this portrayal of God.[61] Here compassion wins out over fierce righteous and justifiable anger. One thing is clear, Yahweh is not portrayed as a deity without feelings, and those feelings are responsive to human behavior and human character in various ways. This, of course, later caused the church fathers no end of head-scratching because they thought God was totally immutable, unchangeable in any way. They certainly also wanted to rule out that God was a being who had irrational and changeable passions. While the Bible certainly does not portray God as having irrational feelings (God's feelings in this passage are perfectly rational, normal, understandable) it does however portray God as having deep and profound emotions, even though at the same time it is said that he is not a human being.

This raises the question of what exactly it means to say God is "the same yesterday, today, and forever" and as I've intimated before, what it means is not that God is not subject to some changes. Surely the Incarnation is a significant change. *What it means is that God's character remains the same always, he is reliable, not quixotic.* He is not just one day and then unjust the next, compassionate one time, and then without empathy the next. But we need to say more about God as a parent.

The first thing to note is that even in Hos. 11, God is not directly called, much less addressed in prayer as father, though the analogy is drawn between God's behavior and a good father's behavior.[62] The same sort of language of analogy is found in Ps. 103.13: "as a father has compassion on his children, so the Lord has compassion on those who fear him." Or we could cite Prov. 3.12, where we learn that God reproves the one God loves, as a father reproves his beloved son. We must be able to distinguish between the use of an analogy, and the "naming" of God as Father. We have already seen in detail how important names, in the case of God the personal name Yahweh, were in those ANE cultures. A name connoted something vital and real about the nature of the one named, perhaps especially when it was a deity being named. If you didn't get the god's name right, you didn't get what you were asking for. It was like dialing a wrong number. You didn't even talk to the right person.

Some scholars will point to Deut. 32.6 as an example of God being "named" as Father. This is a portion of the famous Song of Moses where we hear "Is this the way you repay the Lord, O you foolish and unwise people? Is he not your Father who created you, who made you and established you?" The reference suggests the personal and relational nature of the language. One cannot be a father unless one has one or more children. Thus, when the subject is God's creation of human beings, and in particular his own people, the father language quite naturally would come into play. W. Brueggemann however is right to stress that the imagery does not likely suggest a biological begetting, here or elsewhere in the OT.[63]

---

[61] Abraham Heschel, *The Prophets* (New York: HarperCollins, 2001).
[62] For more details, see Ben Witherington III and L. M. Ice, *The Shadow of the Almighty: Father, Son, and Spirit in Biblical Perspective* (Grand Rapids, MI: William B. Eerdmans, 2002).
[63] Walter Brueggemann, *Theology of the Old Testament* (Minneapolis, MN: Fortress Press, 1997), 244–47.

This same sort of notion of God as father comes into play in Isa. 45.9–11. A father is like a potter who has the right to mold his children and their actions as he sees fit, without giving an account of his actions. While using the language of father, the actual analogy here is with a potter who molds and shapes pre-existing materials. The one reasonably clear exception to the rule that God is not addressed as father in the OT is from Second Isaiah – Isa. 64.7 (8): "You are our father; we are the clay, and you the potter." The image here is of a father shaping his offspring, as opposed to Deut. 32.6, where the image is of a father creating his offspring. The latter idea is also found in Mal. 1.6: "Have we not all one father? Has not one God created us?"

Another text which can possibly be appealed to is Jer. 3.19, "I thought you would call me 'my Father', and would not turn from following me." Ironically, the implication of this verse is that Yahweh wanted his children to appeal to him using that term, but they have *not* done so. Notice as well the assumption of the estrangement of God's people from God, an assumption we also find in the parental passage in Hos. 11. The upshot is, instead of having an intimate and positive relationship with God, characterized in familial terms, just the opposite was happening. While Jer. 31.9 makes clear it is God's earnest desire to relate to his people as father, even after the exile, we hear this, "for I am a father to Israel, and Ephraim is my firstborn."

We may also wish to bring into the discussion the texts where the king is said to be God's son, for instance Ps. 2.7: "you are my son, today I have begotten you," part of a coronation ode used in the ceremony indicating that the king has been officially adopted by Yahweh such that he becomes and deserves the title of and has the position of God's son, at the right hand of God (the place the prince and heir apparent would normally sit). Similar is 2 Sam. 7.14, where David is promised that God will be a father to Solomon and he will be a son to God. In Ps. 89.26–28 we hear that the king will address Yahweh as "Father, God, and Rock of his salvation."

We have now, surprisingly, surveyed all the relevant data from the OT about whether God was called, addressed, or prayed to as father, and as Brueggemann rightly concludes, the images of Yahweh as judge, warrior, king are far, far more prevalent in the Hebrew Scriptures. Yet when we do find the father image or language it suggests God's compassion, care, guidance, shaping, desire for a close relationship with his people and their king. It is God who creates and sustains Israel and her king. The father "image for Yahweh provides a way in which Israel can speak about Yahweh's profound commitment to Israel, a commitment on which Israel can count for special, positive attention."[64]

It is worth stressing, that the language of father–son is *analogical* in character in these examples, as is especially clear when it comes to the king being "God's begotten son." It is also worth stressing that this father language does not really come from patriarchal ideas about God. No human father is seen as the origin of the universe, or of all creatures great and small, or even of a whole people, and yet note the clear associations between God as creator and God as father in various of these texts. Furthermore, one can stress "it is evident that the Father [in texts like Hos. 11] while tender and generous, is not romantic about the relationship but is capable of regret and fierceness. In Jer. 3.19 and 31.9 and Hos. 11.1–9 the metaphor of father is employed in order to exhibit the tension between

---

[64] *Ibid.*, 247.

fierceness and compassion in the inclination of Yahweh. In these texts, as in Psalm 103, Yahweh's compassion prevails."[65]

One possible explanation for the paucity of references to God as father in the OT is the prevalence of use of such language of gods in the surrounding ANE cultures. For example, the king of the Hittites prays to Telephinus and says of him: "Of every land you are Father (and) Mother." Or in a song to Marduk, Anu is proclaimed as "the great Father of the gods." The moon god Sin is addressed as "Father, Nanna, lord Anshar, hero of the gods ... Father and begetter of the gods." So too Amun Re is called Father of the gods in Egypt.[66] W. A. VanGemeren suggests: "Israel was surrounded by nations who held to a mythological understanding of a relationship between the worlds of the gods and men. In this context, the writers of the OT cautiously referred to Yahweh as 'Father'; Yahweh is not El, the father of the 'gods'. He is not Baal, the god of fertility. Yahweh is the Creator of everything and is sovereign (Lord, King, Ruler) over the nations."[67]

As partially helpful as this explanation is, it does not answer the question why the early Christians, many of whom also lived in a polytheistic environment in the Greco-Roman world, and many of whom were Jews like the writers of the OT, did not avoid using the language of God as Father, and to the contrary used it in abundance (120 times in the Gospel of John alone!). There were numerous gods in the Empire called father, and there was as well the rise of the emperor cult with the Emperor being said to be divine and called father as well. In short, the usage of surrounding culture of father language for God cannot entirely explain the paucity of such language in the OT.

A more insightful analysis comes from C. Seitz, who stresses that in the OT things are seen from the Father's point of view, whereas the Father is largely viewed in the NT from the Son's point of view. In other words, the "change has less to do with a matter of culture or even something more personal or psychological, and more to do with the appearance of the man Jesus and a change in perspective: from the Son to YHWH, who is referred to from that filial point of view as 'Heavenly Father'."[68] In other words, it is Jesus himself who places the strong emphasis on God as Father, including emphasizing that his disciples should pray to God as Father, and this better explains why the usage of father language of God is so much more prevalent in the NT than it is in the OT.

Let me be clear that I am not suggesting that God's people did not have, at least at times, an intimate relationship with God prior to the coming of Jesus. Already in Exod. 3, which we discussed earlier in this chapter, we see that Moses has such a relationship with God. But lack of fidelity to Yahweh by God's people in various generations damaged the possibility of such intimacy with God, which is also why we have texts like Hos. 11, where we hear God longing to be called Father and have that close familial relationship, but idolatry and immorality kept interfering with that possibility. Yahweh was prepared to relate to Israel in this intimate way, but all too often they were not prepared to respond in kind. Indeed, a careful reading of the later prophetic use of the Father language shows that it is used to chastise Israel for moving away from "the Holy One of Israel" whether we think of Isaiah, or Hosea, or Amos, or Jeremiah. And it is worth noting that in the

[65] *Ibid.*
[66] *ANET*, 397; 390; 385–86; 365.
[67] W. A. VanGemeren, "Abba in the Old Testament," *JETS* 31 (1988), 392.
[68] C. Seitz, *Word without End* (Grand Rapids, MI: William B. Eerdmans, 1998), 258.

entire Psalter, reflecting the way God's people prayed to and praised Yahweh, the Father language is generally missing in action.

We will have occasion to say a good deal about the "Father" language used of God in early Judaism, by Jesus, and by the writers of the NT, in due course, but following the lead of C. Seitz we will wait on that until we turn to the God of Golgotha, who significantly reoriented the way God language was used. At this point we must go one more mile with Yahweh and pick up the hints we've already seen that Yahweh is not just the creator and redeemer of a people, but the Creator of all things great and small.

An Ode on Creation: Ps. 8

It will seem odd, to many readers of this book, that I have waited until the end of the chapter on Yahweh to talk about God as Creator. After all, doesn't the Bible start that way in Genesis 1? There are several reasons for this. I have done this in part in deference to a large swath of OT scholarship that has suggested that the idea of a singular creator God, who is in fact the only real God, and not just another tribal deity, is an idea that came to the mind of Israelites late in the OT game. So, for example, various scholars have even suggested that Gen. 1 arose in the post-exilic period![69] I am not very convinced by these arguments at all. Whether or not Gen. 1 is a revelation that came late to the mind of an exilic or post-exilic Jew, I do not think this can be claimed for Ps. 8, where we already have a full-blown, beautiful poetic reflection on the God who made it all, who is also Israel's sole deity. Indeed, this seems to be an ode created during the monarchy, perhaps as early as the time of Solomon, and in any case when there was a temple and musical liturgy like this beautiful song.

Ps. 8 is the first praise song in the Psalter, and it is unlike any of the others not only in its structure, but because unlike any other song or hymn in the OT (with the exception of Exod. 15.1–18) it is entirely addressed directly to God.[70] Both Ps. 8 and Exod. 15 have in common that they are songs of an individual addressing God, and in the case of Exod. 15 a famous individual – Moses, as might also be the case with Ps. 8 if it is truly "of David."[71] Sir. 17 could be said to be a further exposition on the same subject, influenced by the theology and character of Ps. 8. This psalm, following as it does the introductory psalms (Pss. 1–2) and the first set of lament psalms (Pss. 3–7) is perhaps put here because the last verse of Ps. 7 says that the speaker vows to sing Yahweh's praise, and Ps. 8 fulfills that promise.[72]

For the director of music. According to gittith. A psalm of David.

LORD, our Lord,
how majestic is your name in all the earth!

You have set your glory in the heavens.

[2] Through the praise of children and infants
you have established a stronghold against your enemies, to silence the foe and the avenger.

---

[69] See Feldmeier and Spieckermann, *God of the Living, passim,* for examples.

[70] J. May, *Psalms* (Louisville, KY: John Knox, 1994), 65.

[71] H. J. Krauss, *Psalms 1–59* (CC; Minneapolis, MN: Fortress Press, 1993), 179.

[72] W. Brueggemann and W. H. Bellinger, *Psalms* (NCBC; New York: Cambridge University Press, 2014), 58.

³ When I consider your heavens,
the work of your fingers, the moon and the stars, which you have set in place,

⁴ what is man that you are mindful of him, and the son of man that you care for him?

⁵ You have made him a little lower than the angels and crowned him with glory and honor.

⁶ You made him rulers over the works of your hands; you put everything under their feet:

⁷ all flocks and herds, and the animals of the wild,

⁸ the birds in the sky, and the fish in the sea, all that swim the paths of the seas.

⁹ LORD, our Lord,
how majestic is your name in all the earth!

One of the major motifs in the Psalms is praising God for his work as Creator.[73] Ps. 8 is the perfect example of this sort of psalm, manifesting the normal structure of invocation (v. 1 expanded by a "who" clause in v. 1c), motive for praise in vv. 3ff., and refrain in v. 9. There is little reason to doubt this psalm was sung in Israelite worship services. The psalm could be said to be a meditation on a particular text from the Pentateuch – Gen. 1.26–28,[74] or alternatively a source for that reflection in Gen. 1

Two of the great imponderables are addressed in this sublime hymn – who God is and what the role of humanity on earth is in light of who God is. This hymn has clear parallels with Gen. 1: the discussion of creation, the mention of humankind in the image of God, and the task of dominion given to humans by God.

If one considers this in light of the ANE background then it is appropriate to remember that in some of those cultures the king was particularly said to be in the image of some god and that deity's plenipotentiary on earth. For example, on a stele of Amenhotep II the Pharaoh is praised as "the beloved physical son of Ra, the lord, the image of Horus on the throne of his father, great in power."[75]

Here, in a sense, the whole race is said to be God's king on earth – called to rule over the rest of creation.[76] This whole line of thinking makes it easier to understand why, for example, the writer of Hebrews was able to see Christ as the one this hymn was primarily talking about. In any case, the *image* theology here suggests that humans have been uniquely made for personal relationship with God, and as persons like unto God, they are able to share some of his majesty, both by being an image-bearer and by fulfilling the task of having dominion over the earth. Verses 6–7 in the Hebrew best reveal the parallels with Gen. 1.

וַתְּחַסְּרֵהוּ מְּעַט מֵאֱלֹהִים וְכָבוֹד וְהָדָר תְּעַטְּרֵהוּ
תַּמְשִׁילֵהוּ בְּמַעֲשֵׂי יָדֶיךָ כֹּל שַׁתָּה תַחַת־רַגְלָיו

The Hebrew terms used for humans in v. 4 (v. 5 in the Hebrew) are אֱנוֹשׁ and אָדָם. The first of these terms is often associated with the frailty of humankind.[77]

The tone of this psalm is set from the opening invocation: it expresses awe, wonder, and joy. The central theme of the psalm could be said to be the majesty and magnificence of

[73] For a much fuller exposition of this psalm and its reverberations in the NT, see Witherington, *Psalms Old and New*.

[74] James Mays, *Psalms* (Louisville, KY: Westminster John Knox, 1994), 67.

[75] Kraus, *Psalms 1–59*, 184.

[76] *Ibid.*

[77] Brueggemann and Bellinger, *Psalms*, 59.

God as it is revealed in nature and human nature and human roles. Verse 2 is the most difficult to make sense of. How could the stammering praises of children and infants in arms be a bulwark against God's enemies, if that's what the Hebrew text means (cf. 2 Macc. 7.27)? Possibly the praise of children drowns out the cacophony of the non-believers? Is true praise what really puts to shame and defeats God's foes?[78] The "free confession of love and trust is a devastating answer to the accuser and his arsenal of doubts and slanders."[79]

In Wis. Sol. 10.21 wisdom is said to "untie the tongue of the little one." Or does true praise and piety bring God's intervention on behalf of his people? Is praise God's weapon of war or at least last line of defense for his people? This whole line of thinking reminds one of the famous story of when Mother Teresa was crossing from Jordan into Israel, and an Israeli guard at the border asked her if she had any weapons, to which she immediately replied – "Yes. I have my prayer books." In any case, this verse is applied by Jesus to the Hosannas of the children as he enters Jerusalem, and their praise confounds Jesus' enemies. It is possible as well, as S. Terrien suggests, that Paul has these verses in mind when he says in 1 Cor. 1.27 that God has chosen the weak things of this world to confound the things which are mighty.[80]

At v. 4 (in English versions, v. 3), the psalmist begins to reflect on creation, which because of its vastness and beauty causes a sense in us of human insignificance. Notice that only at v. 3 do we hear the individual voice speaking, "when I consider," the rest of the song is a group expression. The psalmist is pondering the significance of his personal insignificance, so to speak in the face of so vast a creation.[81] What kind of God could it be that could make all of this? In view of the size and scope of the universe, what are tiny human beings that God should pay any attention to them? The Hebrew here could be rendered "remember and visit." What kind of God remembers and visits human beings? And yet God *is* mindful of his human creatures, not only caring for them but in fact exalting them to a place of honor.[82] We are told that they are made but a little less (or lower) than *elohim*. Now *elohim* might mean angels (this is how both the Greek OT and Heb. 2.6–8 take it; cf. 1 Sam. 28.13; Ps. 82.1–7) or it might mean God or even gods (plural). It is probably not the latter, since our psalmist recognizes only one God, but like other writers of the OT he does recognize the existence of lesser supernatural beings.

We are told that humankind is bequeathed both glory and the functions of God (though on a lesser scale) – to rule over all of creation.[83] Notice that it is God who is the actor in all these actions ("you made … you put"). We are not talking about human accomplishment

---

[78] See Kraus, *Psalms 1–59*, 181–82.

[79] Derek Kidner, *Psalms 1–72* (TOTC; Downers Grove, IL: InterVarsity Press, 1973) 66–67.

[80] S. Terrien, *The Psalms. Strophic Structure and Theological Commentary* (Grand Rapids, MI: William B. Eerdmans, 2003), 129.

[81] See the telling reflections of P. D. Miller "What Is a Human Being?" in *The Way of the Lord* (Grand Rapids, MI: William B. Eerdmans, 2004), 226–36, particularly the phrase "the significance of our insignificance" is James Mays', quoted by Miller (230).

[82] As Kidner, *Psalms*, 67 points out, the term "mindful" when predicated of God doesn't just mean remembering or bearing in mind, but always imply God's movement toward and taking action in regard to the person or group that has come to mind.

[83] Noticing how Job 7.17 draws on Ps. 8.4, with Job lamenting that his suffering amounts to a loss of glory. Could Paul's "we have all sinned and lack the glory of God" (Rom. 3.23) reflect Ps. 8.4 by way of Job's lament?

or what humans deserve, but rather the plan and gift of God. We were meant and made to be rulers over all the works of God's hands.

As B. Anderson reminds us, this stress on human dominion over creation was a revolutionary doctrine. Other ANE cultures saw the gods as part of nature, and all humans as under the sway of the stars (hence the need for astrology).[84] Yet it is not by recognizing nature as humankind's mother, but rather God as our Father, that human beings come to understand why they are here. Only by God's special revelation through his word do humans learn of their true place and task in life. But the psalmist suggests that everyone can know of the existence of an almighty God simply by observing and reflecting on the creation (cf. Rom. 1.20). Humans are to be God's governors or representatives on earth. "The import of these verses is to impress upon the psalm's singers that within the vast scope of divine wisdom, which created and controls the cosmos, God deigns to treat humanity with incredible dignity and respect."[85] Indeed, amazingly enough God has made creation, or at least the human sphere of creation, our galaxy, our sun, our planet, our environment, so that it will support human life. In that sense, God made creation for us – an astounding fact, but perhaps a little less dumbfounding when one takes into account that the sons of Adam are created in God's image, uniquely so.[86]

Interestingly, this hymn does not remind us that we have taken the great power and privilege granted us by God and often used it to exalt ourselves and serve our own ends. While that is a prevalent theme elsewhere in the Psalter, the focus here is not on how "dominion has become domination; rule has become ruin; subordination in the divine purpose has become subjection to human sinfulness."[87] By contrast, this hymn reminds us of the positive character of being God's image-bearer, but at the same time insists "we can say 'human being' only after we have learned to say 'God'."[88] It can be debated whether the psalmist is reflecting on humankind in its pre-fallen state still crowned with glory and honor, or whether the author has no theology of human fallenness, but surely T. Moritz is right that the links with the Gen. 1 material suggests the former rather than the latter.[89] Notice how the reflections on humans are framed by the insistence at the beginning and end of the psalm that the person with the most excellent name and nature throughout the earth is the biblical God who created it all. "Human dignity enjoys its full stature within the grandeur of divine majesty."[90]

One more thing. Though the translation disguises this, it is Yahweh who is called Lord (*Adonai*) in this psalm. This is not some generic psalm imported into Israelite worship. It is a psalm about how the God of Israel is at one and the same time the Creator of all that is, which is to say, he is the only God (with a capital G) in this universe which he has created.

---

[84] Bernhard Anderson, *Out of the Depths: The Psalms Speak for Us Today* (rev. and exp. edn.; Louisville, MI: Westminster John Knox, 2000), 134–37.

[85] E. Charry, *Psalms 1–50* (Grand Rapids, MI: Brazos Press, 2015), 43.

[86] Miller, "What Is a Human Being?" 230–31.

[87] Mays, *Psalms*, 70.

[88] J. Goldingay, *Psalms*, vol. 1: *Psalms 1–41* (Grand Rapids, MI: Baker Academic, 2006), 161.

[89] T. Moritz, "The Psalms in Ephesians and Colossians," in *The Psalms in the New Testament* (ed. S. Moyise and Maarten J. J. Menken; London: T&T Clark, 2004), 184–87. It may be suggested further, that for the author of Hebrews, who assumes a theology of human fallenness, which Christ has not participated in (see Heb. 4.16), Ps. 8 must have been seen as a discussion of unfallen humanity or else it would not have been applied to Jesus.

[90] Charry, *Psalms 1–50*, 41.

Conclusions

We have roamed far and wide in our discussion of the God who first met Moses at the burning bush in the desert near Mt. Sinai. We have examined texts from the Pentateuch, the Prophets, and the Writings, and what we have discovered is a rather clear consistency of portrait of Yahweh who is both the redeemer of Israel and the creator of all things and beings. This God is all-knowing, all-powerful, and omnipresent. But that is not all. This God is also a God who desires relationship with a people, a God who is fatherlike in his care of his people, who is a God of compassion and mercy who keeps intervening on behalf of a people prone to waywardness, prone to listening to the siren song of a dominant polytheistic environment pulling God's people away into idolatry and immorality, even at the foot of Mt. Sinai, as it turns out.

There is a strong emphasis in this literature on Yahweh's deep concern for justice, righteousness, fair-dealing, and, yes, especial concern for the poor, the needy, the oppressed. This concern for justice runs so deep, that as Amos reminds us, there will one day be a Day of Reckoning when God comes in a theophany to settle accounts. Along the way, there are many opportunities for repentance, for renewal, for redemption, for restoration of a father and child relationship between Yahweh and both a people, and the individuals within the people, though the emphasis is always on the relationship of the corporate group, or singular leaders of the group like a Moses or a king, with Yahweh.

Yes, there is some reflection on how it is possible that human beings have any sort of freedom or independence if Yahweh is the Omni-God that Ps. 139 portrays him to be. The answer seems to be God has created humans in his image, with a modicum of power, including the power of contrary choice. This can lead to sin, but it can also lead to freely chosen living of a life that is pleasing to God in praise of God, or at least to being "reckoned" righteous due to trusting God, as was the case with Abraham. The God of the patriarchs, as it turns out, is not re-created in the image of ancient fallen ANE patriarchy, but rather is called father only occasionally and by analogy to draw attention to God's molding of his people, as well as his creating of them and his compassion for them. *HESED* as we saw refers to God's mercy and kindness to people, but it is not a quality that should be translated "covenant love" not least because it is exhibited by the Rahabs and Ruths of the Bible as well, who have no covenant relationship with Yahweh, no bargain with the Omni-God.

God, beginning in Exod. 3, and then regularly, even to the point of being called "the Holy One of Israel" in Isaiah again and again, is pure, perfect, light, and in him is no darkness at all. His presence is a cleansing and sanctifying presence when encountered by a fallen and sinful person. Even a prophet of Yahweh needs cleansing, as Isa. 6 makes very clear. Redemption, as it turns out, involves not just "justification" but also "sanctification" of God's people. God is not interested in their having merely right understanding of God, he wants them to emulate, to radiate his character. They are to be holy, as God is holy, just as God is just, righteous as God is righteous, merciful as God is merciful, compassionate as God is compassionate. Only so, will justice roll down like waters and righteousness like an ever-flowing stream in human relationships. In other words, God is as concerned with ethics as theology, proof of life, as proof of argumentation, and what he really cannot abide is a kind of worship that ignores the ethical demands made on the lives of the worshippers. Lip service will never do or be accepted without life service.

We will have occasion later in this study to discuss covenants, the love command, and so much more, but we have singularly focused on Yahweh, the God of the burning bush, first, the one true, living God, the one who reveals himself and his character through his actions, who will be what he will be in his redemptive actions for his people. This God is a holy God, who demands a holy and not just a worshipping people. Now we must turn to the King who was his only truly begotten Son, foreshadowed in Ps. 2 – the God of Golgotha.

3

The God of Golgotha

The sorrows of God must be hard to bear,
If he really has love in his heart.
And the hardest part in the world to play
Must surely be God's part.
And I wonder if that's what it really means,
That figure who hangs on the cross
…
I remembers, I thinks, thinks I to myself
It's a long time since he died,
Yet the world don't seem much better to-day
Than when he was crucified.

G. Studdert-Kennedy[1]

Jesus, while hanging on the cross, cried out to the God of the Bible, quoting the beginning of the 22nd Psalm, asking why he had been forsaken. The word God in that quotation of course did not refer to Jesus who was reciting the psalm. It referred to Yahweh, and interestingly this is the only time in our earliest Gospel, Mark (followed closely by Matthew), that Jesus called God something as formal or generic as *Eloi*, or as Matthew has it, *Eli*. Everywhere else, Jesus calls God "Father," or as in Mk. 14 in the garden of Gethsemane, *abba*, Father.

For Jesus, as for all early Jews, the term God meant Yahweh, the one prayed to in the Psalms, written about in the Pentateuch, and the one for whom the prophets were the human mouthpiece, saying "Thus says Yahweh." Had the historical Jesus gone around Galilee and Judaea introducing himself as "God" that would have been taken to mean "I am Yahweh," and that is clearly *not* what Jesus wanted to convey about himself. To the contrary, he wanted to distinguish himself from "the Ancient of Days" by referring to himself in terms of the other prominent figure in Dan. 7.13–14 – the Son of Man. As it

---

[1] G. Studdert Kennedy, "The Sorrow of God," in *The Unutterable Beauty* (London: Hodder and Stoughton, 1927), 133.

turns out, however, the phrase "Son of Man" does not mean a mere human being or the offspring of a human being. In the context of Dan. 7.13–14, it means a good deal more than that, as we shall see, in due course. But it is our first task to examine how Jesus related to Yahweh, how he addressed him, and what we can learn about both Yahweh and Jesus by such an examination.

God as Father in Early Judaism

When we search out examples of father language for God in early Judaism, texts like Wis. Sol. 14.3; Sir. 23.1,4 and 51.10; and 3 Macc. 6.3,8 come to mind.[2] Neither Wisdom of Solomon nor 3 Maccabees was originally composed in Hebrew or Aramaic, but rather in Greek, and so they do not provide us with examples of God being addressed as *ab* or *abba*, but they do reveal to us Jews who used father language to talk about God. Wis. Sol. 14.3 is especially striking because here God is actually addressed as Father. In Sir. 51.10 in the Hebrew we find the use of *abi* not *abba* and in the Greek version of Sir. 23.4 we have the double epithet – *kurie pater*, "Lord Father." What is especially important about the Sirach examples is that God is said to be the Father of individuals, not just of God's people or their king (cf. 10.12; 32.13; 33.13; 47.8).[3] We can as well point to examples in the Qumran literature, for instance 4Q 371 and 372, where God is addressed as *abi* (not *abba*), which means "my father," whereas *abba* seems to be a less formal way of addressing God, though it certainly is not slang. It does not mean "Daddy," as we shall see.[4]

Other texts of relevance from the general period, though likely dated a bit later than the NT period, are BT Taan. 23b; Targ. Ps. 89.27; and Targ. Mal. 2.10, with the first of these being the most crucial. Honi ha Neba was a Jewish sage who lived near the end of the first century BC and BT Taan. 23b records how during a drought some schoolchildren came to him crying out "abba, abba, habh lan mitra," which means "father, father give us rain." After this Honi interceded with God, praying "Master of the world, grant it for the sake of those who are not yet able to distinguish between an *abba* who has power to give rain, and an *abba* who has not." In fact, God is not addressed here as *abba*, rather we have a play on words, or an analogy so characteristic of Jewish wisdom literature. God is addressed as "Master of the world," a formal sort of address. Nonetheless, this text is important because it shows that young children could address a teacher as *abba*, though likely it was more common to use it of a father. Targ. Ps. 89.27 is even more intriguing because here God himself promises the future anointed Davidic king that he will be able to call on God, saying "You are *abba* to me, my God." Though this text likely postdates the time of Jesus, nonetheless it is important because it suggests that a special person, in this case the Messiah, would be allowed in the future to address God as *abba*. This is not a big surprise, since already in the Psalms (cf. Pss. 2.7–9 and 89.19–37) the Davidic king is called God's son, in a special sense.

What we should conclude from the material discussed in the last chapter and this material is that the use of father language for God was not very common in the OT times, but

---

[2] Some of what follows can be found in Witherington and Ice, *The Shadow of the Almighty.*

[3] M. Meye Thompson, *The Promise of the Father: Jesus and God in the New Testament* (Louisville, KY: Westminster John Knox, 2000), 51.

[4] Rightly, James Barr, "Abba Isn't Daddy," *JTS* 39 (1988): 28–47.

seems to be on the way to becoming more common in the post-exilic and early Jewish contexts. It was also true that special individuals, namely a king, for example, might be said to have a more intimate or personal relationship to God, such that the king may be said to be "God's son." There is, however, no clear evidence of God being prayed to as *abba* prior to the time of Jesus. Addressing God as *abi* or "my Father" was a more formal way of speaking. That children or students could use *abba* of a parent or a teacher suggests it could be a term of endearment, suggesting a special relationship, and so less formal that *ab*.

I stand by my conclusions from an earlier study where I said: (1) that we do not find clear evidence of God *prayed to* as *abba* either in the OT or in early Jewish literature outside the NT; (2) we do not find any adequate explanation in earlier Jewish literature for the proliferation of the use of father language for God in the NT, which was almost all written by Jews; (3) we do not find any adequate explanation in that literature as to why there was a dramatic increase of the use of this language from the earliest Gospel, Mark (four references to God as father), to Matthew (which has 30 some references), and especially to John (which has some 120 remarkable uses of father language for God). All of this I think makes clear that the early Jewish *context alone* cannot explain the phenomena we find in the NT when it comes to the use of father or *abba* for God.

The Prayers and Personal Piety of Jesus

It will be remembered that in the last chapter, Seitz was cited as suggesting that what we find in the NT is the seeing of God through the eyes of the Son and on the basis of the Son's relationship to the Father, rather than from the viewpoint of God the Father himself, which is what we find in the OT. It was the special relationship the king or messiah was to have with God that provides some precedent in Ps. 2, for example, for Jesus' usage, and that of his earliest followers. Not surprisingly, early Christians came to believe that one came to the Father through Jesus the Son, and that he mediated the special relationship he had with God to his followers. Jesus did not see himself as Israel, but he did see himself as the Son of Man, the redeemer and final judge of Israel and the world.

The term *abba*, as the Honi example cited above shows, was an intimate way of addressing a parent or a teacher, using *family language*. You have permission to use such language if you are in that sort of personal relationship with the person being addressed. When applied to God, it reflects awareness of a special relationship (for example when a king would use such language of God) and is less formal than addressing God simply as God or Master or the like. J. Jeremias' main point (having revised his earlier suggestion that *abba* could mean "Daddy dearest"), I think still stands, namely that the term reflects an awareness on Jesus' part of having a special relationship with Yahweh.[5]

Some scholars would say that it is impossible to probe the relationship the historical Jesus had with the God named Yahweh, just as it is impossible to know how Jesus understood himself. For instance, did he see himself as the Jewish messiah? I disagree with this assessment, and I have given detailed reasons why in various places, beginning with *The Christology of Jesus*.[6] This particular work is a study of biblical theology and here is not

---

[5] J. Jeremias, *New Testament Theology* (New York: Scribner's, 1971), 67; J. Jeremias, *The Prayers of Jesus* (Minneapolis, MN: Fortress Press, 1967).

[6] Ben Witherington III, *The Christology of Jesus* (Minneapolis, MN: Fortress Press, 1990).

the place to rehearse again the reasons for such conclusion. We must concentrate on their theological implications here.

First of all, Jesus was a man of prayer and deep piety. This is perfectly clear in both the Synoptics and in John's Gospel as well. And few scholars would deny that Jesus also took the time to teach his disciples how to pray a particular prayer, which we call the Lord's Prayer, but might better call "the disciple's prayer." Nevertheless, Mark 14 suggests that *that* prayer was also something Jesus himself prayed, for we find in Mk. 14 not only the addressing of God as *abba*, but also the petition "thy will be done," too. It probably goes without saying, but Jesus was not praying to himself. He was praying in Aramaic to the one he called *abba*. Whether he was *unique* in such prayer language or not, it was *distinctive* enough of his prayer language that it was remembered by the earliest Christians, who also emulated the practice, having been told to do so by Jesus himself (cf. Mt. 6 and Rom. 8). And the language was the language of intimacy, of close personal, even familial relationship. Just how important this is can be seen from the following observations.

Whenever Jesus addresses God in the Gospels he always speaks of God as Father with the one telling example of his prayer on the cross, reciting Ps. 22 (Mk. 15.34). To put matters the other way around, Jesus never addressed God as King or Master or by other terms and circumlocutions familiar to early Jews. Secondly, as Mk. 14.36 suggests, when Jesus was in crisis mode, in the garden of Gethsemane, he earnestly pleaded with God in the most intimate way possible. The prayer as exhibited there indicates that Jesus has such a close relationship with God, that he believes he can ask permission to bypass the cross! This is no ordinary early Jewish prayer. Thirdly, Jesus *alone* is depicted in the Gospels as speaking of God as "my Father," and outside the Gospels the phrase "my Father" occurs solely on the lips of Jesus (Rev. 2.27; 3.5; 3.21). Note that Jesus does not pray with his disciples "our Father," rather he teaches them to do so as part of their corporate or group prayer life.[7] The evidence in Rom. 8.15–16 and Gal. 4.6 suggests that early Christians only began to pray this way as a result of having received the Holy Spirit, the prompter of such intimate prayer.

In other words, there seems to be a distinction to be made between the prayer life of Jesus and that of his disciples, during his earthly ministry. Only Jesus is depicted as actually addressing God as *abba* during his ministry, but when the disciples received the Spirit, they too were enabled and prompted to do so. Here M. Meye Thompson is on the right track in saying:

[A] … plausible hypothesis, in light of the restricted use of Father in Paul and its virtual disappearance in Acts [only in Acts 1.5,8 and 2.33] and other New Testament books, is that the usage was deemed characteristic of Jesus and thus was taken over in continuity with Jesus' own usage. Hence the persistent use of "our Father" and the absence of "my Father" from the rest of the New Testament may suggest that both could be traced back to Jesus, with "our Father" as a form of address commended to his followers and "my Father" limited to Jesus himself.[8]

---

[7] Though even this point may be debated since the Lukan form of the Lord's Prayer simply has the address "Father" (Lk. 11.1). Further, there is a tendency in Matthew to turn personal pronouns into something broader involving more than just an individual, for example at the baptismal scene while Matthew is drawing on Mark who has "you are my beloved Son" (Mk. 1.11), Matthew has the public declaration "this is my beloved Son" (Mt. 3.17).

[8] Thompson, *The Promise of the Father*, 65.

For those concerned about multiple attestation issues, note that "Father" is used for God in Mark, Q, M, and L. In some of this material, particularly the important saying in Mt. 11.25–27; Lk. 10.21–22, the intimacy of the Father–Son relationship is stressed. They share knowledge that others do not have *unless the Son dispenses it*. In Mk. 8.38 the Son of Man is said to come in the glory of his Father, which is to say in the living presence of his Father. In other words, there are strong hints in the tradition not only that Jesus regularly addressed God as his Father, reflecting his intimate relationship with Yahweh, but that he distinguished his relationship with God, to some extent, from that of his disciples.

Another helpful aspect of Jeremias' study is the emphasis on the eschatological context in which we should read Jesus' language. "In Jesus' eyes, being a child of God is not a gift of creation, but an eschatological gift of salvation."[9] Here it is apposite to mention Jer. 31.9, where God laments the broken relationship between God and Israel, a relationship which if healthy should have led them to call God Father. In other words, Jesus is not just perpetuating the small amount of previous Jewish usage of father language for God. He is convinced that that relationship needs to be restored, or newly given to Israel, which we can see played out at length in the famous drama in Jn. 3, where Jesus tells even Nicodemus he needs to start over with God, he needs to be born again, spiritually speaking. Jesus was bringing this new possibility of an intimate relationship with Yahweh, through his own person and ministry. Further, I take it that this is the point of the theologizing in Jn. 1.12–13. People are not born "children of God" though they are all created in God's image. No, they become sons and daughters of God when they become born of God, born again. Some scholars have complained that this is making an awful lot out of only a little evidence that Jesus addressed God as Abba, and taught his disciples to do so. Perhaps an analogy will help. If one makes the trip to Arizona to see the enormous meteor crater there, what remains is only small actual traces of the meteoric rock that made that crater. But the size of the crater itself, clearly bears witness to the original size of the meteor. Though the evidence of Jesus' use of *abba* in the Gospels is not plentiful, nevertheless, its importance can be judged by its impact on his earliest followers, including Paul himself, who was converted within a few years of the death of Jesus. And since he was not one of the original disciples, he must have gotten this understanding of Jesus' prayer language from some of the pillar apostles mentioned in Gal. 1–2, perhaps particularly Peter, whom he consulted with. We must turn now to another aspect of Jesus' self-understanding and relationship with God.

Jesus as the Son of Man

It often amazes me that some scholars seem to think you can do a biblical theology without dealing with the theology of Jesus himself, as if just dealing with the theologies of the biblical books was sufficient. But as we have already been intimating, it is more than a little important to understand Jesus's view of Yahweh if we want to do justice to the issue of biblical theology. And one of the keys to approaching that subject is to consider Jesus' preferred form of self-reference, the odd phrase ὁ υἱός τοῦ ἀνθρώπου. The phrase is odd for a variety of reasons. The first of these is the use of the third person to refer to oneself. Most

---

[9] Jeremias, *New Testament Theology*, 181.

people, including most ancients, didn't and don't do that. Secondly, there is the use of the definite article, which definitely must mean something.

Why *the* Son of Man? If Jesus was just using the phrase to mean "a person like me," or "a mere human being" we certainly would not need the definite article. No, the definite article alludes back to something or someone, and as C. F. D. Moule suggested long ago, it likely means "the aforementioned" or "the well-known" "Son of Man."[10] Who is this aforementioned someone? If we work through a process of elimination, it should be noticed that Jesus does not call himself υἱός τοῦ Ἀδάμ, son of Adam. This is in fact what Ezekiel is called in the book that bears his name. Of course, in its Hebrew form it is *ben Adam*. Although Jesus surely spoke in Aramaic, I do not think he used the Aramaic form of the name "Adam" to refer to himself, although it's not impossible, in view of the fact that Paul seems to like suggesting Christ was "the last Adam" (cf. 1 Cor. 15 and Rom. 5). No, the most likely referent for the phrase "the Son of Man" found on the lips of Jesus which refers to "the aforementioned Son of Man" is the Aramaic phrase *bar enasha* referring to one "like a son of man" coming into the presence of the Ancient of Days, who is surely Yahweh under a different name.

There were a variety of thoughts about the coming Jewish messiah in Jesus' day, most of them taking into account 2 Sam. 7.12–16, where God promises descendants to David who will rule, descendants in the first case including Solomon, of course. Jesus, for his part, avoids this text when he refers to himself, and when a Davidic text is brought up by him for discussion, the implication is that it is not enough to say that the Lord's anointed is David's son. No, he is – according to Ps. 110.1 – David's Lord (see Mk. 12.35–37). We are by now very familiar with the Qumran affirmation that there will be both a priestly and a royal messianic figure coming, and we also have Ps. Sol. 17, which is worth quoting at some length here.

You, O Lord, chose David (to be) king over Israel, and swore to him concerning his descendants forever that never should his kingdom fail before you. 5 But, for our sins, sinners rose up against us; they assailed us and thrust us out. What you had not promised to them, they took away (from us) with violence. They in no way glorified your honorable name. 6 They set a monarchy in place of (that which was) their excellency; they laid waste the throne of David in tumultuous arrogance. 7 But you, O God, cast them down and removed their descendants from the earth, in that there rose up against them a man that was alien to our race. 8 According to their sins did you recompense them, O God; so that it befell them according to their deeds. 9 God showed them no pity; he sought out their seed and let not one of them go free. 10 Faithful is the Lord in all his judgments, which he makes upon the earth. 11 The lawless one laid waste our land so that no one inhabited it; they destroyed young and old and their children together. 12 In his blameless anger he sent them away to the west, and (he exposed) the rulers of the land unsparingly to derision. 13 Being an alien the enemy acted proudly, and his heart was alien from our God. 14 And all things whatsoever he did in Jerusalem, as also the gentiles (do) in the cities to their gods. 15 And the children of the covenant in the midst of the mingled peoples surpassed them in evil. There was not among them one that performed mercy and truth in the midst of Jerusalem. 16 They who loved the assemblies of the pious fled from them, as sparrows that fly from their nest. 17 They wandered in deserts in order that their lives might be saved from harm, and precious in the eyes of them who lived abroad was any that escaped alive from them. 18 Over the whole earth were they scattered by lawless men. 19 For the heavens withheld the rain from dropping upon the earth; springs were stopped (that sprang) perennially out of the deeps, (that ran down) from lofty mountains. For there was none among them who did righteousness and justice.

---

10 C. F. D. Moule, *An Idiom Book of the Greek New Testament* (Cambridge: Cambridge University Press, 1959).

[20] From the leader of them to the least (of them) all were sinful. The king was a transgressor, and the judge disobedient, and the people sinful. [21] Behold, O Lord, and raise up unto them their king, the son of David, at the time known to you, O God, in order that he may reign over Israel your servant. [22] And gird him with strength, that he may shatter unrighteous rulers, and that he may purge Jerusalem from gentiles who trample (her) down to destruction. [23] Wisely, righteously he shall thrust out sinners from (the) inheritance; he shall destroy the arrogance of the sinner as a potter's jar. [24] With a rod of iron he shall shatter all their substance; he shall destroy the godless nations with the word of his mouth. [25] At his rebuke nations shall flee before him, and he shall reprove sinners for the thoughts of their heart. [26] And he shall gather together a holy people, whom he shall lead in righteousness, and he shall judge the tribes of the people who has been made holy by the Lord his God. [27] And he shall not suffer unrighteousness to lodge any more in their midst, nor shall there dwell with them any man who knows wickedness, for he shall know them, that they are all sons of their God. [28] And he shall divide them according to their tribes upon the land, and neither sojourner nor alien shall dwell with them anymore. [29] He shall judge peoples and nations in the wisdom of his righteousness. Selah. [30] And he shall have the gentile nations to serve him under his yoke; and he shall glorify the Lord in a place prominent (above) all the earth. And he shall purge Jerusalem, making it holy as of old. [31] So that nations shall come from the ends of the earth to see his glory, bringing as gifts her sons who had been driven out, and to see the glory of the Lord, wherewith God has glorified her. [32] And he will be a righteous king over them, taught of God. And there shall be no unrighteousness in his days in their midst, for all shall be holy and their king the Lord Messiah. [33] For he shall not put his trust in horse and rider and bow, nor shall he multiply for himself gold and silver for war, nor shall he gather confidence from a multitude for the day of battle. [34] The Lord Himself is his king, the hope of him who is mighty through (his) hope in God. He shall be compassionate to all nations who (shall be) in fear before him. [35] He will smite the earth with the word of his mouth forever. He will bless the people of the Lord with wisdom and gladness, [36] and he himself (will be) pure from sin, so that he may rule a great people. He will rebuke rulers, and remove sinners by the might of his word; [37] and (relying) upon his God, throughout his days he will not stumble. For God will make him mighty by means of (His) holy spirit, and wise by means of the spirit of understanding, with strength and righteousness. [38] And the blessing of the Lord (will be) with him: he will be strong and stumble not; [39] his hope (will be) in the Lord: who then can prevail against him? [40] (He will be) mighty in his works, and strong in the fear of God, [45] (He will be) shepherding the flock of the Lord faithfully and righteously, and will suffer none among them to stumble in their pasture.[11]

(Cf. similarly Ps. Sol. 18.37; 1 Qsa. 2.12–20; CD 12.23–24; 14.19; 19.10; 20.1.)

While there is room for debate about the date and provenance of this passage, in all likelihood it comes from well before the fall of Jerusalem in AD 70, and after the exhilaration and then the disappointments of the Maccabean and post-Maccabean eras. Clearly, in this passage a Davidic messiah is envisioned as like David himself in that he will use military might to shatter his foes, whether unrighteous Gentiles or wicked Jews. While this may not have been the dominant expectation among Jews looking for a messiah in Jesus' day, it certainly was a natural and prominent one, and for our purposes what is important is to say that Jesus wanted to avoid any associations with that sort of tradition. Using the mysterious and apocalyptic phrase from Daniel allowed him to carve out his own niche among the messianic pretenders and contenders.

Among the more important points that R. J. Bauckham has made about the monolatry of early Jews is that the issue here at the end of the day is: (1) who shares God's throne and rule and (2) who is the proper object of worship. Even the greatest of angels do not share in God's throne or rule (cf. Dan. 7.10; Tob. 12.15; 4 Q530 2.18; 1 En. 14.22; 39.12;

---

[11] The translation is mine.

40.1; 47.3; 60.2; 2 En. 21.1; 2 Bar. 21.6). They are servants of God, not co-rulers, or co-creators with God.[12] While there are a few early Jewish texts where angels are venerated, the NT at least is clear enough that worship or veneration of angels is inappropriate (cf. Rev. 22.8–9 and 1.17 and Col. 2.18). "Jews understood their practice of monolatry to be justified, indeed required, because the unique identity of YHWH was so understood as to place him, not merely at the summit of a hierarchy of divinity but in an absolutely unique category, beyond comparison with anything else."[13]

The only apparent exception to this rule is found in some of the Son of Man traditions, beginning with 1 En. 61.8; 62.2,5; 69.27,29. Here the Son of Man is said to exercise judgment on God's behalf having been seated on God's throne! And rather clearly, at 1 En. 46.5; 48.5; 62.6,9, he is worshipped. This theology seems surely to have been generated from a reflecting on Dan. 7.13–14 and its implications. And I would submit that Jesus himself interpreted his own mission and ministry out of Dan. 7.13–14. What that text says is that the Son of Man is not only to come to judge the earth, he is to be worshipped by the people of the earth, and he is to rule forever, or put another way, his kingdom, unlike the Davidic monarchy, is to last forever. Notice that in Dan. 7 there is no talk about a series of kings, or dynastic succession. No, in Daniel, quite in contrast to 2 Sam. 7, we are talking about a singular person, personally ruling forever. The author of 1 Enoch seems to have understood this implication rather clearly and there is no reason Jesus could not have done so as well. What this would mean is that Jesus saw himself as part of the divine identity, delegated by Yahweh to judge, to rule, and to be worshipped, and to be seated on the throne that only God should sit on.

Bauckham, in my judgment, is quite right, that later Christian theologians made a muddle of things when they began to distinguish between ontology and matters of function. Such later Greek categories are not all that helpful in analyzing early Jewish statements about God, including those of Jesus and Paul. Reading such a distinction into the NT material is anachronistic and confuses the matter because "the unique sovereignty of God was not a mere 'function' which God could delegate to someone else. It was one of the key identifying characteristics of the unique divine identity, which distinguished the one God from all other reality. The unique divine sovereignty is a matter of *who God is*," not merely what he does.[14] Thus to predicate of Jesus certain divine activities is not merely to claim that he functions in divine ways. It implies that he shares in the divine identity, because early Jews believed that only Yahweh could create, redeem, or judge the world in any ultimate sense of these terms. Unlike later reflections on divinity at the Council of Nicaea and Chalcedon, the concern in early Jewish monotheism was not with *what* divinity is (divine nature) but rather with *who* Yahweh is, the unique and only true God. In short, the issue is divine identity.

Now as both 1 Enoch and also 4 Ez. 13 attest, Daniel was clearly one of the most popular books in early Judaism, including when reflection on the messiah was the issue. It is more than a little intriguing that Josephus himself tells us that it was widely believed during the Roman Empire, and on the basis of some Jewish prophecy, that a major king or ruler would come out of the East, a notion which Josephus, in a stroke of genius, applied

---

[12] Bauckham, *God Crucified*, 13.
[13] *Ibid.*, 15.
[14] *Ibid.*, 41.

to Vespasian himself, saving his own skin during the Jewish war (*Ant.* 10.267–68). I doubt it is accidental that Josephus deliberately omits any direct discussion of Dan. 7.13–14 in his works. After the debacle of the Jewish war in AD 66–72 he did not want to draw attention to earlier Jewish messianic hopes for a Jewish ruler.

If we consider for a moment the context of Dan. 7, several things come to light: (1) this "one like a son of man" is unlikely to be an angel (but see Dan. 8.5–16; 10.16), because the context suggests that the Son of Man figure is one who has suffered like God's people, and so they could identify with him, unlike angels, who, while being God's messengers, have not suffered with God's people; (2) nor does it seem likely "Son of Man" here is simply a cipher for God's people in general (but see Dan. 7.27), because the Son of Man's dominion is being compared to the previous beastly empires described in Dan. 6–7, and in each case the beast has a head, a ruler (cf. 7.27 and 8.21), who runs the empire. The Son of Man is seen not as a group, but as a ruler of a group of worshippers, a king who rules over a kingdom. In both 1 En. 37ff. and 4 Ezra the son of man figure is an individual ruler figure; (3) Dan. 7.13–14 contrasts a human and humane empire of the Son of Man with the beastly and inhumane ones that have preceded it.

One must ask, what sort of person is both like and unlike a human being? Both human and yet so transcendent that God can hand over his throne and functions to this person? While it is often argued that Jews were not conjuring with the possibility of a divine messiah, the speculations in 1 En. 37–71 and 4 Ezra could be said to point to a more than merely mortal figure, not just another descendant of David. It will be remembered that in the Enoch literature, it is Enoch himself who is finally told that he is the Son of Man in question. Clearly, he is not a "son of David." All of this prepares us to consider the use of the phrase Son of Man in the NT including on the lips of Jesus himself.

This phrase occurs a remarkable 81 times in the Gospels, 69 of which are in the Synoptics. *All but three of these instances are on the lips of Jesus himself*, the exceptions being Mk. 2.10, Lk. 24.7, and Jn. 12.34, and I am not at all sure that Mk. 2.10 is an exception. In addition, the phrase is found only three times outside the Gospels (Acts 7.56; Rev. 1.13; 14.14). Within the Gospels it occurs in every layer of the Gospel material – Mark, Q, M, L, and John. The case that this phrase was used repeatedly by Jesus to refer to himself but by contrast was not a phrase his followers were much drawn to, to describe or name him in the earliest days of the Jesus movement, is a very strong one, not least because the phrase is totally absent in our earliest NT documents – the letters of Paul. Perhaps the enigmatic quality of this apocalyptic phrase made its resonances impenetrable to Gentiles who did not know Daniel, and for whom the phrase might be taken to be innocuous. Their reaction to the phrase might be rather like that of some modern scholars who assume it just means "the human one."[15] They might say, "well of course Jesus of Nazareth was a human being. That goes without saying." But the very fact that Jesus kept using it means it is unlikely to have that sort of mundane meaning which would have "gone without saying." The latter would be the natural reaction to the phrase itself, taken out of its Danielic context.

It was certainly not impenetrable to a Jewish follower of Jesus at the end of the first century, namely John of Patmos, who was saturated in the OT Scriptures, and especially

---

[15] For example, the CEB translation of Mk. 2.10.

in the prophetic books. His use of the phrase at Rev. 1.13 and 14.14 shows he knows that the phrase comes from Dan. 7 and refers to a divine figure. In Rev. 14.14 the Son of Man sits on a cloud with a crown on his head and a sickle in hand as the royal grim reaper, the judge of all the earth. The portrait is of someone who partakes in the divine identity.

At this juncture, it will be appropriate to note: (1) that we are told in these various Son of Man sayings that the Son of Man has the authority to forgive sins (and as his interlocutors rightly ask, who can do that but God alone [Mk. 2.10]); (2) according to Lk. 9.44b the Son of Man will be delivered over into the hands of human beings to suffer and be killed; (3) Mk. 10.45 indicates that the Son of Man came to be a servant of human beings and to give his life as a ransom for the many. This saying seems to combine some material from Dan. 7 and from Isa. 52–53 especially; (4) the Son of Man at some juncture is homeless (Mt. 8.20/Lk. 9.58). He partakes of the sufferings of his oppressed people. The Son of Man phrase comes up in a variety of contexts speaking about a variety of aspects of Jesus' life and ministry, words and work.

For our purposes, it is important to focus on Mk. 14.61–62 from the Jewish trial. Here the echoes of Dan. 7 seem very clear indeed. Jesus seems to respond in the affirmative to the question are you the Christ, the Son of the blessed? But it is not such a claim as this that need be seen as blasphemy. Most Jews seem to have believed that the messiah would be like David, a mere, but special, mortal. It might be crazy to claim to be messiah, but it wouldn't be blasphemy. No, the blasphemy comes when Jesus says "and you will see the Son of Man coming on the clouds to judge you." Here Jesus seems to be usurping the role that only God can play, as the judge of all the earth. And, of course, Jesus is turning the tables on those who thought they were judging him. Jesus is not satisfied with a messianism that stops with the Davidic notions and does not go on to talk about the Son of Man in Dan. 7, which refers to a human and yet more than human figure who will bring in the Kingdom of God once and for all upon the earth and be worthy of worship.[16]

We have quite deliberately started our discussion in this chapter with the material that is of direct relevance to Jesus's own piety and self-understanding. What this material suggests is that Jesus, whether early on, or as a result of the revelation at his baptism, or during the earliest days of his ministry, came to view himself as the Son of Man figure referred to in Dan. 7. He believed his job was to bring God's saving and judging final reign to earth, both in the present and in the future, and he believed he would be seated on God's throne and be worshipped by human beings. As such he saw himself as part of the divine identity, but not as the person that in the OT bore the name of Yahweh. He viewed himself as human but more than human, and in either case not simply Yahweh. He saw himself, as we shall see next, as the Son of Yahweh, as well as the Son of Man.

One of the things that is at the bedrock of the Jesus tradition is the conclusion of scholars that Jesus actually was crucified for the crime of high treason, crucified for claiming to be, either directly or by implication, the "King of the Jews," a claim that would be taken to be a direct challenge of either the rule of Herod Antipas in Galilee, or the more direct rule of Rome in the province of Judaea. According to the *titulus* on the cross, written in three languages, Jesus was crucified as *basileus/melek/rex* not as *christos/masiah/christus*. In other words, the charge was a political one with religious implications, not a religious

---

[16] On this and more, see Witherington and Ice, *The Shadow of the Almighty*, 70–82.

one with possible political implications. How Jesus ended up on the cross with that charge has been endlessly debated by scholars, but at the end of the day, the vast majority of them end up agreeing with John Collins when he says:

Herein lies the anomaly of the messianic claims of Jesus of Nazareth. That he was crucified "King of the Jews" cannot be doubted. The claim to Davidic kingship also figures prominently in early Christian sources. The title *christos*, messiah, is treated as a virtual name by Paul. It is unlikely that Jesus' followers would have given him such a politically inflammatory title after his death if it had no basis in life ... The messianic identity of Jesus must be grounded in some way before his crucifixion.[17]

This is right on target, which means that one cannot do biblical theology without raising and answering various historical questions, at least when it comes to the views of the historical Jesus. Theology too often gets abstracted from its historical context and roots, but this is forgetting that we are dealing with a historical religion, a religion that is based on God's activity in human history, not on abstract speculation about God. It is also a religion based in a profound belief in God's self-revelation in words and deeds in human history. That is precisely why one has to talk about the before and after of the progressive revelation of God, his character, his redemptive work, and so on.

Doing biblical theology is not an exercise in pushing theological ideas around a pre-existing theological playing board. It is also not an exercise in reading later theological ideas back into the biblical text, for instance the idea of the later distinction between God's being and his doing, or the later fuller description of the Holy Trinity. What I have said thus far should already make clear that I think that the raw data for the construction of a theology of the Trinity can be found in the Bible, but that articulation is not already present *in detail* in the Bible. And so the person doing biblical theology, or trying to discern the theology in the Bible, must be satisfied with some incomplete answers, some partial conclusions that will and do require further amplification, pursuing the same trajectory but going further than we find *expressis verbis* in the Bible itself.

Some titles were surely applied to Jesus during his ministry, that he himself did not use or favor. Bearing in mind the passage about David and Ps. 110.1 in Mk. 12, it is in order to note that the precise phrase "son of David" is apparently not attested before Ps. Sol. 17.23, but there is evidence from Qumran (4QFlor. 1.11–13), where the promise to David in 2 Sam. 7 is interpreted in light of Amos 9.11 (cf. CD 7.16 and BT San. 96B).[18] Jesus is not the first to cite Ps. 110 messianically and eschatologically if 11QMelch comes from before his day. But Jesus does think the Davidic tradition in itself has been read in inadequate ways. Here we can mention that *the* Son of David, by which I mean Solomon, was believed in Jesus' day to have been given the wisdom of cures, including the wisdom for exorcisms as well as normal healings, and so when for example Blind Bartimaeus cries out to "Jesus 'son of David' have mercy on me," he is speaking on the basis of that Solomonic tradition and asking for mercy. David himself was not viewed that way in the tradition.[19] But Jesus

---

[17] John J. Collins, *The Scepter and the Star: The Messiahs of the Dead Sea Scrolls and Other Ancient Literature* (New York: Doubleday, 1995), 204.

[18] See the still useful older study by D. Flusser, "Two Notes on the Midrash on 2 Sam. 7.1," *IEJ* 9 (1959): 99–109.

[19] On the portrayal of Jesus as a sage and as Wisdom come in the flesh in Matthew and John, see Ben Witherington III, *Jesus the Sage: The Pilgrimage of Wisdom* (Minneapolis, MN: Fortress Press, 2000).

himself doesn't make much of the Son of David connection, unlike say Matthew in Mt. 1–2, who connects him to David through his step father Joseph.

If we wish to probe a bit further into Jesus' own self-understanding and self-presentation, we need to turn to the evidence that Jesus had visions. Here I am not merely talking about when Jesus says "I saw Satan fall like lightning from heaven" (Lk. 10.18) but to his visionary experience at his baptism, and then at his temptation in the wilderness scene. The baptismal scene in our earliest Gospel, in Mk. 1.9–11, is clearly portrayed as involving a vision. The rending of the heavens is a common feature of apocalyptic, the underlying idea being that of a fixed separation between heaven and earth, broken in certain circumstances and conditions by God when God wishes to reveal something not generally known (cf. Apoc. Bar. 22.1; Test. Levi 2.6; 5.1; 18.6; Test. Jud. 24.2; Rev. 4.1; 11.19; 19.11). Notice as well that the voice in Mark speaks to Jesus alone. This is a private experience and revelation, which Matthew in Mt. 3.16–17 has turned into a public announcement, not unlike the even later presentation in John's Gospel.

In Mark, it is only Jesus who is said to see the Spirit descend. Nothing at all is said about receiving the Spirit through the ritual of baptism. Rather, it is just after or while Jesus comes up out of the water that the Spirit descends and the voice of God is heard. Here there is a clear echo of Isa. 64.1, where the prophet prays that the heavens will be rent and God will come down so the mountains might quake at God's presence. In other words, Mark is suggesting this is an earth-shattering event. Jesus is anointed by the very presence and power of God, and so equipped for his ministry, which will be undertaken by means of the power of the Spirit. While this is, at the outset, derived power and authority, it becomes inherent thereafter such that people recognize that Jesus has power and authority independent of any human authorities (Mk. 1.27).

Mk. 1.11 is a composite Scripture citation involving both Ps. 2.7 and Isa. 42.1. The upshot is that Jesus is informed, or better said has confirmed to him, that there is a special relationship between God and his beloved Son, and that Jesus is indeed that Son. The word *agapetos* means literally "beloved" but it often bears the connotation "only" or "unique" (see e.g. Gen. 22.2 and the story of Abraham and Isaac).[20] As God's Son, God's special favor and God's Spirit rest upon Jesus, equipping him for ministry. Jesus must have confirmation of who he is, and be empowered before he is prepared for both testing and ministry.[21] Later Christian theologians would quite rightly see here a scene that involved what came to be called the Trinity. Origen, for instance says the Father bore witness, the Son received witness, and the Spirit gave confirmation and empowerment (*Contra Celsum* 2.72). It may be this story which led in due course to a Trinitarian formula for Christian baptism (see Mt. 28).[22]

The temptation story, in cursory form, is mentioned in Mark, but we get a full-dress presentation of that story in both Mt. 4 and Lk. 4. In all cases, this is a story about a vision

---

[20] One wonders if the fact that Yahweh is called unique *'ehad* in the Shema, is echoed in the NT when Jesus is called "unique" or *monogenes*.

[21] On this passage, see Witherington, *Christology of Jesus*, 148–55.

[22] In all probability, the reason we also hear about baptism in or into the name of Jesus, for instance in the early chapters of Acts, is because in the early days it was simply Jews who were being baptized, and Jews already believed in Yahweh of course, so the new affirmation had to do not with believing in God the Father, but in adding to that a belief in Jesus the Son. On this see Ben Witherington III, *The Acts of the Apostles: A Socio-Rhetorical Study* (Grand Rapids, MI: William B. Eerdmans, 1996).

Jesus had while fasting and praying in the Judean desert regions. Jesus is in a liminal state, and he receives a vision of Satan, who engages in an honor challenge with Jesus. What we need to notice about this honor challenge, or test/temptation is that these are hardly normal human temptations. While I have known human beings who can turn bread into stones, I've never met a sane person who was tempted to try and turn stones into bread. That is simply not a normal human temptation, nor are the other two temptations ordinary. Indeed, we have to pay close attention to what Satan says, namely "if you are the Son of God, then ..." Now this is precisely what God has just or recently confirmed to Jesus in baptism. He is God's beloved Son, God from God, God's only begotten One, and so part of the divine identity. God is, in some not fully delineated sense, quite literally Jesus' Father. It is enough to say he is part of the divine identity. So the main temptation he is experiencing is a temptation to draw on his divine identity in such a way that he obliterates his true humanity.

For Jesus to be truly human, as well as part of the divine identity, he needed to partake of all the natural limitations of being human – limitations of time, space, knowledge, power, and mortality. He was also, according to Heb. 4.15, tempted like us in all respects save without sin. Sin is not a natural human limitation, it is one acquired due to our fallenness, and Jesus does not participate in our fallenness, though he does experience our temptations. And indeed, he is experiencing temptations we do not have, temptations only a "divine" person could have – temptations to turn stones into bread, temptations to use divine power gratuitously and call on one's posse of angels, temptations to make a Faustian bargain to obtain the rulership of this world by bowing down and worshiping the temporary "ruler of this world" who is about to be judged, not to mention the temptation faced in Gethsemane to bypass the cross! Those are temptations only the sinless Son of God might face, tests that only he could pass.

Put colloquially, Jesus' temptation in the wilderness was to push the God button, which he indeed did have; the temptation was to call on his divine identity, which no other human being could do. He resists this temptation, and it will be noted that he relies on the same two resources to do so available to his disciples – the Word of God and the Spirit of God. Notice as well, that Jesus *doesn't* respond to Satan as follows, "I am God; God can't be tempted; ergo away with you Satan!" No, he responds in his humanity, while at the same time being "the Son of God," the only person who could actually do the things he is tempted to do in the wilderness. We will say much more about this "divine condescension" of the Son in order to be truly human, while not giving up his divine identity, when we discuss Paul's Christ hymn in Phil. 2.5–11.

The Relationship of Father and Son Together

Mt. 11.25–27 has already been mentioned, and here we notice that it comports nicely with the notion that Jesus had visions. Jesus is here talking about having a sort of knowledge of God that only an insider would have, indeed, only a child would have of a parent, and vice versa. Some scholars called this saying "the Johannine thunderbolt" and suggested that it is out of character with the Synoptic portrayal of Jesus. This is not so, if one takes into consideration the intimacy Jesus indicated he had with Abba, both in his prayer life and in his visionary experiences, especially the one at his baptism. What the saying also conveys is not merely an exclusive intimate knowledge of God, but, interestingly, a knowledge Jesus can and does share with others. Jesus is no Gnostic, reserving the knowledge of God for the brilliant. He is the mediator of that knowledge to perfectly ordinary people – fishermen, tax collectors, women, and men.

This saying does indeed comport with the portrait of the relationship of Jesus to the Father in the Fourth Gospel in various respects. Though, on the one hand, the Son is clearly portrayed as God in Jn. 1, he is also portrayed in that Gospel as completely dependent on his relationship with the Father. He can only act on the Father's go-ahead, even when a dear friend is in jeopardy of dying (i.e. Lazarus in Jn. 11). He receives revelation, instructions, and more from the Father, and if we note the conversations he has with Yahweh in Jn. 11 and 17, these are no ordinary conversations. Jesus does not merely formally pray, following some rote pattern to address God, he actually has a conversation with the Almighty. And he tells us that the Father always listens to him, listens and responds. For example, we read in Jn. 11: "Jesus looked up and said, 'Father, I thank you that you have heard me. I knew that you always hear me, but I said this for the benefit of the people standing here, that they may believe that you sent me'." Jesus is the first *parakletos*, the Counselor or Advocate/Agent sent from God, sent to reveal the real character and saving plan of God to humanity. Then in Jn. 17 we hear:

After Jesus said this, he looked toward heaven and prayed:

"Father, the hour has come. Glorify your Son, that your Son may glorify you. 2 For you granted him authority over all people that he might give eternal life to all those you have given him. 3 Now this is eternal life: that they know you, the only true God, and Jesus Christ, whom you have sent. 4 I have brought you glory on earth by finishing the work you gave me to do. 5 And now, Father, glorify me in your presence with the glory I had with you before the world began.

6 "I have revealed you to those whom you gave me out of the world. They were yours; you gave them to me and they have obeyed your word. 7 Now they know that everything you have given me comes from you. 8 For I gave them the words you gave me and they accepted them. They knew with certainty that I came from you, and they believed that you sent me. 9 I pray for them. I am not praying for the world, but for those you have given me, for they are yours. 10 All I have is yours, and all you have is mine. And glory has come to me through them. 11 I will remain in the world no longer, but they are still in the world, and I am coming to you. Holy Father protect them by the power of your name, the name you gave me, so that they may be one as we are one. 12 While I was with them, I protected them and kept them safe by that name you gave me. None has been lost except the one doomed to destruction so that Scripture would be fulfilled.

13 "I am coming to you now, but I say these things while I am still in the world, so that they may have the full measure of my joy within them. 14 I have given them your word and the world has hated them, for they are not of the world any more than I am of the world. 15 My prayer is not that you take them out of the world but that you protect them from the evil one. 16 They are not of the world, even as I am not of it. 17 Sanctify them by the truth; your word is truth. 18 As you sent me into the world, I have sent them into the world. 19 For them I sanctify myself, that they too may be truly sanctified.

20 "My prayer is not for them alone. I pray also for those who will believe in me through their message, 21 that all of them may be one, Father, just as you are in me and I am in you. May they also be in us so that the world may believe that you have sent me. 22 I have given them the glory that you gave me, that they may be one as we are one – 23 I in them and you in me – so that they may be brought to complete unity. Then the world will know that you sent me and have loved them even as you have loved me.

24 "Father, I want those you have given me to be with me where I am, and to see my glory, the glory you have given me because you loved me before the creation of the world.

[25] "Righteous Father, though the world does not know you, I know you, and they know that you have sent me. [26] I have made you known to them and will continue to make you known in order that the love you have for me may be in them and that I myself may be in them."

Without question, what we have in John is the sapiential reformulation of various aspects of the Jesus tradition, in the Beloved Disciple's own diction and for a later audience.[23] This explains why there is such a difference in diction between most of this Gospel and most of the Synoptics. But what these texts do attest to, and provide multiple attestation for, is what we've already seen in the Synoptics – Jesus has an intimate communication and communion with the Father, whom he depends upon in all things, and for all things. This comports with the portrait of Jesus as a visionary, and one with an intimate prayer life that the Synoptics already depict. Something is going on here that goes beyond ordinary pious relationships with God, not least in the extraordinary mission that Jesus sees himself as called to, not merely making disciples, but giving his life as a ransom for the many.

My point in stressing all this is that the later Christological developments of the portrait of Christ in Paul, in the first instance, and elsewhere in the NT and beyond, are not developments *away from* or in contradiction to what is already there in the historical Jesus tradition. Whether one thinks that Jesus was right or wrong about himself, it is clear enough that he saw himself as in a very unique relationship with God, and on a very unique life mission. He saw himself as both the Son of Man and the Son of God, called upon to not merely reveal God to those in darkness looking for a little light, but to redeem those in darkness from that darkness. Jesus is not just the revealer in these texts, he is the redeemer as well. And at one point, God himself intervenes to make clear to the inner circle of Jesus exactly how they should view him. Here is yet another visionary experience, but in this case one shared with three disciples.

We Have Seen His Glory

We will start this part of our discussion by looking at what may in fact be a first-hand account of the event that came to be called the transfiguration. It is found in perhaps the latest of all NT books, 2 Peter, and here is what it says. It will be worthwhile to go into considerable detail at this juncture.

For we have not followed cleverly concocted myths (when) we made known to you the power and *parousia* of our Lord, Jesus Christ, but we have been made eyewitness of his majesty. For he received from God the Father honor and glory when a voice came to him in such as that from the Majestic Glory (i.e. God); "This is my son, my beloved, in whom I am well pleased ..." And we ourselves were hearing this voice which came from heaven, being with him on the holy mountain.

One of the small indicators of the character of the rhetoric here is that while Peter uses the term "revelation" to refer to the second coming in 1 Peter, here he uses the term *parousia* or royal arrival/visit (see 1 Thess. 2.19). The emphasis here is on the appearing of the glorious king in the future as he appeared in the past on the Mt. of Transfiguration. Beginning in v. 16b Peter rebuts a false charge. Not only had he not followed myths, he

---

[23] On all this and the wisdom orientation of this Gospel, see Ben Witherington III, *John's Wisdom: A Commentary on the Fourth Gospel* (Louisville, KY: Westminster John Knox, 1995).

had made known to his audience the power and *parousia* of the Lord. Probably here as elsewhere in this discourse we have a hendiadys meaning "powerful coming" or "coming in power," instead of two separate matters. Far from concocting myths, Peter and other apostles had been eyewitnesses of and about the transfiguration.

The word *epoptai* is a crucial one, meaning literally "observers" or "spectators." It is not found elsewhere in the NT, but note that we have its verbal cognate at 1 Pet. 2.12 and 3.2, another little piece of positive evidence that we should see 2 Pet. 1.12–21 as a Petrine fragment.[24] Notably in 1 Pet. 2.12, it refers to being witnesses/spectators of a believer's good deeds, but this is connected to glorifying God at Christ's *parousia*, a clear connection to our present text. Further, this terminology is used nowhere else in the whole NT in any form of the word, so the connection can hardly be accidental here. We must take this as strong evidence that 2 Pet. 1.12–21 is from Peter himself (as is 1 Peter, with the help of Silas).[25]

What is it that Peter had seen at the transfiguration? He says here that he had seen Christ's majesty, a majesty or "glory and honor" (cf. Heb. 1.3; 8.1; Test. Levi 3.4 as descriptors of God, cf. Ps. 8.5 on humans crowned with glory and honor). Christ had received these things from God the Father on that occasion. We are unable here to go into detail but it appears rather clear, as Bauckham has shown at length, that this description of the transfiguration is *independent* of the Gospel accounts. It can either be taken as the author (if it is not Peter) relying on an independent (oral?) tradition, or an eyewitness testimony of Peter. Now the later one dates 2 Peter, the more difficult it becomes to explain this independence from the four Gospel accounts. If 2 Peter was written around AD 90 or later, one must ask where could 2 Peter's author have been to have not known and used the richer, fuller accounts found in the Synoptics? And yet the compiler of 2 Peter knows even obscure and small NT documents like Jude (see 2 Pet. 2), and he knows of a compilation of Paul's letters (see 2 Pet. 3). It hardly seems likely he is totally unfamiliar with at least Mark, the earliest Gospel.

All of this difficulty disappears when we see that Peter himself is likely giving his own remembrances here, which would quite naturally not conform to any second-hand formulations of the event. It is probable that we should see Ps. 2 in the background here (especially Ps. 2.7b–12) which is an enthronement psalm which contains the line, "You are my son – today I have become your father." The import of this allusion to Ps. 2 is this – Peter sees in the transfiguration a depiction of Jesus being installed as eschatological king and judge over all the earth, an office he does not assume until the *parousia*. It is quite probable that the Synoptic evangelists (especially Mark) also saw the transfiguration as a

---

[24] Not surprisingly Jesus Seminar member Robert J. Miller wants to answer no to his own rhetorical question, possibly seeing what we have here as based on the account in Mt. 17.1–8 (Robert J. Miller, "Is There Independent Attestation for the Transfiguration in 2 Peter?" *NTS* 42 [1996]: 620–25). This hardly explains the distinctive features in our account (e.g. the phrase "Majestic Glory"), and it especially does not explain why, if the author of this is not Peter, he did not much more exactly quote at least the divine words from heaven, which here do not match up with any of the Synoptic witnesses. On the Matthean account see Ben Witherington III, *The Gospel of Matthew* (Macon, GA: Smyth and Helwys, 2006), *ad loc*. For a fuller discussion of this entire passage and all its exegetical details see Witherington, *Letters and Homilies for Hellenized Christians*, vol. 2, 314–37.

[25] On the authorship issues, Ben Witherington III, *Invitation to the New Testament* (2nd. edn.; Oxford: Oxford University Press, 2016).

foreshadowing not of resurrection or ascension but of *parousia*. In fact, in Mt. 16.28 there is a direct reference to the coming of the Son in/into his kingdom just before the transfiguration story. And interestingly, later Christian tradition also wanted to connect the transfiguration with the *parousia*.[26] J. Neyrey is even prepared to suggest that the transfiguration is viewed as a prophecy of the *parousia* when Christ comes in glory and honor as the king, the beloved Son of God. He relates this to the later Apocalypse of Peter tradition, where the *parousia* is discoursed on by Jesus in connection with his transfiguration.[27]

Presumably, the reason Peter wanted to set up booths is because he assumed that the great and final day of eschatological celebration was at hand (see Mk. 9.5ff.). If this is a correct interpretation of our text, it explains why Peter refers to the transfiguration to refute the notion that there would be no *parousia*. Peter is saying "at the transfiguration which we saw personally, Christ was given in token an office that he will not fulfill until his *parousia*. Therefore, there must be a *parousia* or else the transfiguration was pointless." N. Hillyer rightly notes that the terms honor and glory do not come up in the resurrection narratives, but certainly they are apropos for both the transfiguration and the *parousia*.[28] Now we are prepared to examine the rest of the particulars of vv. 17–18.

Verse 17b is a reverential way of avoiding two things: (1) saying God spoke directly; (2) saying God's name. The "majestic glory" referred to at the end of the verse, is simply another Semitic way of saying God (cf. 1 Clem. 9.2).[29] The word *toiasde* serves the function of saying the voice was "to the following effect" (i.e. he is avoiding quoting the voice directly, perhaps out of reverence). This reverential approach to the matter makes quite clear that the author of this section was a Jewish Christian who would be likely to use such circumlocutions, which may have the use in the Psalms as a background (Ps. 144.5, 12 LXX). Notice that Peter intends to focus only on the investiture (v. 17a) and what the voice said (v. 17b). The literal rendering here would be "a voice was conveyed from the Majestic Glory."

Unfortunately, we have a textual problem with the key phrase of the voice from heaven. Basically, there are two options: (1) the text as it reads in UBS, 3rd edn.: "my Son, my Beloved, this is" or (2) "This is my Son, the Beloved," supported by Aleph, A, C, K, and a host of others. The problem with the second reading is that although it has good support it appears to be an attempt to conform the text to Mt. 17.5, 3.17.[30] Thus, reading (1) is to be preferred – "This is my Son, my beloved." Some scholars have thought that we should combine the two phrases here and make it, "My beloved son," by which was meant "my chosen Son" or "my only (i.e. unique) Son." However, there is probably sufficient evidence to suggest that "my Beloved" was in fact a separate messianic title for Christ (see Eph. 1.9), meaning "my Elect One."

[26] See Jerome Neyrey, "The Apologetic Use of the Transfiguration in 2 Peter 1.16–21," *CBQ* 42 (1980): 504–19.

[27] *Ibid.*, 519; Jerome Neyrey, *2 Peter, Jude* (New Haven, CT: Yale University Press, 1994), 173–74.

[28] Norman Hillyer, *1 and 2 Peter, Jude* (Understanding the Bible Commentary Series; Grand Rapids, MI: Baker Books, 1991), 175.

[29] See *New Documents Illustrating Early Christianity*, vol. 2 (ed. S. Llewelyn; Grand Rapids, MI: William B. Eerdmans, 2001), 109. Here is where I point out that only in this Petrine testimony do we find a Semitism like this. The rest of the discourse is basically free of them, another clue that a source is being used here.

[30] Bruce M. Metzger, *A Textual Commentary on the Greek New Testament* (1st edn.; London: UBS, 1971), 700–1.

The last phrase in v. 17c is "with whom/in whom I am well pleased." The phrase likely means "on whom I have set my favor" (glory/honor), and Isa. 42.1 may be its source. Bauckham states:

> The very rare construction *eis on* ... probably carries the sense of God's favor selecting Jesus by coming to rest on him, while the aorist indicates an act of election. Presumably the election is considered as having already occurred, in God's eternity; it is now declared at the moment of Jesus' official appointment to the task for which God has elected him.[31]

The point of this is clearly that the transfiguration and that which it foreshadows (*parousia*) is part of God's eternal plan involving the election of Jesus as king and judge over the world. It is thus hardly a humanly contrived myth. Peter stresses that he was with Jesus then and heard all this, so he can vouch for it personally. It happened on the holy mountain. Here we may again see an allusion to Ps. 2.6 – "on Zion my holy hill." Peter then has cast his own experience in scriptural language investing it with such language to indicate that this event was a fulfillment of messianic prophecy in the Psalms.

In its original setting, of course, the event we call the transfiguration served to confirm to the inner core of disciples just who Jesus was, and that they needed to pay attention to him. This visionary experience, however, involved seeing Elijah and Moses as well, who, according to Luke, were consulting with Jesus about his "exodus" or leaving for heaven. Jesus, like Enoch, like Elijah, was going to be taken up into heaven according to this tradition. Notice as well in the Mk. 9 account that it is introduced by a saying that suggests some of the disciples will not die before seeing the coming of the Kingdom with power. This could refer to the transfiguration itself, or it could refer to the resurrection appearances. The transfiguration itself could be said to be a *parousia* preview, and this is apparently how it is viewed in 2 Pet. 1.

But what is the real significance of the glorification of the Son on this mountain? There is of course the confirmation that he is the Son, and that the divine presence is in him. There is also the notion that the Father is vouching for the Son, and so they need to hear and heed the Son, including when he tells them not to recount this experience until after Christ is risen from the dead. Unlike the visionary experiences of Jesus alone, this is a shared experience, but one not to be related until an appropriate time, later. The scene also comports with the emphasis in the Fourth Gospel that the Son is dependent on the Father for all things, but at the same time, his unique relationship with the Father sets him apart from all other mortals as both the revealer and redeemer, the mediator between God and humanity. This theme will be developed further in the later Pauline literature, the Pastoral Epistles (see 1 Tim. 2.5–6). But to fully understand what the Fourth Gospel is suggesting about the relationship between the Father and the Son, one needs to walk down Wisdom's road for a mile or two and take a look at the sapiential landscape.

Jesus the Sage: God's Wisdom

We will not understand the portrait of the relationship of the Father and the Son in the Fourth Gospel, however, unless we step back and take a close look at the sapiential nature of the presentation of that relationship. We will start with the bedrock fact from the life of Jesus himself that he was a sage. His form of public discourse is largely not

---

[31] Richard Bauckham, *Jude, 2 Peter* (WBC 50; Grand Rapids, MI: Zondervan, 2014), 220.

prophetic. He never once says "Thus sayeth the Lord" and then quotes Yahweh. No, his form of public discourse is sapiential. He speaks in parables, aphorisms, riddles, proverbs. The *gestalt* of his speech patterns should be compared to the material in Proverbs, Ecclesiastes, Wisdom of Solomon, and Sirach. But that is not all. He seems also to have presented himself as God's Wisdom come in person. There are several clear indicators that this was part of his self-presentation. Firstly, there is the famous yoke saying, "come unto me all you who labor and are heavy laden ... Take my yoke upon you" (Mt. 11.28). This saying quite deliberately echoes what Sirach says about Torah, which Sirach takes to be God's Wisdom incarnated in the Law. Consider what is said in the autobiographical remarks in Sir. 51:

While I was still young, before I went on my travels, I sought wisdom openly in my prayer.

¹⁴ Before the temple I asked for her,
and I will search for her until the end.

¹⁵ From the first blossom to the ripening grape my heart delighted in her; my foot walked on the straight path; from my youth I followed her steps.

¹⁶ I inclined my ear a little and received her, and I found for myself much instruction.

¹⁷ I made progress in her;
to him who gives wisdom I will give glory.

¹⁸ For I resolved to live according to wisdom, and I was zealous for the good,
and I shall never be disappointed.

¹⁹ My soul grappled with wisdom, and in my conduct I was strict;
I spread out my hands to the heavens, and lamented my ignorance of her.

²⁰ I directed my soul to her, and in purity I found her.
With her I gained understanding from the first; therefore I will never be forsaken.

²¹ My heart was stirred to seek her; therefore I have gained a prize possession.

²² The Lord gave me my tongue as a reward, and I will praise him with it.

²³ Draw near to me, you who are uneducated, and lodge in the house of instruction.

²⁴ Why do you say you are lacking in these things, and why do you endure such great thirst?

²⁵ I opened my mouth and said,
Acquire wisdom for yourselves without money.

²⁶ Put your neck under her yoke,
and let your souls receive instruction; it is to be found close by.

It is hard to doubt that Jesus is deliberately echoing this earlier wisdom material but notice the difference. Wisdom's yoke in Sir. 51 becomes Jesus' yoke in Mt. 11. This is because the historical Jesus presented himself as God's Wisdom come in person to God's people. But this is hardly the only evidence.

Secondly, there is the famous "Wisdom" saying from the same chapter in Matthew – "The Son of Man came eating and drinking, and they say, 'Here is a glutton and a drunkard, a friend of tax collectors and sinners.' But wisdom is proved right by her deeds" (Mt. 11.19). Yes, this is part of the Matthean presentation of Jesus as God's Wisdom, but I would insist that it is grounded in Jesus' own self-presentation. Jesus was not just a sage with independent wisdom and authority. As the yoke saying suggests, Jesus presented himself as the fount of Wisdom or Wisdom come in person, and to understand that, one needed to understand the development of the personification of Wisdom which we first find in Prov. 3, 8–9, then further developed in the Wisdom of Solomon where Wisdom is not merely present and assisting Yahweh at creation or merely calling in the marketplace for God's people to repent (Prov. 9), but also the guide of God's people during its whole history (Wis. Sol. 17–18), and finally the personification of Wisdom takes concrete form in the Torah, where the yoke of Torah is in fact the yoke of Wisdom.

There is in addition the tradition in 1 En. 42 about Wisdom coming to God's people, speaking to them, being rejected, and returning to heaven. It reads: "Wisdom went forth to make her dwelling among the children of men and found no dwelling place. Wisdom returned to her place and took her seat among the angels." It is hard to ignore the parallels between this and the description in Jn. 3.13–14 of the Son of Man who has descended and will ascend, after rejection and crucifixion. But in Jesus the personification of Wisdom becomes not merely incarnate in a book. No, *in Jesus the personification becomes a person.* It is of course hard to know how much of the Wisdom portrait of Jesus in Matthew goes directly back to Jesus himself, though doubtless some of it does, and I would suggest we have independent confirmation of that fact in the Fourth Gospel, which does not draw on Matthew but is rather an independent testimony to and about Jesus, but it also presents us with a Wisdom portrait of Jesus right from the very first chapter.[32]

It has often been remarked that the *logos* hymn in Jn. 1 is the theological key to the Fourth Gospel. The rest of that Gospel is to be read in the light of this Prologue, for this Prologue tells us of the origins and the character of the Son. Here he is not only the only begotten Son of the Father. Here he can even be called God, by way of the comment "and the Word was God." It is very interesting how the Greek reads. It does not say, for example, "the Word was *the* God" for that would imply the Word exhausted the Godhead, and the Fourth Evangelist certainly has no desire to say that. Nor does the grammar allow the translation "the Word was a god," as if there might be other beings worthy of the title – deities or demi-gods. In short, the Prologue says that the Word partook of the divine identity, the word "God" here is used in the generic rather than the titular sense. By this I mean that it is not simply a synonym for Yahweh here. Perhaps for one of the first times in the Jewish tradition, the generic sense is predicated of the real, the living, the genuine God, and not the pretenders, the gods. The Word is the subject of this intransitive verb sentence and can be rendered "God was indeed the Word."

Throughout the Fourth Gospel, knowing where the Son came from is crucial to understanding his identity. It is not just that he came down from heaven, even angels might do that. The point is that unlike all created beings including angels, the Son's origin is in the Father. He is the only begotten Son of the Father. The rest of God's children are children through adoption or through the new birth, as we learn a little further on in Jn. 1 and then Jn. 3. Being a child of God is not a matter of creation, it is a matter of re-creation and adoption.[33]

---

[32] For a detailed presentation of Jesus as God's Wisdom in Matthew and John see my commentaries on those two Gospels, and the relevant chapters in Witherington, *Jesus the Sage.*

[33] Though we may have difficulty understanding exactly what the phrase "only begotten Son" means, it likely suggests at least the following: (1) Jesus is the only "natural" offspring of God, the only one that has "by nature" a connection with the Father; (2) this being the case, and since in the NT we look at the Father language for God through the eyes of Jesus, and how he viewed God, the term Father here is necessary. While Mary was the mother of Jesus, God was his Father, and therefore the Father language is not merely a residue or the result of a patriarchal environment. God is called Father 120 times in this Gospel because the Evangelist wants us to know of the special relationship between the Son and the Father, and through the Son, a relationship that can be had by Jesus' disciples.

It comes then as no surprise when we hear later in John's Gospel that the Son can say and do the very same things as the Father says and does, and we also hear that the Son may label himself by the divine name phrase "I am," and also learn that to reject the Son is to reject the Father. What is important for our purposes is that this is not miles away from what the material from the historical Jesus suggested Jesus thought about himself. It is rather a drawing out in full view of the implications of some of the things he said about being the Son of Man, the Son of God, and David's Lord.

Just how much the Fourth Gospel draws on Jewish Wisdom material to portray Jesus is easily shown. For example, the use of the term *monogenes* of Jesus in Jn. 1 draws on Wis. Sol. 7.22, where we hear that Wisdom is *monogenes*, which can be translated "only one of its kind." In other words, Jesus' sonship is unique, it is not something he can share with other mortals. This includes by implication the notion that he is the only "natural" Son of God. What is emphasized by such language is both the personal uniqueness and the pedigree of the Son. It needs to be stressed that the attributes of God which are personified as Wisdom are necessarily something internal or inherent in God. So, when the Fourth Evangelist predicates these same attributes of the Son this proves to be a simple way of demonstrating that the Son comes forth from the Father, and so is part of the divine identity, just as Wisdom was earlier believed to be. It can be no accident that in the Fourth Gospel and in 1 John (likely from the same person) *only Jesus* is called the Son of God. He is not merely a "chip off the old block," he is one of a kind, as the term *monogenes* indicates.

A further excellent example of the influence of Wisdom material in John that increases the theological and Christological wattage of the Fourth Gospel is found in Jn. 3.14. The Son has come from and is returning to the Father. In Jn. 3.14 we have the notion that when Jesus is lifted up on the cross, he has not only arrived at his hour (cf. 13.31, 17.1) but he has begun his return or ascent back to the Father. Here the Son of Man language is conditioned by what is said in 1 En. 70.2 and 71.1, where Enoch ascends and then learns that he himself is "the Son of Man." These Enochian texts in turn build on 1 En. 42, where it is said clearly that Wisdom descends to earth and returns to heaven rejected (cf. Prov. 9). This same sapiential and apocalyptic influence from earlier Jewish literature can be found as well in Jn. 6.63, where we hear "what if you were to see the Son of Man ascending?" We must keep steadily in view that Jesus himself and the writers of the NT lived at a time when the Wisdom and apocalyptic traditions of Judaism had already cross-fertilized. This can already be seen in Daniel, where we have both sorts of materials. The blending of the Son of Man traditions and the Wisdom traditions in the Fourth Gospel should not surprise us if we are familiar with the larger corpus of early Jewish literature.

So, to understand Jesus in the Fourth Gospel entails knowing he is Wisdom come in the flesh, which entails knowing he has come from heaven and will be returning there. Misunderstanding then amounts to having mistaken notions about Jesus' origins and destiny. For example, in Jn. 1.45–46 even the disciples *think* they know where Jesus has come from and who he is because he is identified as "Jesus of Nazareth" and comes from Joseph's family there. Or again, the people of Jerusalem in Jn. 7.25–27 know about the origins in Nazareth but they do not know where Jesus ultimately comes from (i.e. heaven). Further examples of this sort of misunderstanding crop up in Jn. 7.41, 8.41–48, 9.29, and in 18.5ff. Not knowing that Jesus is the Son of Man/Logos/Wisdom that comes down from heaven amounts to not knowing who he is.

The selfsame error can happen because of not knowing where Jesus is going. In Jn. 7.35 the Jewish officials misunderstand and think Jesus is going into the Diaspora to teach Greeks, or Greek-speaking Jews. Or in Jn. 8.21–22 it is assumed that Jesus is going to kill himself when he says he is going away. Even after Easter in Jn. 20.16–17 Mary Magdalene makes the mistake of assuming Jesus is back to stay. She wishes to cling to the earthly Jesus and simply resume relationship with her *rabbouni*, her teacher, whereas actually Jesus intends to ascend to the Father so a new form of relationship can begin between himself and his followers.

Throughout the Fourth Gospel, Jesus assumes the roles normally attributed to Wisdom in her relationship with Israel (see Wis. Sol. 10).[34] It is Jesus, God's Wisdom, who comes into the world to enlighten God's people. Moses and the prophets were inspired by this Word to write about his future earthly career (Jn. 1.45; 5.46). It is said of Abraham that he saw the Son's day (8.56), for the Son, in the form of Wisdom, pre-existed. Isaiah even saw his pre-existent glory (cf. Isa. 6 to Jn. 12.41). In other words, the Son existed before the incarnation, indeed before all of creation, and he had roles to play before the incarnation. It is hard not to hear loud echoes of Wis. Sol. 10–11 in this material, for it speaks of Wisdom aiding Abraham (10.5), entering Moses so he could perform signs and wonders (10.16), and offer prophecy (11.1, cf. 7.27). Wisdom was present in the wilderness, and sustained Israel with manna and water from the rock (16.26; 11.4, cf. Jn. 4–6 and also 1 Cor. 10.1–10 – "the rock was Christ").

The Johannine Jesus understands himself to be the one who has aided God's people in their trials in all generations. Wis. Sol. 16.6 tells us that the lifting up of the serpent in the wilderness is seen as a sign of salvation, which helps us make sense of the otherwise puzzling saying in Jn. 3.14, which reminds that Moses lifted up the serpent in the wilderness, which even foreshadows the lifting up of the Son on the cross. Notice as well that the author of the Wisdom of Solomon views miracles as symbols or signs of salvation, just as the Fourth Evangelist does (cf. Wis. Sol. 10.16 and 16.6 to the sign narratives in Jn. 2–11).

There has been much debate about the "I am" sayings in the Fourth Gospel (cf. 8.24,28,58; 13.19) and whether they involve the transfer of the divine name to the Son. This question needs to be raised, not least because we are told explicitly in Jn. 17.6,12,26 that Jesus has manifested the divine name found in the Hebrew text of Isa. 51.12 which reads "I am I AM who comforts you." We may compare as well Isa. 52.6, "My people shall know that I Am is the one speaking." In light of our previous discussion of the Burning Bush revelation and the Shema, it is in order to suggest here that perhaps it is just Isa. 52.6 which is the background to the "I am" sayings of Jesus. This would still be a way of saying Jesus is part of the divine identity but it would not be drawing on the burning bush revelation. Notice how in 1 Cor. 8.5–6 the Shema is expanded to include Christ, just not under the term God, but rather under the term Lord.

In Jn. 8.58, and probably in 8.26 and 13.19, Jesus is given the divine name. Yet there are also various "I am" sayings in John that are not free-standing. Rather, they involve a predicate – living bread, light of the world, the door, the life, the authentic vine (6.35,51; 8.12;

---

[34] And herein lies an important point. Jesus is *not* portrayed as Israel in any of these Gospels, including Matthew and John. He is portrayed as Israel's Wisdom. He comes to free Israel not to be Israel, to enlighten those in darkness, not to take their place. He is the unique Son of God, sent to reconcile the world, including Israel, back to God.

10.7,9,11,14; 14.6; 15.1,5). The important point here is that *all these things* were already predicated of Wisdom in texts like Prov. 3.18; 8.38; 9.5; Wis. Sol. 1–8; Sir. 24.17ff. Part of the point of painting the portrait of Jesus in Wisdom colors is that it is being suggested that whatever one longs for or needs from God's Wisdom can be gained from the Son.

Though scholars have often debated why we have discourses in the Fourth Gospel and not in the Synoptics, it seems likely that the comparison with Wisdom literature explains this as well. Jesus offers the teaching of the very mind and wisdom of God, speaking in the format God's people already found Wisdom speaking in, in Prov. 8–9 and elsewhere. The Farewell Discourses in Jn. 13–17 are especially laden with language that encourages the identification of Jesus with Wisdom.

Sir. 4.11–13 is especially germane. It says Wisdom teaches her children (cf. Jn. 14–16). It says Wisdom helps those who seek her (Jn. 14.16ff.). It says whoever loves Wisdom loves life (Jn. 14.15). It says those who seek Wisdom from the early morning are filled with joy (Jn. 15.11). It says whoever holds fast to Wisdom inherits glory (Jn. 17.22). It says the Lord loves those who love Wisdom (Jn. 17.26). Jesus' disciples in these discourses in John are called little children just as is said of Wisdom's disciples in Prov. 8.32–33 and Sir. 4.11 and 6.18. In short, the personified Wisdom tradition is being used throughout the Fourth Gospel to provide a way of expressing Christological monotheism. The Son and the Father are one, just as God and God's Wisdom were of the same mind. To all of this one may also compare the material in Matthew, where Jesus is said in Mt. 1 and 28 to be Immanuel, God with us, and is said to be virginally conceived in Mary by the overshadowing of the Holy Spirit, and is said to be sought by wise men from afar, and so on. The Gospel writers were groping for categories and language grand enough to explain how the Son was part of the divine identity, without suggesting that he was simply Yahweh. They are distinct, and yet they are one. We could also point out how there is a concerted effort even in the Synoptics to predicate of Jesus the very same qualities that are said to be of the essence in God's character, for instance, his *HESED* or mercy and compassion (see e.g. Mk. 6.34; Mt. 9.36 and 14.14, cf. Jn. 11.33).[35] But perhaps the ultimate revelation of his character is seen on the cross.

The God of Golgotha: The Father and Son Apart?

After all this, one may rightly wonder how this comports with the stark and dark portrait of Jesus dying on a cross and crying out in the words of Ps. 22, "My God, my God, why have you forsaken me?" It will be good, as we draw this chapter to a close, that we do some in-depth reflection on that story from our earliest Gospel, that story where this is the only thing Jesus says from the cross, and it comes after Jesus' asking to let that cup pass from him.

The first thing to say is that the starkness of the scene in Mk. 15 should not be damped down by the suggestion that, after all, Ps. 22 ends on a happy note. That is irrelevant since Jesus *only* quotes the opening line of the psalm, and Mark in no way ameliorates the agony and despair of that cry. It has come to be called the cry of dereliction, the cry of abandonment. And what makes it especially difficult is that this is the only place in that

---

[35] For a reading of the whole of the Fourth Gospel in a sapiential light see my *John's Wisdom*.

Gospel (or in Matthew's, which also has this saying) where Jesus simply calls or addresses God as "God" – *Eloi*. He does not cry out with the personal name of God – Yahweh. He simply follows the lead of the psalmist.

Yes, it is true that he says *my* God. The God that he is claiming abandoned him to the cross, is "his God," not just any deity. And furthermore, this God is the one he addressed the night before – no, begged the night before – using the term Abba, to be let off this fate. The contrast in language and in situation could hardly be more clear.

One way to look at this is to suggest that Jesus was experiencing for the only time in his life the general God-forsakenness of fallen humanity. Previously there had only been intimacy with Abba, but not on the cross. Of course, much depends on how you view what is happening on the cross. Is this a scene where "the lamb of God," having been led to the slaughter, is "taking away the sins of the world" in some sort of combination of a Passover sacrifice (an apotropaic sacrifice in which many are passed over because of the blood of the shed lamb) and a scapegoat ritual, where the sins of the humans are laid on the scapegoat, and the animal is sent off into the darkness, into the wilderness? To judge from Mk. 10.45, Jesus not only saw his death coming, he saw it as in some sense a ransom for the many. Ransom from what? Sin and its bondage it would appear.

But Jews did not offer *human* sacrifices. They in fact abhorred such things. But what if it were a self-sacrifice? Here we perhaps have some precedent in the Maccabean literature, in particular the following in 4 Macc. 6.27–29, "As he was about to die, Eleazar prayed 'You know, O God, that though I might have saved myself, I am dying in burning torments for the sake of the law. Be merciful to your people, and let our punishment suffice for them. Make my blood their purification [*hilasterion*] and take my life in exchange for theirs.' " Later on, the book concludes, "Because of them our enemies did not rule over our nation, the tyrant was punished, and the homeland purified – they having become, as it were, a ransom [*antipsychon*] for the sin of our nation. And through the blood of those devout ones and their death as an atoning sacrifice [*hilasterion*], divine Providence preserved Israel that previously had been mistreated" (4 Macc. 17.20–22). It is thus possible that Jesus viewed his death in such a light. But there is nothing in the Maccabean literature to suggest that Eleazar or any other Maccabee saw such a death as involving being abandoned by God. In Mk. 15, we seem to be in deeper waters.

In his classic study *The Crucified God*,[36] J. Moltmann argues that on the cross of Jesus, God is most fully revealed to humankind. He speaks of a God who suffers with his creation, even to the point of experiencing death itself. In fact, Moltmann goes down the road that Bonhoeffer went, quoting one of his letters from prison as follows. "God lets himself be pushed out of the world onto the cross. He is weak and powerless in the world, and that is precisely the way, the only way, in which he is with us and helps us. Christ helps us, not by the virtue of his omnipotence, but by virtue of his weakness and suffering … Only the suffering God can help … That is a reversal of what the religious man expects from God. Man is summoned to share in God's sufferings at the hands of a godless world."[37] This, I think, is getting at something important not only about the nature of God, whom Paul once heard say "my power is made perfect in weakness; my grace is sufficient for you," but about the love of Christ for the world. We will have occasion to talk in some depth about

---

[36] Jürgen Moltmann, *The Crucified God* (Minneapolis, MN: Fortress Press, 1993).
[37] *Ibid.*, 47.

the implications of the death of Jesus for salvation and for dealing with the sin problem later in this study, but here our concern is what this cry on the cross tells us about the relationship between the Son and the Father.

I have already intimated how I view the matter. Jesus is experiencing our God-forsakenness for us, a God-forsakenness he had never experienced before this point in time, and one he himself did not deserve to experience, not being a sinner or ever alienated from God due to some thought, word, or deed of his own. Jesus was the one person who should never have ended up on a cross. He is the one person for whom Jesus did not need to die! And yet there he was, experiencing our God-forsakenness. But here at least we need to ask the question, is the atoning efficacy of Jesus' death a reflection of his being part of the divine identity?

By this I mean, let us suppose that Adam, before he sinned, had been asked by God to die on a cross for the coming sins of the world. That would simply be a human death of someone who was not a sinner. But could it possibly be a once-for-all atonement for all of humankind? I don't think so. I think that in the death of Jesus, something is going on that involves more than just the death of Jesus' sinless human nature. Did Jesus' cry from the cross suggest that he suddenly felt he was no longer part of the divine identity? No longer one with the Father? Could the death of Jesus on the cross have involved both his humanity and his participation in the divine identity, hence Moltmann's title "the crucified God"? And if his "being in very nature God" (Phil. 2) was somehow *not* involved in the death of Jesus, how exactly does that death provide a once-for-all atonement for all sins, past, present and future? These are the sorts of deep questions one is forced to ponder on the basis of Mk. 15 and the cry of dereliction.

Here it may be useful to remind ourselves of the material in Hos. 11[38] and elsewhere that suggests that God does suffer with his people, and even for his people. We may also remember Acts 9, where the exalted Christ asks Saul of Tarsus, "Why are you persecuting me?" I do not intend to give pat or clichéd answers to these deep questions here. Rather, I think it will be worth pondering how Jesus really is "the God of Golgotha" suffering for our sins, and I can think of no better way to further such a meditation than to recite some of Geoffrey Studdert-Kennedy's famous Cockney dialect poem "The Sorrow of God" as we conclude this chapter:

> Yes I used to believe in Jesus Christ
> And I used to go to church.
> But since I left home and came to France,
> I've been clean knocked off my perch.
> For it seemed alright at home it did,
> To believe in a God above
> And in Jesus Christ his only Son
> What died on the cross through Love.
>
> When I went for a walk of a Sunday morn
> On a nice fine day in the spring
> I could see the proof of the living God
> In every living thing.
> For how could the grass and the trees grow up,

[38] See above.

All alone of their bloomin' selves?
Ye might as well believe in fairy tales,
And think they were made by elves.

So I thought that that long-haired atheist
Was nothing but a silly sod
For how did he account for my Brussel sprouts,
If he didn't believe in God?

But it ain't the same out here, you know
It's as different as chalk and cheese,
For half of it's blood and the other half mud,
And I'm darned if I really see
How the God who has made such a cruel, cruel world
Can have love in his heart for men,
And be deaf to the cries of the men as dies
And never comes home again.

Just look at that little boy corporal there,
Such a fine upstanding lad,
With a will of his own, and a way of his own
And a smile of his own, he had.
An hour ago he was bustin' with life
With his actin' and foolin' and fun;
He was simply the life of us all, he was
Now look what the blighters have done.
Look at him lying there all of a heap
With the blood soaking over his head
Like a beautiful picture spoiled by a fool,
A bundle of nothing – dead ...

And the lovin' God he looks down on it all,
On the blood, and the mud, and the smell,
Oh God if it's true how I pity you
For you must be livin' in hell.
You must be livin' in hell all day,
And livin' in hell all night.
I'd rather be dead with a hole in my head
I would by a darn long sight,
Than be livin' with you on your heavenly throne,
Looking down on yon bloody heap,
That was once a boy full of life and joy,
And hearin' his mother weep.

The sorrows of God must be hard to bear,
If he really has love in his heart.
And the hardest part in the world to play
Must surely be God's part.
And I wonder if that's what it really means,
That figure who hangs on the cross.
I remember I saw one the other day
As I stood with the captain's hoss.

I remembers, I thinks, thinks I to myself
It's a long time since he died,

Yet the world don't seem much better to-day
Then when he was crucified.

It's always the same, as it seems to me,
The weakest must go to the wall,
And whether it's right, or whether it's wrong
Doesn't seem to matter at all.
The better you are and the harder it is,
The harder you have to fight,
It's a cruel hard world for any bloke
Who does the thing which is right.
And that's how he came to be crucified,
For that's what he tried to do.
He was always a-tryin' to do his best
For the likes of me and you.

Well what if he came to the earth today
Came walking about in this trench
How his heart would bleed for the sights he'd see
In the mud and the blood and the stench.
And I guess it would finish him up for good
When he came to this old sap end,
And he saw that bundle of nothing there,
For he wept at the grave of a friend.

And they say He was just the Image of God
I wonder if God sheds tears.
I wonder if God can be sorrowing still,
And has been all these years.
I wonder if that's what it really means,

Not only that he once died,
Not only that he came once to earth
And wept and was crucified?
Not just that he suffered once for all
To save us from our sins
And then went up to his throne on high
To wait until his heaven begins.

But what if he came to earth to show
By the paths of the pain he trod,
The blistering flame of eternal shame
That burns in the heart of God? ...

But why don't you bust this show to bits
And force us to do your will?
Why ever should God be suffering so,
And man be sinning still?
Why don't you make your voice ring out,
And drown these cursed guns?
Why don't you stand with an outstretched hand
Out there betwixt us and the Huns?
Why don't you force us to end this war
And fix up a lasting peace?
Why don't you will that the world be still

And wars forever cease?
That's what I'd do, if I were you,
And I had a lot of sons
Who squabbled and fought and spoiled their home,
Same as us boys and the Huns

...

Well maybe that's how it is with God,
His sons have got to be free.
Their wills are their own, their lives are their own,
And that is how it has to be.
So the Father God goes sorrowing still
For his world which has gone to sea
But he runs up a light on Calvary's height
That beckons to you and to me.
The beacon light of the sorrow of God
Has been shinin' down the years,
Flashin' its light through the darkest night
Of our human blood and tears.

There's a sight of things which I thought were strange,
As I am just beginnin' to see.
"Inasmuch as you did it unto one of these,
You did it unto Me"

So it isn't just only the crown of thorns
What has pierced and torn God's head
He knows the feel of the bullet too,
And he's had his touch of the lead.
And he's standin' with me in this here sap,
And the corporal stands with Him,
And the eyes of the laddie is shinin' bright
But the eyes of the Christ burn dim.

Oh laddie I thought as ye'd done for me
And broken my heart with your pain.
I thought ye'd taught me God was dead,
But ye've brought Him to life again.
And ye've taught me more of what God is
Than ever I thought to know,
For I never thought he could come so close,
Or that I could love Him so.[39]

And So?

We began our discussion in this chapter with Jesus' God talk, and his use of the term Abba for Yahweh. We stressed that one of the keys to understanding Jesus was understanding his prayer life and intimacy with Yahweh, the God of the Hebrew Scriptures. We also placed

---

[39] This poem can be found in various of the collections of Studdert-Kennedy's poems. I recommend the collection entitled *The Unutterable Beauty*, reprinted by Pendlebury Press, 2017. This is only an excerpt from the entire long dialect poem.

special emphasis of the origins of NT Christology being in Jesus' own self-evaluation and self-expression. We studied at some length what Jesus meant by calling himself the Son of Man, and then also examined his being called Son of God, Son of David, Messiah, and God's Wisdom. To be sure, some of these traditions reflect later spinning out of the implications of what Jesus said of himself and what he did, but the point throughout is that the Christology of Jesus himself was the basis of such amplifications. It is not the case of later Christians putting royal robes on a non-Messianic Jesus. And this is precisely why, when one turns the page from the life and ministry of Jesus to the earliest Christian evaluations of Jesus found in Paul's letters, in Acts, in Hebrews, in 1 Peter, and elsewhere there is already a remarkable high Christology. This did not show up for the first time late in the first century at the hands of those who were not even first-generation Christians. To the contrary, writers such as John of Patmos, or the compiler of 2 Peter, were building on the earlier witnesses to the Christ event and what they had testified that Jesus said or implied about his own significance.

Furthermore, the sapiential portraits of Jesus in Matthew and John are grounded in Jesus' presentation of himself, not only as a sage who taught in parables, aphorisms, proverbs, riddles, but as he presented himself as God's Wisdom. It is this self-presentation that led to the creation of the Logos hymn, to the discourse format of Jesus' teaching in John, where he speaks again and again like Wisdom, including in the "I am" sayings, offering what Wisdom had previously offered to God's people – life, and light, and a loving relationship with God. Like Wisdom in Wisdom of Solomon, Jesus performs signs that point outside themselves to the Signifier, Jesus himself. Whereas the miracles in the Synoptics are signs of the presence of the Kingdom, God's eschatological saving activity, in John they are signs of the presence of the King.

At the beginning and the end of the chapter, we began to plumb the depths of Jesus' cry of dereliction from the cross in Mk. 15 and par. We suggested that paradoxically this event and the quoting of Ps. 22 reveal not only the sustained closeness of Jesus to God the Father, but also the sudden alienation from God experienced by Jesus on the cross. In his hour of extreme pain and need, Jesus did what any normal pious person would do. He cried out to God, and indeed he called him "my God" despite the sense of being God-forsaken.

What actually transpired on the cross between the Father and the Son? Was there a rupture in the divine identity when Jesus died? Did his death only affect what we would call his human nature, or is this a story which in some mysterious, almost unfathomable sense is a story about "God crucified," the death of the one who would come to be called the second person of the Trinity? Did God die for humankind, or is this just a story about the death of a perfect human being, or the death of the human side of the Son? These are deep waters, but they are stirred up by the Evangelists themselves in the way they presented Jesus and his death. We will be able to discuss these things more fully when we look at the Passion play, the story of the last week of Jesus life. Now, however, we need to turn to the person called the Holy Spirit, the God of the Burning Heart.

4

The God of the Burning Heart

Those in whom the Spirit comes to live are God's new Temple. They are, individually and corporately, places where heaven and earth meet.

N. T. Wright[1]

The dove descending breaks the air
With flame of incandescent terror
Of which the tongues declare
The one discharge from sin and error.
The only hope, or else despair
Lies in the choice of pyre or pyre –
To be redeemed from fire by fire.

T. S. Eliot[2]

We tend to think of him in non-personal terms. At which point our images take over; we think of the Spirit as wind, fire, oil, water – impersonal images all – and refer to the Spirit as *it*. No wonder many regard the Spirit as a gray, oblong blur.

Gordon D. Fee[3]

The "Spirit" in the OT

It is a commonplace amongst OT scholars,[4] and most biblical scholars in general, that the references to God's Spirit in the OT are in fact references to God's spirit – that is Yahweh's presence (רוּחַ). The "spirit of *elohim*" (Gen. 1.2) as it is called at the beginning of the Bible is not seen as a person to be distinguished from Yahweh (cf. Isa. 32.15; Ps. 103.30; Job 33.4; 2 Bar. 21.4). Indeed, the word רוּחַ very much like the Greek word πνεῦμα can mean breath, wind, or spirit, and in Gen. 1 at least the precise meaning is debatable. Or again in Ezek.

---

[1] N. T. Wright, *Simply Christian* (New York: HarperOne), 2006.
[2] From T. S. Eliot, "Little Gidding," *Four Quartets* (New York: Mariner Books, 1968).
[3] Gordon D. Fee, *God's Empowering Presence* (Grand Rapids, MI: Baker, 1994), 6.
[4] In what follows in this chapter I am drawing on a portion of and adapting and adding to my discussion of the Spirit in Witherington and Ice, *Shadow of the Almighty*.

37.5 the prophet is called upon to prophesy to the *ruach* which seems surely here to mean "life breath" which will then animate the corpses of (or spiritual dead among) God's people. The text should likely be rendered "I will cause breath to enter you and you shall live."

What we often do find in the OT is references to God's spirit coming on persons, either to enable them to prophesy or preach (Isa. 61.1, cf. Lk. 4.18; 1 Sam. 10.10) or perhaps to empower or enlighten them to fulfill some office such as king (Isa. 11.1–4) or to give them superhuman strength (Judg. 14.6,19; 15.14) or even supernatural transportation (1 Kgs. 18.12; 2 Kgs. 2.16; Ezek. 2.2; 3.12–14).

There are exactly two references in the whole OT to a "Holy Spirit" and the first is found in a song, Ps. 51.11, where we hear "cast me not away from your presence, take not your Holy Spirit from me," which is surely just two ways of saying the same thing. David or the psalmist is pleading with God not to take his presence away from him. Well might he plead for this after the sins against Uriah and his wife Bathsheba, remembering that God's presence did leave the prior king, King Saul, and in one of the saddest verses in all of Scripture, it is expressed this way: "Now the spirit of Yahweh had left Saul" (1 Sam. 16.10). And yet Saul tragically was unaware of his loss. In Ps. 51 we must notice the distinction between the human spirit of the speaker, and the spirit of God, though in fact when it says "renew a right spirit within me" this could just be a metaphorical way of saying "give me a steadfast and morally upright attitude."

Somewhat more developed is the reference to the Holy Spirit in Isa. 63.10–14, which deserves to be cited in full.

Yet they rebelled
    and grieved his Holy Spirit.
So he turned and became their enemy
    and he himself fought against them.
[11] Then his people recalled the days of old,
    the days of Moses and his people –
where is he who brought them through the sea,
    with the shepherd of his flock?
Where is he who set
    his Holy Spirit among them,
[12] who sent his glorious arm of power
    to be at Moses' right hand,
who divided the waters before them,
    to gain for himself everlasting renown,
[13] who led them through the depths?
    Like a horse in open country,
    they did not stumble;
[14] like cattle that go down to the plain,
    they were given rest by the Spirit of the LORD.

Here for the first time we begin to see the Spirit treated as a person, one who can be grieved, though it is also clearly labeled in this passage as God's spirit, or the spirit of the Lord God. This text provides a minor precedent for the treatment of the Spirit we find in the NT. Basically, however, *ruach* in the OT refers to God's presence, often to his presence inspiring someone, empowering someone, enlightening someone and so on, and occasionally it refers to the presence of God in a holy place (e.g. the temple). See Ezek. 10.18, where the presence is referred to as the כְּבוֹד יְהוָה, the weighty presence or "Shekinah glory" of Yahweh departing the temple, to which must be compared Ezek. 43.4–5, where the "glory" of Yahweh is said to enter the temple. There really is precious little evidence in the Hebrew Scriptures that the spirit of God was seen as an entity or person distinguishable from Yahweh. In each case, the reference is to the presence of Yahweh in a person or place that normally results in the giving of life or the prophetic word or perhaps healing. Importantly, and especially in prophetic texts, the spirit is said to come on a person (or even a place like the temple) sporadically, from time to time, and it could be withdrawn, particularly if a person or group of people became sinful or a holy place was defiled.

Even in a text like Joel 2.28–32 speaking of a "later day" event, it is Yahweh's spirit, called "my spirit," that is promised to come on all flesh, as follows:

And afterward,

I will pour out my Spirit on all people.

Your sons and daughters will prophesy, your old men will dream dreams, your young men will see visions.

²⁹ Even on my servants, both men and women, I will pour out my Spirit in those days.

³⁰ I will show wonders in the heavens and on the earth,

blood and fire and billows of smoke.

³¹ The sun will be turned to darkness and the moon to blood

before the coming of the great and dreadful day of the LORD.

³² And everyone who calls

on the name of the LORD will be saved; for on Mount Zion and in Jerusalem there will be deliverance, as the LORD has said.

Most often in early Jewish literature "the spirit of prophecy" is referred to, a phrase especially common in the Aramaic Targums to refer to the inspiring of speech (Targ. Num. 11.26–27, cf. Josephus *Ant.* 4.119; Jub. 25.14). The spirit provides revelation and guidance (cf. Sir. 48.24; 4 Ez. 14.22; Philo, *Som.* II.252) or wisdom (Josephus, *Ant.* 10.239; Jub. 40.5; Philo, *Vit. Mos.* II.265; Sir. 39.6). The spirit can also inspire praise or other forms of worship (1 En. 71.11; Test. Job 48–50).

Interestingly, when early Jews began to reflect on whether they were in an eschatological situation, they began to think that Joel 2 would be fulfilled in some spirit-endowed messianic figure to come, or even an Elijah like figure (Sir. 48.10) or a messianic priest (1QS 9.10–11; Test. Levi 18), or a prophet like Moses (1QS 9.10–11 drawing on Deut. 18.15–16) or a servant figure who could be a warrior (cf. Isa. 61.1–2 and 11Q Melch). While there is certainly more talk about the spirit and God's association with specific anointed or spirit-endowed figures in the later prophetic literature in the canon and in early Judaism than there is in the older portions of the OT, usually it refers to some "coming one" not to someone already on the historical scene. What we do not find is a treatment of the spirit as a person distinguishable from Yahweh. God has a spirit (presence), God is not a mere "spirit." The comment in Jn. 4.24 probably does not mean God = Spirit, but rather is a comment on the incorporeal nature of God, or at least the implication is that God is not a material being, made of flesh and blood who could be tied down to one specific location.

But what about in the NT? M. E. Lohdahl made the case that the Holy Spirit was not seen as a person even in the NT.[5] While there are some texts in the Synoptic Gospels that could be read that way, and while it is true that there is strong emphasis on the Spirit's functions and activities in the NT, sometimes even stronger than on the personhood of the Spirit, nevertheless, in various parts of the NT, especially in John's Gospel and in Paul, the Spirit is not seen as a mere presence or power, but rather as a person distinguishable from the Father and the Son. In other words, on this subject there seems to be as much or more of a discontinuity between early Judaism and early Christianity on the issue of the Spirit as there is on the issue of the Messiah or Christ. It is the new thing that makes the decisive difference in the NT discussion of the Spirit, for the Spirit is not just treated as personal, it is treated as the personal agent of Christ. For instance, both Christ and the Spirit are called *parakletos* in the Fourth Gospel. The Son is the agent or sent counselor of and for the Father, and the Spirit is the agent or sent counselor of and for the Son.

In some ways, it is less difficult to talk about the Spirit being part of the divine identity than to talk of Christ that way, because of course the Spirit does not have a human nature and did not die on the cross. In short, there are no Spirit texts to eliminate from the discussion because of their focus on the "humanity" of the Spirit. But we can only "flesh out" what the NT says about the Spirit by working through the references to the Spirit in the NT.

The Holy Spirit in the Synoptics

Not infrequently one hears about the paucity of references to the Holy Spirit in the Synoptic Gospels, particularly Matthew and Mark. In one sense, and from a later Christian point of view, this is not so surprising. According to both Lk. 24 and Acts 1–2, and Jn. 14–17, the Holy Spirit did not come on the disciples of Jesus until 50 days after Jesus' death on the cross. So, while in Mk. 1.8 John the Baptizer suggests that Jesus will baptize people with the Spirit (and fire), Mark nowhere portrays Jesus as fulfilling that promise during his ministry, or even promising to fulfill such a prophecy. Instead, we hear of the Spirit descending on Jesus like a dove in Mk. 1.11 and driving him into the wilderness in 1.12. We have Jesus referring to the Spirit in Mk. 3.29 during the discussion about blasphemy, and in Mk. 13.11 a reference to the disciples speaking under the prompting of the Spirit in the future, after Jesus' death. But that is it. It is true that in each case the Spirit is called the Holy Spirit in these texts, but there is no theologizing or discussion of any consequence about the Spirit. Strikingly, when Mark refers to the Spirit in his narrative framework, the adjective "holy" is omitted (Mk. 1.10–12), which is not the case when the Spirit is spoken of by Jesus or John. Perhaps this bears witness to the fact that Mark is not much interested in Christianizing his source material when it comes to the Spirit, nor is it at all likely he added any references to the Spirit that were not in his sources.[6]

In an influential study, C. K. Barrett suggested the paucity of references to the Spirit was because only Jesus had the Spirit in him and on him during his ministry, and his disciples

---

[5] M. E. Lohdahl, *Shekinah Spirit: Divine Presence in Jewish and Christian Religion* (New York: Paulist Press, 1992).

[6] It is striking to contrast this with what happens with the Western text, where the word "Holy" is regularly added to the word Spirit in various places. It is clear from what follows that some early Christians were absolutely interested in expanding references to the Spirit in some early Christian texts. See P. Head, "Acts and the Problem of its Texts" at www.tyndale.cam.ac.uk/Tyndale/staff/Head/TextofActs.htm. But there is not just this

did not (and therefore there was no church before the death of Jesus). "The general gift of the Spirit belongs to the time of the vindication and manifestation of the Messiah and the Messianic Kingdom."[7] A close examination of texts like Mk. 6.12–13 and 9.14–29 suggests that the disciples performed their "mighty deeds" through prayer that God would act (9.29) and by the use of Jesus' name, and not by the power of the Holy Spirit, whom Jesus is not said to have dispensed to the disciples during their preliminary mission activity while he was still ministering himself.

More important is the evidence that Jesus himself sees the Spirit as a person. For example, Mk. 3.29 speaks about blasphemy against the Spirit, but one cannot commit blasphemy against an inanimate force or power. By definition, blasphemy is something one does against God. It is an act of sacrilege. And this same saying makes crystal clear that Jesus as well as Mark views the Spirit as God! Notice as well how closely Jesus identifies himself with the Spirit. To say Jesus "has an unclean spirit" or that he casts out demons by the power of Satan is to blaspheme against the Holy Spirit resident in Jesus himself. This should not lead to the conclusion that Jesus simply identified himself with the Spirit. Clearly not. The Spirit comes upon Jesus at baptism, but both of them already existed. Furthermore, Jesus contrasts taking the name of the Son of Man in vain with blasphemy of the Spirit. And interestingly, unlike Jesus, John in Mk. 1 talks about the Spirit in the more impersonal way characteristic of the OT. He draws an analogy with water, suggesting Spirit is something that can be poured out, or something one can be filled up with, or it is a medium one can be baptized in or with. It is Mark and Jesus, not John, who speak of the Spirit in a personal way in Mark's Gospel. John speaks like an OT prophet, say like Joel.

This brings up an important theological point, which has led to a lot of bad Christian theology about the Holy Spirit. The more impersonal language and metaphors one uses about the Spirit, *the greater the tendency to see the Spirit as a thing or a substance or a power.* Thus, sometimes Christians talk about receiving more of the Spirit subsequent to conversion, as if one received only a portion of the Holy Spirit at conversion. But if the Spirit is a personal presence dwelling within the believer and not just a power or a spiritual substance, one can no more have a little bit of the Spirit than one can be a little bit

---

formal addition of an adjective. Head is able to list substantial alterations involving the Spirit, for example the following:

(1) 6.10: the addition of *tw agiw to pneumati* (Dd Ee gig h p t g² mae eth = TO²). This takes place within the context of a larger addition which emphasises the authority of Stephen (which we shall mention below) 165[102];

(2) 11.17: several Western witnesses attest an addition to Peter's question (which takes three forms): *tou mh dounai autoi" pneuma agion* (467 p vg^ms mae Aug. BarS.) [TO] *t. m. d. a. p. a. pisteusasin ep autw* (Dd) *t. m. d. a. p. a. p. epi ton kurion Ihsoun Criston* (b vg³^mss syr^h* bhm ndl.2 prv tpl).165[103];

(3) 15.7: the addition of *en pneumati* (Dd l Tert. = TO) or *en pneumati agiw* (257 614 1799 2412 syr^hmg Cass.) to the description of Peter: "standing up in the [Holy] Spirit he said to them …";

(4) 15.29: the addition of *feromenoi en tw agiw pneumati* (Dd l Iren^Lat Tert. Ephr. = TO) to the closing statement of the letter from the Jerusalem council;

(5) 15.32: the addition of *plhrei" pneumato" agiou* (Dd alone) to the description of Judas and Silas;

(6) 19.1: an alternative reading for the verse in which the Spirit tells Paul to return to Asia: *eipen autw to pneuma upostrefein ei" thn Asian* (Π38 Dd syr^hmg Ephr. = TO);

(7) an alternative reading in which the Spirit tells Paul to return through Macedonia: *eipen de to pneuma autw* (Dd gig syr^hmg Ephr. = TO).

[7] C. K. Barrett, *The Holy Spirit and the Gospel Tradition* (London: SPCK, 1947), 159.

pregnant. The Spirit can certainly deal with increasingly more aspects of a person's inner being over time, renovating the mind, the will, the emotions, but once believers have the Spirit in their lives, and provided they do not commit apostasy and so quench or grieve the Spirit, they cannot be said to get more of the Spirit over time. The impersonal language of filling or pouring needs to be seen for what it is – metaphorical ways of speaking about the presence or the reception of the Spirit.

We turn now to Mk. 12.36. Here Jesus says that David spoke Ps. 110 through the prompting or by means of the Holy Spirit. The Spirit is the one who inspires prophetic words. It is of course true that in both the OT and NT we hear language like this, but it would appear that Jesus is referring to a more profound theory of inspiration than we find in the OT. Jesus is referring to an inspiration not just of persons, such as David, but an inspiration that results in an inspired or God-breathed text, which he could quote as having divine authority. In other words, he is talking about Holy Writ inspired by the Holy Spirit, not merely inspired or prophetic speech. This idea of course will be further spelled out in 2 Tim. 3.16. There we even have the word θεόπνευστος, God-breathed.[8] Notice as well that elsewhere Jesus contrasts God's Word with mere human traditions (Mk. 7.13), and this theology of the Word likely is implied or stands behind Mk. 12.36. The Holy Spirit is the person who inspired and prompted David to say what he did, which is now preserved in writing which itself partakes of the inspiration and so can be called Holy Writ, a sacred text. The way was paved for this sort of thinking all the way back in the narratives about Abraham, as we saw earlier in this study.[9]

The third reference to the Holy Spirit in Mark is in some ways the most telling. According to Mk. 13.11, the Spirit is the one who actually does the speaking through the disciples when they are dragged before authorities. Jesus is referring to a time when he is no longer around to help or to defend his disciples, and he is saying that then they will have to rely on the Holy Spirit to do the talking! Possibly one could parallel this with what was said earlier in Mk. 5.7–8 about unclean spirits prompting talking when they possess people. The difference between Spirit possession and unclean spirit possession is not that one involves an impersonal force or power and the other does not, for clearly, demons in Mk. 5 are seen as personal supernatural beings with wills and the like. The difference is that the Spirit leads, guides, prompts, directs, but in general respects the personal identity or integrity of the individual person in which the Spirit dwells. It is not like a case of demon possession, where the unclean spirit by contrast coerces, dominates, and in general takes over the control center of a person's being, simply using the person to its own ends, even using him as a mouthpiece to speak its own words.

Turning now to the sayings source used by both Matthew and Luke, called Q, there is not much in this source to help us better understand Jesus' view of the Holy Spirit. Most scholars do think that Mt. 12.28a/Lk. 11.20a goes back to the historical Jesus in some form, but which form? The Matthean form has "If I by the Spirit of God cast out demons …" whereas the Lukan form has "if I by the finger of God cast out demons …" Luke has often, rightly, been called the theologian of the Holy Spirit, for more than the other two Synoptic writers combined, Luke refers to the person and work of the Spirit,

---

[8] See Witherington, *The Living Word of God.*
[9] See above.

and this is only amplified in Luke's second volume, Acts. The point is, if Luke had had a reference to the Spirit in his source for this saying it is hard to believe he would change it to the more arcane and Pentateuchal "finger of God" (cf. Exod. 31.18; Deut. 9.10; Ps. 8.3). This saying probably alludes to Exod. 8.19 primarily and does so in a way that is characteristic of Jesus' way of echoing the OT in his own public speech. He does not quote it directly, usually, but alludes to a famous phrase about a mighty deed of God during the Exodus events that led to the Israelites' deliverance. Thus, it appears we do not have a reference here on Jesus' lips to the Holy Spirit.

By contrast, both forms of Mt. 12.32/Lk. 12.10 do refer to the Holy Spirit, as part of the "Beelzebul" controversy. Matthew seems to have better preserved the original setting of the saying because it clearly distinguishes the Son of Man from the Holy Spirit, and on the basis of this distinction forgiveness against the former is permitted, while forgiveness for blasphemy against the latter is not. In any case, the Spirit is treated here as a person, indeed as part of the divine identity, and just as personal as the Son of Man himself. Both the Spirit and the Son of Man are persons who can be spoken for or against. Jesus is not speaking about someone other than himself having the Spirit, indeed Jesus seems to have rarely spoken of the Spirit at all, prior to the near-end of his ministry, as recorded in Jn. 14–17 during private discussions with his inner circle. And even in that context, it is made clear that Jesus is not baptizing anyone in the Spirit or sending the Spirit prior to Easter.

Furthermore, it is very doubtful that one should even see the scene in Jn. 20 as an example of the bestowal by the risen Jesus of the Spirit on the inner circle. As we shall see shortly, that seems to be a prophetic sign act performed to reassure the disciples that they will, after Jesus departs to heaven, receive the Spirit.

Turning to Matthew, the very first reference to the Spirit significantly enough, comes when we hear about the virginal conception of Jesus within Mary. Mt. 1.18 indicates that the means by which Mary came to be with child was the Holy Spirit, though it is not completely clear who it was that "found Mary to be with child by means of the Holy Spirit." Joseph of course, according to the story, did discover she was pregnant, but the story implies that he did not know that it was conceived by means of the Holy Spirit. Indeed, the resolution to divorce Mary quietly suggests he thought something unholy had happened. The important point in any case about this reference is it indicates the creative power of the Spirit, an ability to generate something out of very little or nothing. In other words, the Spirit is seen here as God at work, much in the same fashion as one sees in Gen. 1. According to Mt. 1.20, it took an angelic revelation to confirm to Joseph he should not refuse to take Mary as his wife, since her pregnancy came from God.

In Mt. 3.11 we find the reference to John saying Jesus will baptize in/with the Holy Spirit and fire. Scholars have debated what "and fire" means, but the First Evangelist at least seems to view it as a reference to judgment, in view of the very next verse. It is possible to read these two verses to mean he will baptize some with Spirit and others with fire, or one can take both references to be to the same action, a baptism by fire through the Holy Spirit (and compare the quotation from the poem by T. S. Eliot at the outset of this chapter). This "baptism" could be seen as purifying as well as redemptive.

As we have already noted, Mark's baptismal scene presents us with a private revelation to Jesus, which Matthew turns into a public event. Mt. 3.16 tells us the Spirit of God is seen descending and landing upon Jesus. Mark does not mention the "alighting" of the

Spirit on Jesus like a dove (not as a dove, but in dove-like manner, so, presumably, gently). Matthew is stressing in a way Mark does not that the Spirit stayed on Jesus, which explains what comes next. In Mt. 4.1 Jesus is said to be led by the Spirit into the wilderness, whereas in Mk. 1.12 the Spirit is said to drive Jesus out into the wilderness. Leading is normally the action of a person and so Matthew even more clearly stresses the personal nature of the Spirit.

Mt. 5.3, "blessed are the poor in spirit," is unlikely to be a reference to the Holy Spirit, as Matthew always uses either the phrase Spirit of God or Holy Spirit to refer to that person. This reading is probably confirmed by the Lukan parallel which just has "blessed are the poor." Note as well that the Holy Spirit is not a subject for discussion anywhere else in the Sermon on the Mount either. And like Mk. 10.1, Matthew says nothing about the Spirit being the agency by which the disciples performed their miracles, including exorcisms.

Mt. 10.16–23 becomes the setting in this Gospel for the saying about being dragged before authorities, and here it is crucial to note the reassurance that "the Spirit of your Father" will be speaking through the disciples, when they have to testify. While this could be taken to simply mean "the presence of the Father," Matthew is surely following Mk. 13.11, which specifies that it is the Holy Spirit that is in view. The emphasis here would be on the Father as the one who gives the Spirit to the disciples, much as in the phrase "the promise of the Father" (Lk. 24.49).

Mt. 12.18–21 involves a quotation from Isa. 42.1–4 which includes the phrase "I will put my spirit upon him," which is referred to what God has done in the case with Jesus. Here the Spirit is viewed in an impersonal way, unlike Matthew's normal way of talking about the Spirit, but since he is quoting the OT here, he is constrained by the form of the quotation, presumably. The discussion about exorcism in Mt. 12.28–31 is interesting because of the three different ways the Spirit is referred to – the Spirit of God, then the Holy Spirit, then in v. 31 simply the Spirit. This makes a total of four different uses of Spirit language in this one chapter, but only in one case, the quotation from Isaiah, is there an impersonal reference to the Spirit. This probably reflects Matthew's faithfulness to what he found in his sources (Isaiah, Mark, and Q), but since he alters Mk. 12.31 it cannot simply be explained that way. For our purposes, the clear difference between the way the spirit language is treated impersonally in the OT and overwhelmingly personally in the NT is yet another good example as to why one must have a sense of progressive revelation to do justice to such a subject when doing biblical theology.[10]

Remarkably, after four, or at least three, references to the Spirit in Mt. 12 there are exactly none in Mt. 13–21. At Mt. 22.43 the Greek literally reads "How is it that David in spirit calls him Lord, saying …?" This could be taken to mean "by the Spirit" referring to inspired speech, but we find the very same phrase, *en pneumati*, at Rev. 1.10, which

---

[10] To be clear, I am not saying that on further review and in light of the NT, all those references to God's spirit in the OT must be references to the Holy Spirit but the OT writers, bless their hearts, didn't understand this clearly. To the contrary, I don't think that is the case. I think spirit in the OT mainly just means God's living, life-giving presence. In other words, I don't think this is a matter of mere perspective, or better understanding in light of later revelation. I think the person of the Holy Spirit first shows up in human history perhaps at the conception and then at the baptism of Jesus, and more clearly, in regard to human beings other than Jesus, the eschatological Spirit invades human history when Jesus and the Father send him from heaven. I think this is what Jn. 14–17 and Acts 2 are getting at, ultimately.

we could call an OT way of speaking of God's spirit, the spirit being the atmosphere or sphere which one enters, leading to inspired speech or a vision. Notice that it is not said in either text that the Spirit was in the speaker. Perhaps the spirit is referred to in an impersonal way here, which would not be entirely surprising since Jesus is citing an OT text, Ps. 110.1, spoken by an OT figure. But it is also possible to see this phrase as a reference to a particular spiritual experience – "in the Spirit he said …" There are no further references to the Holy Spirit in Matthew until the very end, at Mt. 28.19, in the baptismal formula, and so in essence, apart from one OT reference to God's spirit, nothing is said along these lines between Mt. 13.13 and Mt. 28.18.

But it would be hard to overestimate the importance of Mt. 28.19. Here not only is the Spirit spoken of personally as "the Holy Spirit" alongside the Father and the Son, but the Spirit is said to be part of the divine name, the very divine identity. Baptism is to be performed in this tri-personal name. Here indeed, we see the beginnings of Trinitarian thinking. One doesn't baptize a person in some name less than the name of God. It is no accident the First Evangelist depicts Jesus as speaking in this way *after Easter, and as the risen Lord* to whom has been bequeathed all power and authority and, for that matter, all knowledge as the text surely implies. Jesus is now able to reveal the full name, the full identity of God – Father, Son, and Holy Spirit (not merely the spirit of Yahweh). At a minimum, this reveals the Christian speech patterns of Matthew and his community, and note that in many ways Matthew's Gospel is the most Jewish of the four. Matthew does not anachronistically predicate such speech of Jesus or others *prior* to Easter. Indeed, the disciples do not speak of the Holy Spirit even once before the resurrection, in either Mark or Matthew.

The Holy Spirit in Luke–Acts

We have already mentioned that Luke has come to be known as the theologian of the Holy Spirit.[11] Here, and well before Easter, in Lk. 11.13 Jesus says that the Father will give the Holy Spirit to those who ask, and then the risen Jesus urges the disciples quite pointedly to stay in Jerusalem until they receive power from on high which is said to have been "what my Father promised" (Lk. 24.49). Interestingly, however, the place in Luke's Gospel where there is most reference to the Holy Spirit is in the birth narratives, for which material Luke is certainly not relying on Mark, or Q for that matter. Thus, a *prima facie* case can be made that from the outset of both of his volumes (Lk. 1–2, Acts 1–2), Luke wishes to stress the work of the Holy Spirit.

One of the most interesting aspects of Luke's presentation is that Luke, ever the historian, mostly chooses to refer to the spirit in the OT manner in his Gospel, speaking of a power or presence or force or something that fills a person. By contrast, in Acts the Holy Spirit is seen as an actor in the drama, so much so that he is one of the persons who hands down the famous decree in Acts 15.28 – "it has seemed good to the Holy Spirit and to us to impose no further burden …" The Spirit was consulted, and James concluded he was opposed to such an imposition of more requirements for Gentiles. Or again in Acts 16.6 the Spirit is said to forbid Paul to speak the word in Asia. Luke is prepared as well to stress

---

[11] See Joel B. Green, *The Theology of the Gospel of Luke* (Cambridge: Cambridge University Press, 1995), 41–47.

the connection between Jesus and the Spirit, for at Acts 16.7 the Spirit is called "the Spirit of Jesus," in a manner similar to the phrase "the Son of the Father." Luke knows that the personal nature of the Spirit is a Christian issue and emphasis, and so his characters in the Gospel speak like OT folk when they refer to God's spirit, by and large.

Lk. 1.15–17 immediately presents us with intriguing evidence at the outset of the Gospel. The angel tells Zechariah that John will be "filled with the Holy Spirit" (v. 15), but it is not clear (in view of v. 17, which refers to his having "the spirit and power of Elijah") whether or not it is a reference to the Holy Spirit in the Christian sense. Elisha, it will be remembered from 2 Kgs. 2.9, asked for a double portion of *Elijah's spirit*, and in light of this Lk. 1.17 at least would seem not to be a reference to the Holy Spirit.

Lk. 1.35 is the most famous reference to the Spirit in these birth narratives. Mary is told by an angel that "the Holy Spirit will come upon you and the power of the Most High will over-shadow you." This could be taken to be two ways to refer to the very same thing, the power of the Most High being the same as the spirit, which will both come upon Mary and protect her as God's power works within her. Equally Old Testamental is the reference to the Spirit filling a person to speak or sing at Lk. 1.41, where Elizabeth is inspired to proclaim Mary as the most blessed of all women, being the mother of the messiah. Perhaps a bit more personal is Lk. 2.25, where we hear that the Spirit rested on Simeon and that he guided Simeon (2.27), and that the Holy Spirit had revealed to him he would not see death until he saw the messiah (2.26). But as with his language about "the Lord" Luke in his narrative framework speaks as a Christian, but his characters in the dialogue in the Gospel speak as Jews.

At the baptismal scene in Lk. 3.16 there is one new note not found in Matthew and Mark, namely that the Spirit descended on Jesus "in bodily form" like a dove, and this in turn leads to another unique Lukan phrase, namely that Jesus returned from the Jordan, full of the Holy Spirit, a Spirit that leads Jesus *in the wilderness*, as opposed to the Matthean "into the wilderness." Luke is stressing that Jesus was not abandoned by God during the temptation time in the wilderness, and again at the end of that time in Lk. 4.14 Jesus is said to return to Galilee, filled with the power of the Spirit, a note we do not find in Matthew or Mark. All of this prepares us for the declaration in Nazareth synagogue that "the Spirit of the Lord (i.e. Yahweh) is upon me," a citation from Isa. 61.1, not found in the earlier presentations in Mark and Matthew. The Spirit is prompting and empowering his preaching and his miracle-working.

The next reference to the Spirit comes at Lk. 10.21, where in Luke, but not in the parallel in Mt. 11.25–27, Jesus is said to rejoice in the Holy Spirit.[12] Luke combines the reference to the blasphemy of the Spirit with the mention of the promise that the Spirit will guide the disciples in their speech when they are hauled before the authorities (Lk. 12.10–12). It is worth mentioning here that the background for that saying is likely Isa. 63.10, and in general Second and Third Isaiah seem to be the primary OT sources that Jesus and the Synoptic writers draw on when looking for language to describe the work of the Spirit.[13] One noticeable difference between Mark and Luke in that text is that while Mark

---

[12] Interestingly, an early witness P⁴⁵ simply has "rejoiced in spirit," which could refer to Jesus' human spirit (see e.g. Lk. 23.46, a partial quotation from Ps. 31.5, where it clearly refers to the human spirit).

[13] See M. M. B. Turner, "Holy Spirit," in *The Dictionary of Jesus and the Gospels* (ed. Joel B. Green, Scot McKnight, and I. Howard Marshall; Downers Grove, IL: InterVarsity Press, 1992), 341–51. There are also echoes from extra-canonical sources such as Wis. Sol. and Sirach.

says bluntly the Spirit will do the talking when the disciples are on trial (Mk. 13.11), and Matthew refers to the Spirit of the Father speaking through them, Luke on the other hand refers to the teaching of the Holy Spirit. In other words, Luke emphasizes the personal and pedagogical relationship between the Spirit and the disciples, rather than just suggesting the Spirit used them as a vessel to speak through. References to the Spirit are scarce in the rest of Luke's Gospel until Lk. 24.49. Notice that nowhere in Luke's Gospel are the disciples of Jesus said to be full of the Spirit, but John, Elizabeth, Jesus, and Simeon are so characterized. But promises are made to the disciples in this regard in Luke, which distinguishes his account from the two earlier Gospels. In truth, none of the Synoptics has any significant amount of discussion about the Holy Spirit. It is not a topic really discoursed on by Jesus or others, but Luke, like Matthew and Mark, assumes his audience knows the meaning of the phrase "Holy Spirit."

The Book of Acts is a horse of a different color. There is reason why it has sometimes been called the Acts of the Holy Spirit, as opposed to the Acts of the Apostles (who, apart from Peter and Paul, and cameo appearances by James and John, are not really focused on after Acts 1). God in the person of the Spirit is seen as the primary actor or agency in Acts, the prime mover and cause of the positive forward action of the drama in that book. Sometimes, as in Acts 2 and 10, the Spirit simply invades the human sphere and falls upon people before they even know what has happened to them, changing their lives in dramatic fashion.

It is not an accident that the Book of Acts begins with a retrospective that includes the reminder that even the risen Jesus operated on the basis of the Holy Spirit, for it says that Jesus was taken up "after giving instructions through the Holy Spirit to the apostles whom he had chosen" (1.2). There is also the reiteration of the instruction to remain in Jerusalem and await "the promise of the Father" (Lk. 24.49 and Acts 1.4). Notice at Acts 1.5 there is an explicit connection made by the risen Jesus between the prophecy of John and the baptism with the Holy Spirit (1.5). John spoke of baptism with Spirit and fire at Lk. 3.16 and that is exactly how Pentecost's beginnings are described at Acts 2.3–4. Acts 1.8 is to some degree the most important early reference to the Spirit in Acts because it clearly distinguishes between the power that the Spirit will bring and the person of the Spirit who is bringing it – "You will receive power *when the Holy Spirit comes upon you.*" The Spirit is the personal agent who will supply the power the disciples so badly need, power that will enable them to be witnesses throughout the Mediterranean crescent. In the speech Peter makes to the 120 believers, the Spirit is again referred to as a person, who foretold, through David, the demise of Judas (Acts 1.16). The Spirit in Acts is of course "the Spirit of prophecy" but it is also the eschatological Spirit that enables disciples to perform miracles as well.

Without over-analyzing an already over-analyzed account of Pentecost, we need to emphasize just a few key points. Firstly, the sudden coming of the Spirit is described with metaphorical analogies. The Spirit is aptly said to come *like* a violent wind (remembering the word for Spirit and wind are the same in both Hebrew and Greek). Or the divided tongues are said to be *like* fire, in some respect, though no one actually had their hair set on fire! These analogies describe the impression the coming of the Spirit left on the disciples. The description is somewhat impersonal because it is influenced by OT prophecies, particularly the one about to be cited by Peter at 2.17–21 – Joel 2.28–29. Note the language of "pouring out" in the text in Joel.

Having already made clear the personal nature of the Spirit at 1.2 and 1.16, Luke then mixes personal and impersonal language in Acts 2.4 – the Spirit is the person who gave the disciples the ability to speak in other languages, but the description of the process speaks of them being filled with the Spirit, drawing on OT language used when speaking of a prophet being inspired. Notice that the Spirit is said to have filled them all. This was not a mere endowment of a few leaders. Luke wishes to leave the impression that this event was dramatic in its effects, hence the analogy with being drunk at 2.13,15. The disciples are acting in an abnormal, some would say out-of-control, manner, and they are surprisingly loquacious even around a crowd of strangers, and even in foreign languages. Peter explains they are not drunk but rather enabled by the Spirit to miraculously speak in foreign languages, something my Greek students pray for regularly! Note the analogy with Jesus, who also acted on the basis of the power of the Spirit within him once the Spirit came upon him at baptism. Acts 2.22 suggests Luke is comfortable calling the Spirit "God," for by the Spirit Jesus was enabled to say and do what he did (Lk. 3.22; 4.1,14,15).

Notice the close connection between God, the Spirit, and Christ at Acts 2.33 – God gives Jesus the promise of the Spirit, who in turn pours it out on the disciples, motivating and enabling them to speak. Father, Jesus, and Spirit are all in heaven together, acting on behalf of the disciples on earth, enabling them to spread the Good News. At Acts 2.38 we learn that for someone to receive "the gift of the Spirit" they must repent and be baptized and receive release from their sins. The Spirit is not owed to anyone. It is a gift from God, even though it was promised by God and prophesied about by the prophets. Notice that Peter says that the coming of the Spirit on someone produces times of refreshment and renewal, for it is the very presence of God, in the person of the Spirit, the Lord the giver of life, who has come to the person.

According to Acts 4.8, Peter is a Spirit-inspired, and thus prophetic, person who is prepared, as Jesus promised, to speak boldly to the officials based on what the Spirit guides him to say. The Spirit inspires articulate and educated discourse. Notice how the personal agency of the Spirit is stressed again at 4.25 – the Father spoke by the Spirit through the human agency of David. Again, we begin to see a Trinitarian way of thinking about how God acts. Acts 5 provides the remarkable story of Ananias and Sapphira, who are accused of "lying to the Holy Spirit" (5.3), which of course implies the Spirit is a person who can be addressed. Notice at 5.9 it is said that it is the Spirit of the Lord that is said to have been put to the test. It is not clear here whether Lord means God or Christ. It could be either, since later in Acts we hear about the "Spirit of Jesus" (Acts 16.7).

According to Acts 6.3 the leaders to be picked must be full of the Spirit and also of wisdom. This may be an example of hendiadys – full of the Spirit who conveys wisdom. Acts 6.5 says that the first person chosen, Stephen, is full of faith and the Spirit and at 6.8 he is said to be full of grace and power and so enabled to perform great signs and miracles before the people. This provides clues to what the Spirit can give – prophetic speech, wisdom, faith, grace, the power to do miracles. Those who opposed Stephen's evangelizing nonetheless could not withstand "the wisdom and Spirit with which he spoke" (6.10). They were only able to commit libel by suggesting Stephen was blaspheming, which is meant to remind us of what Luke's Gospel says about blasphemy against the Spirit. It is not Stephen who is guilty of this, but his interlocutors. At the end of Stephen's famous speech in Acts 7 and just before his martyrdom at 7.55, Stephen is said to be full of the

Spirit, who inspires Stephen with a vision, enabling him to see the Son of Man in heaven, standing to welcome him there.

Acts 8 chronicles a new stage in the missionary work of the church, with Philip reaching out to the Samaritans. Notice that Philip does not convey the Spirit to them. Rather, it is when Peter and John come down that there is prayer that the Samaritans might receive the Holy Spirit. The reference to prayer here is important and should be compared to Acts 1.24–2.1. The reference to prayer indicates that even the apostles could not dispense the Spirit at will from their own supply, as it were. Rather they must ask God to give it to others. Notice that Simon Magus asks the apostles not for the Spirit but for the power to convey the Spirit (8.19). The Spirit is said to be given through the laying-on of hands but this is only after prayer (8.15–19).

This story is important for several reasons: (1) Luke does not associate the reception of the Spirit with the reception of water baptism. Indeed, the two are clearly distinguished in time and nature here, just as in the Gospel there was a distinction between the reception of John's baptism and the reception of the Spirit through the action of Jesus, though of course the two can be nearly coincident in time, as the story of the Ethiopian eunuch later in this chapter shows (Acts 8.26–40). In the case of Jesus, the water baptism came first, then when Jesus prayed the heavens opened and the Spirit descended (Lk. 3.21–22); (2) for Luke the *sine qua non* of being a Christian is having the Holy Spirit in one's life. Pentecost is the birthday of the church precisely because that is when the Spirit was first received as an indwelling presence in the disciples' lives. The "disciples" in Acts 19 who have never heard of the Holy Spirit but know only John's baptism, are not Christian disciples but rather John's disciples, which is why Paul must start over from scratch with them with water baptism in the name of Jesus followed by laying-on of hands and the reception of the Spirit. This in turn means that: (3) though we are told in Acts 8 that some Samaritans are said to believe, we are not told what or in whom they believed (in Philip? in the truthfulness of his preaching?). In any case, until they receive the Spirit they are not full-fledged disciples of Jesus. Luke is not an advocate of a two-stage process of first having saving faith and then later receiving the Spirit. In this particular case, because of the animus between Jews and Samaritans, there probably needed to be confirmation by the apostles that even the Samaritans were coming to faith in Jesus. Acts 8.39 ends the chapter by portraying Philip to be a figure like Elijah, for the Spirit snatched him away and the next thing he knew he was at Azotus (cf. 1 Kgs. 18.46).

The next reference to the Holy Spirit is in the story of Saul's conversion in Acts 9. Ananias is sent to Saul after his Damascus Road experience, "so that you may regain your sight and be filled with the Holy Spirit" (9.17). Baptism is also mentioned at v. 18, but Luke says nothing about what the connection, if any, might be between being filled with the Spirit and being baptized in water. What we may surmise from Acts 10 is that Luke believed that if one already had the Spirit, water baptism should not be withheld. Acts 9 is most naturally read as assuming a connection between regaining one's sight and being filled with the Spirit.

The summary statement in Acts 9.31 is intriguing. The church in the Holy Land is said to be living in the fear of the Lord (i.e. God) and in the comfort of the Spirit. Notice the parallelism. The Spirit is not simply identified with Yahweh/the Father but is clearly viewed as a person capable of comforting believers. This theme of the personal nature of the Spirit is continued in Acts 10.19, where we hear that the Spirit spoke to Peter after his vision, alerting him to the arrival of Cornelius' messengers (repeated in 11.12). Notice Peter's reference as well to Jesus himself being anointed with "the Spirit and with power" (10.38). The Spirit gives the power but is not simply an impersonal power. Verse 44 refers to the Spirit falling on all of Cornelius' family who heard the preaching of the Good News about Jesus. Peter recognizes this has happened from the fact that he hears them speaking in tongues and praising God, in this case probably referring to glossolalia. Baptism should not be withheld from them.

Notice that in Acts 8 we have seen the order reception of water baptism, then the Spirit, and in Acts 10 the reverse of that, and so we should conclude Luke is not trying to teach a particular order of such events as normative. For Luke, however, it is the reception of the Spirit which makes someone a Christian, not receiving water baptism. In Acts 18, Apollos is certainly a believer in Christ, but he has not yet received Christian baptism. The most important comment of Peter about the Cornelius episode is found at Acts 11.15, where he stresses that it is the same Spirit who fell on these Gentiles as fell on the Jews at Pentecost, and that it happened to them just as it happened earlier in Acts 2 – unexpectedly and at the divine initiative. The contrast in 11.16 between water and Spirit baptism is interesting as well. John offered the former, but Peter says Jesus promised the latter. Actually, this is doubly interesting since Lk. 3.16 told us that John said this, but here Peter says Jesus said this. Perhaps we are meant to think that Jesus later repeated to the disciples what John had previously said at Jesus' baptism. Acts 11.17 says it was God who gave the gift of the Spirit to those who believed in Christ. Note the close connection between preaching, believing in Jesus, and receiving the Spirit.

Barnabas is an important figure in Luke's narrative, as was already evident in Acts 4.36–37, but in Acts 11 he becomes even more important. Acts 11.22–23 describes him in very similar terms to the earlier description of Stephen – "full of the Holy Spirit and of faith" (cf. 6.5, only in the opposite order of mention). Equally interesting is the reference to Agabus the Christian prophet, who "predicted by the Spirit that there would be a severe famine" (11.28). Agabus will reappear at Acts 21.11, this time in Caesarea rather than Antioch, performing the symbolic gesture, a prophetic sign act, of binding Paul. He says: "This is the way the Jews of Jerusalem will bind the man ..." Here again in these descriptions the Spirit is seen as a person, indeed as God, for the standard prophetic formula is modified from "thus says Yahweh ..." to "thus says the Spirit ..."[14]

At Acts 13.2 we have another example of the Holy Spirit speaking, this time commanding that Paul and Barnabas be set aside for a missionary venture. Notice that this "speaking" is said to transpire while the church is worshipping and fasting. Presumably, we are meant to think a prophet spoke this in worship. And notice as well that it is the Spirit who sends these men out. The Spirit speaks, and the Spirit sends out. Yet we also hear of Paul being filled with the Spirit and given spiritual insight into Elymas (13.9). Often, the phrase "filled with the Spirit" is coupled with something else, for example in 13.52 where the disciples are said to be full of joy and of the Spirit.

---

[14] Notice that prophecy is an "inexact" science, for while Paul is bound, it is not by the Jews but by a Roman official who rescues Paul from the mob in the temple and carts him off to Caesarea Maritima, the governor's seat of power.

In Peter's crucial remarks at the council in Acts 15 he says of the Gentiles: "and God who knows the human heart, testified to them by giving them the Holy Spirit." The Spirit in this case is seen as the divine seal of approval, indicating to one and all that they are acceptable. Notice too that it is the Spirit who helps make the final ruling about Gentile Christians and their activities (15.28), just as it is the Spirit who forbids Paul to go into Bithynia (16.7). Here for the only time the Spirit is called "the Spirit of Jesus." Acts 18.25 refers to Apollos as "boiling over in the Spirit," though a less literal translation like "with burning enthusiasm" (NRSV) is possible. Note the interesting discussion in Acts. 19.17 that Paul has with the disciples of John the Baptizer, who had not previously met Paul or heard of the Holy Spirit. In other words, they are not Christians, which is why Paul must go through the entire initiation (baptism) and conversion (reception of the Spirit through laying-on of hands) process with them. They can be contrasted with Apollos at the end of Acts 18 who knows "the way of the Lord" and preaches Christ with zeal but needs further instruction about water baptism. These texts in Acts 18–19 remind us that John continued to have a following long after his beheading, and in lands other than the Holy Land. It also reflects the need for the early Christian movement to be able to distinguish John's baptism and Christian baptism, and both from the reception of the Spirit.

The famous Miletus speech in Acts 20, the only speech Paul gives to those already Christian in Acts, refers to the Spirit testifying to Paul in every city that imprisonment and persecution await him in Jerusalem (v. 23). This presumably refers to prophets telling him what is yet to come (cf. 21.4). The phrasing here is interesting, "through the Spirit, they told him not to go to Jerusalem ..." This would seem to mean in an ecstatic state they spoke, but in any case the odd thing about this is that Paul ignores these warnings of the Spirit, if such they were, believing that God wanted him to go to Jerusalem and deliver the collection (cf. Rom. 15). Perhaps the Spirit is just warning Paul that things will get difficult if he goes to Jerusalem?

It is telling that in the chapters about the legal wrangling over Paul and about the sea voyage there are no references to the Spirit in all of Acts 21.12–28.25, not even in the recounting of Paul's conversion in Acts 22 and 26, which is surprising. The final reference to the Spirit comes in Acts 28.25, where we are told that it was the Holy Spirit who spoke in the ancient prophecies, in this case Isa. 6.9–10. This is important because it confirms that Luke sees the OT as inspired by God, and he stresses that the same Holy Spirit who has been speaking directly to Christians in the early church was the one who spoke to their Jewish ancestors as well. In other words, the coming of the Spirit on Elizabeth or Mary, or the church was not the beginning of the story of the Holy Spirit. The Spirit as part of the divine identity, as a personal being, has a history with God's people. The Spirit is not a mere power or force, though the effects of the Spirit can be powerful, and the Spirit can convey power as well.

The Spirit in the Fourth Gospel as Agent, Advocate, Counselor

The account in the Fourth Gospel of Jesus' "baptism" is, like most other things in this Gospel, distinctive. The actual act of baptizing Jesus is not mentioned, and instead we have John himself saying he saw the Spirit descending and remaining on Jesus (Jn. 1.32). Further, we are informed that John was told that the One on whom he saw the Spirit descend would in turn be the One to baptize others with the Holy Spirit (v. 33). There is a stress here in these first references to the Spirit in this Gospel on the Spirit remaining on Jesus.

The second reference to the Spirit in John comes in the famous dialogue between Jesus and Nicodemus in Jn. 3, where we hear "you must be born of water and the Spirit" and the text goes on to explain this reference by saying "flesh gives birth to flesh, and Spirit to spirit." The term water here has nothing to do with water baptism, much less Christian water baptism. Water was an early Jewish metaphorical way of talking about physical birth, a birth as the text says literally "out of water" to be contrasted with a birth that is "out of the Spirit."[15] Water and Spirit are seen as the mediums or agencies through which such a birth occurs. A person born of the Spirit knows where things come from and where things go, that is he or she knows that spiritual birth comes from above, comes from God, just as Jesus comes from God.

Jn. 4.24 refers to God being spirit, as part of a discussion about the Father's nature, and so this is not a reference to the Holy Spirit. Nor is it clear that Jn. 6.63 is about the Holy Spirit either. Spirit is opposed to flesh here, and is said to give life. But is this the spirit of God or the Holy Spirit? The second half of the verse claims that Jesus' words are spirit and life, which supports the view that the Holy Spirit is not the subject here. Jn. 8.39 indicates that Jesus spoke of the Holy Spirit, but only metaphorically, in terms of rivers of living water flowing out of a person. Far more important, however, is the following comment, which says: "as of yet there was no Spirit for Jesus was not yet glorified" (i.e. believers were to receive the Spirit after the death, resurrection and ascension of Jesus). According to all four Gospels, Jesus offered no public teaching on the Spirit, and only had a private chat with Nicodemus about the Spirit, and a word to the disciples that the Spirit would be coming (but during the ministry the Spirit did not rest on them as the Spirit did on Jesus).

We now come to the five crucial *parakletos* sayings in the Farewell discourses, found in Jn. 14.26; 15.26; 16.7–11; and 12–15. The One Jesus promises to send to the disciples or to have the Father send them (cf. 14.26 to 15.26) is called a *parakletos*, or to be more exact "another" *parakletos*. There is an implied comparison between Jesus and the Spirit. They are both persons who have the same agenda and some shared functions and power. Should the term itself be translated "Comforter," "Counselor," or "Advocate"? An examination of Jn. 14–17 suggests that the Spirit has the following functions: (1) to indwell the believer and convey God's presence and peace, including the presence of Jesus to the believer (cf. 14.17–20,27); (2) to teach and lead the believer into all truth, and to testify to the believer about and on behalf of Jesus (14.26 and 15.26); (3) to enable the believer to testify about Jesus to the world, and with the Spirit guiding the person convicts the world of sin, righteousness, and judgment (15.26–27; 16.8–11). The Spirit is clearly seen as Jesus' sent agent, just as Christ is the agent of the Father on earth (see 16.13–15). There is other judicial language used of the Spirit in these discourses as well, which favors the translation "Advocate" as does (3) above.

It is the task of a legal advocate to speak on behalf of and as a representative of the one who sent him. Only a person can be an advocate, and the comparison with Jesus himself only further supports this conclusion. The Spirit is seen as a person just as the Father and

---

[15] See the full discussion in Witherington, *John's Wisdom*, 94–97.

the Son are, but distinguishable from them, yet working in concert with them as part of the divine identity and the divine plan for humankind. The Spirit is Jesus' surrogate on earth while Jesus is in heaven. He will equip the disciples with the presence of Jesus and the understanding of Jesus' teaching, and give them the power to convict, convince, and convert the world. The Spirit also gives them the strength to persevere through persecution. The ultimate goal of the Spirit is the salvation of the individual through the sanctifying power of the truth, and through such saved persons the salvation of at least some in the dark world.

This brings us to the final reference to the Spirit in the Fourth Gospel at Jn. 20.22. The risen Jesus breathes on the disciples and says "receive the Holy Spirit." Is this the Johannine version of Pentecost as some have thought? Such a suggestion doesn't make sense in that narrative context, for the disciples are still hiding behind locked doors a week later, not boldly proclaiming the Good News hither and yon. They show no effects of the Spirit, any more than they did during the Farewell Discourses and the Passion narrative. Thus, this scene should be viewed as Jesus performing a prophetic sign act, a preview of coming attractions, just as he did in the temple earlier with the turning over of the money changers' tables. He is not yet bestowing the Spirit, for he has not yet ascended to the Father. Thus, the Fourth Gospel agrees with the Synoptics, the Spirit was not given before Jesus ascended. Again, seeing Jn. 20.22 as suggesting a partial giving of the Spirit at this juncture misinterprets John's theology of the Spirit who is a person, and is not distributed piecemeal to the believers. One either has the Spirit in one's life or one doesn't. One does not get some now, and more later, as if the Spirit were like a quantity of water. There is, at the end of the day, very little impersonal language used of the Spirit in John, and the overriding impression conveyed is that the Spirit is a person who dwells within the believer and acts like and on behalf of the Son.

The Spirit in Paul's Letters

One could easily write several chapters about all Paul says about the Holy Spirit. Indeed, Gordon Fee, in his classic study, *God's Empowering Presence*, wrote some 900 pages on this subject without exhausting the topic! We will only be able to highlight some of the most salient points, for there are some 145 uses of the term *pneuma* in Paul's letters and the vast majority of them refer to the Holy Spirit, even though the full phrase "Holy Spirit" is only used some 16–17 times in these earliest of NT documents. In addition to those references we have the phrase "the Spirit of God/his Spirit" some 16 more times, and the terms "Spirit of Christ/his Son" three times (Gal. 4.6; Rom. 8.9; Phil. 1.19). In contrast to Luke, Paul never uses the phrase "filled with the Holy Spirit." Some have seen Eph. 5.18–19 as an exception to this rule, where being drunk with wine is opposed to being full/filled in Spirit. However, the verb here is an imperfect passive, and a literal rendering would be "let yourself be filled" (ongoing action). The author does not say "become filled with the Spirit." It is not a matter of receiving the Spirit or receiving a second dose of the Spirit, but rather is about being filled with the Spirit who already indwells the believer. The idea is of allowing the Spirit to penetrate one's whole being, inspiring one to sing spiritual songs. Furthermore, the verb *pleroo* with the preposition *en* means "be filled by means of the Spirit." That is, the Spirit is not the content of the filling but rather its means. When one is fully inspired by the Spirit, one is led to sing songs, hymns, and spiritual songs.

The primary way Paul speaks about the initial receiving of the Spirit is either of God giving his Spirit, placing it within a person (1 Thess. 4.8; 2 Cor. 1.22; 5.5; Rom. 5.5; Eph. 1.7; 2 Tim. 1.7), or he may refer to the supplying of the Spirit (Gal. 3.5; Phil. 1.19), or he may speak of believers receiving the Spirit (1 Cor. 2.12; 2 Cor. 11.4; Gal. 3.2,14; Rom. 8.15), or finally he may refer quite simply to their "having the Spirit" (1 Cor. 2.16; 7.40; Rom. 8.9).[16] Paul tends to avoid impersonal images for the Spirit (e.g. water, oil, wind, breath, fire).

Many of the Pauline references to the Spirit indicate the personal nature of the Spirit. In Gal. 6.6 the Spirit is said to cry out within us, or in Gal. 5.17 the Spirit has desires that oppose the flesh, or the Spirit leads the believers in God's ways (Gal. 5.18; Rom. 8.14) and the Spirit bears witness with our human spirits (Rom. 8.16). The Spirit intercedes for the believer (Rom. 8.26–27), helps when the believer is weak (Rom. 8.26), strengthens believers (Eph. 3.16), and is grieved by human sinfulness (Eph. 4.30). In addition, the Spirit searches all things and even searches and knows God's mind (1 Cor. 2.10–11). The Spirit dwells among the believing community as well as within the individual believer (1 Cor. 3.16; Rom. 8.11; 2 Tim. 1.14), and the Spirit teaches the Gospel to believers (1 Cor. 2.13).

Notice too that Paul very readily predicates the same activity of the Spirit as he does of God or Christ. For example, 1 Cor. 12.6–11 says that God produces a variety of activities in a variety of people, but v. 11 also says that the Spirit produces these activities. Or in Rom. 8.26 the Spirit intercedes for the believer, but a few verses later in 8.34 Christ is said to intercede for the believer.

The fact that Paul will frequently predicate the same thing of the Spirit as he does of Christ, has confused some scholars into thinking that perhaps Paul equates the two (along the lines of "the Lord is the Spirit"). Here are a few examples: (1) we have life in Christ but also in the Spirit (Col. 3.4 and Rom. 8.11); (2) joy in Christ, but also in the Spirit (Phil. 4.4 and Rom. 14.17), righteousness from Christ but also from the Spirit (Phil. 3.8–9 and Rom. 14.7). It is, however, a big mistake to simply equate the two persons, as if the Spirit were the non-corporeal manifestation of Christ, "Christ's spirit," so to speak. Paul knows quite well that the Son died on the cross, not the Spirit, and the Son rose from the dead, not the Spirit, and the Son was born of woman, not the Spirit, and the Son had an earthly embodied ministry, not the Spirit, and so on. Furthermore, Paul speaks of Christ as a historical paradigm or example that believers should follow in Phil. 2.5–11, but nothing is said like this about the Spirit. Nor does Paul view the Spirit in simply Christological terms.

It is the Father who sends the Spirit (Gal. 4.6; 1 Thess. 4.8; 2 Cor. 1.22; 5.5, etc.). In the three places where Paul uses the phrase "the Spirit of Christ" he is referring to the work of Christ in some fashion, and in any case the phrase "Spirit of God" or "Spirit of Christ" is used to distinguish the Holy Spirit from other sorts of spirits. Notice how the Spirit of God is clearly identified with the Spirit of Christ in Rom. 8.9–11. It is one and the same Spirit. Or notice how in 1 Cor. 2.12–16 having the mind of Christ is the same as having the Spirit of God, or at least the latter is the means to having the former.[17] 1 Cor. 6.17 is to be rendered "anyone united to the Lord is one spirit with him," which is a statement about spiritual connection, not about the Holy Spirit. In 1 Cor. 15.45, the risen Christ is called a

---

[16] Fee, *God's Empowering Presence*, 830.

[17] For a thoughtful refutation of some of the things J. D. G. Dunn suggested in *Jesus and the Spirit* (Grand Rapids: William B. Eerdmans, 1997) see Fee, *God's Empowering Presence*, 831–45.

"life-giving spirit" but note the contrast with the first Adam, who is simply a living breathing human being. The issue in 1 Cor. 15.45 is soteriological, Christ gives everlasting life, not Christological or ontological life. 2 Cor. 3.17–18 is more difficult but probably Paul, who is clearly alluding to Exod. 34.34, is doing exegesis here: "now the term Lord (in this text) means the Spirit, and where the Spirit of the Lord is, there is freedom." Notice the distinction in the second half of the saying between the Spirit and the Lord. The point is, where the Spirit is reigning in a person's life, they have freedom of choice, among other things.

None of this is to deny that Paul believes there is a close relationship, and indeed a close working relationship, between the Son and the Spirit. One could even say that the Spirit turns out to be the means by which Christ (who is still in heaven) lives in the believer on earth. Thus in Gal. 2.20 Paul means "Christ lives in me by his Spirit." And immediately after this he will stress that the Galatians have already received the Spirit, by hearing with faith. For Paul, as for Luke, the Spirit is the *sine qua non* of Christian existence, the very means of that existence at all is the presence of the living Spirit. But the end or focus of that existence is Christ and his example. The Spirit points away from himself, as any good agent or advocate is supposed to do, and to the one who sent him.

1 Cor. 12.13 is a crucial text in many regards. Here Paul says "by one Spirit we were all baptized into one body … and we were all made to drink of one Spirit." Here Paul is stressing there is but one Holy Spirit, not many spirits. It is this one Spirit who joins all believers to the body of Christ, and this one Spirit does not contradict himself when he inspires believers to speak a word of teaching or prophecy or just a word of truth. It is the one Spirit of God who prompts the true confession of Jesus as Lord by the believer (1 Cor. 12.3). Paul is functionally Trinitarian in his thinking about these things, as we can now further illustrate.

The way a person worships speaks volumes about his or her faith. In 2 Cor. 13.13 we have a remarkable benediction – "the grace of the Lord Jesus Christ, the love of God, and the communion of the Holy Spirit be with you all." Here we see rather clearly the dramatic effect the Christ event, especially the death and resurrection of Jesus and the giving of the Spirit, has had on a monotheistic Jew's understanding of God. This can be profitably compared to the "Christianized" Shema in 1 Cor. 8.4–6, where the term Lord, in the phrase "the Lord our God, the Lord is one," is applied to Jesus the Lord, whereas God refers to the Father. The reformulated Father language (he is in the first place the Father of Jesus the Son) is used to introduce Christ into the Shema. In Deut. 6.4 the term God and the term Lord are both used of Yahweh himself, but here in 1 Cor. 8.4–6 there is a bifurcation, with God used of the Father and Lord of Jesus. Notice that Paul acknowledges that there are so-called gods many and lords many, which suggests that he sees the Shema as a statement against polytheism, and in favor of the uniqueness of Yahweh, the only true God, not a statement about God being numerically "one" in the divine identity. We deduce from elsewhere that what Paul means by saying Jesus is Lord, is that Jesus is the risen and ruling Lord, since Easter. It is the passion and resurrection of Jesus that is the game changer, even changing the way one speaks about the godhead. The benediction in 2 Cor. 13.13 refers to the Lord, to God, and to the Spirit all being the source of blessing for the believers, all equally seen as expressions of the divine identity. The grace, love, and communion, or sharing in common, are all gifts of God, yet each person of the divine identity can be said to make their own contribution to the life of the believer.

In fact, it is quite natural for Paul to speak in Trinitarian ways as he does in 2 Cor. 13.13. So, for example, in 1 Cor. 12.4–6 he can refer to a variety of gifts, services, and activities, but one and the same Spirit, one and the same Lord, one and the same God involved. Or notice 2 Thess. 2.13–15, where Paul thanks God because God chose the Thessalonians, the Spirit sanctified them, and they look forward to obtaining the glory of Christ. In other words, Eph. 4.4–6, where we hear of one Spirit, one Lord, and one God and Father over all, does not reflect post-Pauline diction, it is rather clearly in the spirit of the functional Trinitarianism that Paul finds naturally comes to his self-expression (cf. Rom. 8.3–4; 1 Cor. 2.4–5; 1 Thess. 1.4–5).[18] Perhaps most importantly for this chapter, these examples of Trinitarian language show that for Paul the Spirit stands on equal footing with the Father and the Son when it comes to talking about God. This stands in rather strong contrast to later developments in church history where the Spirit seems to have been given short shrift. The council of Nicaea and the council of Chalcedon were in the main all about Christology in various ways, and Christ's relationship to the Father. The Spirit seems to have been treated almost as an afterthought or a stepchild in some cases. How very different that is from what we find in Paul's letters.[19]

The Spirit in the General Epistles and in Revelation

In James and 2–3 John there are no references to the Holy Spirit, and in Jude there is exactly one such reference in v. 20 to "praying in the Spirit," which may correlate with what Paul is talking about in Rom. 8 when he says that the Spirit cries out *abba*, Father. There are but two important passages about the Spirit in 1 and 2 Peter, one in each letter, and both having to do with the fact that the Spirit inspires prophetic speech. 2 Pet. 1.20–21 says "no prophecy of Scripture is a matter of one's own interpretation, because no prophecy came by human will, but rather by men and women moved by the Holy Spirit, spoke from God." The source of the utterance is God the Father, but the One who moved or inspired the person to speak at all was the Holy Spirit, the indwelling presence of God in their lives. The author of this sentence does not believe there is a significant human contribution to the utterance, other than humans are the mouthpieces for God's words. Possibly the author is thinking of Pentecost and the fulfillment of the prophecy of Joel 2, which speaks of both men and women prophesying, which is to say, possibly this reflects a memory of Peter's inaugural sermon at Pentecost.

Even more telling is 1 Pet. 1.10–12, which speaks of OT prophets trying to find out the person and time God had in mind when there was a message about the sufferings and glory the messiah was destined for (here surely he is referring to Isa. 52–53). The prophets were told they were serving a later generation, which is as much as saying that they were speaking predictively, not primarily to their own immediate peers. The inspirer of such prophecy was "the Spirit of Christ" within them (1.11). This is surely a synonym for the Holy Spirit, mentioned in v. 12 as being sent from heaven, who spoke the Good News through human emissaries, bringing Peter's audience the message. The author seems

---

[18] Fee, *God's Empowering Presence*, 841–42.
[19] We will have occasion later to talk about the fruit and the gifts of the Spirit, which is to say the effects of the Spirit in the life of the believer, when we get to soteriology proper.

to believe: (1) since it was Christ who sent the Spirit who inspired Christians like Peter to speak, then it follows that (2) it was the pre-existent Christ who sent the Spirit to OT prophets to speak God's Word. Thus, the Spirit of prophecy is the Spirit of Christ in any and all eras of the history of God's people. And note that the author is not equating Christ with the Spirit, for it is only Christ who was destined to suffer and die.

While there are not many references to the Spirit in the Book of Hebrews, the ones we have are significant. Heb. 2.4 in fact seems to be an intertextual echo of 1 Cor. 12.11; here, however, we are told that it is God who distributes the gifts of the Holy Spirit and does so as part of the testimony about the great salvation first declared by Jesus the Lord. The implicit Trinitarianism of Heb. 2.3–4 should be noted – Jesus the pre-existent one (Heb. 1) is also the risen Lord who first declared the eschatological salvation had come, to which God the Father added his testimony by signs and wonders, and by gifts of the Holy Spirit.

The second reference comes at Heb. 3.7, where, perhaps surprisingly, we are told that it is the Holy Spirit who "says" what we find in Ps. 95.7–11. From a Christian perspective, the Holy Spirit is the Spirit of prophecy in all ages, even though these early Christians believed the Spirit was not given as a permanent possession prior to the time of Jesus. We see this identical phenomenon at Heb. 10.16–17, where the Spirit is the One speaking, offering the material found in Jer. 31.31–34. It should be noted that the author of Hebrews alternates between "the Spirit says," "the Father says," and "the Son says" when it comes to Scripture. All three persons are said to speak in the OT. This is because all three persons are part of the divine identity.

Heb. 6.4 is a crucial text when the issue of perseverance of believers becomes a subject of discussion. We are told that a person who has shared in the Holy Spirit and then turns away cannot be restored to repentance. It is also said of such a person that they have been enlightened and have tasted of the heavenly gift, having tasted the goodness of God's word and the powers of the age to come. A more complete description of the Christian is hard to imagine. For this author, as with Luke and Paul as well, having the Holy Spirit is the *sine qua non* of being a Christian. Notice that here the author doesn't say "having a share of the Holy Spirit" as if it were a thing or substance or power to be parceled out, but literally "having become a participator of the Holy Spirit." One takes part in rather than takes a part of the life in the Spirit. What is being discussed here is apostasy of a genuine Christian, which the author clearly thinks is possible.

At Heb. 9.8, while explaining the tabernacle and the priest's role, and viewing these things typologically, he adds that it is the Holy Spirit who indicates by the existence of the tabernacle that the ultimate and final state of affairs had not yet come to pass. In other words, the Spirit, who inspired the scriptural words about the tabernacle and the high priest, knew in advance that a greater tabernacle foreshadowed by the earlier one, was to come, and the very limitations of the first one were an indicator that more was yet to come. The first sanctuary was but an ante-type of the more perfect and true one, for it dealt only with unintentional sins. Here again is the notion that the Spirit existed before the NT era and was active in Israel's history. Heb. 10.29 has the interesting phrase "Spirit of grace." Notice that the Spirit is said to be outraged (a personal emotion and reaction) by the rejection of Christ and his atoning death by some.

Revelation is our last port of call as we survey how the Spirit is presented in the NT. Here we are immersed in the world of apocalyptic prophecy, where there are always surprises. John, like other NT authors, believes that the Holy Spirit is God, or Christ's agent or representative on earth, since both the Father and the Son are in heaven. This is why it is, for instance the "Spirit and the Bride" say come, bidding Christ to return in Rev. 22.17. The Spirit speaks with and through the church and, notably, from the church's perspective. It appears likely that John's use of the imagery of the seven spirits of the seven churches of Revelation is indebted to Zech. 4.1–14. That vision is intended to teach Zerubbabel that it is by God's Spirit that things can truly be accomplished (4.6). Notice that while the initial image is of seven lamps with seven lips, the metaphor changes when Zechariah also speaks of the seven eyes of the Lord which range throughout the earth. As R. Bauckham rightly stresses, one of the main questions Revelation seeks to answer for its audiences is how God's plan can be worked out on earth, given the beastly empire ruling earth is seemingly irresistibly evil.[20] John answers as Zechariah did – the Spirit of God will accomplish it. Furthermore, it is likely John would connect the seven lamps with the seven-branched lamp stand that stood in the temple (Exod. 25.31–40). In his vision, John sees the seven lamps which he identifies as the seven spirits burning before the throne of God = the mercy seat in the Holy of Holies. The heavenly sanctuary is seen as the model for the earthly one, as in Hebrews, and Exod. 40.25 speaks directly of the seven lamps that burned before the Lord in the earthly tabernacle. The seven Spirits belong to the divine identity as is shown in Rev. 1.4–5, where we find a Trinitarian blessing that includes the seven Spirits before the throne. They are closely associated with both God and with Christ, for at Rev. 5.6 the Lamb is said to have seven eyes which are the seven Spirits of God sent out into all the earth (echoing Zech. 4.10b).

As Bauckham stresses, the eyes of Yahweh not only indicate that God knows everything that happens on earth, but also that he is able to act powerfully whenever he chooses. Thus "the seven Spirits are the presence and power of God on earth, bringing about God's Kingdom by implementing the Lamb's victory throughout the world."[21] By the splitting of the Spirit John indicates that each of the seven churches has the full measure of the Spirit; none is short-changed in terms of power or presence or revelation from God. And here too, as elsewhere, we have an image of the Spirit interceding for believers before the throne of God, in this case on behalf of persecuted churches. Only persons can personally intercede. The Spirit represents the church to God, but also (see Rev. 5.6) represents Christ to the church.

There are 14 other examples of "spirit" language in Revelation. Probably, Rev. 19.10 is not a reference to the Holy Spirit, referring to "the spirit of prophecy," which probably just means the gist or essence or focus of prophecy. All of the other references, however, seem clearly to refer to the Holy Spirit, mainly as the Spirit of prophecy who inspired John's visions. The seven Spirit vision is about the Spirit's mission to the world (5.6), but these other references focus on the activity of the Spirit within and on behalf of the church.[22] Four of these other references refer to the moment of inspiration – John is "in the Spirit" and sees and hears (1.10; 4.1), or he gets carried away in the Spirit (17.3; 21.10,

---

[20] See Richard Bauckham, *The Theology of the Book of Revelation* (Cambridge: Cambridge University Press, 1993), 110–13.

[21] Bauckham, *God Crucified*, 113.

[22] D. Hill, "Prophecy and Prophets in the Revelation of St. John," *NTS* 18 (1971–72): 401–18.

cf. Ezek. 3.12–14). The way this is described suggests an ecstatic or overpowering experience. These four references are indeed carefully placed to make clear that all of John's visions are Spirit-inspired. Perhaps Bauckham is correct that the "Spirit does not give the content of the revelation, but the visionary experience which enables John to receive the revelation."[23] This is not to say that the Spirit cannot speak for himself! He does so at Rev. 14.13. John is quite able to distinguish the Spirit from Christ, and it would be mistaken to see the Spirit as only the mouthpiece for Christ or the Father. The Book of Revelation provides one final example of how a Christian author, while drawing in abundance on OT images and ideas, can in various ways stress the personal nature of the Spirit who is part of the divine identity. In some ways, the Book of Revelation is the most explicitly Trinitarian of all NT books, and thus it paves the way for the post-canonical discussions of these complex matters.

Conclusions

In many Christian circles, the Holy Spirit is the most neglected member of the Trinity, and in some case the silent partner in the Godhead, for those churches which do not indulge in the so-called charismatic gifts. What we have seen in this chapter is that the Spirit language in the NT is basically not the same as in the OT, for in the NT the Spirit is treated as a person, with personal traits – the Spirit can be grieved, can be blasphemed, the Spirit can be angry, the Spirit can speak and act on the Spirit's own initiative, and so on. The Spirit is said to lead, guide, inspire, promote, drive, but not usually to dominate, in contrast to the evil spirits who take over the control center of a person's being and manipulate them.[24] The term Spirit in the NT usually means more than just the presence or power of God, not least because the Spirit is regularly distinguished from, but also grouped alongside, the Father and the Son. But interestingly, the Spirit is not included in the divine name until after the death and resurrection of Jesus, in Mt. 28.19. The baptismal formula tells us that God has a name (singular) but has a tri-personal nature or divine identity.

It is in Acts that we see the Spirit as the primary agent of evangelistic action. Acts 1.8 stresses that the Spirit empowers and inspires believers to speak, to teach, to heal. The Spirit's coming is associated with new and refreshing and everlasting life. As in the OT the Spirit is associated with the coming presence of God who wishes to dwell with and among his people. The Spirit is said to come with the acceptance of Christ by hearing with faith (Gal. 3) or by hearing and making the good confession of Christ (1 Cor. 12; Rom. 10). Paul associates but at the same time distinguishes Christ and the Spirit. It is Christ who died and rose again. It is the Spirit who comes as the helper, the gift and fruit giver. 2 Cor. 13.13 indicates that blessing comes from the Trinity, the divine identity of Father, Son, and Holy Spirit, each contributing in its own way grace, love, and communion. The Spirit is a teacher and a sanctifier. The monotheistic God was understood more fully when it was revealed that not only in Yahweh, but also in the Son and in the Spirit was the divine identity made plain. God, as it turned out, was more complex, and more personal than anyone

---

[23] Bauckham, *God Crucified*, 145.
[24] I say usually, because there is evidence of moments where a person is overwhelmed by the presence of the Spirit and bursts out in speech or song, or simply receives a revelation. But that is an exceptional occurrence, not a regular one.

had imagined before the Son of Man was born of woman and came into the world. Here would be a good place for a brief poetic meditation on the divine identity, which involves three persons, as the manifestation of the one living God.

The Divine Identity

Who can divine,
the divine identity
Of three in one,
and one in three?

Rather than revel
in the secrets of its beauty
I must settle
for the beauty of its secrets ...

Does the word God
Refer to a person
Or instead to a thrice-shared identity?

While I may ponder
until weak and weary
I'll not plumb the depths of that sort of Trinity.

It's not like one clover containing three leaves
It's not like an individual who is father, son, brother
It's not like an atom made of three parts
It's not like the sun with heat, rays, light.
It's not like *anything* in human insight.

But the *via negativa* can only take us so far
We know what you're not,
But not who you *are*.

Unless, serendipitously
You condescend to our sphere
And reveal yourself
While you are here.

If God is spirit, invisible all wise
This is hidden from mere mortal eyes,
Only God with flesh on, real incarnation
Can bridge the gap between heaven and creation.

Made in your image,
There's some similarity
But with You made in ours
A moment of clarity.

Someday I'll see
face to face.
For now through a prism
Refraction takes place.

Perhaps this is needful
For those of our realm
A closer encounter
We'd be overwhelmed.

Only God can be God,
Angel minds don't inquire
So I'll settle for singing
In the heavenly choir.

5

The Stars Align in Constellations: The Storied World of the Bible. Part One

Tell me a fact and I will know, tell me the truth and I will believe, tell me a story and it will live in my heart forever.
Anonymous voiceover on the opening images of the broadcast of the 2006 World Series[1]

When you are dealing specifically with a devout person's religious symbolic universe, which is what our concern is with, you are dealing with something that, while not impervious to change, requires a real Copernican revolution in one's thinking to change in significant ways. By this I mean, it requires what most ancients thought was difficult if not impossible – conversion of the imagination to a new *paradigm*, not just to individual new ideas.
Ben Witherington[2]

Old Testament faith expresses itself initially in narrative. The main bulk of the Old Testament is a narrative account of Israel's story and of God's involvement with it. Its narrative form corresponds to its substance, and theological reflection on its gospel needs to work with its narrative form … the Old Testament tells us who God is and who we are through the ongoing story of God's relationship with Israel.
John Goldingay[3]

As we have already noted, it would seem that the best way to do biblical theology is to start with the symbolic universe that all the biblical writers lived in and were influenced by. In that universe, there were fixed stars like God, revelation, redemption, messiah, holiness, mighty works (or miracles), to mention but a few ideas which were taken for granted by all the authors. We have necessarily focused on just one element in the symbolic universe in the previous chapters – God, with all three persons sharing and expressing the divine identity.

All of our biblical authors were Jews, or perhaps in the singular case of Luke, a God-fearer.[4] Of all these fixed stars, there was nothing more fundamental of course than God, and so we have spent Chapters 2–4 on what the Bible actual says about God – Yahweh/Father, Jesus/Son, and Spirit. More than anything else of any sort, this is both the most

---

[1] See the details in Ben Witherington III, *New Testament Theology and Ethics*, vol. 1 (Downers Grove, IL: InterVarsity Press, 2016), ii.
[2] Witherington, *The Indelible Image*, vol. 2, 69ff.
[3] Goldingay, *Old Testament Theology*, vol. 1, 28, 30.
[4] The other possible exception is the editor of the conglomerate document 2 Peter.

foundational and fixed point, and the proper subject of *theology*. Of course, one can look at this from the perspective that the symbolic universe was formed and shaped by things like the traditions in the books we call the OT, and later the Jesus tradition, apostolic tradition, new prophetic revelation, and the like, not neglecting the experiences of God which are expressed in these various sources. In any case, out of that shared symbolic universe was formed their narrative thought world. And let me be clear from the outset, all the biblical literature is "insider" literature, and in the case of the narratives it is stories told by God's people to God's people, with the reality, the encounters, the revelation of the living God simply assumed, not argued for.

Here I am suggesting that the writers of the Bible not only shared certain big-ticket ideas in common, they also shared a narrative thought world in common as well. They all were convinced, for example, that history was going somewhere, that God was guiding it and working things together for good, and when it comes to the writers of the NT, they believed they were all writing late in the story, trying to get the Good News out in time for the final edition to be published before the "Deadline" was reached. The NT writers all stood on tiptoe, utterly convinced that they already lived in the eschatological age and were looking for a consummation devoutly to be wished. The failure to recognize the common narrative thought world that is presupposed by the various NT writers is a very significant failure indeed. To put things succinctly, when you believe strongly that God acts in human history and interacts with human beings, then it is natural that one would turn to narratives about events in history to tell the story of God and his people. These beliefs co-inhere. The biblical writers in the main are chronicling "the mighty acts of God" in history for his people. Theology is grounded in stories and the history of a particular people. It is not done in the abstract, or simply by logically spinning out the implications of certain theological ideas.

Here we need to also stress, that the OT writers, perhaps apart from some of the exilic and post-exilic ones, were *not* writing in the context of an assumed eschatological state of affairs, nor an assumed Christological state of affairs, as if the messiah and God's *final* saving reign had already broken into human history. And without question, this leads various OT writers to have a different point of view, even when they were gazing further into the future than some of the NT writers. Put another way, they believed they were in a different place in the developing story of the relationship of God to his people, a different place in the unfolding story of salvation history. They are also chronicling a much longer story, with many tragedies as well as some triumphs along the way, whereas Acts, for example, is chronicling a much shorter story which is, overall, much more positive in tone and outcome in various ways, as one might expect from a writer who is part of a successful fledgling religious movement.

This is another reason why one needs to have a clear conception of progressive revelation, and regularly ask oneself, "where are we now in the story?" whether we are reading Exodus or 1 Samuel, or Isaiah, or Daniel or the Psalms, or the Gospels or Acts or Paul's letters or even Revelation. No biblical theology that does not take into consideration this larger historical framework with, and within which, the biblical writers were indeed operating is going to be adequate. The OT writers know part of the ongoing story, the NT writers know *more* of the ongoing story, and are looking *back* at what they see as the crucial turning point in the story, the Christ event and its consequences and sequel. So, what are the crucial story and stories that the Bible is telling? This is the question we will begin to answer momentarily.

Remember: out of that narrative thought world, the biblical writers theologize and ethicize into particular contexts. The commonality lies as much or more at the presuppositional level as at the articulation level. Analyzing only the articulated similarities between the various biblical witnesses is like analyzing and comparing the tips of what appear to be several different icebergs and noticing their similarities in shape and hew and size, all the while failing to note that they turn out to all be united below the surface of the intellectual ocean in which they are floating. In other words, they are all individual peaks of one much larger common mass. This volume then must dwell as much at the level of symbolic universe and narrative thought world, as at the level of articulation into particular contexts. Of course, there are other ways of doing biblical theology but this is our approach here, and we have found it particularly fruitful.

In the Beginning God ...

There are some hints in the Bible about prequels, for instance in Prov. 3 and 8, where we hear of Wisdom being present with God at the creation, and in some sense assisting, or in Phil. 2 we hear about the Son who decided while dwelling with the Father to not take advantage of being part of the divine identity and having equality with God the Father, but instead stripped himself.[5] Whether we start where Jn. 1.1 starts ("in the beginning was the Word ...") or we start where Gen. 1.1 starts ("when God began to create ..."), we are being informed that God existed prior to the space-time continuum, and that there is a back story about the life of the Godhead that the writers of the Bible are largely not telling. And that back story involved the notion that the God of the Bible always existed, is eternal. Further, the back story assumes and to some extent expresses the truth that God the Creator existed separate from and was never part of the creation itself, but rather made the creation, whether out of nothing, or out of pre-formed materials. It should never be missed that the verb *bara*, to create, is only predicated of Yahweh in Gen. 1 and elsewhere in the OT. While humans can *make* things out of pre-existing materials, it may be implied in Gen. 1 that God is so great he can *create* something out of nothing. We will say more about this shortly.

"Genesis" (which derives its title from Genesis 2.4 in the Septuagint), means "creation." Obviously, it is written from the perspective of faith. It does not intend to be a purely neutral or objective view. The author is obviously a believer in the one true God, and he sees things through the eyes of faith. This does not mean that his writing is biased, but that it is selective and written with a definite perspective and purpose in view. It is left to the reader to discern whether the author's faith perspective illuminates or obscures his story. Theological history or theological saga is perhaps the best descriptive label one may give Genesis, that is, history written from a theocentric viewpoint.

The author of Gen. 1 uses the seven-day week framework to describe God's complete act of creation. We may be sure that the text does not intend to tell us how long God took

---

[5] Some of what follows here in the discussion of Genesis and Exodus is found in another form in more detail in Witherington, *Torah Old and New*. Used by permission.

to create, because: (1) we have poetic diction; (2) the Hebrew word *yom* (day) here cannot mean 24 hours, since there are "days" before the sun in our solar system is said to be created (Gen. 1.14) and the seventh day is described as the time when God "ceases"/"rests" from creating, which is for an eternity, not just 24 hours after creation was finished[6]; (3) *yom* is often used figuratively in the OT and in Genesis (Gen. 5.1, "the day when God created" simply means when God created); (4) nor can *yom* mean age here, since it makes no sense to talk about the evening and morning of each age. The author is simply following a week pattern to indicate that God provided an orderly sequence of creation in space and time. Thus, we must be careful to treat the poetic and metaphorical diction as what it is, and have some literary sensitivity as to what means the author is using to convey his truth about God and creation.[7]

Finally, there is the matter of canonical shaping or editing of our material. The organizing principle of Genesis is the *toledoth* ("generations") formula throughout the book: 2.4; 5.1; 6.9; 10.1; 11.10,27; 25.12,19; 26.1(9); and 37.2. The term *toledoth* can mean generation, genealogy, or narrative story. The formula introduces what follows; it is not a conclusion to what precedes. "This is the generation that ensued from the creation of heaven and earth." The formula is followed either by a genealogy (5.1; 10.1; 11.10; 25.12; 36.1) or a narrative (2.4; 6.9; 11.27; 25.19; 37.2). It is sufficient to say here that the author wishes to stress at 2.4 the connection between God's acts of creation of heaven and earth and the succession of human history. Primeval history or saga leads to and is the introduction of all human history. There are two sorts of genealogies, vertical and horizontal. The horizontal (10.1) deals with the relationship of various subgroups within a family. The more critical vertical genealogies trace an unbroken line of descent from Adam to Jacob, and the narratives of individual patriarchal stories fit into this framework. The point is not only that God is interested in and involved in human history, but also that there is one chosen line by which God's purposes in history are carried forward, sometimes even in spite of the conduct of the persons in that chosen line (note Jacob).

As Meredith Kline, my OT professor of many years ago, noted, the author deals with a rejected line, then the chosen line, and the rejected line is dealt with in summary fashion only in a genealogy (Gen. 36). This leads one to the conclusion that Genesis is not intended as a history of all people, but of God's people and his dealings with them in space and time. Though we may note that all humanity is the climax of God's creation and creation is for God's glory, in another sense the history that matters to the biblical author is the history of God's special people. Thus, God's chosen people and eventually God's chosen one, the fulfillment of the Abrahamic promise, is the real climax of creation.

The first Adam began the process which climaxed in the second Adam. This is to see Genesis in a canonical context and in light of the NT, but that is what the NT authors, especially Paul, do. The author of Genesis, however, paves the way for seeing history in a special sense as God's story because he focuses on the story of God's chosen people and

---

[6] Since the author is talking about an almighty God, it can hardly be the case that he thinks the deity is tired after his various acts of creating. Thus, it is likely that the verb from which we get the noun "sabbath" here refers to God's ceasing from his previous activity and admiring his handiwork ("he saw it was very good"), not his resting.

[7] On the genre of the various sorts of literature in the Bible see Ben Witherington III, *Reading and Understanding the Bible* (Oxford: Oxford University Press, 2014).

their progeny. We will deal with the text as we have it, in its final form, and not base any conclusions on its pre-history or possible sources. We can only agree with what George Coats has termed its " 'functional unity' ... the result of this reinterpretation of the tradition is not a literary patchwork but a story whose overall design and dramatic movement make it a work of art, one that even yet stirs and involves the hearer or reader."[8]

Gen. 1.1a is one of the most familiar portions of all Scripture. In the Hebrew, it reads "Bereshit' bara Elohim ..." Already we have a problem of translation. Should we begin the Bible with a subordinate clause and so translate it: "When God began to create the heavens and the earth" (NEB), a clause which would then be completed in v. 2 or v. 3? Or should we take the meaning to be, "In the beginning, God created" (NIV)? In favor of the latter is the witness of all the ancient translations and versions. If we begin the Bible with "when God ..." then some scholars have taken v. 2 to imply a pre-existent chaos independent of God's activity.[9] This is not necessarily the case, since it could mean that when God began to create, the initial act produced a wild and desolate (empty) mass, out of which he fashioned and finished an orderly creation. Certainly, the author would not want to suggest that God created a chaos, which makes no sense anyway,[10] but simply a not-as-yet ordered or organized universe.

Notice that Gen. 1.1 probably implies a creation out of nothing, or in, or even into nothing. In the Genesis version of the creation story there was no co-existent matter prior to God's act. If F. Delitzsch is right, the more likely translation is "in the beginning."[11] This means v. 1 would be a heading to all that follows and would clearly indicate that God was the Creator of all heaven and earth, not merely the shaper of pre-existent matter. God did not need anything to start with to create the universe. However, both usual translations cause the verse to be awkward, and it is reasonable and plausible to suggest a third translation: not "in the beginning God created" nor "when God began to create, he said" (with v. 3 in effect ending the sentence begun in 1.1), but rather "God began to create the heavens and the earth, the earth being wild and empty (or desolate)," and thus v. 3 more naturally follows upon v. 2 as a confirmation of what has just been said.

It should be noted that we must distinguish between what Christians call heaven, the eternal dwelling place of God, and the created heavens, which are part of the material universe. Some scholars have seen a framework in what follows, which may be charted according to D. Kidner as follows:

Day 1 – Light to dark parallels   Day 4 – Lights of day and night
Day 2 – Sea and sky parallels   Day 5 – Creatures of water and air
Day 3 – Fertile earth parallels   Day 6 – Creatures of the land.[12]

The first three days would indicate the forming of these aspects of creation, the last three the completion and fullness of them. If this scheme is correct, then there is no possibility of seeing these days as anything more than a literary principle of organizing the

---

[8] George Coats, *Genesis, with an Introduction to Narrative Literature* (Forms of the Old Testament Literature; Grand Rapids, MI: William B. Eerdmans, 1984), 38.

[9] See B. Childs, *Myth and Reality in the Old Testament* (Eugene, OR: Wipf and Stock, 2009), 31.

[10] Though see Gerhard von Rad, *Genesis* (Philadelphia: Westminster, 1961), 48–9.

[11] F. Delitzsch (and S. Taylor), *A New Commentary on Genesis*, vol. 1 (n.p.: Sagwan Press, 2015), *ad loc.*

[12] D. Kidner, *Genesis* (Downers Grove, IL: InterVarsity Press, 1982), 46.

elements of creation, not real days. However, somewhat against this view is the clear implication of succession or series implied by: (1) "God began to create"; (2) the climax when humanity is made; (3) God's ceasing thereafter. Thus, we should see a succession of events here, though no precise duration or time span is indicated.[13] It is also worth noting that in the sequence here sometimes supernatural creation is indicated, as at the beginning of creation when the creation of sea creatures and birds are mentioned. Notice that thereafter the sea creatures are to reproduce themselves in the normal way (1.22). Also, supernatural creation is indicated in creation of humanity (1.27). But on other occasions God calls upon the earth to produce vegetation and the land to produce living creatures. The significance of this seems to be that creation in some cases came about both by special divine action and also by natural processes set in motion by God. Notice how the author in 2.5 indicates that no shrub or trees yet existed because it had not rained. He simply assumes that a natural process like rain will produce such aspects of creation.

Not least because the creation of humanity story comes up in *crucial* places in the teachings of Jesus and Paul and the author of Hebrews and elsewhere, it is important that we examine rather closely the first creation account about human beings, at Gen. 1.26. Verse 26 begins the climax of God's creative work, the creation of human beings. The term *adam*, which means earth creature here, is a generic and collective term referring to a kind or group, not an individual, as is clear from what follows (male and female he created *them*). The reference to "them" also makes clear that the author does not have some sort of androgynous individual in mind in the first place. Only later in the narrative does *adam* become a name for a particular male individual.

As B. Arnold stresses, here we have a different sort of divine speech than previously in the chapter. Note that the text says, "let us make" whereas before God has simply spoken things into existence. This "us" and "our" (the plural is present even in the verb) may refer either to: (1) a plural of fullness, i.e., God is the equivalent of many and is simply deliberating with himself;[14] (2) a plural of majesty, i.e., a royal "we" as human kings sometimes use; (3) a reference to the heavenly court, i.e., God is consulting with the angels;[15] or (4) in later Christian thought, a reference to the Trinity. On the basis of OT usage of "we" as applied to God, (2) or (3) is most likely here (I Kgs. 22.19–20; Job 1; Dan. 7.10). If (3) is the correct view, as F. Delitzsch argued, then humans are created in the image of God and angels, and we will have to ask in what sense that is so. The text implies the equality of male and female created in the image of God but the text rules out an androgynous or bisexual first human. Humanity is made male *and* female, not male-female together.

We must next ask about the meaning of the phrase "image of God" or "likeness of God." Two different Hebrew words *tselem* and *damuth* correspond to these two English words. The former means "original image or imitation," while the latter means "likeness or resemblance." There seems to be little difference in meaning between the two words. Both refer to a physical resemblance in various contexts, but that is unlikely here. It may be important that *tselem* is also the word used for "idol," so perhaps the author is saying

---

[13] For a critique of the framework hypothesis, see E. J. Young, *Studies in Genesis One* (Philadelphia: Presbyterian+Reformed Publishing, 1999), 43–46.

[14] Bill T. Arnold, *Genesis* (Cambridge: Cambridge University Press, 2009), 44.

[15] C. Westermann, *Genesis 1–11* (Minneapolis, MN: Augsburg, 1984), 144–45; G. Wenham, *Genesis 1–15* (WBC 1; Nashville, TN: Thomas Nelson, 1987), 27–28.

that human beings are God's "idols" on earth, so idols of lesser things like animals or even images of them are inappropriate.[16] Idols were used in worship, and only God should be worshipped, according to our author. We may note that it is said humans are created *in* the image, not *with* the image, as if it could be assigned to some particular part of a person, i.e., his/her form or "soul." Some have suggested that the image consists in our dominion over the rest of the creatures; however, as F. Delitzsch said, this dominion is the *conse-quence* of being in the image, not its *content*.[17]

Perhaps the clue is in the phrase "let us make ..." if this is a reference to the heavenly court. In what regard are we like angels? We share a capacity for relationship with God of a special kind that animals do not have. Because of the image, humankind is not only the representation of God on earth but also his representative, meant to remind all of God's dominion, just as a carved image on a statue or on a coin was intended to indicate who was then ruling. We represent God's presence and rule to and over the world. So serious a matter is it to be created in God's image that God takes an attack on his image-bearer as an attack on himself (note the Cain and Abel story). In ANE literature the king is said to bear the image of the deity he serves, and to rule on his behalf, but here it is not just one person who bears the image but humankind in general, so it is not clear that this parallel provides a clue to the content of the image humans bear.[18]

Being in the image of God not only implies a special relationship to God, but also requires of humans a special respect for all other human beings, who are equally image-bearers, no matter how badly marred by sin that image may be. Humanity as image is then called to the task of stamping God's impression upon the rest of creation (Ps. 8). The word translated subdue, *kabats*, is a very strong one in v. 28. Humans are to govern so as to leave a lasting impression on creation, not for their own sake, but for God's glory. Unfortunately, a human being strives as a fallen creature to make his mark for himself, and not for God, and thus perverts the task of representation and being the representative of God. Gen. 1.31 proclaims not merely that what God had made was good, but that what He made in its completion was *tov meod* or exceedingly good. G. von Rad suggests the translation "completely perfect," just as God designed and planned it.[19] This implies that evil or its consequences were no part of God's creation or plan. God is not the maker or author of evil or evil inclinations or tendencies, much less the author of sin. We will discuss this more in a moment when we turn to Gen. 2.4–3.24.

Gen. 1.26–2.3 concludes with God ceasing from his creation activity. The term so often translated "rested" actually means "ceased" (*shabbat*, from which we get the words Sabbath and sabbatical). The stress here is on both the absence of activity (though no implication of fatigue is involved) and the presence of satisfaction and joy, since the work was completed and the job was well done. Notice here that there is no concluding, "and there was evening and morning, a seventh day." This is intentional. The seventh day goes on; God continues to *cease* from his *initial* work of creation. This cessation does not imply God is bowing out gracefully and leaving the scene. Quite the opposite. His task of

---

[16] Richter, *The Epic of Eden*, 20ff.

[17] F. Delitzsch, *Genesis* (Grand Rapids, MI: William B. Eerdmans, 1988), *ad loc.*

[18] See the discussion of this much-debated question in J. R. Middleton, *The Liberating Image: The Imago Dei in Genesis 1* (Grand Rapids, MI: Brazos Press, 2005).

[19] Von Rad, *Genesis*, 61.

providential governing and intervening for his people begins when the creative task ends. He does not withdraw or take away his interests, his involvement, his governing, his relating, or his helping. As we shall see, this is critical to humanity's ongoing survival.

When we arrive at Gen. 2.4–3.24, we arrive in a different world.[20] The *toledoth* formula in 2.4 refers to the "story" or "account" or possibly "offspring (generations)" of the heavens and earth. This is the only time this formula is used to introduce the *generation* of an object rather than a person. The purpose of the formula seems to be to link this older account of human creation in 2.4–3.24 to the previous account.[21] We are about to be told what came forth from the earth. The account that follows has often been called a second creation story, and, in a sense, it is. Its focus, however, is not on all of creation but on special creation, the creation of humankind from the dust of the ground. It is not really a duplication or replacement or correction of Gen. 1 but an expansion and explanation of Gen. 1.26–27. It is entirely possible that this narrative was derived from a source other than Gen.1, and a host of stylistic and content differences suggest this. The structure in Gen. 2 is less poetic than Gen. 1 (though there is some poetic vocabulary), perhaps because it is connected with the history which follows, which suggests the author wishes us to take this narrative as history of some sort.

Here we see humanity's close relationship to the earth. The text plays on the relationship between the term *adam* and *adamah*, and the latter means "earth." Thus, Adam means earth creature until later it is treated as a proper name. In Gen. 1, humanity is distinguished from all the rest of creation in a proper way. Here we see humanity's points of identification with creation and it is tasked to tend the garden (v. 15). Note that we have the beginning of God's special people, and the concern is to show how God had a chosen one or ones from the beginning. This focus on the chosen line almost to the exclusion of all else explains not only the use of "Yahweh" in this story (God's personal name by which his people knew him), but also why there is no attempt to explain such mystifying questions as where all the rest of humanity came from outside the garden. The author would seem to suggest that God created them as well (cf. the wives of Cain and Abel) but the focus in the story is on the origins of God's people, *not all peoples*. Now we are prepared to examine Gen. 2.4–24 in detail.

---

[20] Here is not the place to debate sources theories in regard to JEPD. Suffice it to say that the character of this story is different enough from the material in Gen. 1 to warrant the conclusion that at least two sources have been drawn on to create this opening to the Bible. As it stands, from the hands of the final editor, the intent seems to be to have the more generic account of all of creation given first, and then an expanded account of the creation of humanity explaining that part of the story in more detail second. Notice that David Carr's recent study *The Formation of the Hebrew Bible* (Oxford: Oxford University Press, 2011) provides actual historical evidence of ANE scribes and how they worked, how they revised existing traditions and transmitted texts, compared with what we find in the OT. And Carr finds clear evidence of pre-exilic texts within the corpus of the OT dating at least as early as the tenth century BC and the early monarchy. This more historical methodology is far more useful than source criticism based exclusively on stylistic considerations that ignores possible historical parallels about how scribes operated in that era. For recent discussion on the composition of Genesis see e.g. K. Schmid, "Genesis in the Pentateuch," in *The Book of Genesis* (ed. Craig A. Evans, Joel N. Lohr, and David Petersen; VTSupp 152; Leiden: Brill, 2012), 27–50 and in the same volume J. C. Geertz, "The Formation of the Primeval History," 107–35.

[21] Arnold, *Genesis*, 55–56. This older account in 2.4ff. introduces a new designation for God in 2.4a – "the Lord God" (*Yahweh Elohim*). This connects the God of the ancestors in Gen. 12–36 with the God of Moses to whom God's personal name was revealed. The God of creation is also the God who made covenant with Israel.

From the start, we note that this narrative appears to be presented as a historical account by the author, hence a saga or legend from hoary antiquity, not a creation myth. Thus, Eden is perhaps seen as a country, though the word means "delight" or "paradise" (the English term comes from the LXX translation of "parkland"). Here Eden is located in the East and from what follows about the rivers, we are to think of a place either in the Armenian mountains or above the Persian Gulf in the area of the fertile crescent, according to some scholars.[22] The mention of the Tigris and Euphrates clearly locates this place in space and time. Eden is usually thought of as a garden. *Gan*, however, can also mean a park or orchard with trees and is originally a Persian word referring to a nobleman's park. The implication is that humanity is getting the royal treatment by God.

God forms *adam* from the ground and gives him the "kiss of life," breathing into his nostrils, as the text says. Humanity is living dust, a true miracle. There is no body–soul dualism in this creation, but body–life dualism.[23] Humanity is not distinguished from animals in being a living being (*nephesh hayah*, cf. Gen. 1.21,24,30), but by being a creature who can relate to God freely and freely choose to respond to His will and word. The capacity of special relationship and the power of moral choice set humanity apart, as the story makes clear by what follows.

Two trees are planted in the middle of the garden: one which could lead to everlasting life, the other to death (whether physical or spiritual or both is not made clear). It seems to be implied that Adam was *not* immortal by nature, but that this gift was available to him for the taking. God said he *could* even eat of the tree of life, but not of the tree of the knowledge of good and evil. It is possible as well that the author views Adam and Eve, while vulnerable to being killed, as not *inherently, due to their very nature*, mortal.

In any case, knowledge (*yada*) here likely implies not mere intellectual knowledge, but the experience of the gamut of good and evil; that is what the serpent offers. Clearly, God has already defined what is wrong for humankind. Not knowledge itself but presuming to be the captain of one's own fate, doing what is right in one's own eyes, is at issue here. God's word has defined one thing that is wrong, eating of the tree which leads to death. The experience of all evil or even the knowledge of it (the wages of sin) leads only to death. Note that God did not make evil; it is not a tangible thing. God, of course, knows all that is good and evil, yet God is not tempted or tainted thereby.

God has provided everything humankind needs: a supportive environment, readily available food, a meaningful job of tilling the soil and tending the garden, and a relationship with God. All *adam* lacks is a mate. The naming of the animals story indicates that humankind is given power and authority over them. In Hebrew culture to name is to define, to order, to organize, and not merely to label. Biblical names normally connote something about the nature of the one named. Verse 20b appears to imply that in this process of examining the animal world, *adam* was also looking for a mate. It indicates how close *adam* is to the animals that he would look amongst them. But, though animals are living beings, they are not to be *one* with humankind. Only woman is bone of his bone and

---

[22] Kidner, *Genesis*, 64.

[23] Arnold, *Genesis*, 58, stresses that *nephesh hayah* refers to the totality of the person. The problem with this explanation is there was already a body formed by God the potter, a body which was not a *nephesh hayah* and it is only when God breathed into that form that a living being existed. I agree, however, that the author is not referring here to the later concept of the "soul."

flesh of his flesh; no animal bears that intimacy and kinship with humanity. God formed them separately.

We must also go on to add that there is no idea of an androgynous Adam in *this* creation story either. Woman is not taken out of man. Rather, she is built up out of a part of him. Adam was looking for his female companion, and she was not simply the other half of his own nature. If man is *ish* in Hebrew, woman is *ishah*, the one who comes out of man. However, as we shall see, calling the woman *ishah* is not giving her a personal name, as later in 3.20, after the Fall, when man tries to take control. Here is not a naming ritual and so an asserting of authority over the woman, but a cry of joy, on finally finding the one for whom you are looking. The key phrase is important here: "it is not good for *man* to be alone," something not said of the woman.

Adam was made for relationship with God, but also with fellow humans. He is made to be a social, not a solitary creature. Indeed, only so can he survive. The phrase goes on, "I will make a helper or companion suitable for (corresponding to) him." Here we should not translate "helpmate." The old King James translation "helpmeet" does not mean a help mate but rather a helper who is "meet," i.e., suitable for the task. Woman is not man's maid, nor merely his assistant, but a "suitable companion," corresponding to him. She is the crown of creation, God's last act which makes it all very good.

Woman is just like man in that she shares the same nature (bone of my bone) and the same capacity for relationship with God. She is also different, a complement that completes human creation, not a duplicate that is redundant. The Hebrew phrase *kenegedo* implies both similarity (correspondence) and supplementariness. Woman is the mirror in which man recognizes himself for who he truly is, a special creature made for special relating. It should be stressed that the Hebrew here for "helper" or "companion" is also used of Yahweh himself in the OT as a helper of God's people, so subordination is *not* implied in the use of that term here.[24] As Arnold notes, Adam's "at last" suggests he has been looking among the animals for a mate, and not finding one until Eve appears on the scene.[25]

Various commentators see here the celebration of the first marriage. God brings the woman to the man. Verse 24 suggests this and also indicates that marriage should lead to the one flesh union, not be preceded by it. Intercourse was the joyous climax of marital sharing, not a result of the Fall, and certainly not the content of the knowledge of good and evil. It was something that would be shared without shame. Adam and Eve were able to engage in this total sharing without shame or self-consciousness or loss of identity, unlike fallen creatures. All seems well, until we turn the page and learn of human infidelity.

Let us be very clear about chapter 3. The problem of theodicy, the problem of where evil came from, is not given any full answer here. This chapter is not about the origin of evil, but about the original sin, its nature and circumstances. We are *not* told that the snake is Satan, that notion first occurs in later Jewish literature (cf. Wis. Sol. 2.23–24; Sir. 21.2; 4 Macc. 18.8; cf. Rev. 1.9; 20.2). The connection is a conclusion one draws in light of later and developing revelation. The snake is called crafty or shrewd (*arum*), surely a wordplay on the description of humans as naked in the immediately preceding verse (*arrumim*). The nudes have been duped by the shrewd, and in their desire to be shrewd they discovered the

---

[24] Arnold, *Genesis*, 60.
[25] *Ibid.*

naked facts about themselves.[26] The first question the snake asks the woman, appearing to seek information but trying to plant a seed of doubt, is: "Did God really say you cannot eat of any tree of the garden?" Of course, the answer to this is no, with one exception. The woman's first reply is a case of stretching the truth or exaggerating it. She adds to the divine prohibition about the fruit that "we must not touch it or we will die." Problems are already brewing here. We are not told that the fruit in question is an apple.[27] Next, we have the frontal attack on God's word. The serpent pretends to know better than the woman or even than God. This is typical arrogance from the powers of darkness. The serpent insinuates that God is jealously guarding his position as deity. The snake is suggesting that there is no metaphysical difference between God and humanity; it is just that God knows more. The text may perhaps be translated, "will be like gods" since the word for god is the plural *elohim* here. In the context of Genesis, however, *elohim* is normally used of the one true God, so it should likely be taken to mean this here. The woman must choose whether to base her decisions about what is best and true on her own judgment or on God's revealed will. This is still humanity's dilemma. It is clear that the woman is free to choose to resist the temptation and obey God. But her eyes are already opened to the possibilities of sin, taking the fruit. It offers physical satisfaction as food; it has aesthetic appeal, being pleasing to the eye. But the best part is that it is desirable for wisdom.

Adam is the silent partner to her sin. First, he commits a sin of omission. If he was with her, why did he not do something to prevent this? Secondly, he commits a sin of commission, for he too eats. Their eyes were indeed opened, but what they saw was not their divinity, but the bare facts about their very frail humanity. The fig leaves are a pathetic attempt to hide their most obvious and vulnerable parts that indicate their full humanity. The issue here is not mere nudity, but rather shameful nakedness, a combination of desire, self-knowledge, disobedience. Our attempt to cover up our nakedness, never mind our sins, is always inadequate and pathetic.

Next, we are told that the couple heard the sound of God coming after them (not the sound of his voice, as some have translated). Their response is fright and flight. Such is always the response of sinful humankind fearful of judgment, not wishing to be revealed or seen for what they are. God does not at this point take a confrontational approach. He simply says, "Where are you?" The creatures God has made personally and specially and given special treatment to are now running from their Maker. It is only sinful humankind who has something to fear from God. Shame is the proper response to sin, but sin also leads to rationalizing.

When humanity is confronted with its sin, rebel humans blame God or other humans. The man blames God and the woman ("this woman whom *you* gave me"), and the woman blames the snake. The all-too-human art of passing the buck has been inaugurated. God judges these three in reverse order, starting with the source of the trouble, the snake, then the first perpetrator of the sin, and finally the accomplice. Gen. 3.15 suggests that

[26] To modify the playful way Arnold renders the storyline here, *Genesis*, 63; following Wenham, *Genesis 1–15*, 72.

[27] Here is where basing a translation on the Latin text got various English translators into trouble. One of the Latin words for apple is *malum*, which not incidentally is also the word for bad, or even evil. If this is about a fruit that conveys the knowledge of good and evil, by rendering the original Hebrew or Greek as *malum* it was possible to conclude that the author was not merely talking about just any bad or enticing fruit, he was talking about a bad apple.

world history will be an ongoing enmity and battle between humanity and the powers of darkness.

Notice, however, that even in judgment there is mercy, because the seed of the woman will crush the head of evil and its source. This is poetic language and conjures up the image of evil snapping at our heels. Some have seen here the first proclamation of the Gospel remedy for sin. Notice also the mercy of God: he does not curse the man or the woman but rather gives them "labor pains" in their primary life tasks – the man in working the ground, the woman in child-bearing. The woman's punishment is not her desire for her husband, which is not bad, but rather that her sinful man will try to take advantage of her and dominate her. The Greek OT has the sense of it right here: "your desire will be for your man and he will lord it over/dominate you." To love and to cherish degenerates into to desire and to dominate. Here is no endorsement of the notion of "male-headship" over women. To the contrary this attempt to "lord" it over women is seen as a clear result of the Fall and the curse on fallenness. It is no accident that the patriarchal narratives come after these stories at the outset of Genesis. Patriarchy begins with the Fall and the curses on fallenness, not with God's original creation design.

Interestingly, what we have here is literally a case of poetic justice, for the sentencing here is in poetic form.[28] For the man, his work becomes toilsome: the ground will produce not just good fruit, but also thorns and thistles. Thus, work indeed becomes wearying, contributing to the shortening of the lifespan. In any event, implied is the ongoing nature of human life. Though humans will die, they will not completely die out. Also, probably implied in God's judgment is that *adam* is dirt (*adamah*) and will return to dust (die) but we are not told whether this involves more than physical death. Painful death, spiritual decay and deterioration, or eternal death may be implied.

And then there is the matter of ongoing struggle – there is wordplay in the verdict on the snake as well – "you will snap (*tensuppenu*) at his heel he will crush (*yesupeka*) your head." Advantage humans. While Judaism saw in 3.15 messianic hope for victory over Satan, the later Church Fathers, Justin and Irenaeus, taking *zera* (seed) to refer to an individual and therefore not a collective noun, saw this verse as a sort of *protoevangelium* – a foreshadowing of the victory of Christ over Satan (cf. Rom. 16.20). It should be clear that the curse on Eve is *descriptive* of the effects of sin, not *prescriptive* of how God intends male–female relationships to be.

No sooner does humankind start dying than he also starts killing. Gen. 4 tells the sordid tale of Cain and Abel. Now all of life is red in tooth and claw. Gen. 5 has as its constant refrain, "and he died, and he died, and he died." The point of all the genealogies is at least in part to remind us of God's faithfulness to keep his chosen ones alive and fruitful because from this chosen royal line will come the one who truly crushes the serpent's head. It may be implied in Gen. 5 that humankind is God's vice-regent upon the earth; he is to govern the earth until he dies and passes the baton to his descendants.

It cannot be emphasized enough that so much of biblical theology is grounded in this theology of Creation and Fall that is enunciated in Gen.1–3. It is not just that this undergirds and makes understandable the urgency of the Christian theology of redemption and the Redeemer found in the NT, but I would argue it also makes sense of so much of the

---

[28] Westermann, *Genesis 1–11*, 257, notes how verdicts were expected to be in verse.

history of God's people recorded in the OT. Both the emphases on the flaws and sinfulness of even the best of patriarchs and leaders (e.g. Abraham and Moses and David and Elijah) and later the judgment of exile of both the northern and the southern tribes added to the constant drum beat of the need for God again and again to intervene and rescue, ransom, or redeem his people, tell us of a God who is consistent in his just and merciful character while his people are only consistent in their inconsistency. At the same time, there are shining moments in the history of God's people when we see why it is said they are created in God's image. Even at its worse, humanity is still redeemable, and God does not give up on his creatures and creation. I would stress that this is not just a Christian view of the OT, it is the view of things found in the OT itself. But the fact that even after many acts of rescue and redemption, God's people continue to go astray, and even after the exile, things are far from perfect, makes evident that some better solution to the human dilemma needed to be attempted, beyond what we find in the OT story.[29]

The story of God's people in OT times vacillates back and forth between positive and negative stages and developments, even within the story of a single person or family's life. Someone will come along who is said to be "righteous in God's eyes" (e.g. a Noah, a Joshua), but then there are people and periods who "do what is right in their own eyes" and do not listen, obey, or truly worship the One God. There are no perfect paragons in these stories, where even a person who could be said to be "a man after God's own heart" (David), is depicted as sinning dramatically against God. And this reminds us not merely that the human figures in the OT stories not only should not be judged by later Christian standards, but even by their own Mosaic standards, they don't hold up their end of the bargain consistently. The complaint about the wilderness-wandering generation echoes through the literature not only of the OT, but again in 1 Cor. 10 as well. The question then becomes what does "redemption" or "salvation" mean in the OT? What it clearly enough *doesn't* mean is "being saved by grace through faith in the crucified and risen Jesus." The historical givenness of the situation is reflected in the storyline. Salvation could not mean what it later meant after the Christ event, because Christ had not yet come.

It would be a mistake however, to suggest that "salvation" meant nothing more than material aid, giving of physical help, rescuing from danger or bondage or the like. The language of redemption certainly can refer to any and all of that in the OT, but it can also refer to the righting of a relationship with God. In other words, to use later language, there is a spiritual dimension to "salvation" in the OT, it just doesn't have a Christological dimension or focus.

Abraham, for example, "trusted God and it is reckoned to him as righteousness" (Gen. 15.6) and Paul takes Abraham to be a paradigm for Christian faith. He even suggests the Gospel was pre-preached to Abraham! These kinds of example from the OT make clear that it is quite impossible to say things like "God is a God of grace in the NT and of Law in the OT" or "the OT is about material blessings whereas the NT is about spiritual

---

[29] From the perspective of various OT writers (see e.g. Ps. 8), the presupposition behind there being a relationship between God and a chosen people is that God is the Creator God who made possible human existence and human history. In other words, the Redeemer God was the Creator God in the first place, and his creation was good, so the flaw was not "in our stars" or in creation itself, but at the level of human behavior and praxis, as the story of Adam makes clear from the outset. Human beings could not complain they had been created defectively, nor could they deny the goodness of creation or the Creator. This meant that the discussion of sin and evil had to take place at the level of human responsibility for human behavior.

blessings including the gift of salvation." In fact, the matter is much more complex than any such caricatures of the OT, or for that matter the NT, would lead one to think. It will be worthwhile, then, in these chapters to review the story as a whole, focusing on a few key revealing vignettes, first in the OT, and then in the next chapter reflecting on how the NT writers and Jesus draw on such stories, and finally considering the stories told about Christians directly in Acts, and indirectly elsewhere in the NT.

Down in the Flood ...

Gen. 6.1–10 can only be entitled, "How low can you go?" As G. von Rad says, we can see that the snowball of sin that started humankind going downhill has now reached avalanche proportions.[30] This narrative in 6.1–4 shows the depth of degradation in creation, so much so that God is pierced to the heart and sorry he ever made human beings. Sadly, but firmly, God resolves to "blot out" humanity. Actually, the verb often translated "blot out" really means "wash away" and likely presages God's means of redemptive-judgment that comes later in the chapter. Yet even here, God provides through Noah a means of preserving his special ones and thus also all humanity. There is a glimmer of light in the darkness, but the darkness is very dark indeed. The text says that human evil is both extensive and intensive. It is extensive in that it affects everyone and perhaps every aspect of human existence. It is intensive in that the impulses are only for evil, for evil continually, and every impulse is tainted. The Hebrew word *yetzer* means more than just imaginations; it means designs and purposes of the heart. For instance, *yetzer hara* means the inclination to evil. Here we have a comprehensive statement of the extent and depth of human wickedness. Humanity was about as low as it could go; however, humankind was still redeemable through Noah and his progeny, but only by God's gracious act of redemption.

As we progress through the OT, remember that the term "heart" (*lev* in Hebrew) refers not only to the seat of emotions, but also to the center of the will and the understanding. Thus, if the "heart" is darkened, the whole control center of human personality is in view – will, thoughts, and emotions. In vv. 6ff. we see that God is no passive deity, but one who cares deeply for his creatures. Here and in Gen. 3, God is described in terms of anthropomorphisms. He walks, he molds humankind, he feels, he grieves. This does not mean God was thought of as human or having body parts. Rather, as L. Kohler says:

The meaning of the many human descriptions of God in the Old Testament is not to bring God from afar to a level like that of man. The human likeness is not a humanization. And these descriptions were never thought of that way except in unfair polemic. Rather they are to make God accessible to man ... They present God as a person. They avoid the error of making God a static, unconcerned, abstract idea, or an inflexible principle. God is a person, full of will, to be found in active discussion, prepared for his communication, open to the impact of human sin and supplication of human prayer and the weeping over human guilt; in a word, God is a living God.[31]

It will be seen that several statements in Gen. 6.9 suggest a worldwide flood: (1) the length of time it rained; (2) the place the ark landed after the waters receded; and (3) the fact that the earth was covered at least 150 days before the ark lands on the mountains (plural) of

---

[30] Von Rad, *Genesis*, 115ff.
[31] As quoted *ibid.*, 118.

Ararat. In addition, Gen. 7.19 says, the water "covered the high mountains (hills) under the whole heavens," and 6.13 says it is God's intent to wash away all humanity (7.4). It is clear that this story appears to be about a worldwide deluge. However, the one factor which strongly counts against this is that frequently the biblical writers, on the basis of their own knowledge, will call their known world of the Middle East the whole world (Gen. 41.56; Dan. 2.38, 4.22).

Notice that in Gen. 10 Noah's descendants repopulate what would have been the known world of Asia, Africa, and perhaps parts of Europe. Remember that frequently the Bible uses *phenomenological or observational* language that expresses a real truth – how things *appear* to the eye of the author or narrator. Thus, frequently we are told of the sun rising and setting, which is not surprising or false language even for us in a post-Copernican world. The Bible is not a scientific, but a pre-scientific account which expresses God's truth about various matters. Thus, Noah's flood may have been confined to the then-known world of the writer, but the text may hint at more than this. One final factor which could favor the universal flood theory is the structure of our narrative, or at least its conclusion.

Beginning with 8.1ff., we see numerous parallels to Gen. 1, where a *ruach* blows over the chaotic waters. Reminiscent of Gen. 1 is the command to go forth with the animals so that they may breed (8.16–19), then God's blessing of Noah and the command to him and his progeny, "be fruitful and multiply and fill the earth." This clearly echoes Gen. 1.28. Following this, there is the reference to humanity made in God's image (9.6). Further, we have a covenantal relationship between God and the creatures and the humans not unlike Gen. 1–3. We have covenant sanctions here, too, as in Gen. 2–3. The promise of blessing also is followed by the prohibition against taking human life (9.6). God promises no longer to curse the ground (8.21). Life and death here as in Gen. 2–3 are clearly the main issues – especially the continuance of human life.

Thus, clearly, we are meant to see Gen. 6–9 as a new start, a new creation, a new blessing by God, a new world being populated by humans and creatures all over again. This does not necessarily mean the author was thinking of more than a massive flood in the then-known world of the ANE, rather than the world as we know it today. We also find that the sequel to creation is once again sin; just as Adam and Eve soon after it all started sinned, so too Noah gets drunk and Ham sees his nakedness (9.21–27). But v. 24 implies that Ham also *did* something. This is not likely a reference to Ham defaming his father by drawing attention to his shameful condition, since it says in v. 25 that when Noah awoke he knew what Ham had done. This would seem to imply that we are dealing with incest or some homosexual act. Elsewhere in the Bible, the phrase "uncover someone's nakedness" can refer to a sexual act of some sort. This would certainly explain Noah's strong response. In any case, sin once again rears its ugly head. All of this leads one to think that the author saw all this in the light of the original creation and thus saw in Noah a new start for all humanity.

Then Came Abraham ...

The author/editor of Gen. 12–50 intends us to see this material as similar to Gen. 1–11, as he deliberately links the two periods by genealogies and other allusions from the former period. Thus, for instance, the genealogies in Gen. 1–11 which begin in Mesopotamia with

Shem end in the same region with Abram, who is from "Ur of the Chaldees." A certain amount of anachronism and/or editorial explanations are to be expected so that Gen. 12–50 will make sense to a much later age that lived after the Exodus. The stories beginning with the genealogy in 11.27–29 come to us as a result of a considerable period of transmission of oral and written stories and traditions. It is obvious the author desires to separate between now and then and appears able to do so. It is also obvious he is dealing on a limited scale with family history, not world history. Before we begin to examine Abraham's call in 12.1, we need to look at his roots as mentioned in 11.27–31.

First of all, the home of Abram is said to be Ur of the Chaldees. Ur is the Babylonian city of dynastic and governmental significance on the Euphrates River. Abram possibly lived there during the third dynasty of Ur, 2060–1950 BC, or possibly at the end of the second dynasty if he migrated by 2092. It is also the city where the moon god Sin was worshipped. Here also the Arameans have roots, for the Chaldeans are an Aramean people, from which we get the word and language Aramaic. Haran not only had trade but also religious links with Ur because it too was a place where Sin, the moon god, was worshipped, and several of Abram's relatives have names associated with the moon (Sarah, Milcah, Terah). This may mean that the reason Terah set out for Canaan but "settled in Haran" was because they were moon worshipers. We should not be surprised if this is so prior to Abram's call, and we cannot assume that Abram began by worshipping the God of the Bible just because he descended from Noah. Descendants can go astray (Josh. 24.2,14).

Abram's call is not located in time in Gen. 11–12, but Acts 7.2–8 suggests he received the call prior to going to Haran. If so, then he did not embark on the final pilgrimage to Canaan until his father died. Notice in 12.4 the indication of a separate trip starting from Haran. Finally, what about the relationship of Sarai and Abram? We are told in 11.30–31 that Nahor married his niece Milcah, the daughter of his brother, and, apparently, it was the custom for Terah's descendants to marry this way (cf. 20.12; 24.3ff.; 29.19). At 20.12 we are told that Sarai is Abram's half-sister, the daughter of his father and another wife who was not Abram's mother. This proves important for what happens in 12.10–20, 20.18. Also, we are told Sarai was barren and had no children (11.30), which is crucial to the story that follows because of the promise made to Abram in 12.1–9. Notice how genealogy prepares us for this narrative.

The Abram cycle may be distinguished from what precedes it in one very important respect: the promises made to Abram are not made to anyone before him. To be sure there is the blessing of fruitfulness for Adam and Noah, but not a promise of the promised land, or the promise that Abram and his seed will be a blessing to those around, part of the major theme. The promise theme runs throughout the rest of Genesis like a clear and ever-present stream, giving life and hope to the story. It is the very heart of the narrative around which all else revolves and can be explained. The patriarchal stories illustrate the numerous obstacles that stood in the way of accepting the promise and the extreme lengths to which God went in order to fulfill the promise. It is not the case that the promises can be seen as a later icing on the cake; without it there is no cake. Further, we have the promise *before* we have a covenantal relationship. If God is faithful to the promise, it reflects in the first instance on his character rather than his loyalty to a predetermined agreement or covenant.[32]

---

[32] On covenants and their nature see the treatment of this matter, pp. 288–305, below.

Kidner says that chapter 12 is the beginning of the story of redemption, for we have the story of the promise. Abram is simply told: "Leave your country, people, and household, and go to an as of yet undisclosed destination." Here is the classic example of moving on faith, not on sight. Thus, Abram in Heb. 11 makes the "hall of faith." Notice that God offers something that could be said to compensate, or at least replace, what Abram was giving up (12.2–3). He leaves a country and is made into a nation. He leaves his people but is promised progeny. He leaves a household, but becomes a household name, a blessing to all peoples.

Canonically speaking, the NT parallel is Mk. 10.28–31, where Peter and the disciples are said to give up all but gain more in due course. Note how the command continues to narrow down what is to be left – country, relatives, immediate family, as the call to obedience becomes more difficult. While it is possible that the move from Ur to Haran was part of a larger nomadic enterprise, here we are talking about the calling of an individual and his family to move; not for economic or political reasons, but due to divine purpose. Abram is like a touchstone or representative of God (12.3). How he is treated will determine how others will be treated by God.

It will become clear that the text does not see Abram as merely a nomad, much less a donkey caravanner; he is or becomes a ruler and a father of rulers (23.5,17,20), a prophet (20.7), and a priest who sets up altars to God (12.8–10 and other places in the book). Not until Abram arrived near the place where Shechem would later be does he receive the word, "to your offspring I'll give this land." Notice God does not say he would give this land to Abram personally (neither does 12.1–3), and the land was not wholly possessed by Abram at any time personally. He would not receive the full benefit of this promise. We have here a theophany, a God appearance, after which time Abram built an altar to honor and worship the God who promised this. Despite appearances to the contrary, for the Canaanites were *then* in the land, God affirms the truth of his word: he was present even in a pagan land; Yahweh was a not a local deity tied to a shrine.[33]

If Gen. 12.1–9 is about *fides* (faith), then 12.10–20 is about perfidy. The author, if he was attempting to glorify Abram and whitewash his story, could not have included this narrative. There are close parallels here to Gen. 20 and 26 which tell a similar story. We can only say in regard to Gen. 26.2, "like father, like son," and in regard to Gen. 20, "if it worked once it might work twice." In Gen. 20 we are given the excuse of Abram, "there is no fear of God in the land; to protect my hide, I did this." In short, these stories are about a fear of human beings by Abram (and Isaac) which does not comport with a fear of God. Whatever the interrelationship of these stories, which may have been edited to appear in similar form by the final editor, we see an Abram who is a man of fear and calculation.

If there was famine it was common to go to Egypt to get food, where the Nile still watered the land and the land could still produce a crop.[34] The famine is said to be heavy. Before Abram and Sarai ever enter the land, Abram decides what he will do to take advantage of his beautiful wife's looks. Abram tells her: "Say you are my sister so I will be treated well, and my life will be spared." Abram wishes to profit by this trip. Verse 16 says he acquired sheep, cattle, donkeys, servants, and camels, because Abram loaned Sarai out

---

[33] Phrases like "the Canaanites were *then* in the land" reflect the clearly retrospective point of view of the person or persons who wrote these stories down at a time later than Abram, perhaps based largely on oral traditions.

[34] J. Skinner, *Genesis* (ICC; 2nd edn. [1930]; Edinburgh: T&T Clark, 1969), 248, refers to inscriptional evidence.

even to Pharaoh. In short, he was willing to compromise his wife's virtue to make money and save his own skin. Abram himself has endangered the promise by giving away his wife. We are to see deceit going on here, for saying Sarai is his half-sister is a half-truth for she is also his sole wife, and he is properly reprimanded by Pharaoh when this becomes known.

We are not told how Pharaoh knew, but Abram has no response, since he knows he is in the wrong. Pharaoh provides Abram an escort out of the country because of his untruth and lack of faith. Abram becomes a curse, not a blessing, to the nation of Egypt, and foreshadows what happens to future Israelites and Pharaohs in that land. It is not implied that the escort was hostile: rather, Pharaoh is trying to make sure Abram goes, to appease God's wrath and send its cause out of the land. Notice how the story is not told for its own sake. What is the point of all this? The point concerns God's wish to be faithful, to protect, and to be true to his promises despite sinful human nature and the obstacles Abram puts in the way. God's sovereignty and control, despite his own people's fears and immoralities, overcome all obstacles.

God is the central actor, and the narrator's intention shows how he brought about his will even through and in spite of scoundrels. It is a word of encouragement to God's people later: "The one who called you is faithful and he will do it." God and his word are vindicated despite the sinfulness of his chosen one. Even the patriarchs were sinners, and what they had, they had by the sheer mercy of God, which they sometimes believed in and accepted. If even an Abram can stumble and still be used by God, then there is hope for all of God's people.

Gen. 14 brings Abram in touch with world history. Abram returns as the victorious conqueror and is met by the priest-king Melchizedek and the King of Sodom, who sees him as a notable conqueror. Note that Abram had 318 men of his household in his military entourage, clear evidence that we are dealing with his tribe, not just a lone individual.

Melchizedek is a mysterious figure. We are given no history about him, and he disappears after this story. He is seen as a prototype of Christ by the author of Hebrews, but even in Hebrews, Melchizedek is *not* seen as a pre-existent appearance of Christ himself. Melchizedek provides hospitality and food for the weary conqueror (v. 18); the bread and wine are part of any normal meal and probably have no sacramental significance. What then is the purpose of this narrative in its original setting? Obviously, it is not told for its own sake; since we are not told anything more than is absolutely necessary about this mystery man, Melchizedek. Three things become evident: (1) Abram prospers only when he does God's will; and (2) even pagan kings and priests must reckon with the works of Yahweh and the validity of his servant Abram. Perhaps we also see how other pagan nations are blessed or bless themselves through Abram, the conquering hero; (3) the name Melchizedek, literally "righteous king," suggests even foreign kings recognize Abram as a formidable figure in the land.

The narrative in Gen. 15 is pivotal in many ways in the Abram cycle of stories because it brings to light covenantal theology in a way we have not seen before (except perhaps with Noah). Covenantal theology has been seen by M. Kline and others as the unifying thread that ties together the OT itself, and the OT with the NT.[35] We can say, looking at matters from a canonical perspective, that Paul in Gal. 3–4 saw a definite connection and

---

[35] See especially M. Kline, *The Structure of Biblical Authority* (Eugene, OR: Wipf and Stock, repr. 1997).

continuity between the Abrahamic and the New Covenant, though of course there are obvious differences (circumcision vs. baptism, etc.).

Here as in the Noah narratives, it is God who initiates, stipulates, and confirms the covenant and its sanctions. Abram is the passive recipient of its benefits. He was in need of more assurance than just a promise, and thus God performed a sacred rite that sealed the promises and made clear that Yahweh was determined to make them come true. Much is learned by studying ancient lord–vassal treaties (Assyrian, Hittite; cf. *ANET*). Such treaties are not between two parties that are equals, but, as the treaty title implies, there is a hierarchical relationship involved, so that the lord dictates terms and benefits. This is, of course, what we find here. God makes promises and by ceremony swears to be faithful to them. There are curse and blessing sanctions in such treaties, curses if the treaty stipulations are not performed, and blessings if they are. *Nevertheless*, the covenant is not unilateral or unconditional.

Gen. 15.6 is significant to NT theology, since Paul draws on it in Galatians and Romans to enunciate the doctrine of righteousness by faith. Notice that Abram believes God's word about the heir on the basis of a promise. In the narrative which begins in v. 7, if this is a second narrative added here, the discussion is about possessing a land, not an heir, and it is about this promise of land that Abram requires further assurance: "how can I know I will gain possession of it?" To this God responds with a covenant ratification rite, indicating an implied curse on himself (!) should it be unfulfilled.

Gen. 15.6 indicates the following: (1) the verb means "trust," Abram trusted God, and thus it is not referring to a set of doctrines Abram believed, but to his trust in Yahweh to do as he said; (2) *saddiq*, righteousness, is a relational term implying right-standing with God, being in a right relation with him. Abram's righteous status is something he receives, not something he achieves, and he receives it through faith; (3) the verb here translated "reckoned" (or better "credited") to him implies a status, not an imparted condition. He is counted as righteous and, in the sense that he is in right-standing with God, he is in the right relationship with God.

It has been said that to come to Christ costs nothing, but to follow him requires everything. We see this same idea of *total dedication* in the two narratives of Gen. 15 and 17, and it is in the latter that the obligations of the covenant incumbent upon Abram are made clear. The point of concluding the covenant at this juncture is that Abram is indeed about to undergo a life-changing event in a year. Isaac will be born and his own identity as father of a multitude will finally be on the way to being established. God appears to Abram and says, "I am *El Shaddai*." We are told at Exod. 6.3 that this was the signature name that God revealed to Abraham, Isaac, and Jacob before he revealed his personal name of Yahweh. Unfortunately, it is not clear what *El Shaddai* means. Some scholars have suggested it is derived from *sadu* meaning God of the Mountains (cf. the psalms that call God "the rock"). This derivation is uncertain. What is more certain is that the word is usually used in situations where God's people are hard-pressed and need assurance (Gen. 17.1; 28.3; 35.11; 43.14; 48.3; 49.25).

This may suggest that it is an assertion of God's sovereignty or might, hence the translation "almighty." In relation to the changing of Abram's and Sarai's names to Abraham and Sarah, D. J. Wiseman argues rightly: "The change of name marks both a new era and a new status and is consistently used in subsequent narratives probably much the same as ...

in a king's assumption of a special throne name."[36] However, here it is God who gives the name and the point is that God is establishing their identity. There is probably wordplay in v. 5. Abram seems to mean "exalted father," while Abraham, if it is not a mere lengthening of the same name, means "father of many."

As so often in the OT, the name signifies something God is or has done for a person or some attendant circumstance involved in a special event in one's life (cf. Isaac, Jacob). Wiseman notes that *no one else in the OT or NT is given this name*. Abraham alone is the father of many for the Hebrews. Abraham is to walk before God in a blameless way, i.e., he is to act in accordance with God's word and will. This is not like Enoch's or Noah's walking with God, which implies a special closeness or relationship. Here the emphasis is on *behavior* in God's sight. The word *tamim* means whole or perfect, and here the meaning seems to be "acting without ulterior motives," wholeheartedly following God's way and word. It indicates complete surrender, not moral perfection. In regard to Sarai's new name Sarah, we can only say that it, like Sarai, seems to mean princess, implying royalty (note that Abraham is called a prince in 23.6, which would strengthen the parallel to the taking of royal names). It is said in 17.6 that kings (17.20b) will come from Abraham, again implying a royal identity.

When God appears to Abraham, he responds like a servant, with complete obeisance, falling down flat on his face. In v. 7 we are told it will be an everlasting covenant (*berith olam*), and we are immediately told how so: this is a covenant not just with Abraham but also with his descendants. If it is for Abraham and his family, then the sign of the covenant must likewise be for all, regardless of age or stage or status. M. Kline stresses that the kind of covenant we are dealing with here is not just master–servant, but high king to vassal king who will serve the high king. The vassal king is under the high king. He has special obligations and duties as well as privileges involved in his position.

When it is applied to God and his royal servant, Abraham, the following has often been said: "The *berith* is neither a simple divine promise to which no obligation on man's part is attached ... nor is it a mutual contract in the sense that the failure of one party dissolves the relation. It is an immutable determination of God's purpose, which no unfaithfulness of man can invalidate; but it carries conditions, the neglect of which will exclude the individual from its benefits."[37] This statement, if it were just about God's character and purpose would be fine. It is *not*, however, true that the unfaithfulness of humankind cannot break the covenant.

As we shall see, Skinner's claim is not quite correct. There are *no* unilateral covenants in the OT, nor are their unconditional covenants that do not require in some measure the appropriate human response. The covenant can indeed be broken by human beings, and God has not obligated himself to keep it if this has happened. Indeed, he is only obligated to enact the curse sanctions he promised to bring if his human partners defaulted on the agreement.

What, then, are we to make of this circumcision to be performed not on believers but on all Abraham's male descendants? Before they are even able to respond God includes them. Thus, their inclusion rests primarily on God's election, not human response, though

---

[36] D. J. Wiseman, *Essays on the Patriarchal Narratives* (Winona Lake, IN: Eisenbrauns, 1983), 159.
[37] Skinner, *Genesis*, 298.

the latter must necessarily follow or else the covenant is broken. Kline takes circumcision here as the oath-sign, i.e., a sign by which one invokes a curse upon oneself if one does not do as the other requires. The curse is related to the promise. If the promise is progeny, the curse is the cutting off of progeny, symbolized by the act of circumcision. The idea is, "if I do not perform this covenant, may I and my descendants be cut off from God's people."[38]

In v. 14 we have wordplay – any uncircumcised one (one without flesh cut off) will be cut off from God's people, by which is meant excommunication, not execution. Elsewhere in the Pentateuch, we have the phrase "cut a covenant" (*karath berith*). Since circumcision is the covenant sign, cutting and covenanting go together in another sense as well (Jer. 34.18; Gen. 15.10). The act of circumcision consecrated someone to the Lord. The point is that one must be willing to accept the consequences (the curse) if one wishes to receive the blessings. Persons are addressed as responsible humans. Some were circumcised before they could exercise such responsibility; however, they are made accountable to God from the start by this act.

What is Abraham's response to the promise of a child? He laughs, asking, "Can old maid Sarah now give birth when she could not previously?" Abraham offers to God a more "reasonable" option. Why not just bless my son Ishmael? But what seems reasonable to us is not always what is right in God's plan. God promises to do this, but here we see that not all that God blesses are his chosen line. Indeed, he promises that Ishmael will be the father of a great nation, but that is not necessarily the sign that God is with them in some special sense.

Prosperity is no clear guide to one's standing with God, even in the OT.

From this narrative, we again see the humanness of Abraham and his seeming disbelief at such stupendous promises. His view of God was too small, for the narrative stresses that nothing is too hard for God. The narrative is also about God's elective purposes, which precede human response and make that response necessary and possible. We see, too, that the covenant involves blessing and curse, promises and obligations, and assumes human responsiveness and responsibility. But God's elective purposes do not require pre-existing ability; in some cases, they may create it. It is worth stressing, however, that what the OT is talking about is not the later Christian concept of salvation through faith in God's Son. Election is one thing, salvation in the Christian sense is quite another. One can be among the chosen people, and not be saved, as the story of the wilderness-wandering generation makes all too clear. Furthermore, election is basically a corporate notion in both testaments – it is "in Israel" in the OT, and it is "in Christ" in the NT. How one gets into the elect group varies, and is not simply a matter of divine fiat, either in the OT or the NT.[39]

All of the Abrahamic cycle has been straining toward the point when Isaac, the promised child, will be born. This great joy is recorded in Gen. 21 with the child being named Isaac, "he laughs," for obvious reasons. In a very real sense, Abraham's life story has gone from the incomprehensible to the incomprehensible. He begins by obeying God and setting out for he knows not where, then he comes to the twilight of his life and God tells him

---

[38] Here and elsewhere in this discussion of Genesis, Kline is Meredith Kline, my OT teacher of many years ago, from whom I learned so much. See his book, *By Oath Consigned* (Winona Lake, IN: Eerdmans, 1968).

[39] See the helpful and detailed discussion by A. Chad Thornhill, *The Chosen People: Election, Paul and Second Temple Jerusalem* (Downers Grove, IL: InterVarsity Press, 2015) and the discussion below.

to sacrifice the one child he had been continually promising him. There have been other tests along the way, but here Abraham is called to act against his lifelong dream and ambition, against his love and affection for his only child born of Sarah.

To be sure, there are interesting parallels between Isaac and Jesus, but at the crucial juncture Isaac is not sacrificed whereas Christ is, and thus it is not entirely surprising that the NT writers make almost *nothing* of the possible parallels. Thus, if you draw parallels, some may ask, is God more merciful to Isaac than to his own son, Jesus? But this is the wrong question to ask. Further, the lamb that is substituted here in Gen. 22 is not said to be a sacrifice for sin; there is no interest in sin or substitutionary atonement in the Abraham story at all. We must *not* turn this story into a Christian allegory and miss its real meaning in its original context.

We are told in v. 1 that God is testing Abraham. This forewarns us as readers, but Abraham did not know that. It is noticeable that Abraham obeys quickly. It is clear that God knows how important this child is to Abraham. "Take your son, your only son, the one whom you love." The redundancy indicates that God knows precisely what is at stake for Abraham. The way the narrative proceeds is indirect. It does not psychologize Abraham or peer into his inner thoughts; we know him only by what he says or does. Isaac is a young boy now, old enough to help with chores, but he could hardly expect that the wood he was carrying would be for his own funeral pyre. Even here we see Abraham's tender care of him to the last.

Abraham takes the knife and the fire which would be dangerous to handle while climbing a mountain. Notice again how Abraham is not told which mountain to go to: "it is one I will tell you about." Not all God's instructions come up front, but often only after we are moving on faith and in obedience.

It is difficult to explain v. 5. Is it merely said so the servants won't follow and interfere, or does Abraham really believe (on the basis of the promise) that he will return with Isaac? The action of the story slows down almost unbearably from v. 6 on. The dialogue between father and son is especially gut-wrenching. Again v. 8 is ambiguous. Is Abraham really hopeful or sure God will provide a substitute, or are these words simply meant to silence his son's thoughts and questions? Perhaps Abraham speaks more truth than he realizes, but even if he is expressing his belief, it is clear he thinks only divine intervention will stop this inexorable process. The words "and the two went on together" (6b, 8b) are a poignant refrain. It is clear Abraham has resolved to go all the way with God's command, and the messenger of Yahweh intervenes only after he has taken the knife to slay his son. Only then come the words, "do not lay a hand on the boy," and only then does Abraham look up and see a ram in a thicket.

Verse 14 indicates that Abraham names the spot, something which would be appropriate. Perhaps "on the mountain it will become clear" or perhaps "on the mountain it will be provided." God reveals himself in his own place and time and in his own way. His will may seem inscrutable on many occasions and very trying, but there will come a time when the truth will become clear. Now we see through a glass darkly. The testing is a most extreme one. In Gen. 12 Abraham had to cut himself off from his whole past. In Gen. 22 he is called to give up his whole future and trust God will provide. Some have seen in this story the mystery of life, apparently so contradictory to the existence of a loving God, yet in this story it is God who provides the apparent contradiction.

Clearly, the story implies God will test his people, even to extreme degrees, but as 1 Cor. 10 says, with the test he will provide a way out. There is something more important than life, and that is obedience to God and the personal integrity of living "with fear of the Lord." Perhaps the best commentary on this is Mic. 6.6–8:

With what shall I come before the Lord? Shall I come before him with burnt offerings, with calves a year old? Will the Lord be pleased with thousands of rams, with ten thousands of rivers of oil? Shall I give my first-born for my transgression, the fruit of my body for the sin of my soul? ... He has shown you, O humankind, what is good; and what does the Lord require of you but to do justice, and to love kindness, and to walk humbly with your God?

Abraham now has the promise of greatness and land reaffirmed. He has finally passed God's ultimate test. He has grown much since he left Ur of the Chaldees, and so have we if we have journeyed with him on his pilgrimages in Genesis.

The Jacob Cycle (Gen. 25.1–33.7)

There are two major sorts of stories in the Jacob cycle: (1) Jacob and Esau stories; and (2) Jacob and Laban stories. Most of these stories are more anthropocentric, more focused on purely human affairs and viewpoints, than in the Abraham cycle, though we do have a few theophanies in this cycle (the Bethel dream, Gen. 28; the encounter with angels, 32.2; the wrestling episode, 32.22 ff.). The promise theme is not as prominent in the Jacob stories as it is in the Abraham cycle. If there were certain unappealing aspects to Abraham's character, we see Jacob in even a less favorable light. The writers do not try to gloss over the bad traits of the patriarchs, and this speaks well for the possibility that we have here some historical traditions and not merely later hagiographic legends that try to do reverence to certain heroes of the faith.

Various other factors support the historicity of the Jacob cycle. First is the fact that we have customs listed in this and the other cycles which were later prohibited by Mosaic Law (e.g. the marriage to two sisters, Gen. 29.15–30, but this is forbidden in Lev. 18.18). Second, in Genesis, the birthright seems to have included virtually all of the father's property, hence Jacob's sullen attitude and his desire to snatch the birthright (Gen. 25.5–6). But in Deut. 21.15–17 the elder son's share is strictly defined as twice that of the other sons, or possibly two-thirds, *but not all*. Third, later Israelite law (Lev. 18.9,11) prohibited marriage to a half-sister as in the case of Abraham and Sarah. All of this suggests these stories are about an age earlier than Moses, not a latter retrojection of Israelite piety. Fourth, the practice of granting birthrights (extra privileges to the eldest son) was widespread in the ANE, but it appears that the practice of *selling* one's birthright is not documented in the parallels of this period. However, selling inherited property is well known at various periods in ANE history.

We are told that Isaac had a taste for venison, and he liked Esau's more manly image and occupation. If Hebrew civilization was going through a period of transition from hunters to semi-nomadic stock breeders and shepherds, then we have a believable historical setting for our narratives. Jacob was "new wave," but his father preferred the old ways and customs. Quite naturally there was tension between the sons because of this and the birthright.

We are now prepared to look at the Jacob cycle in some detail, beginning with Gen. 25.19. Rebekah, like Sarah, was barren. Finally, through Isaac's prayer and God's response she becomes pregnant. Only here and at Gen. 38.27–30 do we have a birth of twins in the OT. The two brothers jostle (literally "crush one another") in the womb, and Rebekah cries: "If it is to be so, why am I ..." but the sentence is incomplete in the Hebrew text; perhaps it means "Why is this happening to me?" (NIV). The Lord told her two nations were struggling within her womb and that they would be divided, i.e., hostile and perhaps incompatible from birth. The text indicates that the pre-natal struggle for dominance foreshadowed their ensuing relationship. Verse 23d indicates the elder will serve the younger, and so once again we see the principle of election operating – neither heredity nor a father's preference would determine the chosen and favored one and his line, only God does. God's choice is apparently not based on any inherent desirability of Jacob, but God in his love decided to set his favor upon him. But again, this election is for a particular historical purpose, the discussion is not about the individual salvation of one or the other brother.

The derivation given in the text of the names Esau and Jacob is difficult, but it appears that Jacob comes from the verb *yakav*, which means to follow at the heel, or snatch at the heel, or overreach, or, if used figuratively, to deceive (cf. 27.36, where the cognate noun means "heel"). The name Jacob means one who dogs another's steps and pulls him down in order to pull himself up, perhaps with the implication of treachery (hence Jacob, "the heel snatcher"). This name could reflect something about the struggle in the womb to be born first.

Jacob, unlike Esau the hunter, who is very much a loner, and not a community person but someone who is irregular and perhaps a bit uncouth in his behavior, stayed close to home. He is "a man who lived among tents" (which could suggest a momma's boy) and we find him cooking lentils. He was the more refined of the two brothers. Esau wandered far, hunting wild animals. Jacob was smooth-skinned. Esau was ruddy and hairy, rough and ready.

The story is episodic; thus, we have nothing about the brothers between birth and manhood. This is not a surprise, since the ancients tended to think that what really matters was one's origins (gender, geography, and generation) and one's adult life. We find Jacob cooking some stew, and Esau comes in from the open countryside starved. Gen. 25.32 probably means, "Look, I'm starving to death." Esau's mental horizons seem fixed on the present and his immediate needs; he doesn't care about tomorrow or his future inheritance. We are even told that Esau despised his birthright (25.34). There are several keys to this story. First, it appears Esau is deceived as to what Jacob is asking. It has been suggested that Esau thought he was going to get blood soup and is deceived and discovers it only to be lentils (a very common dish in the Middle East). Gen. 27.36 says clearly there was deception here.

Second, Jacob does not tell Esau what is cooking, and Esau only says in unpolished fashion, literally, "Let me gulp down some of that red stuff." Jacob makes Esau swear an irrevocable oath to give up his birthright in order to get this food. Jacob insists on an oath (Josh. 9.19), because otherwise the deal could have been rescinded, especially if Esau was deceived. Esau drinks and eats bread given him by Jacob, then gets up and walks off, showing no concern about his birthright's loss. Esau acts impulsively, guided by his sensual needs, which may also explain why he marries the Hittite women, apparently unconcerned about the grief this may bring his family (Gen. 26.34–35).

What is the purpose of this narrative? In part, it intends to show Jacob as he really is, but also, we see how God uses even an unworthy vessel, even in his worst moments, to bring about the divine plan. The explanation given in the Joseph narrative applies equally here. "What you intended for evil, God intended for good." Even though Jacob may be unaware of it (cf. Rom. 8.28), God's sovereign hand is the hidden but guiding force here. Life is one continuous struggle for position and power, blessing and bounty, and in this, Jacob struggles with both humanity and God (noting the comment on Jacob in Hos. 12.3–4).

The narrative in Gen. 27 follows Gen. 25 quite naturally and also has good claims to being a unified whole (at least vv. 1–45) and to having a historical basis. Though the patriarchal blessings of Isaac and Jacob are unique in ancient literature, it should not be alleged that we have a legal matter and Esau could have achieved redress for his wrong, and thus this material must be unhistorical, since Esau can get no remedy.[40] To the contrary, the giving of the blessings is to be seen as irrevocable.

Isaac, whether knowingly or unknowingly, says what God would have him say in this blessing, and he cannot retract it. It is much like Balaam's oracle that was supposed to be a curse but could only be a blessing for Israel (an oracle he could not revoke). Words, especially divine words, are often seen in the Bible as not merely a saying of something but accomplishing or doing something. They are *performative* in nature, enacting what they speak of. We must, however, distinguish between this blessing, which was irrevocable once spoken, and the tangible benefits of inheritance, which were subject to adjudication. Gen. 25 is about the birthright. Gen. 27 is about the blessing that goes along with it, but is not identical with it. Better said, the inheritance is but a small part of the blessing because essentially the blessing is what God will do for Jacob, not what Isaac will leave him (Heb. 12.16,17).

Various scholars have noted the difference between this and the previous patriarchal promises. First, this is by a man, not from God. Isaac is saying, "May God do so and so; may it happen this way." Second, this is a blessing, not a promise. Those are two different sorts of utterances. Therefore, the narrator is under no obligation to include the promise of many generations of descendants or a promised land here. This is a special blessing involving Esau and his status as first-born and his relationship to his brother and neighbors (cf. v. 29). Jacob goes having been blessed, but he is soon to get a dose of his own medicine, deception at the hands of a master-deceiver – Laban.

Occasionally in the Jacob cycle we will get a theophany that is not primarily about Jacob vs. Esau or Jacob vs. Laban, and that is the case in Gen. 28.10–22. As various scholars have points out, these theophanies come where fights and jeopardy are at their most extreme for our central figure, Jacob. What are we to make of this dream revelation? Did Jacob see a real stairway to heaven, or was it merely a dream? Perhaps his surroundings had suggested such a stairway in his mind before he fell asleep.

In any event, we are to think of reality being represented if not depicted in this dream, even if the visual image is only a dream. The word of revelation was certainly real enough

---

[40] But see E. A. Speiser, *Genesis* (AB 1; New Haven, CT: Yale University Press, 1964), *ad loc.*

and stirred Jacob. Also, the presence of God and his messengers who deliver his commands and revelations was a reality that produced this effect on Jacob. He was banished from his home, with an uncertain future. He was alone and about to enter a foreign land, having no roof over his head. Here was indeed a time when Jacob needed some assurance and reassurance from God. Jacob did not seek this revelation, nor had he repented of his deceptions. God does not confront him with his shortcomings here, but only gives a series of assurances. He will have a homeland, others will be blessed through him and his offspring, and God will watch over him wherever he goes and bring him back to the promised land. This promise was an act of pure grace, for Jacob had not changed or prepared for this. Jacob had learned that God was not just located in Beersheba or that area; he could appear elsewhere as well and go with him. Jacob is surprised by this revelation; it was unsought and did not require anything of him. Nonetheless, he responds. We are not in all probability to see Jacob as bartering with God here.[41] Verses 20 and 21 could be read, "since God will be with me ... Yahweh will be my God ... and I will give him a tenth." We close our examination of Jacob with three segments: two about Jacob and Esau, and one theophany in between (Gen. 32.22–32), which once again comes at a crucial juncture and crisis time in Jacob's life. Verses 3–21 reveal Jacob's attempt to placate and soften up his brother for his return. Here we see a clever but fearful man at work, fighting for what may be his life and inheritance. But his struggle is not just with humans; it is also with angels.

Verse 22 begins the theophany. Some may take it that this is an encounter with God, but in a veiled representation. He does not overpower Jacob at first but lets him strive until he learns that it is God's grace and blessing, not human striving, that will produce the desired end. This is something Jacob must find out alone in his encounter with God (cf. v. 24). Jacob comes away lame but blessed, having been made to realize who was God and who defined his identity and future. But no sooner had he encountered God than he had to go on and encounter Esau as well. Having faced God, Jacob may have thought, Esau could hardly be any more difficult. But Esau reacts in a totally unexpected fashion. He accepts Jacob graciously and forgives him.

In these two stories Jacob's two major struggles in life come to resolution. His time with Laban was but a long cooling-off period between two episodes of the Esau conflict. Jacob struggled with God and human beings and came out blessed and reconciled because that was God's plan, not in the end because of his human striving or cleverness. God's blessing, like Esau's forgiveness, was not a *quid pro quo* but sheer grace. Both God and Esau received him favorably, and he has seen their faces and survived. This is all Jacob had hoped for in his encounter with either, but in fact he had gotten much more. Reconciliation in the divine sphere leads to reconciliation in the human sphere. If these narratives are about kinship ties to God and humankind, then here we see the climax: grace and God's work can turn an over-reacher into one who strives with God in a good way and one who can even be reconciled to a hated brother as well as an awesome deity. With God, all things are possible, even reconciling the irreconcilable.

---

[41] It is possible, as David Schreiner has suggested to me, that Jacob is reiterating the terms of the covenant here. In any case vv. 20–21 are a conditional clause: "If God will be with me ... and if I return in peace ... then the Lord will be to me as a god."

Let My People Go ... A Plague on Both Your Houses

The story of God's liberation of the Hebrews from Egypt through the intercession of Moses is in some ways too familiar to need much rehearsing. What is perhaps less well known is the careful literary structure of the material in Exod. 7.8–11.10.[42] Consider the following:

First Cycle

| PRELUDE: | Warning: | Moses stands before Pharaoh. In the morning |
| 1. blood | 2. frogs | 3. gnats |

Second Cycle

| PRELUDE: | Warning: | Moses comes before Pharaoh |
| 4. flies | 5. pests | 6. boils |

Third Cycle

| PRELUDE: | No warning | |
| 7. hail | 8. locusts | 9. darkness/death of the first-born[43] |

Besides this sort of literary analysis of the structure of the material it is also possible to discern indications of another scheme, according to the nature of the plagues. From this aspect, they are divisible into pairs. The first pair (blood/frogs) pertains to the Nile; the second pair (gnats/swarm of flies) comprises two plagues that resemble each other; the third pair (pests/boils) likewise consists of two similar plagues; the fourth pair (hail/locusts) represents two sources of damage to crops; and the fifth group (darkness and plague of the first-born) contains two kinds of darkness, first the darkness upon Egypt lasting three days, and then the darkness of death upon the first-born.

> Plague 1 – Pharaoh is unconcerned and will not let the people go.
>
> Plague 2 – People allowed to go to sacrifice (8.8) but not to leave or take everyone and everything.
>
> Plague 4 – Pharaoh allows Israel to sacrifice within the land, making a specific limitation not seen in 8.8.
>
> Plague 8 – Moses may take the men and go out and sacrifice, leaving women and children and livestock.
>
> Plague 9 – Pharaoh allows people to go but they cannot take their flocks.
>
> Plague 10 – Only now is the capitulation complete, but notice that when the plagues let up, Pharaoh changes his mind and reneges. Pharaoh's character does not change throughout, even though he professes to repent of his sin at various points (cf. 9.27; 10.16).

A third developing theme is the distinction between what happens to the Israelites in Goshen and what happens to the Egyptians. God makes a distinction and protects his

[42] Noting that we dealt at some length earlier in this study with the call narrative of Moses and the material in Exod. 3–6, pp. 22–27, above.

[43] Adapted from U. Cassuto. *A Commentary on the Book of Exodus* (Jerusalem: Magnes Press, 1967), 93.

people or helps them protect themselves. This differentiation appears to begin with the second cycle of plagues, i.e., Plague 4, the flies (cf. 8.22–23; 9.4–6; 9.11; 10.23; 11.6–7). Moses is not clear whether the Israelites also suffered the first three plagues, but since the principle of differentiation is not mentioned until Plague 4, perhaps they did.

The third plague, like the sixth and ninth, comes without warning. It is uncertain how we should translate the Hebrew word at 8.16. It may mean gnat (stinging mosquito) or lice. At this point, Pharaoh's magicians cannot copy Moses' acts. Indeed, *they say*, "it is the finger of God."[44] This phrase is a metaphor used elsewhere at Exod. 31.18 and Luke 11.20, and like the metaphor of God's hand (1 Sam. 5.11) or his arm (Job 40.9), it refers to God's powerful activity. Using the term finger may also suggest that it takes little for God to accomplish what humans cannot; he only has to stretch out his finger.

At the fourth plague, the Israelites are distinguished from the Egyptians. The fifth plague involves beasts, presumably cattle. Exod. 9.6 seems to hint they were all wiped out, but cattle appear again later, so presumably it means all those in the fields. With the sixth plague, not only are the magicians unable to copy Moses, they themselves are afflicted. It will be noted that beginning at 8.19, they began seeing this as God's work. At 9.20–35, Pharaoh's officials fear God's words, and they wish to take the Hebrew God seriously and give him what he wants. Exod. 10.7 says, "Do you not realize Egypt is ruined?" By 11.3 we are told that both Pharaoh's officials and the Egyptian people were favorably impressed and disposed toward Moses. In short, only Pharaoh is unimpressed or unwilling to be convinced of God's will and power. He is seen as an isolated and arrogant and unbending tyrant.

With the seventh plague, we see reiterated the twofold goal of these plagues, to force Pharaoh to let Israel go and to make him see that Yahweh is the only true God. At 10.1–2 we are told that Pharaoh's heart was hardened by God so he could demonstrate his power and nature not only to Israel but also to the Egyptians and Pharaoh. At 9.15 we are told plainly that God could have wiped out the Egyptian court or ended the plagues, but he prolongs them not only to demonstrate his power and nature, but perhaps also so they may see.

Verse 16 indicates that God "maintained Pharaoh alive" out of his forbearance. It does *not* say Pharaoh was created or raised up for the purpose of being hardened, contrary to God's general desire to convince and convict and convert. Notice at 10.2 how the later perspective of the recounting of the oral tradition is stressed. The point of recounting the story is to show who God is, a sovereign God, and how much he loves and redeems his chosen people. Doubtless this might indicate how these stories were kept alive, possibly for a long time, until they were finally written down and edited.

At the beginning of the eighth plague, we are told that God is toying with, or making sport of, Pharaoh. The obstinate Pharaoh is becoming a laughing stock and source of irritation even among his own people. Even after the plague of locusts, Pharaoh will let only the men go. He will keep the rest as hostages, a clearly unsatisfactory arrangement. At 10.16 we see Pharaoh's easy and insincere repentance. A person who does not turn from his sin has not really repented. The ninth plague is described by two Hebrew words that indicate extreme darkness, a darkness that can be felt (v. 21). We are not told when the

---

[44] See G. A. Klingbeil, "The Finger of God in the Old Testament," *ZAW* 112 (2000): 409–15.

darkness ceased – after three days? The argument in verses 27–29 completes the bargaining with a total breakdown of talks. We must not take it too literally. Perhaps it means no more than "I will never appear before you here again." Pharaoh's words prove to be an idle threat.

At 11.1 the tenth plague is announced. It appears from 11.8 that this is still the same occasion as at 10.27–29. Yet 10.29 seems to be a natural conclusion. However, we are still not told Moses left Pharaoh, so it is unnecessary to posit a later meeting contradicting 10.29. Exod. 11.5 is surely meant to say that all first-born males will die, from the highest to the lowest Egyptians, even the slave who grinds the grain. Ultimate disaster will strike them all, but not so much as a dog will growl at Israel. This will show God's sovereignty and ability to save and set apart his people.

The hardening of Pharaoh is sometimes presented as something Pharaoh does to himself and on two occasions what God does to him (10.1; 4.21). The idea seems to be that Pharaoh is hard-hearted, and he hardens his heart. Perhaps it is right to say that God hardens those who harden themselves. We know the plagues are intended to produce the true knowledge of God, even in Pharaoh.[45]

Yet we are told that they fail, as miracles do also. This may say something to us about whether miracles can create faith. However, it also appears that God intends to go on hardening Pharaoh's heart so that the plagues do not have such an effect and so God can go on manifesting his glory. In that case, God is confirming Pharaoh in his hardness of heart and even prolonging it to manifest his glory and sovereignty, but he does not initially create that hardness. He simply uses (and prolongs) it for his glory, "using the wrath of humans to praise him," so to speak.

Passover and Passing Over (Exod. 12; 13.1–22)

The Passover is an event and later a cultic celebration which has special significance not only for the Jew but also for the Christian, since Christ's death is set against the background of the Passover in the Gospels. Exod. 12.1 stresses that, unlike other Israelite ordinances, Passover and unleavened bread were instituted in Egypt. Verse 2 indicates that the new Israelite calendar, whatever may have been followed before, is to date from the time of these events. The month corresponds probably to our March/April and was originally called *Abib* (later *Nisan*, cf. Exod. 13.4; 23.15; Deut. 16.1). This means that Passover became both a spring festival and a new year's festival, but it is a spring festival not because it is simply superseding an older one, but because Israel actually experienced these events in spring.

In v. 3 we have a crucial expression, the *edah*, the gathering or congregation of the people of God. Here we do not have the term *qahal*, which may be the Hebrew background to the NT term *ekklesia* (church). The term "congregation" is not an abstraction, but implies the physical meeting together of the people, usually for a religious purpose. This celebration was not optional but was to involve the whole of God's people. It is an

---

[45] We should also keep steadily in mind that the early portions of the OT do not reflect an understanding of secondary causes other than Yahweh, unlike for example Chronicles, where we have Satan enter the picture as the cause of bad things.

event performed by households, and the head of the household is responsible to get the sacrificial animal.

The Hebrew word *seh* is rather neutral, meaning a head of small stock, whether sheep or goat only the context makes clear. Furthermore, there is no limitation of age inherent in the word *seh*. This we derive from what follows when it is said to be "a son of a year" (i.e. born within the last year). It may be presumed that it was a lamb, not a kid goat, since the latter was less often used for sacrificial purposes on a special occasion.

The fact that Passover is depicted here as a family rite strongly argues for its authenticity, for it originated before temple interests became paramount and central. Each household was to have its own celebration, unless a household was too small to eat the whole animal, in which case another small family would be invited to share the occasion and food. Again, the animal was to be unblemished, and it was to be slaughtered in the evening and eaten on the same night. The roasting over an open fire again suggests the earliness of this narrative since the Israelites were still in their semi-nomadic stage of existence. Furthermore, the mention of the animal being roasted, contrasted with Deut. 16.7, where it is to be boiled, shows that we are likely dealing with a primitive narrative written up primarily before later practical considerations and hygienic rules intervened.

Verse 7 seems to imply that we are dealing with a rite that did not involve atoning for sins, but rather signified protection for God's people, a different though not unrelated matter. It involved a blood ritual to avoid God's last blow against the first-born, an apotropaic sacrifice, or avoidance ritual. Thus, Passover and atonement were not associated at this time, though apparently by Jesus' day such an association was possible. Nothing is said or implied about Israel's sin – this rite is more like an insurance policy. Nor is forgiveness discussed here at all. To be sure, the sacrifice and bloodshed is to avoid a form of God's wrath, but it is not wrath against Israel's particular sins. The Hebrews simply happen to be in the line of fire.

The celebration also involved unleavened bread and bitter herbs. The bread would perhaps be better translated unleavened cakes, still a staple of Bedouin diet today. The Hebrew *massot* gives us the familiar term *matsos*. *Merorim* is translated bitter herbs and may mean lettuce of a wild sort. The Mishnah later included five wild herbs in the list of acceptable and usable types of wild plants for this rite – lettuce, chicory, pepperwort, snakeroot, and dandelion. According to later tradition, but not in Exodus, the bitter herbs symbolized the bitterness of the Israelite bondage in Egypt (Exod. 1.14). The Hebrew *massot* came to be called the "bread of haste." because it symbolized the haste the Hebrews had to use to leave Egypt: there was no time to leaven the dough. As v. 11 states, the Hebrews are to eat fully dressed and be packed to run when the order comes down. Of course, the phrase "bread of haste" comes from v. 11b, telling *how* they were to eat the bread (rather than how they were to bake it).

Verse 12 indicates that this judgment of Yahweh is not only on the Egyptians, but also on their gods. This may be a reference to the fact that Egyptians would often pray for the safety of their first-born in particular (as indeed was customary in many patriarchal cultures), and thus the death of the first-born would be a sign of the impotence (or anger) of their gods. In any event, Yahweh is showing his supremacy over the spirits behind such pagan deities, and thus we should not overlook the supernatural struggle standing behind the battle of wills between Moses and Pharaoh.

The word *pesah* itself is usually translated Passover. The verbal form is found in v. 13 and gives us the origin of the term: no blow will fall on Israel, so, they have been passed over. Leaven was usually a piece of old fermented dough, left over from the previous batch and used as a starter. One reason for the unleavened bread may be that the Israelites were starting out afresh, with a new calendar, new freedom, and whole new way to commemorate God's dealings with them. In the NT, leaven becomes a symbol of corruption (Mt. 16.11; 1 Cor. 5.6–8). There may be a difference between yeast and leaven. Yeast is a healthy raising agent, put into bread, whereas leaven is a leftover piece of cooked bread that still had some yeast in it, and could be used to start the next batch of bread. But such leavened bread was also subject to mold, and contagion, hence the later negative use of the term.

God strikes quickly after giving his own people sufficient and proper warning, and Pharaoh's response is equally quick. He rises during the night, and swallowing his pride, he summons Moses, though he had sworn previously to see him no more. Ironically this is an occasion not when Moses dies (10.28), but when Pharaoh experiences the loss of his special one. In Exod. 12.31–36 we note his total capitulation: "Go as you have said, take it all as you have said." Notice, however, in this last meeting Pharaoh asks for a blessing, perhaps to remove this curse. Pharaoh's words are to the point, and even the Egyptian people try to hurry Israel out of the land (v. 33 "lest they all die").

Verse 37 appears to say that 600,000 men, not including women and children, were their number. If so, then we are talking about several million Israelites leaving, which seems unlikely, since it is doubtful Goshen could have ever supported such a crowd, or that such a group could leave Egypt and cross the Red Sea. Possibly the solution is that *eleph*, which is translated here thousand, may mean "tent group" or "clan" in its early usage; 600 tent groups is believable. Again, a military statement is made, i.e., the Hebrews left armed for battle. Notice that Moses takes Joseph's body, presumably mummified (Gen. 49–50), with him. Joseph had requested eventual burial in the promised land. This is mentioned to indicate that God fulfills such wishes for his people, and to prove that Moses is not planning any trips back to Egypt for things left behind (Gen. 50.25). Finally, the first reference to the pillar of cloud and the pillar of fire is interesting. The cloud is intended to guide them by day, the fire by night, so apparently, they are to travel night and day. It goes before them as a guide, and we are told this was the Lord, or his doing at least (v. 21).

Theophany and Decalogue (Exod. 19–20)

By way of setting the context out of which we as Christians ought to view this material and the Mosaic covenant in general, several remarks are in order. The Mosaic covenant, being for one people, creates ethnic and cultural distinctions. It sets up a protective barrier around one particular nation or ethnic group so they might survive in a hostile world. This is not very different from what we see in certain Christian communities who have this sort of exclusivistic social culture and religion (for example, the Amish). The Amish practice withdrawal from the world like the OT model. In their case, a particular historical and cultural period, the horse and buggy era, is baptized as the best Christian model.

The New Covenant, unlike the Mosaic covenant, is intended to be trans-cultural, for all people on an equal basis. As Gal. 3.28 puts it, "in Christ there is no Jew and Greek, no slave or free, no male and female, for all are one in Christ." This does not mean that all such distinctions automatically disappear in Christ, but it does mean that they must cease to be a determining factor in defining the boundaries of the community. In Christ, Christians are called to set up no particular cultural models as sacred, nor any culturally engendered cultic institutions for worship. NT religion is to be expressed in a wide variety of cultural and cultic settings without baptizing any one way as the only way of doing things. In Christ, there is to be a community not of, nor established by, nor amalgamated with, but expressed in this world. Thus, in the NT there is no attempt to establish *a particular kind* of culture, but to give a Christian a means of living in all cultures and situations.

It is not by accident that those aspects of OT religion which can be applied to all peoples without their adopting a particular culture are the aspects reaffirmed in the NT. It is also no accident that Jesus and Paul both try to take God's people back to a creation order plan, or occasionally to an Abrahamic covenant plan (Gal. 3–4), but *not* to a Mosaic covenantal plan. It is precisely the Mosaic covenant which comes in for the heaviest scrutiny and strongest remarks regarding its permanent validity now that Christ has come. In the NT, we have neither a theocracy nor a merely human monarchy endorsed as the proper model for the kingdom. Indeed, no particular cultural, political, or economic model is baptized.

We may conclude that the NT favors freedom over repression, slavery, and a totalitarian state as a better context for human lives. Historically, and ironically, it has often been the case that Christianity has most thrived when it was in the least free environment, with the blood of the martyrs being seed for the church. One can conclude that no particular human condition is necessary for Christianity to thrive, though some are more conducive and more in accord with Christian values about the sacredness of human life than others. The NT is new wine that constantly needs to be put in new wineskins, not old wineskins. Thus, the church must be constantly in the process of reforming its own structures, adopting and adapting itself to thrive in an ever-changing environment.

From the beginning of Exod. 19, Moses' role as mediator between God and his people is stressed. Verse 4 indicates that Israel's deliverance was God's personal work. The metaphor is used of the eagle carrying something in his pinions. Verse 6 is significant because it indicates how Yahweh views Israel and their role, but it simply continues the terms Yahweh applies to his prized or special possession, i.e., they are also to be a kingdom of priests, a holy nation. We do not find language exactly like this elsewhere in the OT (but cf. Isa. 61.6), but it is clearly important and is picked up in 1 Peter and applied to Christians. It suggests a period before a priesthood was established and set apart from the majority of Israelites.

In the first place, the phrase "kingdom of priests" seems to imply that Yahweh is their proper king, and thus a theocratic situation. Secondly, the phrase "kingdom of priests" applies to every Hebrew and suggests they all have a priestly function. It may be implied that they are to be the ones who represent the world by coming into Yahweh's presence, praying for it, being an example to it. At the least it implies that all Israel was to be devoted to the worship and service of God. This is what was implied in being his special possession. Here the phrase *qados goy*, holy nation (the use of *goy* here of Israel may suggest our text's earliness, since it is usually used of foreign nations), implies that Israel is to be set apart to serve and worship God.

When they indicate their initial willingness, the theophany proper begins: God comes down upon the mountain. Israel, unlike pagan religions, did not see God as dwelling on a sacred mountain like Mt. Olympus. Rather, God comes to them and meets them at various locations. He is a God who can claim "the whole earth is mine" (v. 5b). Verse 9 says "I am going to come to you," and the "you" here is singular, not plural, referring to Moses. Again, his mediatorial role is stressed. The purpose or at least *a* purpose of the theophany is so the people will see what a special relationship Moses has with God, and so they will put their trust in him. The theophany cloud involves a divine disclosure, but at the same time God is hidden from Moses.

The Hebrew refers to "the thickest part of the cloud." The point is that Moses will not see God but rather hear him only. As we saw with Abraham earlier, revelation in the main takes the form of *hearing*. Clouds and darkness are characteristic of theophanies as a symbol of God's presence. Moses was to return to the people and have them prepare themselves to meet God, hence the command "you [Moses] consecrate them." This was to entail a total concentration on getting ready to meet God. Not only were they to wash their clothes and put on their Sabbath best after a long, dirty march, but also, they were to abstain from sexual relations, not because there was anything wrong with such acts, but because it required ceremonial washing after the act (Lev. 15.18), which would take away from the time of preparing to meet God himself.

Verse 11 says God will come down on Mt. Sinai in the sight of all the people, but presumably this means they will see the theophanic indications of his presence. Verse 12 is puzzling. Was Moses to put a boundary around the mountain or around the people? In view of v. 23, the NIV may be correct: "put limits for the people around the mountain." This would protect the people from an unprepared encounter with God and his holiness. Holiness is seen both as a purifying fire and as a deadly power if it encounters the unprepared or unclean. A person who violated these boundaries would be executed. The one who does this cannot be touched but executed from a distance, as if he were contagious.

The signal for all God's people to go up to the mountain was the long blast of the *yobel*, probably the ram's horn. This is where we get the word jubilee. *Shophar* is used in v. 16 of this same instrument. Doubtless this is the origin of the later practice of beginning a festival celebration with the sounding of the ram's horn. On the morning of the third day, they had a close encounter with Yahweh, which involved a spectacular thunderstorm (v. 16) that scared all the Hebrews. Verse 18 indicates that Sinai was covered with smoke caused by God descending on it in fire (cf. 2 Kgs. 1.12). This may mean lightning. We are told it was like seeing a kiln, or a blast furnace, with fire and smoke billowing from it. Not only do the people tremble, but the mountain itself trembles as God descends. As Yahweh gets closer and closer, he sets off all sorts of natural phenomena, and the *yobel* keeps blaring louder and louder.

Verse 19 is somewhat difficult. Should we see the *beqol* as the thunder or as the voice Moses hears? Yahweh is sometimes identified with thunder (cf. Ps. 18.14). Was God's answer given in the thunder itself? Exod. 19.9 refers to God speaking, which would seem to imply that v. 19 records its fulfillment. In any event, the sentence indicates a continuing process, i.e. Moses kept speaking and God kept answering him in thunder (or in a voice).

Exod. 20 is perhaps the chapter of the OT which has been most central to Israel's faith and has had the most effect on Christians. The critical problems raised by this chapter are both greater and lesser than elsewhere in the OT. They are greater because this material is so crucial, and thus proper interpretation is so vital, and there is less margin for error here; lesser because it is generally agreed even by the majority of non-conservative scholars that this material in some form goes back to Moses, though most would insist it has been amplified and edited along the way. There is nothing in the Ten Commandments which could not have originated with Moses. It does not show, as some other supposed decalogues do, the influence of an agrarian background such as we would expect if it originated after the entrance into Canaan. There is also nothing in it which is clearly cultic.

Almost everything has been disputed, from how many commandments there are and how we divide them up to what they mean. Note that while extra-biblical treaties (especially the Hittite suzerainty treaties) are helpful in our study of the form of Israelite covenants in general, we have in Exod. 20 at best a truncated form in comparison to such treaties, and many of the typical characteristics (such as being told where to store and read the treaty) are not found here. These analogies are more helpful with Deuteronomy as a whole than the Decalogue. The treaty form is little help in understanding the content of these verses. At most we can say that the parallels may show a common treaty form, which suggests the antiquity of this covenant and others in the Pentateuch.

Interestingly enough the first actual reference in the Bible to the phrase "Torah of Moses" comes not in the Pentateuch itself, but in Josh. 8.30–34, which reads:

Then Joshua built on Mount Ebal an altar to the LORD, the God of Israel, [31] just as Moses the servant of the LORD had commanded the Israelites, as it is written in the book of the law of Moses, "an altar of unhewn stones, on which no iron tool has been used"; and they offered on it burnt offerings to the LORD, and sacrificed offerings of well-being. [32] And there, in the presence of the Israelites, Joshua wrote on the stones a copy of the law of Moses, which he had written. [33] All Israel, alien as well as citizen, with their elders and officers and their judges, stood on opposite sides of the ark in front of the Levitical priests who carried the ark of the covenant of the LORD, half of them in front of Mount Gerizim and half of them in front of Mount Ebal, as Moses the servant of the LORD had commanded at the first, that they should bless the people of Israel. [34] And afterward he read all the words of the law, blessings and curses, according to all that is written in the book of the law. [35] There was not a word of all that Moses commanded that Joshua did not read before all the assembly of Israel, and the women, and the little ones, and the aliens who resided among them.

Of course, the debate is what exactly, or how much of the Mosaic legislation, does this refer to? Does it refer to "the Ten Words" alone, the so-called Ten Commandments? The reference to blessing and curse sanctions makes it likely it refers to whole original covenant statement with its preamble, promises, stipulations/commandments, curse and blessing sanctions, and concluding remarks. One of the things that makes the Mosaic covenant standout from other ANE treaty documents is the fact that all sin is seen as committed not just against one or another fellow human being, but against God.[46]

That is, sins are not viewed as merely social problems between human beings, they are viewed as a violation of one's covenantal relationship with God, and one is answerable

---

[46] On the entire scenario and content of Exod. 19–24 see the more detailed treatment by T. Dozemann, *God on the Mountain: A Study of Redaction, Theology, and Canon in Exodus 19–24* (Atlanta, GA: Scholar's Press, 1989). He is especially concerned to show that "this study calls into question the opposition that is frequently advocated in biblical theology between Sinai and Zion, Moses and David, law and temple. Our redaction-critical study of Exod. 19–24 would suggest that Sinai and Horeb must be interpreted as theological qualifications of Zion, and furthermore, that Sinai has actually come to represent a tempered priestly theology" (201). Perhaps this may be said more aptly of Deuteronomy than of this Exodus material, but the basic point is correct.

to God, as well as human beings, for such transgressions. This significantly contrasts with the Sumerian Code of Ur-Namu (*c.* 2100–2050 BC), and the more famous Babylonian Hammurabi Code (*c.* 1720 BC). Almost half of the latter deals with human contracts of one sort or another. Not so the Mosaic code. It is worth mentioning in addition that in some of these ANE treaty/covenant documents the king plays a crucial role (e.g. in the documents found at Ugarit), which merely punctuates the fact that Israel was originally a theocracy, and so there is no mention of a king in the Mosaic codes. In other words, the covenant was not with or through a human king, but directly with God the King or Sovereign. It has been said, probably rightly, that no area of OT study has benefited more by comparisons with other ANE literature than the study of law in the OT.[47]

If we consider for a moment the history of OT scholarship on law, including the Decalogue, it has gone through various permutations and combinations, even suggesting at one point that there were two categories of OT law, casuistic and apodictic, with the Ten Commandments falling into the latter category since they involve imperatives, whereas casuistic law was conditional in character and provided a rationale or cause for the directives. Rather clearly, a comparison between the Exodus and Deuteronomy forms of the Decalogue suggests that the code developed over time or was adapted as the times changed. For example, the division into two tables does not occur in Exod. 20 but first in Exod. 34 and Deut. 5. Furthermore, the reference to "Ten Words" does not appear in Exod. 20 but first in Exod. 34.28, Deut. 4.13, and Deut. 10.4. In the Exod. 20 form of the table "covet" seems to have an original connotation of action but in Deut. 5.21 (cf. vv. 12 and 15), it is clear that the emphasis is being placed on the intention or inner attitude.

It is, however, characteristic of OT law in general to juxtapose positive and negative imperatives (cf. Exod. 34.14ff.; Lev. 19.14ff.; Deut. 14.11ff.). The strictly apodictic style of the Ten Commandments is unlike what we find elsewhere in the Pentateuch, where case law or casuistic-style law is mixed with the apodictic (cf. Exod. 22.15ff.; Lev. 19.3ff.). The generalized form of these commandments which have little or no reference to historical specifics or contextually specific concepts and ideas, made them readily transferrable and applicable to many different contexts, including those in the setting of Jesus and Paul.

None of these laws are trivial, rather all of them deal with matters that chart out the ethical boundaries of the covenant community, including its religious or worship boundaries (the affirmation of monotheism, the rejection of idolatry, the affirmation of the Sabbath command). "To transgress is not to commit a misdemeanor but to break the very fiber of which the divine-human relation consists ... The Decalogue serves not only to chart the outer boundary, but also to provide the positive content for life within the circle of the covenant. The Decalogue looks both outward and inward; it guards against the way of death and points to the way of life."[48]

---

[47] D. Patrick, *Old Testament Law* (Atlanta, GA: John Knox, 1985), 8.

[48] In this part of the discussion I am following the helpful reflections of B. S. Childs, *Exodus* (Louisville, KY: Westminster, 1974), 388–401, here 398.

Here is a useful summary of what the *entire* Mosaic Law Code seems to have contained (a helpful outline is found on Wikipedia, accessed on January 27, 2017 at this location, https://en.wikipedia.org/wiki/Law_of_Moses).

Many scholars would see the "forward-looking legislation referencing a king" to be a later addition to the code. The content of the Law is spread among the books of Exodus, Leviticus, and Numbers, and then

The Decalogue is not addressed to just one class of God's people (e.g. the priests), but rather to all of God's people. It seems obvious, at least to this observer, that the Exodus form of the Decalogue is the earlier and more primitive one, which is why we are concentrating on it. These laws presuppose a relationship between God and his people, and it should be clear that they have a correlation to the two great commandments to love God and neighbor – with commandments among the ten in essence falling into one or the other of these two spheres. Idolatry is a violation of the love of God, whereas keeping Sabbath is a form of loving God with one's whole being. By contrast adultery is a violation of loving neighbor and avoiding the inclination to covet is a way of respecting and loving one's neighbor. It probably does not need to be said, but here theology and ethics are intertwined to such a degree that ethics becomes a part of theology, or an expression of its practical implications and applications. The two cannot be radically separated here, or elsewhere in the Bible. Believing in the God of the Bible and behaving in certain ways, including in specifically religious ways involving worship, go together.

In regard to the Decalogue, note that these verses are not called commandments: we are simply told "God spoke all these words." Properly speaking, they should be called the Ten Words, not the Ten Commandments. Here we have general principles, not specific case-by-case rulings, which cover the whole gamut of relationships with God and humanity. They can be divided into two categories dealing with loving God and loving neighbor. The form of these is simple imperatives, and in the Hebrew often it involves just *two* words (e.g. no killing, no stealing). They are not casuistic or conditional remarks, i.e. "If you do this, then …" They are givens, not options, and there are no statements about punishments or rewards if they are broken or kept. Scholars call this form apodictic. As I said, here the general principles are laid down that will be worked out later in the Book of the Covenant (Exod. 20.18ff.) and applied to specific situations.

There are only two positive imperatives – honoring parents and remembering the Sabbath. All the rest are negatives in the form "you shall not." What we seem to have here are remarks necessary for the survival of God's people, if they wish to remain his people and remain distinct from the pagan world. There is little internalization of these words. Most of them have to do with deeds, not attitudes (though see below on covetousness). Here then are the first principles on areas of vital importance for religious life. Most of the

reiterated and added to in Deuteronomy (*deutero-nomy* is Latinized Greek for "Second reading of the Law"). This includes:

- The Ten Commandments.
- Moral laws – on murder, theft, honesty, adultery, etc.
- Social laws – on property, inheritance, marriage, and divorce.
- Food laws – on what is clean and unclean, on cooking and storing food.
- Purity laws – on menstruation, seminal emissions, skin disease, mildew, etc.
- Feasts – the Day of Atonement, Passover, Feast of Tabernacles, Feast of Unleavened Bread, Feast of Weeks, etc.
- Sacrifices and offerings – the sin offering, burnt offering, whole offering, heave offering, Passover sacrifice, meal offering, wave offering, peace offering, drink offering, thank offering, dough offering, incense offering, red heifer, scapegoat, first fruits, etc.
- Instructions for the priesthood and the high priest, including tithes.
- Instructions regarding the Tabernacle, and which were later applied to the temple in Jerusalem, including those concerning the Holy of Holies containing the Ark of the Covenant (in which were the tablets of the law, Aaron's rod, the manna). Instructions and for the construction of various altars.
- Forward-looking instructions for a time when Israel would demand a king.

Ten Words can be paralleled outside the OT, except perhaps for the first two. They are not totally unique, but their combination here and their link to serving Yahweh as one's only God is unique. These Ten Words are addressed to each individual (i.e. "you shall not" is in the singular, not plural). They are not just words for general community behavior collectively, but are also applicable to each of God's children individually.

It would be wrong, however, to take the Ten Words as God's blueprint for all laws in any nation. The presupposition is that these are words for God's chosen people, not everyone, though it would be nice if everyone would obey them. However, the last eight commandments must not be taken out of the context of the first two. They are the things that those who worship the true God are to do or refrain from doing. They are principles for believers. Nonetheless, they are so general that they proved applicable to numerous ages of believers and various of them are reaffirmed in the NT. In this regard, they appear to be viewed by the writers of the NT at least as valuable ongoing guiding principles, unlike what follows in the Book of the Covenant and in Leviticus. I wish to stress once more that what we have here are principles, not laws. They are the basis on which all laws were and could be grounded and extrapolated.

Several general comments about the NT use of this material are important at this point. There can be no doubt that the Ten Commandments, along with the love commandments about God and neighbor, were seen as the most important touchstones of the Mosaic Law. They recur in many forms in early Judaism, and in the NT, even in places where the OT is not being directly quoted but assumed to provide principles for Jewish living. For example, in Lk. 13.14 the indignant synagogue ruler rebukes Jesus for healing on the Sabbath, indirectly, by telling the people observing his act of healing: "There are six days for work. So, come and be healed on those days ..." This of course is an echo of Exod. 20.9 – "six days you shall labor and do all your work" – only there it involves an imperative from God, whereas in Luke it is taken to be a principle for living. In other words, God is commanding a six-day work week, whereas the synagogue leader assumes that is the norm.

According to the earliest Gospel, Jesus explicitly reaffirms the fifth through ninth words of the Decalogue (cf. Mk. 10.1–19). In the Sermon on the Mount, he intensifies several of these, notably those on adultery and murder. Secondly, Jesus seems clearly to reject various Levitical distinctions between clean and unclean (Mk. 7.1–15), or at least Mark was sure that he did (see the parenthetical remark in 7.15). Instead, Jesus wanted concentration on moral purity in light of the Decalogue. One should examine Mk. 7.21–22, where he expands words five to nine and adds various attitudes besides covetousness to the list of prohibitions. Thirdly, it will be noted that neither Jesus nor Paul enjoins the Sabbath on his followers. Indeed, in Mk. 2.28 Jesus appears to change the rules about what is appropriate on such a day and indicates that the Sabbath was meant for the aid and fulfillment of human beings: we were not created to fulfill it. This tells us something fundamental about Jesus' attitude, namely, that he saw all such words as meant for human well-being. They are not eternal principles in the sense that we will always have need of all of them in their OT form.

Jesus felt free to modify, fulfill, qualify, add to, and delete from them as he saw fit, because he was bringing in a new eschatological kingdom situation to which new, as well as some old, rules would apply. In the eschatological age, not all of the Mosaic material was going to be directly applicable, though one can still learn of God's nature and what he wants in general of his children even from that which a Christian is no longer bound to, such as Sabbath observance. One must also realize that believers will hardly need such "thou shalt nots" when the Kingdom fully comes on earth. So, in a real sense, the Ten Words are interim ethics until then. Thereafter we will do by nature what now we must strive to do by will and choice and effort. One cannot help but think that much of what Moses said is based on the premise that we are all fallen creatures, and in some cases, as Jesus makes clear about Mosaic laws on divorce, it allows for human hard-heartedness in a way Jesus does not (cf. Mt. 5 and 19 and par.).

We will be following the Jewish and Protestant, not Catholic, division of the Ten Words: i.e., the second commandment begins "you shall not make a graven image." The prologue is very brief. The first phrase could be read, "I, Yahweh, am your God," but more likely is the translation, "I am Yahweh your God." God identifies himself in v. 2b and reminds them that he revealed who he was in the Exodus deliverance. This gracious act of deliverance precedes this covenanting, and it was not performed on the basis of any covenant or stipulations. The deliverance was pure grace. Thus, we should not see even here the intention of God to provide a way of salvation in these principles. Rather, it is the means of living for those who have already been rescued by God's activity in Egypt.

Word One

The translation of v. 3 is problematic because of the final prepositional phrase. Had the sentence simply read "You shall have no other gods," it would be easier to interpret. The phrase *al-panay* has been translated in the following ways: "before me," "to my face," "beside me," "over against me," "in defiance of me." If this phrase has a hostile connotation, the meaning would be, "You shall not prefer other gods to me." If we take the phrase "to my face" literally, it may imply no other gods in my presence, and some have related it to the prohibition of setting up idols in Yahweh's presence. More likely it is a general statement meaning "I will be your only God." This word does not deny the possibility of other real "gods" existing. This comes later, especially in prophetic literature (cf. Isa. 45.6,14,21). The point is not to debate monotheism, but to state that whatever else anyone may do or have, Israel will have no other gods. Thus, Israel is confined to and defined by monotheism, which made them stand out in the ancient world. As we noted already in the patriarchal narratives, there was a monotheizing tendency already in play even before the time of Moses, and this meant that God's people would be seen as a peculiar people indeed.[49]

Word Two

This word follows logically upon the previous one. The word *pesel* means an image carved from stone or wood, and it later included metal or molten images as well (Isa. 40.19; 44.10). Deut. 4.9ff. clearly interprets this word to refer to images of God. It is of course true that the making of images of false gods would also be unacceptable, but this verse seems to deal with the true God. The point is that this is an improper response to God's self-revelation. God has revealed himself in words and in deeds, but not in an image or a form. The attempt to create such an image is the attempt by human religious imagination

---

[49] On the monotheistic tendency see pp. 29–35, above. On the latter point see Childs, *Exodus*, 402–4.

to define and delimit God. This is both unnecessary and incorrect. God has revealed himself in his own way; human beings must accept him on his own terms, not recreate an image of him as we would like him to be.

We know that at least initially Israel took this commandment to heart. When they invaded and took over Canaan, the archaeology shows that late in the thirteenth century an anti-iconic people entered the land. We must not, however, overlook the fact that the central issue here is the nature of the human response to the true God (i.e. the nature of legitimate worship). Thus, images of the prophets or Jesus or OT or NT saints or even angels in stained glass are not in themselves prohibited here. What is prohibited is the use of images as objects of worship, or objects used to define, delineate, or control God (a regular ancient magical practice). It is an open question what one does with an image or painting outside a worship context, or even in a worship context if it is not used as an object of worship.

Word Three

The taking of the Lord's name in vain has often been misunderstood. The key verb means "swear falsely," but its root meaning is "to be empty" or "groundless." The term almost always has a pejorative connotation. However, it appears from Lev. 19.12 that "You shall not swear falsely in my name" seems to be the primary meaning of Exod. 20.7 as well. Thus, what is being ruled out here is not all use of God's name (literally it reads "the name") but only its abuse. Oaths in OT times were clearly *not* forbidden. Jesus, however, changed this according to the Sermon on the Mount. False or worthless swearing or oaths using God's name are clearly ruled out here. God will not ignore such abuse; he will hold people accountable for it.

Word Four

More attention has been given this commandment by scholars than any other. It is the longest of the Ten Words and the first positive word. At the outset, we notice the different way this word is given here and in Deut. 5.12–15. The word "observe" is used there instead of "remember" here. Deuteronomy adds, "as the Lord your God commands you." In addition, in Deuteronomy the animals are enumerated in a more detailed way. Then too the motive in Deut. 5.15 for Sabbath observance is different: there it is "you shall remember that you were a servant in the land of Egypt and the Lord your God brought you out from there with a mighty hand." In our text, the reason for keeping the Sabbath is God's ceasing from his work of creation. The etymology of the term *sabbat* remains uncertain, but probably the noun *sabbat* comes from the verb meaning "cease from work" or in a derived sense "rest." The major thrust of the word is the stress on hallowing, and here the verb means "make holy" or "remember to make holy" and thus it involves deeds, not just an attitude, and requires an effort. It implies the cessation of normal activities for a special day because the *sabbat* belongs to Yahweh in some undefined way or sense that other days do not.

The question then becomes, is this ordinance also for God's NT people? The vast majority of Christians celebrated worship on the first day of the week, calling it "The Lord's Day," presumably because it was the day the Lord rose. Neither Jesus nor Paul *commands* Sabbath observance of their followers. Paul in fact makes quite clear that it is acceptable to observe one day as sacred or all days alike; each should do as his or her conscience dictates (see Rom. 14.5–7; Gal. 4.10). These earlier observances are viewed as shadows of things that were to come; the reality, however, is found in Christ. In short, Christ's coming has changed the situation in regard to such ordinances. Thus, the Christian is not bound to them anymore. Herein lies a good clue as to how Paul views the OT – it foreshadows things in the eschatological era, but the real substance of God's will and salvation plan do not arrive until the "fullness of time when God sent forth his Son."

Word Five

Here we have the second positive word; however, unlike the fourth word, it does not give a theological rationale for the word but rather includes a promise. Frequently, this commandment has been interpreted to mean that parents are the visible representatives of God for the exerting of his authority. While this interpretation has tended to go far beyond the biblical text, nevertheless it can lay claim to a certain biblical warrant. The command appears to mean that you are to honor your parents whether you yourself are a child or an adult. Many see this commandment as the transition between the commandments involving love of God and love of neighbor.

The promise that goes along with this word is important. It is unlikely the Israelites had a full doctrine of everlasting life at this point, so extension of natural life was considered one of the greatest blessings God could offer. Here, however, the promise is tied to making it into the land and living in it. So now the context suggests that God's promise is to get his people into the land and allow them to enjoy it when they get there. It is thus a promise tied to the specific context of physical Israel as a land and is a heritage of living in one's own land. It is, however, altered in the NT at Eph. 6.2–3 to "the earth" (contrast Deut. 5.6). It is thus applied in a way that does not confine it to the Israelites and their link to a land.

Word Six

There are numerous prohibitions against the taking of life in the OT (Exod. 21.20; Lev. 24.7; Deut. 27.24). There are also numerous crimes for which the death penalty is commanded, not to mention the endorsement of the concept of holy war in the OT. Thus, whatever the sixth word means, it is unlikely to be a prohibition *against all killing*. In fact, it has long been recognized that the Hebrew radical *RSH* refers to a special kind of killing. We cannot simply translate it as "murder" here or elsewhere. It appears that in many cases, this verb has to do with the matter of blood vengeance and the role of the avenger (see Num. 35), including both the initial slaying and the retaliation, as well as the execution of the initial murderer. However, and it is a big however, this verb sometimes refers to accidental killing (Num. 35.11; Deut. 19.4; Josh. 20.3), which by any normal definition is not murder. But more often the term does refer to what we would call murder (Hos. 6.9; Isa. 1.21). Murder involves intent. But clearly here in the Decalogue accidental killing cannot be to the fore, because the brief imperative surely does not mean: "don't accidentally kill someone"![50] D. A. Carson notes that this verb is regularly used of the killing of one person by another, but never in a judicial or military context.[51] In any case, as we shall

[50] See W. Zimmerli, *Old Testament Theology in Outline* (Edinburgh: T&T Clark, 1978), 134–35.

[51] D. A. Carson, "James," in *Commentary on the New Testament Use of the Old Testament* (ed. G. K. Beale and D. A. Carson; Grand Rapids, MI: Baker, 2007), 1001. He also notes how James at least reverses the order of the commands, mentioning killing first and adultery second.

see, Jesus is prohibiting his own disciples from even getting angry with other people, never mind killing them.

Word Seven

The verb *na 'ap* means to commit adultery. It is obviously the purpose of this commandment to protect the institution of marriage in an environment that was profligate. It is usually pointed out that the man can only commit adultery against another person's marriage, and a woman only against her own, due to the nature of ancient patriarchal marriage. We have no mention of punishment here for this crime, but Deut. 22.22 indicates the death penalty for it. Notice that the punishment for fornication with an unmarried woman is not the same (cf. Exod. 22. 16; Deut. 22.28f.), and it suggests this is considered a lesser crime.

Some have suggested that premarital intercourse is never prohibited in the OT, but clearly enough in Exod. 22.16–17/Deut. 22.28–29 we are told that the law about premarital sex requires the couple to marry and it does not allow for divorce![52] One should not infer from its lesser penalties that it was seen as acceptable behavior, not least because these were honor and shame cultures and the protecting of the virginity of young nubile women prior to marriage was an important part of avoiding sexual shame. It may be that its condemnation was so obvious it went without an explicit prohibition. Sexual sin was so serious a matter that even King David falls under the death penalty for his adultery with Bathsheba. Various texts indicate that adultery is also a sin against God, since he created and protects monogamous marriage (Gen. 20.6, 39.9; Ps. 51.4). As is well known, Jesus expands the definition of adultery in Mt. 5 to include attitudes or actions that lead to or lead another into adultery. Further, he also includes divorce and remarriage as adultery.

Word Eight

The verb *GNB* can have as its object either a person or a thing. This particular word is distinguished from other words for theft in that the element of secrecy is involved here. Thus, what is meant is a taking by stealth. Since the word has no object, it must include the taking by stealth of anything that is prohibited.

Word Nine

This word deals with the matter of legal procedures and is a prohibition against giving false testimony. Bearing false witness was a very serious matter in the ANE. Two things were done to discourage false witness. In the Code of Hammurabi, false witness was punishable by death, while in the OT, false witnesses were dealt with by the *lex talionis* (the law of the tooth, "an eye for an eye," etc.). Revenge-taking was to be comparable to what the witness was trying to do to his object of false testimony. In the OT, no one could be put to death on the testimony of just one witness (cf. Num. 35.30; Deut. 19.15). Notice how in Lev. 19.11 the prohibition against false swearing is linked to stealing, lying, and dealing falsely. The prophets also saw this connection (cf. Hos. 4.2; Jer. 7.9).

---

[52] See Dozemann, *God on the Mountain*, 494.

Word Ten

This commandment concludes the list, and here, especially, attitudes rather than actions are in the foreground. The verb *hamad* is repeated with several objects. *Hamad* means literally desire, and in itself is a neutral word. In regard to the objects coveted here, house can mean household, which would include not merely the tent, but also the occupants, perhaps especially the wife. Thus, this word may be related to the seventh commandment. Ox and ass are characteristic of Bronze Age peasant or semi-nomadic societies; slaves are the other prime form of movable property. Childs points out that this list of objects is ancient, which argues for the antiquity of this list of Ten Words in general. The list is intended to be comprehensive, in the sense that it is to include all *types* of things that could be stolen, not all possible items. It is very interesting indeed that when Paul draws on this commandment, in this case toward the end of Rom. 7, he leaves out any object of desire. And as my old mentor C. K. Barrett used to say, this is because the real problem is the sinful desire itself, not the object of desire.

We have now examined the Ten Commandments and seen them in context as a comprehensive set of principles which stand behind all OT laws intended for God's covenant people. We must be cautious how we handle this vital material. We have now worked our way through some of the most crucial parts of the Pentateuch. In a very real sense, all that follows in the OT is a development of what we have already examined. If we keep in mind the major ideas and developments in the Pentateuch thus far, what follows will make a great deal more sense of the narratives that follow and the narrative thought world which supports them.[53] *Here are the ethical principles guiding the selection and presentation of the various narratives in the narrative thought world of the OT writers. Notice that the OT writers are not shy about presenting the sins and foibles of even their major characters in the narrative, such as a David or an Elisha. This is because OT religion was based on God-given principles such as the Ten Words not on personality cults or human hero worship of some sort.*

The Story Continues in the Promised Land

The historical books include Joshua, Judges, Ruth, 1 and 2 Samuel, 1 and 2 Kings, 1 and 2 Chronicles, Ezra, Nehemiah, Ruth, and Esther. This encompasses a wide range of history, from about 1220 BC, when Joshua and God's people entered the promised land, until the post-exilic period. What we hope to accomplish is to present samples and examples of some of the more crucial material in order to convey a sense of some of the major figures and events in the lives of God's people who lived then, and how their stories are told. Bear in mind that we are looking at how these stories are *theologically* configured. We will examine some of the Joshua material and Samson cycle from Judges, consider the early prophet Samuel and the rise of David to kingship, and look at some of the interesting material in the Elijah and Elisha cycles that comes from the north of the land after the time when the monarchy was divided. In this brief review, of key passages, keep in mind three questions: (1) what does this material tell us that the writer thinks about God's character;

---

[53] For an interesting modern treatment of the Ten Words, see Joy Davidman, *Smoke on the Mountain* (Louisville, KY: Westminster John Knox, 1985).

(2) what does this material tell us about human character; and (3) what does this tell us about God's relationship with his people?

Joshua

The Book of Joshua begins with a transitional statement, indicating that the author is picking up the narrative where Deuteronomy left off. We have a consecutive verb form, with a temporal clause. This means that our author appears to have written with Deuteronomy before him, and indeed this chapter has many echoes of the language of the Pentateuch. Here, as in Exodus/Numbers, Moses is called the *ebed*, the servant of God. By contrast, there is Joshua, who is Moses' official or minister. Joshua and all the people, including even those who were going to live on the east side of the Jordan, were to cross the Jordan and inhabit the land. The extent of the land is often described in the OT as from Dan to Beersheba (2 Sam. 24.2–8; 1 Kgs. 4.25).

Perhaps one of the most beloved stories is that of Rahab the harlot and the Israelite spies in Josh. 2. It is a typical example of Jewish humor at the expense of those who do not worship the true God. This story is important for Christians, since in Heb. 11, Rahab is given a place in "the hall of faith." There is the underlying motif of holy war – the city-state of Jericho had heard of Israel's battles against their neighbors and Egypt. In the face of fighting against Yahweh himself, the enemy could only capitulate.

The story suggests that Rahab the harlot was the only smart person among the enemy, for she realized that God was on the side of the Israelites, and so she aligned herself with them. Implicit is a suggestion of the general spiritual imperceptivity of those in the land. The point of the story, in part, is that God can use strange or unexpected people to work out his will. We are not told how Rahab knew of the Lord, nor are we told how she knew the Israelites were going to overrun the land. Yet we do see a miracle of God's power. If God could work and overcome evil with a true confession *even in a brothel*, then anything is possible, and taking the land should be no problem. Rahab calls Yahweh a God in heaven above and on the earth beneath as well. Indeed God is, if he can even reach into this house of ill repute.

Rahab, we are told, exhibited *hesed*, kindness or even mercy to the spies. It is for this reason that she makes it into the Heb. 11 "hall of faith." There are only two intelligent responses to the news that Yahweh is coming – fear or a quick change of heart if you are not already one of the people of faith. God's surprising grace and providence is seen here, working even among the most unlikely people to bring about his purposes. Having heard the tale of the spies upon their return, Joshua responds that surely "the Lord has given all the land into our hands." A God who would go to such lengths to save even these Israelite spies of dubious character could hardly be doubted when he promised the land to them.

The story of the crossing, the memorial, and the conquest is told in Josh. 3.1–7.1. The story of the crossing of the Israelites is a story of a miracle, and without a doubt it is meant to be seen as parallel to the crossing of the Red Sea, not only in its nature but also in the stature it gives to Joshua as a leader of the people. As soon as Joshua had heard from the spies he proceeded to implement the plan to take the land with dispatch. The Israelites advance to the river and lodge there briefly before crossing over.

At v. 3 we hear of the Ark of the Covenant for the very first time in this book. Not only did the ark house the stone tablets on which were inscribed the Law, but also it was the place of God's very presence. We are not talking about a mere symbol, but a real locus of God's presence. It is his presence in the ark which makes the waters stand up so the Israelites may cross the Jordan on dry ground. We are told that the Levitical priests are the ones who carry the ark and go before the people. The restriction of the priesthood to the Levites is mentioned at Exod. 32.26–29 and Deut. 18.5. One of the repeated themes brought over from Exodus is the notion that God's presence is with someone who can part the waters – whether it be a Moses, or a Joshua, or later an Elijah or Elisha, but these were all mere mortals. It's taking it a step further to talk about some who can walk on the waters, as the psalmist says, in a bold metaphor, Yahweh, and later Jesus, does.

At v. 7, we learn that part of the reason for this wonder that God will perform is so the people will follow, obey, and respect Joshua, not because he can perform miracles, but because Yahweh who can do all such things is with him. The miracle at Jordan serves as confirmation of Joshua's claim to divine authority and divine presence with him. Joshua has these as long as he obeys the Lord and his word that came through Moses. Like Moses, then, he is equipped and accompanied by Yahweh. Exactly the same rationale and motif plays out in 2 Kgs. 2.13–15, when Elisha parts the waters with Elijah's cloak and the prophets of Jericho offer to be his servants thereafter, for it is evident God is with Elisha, as he was with Elijah.

We are told at Josh. 4.10 that the people passed over quickly, and as soon as they got out of the river, the priests and the ark also passed over and passed before the eyes of the people, perhaps so they might see the source of their might. No sooner had they gotten out of the Jordan than the river began to flow forth again, clearly indicating that this was a miracle. The effect of this miracle was just as Yahweh said it would be. The miracle inculcated respect and reverence not only for God, but also for Joshua, so that henceforth, as long as he lived, the people stood in awe of Joshua just as they had stood in awe of Moses.

In a very real sense, Josh. 5–6 is the climax of the whole wilderness-wandering period of Israel's life. Just as they celebrated Passover before they left Egypt, so now they do so again once they have entered the promised land. Already, before even a battle is fought, the Israelites enjoy the fruits of the promised land, a sort of proleptic celebration of victory. As before, the story focuses on Joshua, and again there are numerous parallels to the story of Moses, especially as we find it in Exod. 3. Throughout this book, Joshua is cast in the light and shadow of Moses. Again, this is a tale of the authority of God and his Word, and the human response of God's leader and God's people. Obedience leads to blessing; disobedience leads to curse. Does this mean that the promises of God are conditional? In a sense this is true: if a person or even a generation like the one lost in the desert was disobedient, then they did not personally share in the promise received. The promise still stood for the next generation of God's people to participate in. It had not been revoked, but obedience was the key that unlocked the door to their particular and individual participation in it.[54]

---

[54] Sometimes scholars have confused the unconditional nature of some of God's promises with the assumed permanent nature of one or another of his covenants with his people. These are in fact *two different matters*. An OT covenant is never unilateral nor unconditional, as we have already noticed. God's promises, sometimes mentioned in covenants, can be a different matter altogether, for they reflect God's permanent character, his love for his creatures, and more particularly for his own people. This is why God's promises keep appearing in a series of covenants, including finally the new one. God is always the same in his love and mercy, as well

A new generation had come of age, but they were unprepared to receive the benefits of the covenant, much less fight a holy war with God's aid when they did not even bear the sign of the covenant – circumcision. As we have already noted, circumcision was symbolically an enactment of the oath curse on the individual as a way of ratifying the covenant. It was done on the organ of generation to symbolize that Israel would be cut off, their generations cut off, if they disobeyed. The organ of generation and life bore the sign of the covenant which gave life or death, depending on whether one obeyed or disobeyed. It is not true that only Israel practiced circumcision in the ANE. It was a rite known in Egypt and elsewhere, and there is indication that in some cultures it was a puberty rite. Here it is a rite of consecration to God. Notice that just as Moses was reminded to circumcise one of his sons (Exod. 4.24–26) before he entered upon his great task of redeeming Israel, so here with Joshua and his people, circumcision precedes the major task of Joshua's life.[55]

Judges

The Book of Judges deals with the period after Joshua's death, and our focus will be on the familiar story of Samson (Judg. 13–16). We note, however, at the outset that the end of the period of the judges does not correspond with the end of the Book of Judges, for two of the most important judges were Samuel and perhaps even Saul. Thus, the end of the period of the judges should probably be dated to the time when Saul is made king in about 1020 BC. This means there was a period of about 130–200 years when there were judges in the land.

The Book of Judges makes clear that during this period Israel was often at a low spiritual ebb. Hence, we frequently hear about Israel doing what was evil in God's eyes, after which they are punished, enslaved, and beaten by their foes, for God had delivered them into the hands of their enemies, usually for a full generation (40 years). Then, the oppressed Israelites cry out to God, and in due course God has mercy on his wayward people and by his powerful spirit raises up a deliverer for them. The people, after a brief period of fidelity, then fall back into apostasy, and the cycle is repeated. Second verse same as the first, a little bit louder and a little bit worse. Here again it is fair to note that we see the effects of human fallenness, as it affects even God's people again and again, meaning of course that God has to intervene again and again to help them, if his promises to them are to remain stable, and eventually come true.

The second thing to bear in mind, especially in the case of a *sopet* like Samson, is that we must not expect OT figures to live up to Christian standards of ethics and theology. Indeed, Samson falls short of God's mark even by Mosaic standards. There is an important

---

as his righteousness and holiness. Covenants vary according to historical, and then finally eschatological, circumstances. Covenants can be broken and replaced, God's promises are another matter. Promises like grace can be unilateral and not a reaction to something good in the recipient, but just a reflection of the character of the giver. Covenants involve two parties. I remember Victor Furnish once saying that grace is not like a heat-seeking missile, which aims at something inherently attractive in the target.

55 For the interesting theory that the "holy war" was to be waged against the offspring of the *Nephilim* (see Gen. 6.1–4), not indiscriminately, see M. Heiser, *The Unseen Realm: Recovering the Supernatural Realm of the Bible* (Bellingham, WA: Lexham Press, 2015). This certainly makes better sense of some passages. I tend to glean from Peter Craigie, *The Problem of War in the Old Testament* (Grand Rapids, MI: William B. Eerdmans, 1979).

message in this, namely, that God can write straight even with a crooked stick. To put it another way, the fact that God used someone as a deliverer of Israel does not mean that God endorsed all of that figure's conduct or attitudes. Israel had deliverers that in many respects matched her less than perfect character, or as we shall see in the discussions in 1 Samuel, God allows his vacillating people to have a leader, even a king, whom they deserve! Nevertheless, if God can use an enthusiastic sinner like Samson, or say a Rahab, then there is hope that he may use anyone.

Samson is said to be one who "judges" or "delivers" at 13.5, 15.20, and 16.31, but in many ways, he is different from the other judges in this book. For one thing, he is never depicted as leading any other Israelites. Rather, he is a one-man army, a rugged individualist. Nor does he accomplish the task of liberating Israel from the Philistines, in fact, the Philistines do not receive a decisive setback before 1 Sam. 7, when Samuel was judging God's people.

Another factor that sets Samson apart is that he is supposed to be a Nazarite by birth, and it appears that on several occasions his strength is dependent on his observance of the vow, at least in regard to not cutting his hair (16.17,38). On other occasions, it seems he is given extra strength by the spirit of God which falls on him periodically. This means that in some ways he is like the other judges in depending on spiritual endowment from above for his strength, but in some respects, he is not.

Samson was a Danite, and the Danites were a tribe assigned to the southern part of the land. It appears that as the Philistines encroached further and further north, most of the Danites moved to the extreme north of the land. This is why the city of Dan is found in the far north. Yet apparently, Samson's family had chosen not to make that migration, or at least they had not yet been forced to do so. The child was to be a Nazarite from birth, which, according to Num. 6.1–21, involves three requirements: (1) abstinence from all the products of the vine; (2) leaving one's hair uncut; and (3) avoidance of corpses so as to avoid defilement. Any breach of these three requirements nullified the consecration and whatever went along with it. The word *nazir* in fact means one separated or consecrated. It would appear then that Samson is not very obedient to at least two out of the three of these for we find him frequently in contact with corpses (both human and animal), and Judg. 14.10,17 hardly suggests observance of the abstinence requirement. It is probably important to bear in mind that Samson's vow was not voluntary, which may explain in part his failure to meet the requirements of the vow, with the exception of his hair.

Judg. 14 begins with Samson already a young man of marriageable age – no less than 16 or so. He takes the hour or so walk down to Timnah, finds a good-looking Philistine girl, tells his parents it's true love, and demands they get her for him. Samson's concern seems to be with getting what he wants rather than obeying the law of the Lord or honoring his family's wishes.

At 14.6 we are told of the first of Samson's mighty deeds. The spirit of the Lord comes upon him and he tears a young lion in two, as was often done then and now in the Near East with a young cub. We are told that Samson had nothing in his hand when he performed this feat. On a subsequent trip back from Timnah, Samson notices the carcass of the same lion and finds a honeycomb and bees in it. This is extremely unusual unless one assumes it was summertime and the carcass had dried out so much that bees would come near it. Samson cares nothing about the fact that touching the lion's corpse made him unclean as a Nazarite. This is probably why he does not tell his parents where the honey came from – as good Judahites they would not eat unclean food.

At Judg. 15.8 Samson vents his wrath against those who killed his bride, wreaking great havoc on the Philistines. The idiom here is he "smote them hip and thigh," and its meaning is not completely clear, though it seems to connote total defeat. Revenge only breeds more revenge, so the Philistines try to take Samson captive. They go about this indirectly by impelling the Judahites to go and take Samson captive. Samson is seen by his fellow Judahites as a troublemaker who disturbs their peace. Samson comes out and agrees to be bound by his fellow Jews, provided they will not "fall upon him" (i.e. kill him). Apparently, the sight of the bound Samson gave the Philistines courage, for they give a cry of triumph.

Hearing this, Samson has the spirit of Yahweh fall upon him, giving him great strength. He bursts his bonds, picks up a fresh jawbone of an ass, once again making himself unclean, and slays a huge host of Philistines (1,000 as a round number may be hyperbolic, mentioned for effect to convey the idea of a large number). After a hard day at the battlefield, Samson is one thirsty individual, so he prays for God to provide. There is a depression, probably a rock, from which water comes forth and revives Samson's spirit. This appears to be the first really religious act Samson engages in, and though a purely selfish prayer, shows he has some faith in Yahweh and some recognition that he is Yahweh's servant; i.e., he has a task from God to deliver God's people from the Philistines. We must now move on to chapter 16 and the climactic episode in Samson's life.

Samson made a long trip, some 38 miles from Zorah to the southernmost city of the Philistine pentapolis (Gath, Ekron, Ashdod, Ashkelon, Gaza), namely Gaza in order to have intercourse with a harlot there. Notice that he is still foolishly pursuing his penchant for foreign women, even notably immoral ones. The Gazites hear of Samson's arrival and plan his capture. The text appears to mean they kept watch over the gates during the day, but at night when the gate was shut they were less diligent.

Samson was both strong and unpredictable. He arose at midnight and left the harlot. Arriving at the closed gates, he simply took them off their hinges and carried gate and gate bar off in the direction of Hebron, leaving them on top of a hill. The point of the story is to show the impotence of the Philistines.

The story of Samson and Delilah is too well known to need repeating, but certain features require our attention. One of the things that is most strange about this story is that previously one would have deduced that Samson's strength came from the spirit (13; 14.6 and 19; 15.14–5; 16.20), but here it would seem his hair has some sort of magical properties. Why? The reason seems to be this: though Samson had not kept other aspects of his Nazaritic vow, this one part he had kept, thus showing he had some commitment to Yahweh and the task assigned to him. His giving up on the last vestige of the Nazaritic vow meant a forsaking of his life task for the love of a woman. Thus, the giving up of the uncut hair led to God's spirit abandoning him. There is, in short, a connection between the hair and the strength, but it is not the hair *per se* that gave him the strength. When the last link in the chain that tied Samson to God was broken, the rest of the connection fell by the wayside as well. The connection was not re-established until that first link, the hair, regrew, and Samson called upon the Lord again.

Delilah is offered a huge sum for betrayal, 1,100 pieces of silver. This would be worth well over $2,000 dollars, a life's fortune in those days. Notice that it is the lords of the five great Philistine cities who have access to and could provide such funds. Samson had become a menace to the entire people and had to be dealt with at all costs.

First, Samson is tied with fresh bowstrings made from the tendons of animals. The second attempt involves ropes. Notice that the third attempt has something to do with Samson's hair. Probably this is a sign of his mental weakening to the pleading of his loved one. At first it seems Samson is playing a game with the Philistines, but it proves to be a deadly one. Even weaving his hair into a web, probably with a loom, couldn't hold Samson down. Finally, we are told Samson's spirit was vexed to death, and he gave up his secret. Notice it was not Delilah who cut his hair, but a barber whom she had procured. Was she protecting herself lest this be another ruse of Samson?

Delilah then torments Samson with words, arousing him, and tragically he does not even know his strength is gone. He goes out thinking he can once more shake free from his tormentors. Judg. 16.20 is one of the saddest of all verses in the Bible – "he did not know the Lord had left him" – not unlike the story of King Saul (1 Sam. 16.14). The Philistines, rather than killing Samson, take him captive and put him to menial labor. As an insult and an attempt to shame the man, they apparently made him do women's work, grinding the corn. He was bound with bronze fetters and taken to far-off Gaza. As v. 22 hints, the story is far from over, for his hair begins to grow back because the Lord had not utterly forsaken him, however faithless he may have been to his Nazaritic vow.

The final scene of Samson's life apparently transpires in a temple of Dagon in Gaza. From that site has been excavated a temple which was held up by two central pillars. Notice that there were onlookers on the roof peering in on Samson, and this alone could have put considerable strain on the structure. Samson is led out by a small boy servant (another insult) and is displayed like a circus animal. It must never be forgotten that this is an honor and shame culture, and public shaming or dishonor was considered worse than dying in many cases. One preferred to die with honor rather than live with shame.

There is a very large crowd present and Samson asks once more for strength from God, not for God's glory but so he can take revenge on his tormentors. Notice that he invokes God in all three of his basic OT names – *Adonai*, *Elohim*, and Yahweh. Obviously, he is a desperate man, pulling all the religious strings he knows to pull. He also prays to die with the Philistines. The Hebrew suggests he then pushed the columns straight forward and down. We are told that the havoc he wreaked in death was greater than that which he had done during his life (the text suggests he may have killed as many as 1,100 people (cf. 14.19; 15.8,15). Thus ends the tale of this tragic figure. His kinfolk come, take him back, and give him a decent burial.

How then are we meant to evaluate Samson? He was no saint and should not be portrayed as one. It is hard, however, not to feel sorry for a person who is more brawn than brains, more libido than piety. He was a judge of Israel that God's likewise mostly unfaithful people deserved. God takes us as we are and uses us for his purposes. Happy is the person whose character does not betray the work he or she is doing for the Lord. You will, however, also notice the ethnocentric orientation of all these stories.

Not only are the stories told from a Hebrew point of view, but it is simply assumed that however misbehaving a Hebrew may be, he is still God's chosen person, and God strengthens and aids him in his hour of need. This ethnocentric focus and orientation is one of the major things that changes when we get to Paul's mission to the Gentiles and his *magnum opus* – Romans. While Paul is still one to insist that the Good News is "for the Jew first" (Rom.1), his vision of who are the people of God is broader than we find in these texts and includes everyone on the basis of the mercy of God and by grace through faith in Jesus. The writers of Judges and the OT narratives did not and could not imagine such a thing, nor even imagine the way that Paul would look at the Mosaic covenant. The New Covenant was not simply a renewal of the Mosaic one, but at the same time, Israel had an identity outside of Christ and was not identified with "the church" prior to the return of Christ.

1 Samuel: The Rise of the Prophet Samuel

Elkanah and his wife Hannah are depicted as pious Israelites who not only follow the necessary pilgrimages and feasts but also go up at special times on their own. The shrine they visit is at Shiloh, which at that time (1030 BC?) was perhaps the chief shrine in all Israel. Hannah becomes so distraught at the shrine that she weeps and will not eat. Eli was an exceedingly old priest. He was also more than a little near-sighted. Eli sees but does not hear Hannah praying and assumes that she has partaken too much during the feasting at the shrine and is drunk.

Hannah prays that if God will give her a male child, she will dedicate the child to God as a perpetual Nazarite who will drink no wine, never cut his hair, and serve in the temple. Samuel will prove to be a Nazarite worthy of the name, unlike Samson. Hannah replies to Eli that she is not a good-for-nothing woman but is hard of spirit (i.e. persistent). Eli is so impressed by her response that he blesses her and hopes God will grant her fervent request. She responds with, "May I find favor in your eyes," which means "May it turn out favorably as you have said, and may I stay in your good graces."

Hannah goes back to the feast, then returns home, has sexual relations with Elkanah, and later has a child. The child is named Samuel, which probably is a phrase turned into a name and means "he over whom the name [*shem*] of God [*el*] has been spoken." Hannah tells Elkanah she will take the child to Shiloh when he is weaned. It was apparently an Israelite custom to nurse a baby till he was about three years old (2 Macc. 7.27). When she goes up with the child to give him to Yahweh, she also brings a splendid offering. A three-year-old bull is a very valuable gift, and an *ephah* of flour is about a half bushel.

Hannah brings Samuel to Eli, who had been the mediator of the blessing on her. At 1 Sam. 2.11 we begin to see Samuel as a little priest. We are told that the boy, in contrast to Eli's greedy children, carried on the service of Yahweh faithfully. Notice that the word translated "service" here and at 3.1 is used elsewhere to denote the service of the Aaronic priesthood (Exod. 28.35,43; 29.30; Num. 1.50). At 2.35 we have a word from God that when Eli's two sons die, God will raise up a priest forever (literally "all the days"), one who will always be faithful and do God's will. It becomes clear that this cannot simply refer to Samuel since the phrase "all the days" is included. Presumably it means a faithful priestly line walking before the anointed king for all time. It is striking that as this story develops we discover that Samuel has three roles – as a priest, as a prophet, and as one of the last of the judges. He is a crucial transitional figure, and in large measure the rise of monarchy happens through his work.

We turn to the vision of Samuel in 1 Sam. 3. Samuel is still serving an apprenticeship of sorts, ministering under Eli. We are told that the word of the Lord at that time was not commonly given; visions were infrequent in that age. Again, we notice the focus not on what is seen but, on the word which is heard.[56] The phrase "word of Yahweh" is a technical one for the revelation given to the prophets; indeed, many of the prophetical books begin with this very phrase. Since Samuel is a priest designate, a prophet, and soon a kingmaker as well, it is hardly surprising that Luke deliberately portrays Jesus as a latter-day Samuel, though greater, and his mother a latter-day Hannah.[57] Thus, Luke makes clear that Jesus is the one who ultimately combines the roles of prophet, priest, and king. Neither David nor Solomon did this, and thus in some ways Samuel was a greater figure than either of these kings – he was a prophet, a priest, and a kingmaker. It is also notable that in all of 1 and 2 Samuel, Samuel is about the only figure who is portrayed as a totally exemplary character.

Eli's sight had grown dim (3.2), but his insight had not, for he realized that it was the Lord speaking to Samuel, and so he tells the boy what to do. Samuel does not recognize the voice calling him as God's but mistakes it for Eli's. What are we to make of v. 7, which says that Samuel did not yet know the Lord and the Lord's word had not yet been revealed to him? This phrase cannot mean he did not acknowledge God (as it does at 2.12 when used of Eli's sons), nor does it mean he had no relationship with Yahweh. Probably what is meant is that he did not yet have that special relationship with God that a prophet has, in which God speaks directly to the person. This story then is about the beginning of that new phase in Samuel's relationship with God.

Notice how God persistently calls Samuel. It should be stressed that God's message to Samuel is only given when he responds and is ready to receive it, but Yahweh keeps calling until Samuel does respond properly. Eli correctly tells Samuel to say, "Speak, Lord, for your servant hears." Samuel is called God's servant, and we may remember that this was the significant title that Joshua assumed only at the end of his life. Samuel, more like Moses, takes on this title and the task implied at the outset of his ministry.

At v. 10 we are told Yahweh came and stood near to Samuel, so this was indeed a vision that comes in a dream or a trance, a vision which involved seeing and not just hearing. God wishes to tell Samuel some news that will make his ears burn ("tingle" in most translations). The message is about Eli's sons being judged for their sin. Samuel awakes and, not surprisingly, is afraid to deliver this message to Eli, but the old man presses him, and upon hearing the message, Eli resigns himself to it, saying, "It is the Lord; let him do whatever seems good to him" (on acceptance of judgment, one should compare Gen. 16.6; 19.8; Judg. 19.24).

At v. 19 we are told of Samuel's growth and the assurance of divine favor being with him. He is a man of God, and none of his words will return to him void or fail to be fulfilled (Josh. 21.45; 23.14). Samuel's reputation as a man of God spreads throughout the land rapidly (from Dan to Beersheba, north to south). The chapter ends by saying that God revealed himself to Samuel, and through Samuel God's word came to all the people. Samuel is seen as a prophet of national stature and mission, though later he can also function as a local judge (7.16) or seer (9.6–9). Like Moses, he had received a theophany, the

---

[56] On this see pp. 127–32, above, on Gen. 12.

[57] One also notes how John the Baptizer and his mother in Luke bear a resemblance to Hannah and her son.

appearing of God to him. This story then is intended to distinguish Samuel as a singular figure of importance, but also to make clear that it is Yahweh and not heredity that must decide who will lead Israel.

Whether we attribute it to the source material or to the final editors, there is very clearly an attempt in these historical books to convey to the audience that it is the same God, Yahweh, who manifests himself in similar ways in the patriarchal, the Mosaic, and the monarchial periods. The portrayal demonstrates God's consistent character, both righteous and yet compassionate, just and yet merciful, faithful to his word, even in the face of the frequent faithlessness of his people, rescuing and redeeming and restoring his people again and again and again, despite their sins and failures. If there is an exemplary "hero" figure in the narrative thought world of the Hebrews occasionally one can point to a figure like Abraham, on a good day, or Samuel, when he listens to God, but the real One who saves the day, again and again is Yahweh.

The Rise of the Monarchy

1 Sam. 8–10 are some of the most crucial chapters in all the historical books, for they chronicle the rise of the monarchy, which was certainly a mixed blessing. The great problem with kingship was that it could lead to a violation of the first commandment. The king could take on almost a divine status and assume divine and totalitarian powers, as often happened in other nations. Thus, a desire for a king seems to be a form of rejecting the kingship of Yahweh, a rejection of the direct rule of the people by God (theocracy). This also includes the rejection of what goes with theocracy – holy war. Instead, the Israelites want a human king to lead them into battle and fight for them (cf. 8.20 to Deut. 20. 1–4; Judg. 4.14; 2 Sam. 5.24; on the wars of Yahweh, cf. Exod. 14.14; Josh. 10.14,42; 23.3,10). To judge from Saul's case, they also wanted wars where they could take booty and prisoners, not slaughter everything in sight as part of the cleansing of the land.

Samuel is obviously upset by this request for a king and prays to Yahweh. He apparently takes this request as a rejection of his leadership and that of his sons. Yahweh, however, makes clear that ultimately the request for a king was a rejection of him, and not just of the prophet and his family. At 1 Sam. 8.9 the prophet is commissioned to explain the rights and conduct of a king to the people. The description we get most nearly matches the case of Solomon, who copied pagan royal acts and customs. Solomon is known to have used Israelites as chariot commanders, as commanders of horsemen, and as runners to go before the king's chariot and announce his coming. But in addition to the enlistment of Israelites, there would also be confiscation of the best land and royal taxation at a 10 percent rate.

The end result of having a king will be undesirable, but v. 18 indicates that when the Israelites call upon God because of the king's oppression, Yahweh will not respond, for the king is the one the Israelites, not Yahweh, had chosen. Yahweh will not deliver them from what they desired and requested. Despite Samuel's warning, the Israelites still insist on having their own king. The emphasis is on the king being *their* king and *their* choice, not God's. In short, the Israelites typically refuse to listen to the prophet's warning (2 Kgs. 17.14, Jer. 11.10; 13.10). It is hard to escape the conclusion that both the prophet and Yahweh evaluated the request for a king as a form of apostasy, or rejection of God.

David is approved because he is a king of God's choosing, whereas Saul's kingship was the result of a sinful desire and a hasty request. The story from 1 Sam. 16 to 2 Sam. 5 identifies David as the one chosen by God to succeed Saul. Perhaps we may see here a case where God is operating under a situation that takes account of Israel's hardness of heart and lack of faith. God allows them to have a king, though that is not his perfect will, but he takes the initiative because he is gracious and merciful even to his rebellious people. He makes the best out of this not completely desirable monarchial situation by instigating a king of his own choosing – David.

The tale of Saul, the first human ruler, is told in 1 Sam. 9–15. Chapter 9 begins with a genealogy which establishes that Saul came from a good family. We are told Saul is handsome, even as a youth, and that he is head and shoulders taller than anyone else in Israel. He was thus a very striking figure and outwardly an obvious choice for a leader, judging by purely human standards and appearances. The story is both ironic and humorous. The man who went out to find his family's lost asses came back a king, a king who would make an ass of himself. But this is typical of the way God often works, at the least expected times and in unsuspected places throughout this narrative. Some of the narratives, like the tale of Rahab, are probably meant to be humorous, and some are ironic. The tales about Saul are both ironic and tragic. Perhaps one of the main reasons for telling both the good news and the bad news about God's people and even his leaders, is that only God himself is consistently good and of reliable character. Even very pious human beings can be vain, self-centered, and make enormous mistakes. The upshot of such tales is a not-so-subtle push for the reader to place all their trust and faith in Yahweh, not in human beings, for only Yahweh is the same yesterday, today, and forever, always true to his character.

Saul is portrayed in a somewhat positive light, and he even protests against being made the chosen one, hiding from the assembly while the lots are cast. Samuel, who has been told in advance about Saul's coming, is not surprised when he does so. Yahweh instructs him to anoint Saul a *nagid*, a prince over the land. It must be stressed that God does not command that Saul be anointed a *melek*, a king. This suggests that Saul was to see himself as under Yahweh, who was the one true king. A prince is one who knows he is under authority, as well as having royal authority. Notice as well in 10.17–27 that it is the people, *not Samuel or Yahweh*, who proclaim Saul a king.

Anointing was a symbol of God's grace or unmerited favor poured out on a person. Samuel kisses Saul, which may be part of the ritual, but it appears that Samuel is impressed with this handsome young man in the sense that he likes him. Saul is offered a three-part sign to confirm the truth of the word of Samuel to Saul. The first part of the confirmation allays Saul's fears about losing the asses; the second part shows already that he has found favor in the people's and God's eyes. But the focus is on the third part for a very good reason. Verse 6 says that when Saul meets these prophets then the spirit of Yahweh will fall upon him, and he will become a different person (literally "be turned into another man"). The verb translated "turned" here is used elsewhere to mean "overthrow" as in the overthrow of Sodom. Saul will be completely overwhelmed and changed, given the presence, prophecy, and presumably the power of God. This is a sign that is fulfilled within Saul himself; he will know its truth internally.

Verse 7 indicates that Saul is to respond to this endowment by doing whatever his hand finds to do, for God is with him. This appears to mean that whatever he sees that needs to be done, he will be able to do. R. W. Klein says it means he is to act according to the strength he is given (Judg. 9.33).[58] When Saul turned to leave Samuel, he had already been given another heart (i.e. the change was already happening).

Of all the kings in the OT, only Saul and David are called God's elect. But unlike the case in extra-biblical cultures, an elect king could also become a rejected king. Notice the rejection in 1 Sam. 15.23–28, 2 Sam. 6.21. As Klein points out, we have various positive remarks in these stories about Saul, but negative remarks about the Israelites, who lust after a human ruler like the other *goyim* (peoples/nations). This can only lead to the following conclusions: (1) it was wrong to reject God's rule, the theocracy; (2) only because of their hardness of heart did God grant the Israelites a ruler, a prince of his choosing, whom *the people* labeled the king. It would also therefore be wrong to reject God's choice for this position; (3) the ruler chosen was only conditionally elect, as we see in the case of Saul, and could be replaced if he violated God's plan or will. Election has nothing to do with the personal salvation of Saul. He is chosen for a specific historical purpose, just as later Cyrus will be "God's anointed one," to set God's people free from their Babylonian captivity.

David

We find what is called the first part of the "succession narrative" in 1 Sam. 16.1–18.5 (which may run to the end of 2 Samuel). David and Samuel meet only twice – in chapter 16 and at 19.18. It is important at this point to expand our understanding of anointing. Few peoples in the ANE anointed their kings. Some Hittites and some Egyptian officials and vassals were anointed, but in Israel, kings, priests, and prophets were all anointed. Oil could be used in diplomacy, business contracts, nuptial rites, and manumission of slaves, and in the latter case, the act of anointing had a contractual or covenantal meaning. Basically, the persons doing the anointing are pledging themselves to the anointed one and are thereby obligated to him or her. Thus, for instance, when the elders anoint David, it is not because he was not *already* God's anointed but because they are obligating themselves to him.

In the 34 times that "anointed" is used of a royal figure, it always appears with the name of Yahweh or the possessive modifier "his" is attached to it. This means that when one is called "anointed" in the OT, it always means "anointed by Yahweh." By placing the story of David's anointing *here*, the author of 1 Samuel means for us to see all that follow as a manifestation of this initial fact and act of God. God has bound himself to David from the start in covenant and has blessed him. Insofar as good things happen to David, it is a result of this commitment of God. When bad things happen to David, it is because of his own sin or violation of the covenantal relationship with God. Notice that both David and Saul were anointed in private, even in secret, but also note that David is explicitly not picked because of his height or appearance. In fact, God makes clear to Samuel that he is not to judge by that sort of criterion again.

Samuel is told to take a horn of oil, go to Bethlehem, and visit the family of Jesse. Samuel is not told in advance who he is to anoint, only that it is to be one of Jesse's sons. Throughout this passage there is a stress on the word "see." Samuel is to anoint the one

[58] Ralph W. Klein, *1 Samuel* (WBC 10; Nashville, TN: Thomas Nelson, 1983), *ad loc.*

God has *seen*, i.e., the one he has chosen (cf. 16.18; 2 Kgs. 10.3). It is significant that David is to be anointed *king*; but Saul was only anointed *prince*. Samuel has a very human reaction to all this. Since Saul is still alive at this point, this is a very dangerous enterprise. This is especially so since going to Bethlehem required one to pass through Saul's town of Gibeah.

Samuel is drawn to Eliab due to his appearance, but Eliab is not the one Yahweh has *seen*. The Lord sees not as a human being sees. Verse 7 is crucial and we offer a literal translation here: "Human beings look upon the eyes (outward form) Yahweh looks upon the heart" (cf. Jer. 17.10; 20.12). The prophet must learn to do likewise, or at least follow God's lead. One by one the seven sons pass by, but God indicates to Samuel that none of these are the one. Indeed, Jesse had not even considered David as a candidate, but rather left him in the field tending sheep.

At v. 12, David has been fetched, and we are told he is ruddy in appearance, handsome with beautiful eyes. Ruddy may refer to reddish tint of the hair or skin. The name David seems to mean "beloved" or even "darling." In any case, David was not chosen for his looks, but because God was exercising his freedom to choose the youngest and least likely candidate. David is anointed in the presence of his family, but nothing is said to them about the meaning of this event. All they know is that he is chosen by the Lord for *something*. No sooner is David anointed than the spirit rushes upon him, as it had upon Saul, but notice in the case of Saul the spirit's coming is *not* directly connected to the anointing (cf. 11.6). David, unlike Saul, will have this endowment *permanently*, though as Ps. 51 will show, when David has committed a grave sin, he is fearful that God will take his spirit from him. In any case, Saul's good endowment is about to be replaced with an evil spirit. The point of all this is to indicate the superiority of David's endowment. Here we see the key to the whole of David's career. David is the long-foreseen chosen one of God (cf. 15.28). David is a man after God's own heart, the one whom God will be with. After this David is king *de jure*, but only later does he become king *de facto*.

Key Observation

It is worth a reminder that these early stories do not reflect a sense of secondary causes, as do the rerun accounts in 1–2 Chronicles. By this I mean that the tendency is to see whatever happens as coming from Yahweh. So, if Saul suddenly has "an evil spirit" in his life, it came from God, whereas in the later accounts Satan enters the picture, and Satan has a will of his own. Here again, it is necessary to have an understanding of progressive revelation, if one is thinking about these stories as part of a larger biblical theology. In regard to matters of good and evil, God is not the author of evil, nor is God subject to being tempted to do evil, nor does God tempt anyone. God is light and in him is no darkness at all. Unless one realizes that the fuller presentation of God's character from later in the Bible (both later in the OT and especially in the NT) is the one by which one must norm and interpret these earlier presentations, one will make various mistakes in evaluating the more primitive narratives in the OT. Fortunately, already in Chronicles, we begin to have a clear sense of the reality of secondary causes, some of which are indeed evil.

Yes, Yahweh permits such things to happen, but frankly that is the price of and the grand bargain involved in giving a modicum of the power of contrary choice to God's higher beings – both celestial ones (angels, Satan, demons) and terrestrial ones (humans). The Bible consistently, and rightly, holds God's people accountable for their behavior, assuming they have some choice about it. But then, if God wished to have a world in which his creatures could freely receive his love and mercy and freely respond to it, then that modicum of free choice was necessary, even when we are talking about fallen, self-centered human beings who must rely on God's grace to make good choices. That grace enables and empowers them to do the right thing, but it does not take away their ability or need to make their choices without predetermination or manipulation.

Perhaps no narrative in all of 1 Samuel is more famous or better known than the story of David and Goliath, which the narrator tells in considerable detail, and with obvious relish in the telling (1 Sam. 17.1–18.5). The practice of representative single combat is well known in the ANE. We find a similar sort of event in 2 Sam. 21.15ff., indeed four such accounts (cf. 2 Sam. 23.20). The giant in our story is called Goliath only twice; the rest of the time he is "the Philistine." 2 Sam. 21.19 says that Elhanan killed Goliath the Gittite. The reference to the spear like a weaver's beam here and in 2 Sam. 21 makes it likely that we are talking about the same man. 1 Chron. 20.5, written at an even later period, says that it was a brother of Goliath that Elhanan killed. Perhaps this latter suggestion clarifies the matter.

The battle lines are drawn on opposite slopes of the hills at the valley of Terebinth, just north of Socoh. At v. 4 we hear about "the man between the two" (i.e. the representative warrior who stands between the armies and fights). We are told that Goliath is 9 feet 9 inches, or if we follow the LXX, 6 feet 9 inches (which equals 4 cubits and a span). Clearly, he was a large man. The elaborate description of his armor is meant to indicate his apparent invulnerability. He is the quintessential Iron Age infantry man. We are told that Goliath wore an impressive bronze helmet and a coat of mail (literally "plated"), which likely weighed 126 pounds (if a shekel weighed 0.403 ounces). He also has bronze greaves, leg fittings which were probably leather-lined. He had a javelin slung between his shoulders, but some have taken this word to mean a scimitar, which it seems to mean in the Qumran scrolls. He also has a virtually full-length shield, carried for him by his armor bearer. We are told that the spear tip was made of iron, which indicates a technology that Israel did not yet have (cf. 1 Sam. 13.19–22).

Verses 12–30 appear to stand on their own and begin the story of David from scratch. Here David is at home but is sent as a messenger and delivery boy to his brothers, who are in Saul's army, bringing news that the family is well and also bringing food (parched grain, a delicacy that was the ancient equivalent of Wheat Chex, and some cheese). All this is quickly forgotten when David arrives and learns what is happening. At v. 25 we hear of a reward of riches and marriage into the royal family for a victory, but there were no takers. David takes an interest in this, but basically, he shows righteous indignation because the champion of a dead god (1 Sam. 5) was challenging "the living God" (see 2 Kgs. 19.4; Jer. 10.6–10 on this phrase).

It should be stressed that shepherding was not as pastoral or bucolic an occupation as it might seem. The shepherd not only had to watch and guide the sheep, but also had to protect them from wild animals, which sometimes entailed hand-to-hand combat with jackals and lions. Shepherds would engage in such fights because the only way they could be exonerated for stealing a lost sheep was to bring the carcass of the animal to the owner (Amos 3.12; Exod. 22.12–13). Thus, David may have had some skills in life-threatening combat. Indeed, the text says that he claims to have faced and bearded lions (i.e. had taken them by the throat and killed them, perhaps cutting off part of their beard as a trophy).

Goliath had been a warrior since youth, but perhaps so had David with wild animals. The passage about Saul's armor not fitting David is both lifelike and believable and indicates Saul's attempt to help David. Thus, David goes down to the *wadi* (dry creek bed), picks up a few stones, and is ready to do battle. Goliath takes it as a mockery that this beardless young boy would come out to meet him: "Am I a dog that you come after me with such a little stick?" Goliath had size, skill, and armor on his side, but David had Yahweh on his, and Yahweh was the ultimate man of war. Again, we hear the language of holy war. David simply throws the taunt back in Goliath's face. David's motive for fighting is theological, i.e., so that all the world will know there is a God in Israel. Yahweh saves not with a spear, but with his own mighty hand. There are various parallels here with the story of the plagues in Exodus. In both cases, the actions demonstrate who really is the living God. In other words, the story is mainly told to make a theological point.

Slingshots were made of a little bag to which was tied two long leather thongs. The sling would be swung over the head, and then one thong would be released at the appropriate moment. It was a shepherd's chief weapon, but it could be a deadly one (Judg. 20.16; 1 Sam. 25.29; 1 Chron. 12.2; 2 Chron. 26.14). The two most vulnerable spots for Goliath would be in the joint of his armor at the knees or the forehead if it was exposed. It is apparently the latter that David hits with one shot, and we are told the stone "sank in." This is not just luck, but the action of the Lord executing Goliath. It is not clear whether the stone killed him or knocked him unconscious, but David finished the job by decapitating the giant. The Philistines flee and are chased all the way back to Gath and Ekron. This was the Lord's doing, but unfortunately Israel tended to give David too much credit. There is a sense in which God intended such a reaction. Henceforth, David's star would be on the rise and people knew to pay attention to him.

Though 1 Sam. 18.1–15 may not have been a part of the original text, it probably represents authentic early tradition. This narrative tells of a political covenant drawn up between David and Saul's son Jonathan. Jonathan is strongly drawn to David and binds himself to him as a covenant brother, making this clear through the ritual stripping of his own robe and giving it to David. This could symbolically represent giving away the right of succession to the throne (24.5,12 suggest this was a royal robe). Jonathan also gives David his own warrior's belt and garment. David had done a warrior's job and would now be put in charge of some of the military, which seems to please the troops.

Jonathan's covenant is based on his love for David, who is winsome and winning. David thus has the support of the heir from then on, and at Jonathan's death David calls him "my brother" (2 Sam. 1.26) and takes care of his crippled son, even giving him Saul's land (2 Sam. 9; 21.7). David said the love of Jonathan surpassed that of a woman, which indicates a very close relationship indeed. There is nothing at all to suggest there was anything sexual about this relationship, nor does the verb for love (*aheb*) suggest this (cf. 18.16,22,28; 20.17). It will be remembered that the verb *yada* (to know), not *aheb* was used to describe sexual sharing. Jonathan loved David as his very alter ego. Here truly loving neighbor as self was lived out.[59]

Here for the first time we are told that David has men, his own forces, or entourage. Whatever Saul attempts to do, and for whatever motive, it always turns out for David's good. 1 Sam. 19 makes clear that the conflict between Saul and David is now public. The beginning of chapter 19 has Saul telling Jonathan and his servants he intends to kill David, but Jonathan goes immediately to warn him. He serves the role of reconciler or mediator in verses 1–7. We are told at v. 1 that Jonathan took delight (pleasure) in David, so he would not stand for this action, even by his own father. Notice the emphasis on the word "I" (v. 3). David must hide while Jonathan straightens things out. At v. 4 he says that David's deeds are good, which may mean that they are deeds loyal to the king; hence there is no need for Saul's action (cf. 24.18–20).

Jonathan reminds his father that he will incur bloodguilt if he kills David, for it will be the shedding of innocent blood (see Deut. 19.10; 21.8; 27.25). In some contexts, premeditated bloodguilt caused by killing was not atonable by sacrifice. Here we see a significant difference between the Old and New Covenants. In the New Covenant, all sins have been atoned for by Christ's death, and forgiveness is offered to all, no matter how serious their sin. This is not the case in the OT, where some sins, the so-called "sins with a high hand" such as premeditated adultery and murder, could not be atoned for by animal sacrifice. Jonathan also points out that what David did against the Philistines, risking his life, he did for all Israel, not for his own glory or to show Saul up. Saul is persuaded by Jonathan's impassioned speech and Jonathan leads David back to the court. Saul has even sworn on Yahweh not to kill David.

In 1 Sam. 20, Jonathan again shows his loyalty to David. Jonathan's loyalty to David is so great that he promises to tell David all he hears from his father (v. 9), and he seals the promise with an imprecation, a self-cursing formula (v. 13). David is now in the period of his greatest political weakness, yet he is actually the one who is in a position of strength. Yahweh is with him, so he is in the position of power. That the heir apparent agrees that David will actually gain the throne is a clear sign of the ceding of power from Saul's family to David.

David is now also entering the period when he will be a fugitive from injustice. Saul will not rest until David is dead, for as long as David lives he is a threat to Saul's dynastic claim. David never attempts to take over from Saul or kill him. The only thing actually

---

[59] Here Moran's work on Deuteronomy, previously mentioned, is helpful making clear this is a statement about loyalty not sexual love. It is unfortunate that this story has become the playground for speculation about David and Jonathan being gay lovers, or David being bisexual. This sort of speculation ignores a whole variety of ancient cultural factors: (1) same-sex sexual activity was a moral taboo among God's people as the strong prohibitions in Lev. 18.22 demonstrate; (2) in a world of arranged marriages, often the closest bonds were between siblings – brothers or sister, or even between those who covenanted with each other to be a "band of brothers," and it had nothing to do with sexual attraction at all; (3) these were honor and shame cultures, and homosexual behavior was considered shameful, and yes, that is part of what the Sodom story is about. It is our own over-sexualized culture that reads current sexual mores back into these ancient texts. Had the original writers, never mind David and Jonathan, been interviewed about the matter, they would have been horrified by such suggestions. On how *not* to read such texts, see J. W. Knust, *Unprotected Texts: The Bible's Surprising Contradictions about Sex and Desire* (New York: HarperOne, 2012) and D. B. Martin, *Sex and the Single Savior: Gender and Sexuality in Biblical Interpretation* (Louisville, KY: Westminster John Knox, 2006).

preserving the line of Saul this long is, ironically, David himself. Verses 41–42 express the deep feelings between David and Jonathan. They go apart in peace, for theirs is a friendship forever, a covenant forever. We must move ahead in the narrative to when David is already king *de facto*.

The famous or infamous story in 2 Sam. 11–12 begins with King David on the roof of his house in the late afternoon ("toward evening"). Below him, probably in an unroofed courtyard, was a beautiful woman bathing in the nude, presumably in a pool of some sort where the spring water was poured or came forth. David's lust is aroused, and he sends a messenger to find out who this beautiful woman is. Bathsheba's practice of bathing in the open may have been of questionable propriety, for she had to know there were various buildings taller than hers from which she could be seen. Yet it is David who is to blame for succumbing to this temptation, especially because he is in the power position in such a relationship, and all the more so since he is a king in a patriarchal society.

David is told that Bathsheba is a married woman, but that does not deter David as it should have done. She is Eliam's daughter (23.34), but Ahitophel's granddaughter (15.12). The latter was a court counselor of David's, and so this was not an unfamiliar woman. Her husband is called a Hittite, though this may mean Hethite. Uriah was one of David's most prominent commanding officers (23.39, a "mighty man of valor"). Uriah's position and Bathsheba's court connections make this sin all the more foolish. Sin is, for the most part, an act of ultimate irrationality. David wants the woman so much he sends messengers (plural) to get her (v. 4). One suspects that this too was foolish, since word was bound to get out when the action involves more than a few people.

The story in no way explains the frame of mind of David, Bathsheba, or Uriah; it simply recounts the action. Bathsheba comes, whether willingly or unwillingly, we do not know. David sleeps with her (the text reads literally "he took her and she came to him"). Verse 4b must refer back to the fact that when David saw her, Bathsheba was giving herself a purification bath after her monthly period. It was also believed that a woman was more fertile immediately after her period. How ironic that it was an act of purification that led to David's act of impurity!

Bathsheba goes home but she sends word to David that she is with child. David's first solution is to summon Uriah home from the battle against the Ammonites and make it possible for him to have relations as soon as possible with his wife, so no one will suspect adultery. The conversation about the *shalom* of the commander and the way the battle goes is only a pretext for the real issue. Then David appears to make a rather blunt suggestion: "Go down to your house and wash your feet." This probably means, "Why don't you go and have sexual relations with your wife?" as 2 Sam. 11.8 shows. In fact, "foot" or "feet" could be a euphemism for genitals, for example, Zipporah touches Moses' "feet" with the foreskin of their son (Exod. 4.25) or Saul goes into a cave to relieve himself and "covers his feet" (1 Sam. 24.4), or Naomi tells Ruth in Ruth 3.3–4 to go and pull up Boaz's garment and lie down next to his "feet," and so on.

Uriah appears to have suspicions as to what this is all about, and he is clever. He protests that soldiers do not interrupt the *herem*, the holy war, for such things, and besides it would be unfair to the other soldiers who did not have such privileges. How can a mighty man of valor be with his wife while the ark and the troops are out there fighting? It was not unusual for a group of soldiers to take a vow of abstinence during a period of holy war. It is obvious by v. 14 that David is now a desperate man willing to try desperate things to preserve his reputation. His action is both calculating and cruel, for, in effect, he places Uriah's own death warrant in his hand and has him deliver it to Joab. The instructions are explicit. Joab is to act so that Uriah's fellow fighters withdraw; thus, Uriah will be struck down and die.

Joab does not *exactly* follow David's orders to the letter. The troops are not told to withdraw, though Uriah is placed where Joab knows the fighting would be fiercest. Joab is certainly not averse to seeing bloods, even of those on his own side, shed through murder (cf. on Abner and Amasa in 2 Sam. 3.20ff.). The result, however, is more than David had planned. Not one but several men die. David is now an instigator of acts which lead to various deaths at the hands of a despised enemy, the Ammonites. The end of chapter 11 makes clear that trouble is brewing because "the thing that David had done displeased the Lord."

Nathan goes to David only when God sends him. David does not hold this matter against Nathan; indeed, Nathan remains a counselor to the king (cf. 1 Kgs. 1). Nathan gives the rebuke by the most efficient means possible, by indirection, telling a parable so that David will not suspect anything until the application. In other words, he will, if he has any conscience left, be led to see the injustice done, concur with it, and discover that he has been condemned by his own words. The one whom God had so richly blessed, by giving him not only the kingship but also the harem and wives of his predecessor, just could not be satisfied. Yahweh would have given him even more. What David has done is not only a sin against himself and Uriah, but also a form of despising the word of the Lord, an act of rebellion against God, as all sin ultimately is. David is blamed directly for Uriah's death as if he had struck the blow personally. The violence he has unleashed will continue to haunt and hunt David's family line.

To take Bathsheba was a form of despising Yahweh himself, and such sin would be punished in kind. Indeed, the punishment will truly fit the crime. From now on David would indeed live under the cloud of this judgment. He had, in effect, murdered Uriah and must pay (*harag*, the strong word for murder here, not *hikah*). David clearly admits his sin (v. 13), and because it is a sincere admission, Nathan pronounces the word of forgiveness. God does not wish David to perish; he does not wish the death of the sinner (cf. Ezra 18.23,32; 33.11). Yet sin must be dealt with; it will have consequences and punishment. Pss. 32 and 51, if they are from David, give us a look at the turmoil in David's inner being both before and after this sordid affair and the confrontation by Nathan.

It is striking how v. 11 echoes what we heard earlier in words spoken to Saul: he was to hear that the kingdom would be given to a neighbor. Now David is told that a neighbor (in this case Absalom) will despoil his harem. When Nathan left, the baby was struck with an illness, and David goes all out to get God to relent from this death blow. David pleads with God, fasts, and shows the supreme form of obeisance by lying down on the floor (apparently of his own house at night, not the tent of meeting). He refuses all the solicitations of his court aides and servants. In one week, the child is dead. David's response is understandable, if somewhat abnormal. Verse 23b should be examined closely. It probably does not mean that David believed in a positive afterlife for his child or himself. This sounds a bit fatalistic, and it is. There was not yet a clear and full understanding of the afterlife, even by someone as religiously perceptive as David. David had hoped for mercy for the child, but now the child was past prayer and hope.

David then goes to comfort his new wife, and this time God blesses him with a child whom David calls peace (*shalom*), i.e., Solomon. David apparently regards his birth as a sign that he is at peace with God. The Lord loves this child and sends a message to that effect by giving him a second name Jedidiah, which means "loved by the Lord." This was a form of practical declaration by Yahweh, not so much a permanent name, so the child continues to be called Solomon, who was to be a king who reigned in peace. This child enters the world with good prospects.

What can we learn from this sad tale? We know that David will now live under a curse, a cloud, even though he and Solomon will at least initially avoid severe judgment. Secondly, we learn that God does not give up on David in spite of all he did wrong. In this, the situation is different than with Saul. God will reveal his character and advance his cause in spite of the sinfulness of the leader of his people. Still, even with forgiveness, David would have to live with the repercussions or effects of his sin. Sinning can be like opening Pandora's box. One cannot get all the demons back into the box once they are unleashed. The story continues, and in various ways it becomes sadder as we shall see as we turn to 1 Kgs. 2.

In 1 Kgs. 2 we see David as a vengeful old man and Solomon using whatever excuse he can to banish or liquidate his rivals. It is not a pretty picture, and some have wondered whether the conclusion of the succession narrative was meant to pass a very negative judgment on the succession. We must not minimize the problem, for Joab had been very loyal and helpful to David on many occasions, though he had made a mistake with Adonijah. In the case of Shimei, David had already pardoned him under oath. In the case of Abiathar, however, vv. 25ff. seem to take his dismissal by Solomon as a fulfillment of 1 Sam 3.11–14.

Solomon

At the beginning of 1 Kgs. 2 we hear of David's days to die, the idea being that people often died over a period of time. David is aware of his condition and says he is about to go the way of all the earth or, as we would say, the way of all flesh (cf. 2 Sam. 5.4). The narrative suggests that David was now about 70 years old. He charges Solomon to strictly follow the written law and statutes of God (cf. the similar charge in Josh. 1). The *huqqotaw* statutes mean literally the things engraved. The *miswotaw*, the commandments, signify direct orders in the form "thou shalt." The *mishpatim*, judgments, signify *ad hoc* decisions based on particular cases which would be written down to serve as legal precedents. Testimonies, *edot*, mean solemn charges which God is called upon to witness. If Solomon will do it by the book then he will prosper in all he does, and there shall not fail to be a successor on the throne. But all this hinges on faithful obedience to and execution of God's word and ways wholeheartedly.

At v. 5 David shows the anger and hurt that had built up over the years in his heart. Now he is going to have vengeance even on his allies and die a spiteful old man. David blames Joab for putting innocent blood (of Abner and others) on David's girdle and sandals. The point of this metaphor seems to be either that Joab had impaired David's strength by involving him in blood guilt wherever he might go or walk, or that Joab had impaired the strength of his progeny, the bloodguilt being passed down (hence the reference to loins). The latter seems more likely. The term *hokmah* has at least three different meanings. Here it means *savoir-faire*, the knowledge of the ways of the world, the political astuteness, or practical worldly wisdom or cleverness to get rid of one's adversaries.

To be sure Solomon was to reflect some real wisdom and there was a certain brutal sense to eliminating all one's problems at the outset. Here, however, wisdom hardly has the positive and salutary content it has elsewhere when referring to Solomon. There were two other kinds of wisdom spoken of in the Solomon cycle – the capacity of discernment and the ability to decide a case. In the ancient period, when the king was also judge, this was the king's function. This we see Solomon exhibiting in 1 Kgs 3.16–28 in the famous incident of two women claiming one child. Wisdom in this case is the knowledge of a relevant fact and the intelligence to know how to use it to settle a matter under dispute. But in 1 Kgs. 5.9–14 wisdom means yet a different thing. There it denotes encyclopedic knowledge not related to practical administration but rather of natural phenomena. This latter sort of *hokmah* suggests an analogy with Mesopotamian lists of natural phenomena and Egyptian wisdom exercises.[60] In this case we are talking about empirical familiarity with facts.

Returning to 1 Kgs. 2.8ff., the case of Shimei is a disturbing one, especially because David swore not to harm him. Technically he is not doing so, but he gets his son Solomon to "bring his gray head down with blood to Sheol" (i.e. punish him for his curse by bringing him to a bloody end). Cursing a ruler was a capital offense (cf. Exod. 22.28). Sheol is simply the grave or better the land of the dead, the destiny of all whether good or bad. It is possible that we have here the idea that a curse, once spoken, takes on a life of its own so that the person cursed still is under that cloud until the curse and curser is dealt with.

Thus, David likely thought the curse was still potent and could affect Solomon, unless Shimei was dealt with. Tragically, David dies with his last words being "take revenge." Verse 12 tells us proleptically that Solomon sits on David's throne and his kingdom is established, but this verse should be compared to v. 45. It may be the succession narrative ended at v. 12.

Solomon would not be firmly established before he not only dealt with the problems David enumerated but also with Adonijah. Adonijah, however, makes a fatal mistake by requesting Abishag as a wife. Notice at v. 14 when he approaches Bathsheba he is still confident he should have been king and is thus a dangerous man. He says, "You know that the kingdom is mine, and that all Israel expected me to reign," but he recognizes God's hand in putting Solomon on the throne. Obviously, this was a bitter pill to swallow, being the oldest child. Thus, it seems Adonijah asks for a consolation prize, Abishag as a wife. Her former intimacy with the elderly King David gave Abishag a special status, and no doubt Solomon thought that he would have her for himself, as the new king. To give her to Adonijah might encourage more trouble.

Solomon took the request as an indirect claim on the throne (cf. 2 Sam. 16.21ff.). Bathsheba obviously had not thought of that because she goes through with the request, and Solomon pounces on her like a tiger after being especially gracious to her before. She was given the seat at the right hand of Solomon, the seat of authority and power as the queen mother and would be expected to manage the harem and perhaps to act as an

---

[60] See John Gray, *1 and 2 Kings* (Philadelphia: Westminster, 1971) on this passage.

executive when Solomon was absent. But now in Solomon's mind she seems bent on help-ing Solomon's rival. He is obviously insecure about his new position while rivals still live.

"To ask for Abishag," says Solomon, "one might as well also ask for the kingdom." Thus, Solomon in anger sends out his henchman Benaiah to execute Adonijah. He also banishes Abiathar for being on Adonijah's side, but does not do worse to him, only because he bore the ark and the affliction of David. Joab hears of all this and flees to the horns of the altar. When Benaiah goes to get him, he will not come out saying, "no, I will die here," though he was really thinking, "no, I will be safe, as long as I stay here." Unfortunately, Solomon cleverly proposes to take the man at his word, as if he had decreed his own death sentence, "OK, go kill him there then." Solomon does not even have scruples against kill-ing someone in the holy place, which even Benaiah had stopped short of. The ostensible reason is that Joab had bloodguilt on his hands, but really, he was being killed for backing the wrong horse. Solomon is claiming that by that act, Joab's bloodguilt falls upon his own head, not that of David's family, and peace will come for David's line. Benaiah is then promoted to head of the army.

Then we have the case of Shimei, who, on the technicality of violating his parole, is executed because he went to recover his slaves. Thus, we are told Solomon secured the land by heavy-handed violence, none of which was commanded by Yahweh or a prophet. Here we see the human attempt to grasp autocratic and complete power and, despite Solomon's positive accomplishments, there will be a decided spiritual decline in the court and in Israel as Solomon tries to ape the great secular rulers of the day. This document no doubt would have been written by a court person who had to recount Solomon's good deeds, but it is notable the honesty we find here and elsewhere about a king's true character, even his sin and ruthlessness. Israel from now on will give up more and more democracy and tribal freedom and will no longer have charismatic leaders raised up by Yahweh, in exchange for Solomon and all his material glory. It is doubtful this was an improvement. Solomon knew he was not charismatically endowed by God or raised up by him directly. Thus, he felt he had to resort to human machinations to establish him-self as king. What we have seen thus far demonstrates that the story of Solomon is both interesting and disturbing.

If we were to explore the rest of the Solomonic material in 1 Kgs. 3–11 we would see a man both wise and ruthless. We would see a sometimes competent ruler, yet one willing to encourage syncretism by intermarrying with foreign women, especially royal ones. We would see a man capable of great building projects, of consolidating a nation, but also one willing to spend 13 years building his own house and conscripting his own people almost as slaves in the process. Finally, we would see a king that, despite his early clear Yahwism, who apostatized and is judged for going after false gods and causing the disintegration of Israel as a whole.

Those who only concentrate on the stories of Solomon's wisdom with the Queen of Sheba or the baby of the harlot, fail to see the other and much darker side of this man. Sometimes one wishes to say, will the real Solomon please stand up! David had his sins, even adultery and murder, but there was never a time when he truly and fully apostatized. His major sins were caused by sensuality. In Solomon's case, we see a real lust for power and grandeur even at the cost of enslaving his people, and even at the expense of the nation's original tribal unity and spiritual vitality.

The author of the Solomonic material in chapters 3–11 spends the vast bulk of his time relating the major accomplishments of Solomon, the building of the temple, followed by the building of his own cedar palace (chapters 5–7). It is fair to say that Solomon brought boom times to Israel, but was such a sudden and strong dose of centralized materialism what the nation needed? To be sure, the nation had been developed to its maximum economic potential, but at what cost? It must be remembered that Solomon, unlike his father, was not a warrior. The other empires of Solomon's day were weak, as is shown by the fact that Solomon married an Egyptian princess, probably during the reign of Siamun, toward the end of the decadent twenty-first dynasty. As the Amarna tablets tell us, normally Egypt never gave away its princesses for such political purposes. Since Solomon was not a warrior, he was not taking in a lot of booty. Most of what he got came at a cost in land or goods or political alliances. Despite his shrewdness in trade, Solomon could only finance his major building campaigns through wholesale taxation or forced labor, the dreaded *corvée*, though apparently the Israelites did not have to do the menial jobs but were forced to be overseers.

For the purpose of taxation Solomon divided the nation into tax districts with governors, but the districts did not correspond with the old tribal boundaries at various points. Tribal independence was destroyed, as was the old charismatic form of leadership. Instead of tribes being obligated only to each other and to the covenant with Yahweh, now there were districts with people being obligated directly to the crown and the state. The basis of social obligation became the state instead of the covenant.[61]

Along with the boom also came the beginnings of class stratification, as well as the uprooting of many rural and agricultural people to the city for the building projects. At 9.22 we are told that the Israelites were not reduced to actual slavery, as were the Canaanites during the projects. What, however, was the difference between mandatory labor four months out of the year (5.13ff.) and a temporary form of slavery? It appears too that the northern tribes, who bordered on Hiram's Lebanon, were the ones most often used to fell the trees and bring them south, or at least drag them from the port to which they were floated to Jerusalem. All this, in part, led to revolt and the eventual splitting of the nation into north and south.

Solomon also modernized the army by introducing chariots and building certain military bases at strategic spots (9.19; 10.26), which also took manpower and money. We are told that there were 1,400 chariots, 4,000 horses, and 12,000 men. This did not come cheaply (1 Kgs. 10.26). Solomon's basic foreign policy was to forge diplomatic alliances with Hiram and Egypt. Chapter 3 begins by telling us of the alliance with Egypt. Pharaoh means king, but here it is taken as a name. The Egyptian princess was brought to the city of Jerusalem and later given a palace outside the city. This was surely a purely political alliance. We are told at v. 3 that though Solomon followed God's statutes, nonetheless he sacrificed profusely at the high places. These may have been Yahwistic shrines that were in various places throughout the land but at 11.7 Solomon is said to build a high place for Chemosh.

Perhaps Solomon loved Yahweh, but for good measure honored some of the Canaanite fertility gods. This is certainly the case at chapter 11, though it may be implied here too.

---

[61] J. Bright, *A History of Israel* (3rd edn.; Louisville, KY: Westminster John Knox, 1981), 223.

Solomon had earlier gone to Gibeon (1 Kgs. 9) and had a dream revelation from Yahweh at the shrine there. This story is significant since it means that Solomon may have gone there to consult God for help with his large new task. In any case, God tells Solomon to ask him for what he shall give him. Solomon confesses his inadequacy, though calling himself a little child is overdoing it since in the fortieth year of his reign he had a son, Rehoboam, who did not begin to reign until he himself was 41 (cf. 11.42; 14.21). Nonetheless, Solomon is probably referring to being a boy in this new role and lifestyle, needing guidance and help.

Thus, Solomon wisely asks for neither riches, fame, nor land but discernment, the ability to distinguish between good and evil, an understanding mind to govern the people and adjudicate their problems. Solomon literally asks for a hearing heart or listening heart. The Hebrew word *leb* means in part what we mean by mind (i.e. the center of thought and understanding), but it also refers to the seat of emotion and feelings and will. In short, it refers to the control center of the person. This is freely granted by Yahweh, and because he asks well, even more will be granted. This was a dream, to be sure, but for Solomon it was also a dream which had and would come true. Solomon is so grateful that he goes back to Jerusalem, stands before the ark, and offers both burnt (whole) offerings and peace offerings. He was now endowed for the task.

When we survey all of Solomon's life, we come to see that there is both notability and notoriety. Solomon did have some positive accomplishments, but the way he centralized the nation and divided it up for tax purposes, as well as the way he consolidated his power, were surely contributing factors to the division that befell the promised land shortly after Solomon's death. Solomon did love Yahweh, but he also honored false gods and contributed by his example to the spiritual apostasy which the later prophets constantly condemned.

The Elijah-Elisha Cycle (1 Kgs. 17–2 Kgs. 5)

This segment of OT narrative does not place kings or princes at center stage but rather chronicles the words and deeds of two notable northern prophets – Elijah and Elisha. Their realm of activity was Israel, the northern regions of the promised land, which after the subdivision of the kingdom was distinguished from Judah or Judea, the southern part of the land. 2 Kgs. 1–2 suggests that Elijah's ascension took place shortly after Joram became king of the northern tribes. Elisha seems to have lasted until the time of Jehu, whom Elisha told the school of the prophets to go and anoint (2 Kgs. 9.1). Putting these things together suggests the following chronology:

Northern Kings

Ahab 874–853 BC
Ahaziah 853 BC
Joram 853–841 BC
Jehu 841–814 BC

Northern Prophets

Elijah, active 874 (1 Kgs. 16–7) to 852 BC
Elisha 852–840 (±) BC

If this chronology is reasonably accurate then Elijah arose on the scene about 45–50 years after the death of Solomon. There is no mistaking we are involved here in a very troubled time in the history of the ten northern tribes called Israel. 1 Kgs. 17 tells us that Elijah came from Tishbe in Gilead. Gilead is east of the Jordan and just south of the Sea of Galilee. Elisha we find near Jezreel, which is west of the Jordan, not far from the capital city of Samaria. All the activity recorded in 1 and 2 Kings takes place away from Judean soil and Jerusalem, except for the famous pilgrimage of Elijah to Mt. Horeb (1 Kgs. 19) in which Elijah has to pass through the southern kingdom.

There are basically two sorts of stories in the Elijah material: (1) those that record the prophet's activities that had impact upon political and social matters; and (2) those of a more personal or private nature, such as the story of Elijah and the widow of Zarephath in 1 Kgs. 17. Scholars have tended to see the former stories as more historical and the latter as more legendary, as a form of hagiology, the attempt to venerate the great person by telling mostly fictional tales meant to give praise and enhance his reputation. But the actual character of these various narratives seems basically the same. In both Yahweh is involved, and sometimes miracles happen. And some of the personal stories do not show Elijah in the best possible light, so they could hardly be called examples of gilding the lily. I don't think that sort of division of the Elijah material is really justified or all that helpful. Possibly, oral traditions were passed down from Elijah to Elisha and then written down by the school of the prophets, perhaps after the death of Elisha.

Before examining the stories, edited by some unknown Israelite, one feature of the overall cycle needs to be pointed out. There seems to be an attempt to cast Elijah in the light of Moses. Not only does he go up to Mt. Horeb, another name for Mt. Sinai, and do various dramatic things, but the close of Elijah's life is similarly impressive. The ordeal on Mt. Carmel has some parallels with Moses' duel with the Egyptian magicians, in particular Elijah's challenge of the prophets of Baal is like Moses' rejection of the golden calf. Notice also how Elijah, like Moses, is sustained with bread in the morning and flesh in the evening (1 Kgs. 17.6). Of course, in NT times and even before (cf. Malachi), Elijah was seen by some as the forerunner of the messiah. Whoever put this cycle of stories together saw Elijah as a towering figure that could only be compared to the other giants of the faith like Moses.

Some of the most interesting and moving material in the OT is found in 1 Kgs. 17–19. Elijah comes to the fore in the midst of a religious national crisis. Elijah's name bespeaks his very nature – "Yahweh is my God." 1 Kgs. 17 says there was a major drought in the land due to the spiritual unfaithfulness of Ahab and others. Remember that Baal was both a storm and a fertility god. On the one hand, this drought would test faith in such a god, but it would also drive people to pray to such a god since many believed that he controlled the rains. Apparently, the Canaanites had never entirely been eliminated from the northern part of the land during the conquest, and at this juncture there seem to have been many such pagan people in Israel. Their native religion in many cases would have been some form of Baalism, involving a belief in gods who controlled the crop cycle, the rotation of the yearly seasons, and the fertility and rain necessary to having a harvest.

The next episode begins at 17.17 and here the parallel to the story about Elisha in 2 Kgs. 4 should be given close scrutiny. Apparently, Elijah had taken up lodging in the widow's house. He is still staying well out of Ahab's realm. The widow's son falls seriously ill, and there is almost no breath left in him. At v. 21 Elijah cries out, "Yahweh please let the *nephesh* [not the soul but life or life breath] of this lad come back inside him." Thus, here we have a raising of the dead. The widow no doubt had thought that the prophet had brought down judgment on her house, her son's sickness being some form of punishment for some sin in her or her family's life. Perhaps she thought that invoking a holy god's name in her house, which was not sin-free, occasioned punishment by that god (cf. Amos 6.10). The business of Elijah stretching his body out over the child three times is seen by some as an example of contact magic in which the health of Elijah is conveyed by miraculous transfer to the child. But Elijah had already prayed and it is not likely he is attempting ritual magic. Perhaps this is a typical symbolic prophetic gesture indicating to God, "let this lifeless boy's body be as my lively one is through me or my prayer." Alternatively, this may be an instance of "faith healing." In any case, it is the prayer and not simply the contact that is crucial and effectual for healing, thus making clear the ultimate source of the miracle.

1 Kgs. 18 should be seen as a unit, for both vv. 1–16 and 17ff. focus on the issue of the rain and the need for the drought to be broken. The first half of the chapter provides the setting or preparation for the dramatic conclusion on Mt. Carmel. Carmel seems to have been a Phoenician region prior to David's reign and thus it would not be surprising to find Baalism being practiced there, especially because of its view of the coast and the coming weather patterns off the ocean. Baalism had become so prevalent in Israel that Jezebel was entertaining the prophets of Baal and Asherah at her own table (18.19). This implied clear official and royal support for the cult.

At 18.4 we hear of groups or schools of Yahwistic prophets whom Jezebel had expelled but Obadiah had rescued and hidden in caves. Since there are numerous caves on Mt. Carmel, Gray makes the interesting conjecture that they may have been hidden there. The vast number of prophets may surprise us, but it indicates that Elijah was not alone. He had numerous fellow sufferers. It appears that Ahab and Obadiah were looking for fodder for the royal stables, not for grazing land for the animals of the starving people. Obadiah was a sort of royal chamberlain or chief aide to the king. He meets Elijah and does obeisance to him but will not go and tell Ahab he has found the prophet for he fears the anger of his monarch. Thus, Elijah is forced to make himself known in person. At v. 12 we hear of the *ruach Yahweh* carrying Elijah hither and yon, hiding Elijah from the king. This refers to some sort of supernatural form of transportation or activity. As we have noted earlier in this study, the word *ruach* may mean wind, breath, or spirit of God, and probably here it is the latter. Elijah is not merely being blown from place to place!

At 18.17 we get the confrontation between Elijah and Ahab. Ahab calls Elijah the *oker* of Israel, which seems to mean the hex or troubler. It suggests one who has dabbled in spells and has put a hex on Israel. In truth Ahab has consorted with the powers of darkness; he is the real cause for the hex on Israel. How typical it is to blame the judge who punishes the crime for the problems. The text says Ahab had been serving the Baals (the plural probably indicated several shrines of Baal).

Prophets in this era are called *nebiim* (plural) or a *nabi* (singular). The same term is used both for the prophets of Baal and for Elijah at v. 19. This suggests that there may have been a generally perceived similarity in activity, but it is also true that *nabi* is the technical term for the prophetic office. In both cases, there would have been symbolic acts and singled-minded serving of the one thought to be a god. There are also, however, notable differences. The prophets of Baal not only pray but also slash their wrists, making blood flow. This seems to be a rite of sympathetic magic in which the prophet, by letting the life flow forth from his veins, pleads earnestly for their god to let life flow from the sky in the form of rain. The Ras Shamra texts tell us that Baal was assumed to be in control of the sea and the winter rains. Thus, Mt. Carmel was the perfect spot for a shrine to Baal and for a showdown with Baal's prophets. You could see the sea from Mt. Carmel, as well as coming storms.

Elijah asks the now assembled multitude of Israel, "how long will you hobble on two crutches?" (v. 21), i.e., how long will you half-heartedly hop in the direction of one deity and then another. The metaphor indicates indecision by a wobbling motion or action. The people do not respond to Elijah, for they know his complaint is valid. At v. 22 Elijah indicates how badly he is outnumbered. Surely the 450 prophets of Baal can get help more readily than one Yahwist like Elijah. Throughout this whole confrontation, Elijah will mock the false prophets and their god, sometimes in caustic terms. He also allows them all day to accomplish their mission. In addition, he pours water over his own sacrifice to make it very difficult to light. Yet still Yahweh will be decisively vindicated.

Elijah sets up a clear either/or test. If Yahweh lights the fire, then serve only him: "it will be the god who answers by fire, he is the real god." The people can only respond, "the word is good," i.e., so be it. So, the Baalists take practically the entire day, leaving little time for Elijah and his God to act. At v. 26 we are told they leaped about the altar (*pesah*, to leap or to hobble, as in v. 21, thus we have wordplay). The reason Israel has been hobbled is because she is following lame or hobbling priests of Baal whose whole religion is "lame." At v. 27, when no results are forthcoming Elijah begins to taunt the false prophets and even ridicule Baal: "Call louder, for surely he is a god (and can hear); perhaps he is asleep and needs to be awakened, perhaps he is on a trip or away on business." But as v. 29 makes clear, there is no response, no sound, and nobody paying attention. The time had come for the evening sacrifice and so Elijah tells the people, "draw near to me." Elijah repairs the ruined altar to Yahweh on Mt. Carmel, building it in such a way as to symbolize how Israel and Judah could only be one by offering worship to the one true God. The sacrifice is doused repeatedly with water, so much so that the trench around the altar is overflowing. Then Elijah gives a brief lesson in salvation history, trying to connect Israel to her heritage in the patriarchs. This act will vindicate not only Yahweh but also his servant Elijah. There is a vast difference between Israel's personal God and the impersonal and degrading nature of the god, lifestyle, and rites that go with Baalism.

The *es Yahweh*, the fire of Yahweh, falls from the sky (as lightning) and strikes Elijah's sacrifice. Though this probably involves a natural phenomenon, its timing makes clear the providential source of the event. The Ras Shamra texts include the following words: "Baal will send abundance of his rain ... He will utter his voice in the clouds. He will send his flashing to the earth with lightning."[62] Instead of Baal, however, it is Yahweh who performs such an act.

---

[62] The various Ras Shamra texts mentioned in the previous pages are conveniently cited at length in Gray, *1 and 2 Kings*, at the appropriate chapter and verse.

This makes clear to the people that Yahweh the God of history is also sovereign over nature. It is likely that many Israelites assumed that since Yahweh was a God of history, they would have to seek help elsewhere to deal with problems caused by nature. This story makes clear that Israel could no longer hobble in two directions at once if it really wanted help from the one true God. Elijah, seizing the moment, tells the people to seize the prophets of Baal and kill them down at the riverside.

What then follows is the anecdote about seven trips (the number of perfection) having been made up the mountain by the servant to see if a cloud is coming. Finally, he sees a cloud the size of a human hand. Elijah then tells Ahab to hitch up his chariot and ride for Jezreel, the summer home of the northern kings, otherwise he would get bogged down in the mud. The hand of Yahweh is on Elijah so he needs no chariot; rather, he runs 17 miles aided by the *ruach* of Yahweh (moved by the spirit) and gets to Jezreel ahead of the king. Here then is a magnificent story of the vindication of a true prophet and the true God. But the sequel tells a very different tale, of a discouraged and fearful prophet ready to give up on his calling.

1 Kgs. 19.1–18 is a remarkable, even painfully honest story about a true prophet. Elijah, though he was no loser, indeed he had just had a major victory over the prophets of Baal, was in a tense situation. He had been summoned by Queen Jezebel, an ardent supporter of those prophets of Baal, and she had threatened his life. Elijah knew it was a serious threat, and he became very much unnerved and thus he fled. His fleeing could not be called a strategy to get perspective, rather it was an escape plan. Nevertheless, he needed to get away from the problem, and get to a place where he could hear God's answer to the problem. The text says that Elijah fled to Beersheba, which is to say he fled all the way from northern Israel, through Judea, to the southernmost city in Judea, left his servant there in Beersheba, and went off into the desert to pray.

It is very clear that when Elijah wanted to get away, he wanted to get very far away. But what did he pray for? Elijah was apparently so despondent and depressed that he said to God in essence, "there no profit in being a true prophet. Take my life Lord, I don't deserve to live longer than my ancestors." What had so depressed Elijah that he wanted to lie down and die? He tells us very directly: "I have been very zealous for the Lord and yet the Israelites have rejected your covenant, broken down your altars, and put your prophets to death. I alone am left, and now they are even trying to kill me." Elijah is in effect telling God, "it's you and me against the world and I think we are going to get creamed!"

The prophet Elijah sits under a broom tree in the desert and laments that there are no converts, so he asks to die. Contrast him with the prophet Jonah, who sits under his vine and complains to God *because all of Nineveh is converted*, and he asks to die! It's a wonder how God puts up with his messengers – they're not pleased when things seem to go wrong, and they are still not pleased if God fulfills his word, and things go right.

Despite his depression, however, the narrator suggests that Elijah did the right thing. He prayed to God in his hour of need. Elijah doesn't attempt to end his life, he places it back in the hands of his Maker. It is interesting that at this juncture Elijah is showing all the classic signs of depression – he does not take good care of himself, he has worn himself out with fear, running, failing to eat. At the point of both physical and emotional exhaustion, he prays to God and instead of dying he falls asleep.

One of the more fallacious things one could say about the God of the Bible is that sometimes God does not answer prayers. This actually is false. The assumption behind this statement is that only a "yes" or "affirmative" answer counts as an answer to prayer. But in fact, "no" is just as much an answer to prayer as "yes" is. It is characteristic of the biblical God that he answers prayers not always at the point of one's request, but rather at the point of one's needs, for God knows far better than we humans do what is best for us.

Yahweh knew that the real answer to Elijah's problems and his depression was not to take away his life, but rather to strengthen it – to give him sustenance, support, assurance. These sorts of things can get a person back on the right track. God ministered to Elijah not at the point of his request, but at the point of his actual need. So we are told that first of all one of God's angels provided Elijah with food and drink, reviving him physically so he could in fact take a very long pilgrimage so as to deal with the spiritual and emotional parts of his problem.

Mt. Horeb is indeed the same as Mt. Sinai, where God famously had given Moses the "Ten Words."[63] God knew that the gift of physical food, however miraculously provided, was not enough to minister to all of Elijah's problems. Notice that God does not stop ministering to Elijah until he is truly revived and ready to go again. The *shalom* that comes from God involves the well-being of the whole person.

When Elijah got to Horeb, then it was time to minister to the spiritual part of the problem. Notice how God asks Elijah why he has come to Horeb, as if God is trying to stimulate the conversation. Actually, the point is to get Elijah to open up and share what is bothering him so much. God wanted Elijah to realize what he was actually running from so he could see the real source of his difficulties. As it turns out, Elijah's real problem was his own fears – he was afraid of dying a pointless death at the hands of those who should have respected and listened to him as God's prophet. This is not a surprising concern in an honor and shame culture. Loss of honor could lead to loss of life. Put another way, Elijah was afraid of being publicly shamed and feeling as if he had accomplished little in his ministry. Having named his fear, and unburdened his soul, Elijah was finally ready to hear God's solution to the problem.

There follows one of the great passages in the OT where we learn something very clearly about how the narrator believes that God's will and answers can be found, even in troubling situations. We are told that there was a mighty wind, but that God and his will could not be discerned in the wind. There was also a great earthquake, but again God's design and word could not be read from the earthquake. There was a conflagration, but however dazzling it revealed nothing of God's real nature or will for the situation. Then finally there was a still small voice, a bare whisper like a breath of wind, which one had to be totally still and concentrate on, in order to hear it.

At this juncture, God calls Elijah by name (remembering that his name actually means "Yahweh is my God"), and Elijah wraps his mantle around his head, and goes forth from the cave to an open spot. Notice that the first *direct revelation* involves calling Elijah by his personal name. After all this, God reassured Elijah by saying "you are not alone. There are other true believers around, even where you are ministering. Carry on with the tasks I have given you, and I will provide you with some extra help." The God who revealed

---

[63] On which see pp. 145–54, above.

himself to Elijah on Horeb and called him out of his depression, recommissioned him and assured him of aid in his work; Elijah only learned this not by examining nature or obsessing about his circumstance but by hearing the God-whispered words from the still small voice. Here and elsewhere, as we have seen, God's self-revelation comes almost exclusively as a word that is heard, rather than something that is seen, and indeed a word which should be written down, as this story was.

One of the characteristics of Yahweh is that he reveals himself not merely in deeds, but in words. In other words, the writers of all these books believe in a theology of revelation, a clear articulation, often through a prophet, of God's specific word for his people. In this particular story, we are told that even for a prophet, it is necessary to pay attention to the revealed word of God and not judge things on the basis of appearances, or feelings of fear, or analysis of the situation.

The narrative in 1 Kgs. 19.19ff. shows how Elijah fulfilled the commission to anoint helpers. Elisha is engaged in the community effort to plow the community field. Gray says we have here a story about contact magic. Perhaps, in the mantle of Elijah, the power and office are passed to Elisha (cf. 2 Kgs. 2.14). But if so, this story certainly does not make the idea apparent. The mantle was probably a rough woolen robe of coarse or hairy material. Elisha asks to go and kiss his parents goodbye, and it is difficult to say what Elijah's response means. S. DeVries suggests the translation, "very well, but what have I to do with you," i.e., "if you turn back now I will have nothing to do with you." However, Gray's explanation and translation is more helpful and likely: "Go but remember what I have done to you."[64] The emphasis, in any case, is on the uncompromising nature of the call, i.e., all must be given up to follow Elijah. We are reminded of the NT parallels in the teaching of Jesus about the one who has set his hand to the plow.

In any event, with or without kissing his parents goodbye, Elisha performs a symbolic act of his own by breaking up his former tools of the trade (an ox yoke) and sacrificing the beast he was using to work. This is a clear indication of his intention to break with his past. The feast that is shared binds Elisha in fellowship with Elijah, but also benefits the people of the area; thus, we see Elisha already being a blessing to God's people. He is hereby dedicating himself to a prophetic ministry, though we hear no more of it until the cycle picks up again at 2 Kgs. 2.

In 2 Kgs. 2 we have the climax of the Elijah cycle. Ancient Jewish interpreters were on the right track in noting the parallels here to the end of Moses' life. In both cases, they disappear or at least their tomb is nowhere to be found. It is not accidental that Moses and Elijah appear together at the transfiguration in Mt. 17.1ff. and parallels. Most scholars think this story should be seen as the beginning of the Elisha cycle. At 2.1 we have reference to *the* whirlwind, with the definite article, which suggests the whirlwind well known through oral tradition. Perhaps Elisha senses that Elijah is about to depart from him, so he sticks closely to Elijah, dogging his footsteps. Here we may see prophetic premonition. The prophets at Bethel and elsewhere are also aware of what will transpire. Yahweh has already spread the word.

At 2 Kgs. 2.8 Elijah and Elisha come to the Jordan, and Elijah strikes it with his *adderet* or mantle, a long, loose cloak. Though this is somewhat reminiscent of the Joshua story

---

[64] S. DeVries, *1 Kings* (WBC12; Waco, TX: Word, 1985); Gray, *1 Kings, ad loc.*

of the Jordan crossing, the ultimate prototype must surely be the Red Sea crossing, where the waters divided in two. Once again Elijah is seen as a Moses-like figure, but note that Elisha is also, if to a lesser degree (he has to invoke Yahweh, and the text may imply he struck the water twice, once before speaking and once after). In both stories, as in Joshua, they cross over on dry land, indicating a miracle here. Elijah allows Elisha one last request and he asks for a double dose of "your ruach."

This may seem an excessive request until we recognize that here we have the language of Deut. 21.17 and Elisha is asking for the share an eldest son would have a right to. Elijah is seen as both master and father. Notice that Elisha goes on to say *abi, abi* ("my father, my father") at v. 12. A fiery chariot (*rekeb*) and the horse of fire come to get Elijah. Various commentators have pointed out that the horse is the cult animal of the sun (2 Kgs. 23.11), but it is doubtful that it has much relevance here. What we have is a theophany of sorts. Yahweh's army has come for one of Yahweh's warriors, which indicates his uniqueness. He gets a special ride to the sky (cf. 13.14 by Joash of Elisha). There probably is no comparison between Elijah and the armies of Israel here, comparing his worth to them, for instance. Elisha is just remarking on all he sees happening. After Elijah is taken up, Elisha rends his clothes in a sign of mourning or at least of great loss.

The question that Elisha poses at the Jordan may indicate his loss – "where is the presence of Yahweh now to be found?" The answer is in and with Elisha: "The spirit of Yahweh has come to rest on Elisha." Elisha had requested this of Elijah, but rightly Elijah had indicated that this was a difficult request, and indeed only Yahweh himself could decide upon it. It was not like passing a baton or office from one prophet to the next. Elisha had in fact seen Elijah taken up and knew of the conclusion of his life, and so God sent him his spirit, the conditions having been fulfilled which Elijah had stipulated. Thereafter we hear of the prophetic adventures of Elisha.

The story of Naaman's healing in 2 Kgs. 5 is an intriguing one on several counts. First, the question is, what sort of disease does this Aramean have, leprosy or a less severe skin disease? If it is the latter, then it is understandable how he could still associate with public company. In any event, he is unable to get rid of this bothersome disease. He was looked upon with favor by the king. He hears, by way of a Hebrew maid, of a prophet who could help him. This prophet is said to be in Samaria, presumably in the capital. It has been argued that the word *sara 'at* means a skin disease, something not as serious as leprosy. If he had leprosy, presumably he would have been barred from coming into Samaria (cf. Lev. 13.45ff.). The only problem with this theory is that it appears Gehazi gets leprosy and turns white as snow. Was he more stricken than Naaman had been?

Naaman thus writes the ruler of Israel, thinking perhaps the healing would come through the king or that the prophet was a court prophet, or some such idea. The response of the King of Israel, however, is: "Am I god that I can give death or life?" Possibly the king had made request to Israel's king without any mention of the prophet. Israel's king takes this as a provocation for war. Elisha hears about the king rending his garments and says, "send the man along to me." It is not clear whether he heard the whole story; if not, he supernaturally discerned the rest.

Thus, Naaman comes but notice that he treats Elisha as an inferior, and Elisha treats him in kind, only sending out a messenger to tell him to go take a bath in the muddy Jordan, seven times over. Perhaps Naaman thought to "wow" the prophet, driving up in his 842 model chariot with horses. Naaman is obviously insulted and thinks: "At least the prophet could have come out and pronounced the name of Yahweh over me and waved his hand toward the spot(s) where I have this skin disease." He says to himself, "For this sort of advice I could have stayed home and washed in a cleaner stream in Syria! To a person like me he should have come out." This is clearly a sign that he saw himself as socially superior to Elisha; thus, the prophet had a duty to come out.

But perhaps the prophet is putting the man to the test. Thus, Naaman's servants say, "if the man had asked you to do something hard you would have done it, wouldn't you?" Naaman had expected some sort of magical healing ritual, instead he is sent on a self-help program to go wash away his uncleanness in the Jordan. Verse 14 uses the verb *sub* (became), which means his skin *became* something it had not been before, i.e., his flesh was restored and became like a child's skin, fair and clean. Obviously, the man is impressed and goes back to Elisha and says: "I know there is no God in all the earth but Israel's God." And of course, this is the main *theological* point of so many of these stories from the narrative thought world of Israel, making clear that Yahweh alone is the living God. *There then seems to be a two-pronged focus of these historical narratives – to make clear that Yahweh is the only real God, and to reveal what the character of the living God is, and what sort of relationship he has, or desires to have, with his people.*

Naaman now calls himself Elisha's servant; he is in Elisha's debt and wishes to pay. Naaman offers a *beraka*, a blessing or present, but Elisha refuses, even when pressed (*wayyipsar bo*, "he pressed it on him" or "pressed him"). Then Naaman asks for two mule-loads of the promised land, so he may have holy ground on which to give offerings to the one holy God, Yahweh, and no one else. This transferring of holy soil was a widely known custom in the ANE.[65] But the change in the man is not quite total; he asks for pardon when he has to go to the temple of Rimmon (probably Haddad) with the king and the king leans on his arm and he has to bow down to the pagan idol.

Elisha tells the man to go in peace; apparently, he has understood the man's sincerity and takes his going to the pagan temple as strictly *pro forma* from henceforth. Perhaps he was not yet ready to make a total break and give up his whole occupation or even his life by refusing the king. Gray points out that the cult of Rimmon or Haddad already had monotheistic tendencies in Syria so this may have prepared the way for Naaman to recognize the one true God.

We go from one of the more sublime to one of the most odd stories in the narrative thought world of Israel, found in 1 Kgs. 6.1–7. The sons of the prophets complain that their quarters, where they dwell before Elisha, are too cramped. This, like 4.38, likely refers to where they sat before Elisha, i.e., where he taught them, in which case this text does not indicate that Elisha lived with these prophets even for a time.[66] In point of fact, we find Elisha all over the map. He has a house in Samaria, but also is given quarters on the roof in Shunem (chapter 4), and he is at the Jordan (6.1ff.), and then at Dothan (6.13), and again at Samaria (6.24ff.). Needless to say, he was an early version of the circuit rider.

---

[65] See the examples including a Jewish one in J. A. Montgomery, *The Book of Kings* (London: T&T Clark, 1951), 377.

[66] *Ibid.*, 381.

The decision is made to construct a new building nearer to the Jordan (for cleaning purposes possibly). They were hewing down trees at the Jordan when one prophet lost his iron axe-head in the river waters. This problem seemed worse because the axe-head was borrowed. Elisha asks to see the spot where the axe-head went in; he throws in a stick; the axe-head floats; and the axe-head is retrieved by hand. Perhaps the point of this story was to show the man's faith in the prophet's ability to help, and how that faith was seen to be justified, despite an apparently hopeless situation. The story is true to life in some respects – we know poplar and tamarisk trees could be found by the Jordan and it is believable that the prophets might need larger quarters.

Montgomery calls Elisha's act imitative magic, i.e., he throws the stick into the water just as the axe-head went in, and it reverses the effect of the first act. In any case, the author sees this as a true miracle, i.e., the iron floated. Does God defy gravity for so trivial a matter? Perhaps we should again see this as an act of the prophet using the power God gave him at his own discretion to do a deed of kindness.

The Elijah and Elisha cycles suggest that a prophet could be both a miracle worker and a truth teller. It is brutally honest material that portrays the characters as they were, whether good or bad, helpful or harmful, often without moralizing.

What is significant is that these flawed persons stood for and spoke for God in an age when *they* were the closest representatives to a Moses figure, and the most moral examples that one could find. It was a dark age, but the light of monotheistic faith was kept lit by figures such as Elijah and Elisha. Again, it is a mistake to evaluate these OT figures by later Christian moral standards.

And Then …

While there is a good deal to be gained from examining 1–2 Chronicles as a later redoing of some of the material in the earlier historical books, and while one can clearly see how the later texts have a clearer sense of secondary causes (what is attributed to Yahweh in 1–2 Samuel, 1–2 Kings, is attributed to Satan in places in 1–2 Chronicles) and so a sense of progressive revelation emerges from such a detailed comparison of earlier and later historical narratives. On the whole, 1–2 Chronicles is a rerun. And when we get to the classical prophets like Amos and Hosea and Isaiah and Jeremiah, most of them are not by and large storytellers (however, see Isa. 1–39), though occasionally we get glimpses of, or allusions to, or excerpts from the ongoing dysfunctional story of God's people and their constant need to be called to account by prophets, priests, and kings.

It is not an accident that only indirectly, through sources like Esther, or Ezekiel, or Daniel, do we get some sorts of narratives about the exile of the southern tribes in Babylon, and about the exile to Assyria of God's people in Israel, we really hear almost nothing. The story was perhaps too painful to tell, and one can certainly gather from post-exilic material like Ezra-Nehemiah or Third Isaiah and other sources that the attempt to restore normalcy and jumpstart the story again after the return from exile in about 525 BC was difficult, and it is hard to miss the general sense of discouragement. Gone are the great Davidic kings of earlier eras, or even the not-so-great kings of the south or north, be they like Jereboam or Ahab. The monarchy had fallen, and it could not get up. And the later stories about the Hasmoneans and the Maccabees and the short-lived period of liberation from foreign overlords leading up to Herod the Idumean in the first century BC did not provide the ocular proof that the monarchy, and with it the health of God's people, had been sufficiently restored.

It is then no wonder that early Jews began telling tales of a future king, be he like David the warrior (Ps. Sol. 17–19), or a double messiah, priestly and kingly (Qumran), or an odd Son of Man figure (the Enoch literature, and later 4 Ezra). And it is into *this* environment, where foreign overlords are still looming and yet God's people are still hopeful of deliverance, that Jesus of Nazareth walks onto the stage of human history. It was C. S. Lewis who said that when the author of the play walks onto the stage, the play is over. Not quite, in the case of the appearance of the Son of Man, but he does come to inaugurate the eschatological and divine saving activity of God, once and for all, and to form a people of God that could not merely endure but prevail into eternity. There is great value in taking the pains to assess a variety of the stories in the OT, in regard to its theological content and intent. What we have consistently seen is that only God's character is consistently good, and there is a consistent emphasis on monotheizing in a polytheistic world. Further, we have seen the painful honesty of the narrators about even the most positive of characters in the OT. Even just judged by Mosaic standards, "all have sinned," even God's prophets, priests, and kings all had feet of clay – even Moses and Elijah. Indeed, even the "man after God's own heart" provides us with horrible examples of adultery, murder, and revenge-taking. The OT, however, tells a necessarily incomplete story because it is an ongoing story. The writers of the NT, however, will not merely continue the story, but reassess and reinterpret it in light of the Christ event. We must turn to those stories, as found in the NT, now.

6

The Stars Align in Constellations: The Storied World of the Bible. Part Two[*]

On the one hand, this universe will be seen to have a different *form* from theology, for it has the form of a narrative, or at least of a drama that Paul represents in narrative form – as a story about what God and Christ have done, are doing, and will do in connection with the earthly sphere of the other actors in the story. Paul's theologizing refers to this story and provides argumentative elaborations of it, and for this reason we will often have to work through his theologizing to the symbolic universe it presupposes ... Paradoxically, although theological knowledge is about the knowledge we find in symbolic universes, Paul's theologizing is more important for us than his theology because his theologizing takes place as a form of social relations between himself and other actors in the sphere of their social universe. *His theologizing is a means of securing certain kinds of behavior from the other actors by appealing to their shared symbolic universe.*

Norman Petersen[1]

The unity of NT theology is grounded in the implied master story to which these writings witness.

Frank Matera[2]

Your journey begins with you, but your story, the story you become a part of, already existed before you were born.

Dr. Claybon Lea Jr. at the Baylor Preaching Symposium 2017

There is no debating that when one turns the page from the last verse of Malachi, to the first verse of Matthew one realizes something has dramatically changed. The religious ground under one's feet is shaking, and the stars in the sky seem to be realigning in some ways. It is therefore important that we talk about ...

---

[*] Some of this material is found in an earlier and more detailed form in Witherington, *The Indelible Image*, vol. 2, but it is developed here and modified for a discussion of biblical rather than NT theology.

[1] N. Petersen, *Rediscovering Paul* (Eugene, OR: Wipf and Stock, 2008), 30, emphasis added. I would add to this that we have only the theologizing of Paul in his letters, we do not have a theology in the abstract, as Paul wrote no textbooks that we know of.

[2] Frank Matera, *New Testament Theology: Exploring Diversity and Unity* (Louisville, KY: Westminster John Knox, 2007), 427.

The Shift in the Symbolic Universe and Narrative Thought World

My theory is that a seismic shift in the symbolic universe, for example a re-envisioning of the divine identity of God, leads to a shift in the way the earlier stories in the narrative thought world are viewed, used, and retold. And yes, there was such a seismic shift in the minds of at least some of the earliest Christian writers, especially the more creative ones.

Say what you will about Paul, he could see that the implications of Jesus and the Christ event were far more radical than just minor adjustments in the early Jewish world view, particularly because of the implications of Jesus' death and resurrection. It would appear that some of the Judaizers thought that the coming of Messiah, while it did involve the coming of the end-times, did not mean the coming of a totally new covenant. Either they thought Jer. 31 was about a renewal of the Old Covenant, or they did not think that prophecy yet applied. Paul begged to differ. A new covenant implied a new vision of God's people united in Christ and no longer defined by ethnic, social, or gender particularities (see Gal. 3.28).

Somewhere in between was the view of James that while Gentiles did not need to be circumcised or keep food and other Levitical laws, they did need to avoid pagan idolatry and immorality, which was at the heart of the Ten Commandments (see the decree in Acts 15). It may be that James thought Jewish Christians needed to remain Torah-true, unlike Paul, who saw Torah observance as a blessed option for Jewish Christians, even a missional tactic at times (1 Cor. 9), but not required, even of Jewish Christians. What needs to be noticed here is that some of the differences here have to do with ways of thinking about orthopraxy (how then shall we live) and some have to do with orthodoxy (what shall we believe).

I see no evidence that there were any significant number of early Christians who did not think that the death and resurrection of Jesus was crucial to salvation, and that this did not change some things quite drastically. Certainly, none of the NT writers articulate a vision of things without Christ and the Christ event. *It's just that some had not worked out all the implications of the Christ event to the degree Paul had done. Some had a more converted or changed symbolic universe than others, and those that had the most changed view, not incidentally, had the most creative uses of their pre-existing storied world* (cf. e.g. Gal. 4 and the allegory of Sarah and Hagar).

But we have *no NT writers* that represent the extreme Judaizing point of view – not James, not the author of Matthew, not Jude, not anyone. None of them are suggesting Gentiles must get circumcised and become Jews in order to be full-fledged followers of Jesus. To the contrary, all of these NT writers to a very great degree share a common symbolic universe that has a Christologically reformed shape affecting everything from how they view God to how they view matters eschatological to how they view the people of God to how they view the world. The form of the world was passing away, and the new had already come. All the NT writers are convicted about this and they stand on tiptoe waiting for what is next, especially when Christ returns. They are all forward-looking folks, not dwelling on or in the past. The model I would suggest we consider when it comes to the symbolic universe involves circles – intersecting circles.

This is of course a form of a Venn diagram (see Figure 6.1). In this particular form, what we are dealing with is multiple intersecting circles. Now all of the circles share a considerable amount of overlap in the center. And it will be noticed that the outer limits of

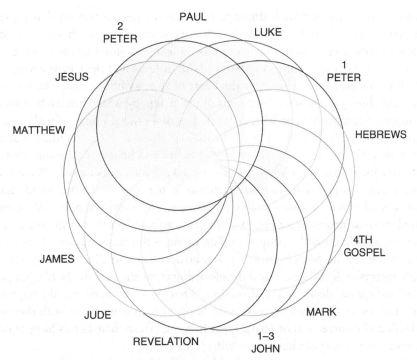

FIGURE 6.1 New Testament Sources and Interrelations

the thought worlds in all cases are not such that one of these witnesses is dramatically out of sync with the others, such that the larger circle of the thought world has a bulge in one direction, ruining the concentric and basically "well-rounded" shape of the larger shared thought world. Because all of the witnesses as we have them are speaking into specific situations, the place where a particular circle is located in the configuration of the whole differs from the other circles.

For example, it will be noticed that the less Hellenized witnesses who are basically addressing Jewish Christians are found at the bottom left of the diagram, from Matthew down to 1–3 John. Jesus is found here as well, though he is addressing Jews on the way to becoming Jewish Christians. Those more in the Pauline orbit, and more clearly focusing on a largely Gentile audience, are found at the upper right of the model from Paul down to Mark, though interestingly the author of Hebrews shares the Pauline perspective but is addressing Hellenized Jewish Christians in Rome. The audience of the Fourth Gospel can be debated, but seems to be Diaspora Jewish Christians by and large. In the case of 2 Peter here finally we have an encyclical to the whole church which reflects influence from both the more Jewish Christian and the more Pauline side of the model. 2 Peter and Paul are at the top of the diagram for a good reason. Here we have the more universalizable form of the NT thought world, a form which could be addressed to Jews or Gentiles equally well.

All of the authors of this material share in common the Hebrew Scriptures, which have prior to their Christian faith formed and furnished their religious symbolic universe and their narrative thought world. This is of course one of the main reasons why there is so much overlap between Jesus and his followers. They share a universe of discourse, though they share a difference in time frame which affects the perspective on that universe. But there is Jesus material, and events in Jesus' story which are also shared in common by these various witnesses as well. The overlap is not simply caused by the sharing of a common sacred text. They also share a common faith in Jesus and the Christ event.

If we ask how we know what is at the heart of their symbolic universe, we can derive an important clue by examining the rituals of the group, by which I mean baptism and the Lord's Supper. Social historians have reminded us of a crucial point – rituals and ceremonies depict and encode at least some of the major values of the community that practices these exercises. We can learn much about the belief and behavior structure that is at the heart of early Judaism and early Christianity by asking such questions as: What is depicted and what is said about rituals like circumcision or baptism on the one hand and what is depicted or said about ceremonies like Passover or the Lord's Supper? What *values* are inculcated by these procedures? For example, it is no accident that both circumcision and Passover are associated with group-founding events – the inauguration of the Abrahamic covenant or the Exodus Sinai events. Nor is it an accident that Christian baptism is associated with aspects of Jesus' death and the cleansing from sin, and the Lord's Supper is also associated with Jesus' death and resurrection. What we see from rituals like baptism is that the Christians believe in *change*/conversion happening in connection with the embracing of the death and resurrection of Jesus. Equally we see from their Lord's Supper ritual that they believe a new covenant has begun with Jesus.

It is also no accident that the talk of real inward spiritual change, of conversion, comes only on the lips of Jesus and his followers. The symbolic universe changes because those who themselves have changed must rethink their world view. Most ancients did not believe in the concept of conversion, not mere resocialization through taking steps like attending synagogue, then accepting food and Sabbath laws, then getting circumcised. Indeed, one is hard pressed to even find stories of such a change either in the OT or early Judaism. The coming of Jesus, his life, his death, his resurrection, the sending of the Spirit, the inbreaking of the divine saving activity, the Dominion of God changed not merely the belief and behavior landscape of some early Jews, it actually changed people, including changing their very capacity to respond to God's initiatives.

Rituals and ceremonies are a form of symbol proclamation, the Word made visible, of the community's most sacred beliefs and values. In the case of both Judaism and Christianity these sorts of rituals and ceremonies are linked to historical and historic events, events configured into a narrative thought world, which led to the foundation of the community in the first place. They are not in the first instances symbols of generic religious experiences. They have to do with historic covenanting acts and foundational redemption events. In this regard, they are very different from various sorts of Greco-Roman religious rituals and ceremonies, including the rites of Isis or the Tauroboleum, or the Dionysian rites, or the Mystery rituals. There is a difference between how rituals and ceremonies function in historically founded and grounded religions and in mythologically grounded ones. But what happens when a meal, or some sort of eating and drinking ceremony, becomes the central symbol of a faith? I use the word "central" advisedly as boundary rituals are one thing, central ceremonies and symbols another. The latter especially allude to the central values and beliefs of a sect or religious group. Meals, perhaps more than any other social event in antiquity, encoded the values of a society, or if it was a sectarian meal, of the sect itself. While we might be prone to calling them rules of etiquette, something Ms. Manners might expostulate on, in antiquity the rules and taboos that applied to meals were serious business. They dictated who would be invited to a meal, where they would sit, what they would eat and the like. Such meals had pecking orders, with the elite guests reclining on the best couches and getting the best food, and the less elite guests further from the head couches and the host of the dinner. As Mary Douglas has put it, if "food is treated as a code, the message it encodes will be found in the pattern of social relations being expressed. The message is about different degrees of hierarchy, inclusion, exclusion, boundaries, and transactions across boundaries ... Food categories encode social events."[3] I would suggest then that we learn a lot about the symbolic universe of the early Christians from examining their rituals, and when we do this we discover that everyone seems to have assumed that the death and resurrection of Jesus was right at the heart of their faith and thought world. It was a given that theology, ethics, and praxis would be done in the light of those central Christological realities. Few were really arguing about or contesting this approach, and when a test or false teaching did arise that touched the Christological core of the faith, such as we see in 2 and 3 John or Jude or 2 Peter, the response was swift and decisive. No challenge to the core values in the symbolic universe was to be allowed.

People who did not believe Jesus was the Christ come in the flesh, died in the flesh, rose again in the flesh, or didn't believe in conversion, or the new eschatological and New Covenant situation would quickly find they were no longer within the bounded circle of the Christian symbolic universe, and were telling the wrong stories, or the right stories wrongly. Sometimes of course people had to be told they were out of bounds, and no doubt some were put out of bounds as well (e.g. Simon Magus in Acts 8 or see 1 Cor. 5). But the fact that we see this boundary-defining kind of behavior in a plethora of the NT witnesses, including by Jesus himself according even to our earliest Gospel, Mark, makes evident that getting the thought world straight was crucial when it came to a variety of theological and ethical and practical subjects. In other words, there was already an incipient sense and form of what would come to be called orthodoxy and orthopraxy in the NT era itself, and it was shared in various significant ways by the authors of these documents. This is not because history is written by the winners. This is because this group of writers represented the full spectrum of the acceptable symbolic universe, and there were no whole Christian communities which represented markedly dissenting voices at this point in time when it came to the core values at the heart of the symbolic universe. There were no Q communities, for example, who focused only on the sayings of Jesus and not his death and resurrection, or Gnostic communities who tried to transmute and syncretize the Jewish substance of the Gospel with Greco-Roman philosophy and other ideas. The latter development would come later in the second century, and the former does not appear to have happened at all.

If we ask the question more particularly of how Jesus' symbolic universe differs from that of his post-Easter followers, several things should be said. Jesus' symbolic universe focuses on the Father, his Dominion and his divine saving eschatological activity happening in and through Jesus' own ministry. While Jesus does have various important things to

---

[3] Mary Douglas, "Deciphering a Meal," in *Implicit Meanings: Selected Essays in Anthropology* (London: Routledge and Kegan Paul, 1975), 249–75, here 249.

say about himself, Jesus' self-understanding is not the only important thing at the absolute center of his thought world, nor is it emphasized as much as these other things just mentioned. Jesus was an early Jew, and of course he does not look back on his own death and resurrection as central to human history in the way his followers do. This is both a matter of temporal perspective but also emphasis. There is also the further issue that Jesus says a lot about Jewish ritual and religious matters (such as the issue of Corban or of gleaning on the Sabbath) which simply does not come up in later Christian discussions, or at least in discussions referred or alluded to in NT documents, so far as we can tell. While it is not improbable that Jewish Christians in Jerusalem continued to talk about these things, their discussions do not appear in the NT. And this brings us to a crucial point.

We can only reconstruct the symbolic universe and narrative thought world of any of these figures with the NT evidence we have, and our evidence is very clearly incomplete. We would love to know what Jesus thought about later issues, for instance the later discussions of spiritual gifts like speaking in tongues, or ethical issues like whether his followers should eat meat offered to idols. Alas, there are many of these sort of issues that Jesus does not address, due in part to the overwhelmingly Jewish context of his ministry. So much of the rest of the NT assumes and addresses a broader audience, or at least an audience no longer (or never) within the orbit of non-Christian Judaism.

The Narrative Thought World of Jesus and the NT Writers

Besides the symbolic universe which the writers of the NT share in common, there is something else they share in common. That universe is drawn up in the context of narratological thinking about life and more specifically about religious life. From the Gospel narratives to the Book of Acts to the stories Paul relies on, to narrative visions of John of Patmos, a storied world is imaged forth by these writers, a storied world which they share in common, though they tell the communal stories somewhat differently depending on the occasion, the audience, and other considerations.

Lest we think that narratological readings of the Bible are something new, Joel Green reminds us that even Israel's first credo took the form of a narrative: "A wandering Aramean was my ancestor" (Deut. 26.5–10). Story is the means by which the meaning of God, and the divine–human encounter, is mainly conveyed from the very first chapter of Genesis.[4] In other words, the Bible itself encourages both the conveying and the reading of its theology and ethics in the context of a narrative. But, as James Dunn has asked, how do we analyze the narratives in and of the sacred text without engaging in a flight from history, by which he means the historical events that stand behind the text?[5]

I agree with Green that an unfortunate choice has often been foisted on students of the Bible – either story or history, either historicity or creativity. But such an either/or is unnecessary. Why not a both/and approach, and particularly one that recognizes the historical character and embeddedness of the grand narrative of the Bible?[6] As Green goes on to point out, recent studies of historical narratives have noticed that they need not be

---

[4] J. B. Green, *Seized by the Truth: Reading the Bible as Scripture* (Nashville, TN: Abingdon, 2007), 165.

[5] J. D. G. Dunn, *Jesus Remembered: Christianity in the Making*, vol. 1 (Grand Rapids, MI: William B. Eerdmans, 2003), 94.

[6] Green, *Seized*, 166.

seen as attempts to create significance through imposing a narrative order and interpretive framework on the messiness of historical events, but the recognition of thematic and causal ties between events in the real world.[7] Green stresses that "Narrative is less about chronicling events and more about drawing out their significance and inviting response. To put it differently, 'narrative' is not just 'story' but also 'action'. Indeed, narration is a particular telling of a story to a particular audience in a particular situation in order to get a particular end. Narrative then is an exercise in influence."[8] He is right that the focus of narrative is not so much on answering the question "Did this happen?" as though the audience were skeptical about the historical substance of the account, but rather on answering the questions "What does this mean?" and "What does it call me to do?" *That is, narrative focuses on answering theological and ethical questions that are the implications of the divine–human encounter.* We have already seen this kind of orientation in the narratives we examined from the OT in the previous chapter. The reader of these stories is invited to enter into such a divine–human encounter, become a part of the ever-flowing stream of God's people, and believe and behave in different ways.

When we turn to the NT itself, it must be admitted from the outset that many of the NT stories are drawn right from the OT, but there are of course the fresh experiences the followers of Jesus had themselves with Jesus and then after the time of Jesus, and these experiences as well become the subject of narratological thinking and storytelling. Without question, eschatological thinking, thinking that history has a purpose, direction, a goal, lends itself quite naturally to narratological thinking about matters of the faith. For one thing, eschatological thinking is forward-looking, believing there will be a resolution to the human dilemma in space and time, and not merely in another world. There is thus a storied world behind the thinking of Jesus and his followers but also a storied world in front of their thinking as well, so to speak.

On first blush, this may not seem as apparent when one is dealing with letters or sermons, but as we shall see, even the theologizing and ethicizing done in those kinds of documents not only presupposes a storied world shared between author and audience, but from time to time those stories are allowed to surface in the discourse, are reshaped and retold for the occasion, and serve as a manner of making theological and ethical points. We must work through some examples from our sources at this juncture.

A few things are immediately apparent from an initial detailed reading through of the NT in comparison to the OT: (1) the Christological emphasis in the material is obvious from Matthew to Revelation, which also means that an eschatological and soteriological emphasis is evident throughout. Salvation takes on a whole new meaning in light of the Christ event; (2) almost as strong an emphasis is placed on the new work of God's eschatological Spirit, and we see this not only throughout a narrative like Acts, but also in our earliest NT documents, the letters of Paul, and this emphasis again and again involves treating the Spirit as both personal, and as distinguishable from the Father and the Son. Here we see in nascent form the beginnings of real Trinitarian thinking long before any church councils, and even before the second century AD; (3) nevertheless, there is no neglect of the heavenly Father, who is called the one God in 1 Cor. 8.6, but the emphasis, especially in

---

[7] *Ibid.*, 167.
[8] *Ibid.*, 168.

John and Paul, is that he should be called Father, and this is so in the first instance because he is the Father of the Lord Jesus Christ. Patrology is not subsumed under the heading of Christology or Pneumatology but continues to have a crucial presence throughout the NT thought world. There are even suggestions of mediation – one comes to the Father through Christ the mediator, but there is also a sense in which one comes to Christ because the Spirit has mediated grace and transformation and new birth making that possible. Salvation becomes something of a team effort, involving Father, Son, and Spirit. And not surprisingly, Jesus himself emphasizes the role of the Father in all these things.

The Storied World of Jesus

It was George Caird who said that Jesus was the starting point and goal of NT theology.[9] He meant this in several ways. For one thing, he meant there is continuity between the Jesus of history and the Christ of faith, and between Jesus and the risen Lord in the thought world of the earliest Christians. He put it this way: "Without the Jesus of history the Christ of faith becomes a Docetic figure, a figment of pious imagination who, like Alice's Cheshire cat, ultimately disappears from view."[10] Unfortunately this happens all too regularly in volumes on biblical theology, which is why we are starting this part of our discussion with an examination of Jesus' narrative thought world, which most certainly influenced that of his earliest followers, who like him were all Torah-loving Jews.

It was Caird's view, and I think he is right, that human experience is the point at which theology is grounded in history. It was the experiencing of the risen Lord or the experiencing of conversion to Christ which led to the Copernican revolution in the thinking of those Jews who became Christians after Easter. Later it was the worshipping of Christ which led to rethinking his significance and how to tell his story.[11] These sorts of things caused the earliest Christians to go back and re-evaluate what the historical Jesus had said and done, and particularly re-evaluate his own teaching. What sort of world view had undergirded and been articulated in Jesus' teaching?

Jesus was without question one of the great sages of all time, and that included being a great storyteller. Whether we consider his original parables or his creative handling of OT stories, he was quite the improviser, to say the least. He lived out of and spoke into a rich, storied world, and he told his own and others' tales in light of the dawning eschatological realities. Not surprisingly his storied world is chiefly populated by OT figures and stories, alluded to, retold, and recycled in various ways, but also his storied world involves the spinning out of new tales, often in the form of parables or visionary remarks ("I saw Satan fall like lightning from the sky"). The function of Jesus' discourse was not merely to inform but also to transform, and that transformation was to involve not merely the audience's symbolic universe but also its behavior, in relationship to God as well as in relationship to each other. In other words, there was both a theological and an ethical thrust to Jesus' teaching. The stories were meant not just to transform the religious imagination of

---

[9] Caird and Hurst, *New Testament Theology*, 346.

[10] Ibid., 347.

[11] On which see the crucial volume by L. Hurtado, *Lord Jesus Christ: Devotion to Jesus in Earliest Christianity* (Grand Rapids, MI: William B. Eerdmans, 2005).

the audience but also to transform their praxis as well, giving them samples and examples of how to believe and behave in the light of the in-breaking Dominion of God.

If there was a difference in thrust in the way Jesus approached the articulation of his eschatological worldview from the way that his predecessor John the Baptizer did, Jesus, even in his more apocalyptic sayings, tended to emphasize the Good News about the coming of the Dominion on earth. "The object of winnowing is not to collect enough chaff to have a glorious bonfire; it is to gather the wheat into the granary; the bonfire is purely incidental."[12] Thus Jesus set about to rescue the perishing and to free Israel from its various forms of bondage. In this, Jesus is not trying to be Israel, any more than the Twelve were set up initially to be Israel. They were all trying to free Israel through a mission of preaching, teaching, and healing. There was, however, urgency and corporate focus to what they did. "The disciples were not evangelistic preachers sent out to save individual souls for some unearthly paradise. They were couriers proclaiming a national emergency and conducting a referendum on a question of national survival."[13] The storm of judgment was looming on the horizon for the Jewish faith centered on Temple, Territory, and Torah. God was intervening in Jesus and his followers before this disaster happened, just as he had already intervened through John the Baptizer. It is this context of social unrest and sense of impending doom that needs to be kept in view when we consider the way Jesus articulates his thought world and the urgency with which it stresses certain things.

This whole line of discussion of course raises the issue of the relationship of Jesus to Israel. I would suggest that Jesus does *not* present himself as Israel, but rather as the Son of Man, and as the Son of Man he is Adam gone right. That is, the scope of his messianic ministry is much broader than just fulfilling the promise of being the ultimate Son of David restoring Israel and her reign in the Holy Land. The temptation scenes make clear that something much broader and more cosmic are at stake – Jesus is tempted as Son of God, not as Israel or Son of David. The issue is what sort of Son of God was Jesus to be? One that comported with his being the true Son of Man of Danielic prophecy, or not?

Jesus of course was speaking to a different audience than his later Christian followers. Every single one of the documents found in the NT is written for Christians, even if in some cases they are written for Christians to use in some form with outsiders. Jesus on the other hand was addressing Jews, even when he was addressing his disciples, and so he was able to *presuppose* the storied world of the OT as something he and his audience shared in common. This perhaps explains why Jesus is able to simply allude to figures like the Queen of the South (Mt. 12.41–42 and par.) or Noah (Mt. 24.36–41), or a widow in Zarephath (see Lk. 4.26) and expect the audience to know who he meant.

It is not a surprise that many of the figures from the past that Jesus speaks of are associated with judgments past and future, including both the Queen of the South and Noah. According to Mt. 12.38–40 and parallels, the only "sign" a wicked generation would get out of Jesus was the sign of Jonah, that reluctant crisis intervention specialist called upon to warn Nineveh of impending disaster if they did not repent. Jonah 3.4 says that the Ninevites were warned that if they did not repent destruction would fall upon them within 40 days. Jesus offers a similar warning in Mk. 13, only the clock is set to 40 years.

[12] Caird and Hurst, *New Testament Theology*, 360.
[13] *Ibid.*, 361.

Luke in his relating of this sort of teaching makes it all the more explicit that Jesus means the destruction of Jerusalem by human armies, namely Roman armies (Lk. 19.41–44; 21.20–24; 23.27–31).

It is interesting, however, that most of the stories that Jesus seems to have told were stories of his own making, stories about contemporaries and contemporary things, such as the coming of God's eschatological saving activity. As you read through even just the narrative parables you find anonymous human figures providing examples of various sorts. Only the parable of the rich man and Lazarus in Lk. 18 presents us with a story about a *named* individual human being.

Even more interesting is the fact that God is portrayed as an actor in various of these parables – he is the owner of the vineyard in Mk. 12 and the forgiving Father in the parable of the prodigal son. Most importantly, we discover that Jesus provides an example of how to do theology and ethics in story form, for these stories are both about divine activity and human responses of various sorts.

There is in addition a dark edge to the stories Jesus tells, when it comes to the evaluation of his own people. By this I mean that they are portrayed as lost (see Lk. 15), and their leaders are portrayed as those who reject God's emissaries the prophets and even his Son (see Mk. 14). The eschatological situation is portrayed as drastic, with all sorts of unexpected persons trying to race through the narrow gate into the Kingdom, while the invited guests have snubbed the host and either refused to come or come late and without the appropriate attire. Pious Jews are going away from temple prayer unjustified whilst tax collectors are being accepted.

There is some sort of drastic reversal of normal expectations happening as the Dominion breaks into human history, and it does not bode well for those who respond negatively to Jesus, it would appear. God is busy vindicating the oppressed, liberating the lost, enfranchising the least and last, and changing the guest list at the messianic banquet. These are stories about the upsetting of a highly stratified world, about the changing of the guard, about new occasions teaching new duties, about both judgment and redemption catching Jews by surprise, and perhaps most of all about the need for repentance by one and all as God's divine saving activity is happening in their midst, and yet many are blind to it.

There is not only a dark edge to the storied world Jesus tells of, there is a strangeness to it as well. Good shepherds don't leave 99 sheep to rescue one straggler. People don't plant a weed like a mustard bush, as it only attracts the wrong sort of birds and attention. God is frankly not like the unjust judge who has to be forced into vindicating the persistent widow, and we could go on. Jesus is offering new perspectives on old images and ideas, and in some cases new perspectives on new vistas and horizons that are coming into view.

N. T. Wright has rightly sensed what is going on in Jesus' ministry, as he says that "the crucial element in his prophetic activity was the story, both implicit and explicit, that he was telling and acting out. It was Israel's story reaching its climax: the long-awaiting moment has arrived! ... To say 'the kingdom of God is at hand' makes sense only when the hearers know 'the story thus far' and are waiting for it to be completed."[14] And precisely

---

[14] N. T. Wright, *Jesus and the Victory of God* (Minneapolis, MN: Fortress Press, 1996), 226. I would say that in fact it is the story of God with a people that is coming to climax and not the story of Israel, which goes on until Christ returns, as Rom. 11 clearly says.

because Jesus is operating in the Jewish ethos of *eretz Israel* he can presuppose a storied world context that most of the writers of the NT cannot presuppose. This may well explain why indeed we don't find parables outside the Gospels. It is because we are no longer speaking into Jesus' specific world, a world where sapiential Jewish thinking, parables and aphorisms with an eschatological twist, made sense. In other words, Jesus' context differs from that of Paul and other NT writers in significant ways, such that Jesus himself and his teaching becomes *transitional* to the new narrative world of the writers of the NT, who do not simply repeat the teaching of Jesus, but rather excerpt it, and build upon it and take it in new directions. As Acts shows, they tell new stories that nonetheless echo older stories both about Jesus, and from the OT itself.

In its own context, then, how would Jesus' articulation of his vision in stories have been heard? Again, Wright helps us by saying that "it would clearly *both* challenge some prevailing assumptions within that Jewish context *and* retain a special focus which would be characteristic only of Jesus' career, not the work of his post-Easter followers. It must be set within Judaism, but as a challenge; it must be the presupposition for the church, but not the blueprint."[15] Just so, and this means that it is crucial to get the balance right between continuity and discontinuity when it comes to assessing the storied world of Jesus and of his post-Easter followers. And again, the point of the parables is to reorder the thinking of Jews: "The parables offer not only information, but challenge; they are stories designed to evoke fresh praxis, to reorder the symbolic world, to break open current understandings and inculcate fresh ones."[16]

A good example to examine closely is the parable of the sower in Mk. 4. Here, as Wright says, we have the revolutionary notion that Jesus is the person who is bringing the story of God's people to a climax in his own ministry. "If we fail to see how profoundly subversive, how almost suicidally dangerous, such a claim was," it is because we have tended to turn Jesus' counter-order wisdom speech into innocuous sermon illustrations.[17] It is right to say that when we are dealing with the narrative parables, we need to follow the narrative logic of the story, not assume that these are thinly veiled allegories of history in detail, much less allegories about Christian virtues. At the same time, there are allegorical elements in Jesus' parables, and especially perhaps this one. Modern distinctions between parable and allegory are not all that helpful when it comes to ancient Jewish storytelling.[18] Who then is the sower in this parable? With most commentators, I agree that it is Jesus, assuming a divine role here of planting God's Word about the Dominion in surprising as well as familiar places.

There are some surprising results of following this narrative logic. For one thing Jesus is not sanguine that most of those who hear him will respond positively in the long term. He is unlike many naïve and overly optimistic preachers of today. But what is perhaps most telling about this parable is that Jesus expects rejection and ephemeral positive responses. He expects too much competition to allow his message to really grow in the hearts of

---

[15] *Ibid.*

[16] *Ibid.*, 229. As we will see in a later chapter, what Jesus says to his disciples is one thing, what he says to non-disciples who are simply continuing in Judaism without following him is another.

[17] *Ibid.*, 235.

[18] On which see Witherington, *Jesus the Sage* and Ben Witherington III, *Jesus the Seer: The Progress of Prophecy* (Minneapolis, MN: Fortress Press, 2014).

many. He expects absolute hard-hearted rejection. And yes, in the good soil he expects good, long-lasting results.

This is an odd message for a person who saw himself in a messianic light, as one who had come to rescue Israel from disaster. In a sense, it is a message about the end of one thought world and the unexpected beginnings of another out of the ashes and remains of the first one. In Jesus' view his world is hell-bent, not heaven-bound, and like John the Baptizer he is here to try and rescue a few of the perishing before the dark night of judgment falls. This parable differs considerably from the one in Mk. 14 about the wicked tenants, as that is a commentary on Jewish leadership in the vineyard, not about the state of the Jewish vineyard in general. Both parables presuppose that things are coming to a climax, and that God's last-ditch efforts to rescue his people are culminating in the ministry of Jesus, who seeks to reclaim God's land, his vineyard before it produces nothing but the grapes of wrath.

With Wright, I think that Mk. 4 and 12 would have been seen as echoing or alluding to Isa. 5–6. In this light, there can be no question but that the vineyard is Israel and Jesus sees himself as fulfilling a prophetic role like Isaiah dealing with hard-of-hearing Israel. But what is most telling when one closely reads Isa. 5–6 together and then thinks of these two parables of Jesus is that already in Isaiah the theme of impending judgment and the exile of God's Jewish people is clear. In this context, the use of parables reflects and indeed presupposes the hard-heartedness of the audience and their refusal to listen. They will not hear and understand unless they turn or repent. Listen as well to some of the Song of the Vineyard: "What more could have been done for my vineyard than I have done for it? When I looked for good grapes, why did it yield only bad? Now I will tell you what I am going to do to my vineyard: I will take away its hedge, and it will be destroyed; I will break down its wall and it will be trampled" (Isa. 5.4–5). The song is really a lament which goes on to bemoan the injustice and bloodshed in Israel.

Here is where I say that this all comports nicely with Jesus' prediction of the demise of the temple and Jerusalem in Mk. 13. In Jesus' view, as his prophetic sign act in the temple showed, Jesus saw this temple as the temple of doom, one that God would judge within a generation. And indeed, exactly one biblical generation after Jesus died in AD 30, the temple fell in Jerusalem to the Romans. Jesus was no false prophet any more than Isaiah was in regard to the demise of Jerusalem and exile in his own era. In light of all this, it is interesting that the later Christian followers of Jesus not only continued to evangelize Jews and see God as promising them much, but, as a text like Rom. 9–11 shows, continued to believe that God, while he might temporarily break off Jews from God's people who did not accept Jesus as their messiah, nonetheless would not replace an unresponsive Jewish people with a more responsive Gentile one. This is only surprising to those who do not know the regular pattern in the OT prophetic oracles of redemption of Israel after and indeed as a result of judgment on Israel (see e.g. Hosea, Amos, and of course Isaiah as well). Perhaps most radically and paradoxically, Jesus was suggesting in Mk. 4 that God's radical rescue of his people would come not by means of military action or a warrior messiah but through the call and response of Jesus' preaching of the Good News, and that of his disciples.

This brings us to the other seed parables in Mk. 4. Jesus seems to think that there will be some "seedy" characters, indeed some characters that Jews would consider "for the birds" (cf. Dan. 4.20–22), in the Dominion to the surprise of the long-time dwellers there. Hence Jesus tells the parable of the mustard seed – a seed no Jewish farmer would ever plant in his garden. While the parable of the mustard seed is a parable of contrast between small beginnings and large, if noxious and surprising, outcomes, it is also a parable that tells us what sorts of persons were going to end up in the vineyard – the wild birds from afar, which should probably be seen as an allusion to Gentiles.

The parable of the seed growing secretly tells us something about the method by which the Dominion is coming – secretly, under the radar, without a lot of human effort and certainly without violence or fanfare.[19] This parable can be fruitfully compared to the parable of the leaven in the dough (Mt. 13.33; Lk. 13.20–21), in that both suggest a sort of automatic process, or process without human aid that produces the result. The hiddenness theme is also evident in the pearl of great price or the treasure in the field stories (Mt. 13.44–46). There are apocalyptic overtones to all these parables as they emerge from a world of opacity, of secrets that require teasing the brain into active thought to figure out, of God producing a crop and a harvest or a treasure as if by sleight of hand. The harvest theme is a dead giveaway that Jesus believed that the eschatological scenario was already in play. And here precisely is where I would differ strongly from Wright. These are not parables about return from exile. If anything, they are parables about the surprising presence of God's saving activity in the midst of occupation and oppression in the Holy Land, a very different message indeed. Jesus did not come to meet the audience's messianic expectations, he came to meet their needs. But ultimately that task could only be consummated through a sacrifice on a cross and its sequel. Redemption would not come on the cheap or even just by a spiritual revival of good preaching accompanied by some miracles. The sin problem would not be dealt with or overcome by those means alone. And this brings us to another crucial point.

Did Jesus tell stories about himself? One could argue that Jesus appears in some of the parables. For example, in Mk. 4 he seems to be the sower and in Mk. 12 it seems clear enough that he is the Son who is rejected, killed, thrown out of the vineyard. We could perhaps also suggest that in the parables of the lost sheep he is the shepherd, or in the parable of the lost coin he is the woman seeking the coin (see Lk. 15). But to be honest, these parables in the main are not about the King Jesus, but rather about the coming of the Kingdom of God. *Jesus' teaching and theology, when it comes to the role of God, is mainly about his Father.*

When Jesus chose to refer to himself, he used a phrase which we do not find in any of the parables – the Son of Man. A close examination of his use of this term shows that at least a good bit of the time he is alluding to the story of that enigmatic "one like a Son of Man" in Dan. 7.13–14, the one who would be given a Kingdom by God and would rule and judge the earth forever, and indeed be worshipped by all nations. This is especially clear in a saying such as we find in Mk. 14.62, but it is also in evidence in other Son of Man sayings, even in the Johannine tradition (cf. Jn. 1.51; 3.31; 8.28). Jesus, it appears, exegeted his own career, purpose, existence, and importance out of various OT stories, and I would suggest this influenced the various Christological hymns his earliest

---

[19] See the discussion in Wright, *Jesus and the Victory of God*, 240–41.

followers created after Easter. The link between the Proclaimer and becoming the One proclaimed becomes clearer when we realize that Jesus also exegeted himself out of the story of Wisdom. This is especially clear in various places in Mt. 11, especially Mt. 11.19, where Jesus calls himself Wisdom directly. Then, too, we must point to a text like Mk. 12.35–37, where Jesus cleverly intimates in his interpretation of Ps. 110 that the messiah is in fact not just David's Son, but even greater than that, he is David's Lord, and in either case he is alluding to himself here. Jesus himself, then, provided the catalyst for interpreting and exegeting his significance out of the prophetic and wisdom literature of early Judaism.[20]

Jesus is not merely telling a story, or carrying a story already in play forward to its logical climax. This becomes ever so clear for example in his yoke saying (Mt. 11.28–30), where it is Jesus' yoke his disciples are to take upon themselves with rigor and vigor, not the yoke of the Mosaic Law. The Mosaic Law, having been fulfilled in the Christ event would not provide the ethical script for all Christian conduct going forward, rather the Law of Christ would. Of course, this would be confusing since some elements of the Mosaic Law would be renewed or reaffirmed or intensified by Christ, for example the Great Commandment. Thus, it would be part of the binding contract known as the New Covenant. But Christ's followers would do these things because they were part of Christ's yoke which he commanded his disciples to take up – called paradoxically a *light burden*. They would not merely continue the story of obedience (and disobedience) of Israel to Moses' Law.

However subversive or paradoxical the later Christian message may have seemed or have been, and however much they may have relied on Jesus' message, even his message about himself, Christian preachers did not by and large follow Jesus' *methodology* of preaching. They told the story straight. Partly this had to do with ethos and social context, since most audiences outside Israel were not well schooled in Jewish sapiential literature. Partly, however, this had to do with the change in symbolic universe from before to after the death and resurrection of Jesus. The proclaimer had become the universally proclaimed, and this was because of the way his life turned out. Apparently, it was felt that the message about a crucified and risen messiah was paradoxical enough in itself, and required enough explaining in itself, so that an evangelistic religion needed to tell the story in a clear and straightforward way. While some of the themes of the Good News song and part of the tune remained the same, the lyrics needed to be less enigmatic and more singularly focused on Jesus himself and his redemptive work.

Here is where I suggest that we can see the modulation of the tune and lyrics best by considering some of the hymn fragments we find in Paul's storied arsenal, and to these we shall soon turn, but we will approach this by looking at the broader contours of Paul's storied world first, and we will see that there is overlap with Jesus' storied world, especially in regard to *abba* and Kingdom language. Paul provides us with the earliest post-Easter examples of the modulations of the tune that Jesus sang.

---

[20] For a full-dress presentation of Jesus' self-understanding see Witherington, *The Christology of Jesus* and see the discussion in Chapter 3, above.

The Storied World of Paul

Because Israel's story speaks of a creator God who claims all people, all lands as his own, Paul is able to reach out from within that story and address Jew and Gentile alike. He thus claims that the story of Jesus fulfills the purpose for which the creator God called Abraham in the first place. Although his telling of the story subverted the narrative world of his Jewish contemporaries, his claim was that it actually reinstated the true sense of the covenant promises.

What had made the difference, clearly, was Jesus; or more fully Jesus and the divine spirit. Paul's theology can, I suggest, be plotted most accurately and fully on the basis that it represents his rethinking, in the light of Jesus and the divine spirit, of the fundamental Jewish beliefs: monotheism ... election, and eschatology. This theology was integrated with the rethought narrative world at every point.

N. T. Wright[21]

This quotation from Tom Wright orients us in the right direction insofar as we seek to answer the question of how Paul dealt with his Jewish thought world once he became a Christian. What it does not do is ask the question about the things Paul derived from his more proximate Christians sources, such as Jerusalem Christians like Peter, James the brother of Jesus and John. We will speak to the latter issue first before considering the former one.

The logical place to start our discussion is by examining Aramaic material found in our sources, as this material must surely go back to Palestinian Christianity, and perhaps back to the earliest Jewish Christian community of all in Jerusalem. Thus, we begin by looking at the use of the term *abba* in two places in Paul's letters – Rom. 8.15 and Gal. 4.6. In both these texts we are told that it is the Holy Spirit in the life of the Christian believer that prompts the invoking of or cry to God as *abba*. It would appear then that Paul is linking the use of *abba* to a form of ecstatic utterance, or at least sees it as an example of the Spirit speaking through the believer.

Yet Paul is addressing non-Palestinian Christians who are doing this praying, certainly including some Gentiles (cf. e.g. Rom. 10.13; Gal. 2.8), and it is very probable that these non-Palestinian non-Jewish Christians did not know Aramaic. Notice too that Rom. 8.15 indicates that *abba* is the common cry or prayer of both Paul and his audience, suggesting its widespread use, even in Rome, where most Christians were likely Gentiles.

The use of *abba* is seen as the sign that the speaker is an heir of God, a joint heir with Christ, a child of God. I would suggest that the reference to being joint heirs with Christ has to do with the fact that Paul knows that Jesus prayed using *abba* and was suggesting that just as this was the cry of the Son who is the heir, so also it is the cry of the sons and daughters who are joint heirs. We discover that Jesus and Paul talk about the Father in the same way. This part of the symbolic world remains unchanged from Jesus to Paul, even to the extent of seeing *abba* as the proper way to address God in prayer.

It is also possible that these texts, especially the Romans text, suggest that the Holy Spirit prompts glossolalia in the form of non-Aramaic speakers addressing God in Aramaic. In fact, Gal. 4.6 indicates that it is the Spirit who is crying *abba*, Father,[22] and this is what

---

[21] N. T. Wright, *The New Testament and the People of God* (Minneapolis, MN: Fortress Press, 1992), 407.

[22] Note, however, that *abba* is clearly translated as Father here, which may suggest that the Gentiles in the audience were told early on the meaning of this word, and in mixed congregations the translation became part of the form of address. It could also be that the translation is not part of the prayer, but in each case is simply Paul's translating of the invocation for his audiences.

Rom. 8.16 suggests as well. Rom. 8.26 may also be about this same phenomenon ("the Spirit intercedes with sighs too deep for words"). In any case, these texts speak of a depth communication with God which suggests a deeply felt intimacy between God and the one who prays. The earliest Christian worship was not only heartfelt, it was Spirit-inspired and probably involved charismatic utterances "in other tongues." The Romans text in particular suggests that it was Jesus, by example and through his mediatorship (joint heirs), who initiated the believer into this sort of filial relationship with God and this sort of prayer language, though now it is the Spirit who enables the believer to pray in this fashion.

Our next Aramaic phrase is found in 1 Cor. 16.22. Here again we seem to have some sort of prayer language in Aramaic. There is debate over whether the original phrase involved just the *marana tha* phrase or whether it was originally *anathema maranatha* in view of v. 22a. However, if, as many think, Rev. 22.20 is a translation and further example of the *marana tha* phrase, then it would seem that *marana tha* stood alone in the prayer (cf. Jude v. 14). How the key phrase is to be translated is in part determined by whether we divide the phrase *marana tha* or *maran atha*. Does the phrase mean "our Lord (has or is) come" or "Come Lord"? In view of the parallels in Rev. 22 and Jude v. 14 it is probably the latter.

The term *mare* of course meant lord, but it is hardly plausible that the term merely means "master" or "respected sir" here. One does not pray to a deceased rabbi or revered master teacher to come! The term here must mean more than lord, more like Lord, with the implication of divinity of some sort. This prayer has not only Christological but also eschatological significance, reflecting not only a belief in Jesus as Lord, but also as a Lord who would return. At a very early date, then, Jewish Christians prayed to Jesus as Lord, but this was not only the language of prayer, it was also the language of the earliest confession.

If we ask how it was that early Jewish Christians came to address Jesus not merely as lord but as Lord, we must consider the confessional fragments found in 1 Cor. 12.3, Rom. 10.9, and especially Phil. 2.11. The confession "Jesus is Lord" was probably one of, if not the earliest Christian confessions, and Phil. 2.11 especially helps us to see what it meant. It meant Jesus is the risen Lord, which is to say this was a brief summary of the story of the risen Jesus, a way of alluding to the whole tale in a shorthand fashion. The title Lord was only appropriate after Jesus had completed his earthly work, including being obedient even unto death on the cross. The hymn in Phil. 2 tells us that the name was bestowed on Jesus by God as a result of the successful completion of his mission. We will say much more about this hymn shortly, but here it is important to remark that we are being told that the name being bestowed on Jesus was God's OT (LXX) name – *kyrios*, Lord, the divine name which is a name above all others. In other words, the earliest confession of Christians was a very high Christological one indeed, and reflecting the church's response to the Easter experiences. But this confession was made without eclipsing or denying that the Father was almighty God and had not resigned his post or been replaced by the Lord Jesus.

1 Cor. 12.3 provides us with a contrast between saying anathema Jesus and "Jesus is Lord." Paul, writing this letter only a little over two decades after Jesus' death, speaks of the confession as something that would be familiar to his Corinthian converts, something that they themselves had probably confessed at conversion. It is the Holy Spirit which

prompts and guides the believer to make a true confession. Only one with the Holy Spirit in his or her life can do so. Again, we have clear evidence that it was only a very high Christological assertion that got one recognized as a Christian, at least in the Pauline communities. At the same time, without the work of the Spirit not only would people not be saved, they wouldn't even be able to make a genuine heartfelt confession of Jesus or the Father.

There were of course many gods and lords in the Greco-Roman world, as Paul admits in 1 Cor. 8.5, but the confession of Jesus as Lord was something different. The Greek and Roman gods or heroes being called *kyrioi* were all either mythological figures or legendary figures from hoary antiquity, whereas Jesus was a historical figure about whom many still had living memory. It is also true that during the first century AD, beginning really with Augustus, many emperors were being divinized, not only after their deaths, but during their lives as well. By the end of the century Domitian felt comfortable insisting that he be called "Deus et Dominus noster" (God and our Lord). It is then possible that the Christian confession was in part an attempt to distinguish the worship of Jesus from emperor worship and other forms of pagan worship. In terms of the Christian storied world, Jesus is seen as the reality of which the Emperor is just the parody.[23]

This particular co-opting of the Emperor's rhetoric or story may also in part explain formulations like "the Lord Jesus Christ," which bears a certain resemblance to "Imperator Caesar Augustus." Notice how in 1 Cor. 12.3 the confession of Jesus is connected with its opposite – cursing Jesus. I suspect the various scholars are right who have suggested that it was not in the first place the study of the OT by early Christians or even the study of Jesus' teachings which prompted this confession but rather the experiences of the risen, and later of the ascended, Lord. Certainly, the *maran atha* confession implies the heavenly position of Christ and his divine ability in due course to come. It was such experiences that led them to search the Scriptures and rethink their understanding of Yahweh and of the role of the Scriptures themselves.

Our third text is Rom. 10.9, which is clearly given in a confessional context. This text is important in several regards. First, we notice how confessing that Jesus is Lord and believing God raised him from the dead are paralleled. This strongly suggests that the confessional formula entailed the proposition *Jesus is the risen Lord*. Secondly, we notice that not just heartfelt belief but confessing with one's lips is in Paul's view instrumental to being saved. We notice here again how the earliest post-Easter Christological discussions seem to have focused on Jesus as Lord. Notice as well that here the connection between the story of the risen Jesus is clearly connected to the confession of him as Lord. This was to become the most paradigmatic of all stories in Paul's storied world.

Rom. 10.9 leads us to examine briefly another text widely regarded as reflecting a primitive confessional formula – Rom. 1.3–4.[24] Here we find two parallel phrases being applied to Jesus: (1) that he was born of the family of David according to the flesh and (2) that he was appointed or installed or vindicated to be Son of God in power according

---

[23] As Tom Wright likes to put it.

[24] For a fuller discussion of this important text see Ben Witherington III, *Paul's Narrative Thought World: The Tapestry of Tragedy and Triumph* (Louisville, KY: Westminster, 1994), 117–19. It is interesting that Paul, Mark, and the speeches of Acts reflect no knowledge that Jesus was born in Bethlehem, and yet all of these sources know of and affirm the claim that he was of Davidic descent.

to the Spirit of holiness by resurrection from the dead. The result of these facts is that he is (3) Jesus Christ our Lord. What is important here is that the story of Jesus' human origins is linked with the story of his divine vindication. This reminds us once more, if we needed a reminder, that in Paul's storied world, as in Jesus' storied world, God is deeply involved and the interaction between the human and the divine on the stage of human history is profound.

Several exegetical notes are necessary at this point. The phrase "in power" likely modifies Son of God, not "appointed." Secondly, the key word *horisthentos* most probably means appointed or installed, not declared. Thirdly, it is possible to interpret the preposition *ek* to mean either by or from the time of (= since). Finally, it is possible to see three clauses here rather than two: (1) "his Son born of the seed of David according to the flesh"; (2) "appointed Son of God in power according to the Spirit of holiness"; (3) "since the resurrection of the dead, Jesus Christ our Lord." The confession then would have three parts, the first having to do with what Jesus was in himself by physical birth and then as a result of the work of God's Spirit in his life after death, and finally what he was to and for believers ever since the resurrection, namely our Lord.[25]

It is clear enough that Paul is not saying Jesus became the Son of God at the resurrection, but that he became Son of God *in power* at that point, having previously been Son of God in weakness. The way the beginning of v. 3 is phrased also suggests that Paul saw Jesus as God's Son already at the point of his physical birth – it was the Son who was born of David's seed. Whether we accept the threefold division of the confession I have suggested or not, it seems clear enough that the text is indicating that Jesus assumed the role of Lord over his followers since (and probably because of) his resurrection from the dead. In other words, *much of Pauline Christology can only be properly explicated in a story or narratival form since we are not dealing with abstract ideas but with events a real historical person was involved in.*

There is a good deal more that could be said about the early prayers and confessions of the first Jewish Christians but we must summarize here the import of this material for a discussion of the storied world of Paul and other of the earliest Christians: (1) it was believed that it was appropriate to pray to or confess Jesus in the same way God was prayed to or confessed; (2) it was believed that it was appropriate to call Jesus, at least after his resurrection, by the title that was used in the LXX of God – *kyrios*. This title denoted a relationship between the believer and Jesus that formerly Jewish believers had only recognized as appropriate to describe the relationship of God and the believer; (3) it was believed that Jesus assumed after his resurrection and ascension a Lordship role that he had not previously undertaken; (4) closely parallel to (3) is the assumption that Jesus was installed (in heaven) as Son of God in power by means of the Spirit and after the resurrection; (5) it was believed that Jesus as Lord would return at some point and this was prayed for; (6) it was believed that the Christian was enabled to be in a relationship to God the Father of the same sort of intimacy that Jesus as a human being had while on earth, such that the Spirit prompted Christians to call God *abba* as Jesus had, and to recognize the filial relationship to God they had which also made them heirs, joint heirs with

---

[25] For the details on this exegesis see Ben Witherington III with D. Hyatt, *Paul's Letter to the Romans: A Socio-Rhetorical Commentary* (Grand Rapids, MI: William B. Eerdmans, 2004).

Christ; (7) it was the Holy Spirit that was said to enable the believer to offer prayers from the heart to God and true confessions from the heart about Jesus to the world. The salvation of humankind was a project that involved the entire Trinity. The relationship with the Father was restored through the death and resurrection of the Son, as implemented and made possible at the experiential level through the ongoing work of the Spirit. But the early Christians not only prayed and confessed they also sang the story of Jesus the mediator of all this. We must now consider these hymn fragments found a variety of places in the NT.

The Christ Hymns Paul and Others Sang

Well before the time of Jesus, early Jews were already singing the praises of God's Wisdom and Word as encapsulated in Torah, as can be seen even in the canonical Psalms (cf. Pss. 1, 119). This praise developed considerably during the intertestamental time to include the praise of the Personification of Wisdom, as is especially clearly seen in texts such as we find in Wis. Sol. 7–8.[26] Thus when we come to the NT hymn fragments we are not dealing with creations out of nothing but with songs that drew on several sources for their material: (1) the OT song book, the Psalms; (2) Wisdom literature and in particular Wisdom hymns; (3) early Christian material about the life, death, and exaltation of Jesus. The story about Jesus was articulated in song long before there were written Gospels, and while it is fair to say that it was not necessarily born in song, it was certainly amplified and proclaimed in song. What I would stress just on the basis of the three points about sources listed above is the creativity in handling Israel's stories and the new Jesus stories and blending them together in various ways. A new storied world was in the process of being born, and we see it in these hymnic texts.

To a large extent Christological storytelling grew out of early Christian experiences of the risen Lord both individually and in corporate worship, as well as out of early Christian reflection upon the Gospel stories and Jesus' traditions. Lest we make too sharp a distinction between the before and after (Easter) factors affecting Christological storytelling, it is important to remember that the earliest Christological prayers, confessions, and hymns were in all likelihood first formulated by some of those who had been a part of Jesus' ministry before Easter and could compare and relate the before and after factors that affected their reflection on and re-envisioning of their Jewish thought world. In general, the material in the hymns about Jesus' death and resurrection seems to draw on the early Gospel source material, while the material about the Son's pre-existence and incarnation draws on the wisdom literature, and finally the material about Jesus' exaltation and roles at the right hand of God tends to draw on the Psalms.

It will be seen from close scrutiny of what follows that the early Christological stories in song had a characteristic "V" pattern chronicling the pre-existence, earthly existence, and exalted heavenly existence of the Son. In short, they were exercises in narrative Christology, tracing the full career of the Son, not just his earthly ministry. What this fuller presentation of Christ involved was discussing his role in creation as well as redemption. That we find these hymn fragments in a variety of sources (Pauline letters, in Hebrews, in the Fourth

---

[26] See my discussion in *Jesus the Sage*, 249–94 and the literature cited there.

Gospel) shows, as Martin Hengel has stressed, that there was a much more unified structure to early Christological thinking done in a variety of Christian communities than some NT scholars are willing to recognize. More to the point for our purposes here we find a clear window into the narrative thought world and symbolic universe of the earliest Christians which demonstrates beyond a shadow of a doubt the enormous amount of shared thought about Jesus and other things of these believers, however little or much they articulated it or exposited about it as they theologized and ethicized into specific situations.[27]

The first hymn for consideration is found in Phil. 2.6–11. This is in some respects the fullest manifestation of the hymnic structure with all three portions of the "V" or perhaps better said "U" pattern manifested.[28] It is characteristic of these hymns that they tend to skip directly from the birth to the death of Christ, focusing on the moments of especial soteriological and Christological importance during Jesus' earthly sojourn (cf. e.g. Rev. 12). We will start with a fresh translation.

[Part I] Who, being in the form of God
Did not consider the having of equality with God
something to take advantage of
But stripped/emptied himself
Taking the form of a servant
Being born in the likeness of human beings
And being found in appearance like a human being
Humbled himself, being obedient to the point of death,
Even death on the cross
[Part II] That is why God has highly exalted him
And gave him the name, the one above all names,
In order that at the name of Jesus
All knees will bend – those in heaven, on earth, and under the earth
And all tongues confess Jesus is LORD
Unto the glory of God the Father.

It should first be said that this hymn is not likely an attempt to contrast Christ with Adam, the latter the disobedient one who grasped at divinity, the former the obedient one who did not. This interpretation is largely based on a dubious rendering of the key term *harpagmos*. Nothing is said here about Jesus making a choice on earth parallel to Adam's choice in the garden. Rather the choice to be a servant was made by the Son in heaven before his human nature was assumed. The language of the last Adam, or about Christ beginning a new race, or about Christ being the first fruits of a new creation by means of resurrection is entirely absent here, indeed even a direct reference to the term resurrection is absent in this hymn. Furthermore, an early Jewish Christian person, being thoroughly monotheistic, would not likely have thought it appropriate to call a human being such as Adam, even the last Adam, *kyrios*. The contrast between being in the form

---

[27] M. Hengel, "Christological Titles in Early Christianity," in *The Messiah: Developments in Earliest Judaism and Christian* (ed. James Charlesworth; Minneapolis, MN: Fortress Press, 2009), 425–48, here 443.

[28] A "U" better represents the notion that Christ came and stayed on earth for a while, he did not merely touch down and then immediately re-ascend into heaven as a "V" might suggest.

of God and becoming in the form of human beings would make little sense if what was being contrasted was two stages in the life of a mere mortal. It is not Adam's tale which is being retold and reformed here, it is the story of God's Wisdom come in the flesh, God's pre-existent Son come in person.

The term *morphē* always signifies an outward form which truly and fully expresses the real being which underlies it. As applied to Christ this means that he not merely appeared to have the form of God but that he had a form that truly manifested the very nature and being of God. This is the reason the further phrase says what it does – Christ had equality with God. He had by right and by nature what God had. In this matter, it is useful to compare the parallel text in 2 Cor. 8.9, where the pre-existent Christ is also said to humble himself and become poor for our sake. What is so important for our purposes is that we are being told that the Son of God is part of both the story of God and the story of humankind. He is not merely the mediator between these two stories, he is an active participant in both stories.

The word *harpagmos* has been the subject of endless debate. Does it refer to something the person has and clutches to himself, or does it refer to something he desires and tries to seize or grab? The clutching interpretation is nearer the mark, but the most probable way to read the word is that it means not taking advantage of something one rightfully already has. The contrasts then between vv. 6b and 7a becomes clear. Christ did not see being equal with God as something he had to take advantage of, rather he stripped himself, which likely means he set aside his rightful divine prerogatives or perhaps his glory in order to be fully and truly human. This need not mean he set his divine nature aside, only that he did not draw on his rightful divine prerogatives while on earth. He took on limitations of time, space, knowledge, power, and mortality while on earth. He did not take on our fallenness, for that is not a God-given or created limitation, not an essential limitation of being human. In fact, Christ went even further, identifying with the lowest sort of human, a slave, a person without any rights. When it says he humbled himself, the term has almost its literal secular sense that he became like a slave, one who must serve all others, one who is obedient even unto death.

The exaltation part of the hymn alludes to Isa. 45.21ff., which says that only God is God and Savior and that one should bow only to God. Christ now is given God's very name and deserves this sort of homage. What we have here is what N. T. Wright calls "Christological monotheism," a form of monotheism which wishes to assert that Christ is part of the divine identity, but without taking away from the glory of the Father and without denying there is only one true God.[29] Nevertheless, when you change the story, it is clear enough that your symbolic world has changed, and something fundamental and basic has changed in the way you view God and the world of reality. For example, whatever it originally meant to confess "the Lord our God is one," once Jesus was viewed as part of the Godhead, it couldn't mean "God has only one personal expression – Yahweh."

The hymn then is divided into two major parts, speaking of what Christ chooses to do (vv. 6–8) and what God has done for him as result of what he did (vv. 9–11). In this hymn, Christ is portrayed not just as a wise man who makes good choices and is rewarded by God in the end, but as God's very Wisdom who comes to earth, is rejected, and yet

---

[29] See N. T. Wright, *The Climax of the Covenant: Christ and the Law in Pauline Theology* (Edinburgh: T&T Clark, 1991), 116.

is exalted by God in the end. Read in light of Wis. Sol. 1–11, or the more general profile of Wisdom or some of the material in Sir. 3 and 11, the text makes good sense. Already here we see a rather explicit Christological affirmation of Christ being part of the divine identity both before and after his earthly career, and presumably during it as well, since the text does not say he gave up his divinity to become human. We shall see that some of these other hymns are no less explicit in their Christological affirmations.

The next hymn is found in Col. 1.15–20 and focuses a good deal more on Christ's role in the work of creation and very little on his role since the resurrection. What we discover about the quotations of these hymns is that Paul and others have adopted and adapted them to serve the specific purposes of the document in which a particular hymn is found. This is the way they theologize out of the shared Christian thought world into specific situations.

[Part I] Who is the image of the invisible God
Firstborn of all creation,
Because in Him were created all things
In the heavens and upon the earth,
The seen and the unseen,
Whether thrones or dominions
Or sovereignties or powers.
Everything [created] through Him was also created for Him.
And He is before everything and everything coheres in Him.
And He is the head of the body, the church.
[Part II] Who is the beginning (source),
The firstborn from the dead,
In order that He might take precedence in all things.
Because in Him is pleased to dwell all the *pleroma*
And through Him is reconciled everything for Him,
Making peace through the blood of his cross
Whether things on earth or in the heavens.

This hymn has a rather clear parallel structure in the two stanzas, especially at the beginning of each stanza. The first stanza is deeply indebted to Wis. of Sol. 6.22–8.1. It is rather clear that the author of this hymn has simply taken various ideas and phrases that were applied to Wisdom in the Wisdom of Solomon and has applied them to the story of Christ's pre-existence, though with certain subtle modifications. Phil. 2 and Col. 1 contain the most similar content of the hymn fragments, though there is no servant discussion in Col. 1, and there is more distinctively non-Pauline vocabulary in the Colossians hymn. It is interesting that the nadir of the "V" pattern in this hymn is not Christ's incarnation or death, but rather the body or church, though Paul goes on to refer to making peace through the blood of the cross. Here as in the Philippians hymn Christ's being the image of God means that he is the exact likeness or representation of God, so much so that it is said that the fullness of God dwells in Christ.

The firstborn terminology is found in each stanza but in neither case should the reference to birth be taken literally. In the first stanza, Christ is said to be the author of all creation, so the term *prototokos* probably doesn't refer to his being created but to his existence prior to all of creation and his precedence and supremacy over it, just as he also precedes all others in the resurrection of the dead.

Verse 16 in fact stresses that Christ created even the supernatural powers and principalities, who all began as good creatures, as did the human race, but then fell, and so with humans are said to need reconciliation to God through Christ. The *Christus victor* idea, or Christ as both creator of and later triumphant over the spiritual beings, is alluded to here.

It seems that the idea of incarnation is already implied in this hymn as it was in the Philippians hymn as well, for the author is saying that the person who hung the stars and created the powers is the same person who died on the cross and was the first to experience a resurrection body and became the reconciler of all things. This is not unthinkable, for already in Sir. 24 we find the idea of the incarnation of Wisdom on earth in the Torah. The new development here is simply the notion of an incarnation of, and in, a person. It is then not true to say that in Jn. 1 for the first time we find the notion of incarnation. It is already at least implicit in Phil. 2 and Col. 1.

Col. 2.9 provides us with the proper commentary on the idea of *pleroma* in this hymn, which says that the whole "fullness" dwells in Christ bodily. This comment is perhaps polemical and meant to counter the idea that there might be a variety of intermediaries between God and humankind, each with a bit of the divine in them. Both here and in Phil. 2, there is a note of universalism at the end of the hymn. In Phil. 2 it is said that all will bend the knee to Christ, but this may mean that some will do so willingly, and some will be forced to recognize Christ's position. Here too the meaning may be that in the end some will experience the *shalom* or peace of being reconciled to God, others will simply be pacified, but in either case all hostilities against God and God's people will cease when the work of salvation is complete. One should compare Wis. Sol. 5.1ff. on all of this. The Colossian hymn emphasizes the cosmic role of Christ in creation and thus implies that he is part of the divine identity even before he became the savior of all higher beings.

Our next hymn fragment, 1 Tim. 3.16, is also found in the Pauline corpus in one of its latest parts and is indeed brief, saying nothing explicitly about pre-existence but rather speaking about the Christ's role on earth and beyond. It reads as follows:

Who was revealed in flesh,
Vindicated by the Spirit,
Seen by angels,
Proclaimed among the nations,
Believed in throughout the world,
Taken up in glory.

The first two lines of the hymn remind us of the statements about Christ in Rom. 1.3–4, but most of the ideas in this hymn fragment can also be found in 1 Pet. 3.18–22. It is not surprising that all the verbs in this particular hymn fragment in 1 Tim. 3.16 are passives, because we have already seen that in the second stanza of the hymn in Phil. 2 we hear of what God does to and for Christ, and the fragment here is decidedly a second stanza, though the verb "revealed" in all likelihood presumes the pre-existence of the one revealed.

It is not clear whether this hymn manifests a clear chronological order, but probably does so, as follows: (1) the first clause alludes to pre-existence and speaks of incarnation; (2) the second refers to Jesus' resurrection by the Holy Spirit (cf. Rom. 1.3–4); (3) the third phrase refers to Christ's ascent to heaven, during which ascent he, according to the early tradition found in 1 Pet. 3, preached to the spirits (i.e. angels) in prison (cf. also 2 Pet. 2.4 and Jude v. 6 – the reference is to the sinning angels referred to in Gen. 6); (4) once exalted to God's side Christ was first preached to the nations and then (5) believed on in the world; (6) which resulted in glory for the Son (cf. how the hymn in Phil. 2 finished on the note of glory). This hymn once again stresses the universal scope of Christ's work, but it also for the first time stresses the role believers play in the finishing of the task of spreading salvation to the world. The allusion to Christ's pre-existence and his glory are the primary portions of the hymn that hint at the divinity of Christ. As we shall see, glory is at the heart of the next hymn fragment.

At this point I am going to take a brief detour from Paul's narrative thought world in order to demonstrate that Paul is not the inventor or only expositor of this Christological story and its thought world. There are others who articulated this same story in equally profound ways, and this strongly makes the point that I have already insisted on – *that there is a large shared symbolic universe and narrative thought world in early Christianity which undergirds the articulated theologies and ethicizing we find in these documents.* Only in the case of the material in Hebrews could we argue that it may reflect the influence of Paul.

The hymnic material we find in Heb. 1.2b–4 includes the entire "V" pattern speaking of the pre-existence, earthly existence, and post-existence of the Son. In the pre-existence portion of the hymn God is the actor, but thereafter Christ is the initiator of the action. A basic translation is as follows:

Whom he appointed heir of all things,
Through whom also he made the aeons (= universe);
Who being the radiance of glory
And the exact representation of his being,
Upholding all things by his powerful word;
Having made purification for sins,
He sat down on the right hand of the Majesty on high,
Having become as much better than the angels as he has,
(He) has inherited a more excellent name in comparison to them.

The hymn fragment is found, as is true of the one found in Jn. 1, as part of the prologue of the document, meant to make clear that God's revelation in his Son was full, final, and definitive in a way that previous revelations were not, and that no other beings, including angels, can compare to God's Son. The Son has more glory, a more excellent name and nature (being the exact representation of God), and he alone has made purification for sins, a major issue in this homily. In the Greek, this fragment is part of one long sentence which stretches from v. 1 to v. 4 and involves alliteration and rhythm not evident in English translations. While the author of Hebrews in the main calls Jesus the Son, in fact in the hymn fragment he is called by no title, and it is striking that in none of the hymn fragments we are examining is Jesus called the Son. Sonship Christology seems to have arisen from some other source or quarter. There are a variety of OT texts being drawn on to compose this hymn (cf. e.g. Deut. 32.43; Ps. 104.4; Ps. 45.6–7; Ps. 110.1; Ps. 2) but it is also clear enough that the author is steeped in later Wisdom material such as that which we find in Wis. Sol. 7–8 and is saying of the Son and his glory what had been previously said of God's Wisdom.[30]

The hymn begins with the affirmation that God had a plan for the redeemer to also be the inheritor of all things, and furthermore to be the agent through whom God created the universe. The theme of the Son as both aide in creation and inheritor of all things is by now familiar. It is the similarity of motifs and concepts in all of these hymns that shows that there was a core set of beliefs about Christ that was widely shared in early Jewish Christianity and was propagated through the use of this hymnic material in various parts of the Diaspora by Paul and others. Not only is the Christ involved in the beginning and end of all things, but he is the one upholding the universe by the word of his power. This is not dissimilar to the notion that in him all things cohere or hold together. In other words, the author does not see the universe as like a watch which God wound up and left to run on its own.

In terms of the Christological story, v. 3a is very important. Here we find two key terms, *apaugasma* and *charakter*. The former can be taken as active or passive in sense but in view of the background in Wis. Sol. 7.25f. it is likely to be active and to mean "effulgence" rather than just "reflection." The difference is that a reflection is like a shadow, but not directly connected to the light source, whereas effulgence suggests a beam coming forth from that light source. The normal referent of the second term is to a stamp or the impression a signet ring leaves on wax or that a stamping device would make on a coin. The meaning would seem to be that the redeemer bears the exact likeness of God's nature. This material is remarkably close to what we have already seen in Col. 1.15–17, though with rearranged clauses.

While the author does not want to lead his audience to call the Redeemer the Father, he does want to make clear the Redeemer is part of the divine identity, is God's final self-expression and exact representation, and is thus higher than any angel in nature. The Son is not merely an act or power of God but a person who is the spitting image of the Father, and so is to be worshipped as no mere angel should be. It may be right, as many have concluded, that this hymn is a rejoinder to those who wished to see Christ as some sort of special angelic being, but it is also possible that our author is stressing that the New Covenant is superior to the one that was mediated by angels, namely the Mosaic covenant (cf. Gal. 3.19; Acts 7.53; Jub. 1.29), because this one is mediated by one of the personal expressions of God, not merely an angel. It is striking that the author withholds the human name of the Redeemer until 2.9, perhaps because he understood that the Redeemer was properly speaking not Jesus until he took on a human nature.

It has been noted by various scholars that there is a closeness between this hymn and the one in Phil. 2 on the matter of Christ's obedience. In Philippians, however, it is discussed as an aspect of his relationship to the Father, while here it is discussed in relationship to the way it benefits the Christian community. The discussion of purification followed by the sitting down of the Son at God's right hand requires a knowledge of sacrificial practices in antiquity. Our author's point is that the purification the Son made was once for all time,

---

[30] It is true that Ps. 2 includes a Sonship motif, but our author's Sonship Christology can hardly be mainly attributed to or drawn from that brief reference.

and so did not require repetition. While other priests had to stand and repeatedly offer sacrifices this priest did the job in such a definitive and final way that he could sit down thereafter (cf. Heb. 10.11–18). Here our author may be drawing on Sir. 24.10, where it is said of Wisdom that she ministered before God in the earthly temple. The author's own distinctive Christological thrusts can be seen and are served here as well, for he wishes to say that Christ is the believers' heavenly high priest even now, and that he is a forever priest, since he is an eternal being. Our author is combining various Christological insights at the end of this hymn, in particular combining the pre-existent Wisdom Christology with the enthronement of the Son at or after the resurrection Christology.

The end of the hymn stresses God's endorsement of what the Son has done. Not only is he given the favored right-hand seat, the side of honor and power next to a ruler, but he is given a divine or throne name as well. This theme of receiving a name is of course also found in Phil. 2, though here in Heb. 1 we are not told explicitly what the name is, only that it is a higher name than angels could have. Notice, however, that here it is a matter of *inheriting* a better name. The concept of a messianic figure not being called such until he has completed his work is found elsewhere in Test. Levi 4.2,3 and 3 En. 12.15. The influence of 1 En. 42 is also possible at the end of this hymn, for in the Enoch text Wisdom takes her seat among, but as one superior to, the angels when she returns from earth to heaven.

This Christological hymn shows how a variety of rich traditions can be drawn on and blended together to present a striking and divine image of God's Son as an eternal being who bears God the Father's exact likeness. It is another example of Christological monotheism, which perhaps receives its ultimate expression in our final hymn text – the prologue in Jn. 1. Equally importantly, it shows how the story of Christ could absorb and transform and transcend other earlier stories.

There are at least four stanzas to the hymn material in Jn. 1 and most scholars would see this material as the apex of the expression of incarnational thinking about Christ in the canon, though we have already seen that the idea of incarnation was likely present in Phil. 2, Col. 1, and Heb. 1, if not also in 1 Timothy. Thus, what we find in this hymn is not a radical departure from what we have already seen in the Christological hymns, but a further development thereof. There are several major themes in this hymn, including: (1) the pre-existent Word (*logos*); (2) the Word and creation; (3) the response of those created (rejection); (4) incarnation and revelation; (5) the response of the faithful community ("we have seen his glory"). The first two stages of the "V" pattern are what this hymn concentrates on (pre-existence and earthly existence). Like the hymn in Heb. 1, the material in Jn. 1 is used to establish at the outset the character and career of the main character of the book. The author of the Fourth Gospel is, however, concerned about where the Word is going as well as where he came from, and indeed especially in this Gospel it is made evident that one cannot truly understand the Christ and his character unless one knows about his divine origins and destiny. In all probability vv. 6–9 on the Baptizer are not an original part of the hymn and so it likely originally read as follows:

In the beginning was the Word
And the Word was with God,
And the Word was God.

He was with God in the beginning.

Through Him all things were made.

Without him nothing came to be.

In him was life,

And this life was the light of humankind.

The light shines in the darkness,

And the darkness has not overcome/understood it.

He was in the world,

And though the world was made by Him,

It did not recognize/respond to Him.

To his own he came.

Yet his own did not receive Him.

But all those who did accept Him,

He empowered to become children of God.

[Verses 12b–13 are the author's explanatory insertion about how one becomes such a child.]

And the Word became flesh,

And dwelt among us.

And we beheld his glory.

The glory of the only begotten Son of the Father,

Full of grace and truth.

It has often been noted that this hymn is indebted to Gen. 1 but less frequently has it been recognized that in fact what this hymn is most indebted to is the sapiential interpretation of Gen. 1 that we find in places like Prov. 3 or Prov. 8.1–9.6. It must also be borne in mind that Torah and Wisdom are seen as interrelated, the former being the consummate expression on earth of the latter according to Wisdom literature (see Sir. 24). One needs to keep in mind also the interplay of Wisdom and Word in the Wisdom of Solomon. The two terms are used in parallel in Wis. Sol. 9.1–2, in 9.10 it is Wisdom that is said to be sent from God's throne by God, and in Wis. Sol. 18.15 we hear that God's "all-powerful Word leaped from heaven, from the royal throne into the midst of the land …" At the very end of this hymn we learn, however, that the Son or Word eclipses this Torah. Interestingly, in Sir. 24.8 Wisdom is said to tent in Israel in Torah. In other words, what has been previously said about Torah as the repository of Wisdom is now being said of Christ. That phrases are being used in this hymn that were familiar in early Judaism can be seen by examining 1QS 11.11: "All things come to pass by his knowledge. He establishes all things by his design, and without Him nothing is done [or made]." The phrase "full of grace and truth" is reminiscent of the Colossian idea of Christ being the *pleroma* or fullness of God, another hint that all of these hymns likely came out of the same sort of situation in life.

The very first verse of the prologue is in some ways the most important verse of it, and indeed of the whole Gospel. The author wants to make clear from the outset that the deeds and words of Jesus, God's Word and Son, are the deeds and words of someone that can be called God, and not a created supernatural being either, for he existed prior to all creation. That he is said to be the *monogenes* Son may mean he is the unique Son, but more probably means that like produces like and that the Son has come forth from the Father sharing the divine identity, not like those other distinct beings who were *made* by the Father and the Word. Jesus then is seen as the natural Son of God while others are the adopted sons and daughters of God through the new birth.

The Word is said to be involved in the whole scope of the divine work. Nothing was created and nothing is saved without him. Light and life are benefits of both the creation and the re-creation that comes from and through the Word. There is great irony in what is said in stanza three, namely that the creatures rejected the one who created them when they rejected his offer of salvation. In fact, the real statement of the incarnation does not come until v. 14, when we are told that the Word took on flesh or reached the human stage. The point is that the Word became more than he was before, *not less*, adding a human nature to his divine identity. There is no emptying language here. As E. Käsemann once said, in this whole Gospel Jesus bestrides the stage of history like a God and there is truth to this claim. While the stay of the Word on earth was of limited duration so that only some saw his glory, nonetheless all have an opportunity to benefit from the Word's coming, all can receive grace and truth at any time by believing. Truth in this Gospel always refers to saving truth, not just accurate information. While Moses and Torah gave accurate information about God's will and plan, the Word gave the ability to perform God's will and truly understand that plan. Though it is a bit of an overstatement, E. D. Freed was basically right when he remarked: "It may not be going too far to say that the writer of the *logos* verses in John has scarcely done more than add the technical term *logos* to a Christology which had already been formulated by Paul and others."[31]

It would appear that the creators of these various hymns were concerned to make clear that the subject being discussed was a *person*, not merely a divine attribute or power of God. In each of these hymns in one way or another whether through reference to death on a cross or making purification for sins, or by reference to flesh, the author makes clear that he is talking about a real human figure who acted on the stage of history. In other words, there was an attempt to guard against these hymns being understood as mere myth-making.

When Jewish Christians composed these hymns, they were looking for and found exalted language from their Jewish heritage that they believed gave adequate expression to their faith in Christ. They found particularly appropriate the use of earlier hymnic material praising God's Wisdom found in places like Prov. 8–9 or Sir. 24 or Wis. Sol. 7–9 to praise Christ. It seems probable that these hymns were first composed in Greek, especially in view of their indebtedness to Wisdom of Solomon, which may mean they arose in the Diaspora, but this is by no means necessarily the case, not least because there were already Greek-speaking Christians that were part of the earliest Jerusalem church, if we are to believe Acts 6–7. In any case, there is no reason to see any of these hymns as reflecting later Gentile thinking about Jesus.

The hymns are thoroughly Jewish in their concepts and phrases, and even in the "V" pattern they are indebted to earlier Jewish literature about Wisdom. The earliest Christians were groping for a way to adequately praise Christ and at the same time not relinquish a belief in the one true God. The early Jewish discussion of the relationship between God and God's Wisdom facilitated this sort of Christological development, and this surely

---

[31] E. D. Freed, "Theological Prelude and the Prologue of John's Gospel," *SJT* 32 (1979): 257–69, here 266.

transpired well before the Gospels were ever written. This in turn reminds us, as we return to the discussion of Paul's storied world, that Paul was not a unique innovator of this sort of complex theological storytelling. Other had gone before him and stood beside him and were doing the same sorts of theologizing.

The Stories Paul Knew and Told

There are myriad other ways to examine Paul's storied world, but of course one of these that is fruitful is to see the way he handles OT stories. Occasionally Paul will retell some of these stories, occasionally they bubble up to the surface in a relatively full form (see e.g. 1 Cor. 10; Gal. 4), but by and large they function as the presupposition, the subtext, of what we actually find in Paul's letters. Like a tune always playing in Paul's head, which occasionally we hear the apostle humming or singing, Paul's storied world provides the music, the harmony, the inspiration of and for his life and thought processes. Just as we might overlook the revealing tune a person was humming, as we walked or talked with them, so in the past many have overlooked this important and revealing dimension of the apostle's thought world.

It needs to be emphasized that this approach to Paul, like this approach to Jesus' thought, does not arise out of the post-modern interest in story and the logic and discourse of narratives, though that is surely in some cases a contributing factor. To the contrary, it arises to a substantial degree out of the recognition that Paul was an ancient person. Neither he nor the other writers of the NT were post-Enlightenment theologians or ethicists or philosophers, and the attempt to reduce their thought world to these sorts of categories is anachronistic. This is not to say that Paul did not use ancient Greek forms of syllogistic logic from time to time (cf. e.g. 1 Cor. 15.12–19), but by and large Paul's logic is a narrative one. It has to do with stories about Adam, Abraham, Moses, Israel, Christ, himself, and Christians. Unless one has a sense of the scope and dimensions of the drama out of which Paul lives and thinks, it is difficult to understand how the individual parts or details of his thought world fit together.

Prior to the rise of narratological studies of Paul it had often been suggested by Pauline scholars that Paul's thought is essentially *ad hoc*, essentially a response to a situation in the life of some church which he finds he must address. It would be closer to correct to say that his theologizing and ethicizing is prompted by *ad hoc* situations, but is being done out of his narrative thought world and symbolic universe which are givens, presupposed.

Here below, in a nutshell, are the formative narratives I see Paul grounded in, reflecting on, and using. *They are five interwoven stories comprising one large drama: (1) the story of God, the one who existed before all worlds and made them; (2) the story of the world gone wrong in Adam; (3) the story of God's people in that world, from Abraham to Moses and beyond; (4) the story of the Jewish messiah, the Christ, which arises out of the story of both humankind and of Israel, but in the first place arises out of the larger story of God as creator and redeemer; (5) the story of Christians, including Paul himself, which arises out of stories (2)–(4).*

The stories of Christ and Christians are in various ways closely knit together, such that they begin to tell the tale of how the world is being set right again. Christ's story is the center in the middle of this narrative tapestry, or to put it another way is the hinge, the crucial turning point, bringing to a climax the previous stories and determining how the rest of the story will play out and turn out. The story of God's own people in effect contracts to that of the Christ, the seed of Abraham when he comes, but expands again to include Christ's followers. Let us consider briefly each story in turn. Storytelling, and getting the story straight, is in order.

It may come as something of a shock to us, but Paul does not spend a good deal of time on "theology" proper in his letters. By this I mean he does not spend nearly as much time as we might expect discussing the one whom he calls God the Father. This is of course in part because, for Paul, Christ is part of the story of God. In fact, Christ is the most crucial part for someone like Paul who is concerned about the salvation of the world, and not merely abstract or philosophical reflections on the creator God of the sort we sometimes find, for example, in Philo. The soteriological and eschatological urgencies dictate in large measure the way Paul deals with the story of God. And it is probably the case that because Protestant theology has been so focused on Paul's letters that a good deal of it has neglected patrology for the sake of Christology, and in the case of non-charismatic, non-Pentecostal Protestant theology pneumatology has been neglected as well.

What then do we know from Paul about God's own story? Firstly, Paul has a very clear understanding that God created the world, created it good, created human beings in that world, made them male and female in the divine image (cf. Rom. 1.19–20; 1 Cor. 11.8–12). As 1 Cor. 11.12 says – all things come from God. Paul is no advocate of two divinities or powers in heaven, no advocate of ontological dualism with a good God and an evil one fighting it out for control of the universe. Nor does he make the mistake, like the later Gnostics, of divorcing God from the creation by making God and spirit good, but matter and the material universe evil or tainted. He is very firmly committed to monotheism, as his adoption and modification of the Shema (the credo of Israel – "Hear O Israel, the Lord our God, the Lord is One") in 1 Cor. 8.5–6 shows. It is just that Paul's understanding of Christ and his activities have caused a re-evaluation of what or who is included in or meant by the term God or Lord.

But it is not just a matter of "in the beginning God ..." for Paul. As Paul says in 1 Cor. 15.28, when all is said and done and when Christ has completed all his tasks after the second coming, "then the Son himself will also be subjected to the one who put all things in subjection under him [cf. Eph. 1.22], so that God may be all in all." Nor is it just a matter for Paul of God the Father having a role at the beginning and at the end of the drama, with Christ and the Spirit doing everything in between. William Paley's watchmaker God who starts things going, winds up the clock, and then lets it tick on its own is not the God of Paul the apostle.

Paul's God is continually involved in the work of creating and sustaining. For example, Paul stresses that it was God who raised Jesus from the dead (1 Cor. 15.15), Jesus did not raise himself. This event in space and time shows that for Paul, God is still working, indeed continually so. Furthermore, the Father is the one who answers prayer, is the one whom the believer (and the Spirit within, prompting the believer) seeks to provide succor or salvation, comfort or consolation (Rom. 8.15). Gal. 4.6 informs us that God is the one who sent the Spirit of his Son into our hearts so that we might cry out *abba*. We also learn that it is God who was in Christ reconciling the world to himself (2 Cor. 5.18–19). Notice the stress that, ultimately, even redemption and reconciliation come from God, not just from

Christ: "All this is from God, who reconciles us to himself through Christ and has given us the ministry of reconciliation" (5.18).

When Paul reflects on his own story as well, he stresses that it was God who had set him apart before his birth and called him by grace and was pleased to reveal his Son in him (Gal. 1.15–16). Much more could be said along these lines, but this will have to suffice. Paul, in the vast majority of the cases in his letters, uses the term *theos* for God the Father, not for Christ or the Trinity, though occasionally, as we shall see shortly (cf. below on Rom. 9.5), Paul is very willing to use the term *theos* of Christ. In Paul's view, God the Father has always been the instigator and sustainer and redeemer and is no absentee landlord in a universe he has left to its own devices. Not only is God continuing to create, sustain, redeem, he is also busy judging (cf. Rom. 1.18), goading and guiding, and answering prayers. The story of the Christ and of the Spirit which is called the Spirit of God or of the Lord (2 Cor. 3.17–18) is to some extent just a subset of the story of the Father. They are both part of the one divine identity. This needs to be borne carefully in mind. Paul believed that he had not given up monotheism when he became a Christian. He believed that his understanding of what monotheism entailed had simply been broadened through his conversion. In our earliest NT writings, the letters of Paul, we already see the beginnings of Trinitarian thinking.

The story of humankind is, in Paul's view, the story of three universals. All live in this present age and are subject to its spiritual and even supernatural wickedness and problems. Indeed, even the creation itself experiences the fall (Rom. 8.19–22). All are sinners, so none can be justified by their works (Rom. 3.23–25). All are subject to death. Outside of Christ, one experiences the unholy trinity of the fallen world, the flesh, and the devil, and that trinity rules in a human being's life. There is only lostness outside of Christ, and a complete inability to save oneself.

But how had humankind come to be in such a drastic and dark state of affairs if God had in fact created all things good? Paul's answer is to tell the story of Adam. It is interesting that we do not find Paul saying much about original righteousness or the pre-fallen condition. He focuses on the world as he finds it since Adam, the world whose form is passing away (1 Cor. 7.31), and Adam is only brought into the discussion to explain the present malaise (Rom. 5.12–21; 2 Cor. 11.3). Of course, Paul knows the story of man created from the dust and given a natural life-animating principle (1 Cor. 15.47–48) and the story of being created in the image of God with Eve originally coming forth from Adam, but man coming forth from woman ever since (1 Cor. 11.7–12). Paul does not say more about this precisely because his audience doesn't live in that world any longer. They live in a world of dark shadows of disease, decay, death, and the devil. To be sure humankind is not as bad as it could be – the image of God has been defaced, but not erased, not entirely lost. The point, however, is that humankind has fallen and cannot get up on its own. Salvation is not for Paul a human self-help program.

What is of prime importance to Paul about the story of Adam and Eve is the effect they have had on the rest of the race. Paul mainly holds Adam responsible for the fall (Rom. 5.12; 1 Cor. 15.21–22); as for Eve, she was deceived (2 Cor. 11.2). Paul believes that the story of Adam and Eve is more than a personal tragedy, their story is representative and affects the entire human race. The original couple not only committed the original sin but as a result of the curse placed on them which affected the whole race, the inclination and the determination was present to go and do likewise. Paul concludes, "just as sin came into the world through one man, and death came through sin, so death spread to all *because all have sinned*" (Rom. 5.12). The race is like their representatives in their tragedy.

One of Paul's most creative moves in telling the story of human fallenness is found in Rom. 7.7–13. He tells the story in the midst of commenting on the Law. It appears Paul thought that the original sin was a violation of the tenth commandment, the one against coveting. In Rom. 7.7–13, Paul is dealing with the paradox that while God's command-ments are certainly all good, yet human beings would not have known what transgression fully amounts to had there not been commandments – "I would not have known what it is to covet if the law had not said, 'You shall not covet'."

For dramatic purposes, Paul has chosen to retell the tale of Adam in the first person and has chosen to personify Sin as the snake. One can then read Rom. 7.8–11 as follows: "But the serpent [sin], seizing an opportunity in the commandment, produced in me all kinds of covetousness … But I [Adam] was once alive apart from the Law, but when the com-mandment]singular] came, sin sprang to life and I died, and the very commandment that promised life proved to be death to me. For sin [the serpent] seizing an opportunity in the commandment, deceived me and through it killed me." Here is the by now familiar primeval tale of life apart from sin, then comes a commandment, deception, disobedience, and ensuing death.

There are strong reasons for reading Rom. 7.7–13 in this fashion: (1) in vv. 7–8 there is reference to one specific commandment, called *the* commandment in v. 8, and Adam was only given one; (2) v. 9 says, "I was living once apart from the Law," but certainly the only persons Paul believed lived both before or apart from any law are Adam and Eve; (3) in v. 11 sin is certainly personified as a living thing that seized an opportunity and deceived a human being. This is surely the tale of Eve and Adam and the snake; (4) the same verb used for deception here is the one used to speak directly about Eve being deceived in the garden in 2 Cor. 11.3; (5) in v. 7 Paul says sin was not known except through the com-mandment. But everyone since Adam has had personal or experiential knowledge of sin. The view that best makes sense of all the nuances of Rom. 7.7–13 is that Paul is reflecting back on the primeval story of Adam and how human sin and fallenness began.

If Rom. 7.7–13, which involves all past tense verbs, is about Adam, whose story is told in Rom. 7.14–25, where we find present tense verbs? I would suggest that it is a dramatic presentation of the present fallenness of all humanity who followed in Adam's footsteps, with perhaps the story told primarily from the point of view of a Jewish person outside of Christ or even a person at the point of conversion and under conviction of sin, recog-nizing his bondage. Paul has prepared for this discussion earlier in Rom. 5.12, where he explained that not only did sin enter the world through Adam, but that all humanity went on to sin as well, both Jews and Gentiles. Indeed, as Rom. 2.9 says, judgment for sin will begin with the household of God. Rom. 5.17 says sin and death came to reign over all humankind, and Rom. 6.17 says those outside Christ are slaves to sin, unable to avoid sin or escape its bondage.

It must be stressed once again that the context of the discussion found in Rom. 7.14–25 is the discussion of the Law. Notice the important statements that prepare for this section in Rom. 7.5–6, where Paul speaks of what believers were in the past in the flesh, and what they have now been made in Christ (v. 6). Believers have been released from the Law, as the analogy with the death of the husband makes clear. One is no longer under its jurisdiction, no longer obligated to it. Notice too how in Rom. 8.8–9 Paul uses the phrase "in the flesh," just as he did in Rom. 7.5–6 to characterize what *was* true of a person before they became a Christian. Yet the person described in Rom. 7.14–25 is said to be fleshly and sold under sin (v. 14) and cries out for deliverance. This is not a person who is free in Christ.

I have discussed elsewhere in detail who Paul sees the "I" to be in Rom. 7.14–25, considering all of the major options,[32] and there are really only two that make sense of the context of Rom. 7.14–25. Paul may be discussing the Jew who knows and strives to obey the Law, but the Jew as now seen by Paul with twenty-twenty hindsight and Christian insight. This person knows the Law of God is good, but his fallen nature leads him to do what he ought not to do. The other possibility is that Paul is describing the plight of any person outside of Christ who is under conviction, having heard God's Word, in particular his Law, and yet is still in the bondage to sin. It must be borne in mind that Paul had earlier said in Rom. 2.14–15 that the essence of what the Law requires is written on Gentile hearts. Thus Rom. 7.14–25 would describe the person under conviction of sin and crying out for redemption, and Rom. 8.1–15 would be the response of God to this cry and the description of the transformation that happens once one is in Christ.

Notice that Rom. 8.1–10 not only makes clear that the verdict of no condemnation has been pronounced but that the Spirit has entered the person's life and has set him free from the bondage to sin. The spirit of slavery has been replaced by the spirit of adoption, and what this Spirit prompts the person to say is not "Who will deliver me from the body of this death" but "Abba Father" (contrast 7.24 and 8.15). Paul is of course not saying that believers instantly become perfect or are not still tempted to sin after conversion. The point is that while the temptation to sin remains, it no longer reigns (see 1 Cor. 10.13, "no temptation has overcome you …"). But in fact, having taken a journey through Rom. 7–8, we have given a preview of coming attractions. We have gotten ahead of the story and shown where it is leading. The next story after the story of Adam that is crucial in Paul's narrative thought world is the story of Abraham.

It comes as something of a shock that Paul, the former Pharisee, while devoting a great deal of time and space to the discussion of Abraham and his story (cf. Gal. 3.6–18; 4.21–31; Rom. 4; 9.6–15; 11.1), gives Moses far less ink. For Paul, Abraham is the critical example of faith prior to the coming of Christ. Gal. 3.8 puts it this way: "And the scripture, foreseeing that God would set right the Gentiles by faith, declared the Gospel beforehand to Abraham." Abraham is the prototype or exemplar of Christian faith because he heard the first preaching of the Good News about righteousness by faith and he responded appropriately.[33] Abraham thus is seen as the ancestor of both Jew and Gentile. Even Gentiles share the faith of Abraham (Rom. 4.16) and become, with Jewish Christians, his heirs and the beneficiary of the promises given to him through Christ (Gal. 3.14). This is only appropriate since Abraham began life as a pagan.

As is true with all the stories of the Hebrew Scriptures, Paul looks at the story of Abraham through Christological, eschatological, and to a lesser degree ecclesiological

---

[32] See the commentary in Witherington, *Paul's Letter to the Romans*.
[33] One could even argue that Abraham received credit for righteousness after and as a result of believing the promise.

glasses. The elements in the stories that he stresses are those most germane for his Christian audience. Yet what Paul omits from his discussion (the sacrifice of Isaac, the Sodom and Gomorrah story, the entertainment of angels, the Melchizedek incident) is as telling as what he includes. Paul's concern is to show that Abraham is a paradigm and a paragon of faith, and that the promises to him are fulfilled in his seed Christ and by that means to those who are in Christ. In part this means that one of the most crucial aspects of the Abraham material is its chronology.

It is crucial not only that Abraham is already promised many offspring in Gen. 12.2–3, but also that God's covenant with him is already initiated in Gen. 15. The most crucial remark is, "And he believed/trusted God and it was reckoned to him as righteousness" (15.6). All of this transpires *prior* to any discussion about circumcision as a covenant sign, which appears in Gen. 17. Note also that the discussion of Hagar and Sarah does not show up until after Gen. 15.6 (see Gen. 16 and 21.8–21). This order of events allows Paul to appeal to God's original dealings with Abraham over against any later institution of circumcision, whether Abrahamic or Mosaic. This leads to conclusions like we find in Rom. 4.11–12 – circumcision is only the seal or sign of a righteousness or right-standing that Abraham had *already obtained* through faith in God. Paul also sees this order of events as implying that Abraham can be the father of Gentile believers as well as Jewish ones, for like them he believed without having already been circumcised and he was accepted on this basis (see Rom. 4.1). But is he also the forefather of all believers according to the flesh? One could argue either way. On the one hand, clearly Paul is emphasizing that people who believe the Gospel are the heirs of Abraham by faith. On the other hand, Abraham started life as a pagan living in Ur before God called him, and so he could even be said to be the forefather after the flesh of Gentiles (by birth) and Jews (by circumcision). In any case, there is a further corollary. Not all of Abraham's physical descendants are true children of God, for it is not the children of the flesh but those of the promise who are true descendants, whether they are Gentiles or Jews (Rom. 9.6–7).

The paradigmatic character of Abraham comes to the fore in a text like Rom. 4.23–24. Abraham is Exhibit A of relating to God on the proper basis of eschatological faith: "Now the words 'it was reckoned to him' were not written for his sake alone, but for ours also. It will be reckoned to us who believe in him who raised Jesus our Lord from the dead."[34] It needs to be stressed that of course this is not just any story but a scriptural story, and as such it provides a normative model for the people of the Book. Abraham is not merely analogous to Christians, he is their scriptural model or prototype.[35]

The story of Abraham takes a surprising turn in Gal. 3.16, where, in a *tour de force* argument, Paul will maintain that the term "seed" in the Abraham story refers in particular to Christ. Wright is correct to repeatedly stress the twists in the tale that Paul administers to his foundational Jewish stories.[36] Gen. 17.6–7 seems to lie in the background here. It is this version of the promise to Abraham that refers to the fact that kings will come from

---

[34] The term "Jesus" rather than "Christ" is used here probably to punctuate that it was a human being who was raised by God, albeit a very special and unique one.

[35] See S. Fowl, *The Story of Christ in the Ethics of Paul* (Sheffield: JSOT Press, 1990), 94. Notice as well that it is Abraham's faith that is reckoned as Abraham's righteousness. Nothing is said about Christ's righteousness being imputed to him. On this subject see below.

[36] Wright, *The New Testament and the People of God*, 405–9.

Abraham, and it is this version that also says the covenant is between God and Abraham and his offspring. Rom. 9.6–7 shows that Paul knows quite well that "seed" is a collective noun, but the larger context of Gen. 17 has provided Paul with the legitimate opportunity to talk about the most important Jewish king that was to be the descendant of Abraham. What we learn from this discussion is that in fact Paul sees the risen Christ as, like God, an inclusive personality, one in whom many can abide or dwell. Christ is the seed, and believers in Christ are also that seed if they are in him. They become heirs through being *in* the seed who is Christ. "Seed" then in Gal. 3.16 has both a particular and a collective sense (Christ and those in him), just as it did in the case of Abraham (Isaac and subsequent descendants are promised). What this means is that if Gal. 3 is read carefully in light of the larger context of Gen. 17, if one hears the intertextual echo, then Paul in the end is not guilty of exegetical legerdemain here.

Of crucial importance for understanding Paul's narrative thought world is the connection mapped out between the Abrahamic and New Covenants in Gal. 3–4. The Abrahamic covenant is seen as being fulfilled in Christ, and thus the covenant which he began is the consummation of the Abrahamic one. Both covenants involved both the circumcised and the uncircumcised. From Paul's perspective, circumcision is not the essential thing, faith is, for Gen. 15 precedes Gen. 17. Both covenants involve children given by the grace of God, both involve an everlasting covenant, both have to do with the fact that in this context all the nations of the earth will be blessed (see Gen. 17.6).

In terms of the narrative flow of Paul's thought, the cost of closely linking the Abrahamic and the New Covenant is high. It means that for Paul the Mosaic covenant must be seen as an *interim* arrangement, a parenthesis between the promises given to Abraham and the promises fulfilled in Christ. This of course would not mean that the Mosaic Law was a bad thing, just a temporary one, a temporary guardian or childminder to keep God's people in line until Messiah should come.

When Paul thinks of Adam he thinks of the entire story of sin and the Fall, when he thinks of Abraham he thinks of faith and the promises that went with it, but when he thinks of Moses, he thinks of the Law, and in particular the Law as something given *pro tempore*. Nowhere is this more evident than in Gal. 3–4, though Romans suggests the same thing.[37] Because Paul thinks Christologically about the timeline of salvation history, when Christ came the situation in regard to the Law and God's people also changed: "But when the fullness of time had come, God sent forth his Son, born under the Law, in order to redeem those under the Law, so that we might receive *adoption* as children" (Gal. 4.5). The Mosaic Law is not seen as opposed to the promises nor as annulling the Abrahamic covenant (Gal. 3.17–21), it was simply given for different times and purposes. Notice the language of adoption as well. Both Jew and Gentile need *adoption* to be part of the New Covenant, and furthermore Jews need to be redeemed out from under the Mosaic law covenant.

Perhaps Paul makes clearest his views on the Mosaic covenant in 2 Cor. 3. We have here a retelling of the story of Moses' visit to Mt. Sinai, and if one does not know this story, one will not understand the nuances of Paul's interpretive moves here. 2 Cor. 3 can also be

---

[37] See the more detailed substantiation of this line of argument in my *Grace in Galatia: A Commentary on Paul's Letter to the Galatians* (Grand Rapids, MI: William B. Eerdmans, 1998), 197–341.

said to be a tale of two ministries of two called servants of God (Moses and Paul), which leads to comments on two covenants, the Mosaic one and the new one. This tale is clearly not about the Hebrew Scriptures themselves, nor is Paul suggesting we should adopt a particular hermeneutic here – spiritual vs. literal – in the interpretation of the text. Nor is Paul pitting the written word (here written in stone because the Ten Commandments are meant) against the Spirit or even the spoken word. Rather, he is comparing and contrasting ministries and the covenants on behalf of which these two ministries were undertaken.[38]

Moses ascended Mt. Sinai and came back down with the Ten Words, trailing clouds of glory. The Ten Commandments, like the Law as a whole, was seen by Paul as holy, just, good, and even spiritual (Rom. 7.12,14). Paul in no way disputes that the Law came attended with splendor. The fact is, however, that its glory or splendor and that of Moses have been eclipsed by the greater splendor of Christ and the New Covenant. Thus, not only the glory on Moses' face but the Mosaic covenant itself is being annulled (2 Cor. 3.11). Unfortunately, though the intent and purpose was otherwise, the direct *effect* of the Law on fallen human beings was death-dealing rather than life-giving. The problem with the Law was that it could not give life, it could not enable one to obey it, which meant it could not but condemn fallen human behavior over and over again. What was to be done about this?

The crucial verb in 2 Cor. 3.7, 11,13,14 is *katargeō*. Twenty-one of the 27 NT uses of this verb are found in the Pauline corpus, and in other Pauline texts the word *always* refers to something replaced, invalidated, abolished, not merely something that is faded. The deliberate contrast between the ministry of life and that of death in 2 Cor. 3 strongly suggests we must interpret the verb similarly here. The coming of the glorious Christ has put even former glories in the shade, in effect making them obsolete. Paul's argument is one grounded in his reading of the way salvation history has progressed. It is not about human attitudes or approaches toward the Law, nor is the Law itself seen as defective. The defect lies in fallen human beings. The effect of the Law on such fallen ones is contrasted with the effect of the Spirit on them. The written code kills, the Spirit gives life. Gal. 3.19 then makes clear that a change of guides or guardians was needed. The Law was only until Christ came.

Thus, once again, as was true when Moses came on the scene, the story of humankind takes a decisive new turn when Christ comes on the scene. Yet Christ himself came on the scene, like Moses coming down from the mountain, trailing clouds of glory. Ironically enough though, Christ chose to leave his glory behind in order to fully take on the human form, indeed the form of a servant among human beings. The story of the Christ, the plot of his career, is most ably and nobly summed up in the Christological hymn material found in Phil. 2.5–11, which we have already discussed.

Here it is important to stress that Phil. 2.5 does deliberately draw a parallel between the frame of mind and decision making of the pre-existent Son of God, and that of Christians. This exalted piece of theological discourse has an ethical function meant to produce the imitation of Christ in and by believers. Christ deliberately stepped down, he deliberately did not draw on his divine prerogatives, he deliberately took a lower place, he deliberately

---

[38] I am taking a quite different line here from Hays, *Echoes of Scripture in the Letters of Paul*, who does think hermeneutics is at issue in this passage.

submitted even to death on the cross. Of course, the analogy drawn here between the behavior of Christ and that of Christians is just that – an analogy. But it is a potent one.

The essence of the analogy is that believers ought to follow Christ's self-sacrificial life style so others may benefit. The first half of the hymn has a paraenetic thrust. It may also be that the second half hints that God will do for the believer what he has already done for Christ – provide a resurrection, saying "come up higher brother or sister" and the like. The crucified conqueror's story is to be recapitulated in the life of his followers, as Paul himself was in various ways experiencing.

It is in this same letter Paul says "I want to know Christ and the power of his resurrection and the sharing in common of his sufferings by becoming like him in his death, if somehow I might attain the resurrection of the dead" (Phil. 3.10–11). Paul mentions this not least because he sees himself as modeling Christ so that his converts will do likewise. This is made very clear in 3.14–17, where Paul pleads directly "Brothers and sisters join in imitating me" (cf. 1 Cor. 11.1). The context must be remembered, however. This is not hubris, it is the modeling a good teacher was expected to do. Paul is not claiming to be *the* pattern, only a good example of how one follows the Christ pattern.

Paul assumes that the gift of right-standing with God is the platform or basis for exhorting his charges to Christ-likeness and promising them the completion of the process if they remain faithful to the end. To "gain Christ" (3.8) is not merely to gain right-standing with God, it is to gain full Christ-likeness at the resurrection (3.10–11). It is thus the human career of Christ, beginning with the taking on of the form of a servant and continuing on through death and resurrection, which is said to be analogous to the plot of the story of Christians. Christ not only stripped himself but also shunned any rightful human accolades or dignity, taking on the form of a servant or slave. How very differently he lived than most ancient persons, caught up in honor challenges and striving for more public recognition. Yet in the end he was honored.

Christ's story is the crucial *hinge* story in the whole human drama which indicates how the story will end.[39] Paul is able to retell this story in many other creative forms (see e.g. Col. 1.15–20), but the essence of the story is the same in each case. It is about a pre-existent divine Son of God who stooped to conquer. The means of triumph was not just taking on the form of a servant, but also dying a slave's death on the cross, and then being vindicated by God through the resurrection (cf. Rom. 1.3–4). This story has in fact a sequel, involving the return of Christ to earth once more. This in turn means that the follower of Christ must live between the advents, keeping one eye on each horizon. There is an "already and not yet" character to the story of Christ, and so to the story of his followers. As we draw to a close our discussion of Paul's narrative thought world, the thought world which undergirds and guides all of his exegesis, ethical remarks, and theologizing, we will look briefly at Paul's telling of the story of Christians.

Paul is interested in the entire story of humankind from beginning to end. When he reaches the climax of the story, the story of Christ, it is notable that he focuses overwhelmingly on the end of the Christ story – the death and resurrection, though the coming and true humanity are also emphasized. Paul's gospel about Christ is a passion and resurrection narrative with a short introduction, whereas the Gospels themselves, while spending

---

[39] Wright, *The New Testament and the People of God*, 406–7.

about a third of their extent on the passion and resurrection, have much more about the life and ministry of Jesus.

Yet Paul also does not neglect the cosmic origins and ends of the story, not least because the latter has direct effect on the believer's story now. If it is true that Christ has led super-natural captivity captive (Eph. 4.8), and believers are no longer in the thrall of demons (though they may still be pestered or persecuted by such foes), then Christians need to know this and not live as those without hope or help.

The story of humankind was narrowed down to the story of God's chosen people, in the persons of Abraham and Moses and their successors, which in turn was further nar-rowed down to the story of the Jewish messiah, the Christ, and thereafter the story widens again to embrace the story of those who are in the Christ, and of course this includes Paul himself, who believed that his own story had been radically changed through a Damascus Road encounter with the Christ. A much-neglected text in the study of Paul's conversion is 2 Cor. 4, particularly 4.6. Here we find a partial citation of Gen. 1 that refers to God making light to shine out of darkness. Paul wishes, however, to connect the text with the fact that "Christ has shone in our hearts to give the light of the knowledge of the glory of God in the face of Christ." What Paul is saying is that conversion is the beginning of a whole new world for the convert. He or she becomes a new creature, or part of a new crea-tion. This new world of illumination dawned on Paul on Damascus Road when he saw the risen Lord, or as he puts it here, he saw the very presence, the very glory of God in the shape of the face of Jesus. The new creation then is very much like the first one, a matter of God "calling into being the things that do not exist" (Rom. 4.17b). This implies a radical departure from the past, a truly new and fresh start. The emphasis is on discontinuity with the past. While it may be in part that Paul is envisioning here his story in terms of the story of the first Adam (see above), it is clear enough that he envisions it even more in terms of the story of the last Adam – the one who gave up much and took the form of a servant.

This is very much how Paul sees himself, as is clear from an autobiographical text like Phil. 3.4–10, and it is not an accident that Paul tells his own tale here with echoes of the way he had told the story of Christ in Phil. 2. Paul's status and standing and prerogatives in Judaism were considerable, and he was advancing in it well beyond his peers, as he tells us in Gal. 1. He was on the way up, not on the way to become a servant among human beings. Yet as a Christian, Paul is prepared to count all of that as in the loss column in comparison to the surpassing privilege of knowing and being known by Christ and being conformed to his image. Thus Paul, in a text like Gal. 6.15, is clearly able to distinguish between the things that once mattered greatly to him, such as whether one was circum-cised or not (cf. Phil. 3.5), and the things that now matter – namely the new creation. As R. N. Longenecker has rightly stressed, Paul is not just talking about re-creation, but a new creation, with an emphasis on the word *new*.[40] This comports with the fact that Paul is not simply talking about a *renewed* covenant either, but rather a new one which eclipses, brings to closure, and in various senses fulfills or completes the old ones and the whole process of God's covenanting with his people.

1 Cor. 5.17 of course describes the fact that when a person is in Christ they are a new creature. Among other things, this changed dramatically Paul's view of Jesus. Whereas

---

[40] R. N. Longenecker, *Galatians* (Grand Rapids, MI: Zondervan, 2015), 296.

formerly he evaluated Jesus from a fallen and worldly point of view, he certainly does so no longer. Yet it would be a mistake to think that Paul sees conversion as only involving a trans-valuation of values and attitudes about various matters. He believes that conversion also entails a change in one's spiritual makeup. One's life becomes christoform in shape.

It is not an accident that one of Paul's favorite descriptions of himself is servant (Phil. 1.1; Rom. 1.1). Paul's story is analogous to that of Christ and is modeled on it. But this is not just a matter of imitating Christ, it is also a matter of being conformed to the image of Christ by God. Thus, Paul speaks of suffering the sufferings of Christ in 2 Cor. 1.5. In Paul's view, the trajectory of his own life is much like that of his Master. Paul's hope is to be completely conformed to Christ's image by means of obtaining a resurrection like his. It can be added as well that Paul does not just draw on the pattern of Christ's life for his ethical and theological exhortations, he also from time to time draws on Christ's actual teachings as well for these purposes (see Rom. 12–15; 1 Cor. 7).

It appears quite likely, in view of 1 Cor. 15.8–9, that what was being said about Paul is that his transformation from persecutor of the church to apostle of Christ was something that happened with unnatural haste. Early Jews were used to persons becoming proselytes to Judaism gradually, after first having been inquirers or God-fearers for a period of time. Paul by contrast seemed to have had a sudden change of character. Ancient persons were naturally suspicious of claims about people changing their nature or character, for character was seen as innate, something one was born with, and then manifested over the course of one's life. It is thus not surprising if some were calling Paul an *ektroma*, and therefore someone unfit to be or be called an apostle of Jesus due to his persecuting activities (15.8–9). An *ektroma* was a miscarriage, perhaps due to having a stillborn or due to an abortion, in short, a child rushed prematurely into the world. The image is connected here by Paul with his being last to see the risen Lord. The implication would seem to be that had this not happened quickly, it might not have happened at all.

It is not clear whether Paul just means that people saw his conversion as something that happened too suddenly, with ungodly haste, or that they also saw his sudden adoption of an apostolic role as also too hasty. It may also be that Paul means that the appearance he received from the Lord happened out of due season, indeed apparently well after the other appearances to judge from Acts, and so had it not happened as it did, out of due season, it would not have happened at all. In any case, it is clear that both Paul and his critics saw him as unworthy to be an apostle. But it wasn't a matter of worth or works, it was a matter of grace.

Being born a new creature in midlife was of course no easy thing, as it meant giving up much that one had worked for and loved. It meant in one sense dying to one's past and being born again. Paul spoke for himself and other Christians when he says in Rom. 6.2–4 that conversion means a being buried with Christ in baptism, being baptized into his death, and so beginning to be put into the story of Christ. The heart of the creed for Paul was that Christ died for our sins according to the Scriptures, was buried, and was raised on the third day (1 Cor. 15.3–5). Interestingly, this becomes the heart of his description by means of analogy of what happens and will happen to Christians in Rom. 6.2–4.

Just as Christ died for sins, so believers die to sin (6.2). Just as Christ was buried, so the believer has been buried with Christ in his death (6.4), and just as Christ has been raised, so too the believer can now walk in the Spirit, walk in newness of life and look forward to their own future bodily resurrection. Of a similar sort is what is said in Col. 2.6–11. When Paul refers to the circumcision of Christ in 2.9 is he referring just to what happened to Christ or also to what happens in general to the believer in Christ? The believer is raised together with Christ "through faith in the effective working of God who raised him from the dead." Christ's story is efficacious for the believer when by analogy it is recapitulated in that believer such that they go from being dead in trespasses to being made alive in him. What Christ has done *for* the believer on the cross and in the resurrection is the basis of what he later does *in* the believer. Christians experience Christ-likeness in the Spirit only because Christ himself first experienced death and resurrection.

The story of Paul's and other's Christian lives does not stop at the point of right-standing by grace through faith, though a text such as Gal. 2.15–21 makes clear that this is the crucial beginning point.[41] One must go on to work out one's salvation with fear and trembling, one must go on to grow in grace and in holiness. One must consciously choose to walk in the Spirit and not indulge the works of the flesh (Gal. 5). One must have a sense of the already, but also of the not yet of one's Christian existence – suspended between new birth and new body, between inner renewal and outer decay.

The two crucial things remaining to be said about the Christian's story are that one should not expect to be exempt from suffering in this life, since Christ and his apostles were not, and secondly one must have a clear vision that Christ's history is the believer's destiny. This is precisely what Paul has in mind when he talks in 1 Cor. 15 about the believers being the latter fruit of a crop of resurrection persons of which Christ was the first fruit. This is also what he has in mind when he speaks of believers being destined in advance to be conformed to the glorious resurrected image of God's Son (Rom. 8.29). The moral conforming is happening now, the physical conforming later.

Thus, Paul himself sees his life as a pilgrimage toward resurrection: "I want to know Christ and the power of his resurrection and the sharing of his sufferings by becoming like him in his death, if somehow I may attain the resurrection of the dead" (Phil. 3.10–11). Paul knows this latter will not happen before the Lord returns. This means that the present is a time for striving and pressing on toward the goal. Every Christian, like Paul should have the honesty to admit "not that I have already obtained this or have already reached the goal; but I press on to make it my own, because Christ Jesus has made me his own" (Phil. 3.12). This sounds neither like eternal security nor eternal optimism of the wrong sort, but rather a quiet confidence and assurance that one is headed toward the desired goal, but there are miles to go before one sleeps in the Lord, and so one must make every effort to press onward. What the Gospel promises is not "eternal security" in this life, but rather "the assurance of things hoped for and a conviction about things not seen" that we press on toward.

The mark on, and of, the Christian is the mark of Christ. A Christian belongs to Christ and imitates his Master and is spiritually conformed to the image of that Master. This involves both tragedy and triumph, sorrow and joy. The words of William Penn would have been heartily endorsed by Paul as a description of the Christ-like life: "no pain, no palm, no thorns not throne, no gall, no glory, no cross, no crown," and indeed no final resolution until the author of all these stories brings down the curtain himself on the

---

[41] See Witherington, *Grace in Galatia*, 169–94.

human drama in the person of his Son when he returns. Then the human story, the story of Israel, the story of Christians will be finally and fully gathered up into the story of Christ, and every knee shall bow and every tongue confess, whether willingly or unwillingly, that Jesus Christ is Lord, and the glory will be to the Father, whose story began this discussion.

This retelling of Paul's fundamental stories leads to the conclusion that there is still much to be learned about Paul from such an analysis. For now, it is sufficient to say that Paul lived in and out of a storied world, and his thought cannot be understood apart from these foundational narratives. Not surprisingly the one story by which Paul exegetes all the others is the story of Christ, *which is not a story in the OT, but a retelling of the kerygma of the early church. This is one reason why intertextual studies will not in the end alone suffice to plumb the depths of Paul's thought world.*[42]

I also doubt that we can confine Paul's thought world to the story of Israel or insist that Israel's story is *the* central one for him. Paul spends next to no time on the story of David, and the Davidic character of Christ, and much more time on the Adam/Last Adam tandem. He spends more time on Abraham than on Moses, which is to say on the forefather of Israel, but not on Israel proper as it came forth from Egypt and became a people called Israel at Sinai. When Paul does focus on Moses and the Law in Galatians and in 2 Cor. 3 the discussion is more about obsolescence than fulfillment, more about the newness of the new ministry than its continuity with the old, more about the surpassing glory than the fading glory. For Paul, all humankind stands not between Sinai and the Promised Land, or between exile and return to old Jerusalem, but between Adam and the eschatological Adam and must live out of the story of one or the other of these Adams and their respective stories. The center of Paul's story is Christological, not ecclesiological or "Israelogical" if we may coin a term, or more broadly the center of Paul's story is theocentric – focusing on God's redeeming work in human history, including the might acts of Yahweh, Christ, and the Spirit. My reading of Paul's narrative thought world differs considerably from Wright's, even in its most recent iterations.[43] For now it must be said that he needs to heed the strong stress on Christocentric and more broadly theocentric universalism in Paul's thought rather than on the Israelogical or Israelocentric character of that thought.

We cannot understand Paul the exegete, or for that matter Paul the ethicist or theologian, unless we have clearly in mind the sort of synopsis of Paul's narrative thought world we have just briefly presented. These stories are sacred stories taken from the Hebrew Scriptures and from the Christian tradition. Yet the old, old stories have been reconfigured in the light of the Christ story. Paul's hermeneutic is both theocentric in terms of its guiding force and aim, and also ecclesiocentric in terms of its scope and application. Christ is the hermeneutical key to a right reading of the Scriptures, the church is the primary audience for hearing this rereading. Thus, Paul reads the sacred traditions through the eyes of the Christ primarily for the sake of the Christian community and its edification. A few illustrations of Paul's use of the OT stories for Christian purposes is in order.

---

[42] This in no way is to diminish the importance of intertextual studies but to explain the right framework in which they bear fruit. What they show is that the NT writers were mainly not exegeting the OT when they used it nor striving for metalepsis assuming their audience knew the OT by heart, but rather were using it in homiletical ways to make their own points about the Christ story and the subsequent eschatological situation. See my *Isaiah Old and New*; *Psalms Old and New*; and *Torah Old and New*.

[43] On which see Ben Witherington III, *Paul and the Faithfulness of God* (Minneapolis, MN: Fortress Press, 2013).

It probably does not need to be said, but Paul sees all of the Hebrew Scriptures, including the Law, as God's Word, and therefore profitable for learning and teaching. Even the ritual law (cf. 1 Cor. 9.8–9) has lessons for the Christian. Paul believed it was crucial to know where God's people were in the working out of the story of salvation history, that is beyond the era of the Law and under the reign of Christ, if they are to properly understand the significance of Scripture for them. While they are not under the Mosaic covenant, they are under the guidance of the Scriptures which are fulfilled in the messianic age. More often than we might realize, Paul the pastor is busy using and applying the text in creative ways, rather than simply interpreting the text. In other words, he is engaging in what has been called a *pesher*, or contemporizing of the text, a skill he may have learned in part while he was a Pharisee.

In his magisterial study of the intertextual echoes of the Hebrew Scriptures in Paul's letters, R. B. Hays has shown in detail that even when Paul is not formally quoting Scripture he is often alluding to it, and occasionally relying on echoes to conjure up the larger whole of the particular OT context.[44] If we take into account not only the formal quotations but also the allusions to the OT we quickly discover what a crucial role Scripture played in forming Paul's thought world and symbolic universe. Yet of course this mental furniture underwent some drastic rearrangement and reconceptualization when Paul accepted the story of the crucified and risen one. He sees both the Father and the Spirit through the lens of his new Christological understanding of Jesus. Remember that we noted how the writers of the NT, grounded in Jesus' own way of viewing things, saw the Father through the eyes of the Son.

There is indeed a sense in which Paul sees the whole of the Hebrew Scriptures as a giant repository of largely prophetic texts that have some key lessons to teach Christians. Even seemingly unpromising texts like Deut. 25.4 can, in the hands of the master applier of the Word, be seen to teach us something about God's ways with his New Covenant people (see 1 Cor. 9.8–12). The principle of analogy brings the text to life again and again because Paul assumes it is the same God, operating in the same ways, in his own day as in OT times. *The form of the community has changed, but the character of God and God's ways with humankind have not.* Yet we must be able to distinguish, as Paul himself does, between the original meaning of the text, and its larger significance and relevance to the eschatological community of God's people in Christ. As a representative example of Paul's use of the principle of analogy and the rhetorical device known as *synkrisis* or historical comparison, let us consider for a moment the typological use of Scripture we find in 1 Cor. 10.1–13. Paul believes fervently that the things that happened to God's people in OT times really happened, they are not cunningly devised fables, and furthermore he believes that at least part of the reason various of these things happened and were recorded in Scripture was as "types" for the Christian community. There is a strong sense in which Paul would claim that the Hebrew Scriptures is the book of and for Jews and Gentiles united in Christ, intended especially for the instruction, edification, and exhortation of that eschatological community. This is because he sees the whole as to some degree a prophetic corpus. It was of course the Scripture for those who came before Christ as well, but Paul believes that he now lives in an age when the true

---

44 See Hays, *Echoes of Scripture in the Letters of Paul*; Hays, *Echoes of Scripture in the Gospels*.

implications and significance of these texts can more fully be seen, as was never fully the case before that time.

The fundamental idea behind typology is that since God's character never changes, God acts in similar ways in differing ages of history, and perhaps more importantly provides persons and events that foreshadow other later persons and events in salvation history. In other words, it is *not* an ahistorical reading of the text, but one which compares what has happened before to God's people and what is happening now. Cognizance of both stories is crucial if the analogy is to be drawn. There is also the sense as we have said that all that has come before Christ was preparatory and pointing forward to what has been happening since Christ appeared.

Typology as we find it here in 1 Cor. 10 does not involve a point-by-point comparison in all matters. For example, Paul does not believe the Corinthians have yet perished in the spiritual desert of the pagan world, indeed the whole point of the analogy is so they will not do so. Yet Paul entertains the possibility that some of his converts may yet end up like the wilderness-wandering generation of Israelites. Paul wishes to use the OT to show Christians how they should and should not live, in view of God's consistent judging of idolatry amongst his people. Notice how Paul begins 1 Cor. 10 with reference to "our ancestors." The story of the Israelites is "our" story, because in Paul's view, Jew and Gentile united in Christ is the continuation and true development of the OT people of God at the present, but he also believes that God is not finished with non-Christian Israel, as Rom. 9–11 makes clear.

Paul's way of handling this text in 1 Cor. 10 works two ways. He will interpret the OT events in a Christian and Christological manner, and he will interpret contemporary events in light of the OT stories. In other words, he will move in both directions at once – from experience to text and from text to contemporary experience. When Paul says in 1 Cor. 10.4 "and the rock was Christ," it is to be noted that he does not say "the rock *is* Christ" nor does he say "the rock signifies Christ." In Paul's view, it is appropriate to read the OT in the light of his knowledge of how these texts were interpreted in Jewish sapiential literature where it was argued that Wisdom was the rock that provided water for thirsty Israel in the desert (Wis. Sol. 11). Paul believes Christ who is the Wisdom of God was in fact really spiritually present as the pre-existent one, with Israel and providing them with benefits. This is not an interpretive or merely a hermeneutical move so much as a theological reflection on what was believed by Paul to be actually the case during the OT times.

The very reason this analogy works so well in Paul's view is that both his present audience and the one referred to in the OT text had benefits from Christ. Yet those benefits didn't spare the Israelites from judgment, any more than partaking of the Christian sacraments would spare Corinthian Christians who were attending idol feasts from being judged by God. Notice how in 1 Cor. 10.1–4 Paul stresses, using deliberately Christianized language, that all the Israelites partook of the so-called Mosaic sacraments. Now Paul knows very well that the Red Sea crossing was no baptismal rite (v. 2) for he knows the Israelites went across on dry ground! Nor is he really suggesting that the partaking of manna had the same sacramental character as the Lord's Supper. His point is simply this – the Israelites had the same general sort of spiritual benefits (cf. v 3 – food spiritually provided) from the same God, and it did not save them from judgment!

We may pause to ask here, in what sense was the rock, or the food, or the drink the Israelites had "spiritual"? I would suggest the term is chosen to indicate the source of this sustenance, namely that it came from God, who is spirit. Paul may also be assuming that spiritual people like himself should be able to discern the deeper spiritual lessons to be drawn from these sorts of analogies. The food was no more figurative or allegorical than the Corinthians' sacraments. However, the spiritual significance of that reality needed to be seen.

Verse 11 is an important one for it reveals something of how Paul views the OT text. He says these things happened as a warning to himself and his audience, "on whom the ends of the ages have come." Paul believed that he lived in the eschatological age when one would see the significance and the beginning of the completion of the divine designs for humankind. The goals to which history had been pressing had in his day begun to be realized.

Now if one grants Paul his theological assumptions – (1) that the pre-existent Christ really had a hand in the affairs of the Israelites and (2) that Paul and his converts were living in the eschatological age when all the promises and prophecies and paradigms were coming to pass and to fruition and (3) that the Scriptures were written for God's people, and perhaps especially for the eschatological gathering of God's people – then what Paul does with this text makes very good sense. It is not a matter of exegetical legerdemain, or hermeneutical hocus-pocus. It is a matter of having the right eschatological and Christological and ecclesiological perspectives to see the new significance these historic texts had for Paul's own audience.

When Paul seeks to do typology, he announces his intentions so the audience will see how he is proceeding by analogy. Likewise, when he uses another major hermeneutical technique, allegorizing a non-allegorical text, he announces his intentions. We see this clearly enough in Gal. 4.21–5.1, where in the midst of the discussion Paul says quite clearly "Now this is an allegory" (4.24). It needs to be borne in mind that the term *allegorein* can mean to either speak or to interpret allegorically, and in that case, one must be able to distinguish between: (1) a text created as an allegory; (2) an allegorizing of elements or portions of a text; (3) allegorical interpretation of a non-allegorical text. Surely, Paul is well aware that he is doing a creative allegorical interpretation of a text that is not in itself an allegory and in fact he is also allegorizing only certain elements in the text. Again, this falls into the category of hermeneutics rather than exegesis, a distinction too often overlooked.

While typology is more firmly grounded in the actual characteristics of the type and antitype displayed in the narratives, and it is normally persons or events, not things, that are set up as types or antitypes, in allegory, persons, places, things can all take on symbolic or secondary connotations. I suspect that if asked, Paul would freely admit that Hagar was not a "type" of either Mt. Sinai or the present Jerusalem. Only the concept of bondage or slavery binds them together and it is this linkage that allegorizing the text brings to light. Paul is not really doing exegesis here at all but presupposes a basic understanding of the story and then creatively uses elements of the story for pastoral hermeneutics and application. This falls into the category of a pastoral or homiletical use of a text and should not be evaluated as a bizarre attempt at contextual exegesis. Paul's allegorizing of the historical narrative is perhaps closest to what we find at Qumran (cf. CD 6.3–11, where

Num. 21.18 is similarly allegorized). In both cases, contemporary events outside the text (e.g. in Paul's case the presence of Jewish agitators in Galatia) led to creative handlings of the text.

At this point we must call upon R. B. Hays as a dialogue partner as we attempt to assess Paul's exegetical and hermeneutical techniques. Hays argues that Paul believes in the concept of a *sensus plenior*, that the text has a deeper or latent or even metaphorical meaning that can be liberated or ferreted out by a creative "spiritual" handling of the text.[45] I would suggest that this confuses the issues of meaning and significance or application.

To a large extent, Hays reaches his conclusion on the basis of a certain reading of 2 Cor. 3, which he takes to reveal Paul's hermeneutics. Christians are freed from the bondage to a circumscribed reading of the Old Covenant and empowered to read it with freedom, indeed even with reckless abandon. This conclusion comes from a fundamental misreading of the contrast between letter and Spirit by Hays. Paul is not saying that one sort of interpretive move in handling the OT is death-dealing, while another more freewheeling one is life-giving. Paul is saying that the effect of the Law, even the Ten Commandments, on fallen persons is condemnation, is death-dealing. By contrast the effect of the Spirit on fallen persons is that it gives life.

Paul says much the same thing elsewhere in Romans and Galatians about the effect of the Law on fallen persons (see e.g. Gal. 3.21). Not exegesis nor hermeneutics but spiritual experience is the issue here. V. P. Furnish sees this quite clearly: "the description Paul gives of the *new covenant* does not so much reflect his hermeneutical perspective on the law or scripture in general as it does his eschatological perspective on God's redemptive work in history."[46] Paul is offering a tale of two ministries and two covenants, not a discussion of two ways of reading or two kinds of attitudes toward the OT or the Law. Paul the exegete is a second-order issue to Paul the storyteller. Paul thinks these stories are coming true by the power of God and so the primary thing is always spiritual experience not spiritual exegesis or hermeneutics.

What about a text like Galatians 3.8? Here clearly Paul personifies Scripture as a prophetic book. Scripture saw in advance that God will set right the Gentiles by faith, and so "pre-preached" the gospel to Abraham. The point here is again not about a deeper meaning in the OT text. The point is that Paul actually believes that Abraham heard the essence of the Gospel message of acceptability to God through faith reckoned as righteousness and responded positively. This is not anachronism but analogy. In particular, it is an argument, like we find in 1 Cor. 10, based on analogous experience. Salvation historical experience shared in common by Abraham and by Paul's converts is the point. The only anachronism is calling this message which Abraham heard and responded to "the gospel." The Gospel message is not "hidden in OT Scripture," rather it is in plain sight as a message once given to Abraham.

Let us consider another of Hays's key texts, Rom. 10.5–10. Here Hays has more of a case, to be sure. But is Paul really arguing that there is a concealed or hidden meaning in Deut. 30.11–14? To the contrary, he is arguing that there is a revealed meaning *in* the text, not behind or beneath it. Just as the word was near to them, it is all the more near to the eschatological community of faith. The phrase "the word is near you, in your mouth

[45] Hays, *Echoes of Scripture in the Letters of Paul,* 154.
[46] V. P. Furnish, *II Corinthians* (Garden City, NY: Doubleday, 1984), 200.

and in your heart" provides Paul an opportunity to talk about the word of faith which he preaches and his audience believes in their hearts and confesses. Paul clearly here is using the *pesher* technique of contemporizing the text. He believes that the phrase had meaning in its original setting, but now Paul will use these scriptural words to speak about something that is true of Paul's preaching and the Christian's experience.

The personified "Righteousness from Faith" has caused no end of debate. Whoever or whatever this is, it cannot be Moses, for it is contrasted with Moses, who wrote concerning the righteousness that comes from the Law (10.5). "Moses *writes* concerning legal righteousness ... *but* the Righteousness from Faith *says* ..." This may be a reference to Christ and the way he spoke the gospel, using OT phrases, when he was on earth.[47] Alternatively, this may refer to the Christian oral tradition about righteousness from faith and the way it uses the OT text to make its points. Still another possibility would be that the abstract concept "righteousness from faith" has been personified (just as elsewhere Paul has personified Scripture) and is speaking the inspired word of God for today, using OT phrases. This personification is in fact the personification of what Paul calls the gospel, the oral message summarized in places like Gal. 2.15–21. This last seems most likely here.

In any event, we must be able to distinguish between a contemporizing use of scriptural phrases as here, and a theory about how Paul believed the OT text had a hidden or deeper meaning. The meaning of the text is one thing, how it is used hermeneutically is another. It is hermeneutics when one is seeing a further significance of the text for some application today that goes beyond its original meaning. This, I submit, is what Paul is doing here. It is thus not warranted to conclude from such pastoral uses of the text that "Paul's readings of Scripture are not constrained by a historical scrupulousness about the original meaning of the text. Eschatological meaning subsumes original sense."[48] I would say eschatological *application* extends original meaning and application, following the principle of analogy. Sometimes, especially when the Scripture is used by way of echo or allusion, what we are actually seeing is the use of biblical language for purposes other than those which the language was originally used. I call this a homiletical *use* of the OT. NT writers often speak in "Biblese."

Yet in the end we must agree with Hays that Paul's hermeneutic is narratologically oriented, which explains the importance of typology for Paul. "Paul reads Scripture under the conviction that its story prefigures the climactic realities of his own time."[49] In other words, Paul is basically not an allegorist looking for some abstract eternal truth of philosophical profundity buried in a narrative (unlike Philo). Paul thinks in terms of historical progressions, and the breaking into space and time of God's divine saving activity. The narratives in Paul's thought world are founded and grounded in God and in history, and this of course includes the narratives about Christ and Christians. Typology is the technique of one who has a profound belief in the historical substance of what he speaks and a profound belief in the God who is sovereign over history and relates in a consistent way to his people age after age.

Paul's allusive handling of Scripture shows repeatedly that he believed that one needed to know the whole story to appreciate the parts. As an exegete and applier of the text, Paul was

---

[47] See Rom. 3–4, where it is argued that God has shown forth his righteousness in a new way in Christ, the paradigmatic example of faith and faithfulness.

[48] Hays, *Echoes of Scripture in the Letters of Paul*, 156.

[49] *Ibid.*, 161.

creative, using typology and even allegorizing to relate the Scriptures to the situations of his converts. Yet it would be a mistake to see him as an early predecessor of Augustine or others who were constantly looking for a *sensus plenior*, a deeper or hidden sense to Scripture. Paul to the contrary believed he lived in an age when the hidden had been brought to light, and the meaning and truth of Scripture made plain. He believed he lived in the eschatological age, when the ends and goals and aims of all the ages were coming to fruition through Christ and his body. What Paul was looking for was new ways to apply the old meaning to his converts, and it is his hermeneutical creativity that helps him find these ways.

Paul reads Scripture with a historical and narratological consciousness dictating how he views the befores and afters in the story. He is not Philo looking for abstract or eternal Platonic ideals in the midst of the maze of historical particulars. For Paul, history and experience are the realms that Scripture speaks of and to again and again. One needs to look into history and into the sacred story, not beyond or behind it to find the meaning and purpose of life and the explanation for what transpires.

Paul's hermeneutic was Christologically determined and focused, the Christ event being the lens through which all must be seen and understood, including God. Yet it was ecclesiologically directed. It was also eschatologically generated, as Paul sees himself living in the age when the prophetic and the promissory comes to pass. The story which summed up all that came before and encompassed all that was to follow was the story of Christ. It was the key that unlocked all the secrets, the key that opened the door setting the prisoners free from fallenness, from slavery to the powers of darkness, from servitude to the Law. Paul believed that the story had reached its climax, and he was living in the denouement. He believed the story was being replicated in his own experience and that it was calling him to the imitation of Christ.

But was Paul some sort of anomaly, or did other NT writers also do theology in a narratological mode? We must turn to Hebrews next to begin to answer this question but let us remind ourselves once more of the stories that Paul most used and emphasized in articulating his symbolic universe. They are five interwoven stories comprising one large drama: (1) the story of God, the one who existed before all worlds and made them; (2) the story of the world gone wrong in Adam; (3) the story of God's people in that world, from Abraham to Moses and beyond; (4) the story of the Jewish messiah, the Christ which arises out of the story of both humankind and of Israel, but also in fact arises out of the larger story of God as creator and redeemer; (5) the story of Christians, including Paul himself, which arises out of stories (2)–(4).

The Narrative Thought World of the Author of Hebrews

Entering the world of the letter to the Hebrews after a close study of Paul is a bit like listening to Monteverdi after listening to Bach. We are clearly in the same world, but the texture is different, the allusions are different, the whole flavor is changed.

N. T. Wright[50]

---

[50] Wright, *The New Testament and the People of God*, 409.

I have demonstrated elsewhere that the author of Hebrews seems very likely to have been part of the Pauline circle of evangelists and co-workers, and indeed may have even been Apollos.[51] Whoever he was, he was as formidable a thinker as Paul himself, and shows some indebtedness to Pauline thought at points, but he has made such concepts and readings of the Christian story his own, and given them his own focus and emphases. He is no mere imitator, and nothing about his homily can be said to be derivative in any way. For one thing, he wants to retell the story of Israel differently than Paul and emphasize much different aspects of it. The tabernacle, Moses, Melchizedek, the priesthood in general and much more play roles in this author's Christian thought world in ways that they do not in Paul's.

Furthermore, the author of Hebrews is indebted to some different Jewish sources of material than Paul, for example the end of Sirach. As Wright shows, Sir. 44.1–50.21 is profitably compared to Heb. 11–12. However, in Sirach the list of heroes culminates when the history of the world and of Israel climaxes in the worship of Yahweh in the Jerusalem temple, especially in the spectacular ministry of the high priest Simon ben Onias. "This is where Israel's history has been leading: a great high priest, magnificently robed, splendid in his liturgical operations, coming out of the sanctuary after the worship to bless the people."[52]

Strikingly, this is echoed in Hebrews. Only now, Jesus is the great high priest, the holy of holies is the heavenly sanctuary, the sacrifice was Jesus himself, and when he comes forth from that heavenly sanctuary it will be to save those who eagerly wait for him. The story Jesus ben Sira was telling is subverted by the story that our author is telling such that Jesus of Nazareth becomes the focus of worship, the creator of a new sort of worship that is not tied to an earthly sanctuary be it the ancient tabernacle or the temple in Jerusalem. The true worship of the true God now is both facilitated by and directed toward Jesus. We need to unpack this some by looking at a few elements of the narrative thought world that makes Hebrews stand apart from Paul and other NT writers.

When we spoke of the Christological hymn fragment in Heb. 1 earlier in this chapter we dealt with how our author chooses to present the story of the pre-existent Son of God, who is indeed properly called God, and has various of the divine attributes and the trajectory of his story, including his making purification for sins and then returning to heaven. Here it will be useful to deal with a passage that talks about his humanity, and its necessity in order that he could be a human priest – indeed the believer's high priest now and forever – Heb. 4.14–5.9.

First of all, in Heb. 4.14 we hear about Christ's journey to heaven, which is described as a "passing through the heavens," perhaps echoing the idea of the high priest passing through the curtains into the holy of holies. More pertinently, early Jewish listeners would think of the earlier experiences of Enoch (cf. Gen. 5.24 and 1 En. 14–19; 70–71) or Elijah perhaps (2 Kgs. 2.11), or the post-OT traditions about the ascension of Isaiah (Ascen. of Isaiah 6–7). We may also notice that the phrase "great high priest" is not unprecedented (see 1 Macc. 13.42 of Simon; and the high priest is often called a great priest in the

[51] See Ben Witherington III, *Letters and Homilies for Jewish Christians: A Socio-Rhetorical Commentary on Hebrews, James, and Jude* (Downers Grove, IL: InterVarsity Press, 2007).
[52] Wright, *The New Testament and the People of God*, 410.

LXX – Lev. 21.10; Num. 35.25–28; Zech. 6.11). But our author means something special by the appellation – he means one of a wholly different ilk and priestly line. The audience is urged to "hold fast" to their confession already given about this great high priest. Though his methodology is more subtle, our author's argument is not different in thrust from Paul's – namely you already have in Christ all that you might look or long for from OT religion.

One of the things that our author makes clear here is "Christ's full humanness and his sinlessness are not contradictory. Being sinful is not intrinsic or necessary to being fully human, nor, to state the opposite, is being sinless an obstacle to full humanness."[53] It is a modern notion that sinning makes one more human or approachable, a notion not shared by our author or other early Jews. There was in early Judaism in any case the notion of a righteous messiah who would come (see Ps. Sol. 17.36). The phrase "tested in every respect/way" probably does not mean that Jesus endured every basic temptation that humans undergo, but rather that he underwent the full gamut of types of temptation we experience. He is thus able to sympathize with his fellow human beings' struggles and weaknesses.

The phrase *kat' homoiomati* could mean "tested according to the likeness of our temptations" or "according to his likeness to us." The phrase could be interpreted either way. The point in either case is that he has experienced all the sorts of temptations we have, and being like us, he thus understands what we go through. The final clause in 4.15 means literally "without sin." There has been some controversy as to what this means. Christ went through the same sort of temptations as we do but came out unscathed. In view of 7.26 this assertion of sinlessness applies to Jesus not only in heaven and as a result of his death, but in fact before it when he offered a pure and unblemished sacrifice. He was not only a high priest without sin, but a sacrifice without sin as well, so that he did not have to die for himself but could offer the perfect and full sacrifice that brings final atonement.

In regard to the exhortations in these two verses, "holding on firmly" to the confession and "drawing near" to the throne of grace, the second verb *proserchometha* (cf. 7.25; 10.22; 11.6; 12.18–22) is almost a technical term for the liturgical work of the priest drawing near to the altar or worshippers drawing near to God (Lev. 9.7; 21.17,21; 22.3; Num. 18.3 LXX). It is a mirror opposite of the warned-against "shrinking back" or "turning away" (3.12; 6.6; 10.38–39). While the audience may feel alienated from the macro-culture at the moment, or even from the Jewish subculture, our author is stressing they are right where they need to be, in the center of God's will, having already arrived at the doorstep of Zion and are in the process of "entering in" to God's blessed rest and eternal salvation.

Now is no time to look back with longing, or to shrink back from the finish line. Of course, our author, in order to justify the use of the image of high priest applied to Jesus, must resort to the novel idea that Jesus is a priest after the order of Melchizedek, which is not a hereditary priesthood, but a forever one. This comports nicely with the way the author will insist that Jesus' sacrifice is once for all time as well. The story of priesthood and sacrifice has been tailored to fit the specific theological points our author wants to make about Jesus.

---

[53] Donald Hagner, *Encountering Hebrews* (Grand Rapids, MI: Baker, 2004), 78.

It would not be at all obvious to the audience that Jesus was a high priest. Jewish Christians would query such an assertion on the basis of Jesus' genealogy, the geographical locale and character of his ministry, not to mention the "temple tantrum" in the temple in Jerusalem when Jesus overturned the tables of the money changers. Jesus went through none of the following, which normally accompanied investing someone with the office of high priest: purification bath, donning sacred vestments, being anointed with oil, offering sacrifices and especially going into the holy of holies on the Day of Atonement (cf. Exod. 28.41; Exod. 29; Lev. 8). Thus, rhetorically speaking, our author must exercise no little amount of persuasion (off and on in the entire section between 4.14 and the end of Heb. 10) to make a convincing case that Jesus was a priest at all, much less a high priest. One could say he does so by a *tour de force* argument where he in essence argues that Jesus was a high priest on a whole different level – in heaven, not on earth. Although Jesus offers himself as the sacrifice while on earth, he assumes the mantle of full-fledged priest in heaven.

We do not know where our author got the ideas he shares here, though perhaps there are some parallels with the Qumranite concept of a priest/king or priest/messiah. For the Hasmonaens and, later, the Sadducees, Melchizedek was the prototype of their priestly-kingly view of rulers. For the Pharisees, he was to be identified with Shem and to be demoted for his irreverence from any continuing priestly succession. For Philo, he was mainly the manifestation of the eternal logos; for Josephus, he was a Canaanite chieftain who became God's priest at Jerusalem due to his piety, and most importantly for Qumran (11 QMelch.) he was a heavenly and eschatological figure, even perhaps an archangel redeemer who exercised certain priestly characteristics in atoning for sin. In view of the Qumran finds, it is easy to see how our author might be able to argue for the superiority of Christ over the Levitical priesthood, on the basis of a connection to the order of Melchizedek, since there were some Jews who viewed him as a heavenly redeemer figure.[54]

But in fact, one need look no further than the OT example of the king-priest Melchizedek, which is probably the source of our author's thought. Jesus will be presented here as both royal Son and priest, after the order and fashion of Melchizedek but greater. Whatever the source of the ideas, our author has made them his own, and turned them into a unique and specific commentary on Jesus, with elements such as the self-sacrifice, which could only have come from his knowledge of Jesus' own story.

Obviously the most fundamental requirement for Christ to be a priest is that he had to be a human being. Angels may play the role of messengers or even warriors, but they are not mediators, because they do not partake of human nature. Priests then are a different sort of intermediary from angels, not least because they primarily represent human beings to God, whereas angels do the reverse. The priest's most basic role is said to be offering gifts and sacrifices to God (a stock phrase and so we should not differentiate between the two terms – see 1 Kgs. 8. 64, cf. Heb. 8.3), and in due course one hears about the special form that takes with the high priest (Heb. 9.7,25).

It is not expected that a priest be perfect and without sin, though it is expected that he be cleansed, forgiven, shriven of sin when he takes up his holy tasks. But one of those tasks is in fact offering sacrifices for himself and his own sins, as well as for the sins of others.

---

[54] J. A. Fitzmyer, "Further Light on Melchizedek from Qumran Cave 11," *JBL* 86 (1967): 25–41, here 41.

On the one hand, it is a good thing that the priest is weak and knows his own shortcomings as he is better able to identify and empathize with other weak mortals, but at the same time his weakness is not a strength in another respect, namely that he must sacrifice for his own sins. Here only in the NT do we have the verb *metriopatheō*, which literally means to moderate the pathos, or to control one's deeper emotions. The issue here is not sympathy, but the ability to control one's anger with ignorant or spiritually wayward people. While the ordinary priest controls his anger, Jesus is said to actively sympathize with his fellow humans.

In the OT, sacrifices for sin were efficacious if they were offered for sins of ignorance or for sins which were unwitting or unintentional in nature (see Lev. 4.13; Ezek. 45.20). These sins are viewed differently from sins committed intentionally or willfully, or as the OT puts it "with a high hand" (Num. 15.30–31). Acts 13.39 states clearly that through Christ's death, atonement is now possible for intentional sins which were not covered under OT law. This is one of the reasons our author will emphasize that Christian believers have a very merciful high priest. He will also stress, in making clear the mercy of Christ, that in the OT deliberate sin was viewed less mercifully (see Heb. 6.4–8; 10.26–31; 12.17). Thus, when our author speaks of how gently Jesus deals with his audience, there is an implicit contrast with other priests and earlier sacrificial systems. Just how merciful is further demonstrated by the fact that he was not a sinner, unlike all other priests. At Heb. 7.27 our author will make much of the fact that Jesus is unlike other high priests in respect to not needing to sacrifice for his own sins. Jesus was the one person for whom Jesus did not have to die to atone for his sins.

At v. 4 our author will make the further point that priesthood is not an office and an honor earned but rather one granted by God who "calls" priests. Aaron is singled out as the example (Exod. 28.1) of this process of divine selection, and our author totally ignores the fact that in Herod's temple there were a whole series of high priests who were not divinely chosen, to say the least, but rather were appointed by human rulers, involving a political process. Indeed, the controlling of who became high priest was one of the most vital and volatile political issues that a Roman procurator had to supervise, without appearing to interfere or control.

According to v. 5, Jesus met the essential requirement of being selected by God, not being self-selected, to be priest. Here Ps. 2.7 comes to the fore as it did in Heb. 1.5, only this time the issue is God selecting the Son to be a priest, rather than for a different sort of royal role. Our author moves on to consider another psalm again as well, this time Ps. 110, and it is fair to say that he reads Ps. 110.4 in light of Ps. 110.1, and in fact it is Ps. 110.1 which links our author's reading of Ps. 2.7 to that of Ps. 110.4. The logic of v. 5 and v. 6, which involve the quoting of phrases from Ps. 2.7 and Ps. 110.4, is just this – because the Son has been exalted to rule from God's right hand, he is in the place and condition where he can be the perfect heavenly high priest, a forever high priest always in the inner sanctum, right in the presence of God forever. His exalted Sonship role allows him to play the role of heavenly high priest.

Perhaps surprisingly and suddenly our author seems to turn in v. 7 to the Gethsemane scene, with Christ struggling to obey God's will for him. The description is full of pathos and meant to evoke the deeper emotions of the audience. Presumably part of what is going on here is demonstrating how Christ can identify with the audience in their own struggles, and in their own pressure-packed situations, which may lead to their suffering and death. Actually, here we have another dimension of the priestly portrait of Jesus, for prayers were something the priest was supposed to offer to God, for himself and for others.

Here is where we note that while *eulabeias* can mean piety or devotion in a general sense both here and at 12.28 (the only other occurrence of the term in Hebrews), it is used in the context of talking about Christ's priestly service. Thus, it suggests the attitude of reverence appropriate to priestly service. In any case, *eulabeias*, since it carries the connotation of a pious attitude such as godly fear, is not the term for ordinary fear (when our author wanted to talk about deliverance from the fear of death he used *phobos* – see 2.15). It is thus far-fetched to think this refers to Jesus' fear of death.

There has been great debate about what it means here to say that "he was *heard* because of his reverence"[55] when he had been pleading that he be spared from death. This verse has been debated since the times of the church fathers and is still debated today. Perhaps our author means that when Jesus said "nevertheless thy will be done" that that part of the prayer was heard. This may be correct, but our author then would be assuming his audience knows the fuller Gethsemane story beyond his dramatic characterization of it here and knows about the "nevertheless" remark.

This sermon called Hebrews was likely written before any Gospel account of the Gethsemane episode was written down, and so it is interesting to compare this, to the account in Mt. 26.36–46 or Lk. 22.43–44, for example, found only in some manuscripts of Luke, which in some respects most resembles what we have here in terms of the pathos expressed there: "and being in anguish he prayed more earnestly, and his sweat was like drops of blood falling to the ground." Possibly this Western text of Lk. 22 is drawing on some traditions also known to our author. They could reflect an early authentic tradition, one that was not originally part of any canonical Gospel.

If one draws this conclusion, what is added to our understanding of the Gethsemane story? First, it increases the emphasis on the humanity of Jesus and his great distress in the garden. An angel appears to him and strengthens him so he can survive the test (cf. Mk. 1.13). Secondly, it shows that Jesus is a man of prayer, dependent on the Father for help. Thirdly, the text does not speak of Jesus having bloody sweat, it speaks of his sweating being like or presumably being the size of blood droplets. Fourthly, we are told Jesus was in anguish, which is compatible with the picture of Jesus praying for the cup to be taken from him. In other words, rhetorically speaking, this Lukan text serves much the same set of purposes as does our brief telling of the Gethsemane moment of testing here in Hebrews. Jesus was tempted to bail out but passed the test.

Thus, this brief vignette from the life of Jesus serves to illustrate our author's point about his being tempted/tested in every respect like us, save without sin and his ability to identify with human struggles to remain faithful and obedient to God. The scenario envisioned here involves multiple prayers, not merely a cry of anguish. If we ask why our author has chosen this episode from the life of Jesus to refer to, the answer is likely to be because it provides a paradigm for the audience to follow in their own trials, suffering, and possibility of facing a martyr's death. Here is simply another way that Jesus is seen as

---

55 Some have even translated here "he was heard and delivered from fear of death" but this translation labors under the difficulty that words with the *eulab* root indicate reverence, not abject fear, such as a fear of death.

their pioneer or trailblazer. One can also point to the material in the Maccabean literature, where earnest prayer is described as involving loud cries and tears (cf. 2 Macc. 11.6; 3 Macc. 1.16; 5.7,25), however this material simply reflects the fact that this is the way early Jews did indeed entreat God when they were in a crisis situation. It need not suggest any literary dependence between this material and what we find in Hebrews, though I would not rule out our author knowing the Maccabean literature.

Verses. 8–9 say that Jesus learned obedience through his suffering (noting the neat aural play on words here with *mathein* and *pathein*, learn and suffering) and that he was made complete, that is fully equipped and enabled to play the role of heavenly high priest and thus a source of salvation, having himself been the perfect sacrifice that makes atonement for sin and can be the basis of interceding with the Father in heaven. One should compare 2.10 on the issue of perfection, and here we are in fact talking about a sort of completion of ministerial training, his preparation to be high priest in heaven. Instead of a "trial sermon" he had a trial sacrifice – of himself! Notice that in Lev. 4.5; 8.33; 16.32; 21.10 and Num. 3.3 the appropriate translation of this perfection terminology used of priests in the LXX is "consecrated." Jesus was "consecrated" to the ministry of being heavenly high priest by his suffering and death. In this sense he was made holy, set apart, complete, perfect through suffering. It is not a statement about his moral condition.

Notice as well that there is a proviso in v. 9 – he is the source of salvation for all who obey him. Of course, our author is not just satisfied to say Jesus is our high priest, he wants to make clear that he eclipses all previous ones, and one of the ways he accomplishes this is that he makes clear that unlike ordinary high priests, Jesus is actually the source of salvation, and the salvation he offers is an eternal one (only here in the NT do we have the phrase eternal salvation), not the temporary expedient of short-term atonement by one sacrifice after another. The "how much more" or "can you top this" motif in the earlier comparison with Moses (see Heb. 3) is carried out here as well, not only in the two ways just mentioned but also by means of stressing that Jesus was of a greater priestly order than Aaron – namely the Melchizedekian one, a theme to which our author will not return until Heb. 7. Here our author is content to say Jesus exceeds the high priestly job description and surpasses all rivals and comparisons. Through his death, he became fully qualified to be appointed a priest, and God did so, assigning him a forever priesthood according to v. 10. Nobody before or since has been assigned a job quite like that.

What is so remarkable about all of this is that our author creatively combines the OT stories about the role of priests, and perhaps also even here the descriptions in Sir. 44–50, with the story of Jesus' Gethsemane experience in order to make clear the suitability of Jesus to be our high priest forever after the order of Melchizedek. The Gospel story is fitted nicely into the larger story that the author wishes to tell about Jesus and his impact and significance. Typological use of the OT, combined with the notion that the climax of revelation comes in God's Son, and that his human story is a crucial part of how he came to be our heavenly high priest, is all melded into one fluid presentation.

When we think of our author's narrative thought world we cannot simply think of his revising OT stories, when in fact it is his story of Christ which causes him to revise how he views all OT institutions and stories, even the stories of the OT patriarchs, prophets, and heroes. And it needs to be stressed that our author does not try to suggest that there is a heavenly climax to this story. As is the case with other NT writers, the climax comes when Jesus returns from heaven to bestow everlasting salvation, a consummation and theophany described at the climax of the discourse in Heb. 12 and contrasted with the theophany at Sinai which Moses and the people of Israel endured and did not enjoy. This is truly a remarkable example of bold storytelling, subverting and revising old stories, especially when one takes into account that this is written to Jewish Christians in Rome thinking of going back to being non-Christian Jews![56] Despite dwelling a lot on what is true now in heaven, our author agrees with and ends with the usual eschatological climax to the story that we find in so many places elsewhere in the NT. He is not into providing alternate endings to the story of Christ and his people and their salvation.

If we compare this material with what we find in the Jesus material and in Paul's letters, a pattern has emerged involving: *(1) focus on Christ; (2) Christological or Christotelic interpretation of the OT, a rereading not only of the prophetic material but even the priestly material in light of the Christ-event; (3) a focus on both the humanity and the divine identity of Christ; (4) a belief that Christ the Messiah has brought in the beginning of the eschatological realities called Kingdom or salvation, or both; (5) an expansion of monotheistic ideas now to include Christ; (6) a belief that the eschatological Spirit has been bestowed, amongst other benefits, by the exalted Christ on his people; and (6) the people of God are viewed as Jew and Gentile united in Christ, and in this people we find the culmination of the mission of Israel to be a light unto the nations.*

We will hear of more on this last point when we turn to Luke-Acts, but here it is important to stress that at the heart of our author's biblical theology is indeed Christology, and not just any sort of messianic thinking, but messianic thinking focused on a historical person named Jesus of Nazareth who suffered at Gethsemane and then on the cross. This is what most distinguishes these documents from other early Jewish documents, and at the same time most makes clear that these authors are sharing a common Christ-focused worldview that has changed the way they view their own storied world, and the stories they learned growing up from the Hebrew Scriptures, not to mention their whole understanding of God the Father and the Spirit as well.

The Narrative Thought World of Luke-Acts

The idea that history is story is widely held among critics from a number of disciplines, including history, although it is fair to say that it is not a prevailing idea, especially among historians ... [H]istory as it happened is something that can only be grasped by telling stories about it. History in the strict sense is a story about events, not the events themselves, or even a verbal representation of them, since it is impossible to represent the enormous mass of "events" we perceive even in a given day.

Norman Petersen[57]

Luke was no ordinary storyteller, and we are fortunate to have two volumes of his work in the NT which make up about a third of that corpus. In fact, Luke was a master storyteller, and a master editor of his sources as well, as even a cursory examination of his handling of the material he derived from Mark makes so very clear. And to Luke we owe

---

56 Witherington, *Letters and Homilies for Jewish Christians.*
57 Petersen, *Rediscovering Paul*, 10.

the widest vista when it comes to telling the story of the rise and spread of the Good News, as Luke situates the story so very clearly in the larger context of God's saving activities in the world and for his people. There is a reason why he has been called the theologian of salvation history.[58]

It ought to be stressed from the outset that Luke is operating differently from the other Gospel writers, as he is offering a two-volume historical monograph indebted not only to biblical history, but also to ancient Hellenistic historians in terms of methodology and approach as well. He does not give us a biography of Jesus in his first volume any more than he gives us a biography of the apostles in the second one. His focus is actually on the narration of the "things which have happened among us" (Lk. 1.1–4) and what they mean. One would not know that Luke's Gospel was going to be about Jesus at all from the first column or so of the document, for there we have a brief prologue in which Jesus is not mentioned, and then we are introduced to the story of Zechariah and Elizabeth and the divine intervention that happened in their lives. Luke feels he must get a running start before engaging in telling stories about Jesus and his family and followers. In other words, the story is ongoing by the time we get to Jesus, and indeed has been going on for quite some time before we get to the ministry of Jesus.

Luke conveys this sense of continuity with the past in a very different way from Matthew, who begins with a genealogy. Luke, by contrast, begins by indicating his historian's approach and then tells of the sequence of events which led up to the angelic visitation to Mary. Divine intervention, salvation history, is already in process when Mary is called upon by God's messenger. God has a plan, a long-term plan, and it is working itself out through various historical persons and processes. At a few points along the way Luke will show how the macro-history of the Empire interfaces with the micro-history of salvation history which happens in particular places involving particular persons at particular times (see e.g. Lk. 2.1–2; 3.1–2; and Acts 18.2), but by and large he is content to tell the story of the Good News spreading from Galilee to Jerusalem, and then from Jerusalem heading west to that whole part of the Empire. Instead of synchronisms, or the use of formula quotations, Luke will establish contact with the longer sweep of biblical history by means of allusion, echo, occasional Scripture quotation.

Thus, for instance, in the story of Zechariah and Elizabeth, it is surely right that we are meant to hear echoes of the stories about the birth of Samuel and the beginnings of the Israelite monarchy.[59] A new king is coming and preceding him will be a new herald whose mother had a Hannah-like experience (see 1 Sam. 1–2). So, as Wright says, John the Baptizer will play Samuel, to Jesus' David and the climax of their interaction comes when Samuel anoints David and the spirit of God comes mightily upon him (1 Sam. 16.13) and when John baptizes Jesus and once more the Spirit comes down mightily and remains on Jesus. "The story of salvation continues in parallel. David's anointing is followed, in the narrative of 1 Samuel, by his taking on Goliath single-handed, as the representative of Israel. Jesus' anointing is followed at once by his battle with Satan."[60] The game's afoot, and the king is abroad in his land, though incognito at first. We would be remiss not to

[58] For a detailed study of Luke as a Hellenistic historian see Ben Witherington III, *The Acts of the Apostles: A Socio-Rhetorical Commentary* (Grand Rapids, MI: William B. Eerdmans, 1998), especially the Introduction.

[59] See Wright, *The New Testament and the People of God*, 379.

[60] *Ibid.*, 380.

also hear repeated echoes of the story of Abraham and Sarah in the Lukan birth narratives, especially in the poignant story of Elizabeth and her plight, only Elizabeth in this tale must be her own Abraham, as her husband is struck dumb for lack of faith and trust in the angelic announcement, in contrast to Mary's response.

The point of such parallels is not to suggest recapitulation of an old story, but rather foreshadowing and climax to the story of salvation history. It suggests a God who operates with his people following a consistent and persistent plan and pattern, and Luke is all about displaying the patterns of salvation history, including many parallels between the Gospel and his Acts volume, as we shall see in a moment. Yet it would be a mistake to think that Luke's storytelling is simply like that found in Hebrews. Our author is not merely doing typology and saying this later person/action is better than that older one. Luke is saying this is the climax and fulfillment of a long historical process only dimly foreshadowed before.

Luke, more than the other two Synoptic writers, wants to stress that Jesus is the savior of the world (Lk. 2.10–11), and his coming proves to be the reality of which the Emperor's coming and "Good News" is only a parody. Thus, Luke is not interested in simply saying Jesus will save his own people, nor is he interested in saying Jesus will lead the revolt which will throw off the yoke of Rome and liberate God's oppressed people. This is because there is no need either to ghettoize the Gospel or to politicize it because God is directly intervening in Jesus and will go on doing so. Wright puts it this way:

The End has happened in Calvary, Easter, and Pentecost; one need no longer fight for it, since it has already happened. At the same time, the End is yet to come, with the return of Jesus (Acts 1.11) ... If this double End enables Luke to avoid the false antithesis of the ghetto and the sword, it also enables him to avoid the bland triumphalism of Eusebius, who in turn subverts Luke's story by combining the story of the kingdom of Israel's god with the story of the kingdom of Constantine.[61]

Luke is not interested in merely telling how the story of Israel and its Davidic monarch came to climactic fulfillment. It is clear not only from Lk. 1–2, but also Lk. 3 that this story has a more universal scope than that. This is why the genealogy in Lk. 3 traces Jesus back to Adam and from thence even to God. Jesus is son of Adam, and son of God. This affects the way one can and should read the Son of Man material in Luke's Gospel, which, like Mark, he chooses to use as the main way of revealing who Jesus was during his ministry.

In Lk. 4 as well something remarkable happens. God's dealings with Israel, including "this present generation," are coming to the point of judgment, as Isaiah had foreseen. It is thus no accident that Jesus will cite Isa. 61.1–2 and then go on to say to those who have rejected the idea that it was being fulfilled in their hearing by Jesus, who is, like former northern prophets Elijah and Elisha, not accepted in his own region by his own folks. And so, healing and blessing ended up going to someone from Sidon or Syria, neither of whom were Jews. Luke prepares us for a large rejection of Jesus by Jews, and then a turning to Gentiles already in Lk. 4. This will play itself out in Acts in the "to the Jews first, and then if and when they reject the Good News to the Gentiles" motif that is said to characterize Paul's missionary work (see e.g. Acts 13–14). The Good News story goes on, on the larger stage of world history, as is revealed in Acts. This is not because the Jewish story or appeal to Jews has been left behind, even in Acts 28. It is because the Jewish story has been taken

---

[61] *Ibid.*, 382.

up into a larger story of world redemption in the hands of Luke. It is not surprising that Luke made this rhetorical move with his presentation, since he seems to be writing for his patron Theophilus, a high-status Gentile new convert to Christianity.

It is interesting that in the plotting of the narratives in Luke and in Acts there is a paradigmatic speech in each volume which sets in motion the mission of the Good News – the speech of Jesus in Nazareth in Lk. 4, and the speech of Peter in Acts 2 in Jerusalem. The living Word of God changes things either by transforming or scandalizing the audience, over and over again. It is not an accident that Luke presents us with as much speech material in Acts as he does in his Gospel. In fact, one can find a remarkable parallelism between the speeches and deeds of the Apostle to the Jews, Peter, and the Apostle to the Gentiles, Paul, in Acts:

PETER	PAUL
2.22–29	13.26–41
3.1–10	14.8–11
4.8	13.9
5.15	19.12
8.17	19.6
8.18–24	13.6–11
9.36–41	20.9–12
12.6–11	16.25–41[62]

These parallels are interesting and telling, reassuring Theophilus that God is no respecter of persons and was doing the same sort of saving work with Gentiles as with Jews. But one could also note the parallels between the trials of Jesus (before Judeans, and then the hearing with the Galilean king, and then before Pilate) and the trials of Paul. Paul, like Jesus, is said to be guilty of no crime, over and over again. Just as the centurion beneath the cross in Luke proclaims Jesus a righteous man, so at one of the trials of Paul the judge says he can find no crime that Paul has committed. The Gospel, then, is not presented as a challenge to the social authority of the Emperor and the Empire, nor preaching the Good News as a violation of Roman law. Christianity, then, is not a religion of and for felons or just for the least, the last, and the lost, though it is certainly for them as well. Jesus was crucified out of ignorance, say the speeches in Acts, and Paul is wrongly incarcerated in Philippi (and elsewhere), as he is a Roman citizen.

But it is more than an emphasis on the social benefits and political expediency that prompts Luke to tell the story of salvation history the way that he does. The crucial theme of God's plan and Scripture fulfillment had to be emphasized to show that the "Way" of Jesus was no innovation, but all along was intended by God. God's plan was to spread the Good News involving Jesus from Galilee to Samaria and from Samaria to Jerusalem and Judea during the lifetime of Jesus (as chronicled in Luke's Gospel) and then to show in Acts how the Good News spread in and around Jerusalem (Acts 1.1–6.7), to Judea and Samaria (6.7–9.31), to Gentiles (9.32–12.24), which paves the way for it spreading then

[62] I owe this list to my fellow Durhamite James Dunn. See the discussion in Witherington, *The Acts of the Apostles*, 72–73.

to Asia (12.24–16.5), Europe (16.5–19.20), and finally Rome (19.20–28) at the heart of the Empire.

One of the interesting ways Luke gives a sense of motion and growth to his story, particularly in Acts, is by little summary statements of change and growth (cf. Acts 6.7; 9.31; 12.24; 16.5; 19.20) which divide his second book into panels of a sort. Notice especially the remarkable language in Acts 6.7 and 12.24 about how the Word of God grew – it being viewed as a living thing. This is not merely a recapitulation of an OT story, nor even merely the fulfillment of the hopes and dreams of Israel, though it entails that as well. The former stories have been fulfilled, filled out more fully, extended, stretched, brought to a climax, and then in Acts even gone beyond. For Luke, as for our other NT writers the story of Christ is the linchpin or hinge of the whole human drama. Salvation is of the Jews, but it is Good News for all peoples.

One of the notable parallels of course between Luke's Gospel and Acts is the references to the eschatological Spirit being at work. In the Gospel, the locus of this is primarily Jesus (see Lk. 3.22; 4.1; 4.14,18) and in Acts the locus is Jesus' followers and those who become his followers, beginning in Acts 2. With reason, Luke has been called the theologian of the Holy Spirit and his second volume is actually better titled the Acts of the Holy Spirit. For Luke, of course, this makes clear that he thinks he lives in the eschatological age when the Dominion of God's saving reign is already breaking into human history but is yet to be completed. Like all the NT writers, he has a sense of eschatological already and not yet, and it is simply not true that he ignores the "not yet" dimension of things, for he speaks of the return of Christ in both his volumes (cf. Lk. 17.22–36; Acts 1.11). Yet operating as a historian his focus must be on the past and the present, not the future, and rightly so. Luke's work is not a book of prophecies, but rather a work of salvation history writing. Luke then places an especial emphasis on the new factor in Acts, the coming of the Spirit on all God's people, and thereby drives the story in a Trinitarian direction. The Gospels, including Luke's Gospel, had already established the revelation of the messianic figure Christ as the divine Son of God, but now the last person in the divine identity shows up on the stage of history in a continuous, indeed permanent manner.

It speaks volumes that the Synoptic Gospel writers share so much common material about Jesus and his exploits. This is of course because they believe much the same things about Jesus and what he said and did. Each of them in their own way seeks to set the story straight about Jesus, especially about the end and import of his life, and they all can be called Passion narratives with a long introduction. In fact, all four Gospels are this way because ancient people believed that how a person died most revealed his character and Jesus died in a shameful and shocking manner.

The storytellers had to explain how Jesus could indeed be the Jewish messiah, and even the Savior of the world, in spite of the fact that he died on a Roman cross. This required a great deal of explanation. Hence all four Evangelists spend almost a third of their storytelling on the last week of Jesus' life, showing how it was a fulfillment of Scripture, of God's divine plan for his Son. Since this was not an outcome expected by most early Jews when they thought of their messiah, much less by Gentiles looking for a savior, much of the story had to be devoted to explaining such a thing. And furthermore, it was needful to show that Jesus was vindicated beyond the crucifixion, so the cross did not have the last word about him, and his story carried on.

All four Evangelists agreed that the story of Easter had to be told, or else the story would hemorrhage and die, coming to an abrupt, untimely, one could even say ungodly, end – with Jesus screaming "My God, my God why have you forsaken me." All four of them agreed that the resurrection of Jesus involved, indeed necessarily entailed, an empty tomb, for resurrection meant something miraculous that happened to a human body. Indeed, all four of them told recognizably the same story about the same Jesus who was baptized by John, had a brief ministry involving preaching, teaching, and healing, and then chronicled the demise and rise of this man.

But it was not just the Evangelists for whom the Christ tale, at least in summary form, was the hinge and basis for a reordering of the way one viewed the story of God, Israel, and the world. Peter stood up on that first Pentecost and said (Acts 2.22–36):

People of Israel, listen to this: Jesus of Nazareth was a man accredited by God to you by miracles, wonders, and signs, which God did among you through him, as you yourselves know. This man was handed over to you by God's set purpose and foreknowledge; and you, with the help of wicked people put him to death by nailing him to the cross. But God raised him from the dead, freeing him from the agony of death … God has raised this Jesus to life and we are all witnesses of this fact. Exalted to the right hand of God he has received from the Father the promised Holy Spirit and has poured out what you now see and hear … Therefore let all Israel be assured that God has made this Jesus whom you crucified both Lord and Christ.

Some such summary of the life and work of Jesus as this was repeated innumerable times across the Empire in the first century, was expanded into full Gospels, was the basis for preaching and teaching by Paul, Peter, James, Jude, the Beloved Disciple, John of Patmos, and many others.[63] The Christ story was what set apart the followers of Jesus, and it became the basis of the reordering of their symbolic universe and their narrative thought world. And to be sure, because it was such a surprising, unexpected, and in various respects problematic story, they felt a need to get the story straight, and did so. This story was shared by all the writers of the NT and was a fount to which they returned again and again to draw living water. It is interesting that the story of the coming of the eschatological Spirit prophesied in Joel was far less controversial or unexpected. It had been presaged in various ways in the prophetic books of the OT. There was nothing scandalous about God's Spirit coming to help, to heal, to empower, to gift his people. No, it was not the story of the Spirit that needed extended apologia and explanation, it was the story of Jesus of Nazareth, virginally conceived, crucified, and risen, and coming again in due course.

The Narrative Thought World of the Wisdom Gospels

The Johannine Jesus bestrides the stage of history like a God.

Ernst Käsemann[64]

Matthew did not write his Gospel without forethought: he was a historian-biographer and interpreter, not just a storyteller.

Craig Keener[65]

---

[63] As was noted long ago by C. H. Dodd in his classic study *The Apostolic Preaching and its Developments* (New York: Harper & Row, 1964). The original lectures were given in 1936.

[64] E. Käsemann, *The Testament of Jesus* (Philadelphia: Fortress Press, 1968), 22–24.

[65] C. Keener, *A Commentary on the Gospel of Matthew* (Grand Rapids, MI: William B. Eerdmans, 1999), 23–24.

Both the First and the Fourth Gospels approach telling the story of Jesus differently from either Mark or Luke in this respect – they intend to emphasize in two different ways that Jesus is both a sage and the Wisdom of God come in person. Matthew's presentation focuses on Jesus as son of David like unto but greater than Solomon, and so there is a strongly Jewish flavor to the presentation.

The Fourth Gospel writer chooses a broader approach – Jesus is the Logos of God come in the flesh, Wisdom incarnate, so to speak. The former presentation would work better with more traditional and less Hellenized Jews who lived in a world where scribes and Pharisees abounded – namely in Galilee. But the Fourth Gospel is written for Hellenized Jews who live in a largely Gentile environment. The latter's ethos was not one where demons were a regular concern and Jewish parables were not a regular teaching technique there, either. There was a need for greater clarity about the identity of Jesus in that Asian environment, while in the former environment the true Jewishness and messianic character of Jesus had to be demonstrated. Nevertheless, the same basic story and narrative thought world is drawn on to present Jesus.

The Gospel of John of course has more scope than Matthew's Gospel. It begins with a retelling of the story of creation in Gen. 1, only it is Genesis as filtered through the Wisdom interpretations we find in places like Prov. 3, 8–9, or the Wisdom of Solomon. Jesus is presented as the Wisdom who was the co-creator with the Father before the space-time continuum existed. The story of the historical Jesus is suddenly viewed through a much wider-angle lens.

There is this further difference as well. Though both John and Matthew share a sapiential approach to Gospel writing, the focus in John is more personally on Jesus as Wisdom as is clear from the I am discourses ("I am the way, the truth, the life …"), whereas the focus in Matthew is on wise teaching for life, which is more in accord with traditional Jewish wisdom literature. Bear in mind that there are few if any real "parables" in the Fourth Gospel, whilst parables, aphorisms, riddles, proverbs proliferate prodigiously in Matthew. Both offer something of a counter-order sort of wisdom, and both rely primarily on revelatory wisdom, the wisdom that comes not from examining nature or human nature but rather the wisdom which comes from above.

Focusing on Matthew for a moment, one of the things that distinguishes this Gospel from John's is that it is the work of a careful scribe, who has taken over some 95 percent of the material he found in Mark and then re-audienced it for his Jewish Christian listeners in Galilee (or Antioch). This contrasts with the eyewitness approach we find in the Fourth Gospel, where the author is not following a tradition carefully but rather writing up his memoirs in his own manner and style.

Matthew stands in the scribal tradition that wants to correlate things carefully with the OT text and show fulfillment of prophecies and the like, thus stressing continuity with the Jewish past, but this is far less of a concern in the Fourth Gospel. The greater concern in the latter document is how wisdom involving and focusing on Jesus could be conveyed to an audience of highly Hellenized Jews in the Diaspora.

The First Evangelist sees himself as standing not primarily in the mold of latter rabbinic scribes doing midrash on the OT but rather in the mold of the older sapiential scribes described in Sir. 39.1–3: "He seeks out the wisdom of all the ancients, and is concerned with prophecies; he preserves the sayings of the famous and the subtleties of parables; he seeks out the hidden meaning of proverbs." In Matthew, the focus is on Jesus' teaching being the culmination and fulfillment of all older wisdom. In John, the focus is on Jesus offering new wisdom, new revelation, repeatedly. This is not to say that there isn't concern for the new in Matthew as well, as Mt. 13.52 shows, but the larger issue is continuity with older Jewish wisdom and fulfillment and extension of Torah wisdom. The First Evangelist skillfully weaves together the old and the new to portray Jesus as both sage and Wisdom, as both the revealer of God and Immanuel. The Fourth Evangelist takes this a step further by revealing Jesus as the logos, the Word of God who existed before all of creation. One other interesting fact is that the First Evangelist seems to have seen himself as a scribe, not a sage, and so as a conserver and combiner of the past wisdom. The Beloved Disciple, if, as is likely, he was also responsible for 1 John, is himself a sage, conveying Christian wisdom for life. He follows in the footsteps of Jesus, he does not merely stand in his shadow.

Without question, the *gestalt* of these two books differs in part because they were meant to serve different purposes. If we take Jn. 20.31 seriously, then it seems that the stories in the Fourth Gospel were meant to be winsome tools to be used in spreading the Good News in order that people may believe in Jesus. This contrasts with the apparent purpose and function of Matthew's Gospel, which is probably a training or teaching manual for Jewish Christians being socialized into the Jewish Christian ethos and taught how to distinguish themselves from other groups such as the Pharisees. The difference of social context (Galilee/Antioch vs. Ephesus or the province of Asia) explains in part why the story is told differently, but the difference in purpose also comes into play. The Jewishness of Jesus must be stressed in the Galilean context, where the more universal character of Jesus and his Wisdom must be stressed in Asia Minor. In Galilee one hears about Jesus being greater than Moses and greater than Solomon and the like. In Asia Minor we hear about Jesus being greater than the Emperor, as being the one who deserves to be called "my Lord and my God" (Jn. 20), usurping the claims of Domitian.

What is most important for our purposes despite all these differences is this – *the basic outline of the story of Jesus is the same in these two Gospels.* There is a Galilean ministry involving teaching and miracles, there is a final fateful trip up to Jerusalem, there is a long focus on the last week of Jesus' life including the triumphal entry, the final meal(s) with the disciples, the betrayal, the trial(s) the crucifixion, the resurrection and resurrection appearances. There were some parts of the story which simply could not be left out. It is so very telling that the Fourth Evangelist feels he must include the story of the cleansing of the temple like all the Synoptic writers, even though he feels free to push it forward to near the beginning of the ministry so that it supports his theme of Jesus fulfilling the institutions of Judaism in himself (i.e. he is the Passover lamb, he is the temple where God resides on earth, he is the light, life, bread, liberation which other Jewish festivals celebrate and so on). The basic template of storytelling is the same in these two Gospels – an account of Jesus' origins, his relationship with the Baptist, the Galilean ministry, the final week of his life, and its outcome. Within that larger script various different ways to tell the story are implemented.

Matthew wants to focus on Jesus as the royal son of David like unto but greater than Solomon. The Fourth Evangelist wants to insist that Jesus is both the Word/Wisdom of God and the Jewish source of salvation for the world (Jn. 3.16) since salvation is "of the Jews" (Jn. 4). Especially when one compares what Jesus says about himself in a chapter like Mt. 11 and what he says about himself in the "I am" discourses in John, it is recognizably the same Jesus – who is and conveys God's Wisdom. But the Fourth Gospel is not a rewrite or variation on a Synoptic theme. It is a taking of the basic score about the life of Jesus and composing a whole new oratorio. What Matthew and John show us is the limits of the possible while still trying to present Jesus within a sapiential framework and while being faithful to the basic Jesus story. These are two different portraits of Jesus, but recognizably the same wise person, the same divine person who can be called God's Wisdom come in the flesh – Immanuel.

The Narrative Thought World of Mark

[A] strong argument can easily be made that Mark – whoever he may have been ... is the most original narrative writer in history, an apparently effortless sovereign of all the skills and arts of durably convincing storytelling.

Reynolds Price[66]

Mark's Gospel, so far as we can tell, was the first attempt to narrate in written form at length the story of Jesus, and, to some extent, it seems to have provided the template for Matthew and Luke's presentations. Each of them chose to do much more than just replicate the Mark outline, but they did in fact follow the skeletal chronological outline which Mark sets up, often in detail. This is especially the case with the Matthean use of some 95 percent of Mark, whereas Luke takes over only a bit more than half of the Markan material. But what is more telling than the amount of common material is the fact that neither Matthew nor Luke chose to tell the story in the apocalyptic fashion that Mark did. If Matthew was indebted to sapiential ways of looking at narrative, Mark resonates far more with the material we find in Daniel or Zechariah.

Mark's biographical portrayal of Jesus and his ministry is both dark and stark. There are commands to silence interspersed with moments of disclosure of Jesus' identity. The disclosure moments punctuate the narrative at its outset (at the baptism of Jesus), at the climax of the first half of the Gospel (Caesarea Philippi), at the Mt. of Transfiguration where Jesus, Elijah, and Moses appear to Peter, James, and John, at the Jewish trial, at the crucifixion, and indeed at the empty tomb as well. Ched Myers, in a particularly helpful study, shows how very apocalyptic is the approach of Mark in the unveiling of the secret of Jesus' true identity. The audience lives in a benighted world and condition, lacking faith and understanding unless there is revelation from on high.

BAPTISM	TRANSFIGURATION	CRUCIFIXION
Heavens rent	Garments turn white	Sanctuary veil rent
Voice from heaven	Voice from cloud	Jesus' great voice
"You are my beloved Son"	"This is my Son the Beloved"	"Truly this man is the Son of God"
John the Baptist as Elijah	Jesus appears with Elijah	"Is he calling Elijah?"[67]

---

[66] R. Price, *Three Gospels* (New York: Touchstone, 1997), Introduction.
[67] Ched Myers, *Binding the Strong Man: A Political Reading of Mark's Story of Jesus* (Maryknoll, NY: Orbis, 1988), 390–91.

As Myers points out on the basis of this chart, these disclosure moments are meant to focus the audience's attention on the identity of Jesus. This is not a surprise, of course, in an ancient biography, but what is a surprise is that there is a messianic secret motif involved here. Apparently, Mark is telling us that the narrative can only go forward, and Jesus can only be understood, if there is periodic revelation of his identity from on high. Clearly this is not something that "flesh and blood" could deduce on its own, however sagacious one might be. We can perhaps distinguish between the more apocalyptic moments which involve a vision at the baptism and the transfiguration, and the disclosure moments, but both point to a world, and even a group of disciples, that is in the dark about who Jesus is. Thus, the entire first half of the narrative of Mark involves the raising of who and why questions about Jesus (cf. 1.27; 2.7; 2.16; 2.24; 4.41 [especially]; 6.2; 7.5), and the who question is not answered until Caesarea Philippi, even for the disciples themselves. And only at that juncture does Jesus reveal in a fourfold manner in three straight chapters (Mk. 8.31; 9.31; 10.32) that he is the man born to suffer many things, be killed and rise again, or as Mk. 10.45 puts it, he is the one who has come to be a servant and give his life as a ransom for the many. In this sort of narrative plotting, then, the Passion and Easter narratives which take up Mk. 11–16 are the chronicling of the accomplishment of the mission set out in the Passion predictions in Mk. 8–10.

This whole structure in turn suggests that Mark is telling his audience that until they answer the "who" question about Jesus, they could not possibly understand why he had to die and rise again. Thus, the Caesarea Philippi and the transfiguration stories become crucial at the heart of the narrative because there is repeated effort to make clear to the disciples precisely who Jesus is before the Passion events ensue. With knowledge is supposed to come power and responsibility, but it is not an accident that when push comes to shove Jesus envisions a fulfillment of the apocalyptic sayings in Zechariah not only about the striking of the shepherd, but also the scattering of the sheep (Mk. 14.27) and Mark most emphatically presents us with a tale of woe of how the Twelve betrayed, denied, or deserted Jesus in his hour of need, fulfilling this very prophecy that all would fall away. We have a failure of monumental proportions and restoration only comes at and after Easter, when Jesus appears to his disciples, going before them into Galilee and revealing himself there.

One of the things that is certainly shared in common in all four Gospel portrayals of the last week of Jesus' earthly life before Easter is that all are in complete agreement that a full explanation had to be provided for why Jesus' demise happened as it did. There is a sense of urgency in providing scriptural support for all this, down even to when Jesus says "I thirst" on the cross. This is, in part, caused by the disconnect which would be felt in talking about a crucified messiah, never mind a crucified God. It was caused in part because this outcome was, while not unforeshadowed or unannounced, nonetheless unprecedented and unexpected even by the closest disciples.

Few if any had talked about a crucified messiah in those terms before, Isa. 53 not being interpreted that way in early Judaism so far as we can tell. When you believe, as many ancients did, that how a person dies most reveals their character, then of course the death of Jesus required major explanation, especially if you wanted to claim that it somehow unexpectedly atoned for the sins of the world![68] Mark set the other Gospel storytellers

---

[68] Mark, it will be seen, since he takes a more apocalyptic or revelatory approach to the Christological storytelling, not surprisingly focuses on materials from Daniel and Zechariah and some messianic psalms in his bringing forward of the OT stories in order to exegete the Christ event and explain its peculiarities.

a benchmark, making clear that a full explanation of that last week, and especially of its salvific import, was crucial to making a good case for the Good News, especially in a world which viewed crucifixion in no redeeming light at all, indeed viewed it as the most shameful of all ways to die.

Notice that I have said very little about the theologizing and ethicizing that is done out of the core narrative about Jesus' life. I am talking about the powerful and extensive shared story that all four Evangelists felt compelled to tell in their various ways and with their varying emphases. But the Christ story is a huge block of common material that they shared, and not only did the Evangelists share it, but in the oral culture in which they lived, long before it was written down by Mark, it was being summarized and epitomized by teachers and preachers in various places and ways, as Acts makes so clear. C. H. Dodd well over a half century ago was correct to emphasize the apostolic preaching of the Good News and its carrying forth of the story, as we find in certain summaries in Acts and in some of the epistolary literature in the NT.[69] There is a good reason why Luke in his prologue in Lk. 1.1–4 tells us that he had been listening to preachers and eyewitnesses tell this tale for some long time. He had! And he did not need to rely purely on Mark to know the story and get it straight and give an orderly account of it. Mark was only one teller of the common tale shared and highly valued by all early Christians in many places.

And this brings us to a point where we can draw a crucial conclusion. *Too often the study of "NT theology" has been viewed as a matter of assembling the disparate pieces of a complex jigsaw puzzle, or to use another metaphor winnowing a large pile of contingent chaff to get at the coherent kernels, the core, the substance shared by NT writers, and then having done that, attempt a synthesis of these nuggets. What this whole process ignores is that these writers are operating out of a fundamental unity which in fact makes them Christians, and sets them apart from non-Christian Jews. Furthermore, they also shared a common approach to biblical theology which gave due attention to Father, Son, and Spirit.*

The writers of the NT share a common story and belief system, a common symbolic universe and narrative thought world, out of which they do their theologizing and ethicizing into particular situations. The unity primarily exists in that shared narrative thought world and highly Jewish symbolic universe. There is of course also some unity of theological and ethical expression, of articulation of that thought world, but that is less profound or vast in scope than their shared commitment to the OT and its stories, to the story of Jesus and of his earliest disciples, and the like. They share the conviction as well that God's eschatological Spirit has been sent as a permanent Advocate, advisor, anointer of his people.

Occasionally, of course, we get glimpses of just how true it is to speak of a large shared unity of thought world. For example, Paul tells us in the early 50s that he passed on to his Corinthians the very narrative he himself had received as sacred story about the death, burial, and resurrection, and appearances of Jesus (see 1 Cor. 15.1–4). He does not need to mention this more than in passing because his audience has already learned this story, has heard it on repeated occasions, and indeed has embraced it.

It must not be forgotten that the whole of the NT is addressed to those who already are Christians and have already heard their story told in many ways and on many occasions.

---

[69] Dodd, *The Apostolic Preaching and its Developments*.

The narrative thought world, including the way the Christ story has reconfigured the Jewish thought world, is simply presupposed as a baseline assumption, a fundamental unity, from which all such Christian discourse should begin. And when the Christ story is challenged in any crucial way, the response is swift and particular – to not believe that Jesus Christ has come in the flesh, has died, has come forth in glory, and has been seen and touched and known beyond his death is already called false teaching in a sermon like 1 John. We do not need to wait until the second century to find out that the early Christians had a sense of the boundaries of their thought world, and would recognize when someone had misrepresented the Christ story. The unity behind, beneath, and undergirding these NT texts is certainly vaster than the unity that can be shown from comparing and contrasting the articulation of theology and ethics on the basis of the shared narrative thought world, and yet that outward visible edge of the unity as expressed by various authors is impressive and substantive as well.

And from our earliest NT writer, Paul, we already see a strong belief that since God has sent the eschatological Spirit, new creation, the overcoming of sin, new fruit and new gifts can be found in the lives of believers, and they can be called to a higher ethical standard than even the heroes of the OT were expected to model. For, example they are called to absolute fidelity in marriage, and to absolute non-violence in relating to other human beings.

Obviously, the thought world shared by the writers of the NT is more homogenous than that shared by all the biblical writers taken as a whole. This is in part because the Bible is a book of progressive revelation, and "to whom more is given, more is expected," which is to say that one should not read the OT as if it were the tale of proto-Christians who already knew Jesus and had the eschatological Spirit as an ongoing source of illumination and power.

What the biblical writers as a whole share is a belief in the living God of the Bible and in his chosen people, and in the numerous attempts by that gracious God to redeem, restore, renew that people, and through them renew a relationship with all of humanity, all of whom were created in the image of the one living God. In all these writers, there is a sense of God acting in human history and history having a purpose, and going somewhere, though at times some of the writers despair of a positive outcome (see Ecclesiastes). What none of these writers do is theology in the abstract. It is always done out of their symbolic universe and narrative thought worlds, which is to say it is always done differently from modern attempts at theology since the Enlightenment taught us that a history of ideas or a logical arrangement of ideas was the appropriate approach to such things in philosophy and theology. It is my view that we are the poorer for being children of the Enlightenment rather than following the lead of the biblical theologians we have in the Bible itself.

The Narrative Thought World of 1 Peter

For all its Pauline echoes, however, 1 Peter also has close affinities with the synoptic tradition and to a lesser extent with the Gospel of John, Hebrews, and James. There are remarkable convergences with Peter's speeches in Acts. Since 1 Peter resonates with such a wide spectrum of early Christian witnesses, some scholars have suggested, only half-jokingly, that its author knew the whole NT! ... Part of 1 Peter's enduring appeal stems from the breadth and depth of common tradition on which it draws and its appropriation of the earlier, apostolic consensus in giving authority to its distinctive voice.

Carl Holladay[70]

1 Peter, as much or more than any other NT text, is a meditation on suffering, trying to steel the audience for what they have endured and would endure. The rhetorical strategy of the author to deal with this pastoral problem is to remind them of the story of the suffering servant of Isaiah (and the Psalms) and the particular embodiment of that story in Jesus' own story, and then to suggest that the audience is called to the imitation of those stories, should it come to that. But there is so much more to say about the tradition and narrative-rich Petrine legacy.

It has been said that Christianity in the first century was a social world in the making.[71] This is of course true, but the question is what sort of social world was being constructed by the external evangelistic program, the Good News storytelling, and the internal ordering of Christian communities based in house churches? Was it an ordering that baptized various forms of the social status quo and called it good? Was the aim to make clear that Christianity was not a revolutionary new religious sect in the Roman Empire? Was it an attempt to extend largely Jewish values and beliefs to a wider audience? And what role was 1 Peter meant to play in this social constructing of a "new world" or at least a new Christian society and subculture?

Often missed in such a sociological study of 1 Peter is the fact that the author is also busily constructing a rhetorical world, a world of advice and consent, of persuasion, of dissuasion, where certain beliefs and behaviors are inculcated not merely for social reasons but also for theological or ideological ones as well. When we analyze 1 Peter as rhetoric, what do we learn about the aims and purposes of this document, broadly speaking? Is it meant to steel the audience for persecution by persuading them about the value of Christlikeness? Is there some considerable rhetorical exigence or problem this discourse is meant to overcome? And what do we make of the intertextual echoes in this document, not only of the OT but of material from Jesus' rhetoric, James' rhetoric, and Paul's rhetoric as well?

Where was our author placed, geographically, socially, temporally, rhetorically, that he would have known all of the material mentioned by Holladay in the quotation above, and does such evidence provide clues to the authorship of this document? Could 1 Peter really be the masterpiece and last grand act of the great apostle who had known personally, and known the rhetoric of, Jesus, James, and Paul and now was making their contributions serviceable for his own audience? Was our author at the fount from which the apostolic tributaries flowed forth, and so in touch with the origins of Jewish and Gentile Christianity and its leaders, or was he at the place where all those tributaries came back together at the end of the first century and the beginning of the second? For now, it is interesting to note that though 2 Peter is a composite document deeply indebted to its predecessors, this also characterizes 1 Peter as well, though in a very different way. The Petrine legacy in the canon is tradition-rich and not story-impaired, either.

---

[70] C. Holladay, *A Critical Introduction to the New Testament* (Nashville, TN: Abingdon, 2005), 485.
[71] See John H. Elliott, *A Home for the Homeless: A Social-Scientific Exegesis of 1 Peter, Its Situation, and Strategy* (Philadelphia: Fortress Press, 1981), 2.

Commentators have often stressed that 1 Peter is more of a theocentric than Christocentric discourse, but if we ask what has caused the reconfiguration of Peter's thought world, there can be no doubt that it is what he thinks about Christ that has caused the shift. He operates with a Christocentric or Christotelic[72] hermeneutic when it comes to his handling of the OT (see e.g. 1 Pet. 1.10–12) which is by no means unique in the NT (cf. Lk. 24.25–26,45–47), and not only does the teaching of Christ echo in his words, and the figure of Christ entirely shape his theology of sacrifice and atonement, Christ provides the ethical pattern set forth for his audience to emulate. And this brings us to a further critical point. The longer I work with the Bible, the less and less satisfactory it seems to me to divide theology and ethics from one another as if they were discrete subjects. By this I mean, the figure and pattern of Christ binds the two together in the NT and grounds both the indicative (what Christ was and did) and the imperative (what his followers should do and be). Likewise, the theology of the redemptive work of Yahweh grounds the imperatives in the Ten Commandments as we have seen in the exposition of the Ten Words in Deuteronomy. In one sense, the ethics of 1 Peter is just a playing out of what it means to be like and to follow Christ. They participate in the sufferings of Christ in some sense, they look forward to an exaltation like Christ's as well, and the "V" pattern (humbling self and being exalted) is repeated in the life of the disciple (cf. 1 Pet. 4.13; 5.1–6).

The Christological language, indeed the whole theological language set, is suffused with the eschatological and apocalyptic worldview of our author. It is, then, no surprise that Jesus' second coming is referred to in 1 Peter as a "revealing" or "unveiling," with the same language being applied to the Day of Judgment that comes at and with and by means of the return of Christ (cf. 1.3–7,13 to 1.5; 4.13; 5.4). Christ is exalted, having entered heaven, and so now is hidden but one day will be revealed at which juncture believers will see him once more (1.8; 4.13b). Interestingly Peter is even prepared to call the first coming of Christ an "appearance" (1.20). It was *that* appearing which set the eschatological clock ticking, and our author lives in the exciting atmosphere of expectation about the return of Christ, possibly his near return, though expectation never degenerates into calculation in 1 Peter. This is in some ways no surprise, since we find much the same sort of orientation in Mark's articulation of things, and Mark is dependent to a degree on Peter's telling of the Christ story.[73]

We must be satisfied here by examining two ways that Peter articulates his narrative thought world. The first involves the re-evaluation of the meaning of OT texts in the light of the Christ event, and the second involves a brief comparison of Peter's speeches in Acts and what we find in 1 Peter. The latter provides us with one more piece of evidence, if we needed it, that shows how even as diverse figures as Peter and Luke share the same narrative thought world, and Luke has a concern to articulate that world in a way that is faithful to how Peter actually preached.

Let us closely consider how Peter uses the OT in 1 Pet. 2.6. First, he quotes the OT in v. 6, and in part confirms what he has said in vv. 4–5, but also he goes on to advance his

---

[72] A term I borrow from my friend Richard Hays, which refers to how Scripture is seen as pointing to or having Christ as its goal or fulfillment.

[73] On which see Ben Witherington III, *The Gospel of Mark: A Socio-Rhetorical Commentary* (Grand Rapids, MI: William B. Eerdmans, 2002).

argument (not just proof-texting his point) using OT phrases after that. Sometimes Peter, like other NT writers, uses the OT to mean things that probably were not the main point that the OT writer had in mind. Verse 6 is a quotation from Isa. 28.16 (LXX, cf. Rom. 9.33). The phrase "in him" is not found in the MT, but only in some LXX versions. Our author cites the version which makes the Christological point clearest. During the whole course of this argument Peter seems to have Jesus own words about "the stone the builders rejected" in mind (cf. Mark 12.10–11; 13.1–2; 14.58). Notably Mark, Peter's interpreter, highlights Jesus' use of these terms near the end of his Gospel. I am inclined to agree with the suggestion that Peter learned how to handle texts in these Christological and ecclesiological manners from observing the praxis of Jesus himself.

It is quite striking that the quotation here is introduced by a unique phrase which literally reads "for it says in writing," but of course Peter is not talking about just any kind of writing. He is talking about the OT. The question about the phrase is whether Peter is implying that because it is in writing it has more authority. This would depend on his theology of sacred texts, but I think the answer to this question is yes. In an oral culture, texts, especially religious texts, take on an even more sacred aura then they do in our culture of endless texts.

The quotation refers to God laying a stone in Zion – which is a synonym for Jerusalem in general, and more often indicates the city of God, the place of his indwelling, or his sanctuary, the temple hill being called Mt. Zion (cf. Pss. 20, 48, 74). Here the usage makes sense because Christians look forward to a new Jerusalem. They *are* the new temple, but they expect a new Zion (cf. Rev 14.1).

By etymology the Greek word in question means "extreme" (*akro*) "corner" (*gonias*) and so certainly cornerstone is a possible meaning here. But is it a bottom corner, like a modern cornerstone (for which there is little ancient evidence) or a "top corner"? I would suggest that *akrogōniaion* probably means a stone designed for the top corner of a wall, not a capstone of an arch, but it could be the latter. This interpretation has the advantage of matching up with the Scripture citation in v. 7 and means that there is not a different sort of stone in view when one compares Ps. 117.22 and Isa. 28.16. This interpretation also has the advantage of matching up with Test. Sol. 22.7–9; 23.1–4, which speak of Solomon's erection of a temple in which "there was a great corner stone (*lithos akrogōniaios*) that I wished to put at the head of the corner (*kephalēn gonias*)." The stone then is set on the pinnacle of the temple at the top and juncture of the two walls.

It would be impossible to stumble on a capstone or a head of the cornerstone unless of course it is envisioned as being on the ground and not yet in place in the building which is why various commentators think a cornerstone is meant.[74] Also a foundation stone which is below ground is not likely in view. We are not talking about the foundation here, but a special stone around which the rest of the edifice is built which could be either a cornerstone, a keystone, or a head of the cornerstone, which is clearly referred to in the second part of the quotation. So Christians are viewed as being built into the community which is vitally linked to and designed around Christ. Christ is the elect and precious one, or one held in honor, who makes it possible for believers who are "in Christ" to be elect

---

[74] Unless of course one was standing on the pinnacle of the temple, as Jesus is envisioned doing in the temptation tales.

and precious to God. Indeed v. 7 even refers to honor that comes to the one who believes in Jesus. It is interesting to contrast the discussion here with that at Qumran, where the Qumran community itself is characterized as the "precious cornerstone," using this very same text from Isa. 28 (1 QS 8.7, cf. 1 QH 6.26).

The quotation itself also says that those who believe in him will not be put to shame. This is an OT idiomatic expression referring to being condemned by God at the last judgment, the ultimate disgrace one can undergo, which results in shame rather than honor for that person involved. Believers share in the honor that belongs to Christ. But to unbelievers, those who build the edifice of their life rejecting the *key* or crucial stone, Christ, it becomes a stone which they stumble over, i.e., sin (just as walking implies obeying in OT). Christ is said to be a rock that is a stumbling block. The Greek term here is *skandalon*, from which we get scandalous. It here means that which occasions sin or stumbling – generally an obstacle in the way of the sinner. The irony, of course, is that these builders rejected the very one whom God selected and made into the head of the corner. Far from being a castoff he was the one of chief importance, the head of it all, particularly in the matter of salvation.

Peter is developing his argument here by drawing on two other stone passages – Isa. 8.14 and Ps. 118.22. Notice that both Rom. 9.33 and our text here are closer to the MT than to the LXX, perhaps because the LXX leaves out the notion of offense or scandal. There was another reason to follow the MT for several of these texts as well – in the LXX of Isa. 28.16 there is reference to the stone in question being sunk in the foundations, and therefore something one could not likely trip over. This has led some to suggest that Peter is following here a catena of "stone" texts which he and Paul shared in common. This is possible, but it is also possible that Peter, in Rome, had read Romans or knew of its argument, especially since Romans had been available to that community for some years, since about AD 57 or 58. In favor of the testimonia view is Ramsey Michael's point: "If Peter were using Paul [here], it is unlikely he would separate out two quotations that Paul had so carefully integrated into one. Moreover, his middle quotation Ps. 117[118].22, is not found in Paul's epistles ... but (within the NT) only in 1 Peter and the Gospels (cf. Mark 12.10//Matt 21.42//Luke 20.17; cf. the paraphrase attributed to Peter in Acts 4.11)."[75]

In v. 9 Christians are seen as a chosen race, a holy people for God's possession – Exhibit A, revealing the mighty acts of God. Indeed, they are chosen for the specific purpose of proclaiming God's mighty acts. What has happened to believers has happened so that these acts might be proclaimed, and thus God be glorified. Redemption is for the believer's succor, but it is also for God's glory. God is the one who called persons from the darkness of sin and spiritual blindness into his marvelous and everlasting light. There is nothing here about an old Israel that is being replaced by a new one. To the contrary, Peter's view is that the one people of God has kept going all along, only now the true expression of it is found in Jew and Gentile united in Christ. This is more of an eschatological completionist schema than a replacement schema.[76] There is certainly no anti-Jewish sentiment in this

---

[75] J. R. Michaels, *1 Peter* (Grand Rapids, MI: Word/Zondervan, 2015), 94.

[76] It is true that on my reading 1 Peter is not by and large addressing Gentiles. As I have said, however, it is very likely that some God-fearers came into Peter's churches through evangelism of Jews, as was true with other apostolic work. Thus, Peter is thinking of the true people of God as Jew and Gentile united in Christ the living stone.

discourse, nor even any polemic against the synagogue. But Exod. 19.6 is being appropriated and applied to the community of Christ here. *Here as in Hebrews, Christ and his
people are seen as bringing to completion the mission of Israel.*

One phrase calls for close scrutiny in v. 9. Is *Basileion hierateuma* an adjective and a
noun or two nouns? Does it mean: (1) royal priesthood; or (2) house of the King, body of
priests; or (3) a priesthood in service of the king; (4) a kingdom of priests; (5) a group of
kings, a body of priests? In favor of (4) is the OT background – Exod. 19.6 as translated
in the LXX. The Hebrew reads "a kingdom of priests" but the LXX translates it as two
substantives, two nouns in apposition to one another – kings and priests. It may seem odd
to stick two nouns side by side, but if the LXX could do it, so could Peter. Now, if view
(4) is the right rendering, it does not imply believers are kings, only priests in service of
the king. Against view (5) we may argue that there is no precedent for the word *Basileion*
meaning a "group of kings."

Against views (1) and (3) we must argue: (a) if *Basileion* was an adjective, it would
normally follow its noun as *eklektos* follows *genos* and *hagios* follows *ethnos*; (b) in the
only other use of *Basileion* in the NT (Lk. 7.25), it means a palace or king's house, and
is not an adjective, and in parallel Hellenistic literature it is normally a noun (cf. 2 Macc.
2.17; Philo, *de Sobr.* 66l and *de Abra.* 56); (c) what precedes this in v. 5, a reference to a
spiritual house, may suggest a parallel here – king's house. Thus, perhaps we should see
this as two nouns in apposition, and if so, view (2) "house of the king, body of priests" will
be the best translation. If the LXX and Hebrew background is in view, as the other terms
in the list may suggest, perhaps we should translate as a kingdom of priests or even a royal
priesthood, because the other four honorific phrases here involve a noun and a modifier. If
the latter, it is simply affirming that all believers are priests, if the former it stresses believers are both collectively God's house, and his priests.

Notice the contrast in v. 10, "you who were once not a people are now a people." Here
E. G. Selwyn urges:

What Peter's words conveyed to people so placed was that they now once again belonged to a community which claimed their loyalty; and it was something which could give all their instincts of
patriotism full satisfaction. In short, the term connotes in Greek, community. In the mixed society
of the Roman Empire, where freedom of association was suspect and subject to restrictive laws,
as in modern despotic states, this sense of community must have worn very thin, and produced a
widespread feeling of homelessness.[77]

These words from Hosea, however, originally referred to Jews, and there is no reason why
they can't refer primarily to Jewish Christians here either.

Notice as well the "now" in this text. Peter emphasizes both what God has now done
and what he will yet do. To be a people, a community, means believers have experienced
the mercy of God. Many commentators think that v. 10 could not have been spoken of
Jews. Peter can only be talking about Gentiles here who are now included in God's new
chosen race. This is forgetting that Peter's view is that when Jews have rejected Christ
they at least temporarily cease to be part of the people of God (cf. Rom. 11). Peter is here
quoting Hos. 1.6–7 and probably Hos. 2.25b as well and these texts were certainly being
applied to Jews there, as they likely are here as well. What we have seen in this section of

---

77 E. G. Selwyn, *First Peter* (London: Macmillan, 1946), 101, col. 2.

the discourse is the very sort of *tour de force* use of the OT as a basis for argumentation, loaded with allusions and partial quotations tailored to fit the context here, and as such it rivals what we find in Rom. 9–11 and the use of the Scripture there.

For Peter, it was essential to ground his argument in such a way that he could say, as he does in v. 6: "for it is contained in Scripture that ..." For him this is the final and irrefutable authority which clinches the arguments and makes the case. No audience would be more likely to pronounce the Amen to that theology of the Word than Jewish Christians who also knew and resonated with these very texts. But how poignant must these texts have been for Peter himself, who was called Cephas, but also a "stumbling block/*skandalon*" on the same occasion when he confessed Jesus as the Christ. One can understand his wrestling with these very texts to understand not only Jesus' identity but his own. This argument is brought to a close by a reminder to the audience that they have a high calling, they are a temple, and indeed they are a royal priesthood, and as such they are God's option in their own pagan environment, and so they must live in a fashion that makes them good witnesses, good neighbors, good people.

Almost from the very beginning of 1 Peter it becomes apparent to any close reader of Acts and 1 Peter that there is some connection between the speeches of Peter in Acts and 1 Peter. In 1 Pet. 1.2 we heard about the elect who had been chosen according to the foreknowledge of God and Acts 2.23 contains the only other reference to *prognosis* in the NT, where we hear about "this Jesus delivered up according to the foreknowledge and plan of God." Were this the only correspondence one might pass it off as a coincidence.[78] But in fact there are many others that one discovers as one works through 1 Peter, and it is always with the speeches of *Peter* in Acts, not with Acts in general or speeches in Acts in general, that we find correspondences.

I have dealt at length with the speeches in Acts, including Peter's speeches in my Acts commentary.[79] These speeches present the largest challenge to the student trying to evaluate the historical substance of the Book of Acts, since in many cases Luke could not have been present to hear these speeches, and in all, or nearly all, cases, what we have is summaries of speeches, not a transcript of whole speeches. These speeches make up some 365 verses of Acts or about a third of the whole book. The goal of a good Hellenistic historian was to present the major points of a speech, not just the singular main point, and to do so in a style and form that comported with Peter and his own ethos. Luke has made his source material his own, but precisely because there are correspondences between the Petrine speeches in Acts and the diction in 1 Peter it becomes clear that he must have been rather faithful to those sources and their style and substance. I have made the case elsewhere that Luke was a careful Hellenistic historian following the conventions of his predecessors like Thucydides and Polybius.[80] This result will be assumed here, not argued for. One of the important conclusions of that study was that since Luke believed that the early Christian movement was in one sense created and carried along by evangelism, the spreading of the Word (cf. e.g. Acts 6.7), he spent disproportionately more time on speeches in his work than his Hellenistic predecessors did.

---

[78] See Elliott, *Home for the Homeless*, 376.
[79] Witherington, *The Acts of the Apostles*, 116–23.
[80] *Ibid.*, 1–65.

We have some eight speeches by Peter, all of them in the first half of Acts (Acts 1, 2, 3, 4, 5, 10, 11, and a bit in 15) and there are a further nine speeches by Paul (Acts 13, 14, 17, 20, 22, 23, 24, 26, 28) and thus we see that Paul is sort of depicted as picking up where the trail of Peter goes cold. These two are given by far the most space for speeches in Acts, the next closest being the one long speech by Stephen in Acts 7 and two speeches by James in Act 15 and 21.

What is especially interesting about the place where Peter's speeches stop is that this is the juncture where Peter apparently went to the very places listed in 1 Pet. 1.1–2. The correspondences between 1 Peter and these speeches, as we are now about to see, suggest that Peter continued to preach in the same fashion and using the same subject matter as he had earlier. Three important impressions stand out from reading through Peter's speeches in Acts: (1) *Peter is always addressing Jews or in one case God-fearers like Cornelius in these speeches. There are no representative speeches to pagan Gentiles;* (2) *Peter in the paradigmatic speech at Pentecost in Acts 2 which sets the tone for all that follows in Acts uses the OT in much the same Jewish and messianic ways that we find him using it in 1 Peter;* (3) *as has often been noticed the rough Semitic style and primitive doctrine in these speeches (e.g. especially Acts 10.34–43) comport with both what we know of Peter elsewhere in the Gospels, in Paul's letters, and in 1 Peter.*

E. G. Selwyn over fifty years ago pointed out in detail the correspondences between the speeches of Peter in Acts and 1 Peter.[81] It will be well if we review that data here.

ACTS 2.14–40: The reference to the Spirit that Christ sends falling on the Church as the signal of the eschatological age being in process should be compared to what is said about prophets in 1 Pet. 1.10–12. Christ's death, in this speech, is said to take place according to God's counsel and foreknowledge (cf. 1 Pet. 1.20 and 1.2). The statement that Christ was not left in Hades and his flesh saw no corruption but rather he was raised from the dead (Acts. 2.31 and v. 27) should be compared to 1 Pet. 3.18 and also 4.6. Notice how Christ's resurrection and ascension are closely linked in Acts 2.32–36 and we can compare 1 Pet. 1.21; 3.22. The purpose of baptism according to Acts. 2.38 is said to be remission of sins, which should be compared to 1 Pet. 3.21. The universality of grace promised in Acts 2.39 becomes a theme that runs through 1 Peter – see especially 1.10–12; 2.9–10.

ACTS 3.11–26: Here we have the references to Jesus as God's servant (3.13,26 and 4.27–30), which seems clearly enough to echo Isa. 40–55, a source text used Christologically which certainly crops up in 1 Peter with some regularity. Particularly, the language Peter uses about the death and vindication of Jesus seems to echo Isa. 53. Equally interesting and telling is the theme of *agnoia* found in Acts 3.17 (cf. 1 Pet. 1.14). What is especially telling about this is that the ignorance in the Acts passage is predicated of Jews, as is probably the case in 1 Pet. 1.14. The various general parallels between these speeches and 1 Peter provide support for seeing a close parallel on the ignorance issue. Notice as well the parallel references to the Second Coming in Acts 3.20 and 1 Pet. 1.7,13, and 4.13, and to the rejection and slander of believers (cf. Acts 3.23 and 1 Pet. 2.7.10). Notice also the parallel reference to the inevitable nature of Christ's suffering (cf. Acts 3.18 and 1 Pet. 1.11 and 20).

---

[81] Selwyn, *First Peter*, 33–36.

ACTS 4.9–12: This is only a brief speech but notice the use of the OT stone material here in Acts 4.9–12 and in 1 Pet. 2.7, in both cases drawing on Ps. 117.22.

ACTS 5.29–32: Here and in Acts 10.39 the cross is called *to zulon* or a tree (cf. 1 Pet. 2.24 and Acts 13.29). This, undoubtedly, echoes Deut. 21.23. In Acts 5.32 the disciples are called witness of *tōn rēmatōn*, i.e., these things, where things refer to actions or events or even words (cf. 1 Pet. 1.25).

ACTS 10.9–16,34–43: Notice the use of *prosōpolēptēs* in v. 34 of this speech and see 1 Pet. 1.17, the use of *aprosōpolēptōs*. One can also compare the phrase "the judge of the living and the dead" referred to Christ in v. 42 and what is said in 1 Pet. 4.5.

ACTS 15.7–11: Compare the emphasis on God's choice in 15.7 and in 1 Pet. 1.1 and 2.9, and on the cleansing power of faith in v. 9 and 1 Pet. 1.22.

In addition to the above it is striking that we have the reference to the name *christianos* (Acts 11.26; 26.28) and in 1 Pet. 4.14–16. The "name" arose when Christians lived in a predominantly Gentile environment. After reviewing this evidence, Selwyn concludes:

Few would suggest that the parallels of thought and phrase between the speeches and 1 Peter are based upon St. Luke's reading of the Epistles: for in both documents they clearly belong to their contexts, and the doctrinal issues in the speeches, notably the idea of Christ as *pais Theou* are obviously original and not deductions from the Epistle. On the other hand, they are what might be expected if both alike are utterances of the same mind, given on different occasions. The connection, that is to say, is not literary but historical: the common ground lies in the mind of St. Peter who gave, and was known to have given, teaching along these lines and to a great extent in these terms.[82]

I would phrase things a bit differently, while being in strong agreement with Selwyn. The evidence that we have considered here is sufficient to say that the implied author of 1 Peter certainly reflects various of the speech traits and thematic interests of the Peter who speaks in the sermons in Acts. The question is – How do we explain this? Carl Holladay suggested that the author of 1 Peter wrote so late in the NT era that he knew various earlier NT works. This is not impossible, but of course this could even be true at a time well before the ninth decade of the first century – *it depends on the dating of the other NT books*. But in fact, what neither Holladay nor others have been able to show is a "literary relationship" between 1 Peter and Acts or with various of Paul's letters or the Synoptics. It seems rather to be more on the level of oral tradition or familiarity of the author with some of this material directly, by which I mean that the author of 1 Peter knew some of the people who wrote these books – for example Paul and Mark, and perhaps the author of Hebrews.

Here is where the issue of social location comes into play. The author of 1 Peter is in Babylon (aka Rome). Whether he is Peter or some later figure writing in Peter's name, he is a Christian who could have had access to Christian documents written in or sent to Rome – such as Romans, Hebrews, Mark, and perhaps even Acts, to judge from Acts 28, where the narrative breaks off. In my view, the correspondences between 1 Peter and the Petrine speeches in Acts are too subtle and convincing to be the work of a mere copier or imitator who decided to mimic the Petrine style of the speeches when he wrote 1 Peter.

It is a far better and more economical thesis, and one that avoids the serious problems of seeing 1 Peter as a pseudepigraph, and therefore a deceptive work, to suggest that the

[82] *Ibid.*, 36.

Peter who was a disciple of Jesus and knew his teaching, was an associate of James and knew some of his teaching, was an associate of Paul and knew some of his teaching, and had Mark, the author of the earliest Gospel, as a co-laborer in Rome is responsible for 1 Peter. Furthermore, we must consider the possibility that Luke as well finished in Rome, and perhaps had access to Peter while he was there during the period of Paul's house arrest in Rome between AD 60 and 62.

If so, then Peter is the source of the summaries of his own sermons in Acts, and it is accordingly no surprise at all that 1 Peter, then, sounds like some of that sermonic material. This is not because Luke is a good imitator and editor. It is because, while he is a good editor, in the case of Peter's sermons at least, he had a good eyewitness and original preacher source (just as he claims in Lk. 1.1–4) and it was the man called Cephas. While all roads may not lead to Rome, all these rabbit trails and echoes of other Christian sources in 1 Peter eventually lead back to the historical figure of Peter himself. He is the best candidate, perhaps with the help of Silvanus, for the authorship of 1 Peter, just as he is the one who spoke of these things on many occasions to Jews in Jerusalem and elsewhere during the first decade of the life of the church, and beyond.

This brings us to a further crucial point. We could also go on to point out the various parallels between Paul's letters and 1 Peter, including the use of the phrase "in Christ" among other things. *Not only did the NT writers share a common thought world grounded in their shared sacred text, the OT, they also exchanged information, shared stories, built up the new Christian thought world together. This involved not merely a social world in the making, but a Christian thought world in the making. The fact that there are so many similarities in the way the OT is used and the way the Christ story is articulated between so many of these witnesses suggests a movement with considerable social networks and obvious dialogue. The unity is not limited to just the obvious shared ideas that lie on the surface of various of these NT texts. It is appropriate to add that these various correspondences provide an open invitation to reflection on a larger biblical theology, indeed they encourage such thinking, as the authors themselves are already doing a form of biblical theology themselves. Notice that one must consider not only the intertextuality of these texts in their use of the OT, but also the intertextuality involved in the NT itself, as the various authors use each other's materials, or their own materials in several ways and places.*

Here it is well to remember what Paul tells us in Gal. 2. He says that he set his Gospel before the pillar apostles so that he would not be running in vain. He says he received the right hand of fellowship from these pillars and his mission to Gentiles was recognized and endorsed. Whatever differences of praxis that would and did arise between Paul, and some Judaizers from Jerusalem (some men from James, but not James or Peter or John in particular), *it did not have to do with the articulation of the Gospel, the story of Christ, nor have we any reason to think it had to do with the Christological and ecclesiological way the OT was now being read. Acts 15 shows that James is just as busy offering such readings as Paul or Peter or any other early Christian writer.* Out of the many and divergent articulations of theology and ethics in the NT there was a considerable unity of narrative thought such that wherever one went in the Empire and spent time with Christians, the Gospel and its new way of reading the OT was shared in common.

And this brings us to just a few comments about 2 Peter. 2 Peter is a composite document assembled likely in the last decade of the first century AD. It is indebted to 1 Peter and an otherwise unknown Petrine fragment recounting his reaction to the transfiguration. It is indebted to Jude, and it is indebted to Paul. The editor of this material is not an innovator nor does he seek to be. He is a collector and consolidator of earlier Christian traditions. But what 2 Peter shows is that he assumes that the earlier traditions are not in any way discordant. He assumes that they work very well together to address his own Christian audience. He assumes that they all have their own stories straight, and indeed they are all telling the same Christian story, unlike the false teachers against whom he is doing polemics. The apostolic tradition is already in play and a living reality in his discourse.

This attention to and dependency on shared sacred tradition should in no way surprise us, since the author like all the other NT authors, except perhaps Luke, is probably a Jew. But it tells us a great deal about the early Christian movement that so much material was shared, including of course both the OT and the Gospel. It then comes as less of a surprise that all these writers articulated their theology and ethics in ways that are harmonious with, and sometimes even identical with, what we find in other NT writings. Christianity after all was a fledgling minority movement in the first century AD, regarded by many as a pernicious religious superstition, not a licit religion. Under such circumstances, it is not a surprise that these Christians hung together in the way they thought, taught, and preached, lest they hang separately, and of course they did that together as well. This too is an invitation to see and articulate the larger biblical theology in the Bible.

The Narrative Thought World of Revelation

Those first ancient auditors of the Apocalypse came together not merely to be informed but to be transformed, to undergo a collective change in consciousness.

A. D. Callahan[83]

While we could spend some brief time on the narrative thought world of James, Jude, 1–3 John, in truth it is so allusive that in James we have bare references to Job and Elijah and a little more about Abraham, in 1 John we have a passing reference to Cain, in Jude we have colorful references to a group of the bad boys of the Pentateuch coupled with references to extra-canonical traditions about Enoch and Moses. But in all cases these stories are taken for granted as shared with the audiences, known to the Jewish audiences, and so there was no need for elaboration at all. Furthermore, in each case the names arise or are alluded to in order to make ethical points, not theological ones. The issue is praxis and behavior, not primarily the thought world in each case. In addition, of course there are the allusions to and echoes of Jesus' teachings, particularly in James. But in these more paraenetic discourses the thought world is not much in play or articulated, and this is even less the case in brief personal letters like 2 and 3 John. Thus, this brings us to the very rich and complex last volume in the canon – the Book of Revelation

Revelation is different from all of the rest of the NT in providing us with a book of apocalyptic prophecy within an epistolary framework. The narrative thought world of this

---

[83] A. D. Callahan, "The Language of the Apocalypse," *HTR* 88 (1995): 453–67, here 460.

book is more extensive than many NT books, especially in relation to the future of Christ's story and the story of the world and of his people.

One of the interesting features of John's narrative thought world is that clearly John's mind is a Scripture-saturated one. There are literally hundreds of allusions, echoes, or partial quotations of the OT in this book, but they are used in the service of a Christological vision of the present and the future. Once again, the Christ story reconfigures how the OT is viewed, and more importantly how it is used. John believes he knows how all those prophecies in the OT will be fulfilled, and by whom, and the answer is through and in Christ and his people. A unique feature of course of John's visionary rhetoric is that he recounts not only the story of what is and will transpire on earth, but also what *is* transpiring in heaven as well. As George Caird suggested long ago, John gives us a glimpse into the control center of the universe, into the heavenly court where we find the divine situation room and learn of how God is and will manage the crisis of sin and evil on the earth by bringing both temporal and eternal judgments and acts of redemption to those on earth, though ultimately the real solution to the human dilemma has been provided already by a slain lamb and the Word of God. John also will recount how what is currently "up there" will someday be "out there" when Christ returns and the new heaven and new earth follow. The other world and the afterlife effect a corporate merger.

We should not be led astray by the hyperbolic, bizarre, and sometimes even mythological images in this book to assume that John's revelation is not referential and is not intended to speak about the future. This is in fact not true. John believes in a literal return of Christ in space and time and there is no reason to doubt he also believes in a series of redemptive-judgments which will fall upon the earth prior to that consummation. It is of course true that the overall message is that God is in his heaven and all will be right with the world because God's divine reign will come fully on earth when Jesus returns, and before then God will already be dealing with rescuing his people and judging their oppressors. There is a strong stress on the sovereignty of God over the historical process, including the future. No one should see this as ephemeral idealist rhetoric, the ancient equivalent of insubstantial comfort food. John is in deadly earnest about the coming judgments and redemption wrought by God.

The arc of the narrative John tells mostly begins and ends with the story of a Christ who is Alpha and Omega, and so present in the beginning and at the end, but is born of a woman at a particular point in time and is snatched back up into heaven just when Satan had thought he was going to snuff out his life for good (Rev. 12). This story is juxtaposed to the story of the threefold fall of Satan, who not surprisingly tries to do away with this Incarnate One, but himself ends up not only falling from grace and heaven to earth, but falling into the pit, and thence into the lake of fire. But between the fall from heaven and the fall into the pit, Satan chases the woman, the emblem of God's people. She is protected on the earth, not raptured into heaven, as Rev. 12 makes so very clear. It would be remiss not to also note the Trinitarian character of John's discourse. The Father also is called Alpha and Omega in Revelation, and the Spirit is quite specifically associated with the seven churches mentioned in Rev. 2–3, with each church having the Spirit.

John's story has not only more scope than most of the tellings of the story in the NT, but it also has more texture and scope and depth. For example, John is concerned to contrast the evil empire with the godly one. So, we will hear about the emperor under the figure of Mr. 666, and there is his imperial cult apparatus under the figure of the false prophet/priest and the land beast. The emperor and empire are as one in the image of the beast with multiple horns and wounded head. We have in addition a tale of two cities, not Jerusalem vs. Rome, but rather Rome the harlot vs. the new Jerusalem which will come down from heaven. Despite all the stress on three sets of seven judgments, which takes up the largest single bit of the plot, John has an expansive vision of saved Jews and myriads of Gentiles, of 144,000 of the Jewish saints saved, but also the Gentile ones, of OT saints and NT apostles being foundational to the heavenly city not made with human hands. The political nature of this coded rhetoric far outstrips the allusions we find from time to time to the emperor cult in Paul's writings and elsewhere in the NT. This book is certainly not mainly about pie in the sky, by and by – it's about justice and redemption being done upon the earth. It is not the ancient equivalent of escapist fiction, and no, John does not affirm a rapture into heaven for Christians, just when the going gets rough on earth. Rather, Revelation is the book of the martyrs, and the word *martus* here, perhaps for the first time, refers not just to any kind of witness, but one who witnesses to Christ faithfully unto death.

John believes in the interface between the material universe and a spiritual one, between earth and heaven. Thus, he does not believe that human history is a self-contained homogenous process where the normal lines of historical cause and effect apply in all cases. Divine governance is a perpetual condition and divine involvement in history is a regular occurrence. For John, the most important events in human history have already happened – the death of the Lamb and his resurrection and exaltation to the right hand of God the Father. John believes that the end of history has already broken into space and time and so his is an eschatological perspective, not an ordinary salvation history perspective. God's eschatological judgment on history, not a normal chronicling of history, is going on here, and of course it is future history which is being prophesied and commented on in this book. In this telling of the story, history receives its final meaning from what is yet to come. The comfort for the suffering audience comes not mainly from the reassurance that they will go to be with the Lord in heaven, though that is certainly believed and spoken of, nor even that God will judge their oppressors before the end, but rather it comes from the vision of the end itself, which involves new heaven and new earth and the final elimination of sin, suffering, sorrow, disease, decay, and death, and evil as well. John's focus is not on the meaning of history, but rather on the meaning of suffering and the response of God to it, showing that God remains sovereign even in this vale of tears.

Like Luke, John of Patmos believes that the story of the church is a continuation of the story of Jesus in various senses. Thus, for example in Rev. 12.1–14.20 and in 15.2–4 we have the story of God's people in the present (and future) in conflict with evil and dealing with suffering, and the pattern of Jesus' suffering is replicated in the saints who are martyred and end up under the altar in heaven (Rev. 6.9–11). John believes that there is one continuous history of God's people from the patriarchs to the consummation, but, obviously, the nature of that people changes, becoming Jew and Gentile united in Christ once the Lamb is slain and then exalted on high. There is no separate history for Israel and the church, but one ongoing tale. This is not in any way to deny the constant divine interventions in the tale, though "interventions" is not the right word since God is governing the tale all along. Better is the suggestion that we talk about the divine *participation* in the history of God's people all along.

The macro-story of God's people helps give perspective on the trials and tribulations of the particular churches which John is addressing in Rev. 2–3. Their travails are set against the backdrop of those of God's people before and after them. What we learn of the story of John's churches is that they have existed for a considerable period of time, have had various ups and downs, various temptations and triumphs and they are ongoing. Some of these churches are doing better than others, but John tells them the cautionary tale in Rev. 12 to remind them that they have protection from obliteration but they need to be vigilant as well. If the two lampstands in Rev. 11 are two of these churches, then there is the reassurance that "if anyone tries to harm them, fire comes from their mouths and devours their enemies." Fire-breathing churches is a rather fierce image of the church's ability to endure through persecution, prosecution, and execution.

The intersections of the stories of Christ, the church, and the known world's empire are various, and much is woven together. But not surprisingly it is the Lamb who is also the Lion who is also the Lord who has the first and last word about both his church and his world, as Rev. 21–22 make clear. This story is only foreshadowed and alluded to in the little apocalypse in Mk. 13 (and par.), but what John says here is consonant with what we find there, and for that matter with what we find in 1 Cor. 15 and 2 Thess. 2. The shared eschatological and Christological worldview of all the NT writers is presented to us in detail and Hi-Definition in Revelation.

Jesus too, in his discussions of a future coming of the Dominion involving a messianic banquet, the patriarchs, himself, and his converts, suggests that he envisioned a future millennial messianic kingdom on earth not unlike what Rev. 20 has in mind, a not-uncommon view of early Jews, such as Pharisees and Qumranites, who subscribed to an eschatological afterlife view.

The final vision in Rev. 22, like the vision at the outset, reinforces that the author has a Trinitarian view of God. The throne of God and the Lamb will be on earth in the new Jerusalem, the locus of worship without the mediation of a temple or priests. And it is the third member of the Trinity who has been with God's people, the bride, all along since Pentecost who beckons with the bride for this final eschatological conclusion to happen. The Spirit proves to be the means and empowerment of worship of God and the Lamb, just as it was only "in the Spirit" and especially "on the Lord's Day" that John saw all these remarkable visions in the first place. It was the Spirit that transported John in these visions so that he might glimpse the inner workings of heaven and the future, peeling back the opaque canvas of history, of space, of time. As we have said before, the beginnings of a Trinitarian way of thinking about the divine identity are already present in the NT, including in unique ways in the climax of the NT in Revelation. It only remained for later Christians to reflect on and elaborate what was already present in the NT books themselves.

And So?

We have by no means covered the entire shared narrative thought world spoken of or alluded to in the various NT books and in the teaching of Jesus, or those in the OT, either. There is a great deal more that could in fact be said. My goal in this chapter was to present a representative sampling to show the depth and scope of this narrative thought world, and the degree to which it is shared by all these writers, and with Jesus as well. Monotheistic, messianic, eschatological, and even proto-Trinitarian thinking characterized the thought world of all these early Jews. They believed they lived in the age of the fulfillment of prophecy, the climax of history, the arrival of final redemption and judgment which would begin with the household of God. This was not just the perspective of John of Patmos, who was merely the most obvious example of this sort of thinking, bringing it to its fullest and most vivid expression. The revision of monotheism in a Christological and, to a lesser degree, in a Pneumatiological light characterizes all of this literature's narrative thought, even beginning with Jesus himself. In some respects, they shared eschatological notions with the exilic and post-exilic prophets – Ezekiel, Daniel, Zechariah, Third Isaiah and others.

We can and should reiterate here some of the salient conclusions drawn earlier in this chapter. *If we compare all this material a pattern emerges involving: (1) focus on Christ; (2) Christological or Christotelic interpretation of the OT, a rereading not only of the prophetic material but even the priestly material in light of the Christ event; (3) a focus on both the humanity and the divine identity of Christ; (4) a belief that Christ the Messiah has brought in the beginning of the eschatological realities called Kingdom or salvation, or both; (5) an expansion of monotheistic ideas now to include Christ and the Spirit; (6) a belief that the eschatological Spirit has been bestowed, amongst other benefits, by the exalted Christ on his people and the people of God are viewed as Jew and Gentile united in Christ. In this people, we find both the culmination of the mission of God to the world and the completion of its formation as a people awaits the return of Christ when "all Israel" will also be saved, by the mercy of God, by grace through faith in Jesus. Here it is important to stress that at the heart of NT theology is indeed the doctrine of God – Father, Son, Holy Spirit – and this involves taking up into this understanding of God much of what the OT said in the first place about the character and nature of Yahweh. This is what most distinguishes these documents from other early Jewish documents including the OT, and at the same time which most makes clear that these authors are sharing a common Christ-focused, Spirit-illuminated worldview which has changed the way they view their own storied world, and the stories they learned growing up from the Hebrew Scriptures.*

7

The Passion Play and its Sequels without Equal

Nothing in the New Testament authorizes Biblical theologians to work backwards from the New to the Old and pour a developed Christology or Trinitarian theology into every messianic reference or every text about the Spirit. But the New Testament references do reveal that their authors were working in the opposite direction, affirming that God's Spirit was still at work in Israel and that what was true about Yahweh in the Old Testament was true of Jesus in the New.

James K. Mead[1]

The ability to distinguish correctly law from gospel is what makes a theologian a theologian.
Oswald Bayer, following Luther[2]

It is a commonplace in NT scholarship that probably the very first portion of the story of Jesus that came to have a written and reasonably fixed form is the Passion narratives. 1 Cor. 11, where Paul, in about AD 52 or so, quotes a bit of the story about Jesus' last night before the crucifixion, is probably evidence that this conclusion is correct. What is beyond cavil is the fact that almost a third of the Gospels are devoted to the last week of Jesus' life. This might seem to us a lopsided way to tell the story of Jesus' entire earthly life, until we realize that the ancients believed that: (1) how a person died revealed essential things about that person's true character and identity, and (2) death on a cross had no positive valence at all in early Judaism, indeed it could even be said to be evidence that the person in question had been cursed by God, for crucifixion was seen as the most horrendous and shameful form of death – something reserved for the very worst elements in the Empire, rebellious slaves, and hardened criminals guilty of treason. In other words, explaining the surprising and unexpected and premature nature of Jesus' death became a necessity, especially for an evangelistic religion that hoped to win over both Jews and Gentiles to the following of Jesus of Nazareth. We have reserved several crucial elements of the narrative thought world of various NT writers for this chapter because they especially deserve to be given more attention and more focus than the survey of the narrative thought worlds of NT writers could encompass.

---

[1] Mead, *Biblical Theology*, 175.
[2] Tübingen Luther scholar Oswald Bayer is here echoing Luther himself. See Luther's own words in *Luther's Works* 26:113 (Lectures on Galatians), in Oswald Bayer, *Martin Luther's Theology: A Contemporary Interpretation* (Grand Rapids, MI: William B. Eerdmans, 2007), 65.

This chapter will be divided up in a sort of chronological order, dealing with the death of Jesus on the cross, some of the other famous last words of Jesus (other than the one sentence found in Matthew and Mark), the resurrection accounts, and the later reflections on them by Paul in 1 Cor. 15 (which are actually our earliest such reflections chronologically speaking since 1 Corinthians was written before the Gospels in all likelihood), and we will examine the "spiritual" benefits of the death, resurrection, and Spirit-sending of Jesus. We will finally turn to the even later reflections in 1 John on the death of Jesus and its spiritual benefits. What this chapter will show is the various writers of the NT were indeed theologizing and ethicizing *especially* out of the Christ story, and especially out of its conclusion – the death and resurrection of Jesus. They believed that the Christ event had an ongoing impact not only on the lives of Jesus' followers, but by way of the proclamation of the Good News also on the lives of Jews and Gentiles who did not yet believe the Gospel. They also believed that had the death and resurrection and ascension of Jesus not happened, there would have been no eschatological sending of the Holy Spirit on Christ's followers.

Famous Last Words

The backdrop to Jesus' famous last words in context is of course the betrayal, threefold denial, and desertion of Jesus by his various Galilean male disciples. Particularly egregious was the behavior not merely of Judas, but of the leading male Galilean disciple, Peter. And by general account of the Synoptic writers none of the Twelve were present to witness the crucifixion. This might seem to be contradicted by the Johannine account, except when one realizes that the Beloved Disciple is not portrayed as one of the Twelve in the Fourth Gospel, a Gospel which does not mention the Zebedees' brother *at all* prior to the appendix in Jn. 21. Judging strictly by the content of that Gospel, the Beloved Disciple appears to have been a Judean follower of Jesus who did not itinerate with Jesus in Galilee and had a different tale to tell in his Gospel.[3] This brings us to the vital point that *so far as the Galilean disciples who itinerated with Jesus there and came with him for the festivals to Jerusalem are concerned, it was only the female disciples who were last at the cross, first at the empty tomb, and first to see the risen Jesus.*

We can confidently say that no evangelistically inclined early Jewish movement that wanted a broad audience for its Gospel would be likely to make up the notion that women, in the first instance, were the primary witnesses to the most crucial parts, the climactic parts, of Jesus' earthly ministry. And the *ocular proof*, to borrow a phrase from Shakespeare's *Othello*, that these facts were *not* made up by later Gospel writers is the very fact that the list of eyewitnesses in 1 Cor. 15 does not mention these women directly (perhaps indirectly in some group appearance to the 500?).

In other words, the Gospel writers felt compelled to tell the end of Jesus' story straight, even though it was quite unflattering to the Twelve. No writer in his right mind, writing at a time when Christianity had already received some persecution and pushback (and would

---

[3] For a detailed study of who this person was, in my view it was Lazarus, as Jn. 11.1–4 suggests, but even if not, surely a Judean disciple who is not among the Twelve, see Witherington, *Invitation to the New Testament* and also in more detail Ben Witherington III, *What Have They Done with Jesus? Beyond Strange Theories and Bad History: Why We Can Trust the Bible* (New York: HarperOne, 2007).

later be criticized for being a religion whose primary adherents were mere women and children and slaves) would have written in the last third of the first century AD that Jesus appeared first to a Galilean woman from a fishing village on the Sea of Tiberias whom he had cast seven demons out of previously (cf. Lk. 8.1–3 and Jn. 20). No, the Gospel writers felt compelled to speak of the role of women at the end of Jesus' life, including of course his own mother. So, let us consider the things that happened and were said according to Luke and John, probably our latest two Gospels, about the Passion and Jesus' famous last words.

We pick up the story at Lk. 23.32–55, noting the pointed reference to the women watching the crucifixion from afar, who will then be mentioned again at Lk. 24.1–11, by name as Mary Magdalene, Joanna, Mary the mother of James, and other women who "remembered Jesus' teaching" (cf. Mk. 15.40–41), but whose report was considered an idle tale by the male disciples when they came and told what they found at the tomb and what the angels said about the risen Jesus. The word "remembered" is meant to remind Theophilus that the women had been taught this previously – they too were disciples. In that larger context, we can best appreciate Lk. 23.32–55.

Jesus is crucified between two malefactors, probably revolutionary bandits, since mere "thieves" did not receive capital punishment for their crimes. This only increases the general *pathos* of the account, for Jesus ends up telling the "penitent bandit" he can share Paradise, the blessings of heaven, with him. There is as well the famous "Father forgive them for they know not what they do," but about whom is this said? It could be about the executioners, for they are indeed ignorant of who Jesus genuinely is, or it could be about the Jewish authorities who handed Jesus over, as well as the executioners (see Peter's speech in Acts 3). There is in addition a textual problem here. Various early witnesses, including P75, B, D*, W, and others, do not have this "last word" of Jesus from the cross. Nevertheless, the textual experts still think it likely that this is a dominical saying of Jesus, and it certainly comports with what he says about forgiveness, ironically to Peter, in Mt. 18.21–22, and what he says in the Sermon on the Mount about loving enemies and praying for those who persecute you in Mt. 5.33–34, and his actual praxis as depicted in Jn. 21, where Peter is restored to a leadership role.[4]

The famous exchange between two crucified men in Lk. 23.42–43, like the saying we have just mentioned, is also uniquely Lukan in character, emphasizing in a further way the gracious and compassionate nature of Jesus even while dying on the cross. One could even say that Jesus was busy saving the least, the last, and the lost, including even notorious sinners, even on the cross. There is some uncertainty about whether the Greek suggests an immediate departure to Paradise "today" or whether Jesus is simply reassuring the man "today" that he will in due course enter Paradise. Either way, the outcome is shockingly positive, revealing the extreme graciousness of Jesus. In the case of the criminal himself, this might well be called the first genuine deathbed conversion.[5]

The final word from the cross is of course "Father, into your hands I commend my spirit." Jesus believes that he has a spirit that will survive death, and he is going back to the

---

[4] On the textual problem, see Bruce M. Metzger, *A Textual Commentary on the Greek New Testament* (2nd edn.; Stuttgart: German Bible Society, 1994), 154.

[5] On all this Lukan material see now A.-J. Levine and Ben Witherington III, *The Gospel of Luke* (Cambridge: Cambridge University Press, 2018).

Father, giving his life back to its very source. There is no agony on the cross in Luke, and indeed Jesus dies in such a noble way that in Luke, the centurion on duty at the cross says "Surely this was a righteous man," which presumably means not only that he died a noble death, not cursing God, but perhaps even intimates a recognition that he was crucified in ignorance, done wrong to in the end. Notice that even this utterance by the centurion is different from the earlier Gospel accounts, which have "surely this was a son of God" (Mk. 15.39).

It cannot be stressed enough that while the "last words" of Jesus in Mark and Matthew are stark and dark, here we see a very different side of Jesus, who seems to be in control of the situation, as is even more evident in John. No one takes away Jesus' life, he simply gives it up to the Father. Since it was true that people took very seriously a person's last words, and how they died, Luke is undoubtedly trying to stress that though Jesus was crucified he: (1) did not deserve it, on the testimony of even his executioner, (2) expected Paradise thereafter, a positive outcome in the end, and (3) was still about the business of saving the lost even on the cross! This is not unlike "having loved his own who were in the world, he loved them to the bitter end" (Jn. 13.1), only here, extraordinarily, he is even loving a last-minute convert.

Turning to the Johannine account in Jn. 19.25–30, we have a sort of last will and testament scene. There is some evidence that a person could even make such a will while being executed,[6] but we should notice immediately that while several Marys are there at the cross when Jesus dies, he addresses only the two persons who apparently were standing closest to the cross – his mother and the Beloved Disciple. Notably missing in action are any of the rest of Jesus' family, perhaps scandalized by the shameful outcome of his life, and notably having nothing to do with the burial rites, which was normally a major duty for siblings of their elder brother. We learn in Jn. 7.5 that the brothers didn't believe in Jesus, and in 1 Cor. 15 that it took an appearance of Jesus to his brother James for him to become a disciple, and then we hear about Mary and other family members (brothers) in the upper room awaiting Pentecost in Acts 1.14. All that makes the words of Jesus here all the more surprising and poignant.

Jesus says to his mother, "woman behold your son" and then to the Beloved Disciple, "here is your mother." And we are told that thereafter the Beloved Disciple (hereafter BD) took her into his own home. Since the BD was a Judean disciple, indeed, I would say one who lived in the Jerusalem suburbs of Bethany, it then becomes understandable why Mary is still in Jerusalem according to Acts 1.14. Jesus wished not only to take care of his mother, but to integrate her into the family of faith. The BD is to become her spiritual son, and she is to become his spiritual mother. Even from the cross Jesus is creating his community, which will survive his death.

The final saying of Jesus from the cross, "I thirst," reflects the concern to depict everything that happened to Jesus, even his death on the cross, even how it all ended, as being part of God's plan, thus "I thirst" is seen probably as a fulfillment of a text from the Psalms (cf. Pss. 22.15 and 69.21).[7] Jesus once again is seen to be in control, and the soldiers do not in fact take or shorten his life by breaking his bones. Before the spear thrust, he had

---

[6] On the historical particulars see Witherington, *John's Wisdom*, on this chapter.

[7] On the focus on Jesus fulfilling the Psalms in the Fourth Gospel, a trend not nearly so noticeable in the other Gospels, see Witherington, *Psalms Old and New*, pp. 69–107.

already freely said "it is completed" and bowed his head and given up his spirit. In short, the portrayal of the death of Jesus in Luke and John is dramatically different than in the earliest two Gospels. Both Luke and the Fourth Evangelist have a concern to show that Jesus' life did not end in shame, disaster, much less that what Pilate had done to him was fair, in terms of human justice. Also note that none of the four portraits of Jesus' death directly suggest Jesus was cursed by God, as Paul was later to do, though Paul's view is that Christ endured the curse on sin for others as a fulfillment of Scripture (see Gal. 3.13 and Deut. 21.23).

Throughout the four Passion narratives there is a concerted effort to show that the shocking things that happened during the last week of Jesus' life, including his death on the cross, were foretold in Scripture and all along part of God's plan. *Nothing* in that last week happened by accident or against the will of God is the message of the Evangelists, not even Jesus' death on the cross. This was the cup Jesus was asked to drink to the dregs by God his Father, and he did so. But all of this remarkable scriptural interpretation of the events of the last week of Jesus' life would never have even been attempted if there had not been a sequel without equal to that horrible end on the cross. The cross would have been nothing more than yet another tragedy of Roman making, yet another act of ruling oppressors, without the resurrection, to which we now turn.

It is admittedly odd in some respects, that while there is great effort in the Passion narratives to chronicle the events and frame and interpret them in light of OT ideas and phrases and quotations, there is very little attempt in these narratives to provide a theological interpretation of the meaning of Jesus' death, with some rare exceptions. Yes, Jesus' reinterpretation of the bread and wine at the Last Supper is such an exception, and yes, the pre-Passion explanation that Jesus came to give his life as a ransom for the many in Mk. 10.45 helps. Perhaps this paucity is partially explained by the fact that early Jews didn't view execution of a Jew by capital punishment in relationship to atonement for sins.

The Maccabees were voluntary martyrs, and they did not die on crosses for others' sins. There is a focus, in a text like Mt. 27, on indirect suggestions as to who Jesus is, *in spite of his hanging on a cross*, for instance in v. 44, where we hear him called Son of God and King of Israel. Perhaps more suggestive is the odd, uniquely Matthean statements that just as Jesus died, tombs were opened of the OT saints who had died. Nothing happens other than this at that juncture, but then later, "after his resurrection" (see vv. 52–53), they came out of their tombs just as Jesus did, entered Jerusalem, and appeared to many. I would suggest that this bit of narrative theologizing is a way of saying that Jesus' resurrection triggers or is at least linked to the eschatological resurrection of the saints. Perhaps we see this idea in Paul as well in 1 Cor. 15, where he calls Christ's resurrection the first fruits of the resurrection, by which he means, that when Christ returns, the dead in Christ will rise – not everyone, just the saints, just the dead in Christ. We will say more about the resurrection in a moment.

There is one more possible explanation for the failure to provide any sort of detailed theological explanation of the meaning of Jesus' death in the Passion narratives. If it is true that these documents were written in the last third of the first century, then they were written after Paul's letters, after Hebrews, probably after 1 Peter as well. In other words, there had already been some deep reflection on the meaning of Jesus' death in these other early Christian sources. Lk. 1.1–4 tells us that many had been trying to deal with the story before him. He is aware of such attempts, and, I would suggest, he is aware of Paul's theologizing, as a comparison of the Lukan Last Supper account with 1 Cor. 11 would suggest. So perhaps the Evangelists didn't see themselves as acting and explaining in a vacuum. Perhaps they felt their contributions were just to tell the story with the help of the OT. This they do remarkably well. What then of the resurrection?

Rising to the Occasion

What should be clear from all four Gospel accounts, even if one thinks Mk. 16.8 is the original ending of Mark's Gospel, is that they are all in agreement that resurrection involves something that happened to the dead Jesus' body. The empty tomb in itself could be explained variously, but it is precisely connected to his resurrection. "His body is not here" and that is because "he is risen." Resurrection in early Judaism, as is amply demonstrated in N. T. Wright's *The Resurrection of the Son of God*, did not refer to someone's spirit going to heaven. Nor did it refer to the immorality of the soul. No, it referred to something that happened to the body or ashes of a deceased person. It was a remarkable, indeed miraculous, something that happened to the dead person.[8] Furthermore, it did not refer to a person coming back from the dead with some ethereal and non-material form. No, it referred to a raised physical body, though with various different properties than it had before, for example it was no longer subject to disease, decay, death, or, in general, mortality.

It is the conviction of Paul in 1 Cor. 15, our chronologically earliest Christian testimony about resurrection, that: (1) Jesus was raised "from out of the dead ones" in a body (the rest being still in the land of the dead); (2) he was the first fruits of the resurrection, which is to say, he was the first one to get a glorified or resurrection body; (3) he saw this as the precursor and first installment of the eschatological resurrection but that nothing more would happen until Christ returned and the dead in Christ then would be raised; (4) the resurrection body would be everlasting as opposed to mortal, imperishable instead of perishable, it would be powerful as opposed to weak, it would be fully sustained by the indwelling of the Spirit, which is what Paul means by a "spiritual" body in contrast to a body like Adam's that merely had life-breath in it. In addition, it would be fully conformed to the image of Christ, as the old body was conformed to the image of Adam, *and finally* while the old body was nothing to brag about, was all too inglorious, the resurrection body would be glorious. While there had been those before Jesus who had been raised from the dead, none had partaken of a resurrection body, and so they came back into their mortal frame, and eventually died once more.

Precisely because the resurrection of Christ had already happened "according to the Scriptures" (1 Cor. 15.3–4), the eschatological age had clearly already dawned. Early Judaism was not looking for an isolated resurrection of their messiah prior to the end of the age when all the righteous might be raised, and so what happened to Jesus was a game changer, with all sorts of theological and ethical implications. It is Paul who first spins these out in 1 Cor. 15 at some length.

---

[8] See N. T. Wright, *The Resurrection of the Son of God* (London: SPCK, 2003), pp. 1–150.

For one thing, it definitely meant that God had vindicated Jesus after his death on the cross. Pilate's no to the life of Jesus had been overcome by God's yes. If indeed God had raised him from the dead, then what Paul says in Rom. 1.4 – he was vindicated to be the Son of God in power by means of his resurrection from the dead – was surely true. This meant not only that Jesus' claims about himself were true, it also meant a negative evaluation of his death on the cross was wrong. It could not have been a case of Jesus being judged by God for his own sins and wickedness. And again, it is Paul, our earliest witness, who tells us in Rom. 3 that his death was a propitiatory sacrifice for sins, absorbing the punishment and bearing the guilt. Jesus was both the Passover lamb, whose shed blood protected God's people from a death verdict, as in the first Passover, but also the scapegoat, who took away the sins of the world. *There would have been no positive evaluation of the cross without the risen Jesus.*

Paul is also quite careful to make clear to say that the risen Jesus "appeared" to various people at various times, in various places, both to individuals like Peter and James, and to small and large groups of disciples. Notice that he does not say that the disciples *thought they saw Jesus or had visions.* No, he says the initiative was with Jesus, he chose to *appear* to certain people, over a 40-day period (according to Acts 1.3). And notice that he appeared to at least two non-disciples of Jesus – Jesus' brother James, and also Saul of Tarsus, an opponent of the Jesus movement. Paul does everything he can to make clear he is not talking about visionary experiences. That being the case, a non-miraculous interpretation of history becomes impossible.

The resurrection of Jesus meant the beginning of the End, and no one knew when the thief in the night might return to bring the End-times to their conclusion. It was the combination of the certainty that Christ would return and the uncertainty about the timing that meant believers needed to always be prepared, knowing not the day nor the hour of their visitation. The ethical outcome would be final conformity to Christ's own image, by means of the resurrection of believers. Theological anthropology and ethics would both be consummated at the consummation. But what of the interim? Had God not sent his eschatological Spirit already, the Advocate, the Agent, the Counselor, the Comforter, the Convictor, the Convincer, the Inspirer, the Gift Giver? What tokens and pledges of things to come had the Spirit already given the church for the interim period?

The Fruit and Gifts of the Spirit

The term *pneuma* occurs in Paul's letters an astounding 145 times, and even if one eliminates the cases where it probably doesn't refer to the Holy Spirit, one still ends up with at least two references to the Holy Spirit per page, bearing in mind again that Paul is our earliest Christian witness to this matter. Here we are concerned with what was seen as the benefits or effects of the eschatological Spirit-giving as a result of Jesus inaugurating the eschatological age.

Perhaps the first observation of importance is that Paul, unlike Luke, never speaks of being "filled" with the Holy Spirit, and Eph. 5.18–19 is not an exception to this rule for it is speaking of an ongoing action of persons who already have the Spirit in their lives. It is interesting that in the main Paul talks about God the Father giving the Spirit, not Jesus (cf. Rom. 5.5; 2 Cor. 1.22; 5.5; Eph. 1.7; 1 Thess. 4.8; 2 Tim. 1.7), and of God supplying the Spirit (Gal. 3.5; Phil. 1.19). Paul tends to avoid impersonal images for the Spirit, which might suggest it was a substance like water or oil, or a mere impersonal power like wind or fire. Further, the Spirit is often depicted as working in tandem with Christ and also with the Father. Notice for instance the rather natural Trinitarian character of the language in 1 Cor. 12.4–6 – a variety of gifts, services, activities but just one and the same Spirit, one and the same Lord, one and the same God involved in all of it. Or 2 Thess. 2.13–15 – God chose them, the Spirit sanctified them, they look forward to obtaining the Lord's glory (probably a reference to his glorious resurrection).

Because of the current popular nature of the discussion, it is sometimes assumed that Paul focuses his discussions on the gifts of the Spirit but his references to the fruit of the Spirit are more infrequent. This is overlooking the fact of how much evidence there is of Paul showing concern about the character of his converts. In any case, it needs to be emphasized from the outset that Paul's view of the Spirit's work is not limited to how the Spirit converts people ("by one Spirit we were all baptized into the one body" – 1 Cor. 12). No, he views the work of the Spirit in the believer's life as ongoing, involving: (1) the freeing of the believer from the bondage of sin (see Rom. 8.1–4), and (2) the ongoing dispensing of gifts and fruit reforming the character and empowering and even creating the abilities of the believer.

From an anthropological point of view, Paul sees the tension in the Christian life as a "flesh" vs. Holy Spirit tension, and also an inner vs. outer tension. Inwardly the believer is being renewed day by day (2 Cor. 4.16) but outwardly he or she is slowly wasting away. But the inward struggle between flesh and Holy Spirit is a struggle between the *yetzer hara* (the inclination to do evil) and not a natural inclination to do good (*yetzer tov*), but rather the tugging or leading of the Holy Spirit according to Gal. 5. *Sarx* in Paul can mean as little as just the skin or physical form ("flesh and blood shall not inherit" – 1 Cor. 15.50), but it does not simply mean the whole person any more than *soma*, body, means the whole person in Paul's thought.[9] R. Bultmann and his disciples were wrong about this. The Spirit is trying to pull and guide the Christian in the direction of a more Christ-like character. So, the believer who chooses to walk by the Spirit will not indulge the desires of the flesh. The implication is that the believer must continually submit to the Spirit's leading and guiding. The Spirit has a personal relationship with the believer, it is not like a calibrated GPS device that works automatically.

It has become a commonplace, but is still ignored, that Paul doesn't speak of "fruits" (plural) of the Spirit, but rather "fruit" (singular) in Gal. 5. All of the traits he lists (love, joy, peace patience, kindness, self-control, and much more) he expects to be manifested in each Christian in due course. And notice that these attributes or fruit have to do with interpersonal behavior. We could point out how Paul deals with individual aspects of the fruit in numerous texts, such as Rom. 5.5, where he talks about the love of God being poured into the believers' hearts. That text is crucial as it reminds us that Paul is *not talking about the enhancement of natural character traits. He is talking about the Spiritually reformed character, which may or may not have much to do with a person's natural inclinations or traits.*

---

9 See the older but still pertinent study by Robert Gundry, *Soma in Biblical Theology: With Emphasis on Pauline Anthropology* (Cambridge: Cambridge University Press, 1976).

Nor is Paul talking about traits produced by normal circumstances, such as when a parent rejoices at the birth of a child. The joy Paul refers to in Gal. 5.22 is not the product of temporary circumstances but rather of the internal working of the Spirit in the life of the believer and may be in evidence even during adverse external circumstances, even during severe suffering. This joy is neither given by the world, nor can the world take it away. Similarly, the peace Paul talks about in Gal. 5.22 is not primarily about the absence of turmoil or negative circumstances in the believer's life, but rather about the living presence, the *shalom* of God's presence, through the Spirit in a person's life, and in Col. 3.15 it is connected to the death of Christ. It involves both peace with God and peace between human beings as well.

Much more could be said along these lines,[10] but this is sufficient to make quite clear that Paul is talking about internal dispositions which lead to certain patterns of behavior that are Christ-like. 1 Cor. 13 has sometimes been said to be a picture of the character of Christ, one that Paul himself is striving to emulate with the empowerment and guidance of the Spirit and one which he longs for his converts to imitate. If Christians walk in the Spirit, the corollary is that they will not only avoid the temptations of their sinful inclinations, they will actually exhibit on a smaller scale the character of Christ himself. The Spirit is forming Christ-like character within, in tandem with the deliberate efforts of the believer to imitate Christ in their thoughts, words, and deeds. It is interesting how the Spirit and his work points away from the person of the Spirit and toward Christ. Perhaps this is because the Spirit in Paul, as in Jn. 14–17 is seen as the agent or advocate of Christ. So, we do not hear in Paul about having faith in the Spirit or following the example of the Spirit. The Spirit points away from himself toward Christ and forms Christ-like character in the believer.

Paul thinks and speaks very differently about the gifts of the Spirit than he does about the fruit of the Spirit. Every Christian must manifest the fruit of the Spirit, another way of saying must manifest a Christ-like character. But as for the gifts of the Spirit which are distributed by the Spirit (and which believers do not necessarily get to pick and choose from – see 1 Cor. 12) different persons are given different gifts, and apart from the gift of saving faith and the living presence of the Spirit in one's life, there is no singular *charisma* or grace gift that *all* Christians should expect to be given to them.

The negative rhetorical questions in 1 Cor. 12.29–30 make this very clear – "not all speak in tongues, do they?" Any such rhetorical question which begins with the negative particle "not" can only be answered "no." And Paul is not just stating an obvious fact, he is speaking about how the Spirit works, distributing different gifts to different members of the body of Christ in order that the body as a whole might be fully functional, fully gifted. Paul has a corporate vision of how the gifts should be viewed and function. They are given not to puff up the individual, but rather to build up the body of Christ. The way they may enhance the personal spiritual life of the individual is a by-product, but not the main intended purpose. A person is given gifts to use for the benefit of others. *The fruit of the Spirit must norm the gifts of the Spirit and how they are used.*

The Spirit, as a rational divine person, chooses who gets which gift. Notice that in 1 Cor. 12.28–31 Paul ranks the intelligible gifts of proclaiming, prophesying, teaching ahead

[10] See Witherington, *Indelible Image*, vol. 2, 367–76.

of gifts of healing, wonder-working, or speaking in tongues. In 1 Cor. 14.1 he urges the Corinthians to seek the gift of prophecy, which presumably means one can petition the Holy Spirit for such a gift, but it will be up to the Spirit to decide whether the gift is given. Paul emphasizes that God is a God of order, not of chaos, and so one could say that all of 1 Cor. 11–14 is an attempt to bring order to the chaotic Corinthian worship services, without quenching the Spirit.

As for speaking in tongues, it seems to refer to something different from what we found in Acts 2.[11] 1 Cor. 13.1–2 suggests that we are talking about an angelic prayer language, which can be spoken in worship if there are those present who can interpret it so all can be edified in the worship service. The goal is the glorification of God by all, and the edification of all by the expression of the gifts. The function of the gifts, even the more private gift of speaking in angelic tongues, is building up the body of Christ, not going on a personal ego trip of self-expression.

Notice as well the evangelistic potential of the gift of prophecy in 1 Cor. 14.16–17. An outsider or uninitiated person (*idiotes*) is allowed into the Christian worship serve and may be convicted of sin and repent under the influence and impact of Christian prophecy. It is also to be noted that Christian prophecy seems to be unlike OT prophecy in several regards: (1) Paul in 1 Cor. 14 suggests that it needs to be critically evaluated as if it could be 80 percent inspiration and 20 percent mere perspiration; (2) Rom. 12.6 insists "we have gifts that differ according to the grace given us; prophecy [which should be done] in proportion to one's faith." In other words, there was danger of a person, in the thrill or exuberance for one's own verbosity, going beyond what the Spirit inspired the person to say. This seems (3) rather different from OT prophecy, where Yahweh is quoted verbatim. Perhaps this difference between OT and NT prophecy has to do with the fact that the earliest Christians not only had written guidance from God in the OT itself, unlike many or most of their predecessors in the OT period when oral cultures prevailed (noting how even pious young King Josiah [641–609 BC] had to be informed of the Mosaic code which had been forgotten or left in storage for a long time – 2 Kgs. 22.8–13), but in addition Christians lived in the eschatological age when the OT prophecies and institutions were being fulfilled, and so predictive prophecy was less the focus and less necessary. We do of course have prophecies by Jesus in Mk. 13 and parallels and also of course the apocalyptic prophecies in Revelation, but overall the NT has but one whole book of prophecy, in stark contrast to the OT, which strongly suggests that prophecy functioned differently in the NT era than in the OT era. It served to convict, convince, and help convert the non-believer, and convict the believer of ongoing sin. Prophecy in the OT could hardly ever be said to be an evangelistic tool. It is rather a way of convicting and guiding those who are already God's people.

It is worth stressing and reiterating that 1 Cor. 12 makes quite clear that the person of the Spirit is not only responsible for joining the convert to the body of Christ but Paul says in that same process each believer is given the Spirit from which is drawn spiritual life and nourishment. In other words, the Holy Spirit is in the believer's life fully, as a personal presence, from the beginning of that spiritual life. The Spirit is not distributed in doses throughout the Christian life. You do not get more of the Spirit later in your spiritual pilgrimage, though the Spirit may get hold of more aspects of the believer over time. This is called progressive sanctification.

---

[11] See pp. 240–5, above.

So emphatic about all this is Paul that he says that no one can even truly be a believer and truly confess Jesus is Lord from the heart except by the Holy Spirit prompting this in a Christian life (1 Cor. 12.3). In short, the relationship between the believer and the Spirit is a personal one, which must involve openness and obedience to the leading of the Spirit, and it can go in other directions. One can grieve the Holy Spirit, one can even quench the Spirit or its gifts in one's life. One can also allow the Spirit to fill one up with adoration, prompting praise and thanksgiving (see Eph. 5.18–20). And of course, the Spirit can choose to add gifts to a person's life as the body needs them, and as a person is open to them. Like the believer's relationship with the Father and with the Son, it is something freely given and freely received and must for the most part be freely participated in, although of course there are times, like Paul's experience on Damascus Road, where one may be overtaken, overwhelmed, overcome by the dynamic presence of God in one's life.

The Amplified Version: 1 John on the Further Impact of the Christ Event

1 John is a sermon, not a letter. In fact, it is a form of amplified exhortation that rhetorically speaking keeps ringing the changes on certain key theological and ethical concepts and truths. It will pay us dividends to examine some of this material in some detail to get a flavor of how the death and resurrection of Jesus reconfigured discourse about sin and the believer's life. That this is not a mere ethical harangue should be clear from the outset of this little sermon:

1a What was from the beginning
1b What we have heard
1c What we have seen with our eyes
1d What we contemplated
1e What our hands felt
1f about the word of life
2a and the life was revealed
2b and we have seen and testify
2c and we proclaim to you
2d the everlasting life
2e which was with the Father
2f and was revealed to us
3a what we have seen and heard
3b we proclaim also to you
3c so that you too may share it in common with us
3d and indeed it is sharing in common with the Father
3e and with his Son Jesus Christ

The author, the Beloved Disciple, has been an eyewitness of the life of Christ and an earwitness to the ongoing testimony about him.[12] The character of this document is sapiential, and the echoes and overlaps with the Fourth Gospel are so substantial that one cannot doubt they are drawing on traditions that come from the same person, even if a third

---

[12] For a detailed exegesis of this wonderful book see Ben Witherington III, *Letters and Homilies for Hellenized Christians*, vol. 1: *A Socio-Rhetorical Commentary on Titus, 1–2 Timothy and 1–3 John* (Downers Grove, IL: InterVarsity Press, 2006), 393–562.

party assembled the final form of the Fourth Gospel itself. The exordium above involves announcing three themes which will undergird the ethical exhortations that follow: (1) everlasting life through Christ; (2) the historical reality of Christ; (3) the theme of eyewitness testimony. It is assumed, taken for granted, that the story of Christ, the Passion play and its sequel, are well known by the audience. This is why the author can use shorthand phrases like "Christ come in the flesh" to refer to profound ideas like the Incarnation of the pre-existent Son of God, or for instance in 1 Jn. 5 he can talk about the three witnesses – the water, the blood, and the Spirit – which translated refer to the birth and death of Jesus, and the Spirit.[13] Like Paul with his *pistis Christou* phrase, which turns out to be shorthand for Christ's faithfulness even unto death on the cross, the Beloved Disciple can also refer to key elements in the salvation story in telegraphic and even metaphorical ways. This is not unexpected in the context of a sapiential discourse heavy on figurative language.

There is a strong emphasis, then, from the beginning of this sermon on the total impact Christ had on our author and others while he was on earth.[14] He was listened to, he was observed, the meaning of his words and works and person were contemplated, and close fellowship was had with him – he was even touched (on the verb here cf. Lk. 24.39 and Heb. 12.18 of physical touching). A. Plummer puts it this way: "A climax: seeing is more than hearing, and beholding (which requires time) is more than seeing (which may be momentary); while handling is more than all."[15] The phrase "word of life" probably is an objective genitive, the word about everlasting life, since that is a major theme in this sermon, but since Jesus embodied both the everlasting life and the word, it is appropriate to use it as a way of describing his impact. He is preeminently the word of life beyond all ordinary speech or persons.

But the point here is about how he came across, how he impacted our author and others – how he was encountered and perceived and received. Everlasting life, here as elsewhere in the Johannine literature, does not merely refer to life *everlasting*, though that is meant as well, but also to a different quality of life, an unending spiritual life which has unlimited potential and is full of *joie de vivre*. It is a life that binds the believer forever to God and to other believers. As such it already transcends time, for we have it already in time, but it will go on beyond the temporal existence we now experience. The Son is not simply identical with this life, since it exists in his followers as well, but he clearly most fully embodies it and also bestows it. The person who has the Son has life with a capital L, but also a lot more, including endless joy.

In 1 Jn. 1.5–2.17 we have the initial salvo of this discourse, which in some respects reads like a two-way discourse found in early Judaism, talking about the differences between walking in the light and walking in darkness, and the consequences of each course of behavior (cf. 1 QS 1.9–10; 3.13–4.26 on the sons of light and the sons of darkness; cf. Epistle of Barnabas 18.1–21.9). *The focus is primarily on behavior in this section, with theology and Christology brought in to deal with behavioral issues (e.g. if anyone sins we have an Advocate, namely Jesus).* I emphasize this last point to make clear that the story is the basis for the amplified ethical exhortations, and again, the author assumes the audience knows the story.

---

[13] On the Johannine language of "birth out of water" referring to flesh giving birth to flesh see Jn. 3.5–6.

[14] On "Word of Life" referring to a person here see e.g. J. Emmette Weir, "The Identity of the Logos in the First Epistle of John," *ET* 86 (1974–75): 118–20.

[15] A. Plummer, *The Epistles of St. John* (Grand Rapids, MI: Baker, 1980; first pub. 1886), 15.

Consider for a moment how the author intertwines theology and ethics at the end of chapter 1 and the beginnings of chapter 2, saying:

And this is the message which we have heard from Him and which we proclaim to you – that God is light and darkness is not in Him in any respect. If we say that we have communion/sharing in common with Him and we are walking in darkness, we are lying and we are not doing the truth. But if we are walking in the light, as He is in the light, we have communion with one another and the blood of Jesus his Son cleanses us from every sin. If we say that we have no sin, we lead ourselves astray and the truth is not in us. If we confess our sins, faithful is he and righteous in order that he forgives us the sins and cleanse us from all unrighteousness. If we may have said that we had not sinned, we are making Him a liar and his word is not in us.

My little children, I write this to you in order that you may not sin, and if anyone sins, we have an Advocate with the Father, Jesus Christ the righteous one. And he himself is the propitiation concerning our sins, but not only concerning ours but also concerning/for the whole world. And in this we know that we have known Him – if we keep his commandments. The one saying "I have known Him" and not keeping his commandments, is a liar, and in this one the truth is not. But whoever keeps his word, truly in this [act] the love of God is fulfilled/completed. In this [act] we know that we are in Him. The one saying he ought to remain in Him, just as He himself walked, also he ought to walk.

Here we should go into some depth of exposition to demonstrate just how much the theology leads to the ethics, and how the story of Christ is the basis for the theologizing as well as the ethics.

Verse 5 begins the discourse proper with a statement about the character of God, namely that God is light (cf. Ps. 104.2 to Ps. 27.1; Ps. 36.9; Isa. 49.6; Philo, *de Somniis* I.75). This "means that he is absolute in his glory (the physical connotation of light) in his truth (the intellectual) and in his holiness (the moral) ... To describe God as absolute 'light' presupposes that God and darkness (error or evil) are mutually exclusive."[16] It is the character of God as light that provides the basis of the exhortation which follows.[17] The source of this message is said to be "him," in this case surely Christ, and we may compare 1 Jn. 4.21, where Jesus' formulation of the double love command is rehearsed. This verse should be seen as a transition to what follows, further establishing the ethos and authority of the speaker, who here claims to have heard about God's character from Jesus himself.

It is interesting to compare a similar sort of contrast between light and darkness applied to God in another sapiential homily in James 1.17, where we hear of how every good and perfect gift comes down from the Father of light in whom there is no variation or shadow of change. The implication is of course that believers should mirror the character of God, as well as of Christ. Unlike "many forms of hellenistic and Gnostic piety, association of light with divine being did not mean that people were to seek a personal, private, interior vision of that divine light. It meant, as the author will go on to spell out, that they were to conduct their lives in obedience and fidelity to the community which that God had acted to establish (1.5f.; 2.10f.)."[18] Darkness contrasted to light is typical of Johannine antitheses, but notice

---

[16] S. Smalley, *1, 2, 3 John* (Waco, TX: Word, 1984), 20.

[17] See Plummer, *Epistles of St. John*, 23: "We are not told that God is *the* Spirit, or *the* Light, or *the* Love: nor that he is *a* Spirit, or *a* Light ... spirit, love, light are His very Nature. They are not mere attributes like mercy and justice: they are Himself. They are probably the nearest to a definition of God that the human mind could frame or comprehend ... The simplest intellect can understand their meaning; the subtlest cannot exhaust it."

[18] P. Perkins, *The Johannine Epistles* (Wilmington, DE: Glazier, 1984), 15.

how strongly the matter is stressed by using the double negative: "no darkness ... none at all." The net effect is that our author is saying in him there is not the least bit of darkness. It is important to note that the term *skotia* is characteristic Johannine vocabulary (Jn. 1.5; 2.8–11; 6.17; 8.12; 12.35,46; 20.1) and is rarely found elsewhere in the NT (cf. Mt. 4.16; 10.27; Lk. 2.3). It is worth quoting 1 En. 92.4–5 here: "God will be gracious to the just person ... and he shall walk in light, while sin shall perish in darkness forever."

Verse 6 should be seen as forming an *inclusio* with v. 10, and in fact it will be useful to set out the whole series of conditional statements that are found in vv. 6–10 so that we can see the progression of the argument or discourse.

Protasis
6ab – If we say, "we have communion with him" while we are walking in darkness
8a – If we say "we have no sin"
10a – If we say, "we have not sinned"

Apodosis
6cd – we are liars and are not doing the truth.
8bc – we lead ourselves astray and truth is not in us.
10bc – we make him a liar and his word is not in us.[19]

It is possible to see a progression of thought here both in the protasis and the apodosis of these conditional remarks, but it is crucial first to note that "we" are the ones referred to in both halves of each conditional statement – it is "we" who are making the claims or boasts, and it is "we" who are guilty of falsehoods of several sorts. In the protasis, we move from claiming to have communion with God, to claiming we have no sin (currently) to claiming we have never sinned, which is a series of claims which certainly do not comport with the Wesleyan idea of going on to perfection! In the apodosis here, we can also see a progression which is no better than the progression of boasts in the first half of each remark. Firstly, it is said that "we" are liars not doing the truth, then it says we have believed the lie ourselves and so are deceived and the truth is not in us, and then worst of all we make God out to be a liar and his word itself is not in us.

Here is a description of pilgrim's regress into darkness, involving both arrogance and wickedness. Our author is warning the audience about the dangers of apostasy already here at the beginning of the sermon, a matter which will certainly come up again toward the end of the discourse, when we will even hear about the sin unto spiritual death. Our author clearly believes both theological and ethical apostasy are possible (see 1 Jn. 5) and is warning against it throughout this discourse.

Verse 6 provides us with the first of a series of conditional statements. It is "we" who are in danger of acting like this, and the "we" in question encompasses the author and his audience, not the author, audience, and the secessionists. The latter are no longer part of the "we," indeed our author will claim they never really were part of it.[20] He is not likely rebutting the claims of those now gone who cannot be included within the "we" who are critiqued.

[19] See R. E. Brown, *The Epistles of John* (New York: Doubleday, 1982), 231, whose chart I have modified here.
[20] See rightly B. F. Westcott, *The Epistles of St. John* (Grand Rapids, MI: William B. Eerdmans, 1966; first pub. 1908), 19, who says our author considers only the case of true and confessing Christians here.

The kind of conditional remarks we have here are *ean* plus a present subjunctive verb, which suggests a very possible though *hypothetical* condition. We could even translate it "if anyone should say ..." or we could translate the present subjunctive *peripatomen* "if we might be walking." Our author has his concerns and pastoral anxiety about what his "children" might be doing or attempting to do in the wake of the schism, but *he realizes he is subject to the same temptations (hence "we")*. We would expect *ei* plus the present tense verb if the author wanted to speak of a clearly real condition. "With great gentleness, he states the case hypothetically, and with great delicacy he includes himself in the hypothesis."[21] That which troubles our author is the inconsistency between one's faith talk and one's faith walk. Claiming to have communion, a sharing in common with God, and yet walking in darkness. In other words, a radical disjunction between one's theology and one's ethics is a sure sign of spiritual danger. Two things are said to follow from this inherent contradiction – one is both a liar and one is not "doing the truth."

Talk of behavior as a matter of walking or doing the truth is typically Jewish (cf. Gen. 17.1; 1 Kgs. 2.4; 2 Kgs. 20.3; 1QS 5.25; 7.18; 8.5; 1QH 16.7), and it reflects the fact that for our author there is no hard and fast line between belief and behavior, between theology and ethics. Ethics is just putting one's theology into practice, doing the truth (cf. Jn. 3.21; 2 Chron. 31.20; Neh. 9.33; 1QS 1.5). Furthermore, as the next few verses will make clear, our author is perfectly well aware that real Christians sometimes fail to do the truth, indeed they sin. He is neither an idealist nor in the modern sense a mere realist. Here he is simply making clear that such is not a legitimate option for a believer. Behavior matters just as belief does, and aberrations in either sphere can sever one from fellowship with the community and with God.[22]

The strong connection between belief and behavior, and the belief that aberrant behavior was in fact a denial of one's credo, and perhaps even proof that one was not a true believer, is typical of Jewish sapiential rhetoric. Notice too that like so many wisdom maxims we have carefully balanced terms and clauses – lying parallels saying and doing parallels walking. R. G. Loader is quite right about the focus on praxis that comports with one's relationships with God and others. For our author, "the focus of the Christian gospel is not a future place or a spiritual sphere, not a guarantee of security or a gift of ecstasy, but a relationship that is ongoing. It has implications for every area of life. To be *sharing in God's life* (1.6) is to be involved in loving, as God loves, and that is something concrete which affects the way we relate to others."[23] One might say that our author believed that as one acts, one is.

Notice further that the verb "walking" is in the present continual tense, indicating ongoing activity, perhaps even habitual activity, and in any case a course of action and trajectory pursued over a period of time, not just for an instant. Walking in darkness is more than just taking a step in the direction of darkness. If one is walking in darkness one is already "in the dark" (cf. 2 Cor. 6.4). "A life in moral darkness can no more have communion with God than a life in a coal-pit can have communion with the sun."[24]

---

[21] Plummer, *Epistles of St. John*, 25.

[22] C. H. Dodd, *The Johannine Epistles* (London: Hodder and Stoughton, 1946), 20: "Religion is not just 'morality tinged with emotion', but on the other hand, there is no religion in the Christian sense of the word unless it includes moral endeavor and the criticism of conduct."

[23] R. G. Loader, *The Johannine Epistles* (London: Epworth, 1992), 11.

[24] Plummer, *Epistles of St. John*, 25.

Verse 7 stands in deliberate contrast with the immediately preceding verse, and we should take the "but" here as more than perfunctory – an antithesis is being stated. But as Brown points out it is an antithesis that is the beginning of several conditional statements which can be delineated as follows:

Protasis

7ab – But if we walk in the light as He Himself is in light

9a "But if we confess our sins"

2.1b – But if anyone does sin

Compound Apodosis

7c–e – we have communion with one another and the blood of Jesus cleanses us from all sin

9b–d – He who is faithful and just will forgive our sins and cleanse us from all unrighteousness

2.1–2 – we have an Advocate with the Father, Jesus Christ the Righteous One, and he himself is a propitiation for our sins, and not only for our sins but also for the whole world.[25]

The first conditional remark is quite interesting because it not only implies that Christians who are walking in the light have communion with God but also that they sin and are forgiven. The subject of cleansing from all sin, or expiation, comes up in both the first and second apodosis listed above. Both the second and third protasis deals more directly with what to do when a Christian sins. The second apodosis makes apparent that forgiveness alone is not the solution to the problem, *cleansing* from the effects of sin (e.g. presumably guilt) is also necessary, and the third apodosis delves into atonement theology proper.

This last compound apodosis is rich and will require more detailed treatment, but here we note that since it is about what Christ does in relationship to the Father (be our advocate) it is natural to see the key Greek term here to refer to propitiation – the satisfying of God's just requirements in regard to sin and so the assuaging of God's righteous anger against it. The final clause is even more remarkable because it shows that our author is not a pure sectarian in his thought – he believes that Jesus' death atones not just for believers, but also for the sins of the world.

Verse 7 has several dimensions to it. Notice that here God is said to be "in the light" so light does not just describe God's character it also describes God's behavior – it can stand the light of day or close scrutiny. Our author adds that moral integrity (aka walking in the light) is a prerequisite to truly have communion or fellowship with one another. It is difficult to fully love and commune with someone you can't fully trust. We might have expected our author to say that if we walk in the light we will have communion or sharing in common with God,[26] but instead he speaks of sharing in common which results in

---

[25] Brown, *Epistles of John*, 237.

[26] In fact, Tertullian in the second century knows of a text or texts containing this verse that says this very thing (*De Pud.* 19). Clement of Alexandria seems to know of this reading as well. This suggests quite rightly to Plummer, *Epistles of St. John*, 26, that the Johannine Epistles must have been circulating for a considerable period of time before Tertullian for such poorly attested variant readings to show up in such diverse places. Plummer is also right that there is no need to try and make this verse an exact parallel to v. 6 (which Augustine

communion and fellowship with each other. Cicero would have agreed with some of the logic here, for he says that real friendship is impossible without virtue (*De Amic.* 6.20). Notice as well that it is only after sharing in common is mentioned that we hear about the blood of Jesus cleansing us from all sin. It was not just the blood of any righteous person or any ordinary sacrifice that provided the ongoing cleansing our author refers to. No, it was only the blood of the Righteous One that provided this perpetual benefit.

The verb "cleanse" is present continual tense, referring to an ongoing activity. It is worth pondering whether our author is saying that cleansing happens in the course of Body of Christ life, in the context of our communing with one another. Clearly, he does not see it as a purely private matter between the individual and Jesus – it is "we" who have communion and are cleansed by the blood. Though it may seem something of a paradox, it is precisely those who are walking in the light who are most likely to *see* their flaws and sins and know their need for ongoing cleansing from the effects of sin.

The reference to "all" sin means even the gravest sins can be expunged and even the worst of sinners cleansed. It is probably also the case that the implication here is similar to what is stated clearly in Acts 13.38–39, namely that there were deliberate sins for which there was no atonement in Mosaic Law, but in the case of the atoning death of Jesus, all sins, and all kinds of sins, have been atoned for. It is not clear whether we should translate *pas* as "all" here, or in the distributive sense of "every" but in either case the meaning is the same. Christ's blood cleanses from each and every, and therefore all, sin. Cleansing is necessary because God is a holy God who longs to have *koinonia* with his children. Furthermore, the cleansing is something that only Christ can bring about within the believer. Our author is not talking about a process of purgation by which the sinner can cleanse himself.[27]

Verse 8 brings us to a new conditional remark, once more with *ean* plus the present subjunctive, "if we should say …" The remark is hypothetical but seen as a possibility and a danger. Here the claim or boast is "we have no sin." Such a claim is seen as an ultimate form of self-deception and a clear sign that the truth is not in the claimant. Our author is clearly not a perfectionist. Bede says of this particular verse: "This verse refutes the teachings of the Pelagians, who say that babies are born without sin and that the elect can make such progress in this life that it becomes possible for them to attain perfection" (*On 1 John*, PL 93.88).

But what is meant by claiming "we have no sin"? Is he referring to sin as a condition or sin as activity or sin as attitude? These questions are all the more pressing since we know the author is using the technique of amplification and it is thus possible that he is saying the very same thing in several differing ways in vv. 8–10. There is some progression of thought, however, in the apodoses (see above), but what about in the first half of this and the succeeding "if" clauses in vv. 8–10?

I agree with Perkins that "nothing in the context suggests that members of the Johannine community were following a libertine interpretation of Christianity."[28] As we have said

---

and Calvin both attempt to do). When one recognizes the rhetorical technique of amplification one knows that part of this technique is to make small variations and changes, some synonymous, others with some substantive difference, reiterating some of the previous content.

[27] See Dodd, *Johannine Epistles*, 21. It is right to add as Smalley, *1, 2, 3 John*, 25, does that our author does not tell us *how* Christ cleanses us from sin.

[28] Perkins, *Johannine Epistles*, 18.

this conditional sentence is hypothetical, but it reflects a concern the author has about some possible problems that could arise.

Brown suggests getting beyond some of the quandaries this text raises by translating the phrase "have sin" as "be guilty of sin." He points to the use of the phrase in Jn. 9.41; 15.22; 19.11.[29] If this is right, then it would appear clear that this phrase means nothing different from the one in v. 10 which refers to having not committed acts of sin. "No New Testament writer manifests the tension between the reality of sin – even in believers – and the demand of Christ for perfection more dramatically than 1 John."[30] Also in favor of this conclusion is the fact that "sin" (*hamartia*) is in the singular in v. 7, where it clearly means acts of sin, indeed every or all acts of sin.

So, the singular here need not connote something like sin nature or a mere attitude or inclination toward sin. Thus, the old suggestion that our author says acts of sin are avoidable by the Christian but the sinful inclination is always with us, does not quite do justice to what is being said. At the least, sinful acts in the past are being alluded to here as needing to be confessed and from which one must be purified. As Brown points out, in the Gospel parallels of the key phrase, in each case a sinful action has already been committed or a sinful attitude already exists.[31]

The verb *planomen* coupled with "ourselves" can certainly be translated "we lead ourselves astray," which is more than saying that one errs or is deceived. Here one is the agent of one's own demise and pilgrimage into darkness. This language will come up again at 2.26 and 3.7 (cf. Jn. 7.12), and if we take these texts together they suggest that this verb is a strong one and so the author is talking about a serious departure from truth. Had the author really wanted to speak about just self-deception he would have used *apatan*, as we find in James 1.26.[32]

But what does it mean to say one has the truth in oneself? Our author has already spoken of doing the truth, but now we hear of it dwelling within. Perhaps the idea is analogous to when a modern musician says "I have the music in me," by which she means that she is so saturated with and has so imbibed music that it permeates her thoughts and dreams and even the rhythms by which she walks and moves. A person capable of self-deception on so large a scale as to say "we have no sin" is a person who does not have the truth resident in their being and constantly illuminating them about their errors and shortcomings and missteps.

Verse 9 focuses on confession and its beneficial outcomes, but we are also told something about the character of God – that God is faithful and righteous. There may be an implicit contrast here with various of the pagan gods who were portrayed in the myths

---

[29] Brown, *Epistles of John*, 205–6.

[30] D. M. Smith, *First, Second, and Third John* (IBC; Louisville, KY: John Knox Press, 1991), 45.

[31] Against Brown, *Johannine Epistles*, 206, however, this phrase surely means more than "I have no guilt from sinning."

[32] While it is an artful dodge, it is nonetheless a dodge to say that here the author says plainly that Christians sin and must confess their sins, while later in 1 Jn. 3.6 he says sin can and must be avoided by Christians and so he is referring to avoiding habitual sin (see Smalley, *1, 2, 3 John*, 30). This is to overlook the hypothetical character and conditional form of the remarks here. Here the focus is on having not committed sins in the past. In 1 Jn. 3.6 the point is that sinning is not a valid option for Christians and conscious willful acts of sin in the present or the future can be and must be avoided.

as being fickle rather than faithful, and immoral rather than moral.[33] It is indeed remarkable that God's forgiveness is grounded here on not only God's faithfulness (cf. 1 Cor. 1.9; 10.13; 2 Cor. 1.18) but also on his righteous nature. Some have viewed God as having to forfeit his righteous demands in order to be able to forgive. Nothing could be further from the truth. It is precisely because God will always do what he has promised and at the same time do and be what is right that he forgives. C. H. Dodd puts it quite eloquently:

God's attitude to us, His purposes for us, do not alter because we sin against Him. When we turn to Him again, we find Him still the same. If we confess our sins, and in confession repudiate them, then God forgives, not (as a man might) because He chooses on this occasion to be indulgent or considerate, or tolerant, but because no other course would be consistent with the perfectly good will by which the whole universe is created and sustained. It is this, and this only, in the last resort, that justifies our confidence of being forgiven our repeated offences against the law of God. We believe in the forgiveness of sin, not by convincing ourselves that our sins were excusable or remediable, or that we meant well, or that "we won't do it again." It is because the principle of forgiveness is built into the structure of a moral order created and determined by the character of a just and faithful God ... The probability is that an effective appreciation of our own sinful condition is in most cases not (as is often supposed) a preliminary to the hearing of the Gospel, but a consequence of it.[34]

To the above one can only add that it is the death of Christ which makes it possible for God to be both righteous and the one who sets right sinful human beings. We are being told that what God demands of us is truthfulness, truthfulness even about our sins, and that God is ready and eager to respond to such truthfulness and to forgive and cleanse. We do have an aorist verb here, which suggests that completed actions are in view – the one who confesses is forgiven and is cleansed. What is not made absolutely clear here is whether a public confession to God before human witnesses is in view (as in James 5.16; Didache 14.14) or simply a private confession to God. It could be either one on first impression.

But in fact, if we compare the use of the term *homologeo* elsewhere in the NT it refers to a public confession of some sort (cf. Mk. 8.38; Rom. 10.9) and thus it is likely that is meant here as well (cf. Lev. 5.5; 16.21; Isa. 7.19; Ps. 32.5; Prov. 28.13; Dan. 9.20 and for public confession at Qumran, see 1 QS 1.16–3.12 and CD 20.28–30). It may be of some relevance that the only reference to confession of sin in Acts comes in the context of Ephesus in Acts 19.18. Loader makes a good point when he indicates what happens when a person thinks they are faultless or perfect when it comes to sin.[35] "Believing in one's own infallibility or faultlessness makes facing failure and accepting forgiveness a threat."[36] We do not find the Pauline language of grace in 1 John, indeed in the Johannine epistles in general except in 2 Jn. 3. There is, however, much convergence at the level of thought between our author and Paul, but the way of expressing these things is distinctive in each case.

---

[33] Dodd, *Johannine Epistles*, 22: "It is because God is faithful, or trustworthy, that He can be the Object of faith or trust. God is also just, or righteous: without this conviction, there is no ethical religion."

[34] *Ibid.*, 23.

[35] Since our author distinguishes between forgiveness and cleansing, perhaps we should see cleansing as referring to not just the removal of guilt but also the destruction of sinful desires. This may be correct.

[36] Loader, *Johannine Epistles*, 13. He is also right that it is not surprising that this homily was so crucial to John Wesley and the setting up of his class and band meetings, where open confession in a confidential circle of believers was one of the key features that led to genuine Christian community during the Wesleyan revival in the eighteenth century.

Verse 10 has a perfect tense verb – "we have not sinned." This amounts to more than a claim that there are now no lingering effects of past sin. It apparently indicates no past acts of sins have been committed, but again we must bear in mind the rhetorical and hypothetical nature of these conditional remarks. Our author is laying out a map and showing his audience various directions they should not allow their thoughts or lives to pursue. Plummer suggests the claim is "we are in the condition of having avoided sin."[37] But to make that claim is to make God into a liar, which is an even more serious sin than lying or leading oneself astray. The latter two reveal the character of the individual, but v. 10 is referring to libeling the character of God, who is true and synonymous with the truth.

1 Jn. 2 continues to further the themes of the first chapter but moves forward to other issues as well. Our author pleads with his audience to renounce sin, in fact he says this is one of the reasons, if not the main reason, he is writing this sermon. Here the verb is in the aorist subjunctive and refers to definite acts of sin rather than a habitual state. Our author is not suggesting that his audience will cease to have the inclination to sin or cease to be tempted, only that they should renounce any such inclinations and not let them lead to action. We are reminded once more by this purpose statement that this homily is primarily hortatory in aim and character, but intertwines theology with its ethical exhortations. Notice as well how very personal matters become. Not only is the audience addressed as dear children, but the author speaks now as "I," explaining why he is writing this urgent appeal.

We have a variety of conditional statements in 1 Jn. 2, here in v. 1b we have a future, more probable conditional statement – but "if anyone should (as is likely they will) commit definite acts of sin." Our author is a realist. He believes that the audience will at some juncture in the future probably fail to restrain themselves from sin. Should that happen, he says, we have an Advocate with the Father – Jesus Christ. The term used here of Jesus is *parakletos*, which in Jn. 14–17 is used on various occasions of the Holy Spirit, though the Spirit there is called "another advocate" (14.16), implying that Jesus is one as well. The basic meaning of this Greek term is someone who pleads a case, a legal advocate or one who intercedes for another. This is especially the likely nuance in a rhetorical discourse such as this one.

Jesus, then, is the sinner's advocate in heaven, pleading his case with the Father. This image, while similar to what we find in Hebrews, also has its differences to the heavenly high priest theology there. For one thing Christ is depicted as a priest in Hebrews and he is praying, seeking to help us avoid sinning (Heb. 2.18; 4.14–16; 7.25). Here, however, Christ is playing the legal advocate for someone who has already sinned. It is not just anyone who is the sinner's advocate – it is the Messiah, and indeed it is a totally righteous person. If he advocates for the sinner, it must surely be a successful appeal. In ancient rhetoric, the ethos or character of the advocate was all-important if the rhetoric was to be persuasive. The implication here is that the sinner need not worry, especially since the Father is a loving Father desiring to forgive and be reconciled to his children. Notice as well that the author breaks the flow of the pronouns to stress that he, like the audience, is in need of the Advocate ("if anyone has sinned ... *we* have an Advocate").

---

[37] Plummer, *Epistles of St. John*, 30–31.

It is striking that in the Jewish tractate Pirke Aboth 4.13 we find this very Greek word, now transliterated into Hebrew and used to speak of a man as a defendant before a heavenly tribunal: "He who fulfills one commandment has gained for himself one advocate; he who commits one sin has gained for himself one accuser." How different this theology is from our author's, who is suggesting that Christ and his death pleads for the believer because his own works cannot do so.[38] Notice as well that our author individualizes matters in this verse "but if anyone should sin …" Sin is seen as an individual matter here and refers to behavior of the individual, not some sort of collective guilt.

Jesus Christ is also called here the Righteous One, an early Jewish Christian title for Jesus (Acts 3.14; 7.12). Here the implication seems to be that he is of impeccable character and therefore his advocacy carries supreme weight. As a secondary notion, there may also be the idea that he was the innocent one who did not deserve to suffer but did so on the behalf of others. He did not need to atone for his own sins.

Verse 2 gives us the first full indication of our author's theology of the cross, which surprisingly is very little in evidence in the Fourth Gospel, despite the emphasis there on the cross being the ultimate sign and moment of glorification of Jesus. Here we are told that Jesus himself is the *hilasmos* for our sins. Notice that it does not merely say that he provides this, but rather he *is* this. The big question is how to translate this term – propitiation or expiation, or should we choose a more comprehensive term like atoning sacrifice? Propitiation is an act which appeases the wrath of God against sin or some offense, offered by a human being.

Expiation by contrast is not something which God is the recipient or object of, but rather the subject of, referring to the divine act of removing the defilement of or cleansing someone from sin, or covering or protecting someone from the consequences of their sin.

In part the meaning here can probably be determined by the preposition used – *peri* not *huper*. The former preposition means with respect to rather than on behalf of. This suggests that propitiation is at least one of the things in mind here. If so, the picture would be similar to what we find in Hebrews, where we learn of Jesus the High Priest in heaven offering intercession, indeed offering himself as a sacrifice to God, his death doing the pleading for sinners. On the other hand, in 1 Jn. 1.7 the idea seems to be of expiation, of the sinner being cleansed of sin by God through Christ. Here however in vv. 1–2 we are talking about God being offered something and so here propitiation is more likely in view. Some have resorted to translating this term as atonement or atoning sacrifice, and Brown may well be right that the language here has in mind the sacrifice offered by the High Priest on Yom Kippur, the Day of Atonement.[39]

In any event, we must note that the verb tense is present continual – Jesus is now and always will be the believer's offering for sin. But notice the stress that Jesus' atoning death was not merely for the sins of believers, but for the sins of the world. He is not merely the Savior of the community, but of the world, a thought that is developed further in 1 Jn. 4.9–14, showing that a narrowly sectarian reading of 1 John is wrong.[40] Furthermore, in

---

[38] See rightly Dodd, *Johannine Epistles*, 24.

[39] Brown, *Epistles of John*, 217–19.

[40] The term *kosmos* can of course have various nuances in the Fourth Gospel and the Johannine Epistles, as Brown, *Epistles of John*, 223–24, has demonstrated. It occurs some 78 times in the Gospel and 23 more in 1 John. For our purposes, what is important is that when the issue is about God's salvific intent and desire, the whole world is included, as Jn. 1.29; 3.16–17; 4.42; 6.33,51; 12.46–47; 1 Jn. 2.2 and 4.14 make evident. The

the Johannine literature it is perfectly clear that it is not God or Christ that limits the scope of the atoning death of Jesus (cf. Jn. 3.16–17). This entire language of atonement requires closer scrutiny, however, which we will devote to it elsewhere in this study.[41]

And So?

We have taken the time to look in some more detail at how the story of the Passion and resurrection of Christ informs subsequent Christian theologizing and ethicizing into particular contexts, in this latter case a Johannine context. What we have seen in this brief, yet more detailed consideration of 1 John is that indeed the theologizing and ethicizing, which are necessarily intertwined (not simply the latter built upon the former), are done presupposing and out of the author's Christian narrative thought world. We have also seen how that Johannine thought world overlaps with Paul's at certain junctures. While the means of expression often differ, there is a shared story and way of approaching the theologizing and ethicizing out of those stories, especially the story of Christ himself.

And we may add that even the famous last words of Jesus about forgiveness and everlasting life also are informing these sermonic thoughts here. We will turn to some concluding thoughts about the impact of the Christ event on later theologizing in a subsequent chapter. Here it is sufficient to note that the narrative thought world of early Jewish Christians was reconfigured by the story of Christ himself, especially the story of the last week of his life. The Gospel story, however, didn't do all the theologizing and ethicizing that was required to guide and norm the fledgling Christian communities and the individual spiritual journeys of its members. To that end, various sermons, discourses, letters, and a historical chronicle of the beginnings of the movement, and even a book of apocalyptic prophecy, had to be written. But in every case, it presupposed the Christ story, and the larger storied world of the Bible, and most of these writers clearly presuppose that the audiences know the "old, old story" and how Christ's story has reshaped the way the biblical narratives should be viewed, and what they were intending and leading up to, all along.

term "world" does of course sometimes mean in these documents, when focusing on human response to God, "humanity organized against God," and even rejecting the light. This is why we also hear about the judgment of the world and of Satan being the prince of this world, and of the hatred of the world for Jesus, and of Christ's not praying for the world, and of Christ's kingdom not being of the world (cf. Jn. 1.10; 7.7; 15.18; 17.7,9,25; 1 Jn. 2.15–17; 4.3–5; 5.19; 2 Jn. 7).

Brown sums up aptly: "the divine intent is initially salvific toward the world, but people prefer darkness to light ... and so 'the world' becomes the name of those who refuse Jesus and choose Satan as their father" (224).

[41] See Appendix B, below.

8

Covenanting and Theologizing after the Fall
and before the Incarnation

BEN WITHERINGTON III: So, what does *HESED* really *mean*?
WALTER BRUEGGEMANN: Tenacious loyalty. Loyalty to the covenant and covenant people.
Conversation at the 2017 Baylor Symposium on Preaching

It probably goes without saying that one of the ideas that has dominated OT theology and NT theology over the last century or so is the idea of covenant. It affects, and is affected by, one's view of salvation history and progressive revelation. On the one hand, there are those scholars, mostly of the Reformed camp, who want to talk about covenantal continuity, or better said, one covenant in various different administrations, such that the New Covenant is not a genuinely new covenant, it's a renewal of the Old Covenant and in particular the Mosaic covenant. Furthermore, the Abrahamic covenant is not distinguished in any dramatic way from the Mosaic covenant in some of these discussions. In fact, in early Judaism, the Abrahamic covenant seems to have been read and over-read in light of the Mosaic covenant, so that we hear things like Abraham *obeyed* God and it was credited to him as righteousness, reading the later episode about sacrificing Isaac backwards into Gen. 12 and following. Never mind that Abraham trusted God and only later was there circumcision, and never mind that Abraham was not a Jew to start with, but rather a pagan from Ur.

On the other hand, there are those scholars who want to emphasize the newness of the New Covenant (more often NT scholars than OT scholars) and think that one cannot see the New Covenant as simply a renewal of the Mosaic one, though there are commandments that the two covenants share in common. Underlying all these discussions are certain assumptions about the nature of covenants between God and his people, often coupled with assumptions about the nature of election, salvation, and a cluster of other ideas. In this chapter, we will be focusing on the *berit* itself, the nature of covenanting itself, and in particular, covenanting in the OT.

The Framework

OT scholars have long recognized that the discussions about covenants in the OT seem rather clearly to be similar to or parallel with discussions about covenants or treaties in the ANE. Sometimes the discussion is nuanced by a conviction that since Yahweh was a unique deity, there couldn't be just a straightforward analogy with, say, Hittite suzerainty treaties between a lord or king and some vassal or vassal state. In particular, it was assumed that Yahweh, practicing "tenacious loyalty" to his covenant and covenant people, had made a permanent treaty with them, regardless of their response or behavior. In that sense, though the covenant was between two entities, nevertheless, it was basically a unilateral treaty. Not only did Yahweh draw up the contract, and lay down all the stipulations, commandoments, potential blessings and curses, but he stuck to the deal, through thick and thin, even when God's people continually broke the covenant. God was faithful even when the people were fickle and faithless.

There are some problems with this logic at various points. For one thing, there are repeated statements in the OT indicating the *conditional* nature of this or that covenant. For example, consider the following text from 2 Chron. 7:

When Solomon had finished the temple of the Lord and the royal palace, and had succeeded in carrying out all he had in mind to do in the temple of the Lord and in his own palace, the Lord appeared to him at night and said:

"I have heard your prayer and have chosen this place for myself as a temple for sacrifices.

"When I shut up the heavens so that there is no rain, or command locusts to devour the land or send a plague among my people, *if* my people, who are called by my name, will humble themselves and pray and seek my face and turn from their wicked ways, *then* I will hear from heaven, and I will forgive their sin and will heal their land. Now my eyes will be open and my ears attentive to the prayers offered in this place. I have chosen and consecrated this temple so that my Name may be there forever. My eyes and my heart will always be there."

The context is the relationship between Solomon and God, a Solomon who has just built the temple and the royal palace. Notice in particular God's remark that the receiving of forgiveness from God and the hearing of prayers of the people is *conditional* upon the repenting and turning of God's people back to God. The relationship is a living one, and both parties have to freely participate in it, and in particular the people have to participate in it in the right manner if they want the right outcome. The promises, the blessings, the hearing of prayers are conditional upon repentance and a turning back to God. This discussion of course comes late in the game. Gone is the theocracy that existed in Abraham's and Moses' day, and we are at the height of the monarchy sometime after 1000 BC, with the reign of Solomon, who is busily acting like various other ANE kings, with vast building projects, military conquests, fortifications of borders and walled cities, acquiring of military hardware (e.g. chariots), so that Israel may be a nation "like unto other nations." And it needs to be noted that according to 1 Samuel, God was not best pleased with the demand for a king, a ruler like other nations had, and initially he gave them only a "prince," Saul, who was the sort of king a fickle people might well deserve.

Another rather clear indicator that certain covenants were seen as *conditional* in nature comes from the very promise we find Yahweh making to David in 2 Sam. 7. The two passages (2 Chron. 7 and 2 Sam. 7) are similar in various ways, but in the former, Solomon has already built a house for God, and receives a direct revelation from God in a dream, whereas in 2 Sam. 7, the revelation comes to the prophet Nathan, who must explain why David is not supposed to build a house for God. Here is the text and the relevant context:

Now then, tell my servant David, "This is what the LORD Almighty says: I took you from the pasture, from tending the flock, and appointed you ruler over my people Israel. 9 I have been with you wherever you have gone, and I have cut off all your enemies from before you. Now I will make your name great, like the names of the greatest men on earth. ¹⁰ And I will provide a place for my people Israel and will plant them so that they can have a home of their own and no longer be disturbed. Wicked people will not oppress them anymore, as they did at the beginning ¹¹ and have done ever since the time I appointed leaders over my people Israel. I will also give you rest from all your enemies.

The LORD declares to you that the LORD himself will establish a house for you:
¹² "When your days are over and you rest with your ancestors, I will raise up your offspring to succeed you, your own flesh and blood, and I will establish his kingdom. ¹³ He is the one who will build a house for my Name, and I will establish the throne of his kingdom forever. ¹⁴ I will be his father, and he will be my son. When he does wrong, I will punish him with a rod wielded by men, with floggings inflicted by human hands. ¹⁵ But my love will never be taken away from him, as I took it away from Saul, whom I removed from before you. ¹⁶ Your house and your kingdom will endure forever before me; your throne will be established forever."

¹⁷ Nathan reported to David all the words of this entire revelation.

Here we have a clear promise of Davidic dynastic succession. But was this an unconditional promise from Yahweh to David? A better way of asking the question is, "How did this turn out when in fact God's people went after foreign gods, whether we think of Rehoboam in the south or say Ahab and Jezebel in the north?" In fact, there was not a "forever" succession of Davidic kings leading up to the time of Jesus. To the contrary, in 722 BC and in about 588 BC both the northern and the southern leadership cartel were carted off into exile, and even when they returned to the land there was no Davidic king. Nor later did the Maccabees qualify as such, much less Herod the-not-so-Great, who was one part Idumean and one part Jewish. And in fact, we have already seen in Genesis itself the conclusion of Bill Arnold that the covenants were not unilateral, and they also were not unconditional, either.[1]

One of the problems with discussions about covenant, in both OT and NT scholarly circles, is that the discussion doesn't always, and in some cases doesn't often, take into account history. It is an abstract theological discussion, based on a certain kind of view of God's *HESED* or his tenacious loyalty to a covenant or covenants with his people. This, I would suggest, is a mistake, because covenants are always historical agreements, in this case between God and his people. The biblical writers did their theologizing out of their narrative thought world, *but* that thought world was not grounded in some idealized version of their story, but rather was based in their understanding of how that story worked out in the actual history of God's people.

Covenants in antiquity, including biblical ones, were two-way streets. The very reason there were curse and blessing sanctions was because it was expected that God's people would respond appropriately, and if they didn't, they could expect punishment. A God of righteousness and holiness could not overlook or pass over sin forever. It had to be dealt with. And if the covenant was flagrantly, knowingly, and repeatedly broken by God's people, God was under no obligation to: (1) keep the Old Covenant, or (2) renew that covenant, or (3) inaugurate an entirely New Covenant. It was entirely up to Yahweh how things would be going forward, or whether the relationship would go forward at all.

And this brings us back to the word *HESED* once more. As we have already noted in this study, *the basic way this word is repeatedly translated in the LXX is "mercy."* Now,

---

[1] See pp. 20–2 above.

mercy is not an obligation, much less a covenantal obligation. Mercy is when you don't get what you deserve, and in this case, that would mean when God does not enact the covenant curse sanctions or simply cut himself off from his wayward people. Hos. 11, a text we have already discussed,[2] tells us that God is not like human beings, and he will have mercy on his wayward people. *What needs to be stressed about this is that this is not because of a covenantal obligation to do so. Indeed, it is in spite of an extant covenantal curse sanction! Rather, this is an expression of God's character! God is not obligated to have mercy on his sinful people. HESED means mercy or loving kindness, even on those who do not deserve it, and to whom God has no duty to show mercy.*

The fact that God, again and again, like the proverbial "hound of heaven" in the famous poem by Francis Thompson, comes after his straying people, and renews his relationship with them again and again, speaks volumes about the *character* of Yahweh, but implies nothing about covenantal continuity, nor about whether or not the New Covenant is a renewal of some form of the Old Covenant. And in any case, *renewal* is not the same thing as *fulfillment*. Paul certainly does suggest in Gal. 4 that: (1) the Abrahamic covenant is fulfilled in Christ and in the new covenant he inaugurates, and (2) the Mosaic covenant is one of fading glory and increasing obsolescence (see 2 Cor. 3–4 and also Hebrews), but the way he talks about these matters makes clear that at least the Apostle to the Gentiles does not see the New Covenant as a renewal of the Mosaic covenant at all.

So, the story of covenanting between the Fall and the Incarnation has various chapters.

There is a Noahic covenant, there is an Abrahamic covenant, there is a Mosaic covenant, there is a Davidic covenant, and the element of continuity which connects these various covenants is God's merciful will to continue to have a chosen people who continue to be called to be a light and blessing to the nations. It will be useful if at this point if we work through these various covenants one by one, noting the differences in the covenants as well as their points of contact.

The Covenant with Noah: Gen. 9

Then God blessed Noah and his sons, saying to them, "Be fruitful and increase in number and fill the earth. [2] The fear and dread of you will fall on all the beasts of the earth, and on all the birds in the sky, on every creature that moves along the ground, and on all the fish in the sea; they are given into your hands. [3] Everything that lives and moves about will be food for you. Just as I gave you the green plants, I now give you everything.

[4] "But you must not eat meat that has its lifeblood still in it. [5] And for your lifeblood I will surely demand an accounting. I will demand an accounting from every animal. And from each human being, too, I will demand an accounting for the life of another human being.

[6] "Whoever sheds human blood, by humans shall their
blood be shed; for in the image of God
has God made mankind.

[7] "As for you, be fruitful and increase in number; multiply on the earth and increase upon it."

[8] Then God said to Noah and to his sons with him: [9] "I now establish my covenant with you and with your descendants after you [10] and with every living creature that was with you – the birds, the

---

[2] On *HESED* see pp. 288–91 above and on Hos. 11 see pp. 49–55 above.

livestock and all the wild animals, all those that came out of the ark with you – every living creature on earth. ¹¹ I establish my covenant with you: Never again will all life be destroyed by the waters of a flood; never again will there be a flood to destroy the earth."

¹² And God said, "This is the sign of the covenant I am making between me and you and every living creature with you, a covenant for all generations to come: ¹³ I have set my rainbow in the clouds, and it will be the sign of the covenant between me and the earth. ¹⁴ Whenever I bring clouds over the earth and the rainbow appears in the clouds, ¹⁵ I will remember my covenant between me and you and all living creatures of every kind. Never again will the waters become a flood to destroy all life. ¹⁶ Whenever the rainbow appears in the clouds, I will see it and remember the everlasting covenant between God and all living creatures of every kind on the earth."

¹⁷ So God said to Noah, "This is the sign of the covenant I have established between me and all life on the earth."

If some of this sounds strangely familiar, then it should. There are clear echoes here of the so-called Adamic covenant in Gen. 1–3, in terms of the command to "be fruitful and multiply," but notice the obvious differences as well. Noah's kin are allowed to stop being vegetarians and God promises not to destroy the world again by flood. There is the further point that this covenant is not just with Noah and his descendants but also with every living creature on the earth. One may also perhaps point to the fact that God makes explicit in this covenant "no killing of fellow human beings," and if one does so, its sets in motion the in-kind response.

While various scholars have spoken of the covenant with Adam and Eve, actually the language of covenant does not appear in Gen. 1–3. The term *berit* first appears here in the cycle of stories about Noah in Gen. 6–9, and I am in agreement with Bill Arnold that the language of "establishing" the covenant is not the same as "cutting a covenant," the latter being the phrase speaking of the inauguration of a covenant (cf. Gen. 15.18; 21.27,32). The "implication is that Noah is already in a covenant relationship with God, which further explains that his righteousness (6.9–10) is derivative of that relationship. This interpretation can be confirmed by the syntax of 6.17–18 which can be taken sequentially rather than following NRSV's disjunctive: 'I am going to bring a flood of waters on the earth … *and then* will confirm my covenant with you.' "[3] This covenant, like other covenants that involve God, is of course not a parity agreement, negotiated between two equal parties, but rather a lord–vassal asymmetrical covenant. All such covenants involve both promises and obligations, some focusing more on the former (e.g. Noahic and Abrahamic covenants), some more on the latter (e.g. Mosaic covenant).

One may ask at this juncture, why the ban on eating flesh with the blood in it (Gen. 9.4). The answer is that the blood is "the life" and life itself is viewed as sacred, which is also the reason to ban killing humans. There are various texts in the Pentateuch that stress that the blood is (the source of) the life and human life is sacred (cf. Lev. 17.11,14; Deut. 12.23; Lev. 3.17; 7.26–27; 19.26; Deut. 12.15–16).[4] On the *lex talionis* or law of proportionate or equivalent response one can consult Exod. 21.12 and Lev. 24.21. With the term covenant coming up some seven times in just ten verses (9.8–17), and never before this occurrence in the text of Genesis, it likely makes evident that God's covenant with Noah and his descendants is critical to the ongoing existence of the world order after the flood.

³ Arnold, *Genesis*, 100.
⁴ Cf. Westermann, *Genesis 1–11*, 464–65 and Wenham, *Genesis 1–15*, 193, for various interpretations of this prohibition.

Most covenants do have "signs" and the one given with the Noahic covenant is a surprise, for normally a sign is a reminder to humans of their obligations in the covenant, but here the sign is a reminder to God himself of his obligations (9.15–16). It needs to be stressed that this particular covenant is said to be an *olam* or forever covenant (9.16), but this is *also* said of the Abrahamic, the Mosaic, and the Davidic covenants as well (cf. Gen. 17.7,13,19; Exod. 31.16; Lev. 24.8; 2 Sam. 23.5). Clearly, all these covenants are not the same, do not all have the same sign, and cannot all run simultaneously with the same group of people. So, the question is – what does *olam* really mean?

I would suggest it means "ongoing" rather than "forever." In other words, it isn't put on the clock from the outset, there is no inherent time limit to the covenant. The covenant can be broken, annulled, replaced by God, but there is no built-in obsolescence to the covenant itself. It is not on set up for a specific duration. Much depends on how God's people respond to this or that covenant, and whether they break it or not. If it is broken, then God must decide whether simply to apply the curse sanctions and stop relating to that group of people, or renew the covenant in some way, or inaugurate a new covenant. The matter is in God's hands, since he inaugurates all the covenants with his people. The relationship and covenant is asymmetrical. Arnold helpfully puts the matter this way. "God's perpetual covenant is of 'long duration' although it is not necessarily unconditional, which … would not be the nature of a bilateral covenant."[5] Just so, but to avoid confusion, it would be better to not use the term "perpetual" for such a covenant, which is bilateral and can be broken or abolished. "Ongoing" or "of long duration" is more apt and meets the historical and theological presentation of covenanting in the Bible during the era between the Fall and the Incarnation.[6]

This passage has been viewed as of importance not just in itself, but also in biblical theological terms because it has been assumed to be the background for the decree of James in Acts 15 about requirements for Gentiles who have become followers of Jesus. R. J. Bauckham, for example, has argued that the decree is James stating what Torah requires of Gentiles, as opposed to Jews.[7] Bauckham argues that the basis for the decree is the Scripture quotation in Acts 15.16–18, but the question is in what way, or what part of that quotation is the basis? Is it just the fact that the quotation refers to the coming of the Gentiles to the living God, which James asserts is now happening, based on the reports of Peter and Paul and Barnabas? Or is he also alluding to a *different* OT text from that cited from Amos 9.11–12 (LXX), perhaps the text of Gen. 9 cited above or perhaps Lev. 17–18? Bauckham suggests that the four things prohibited to the "alien in the land who sojourns in your midst" correspond to the four prohibitions of the apostolic decree in the same order as is found in Acts 15.29, so "things sacrificed to idols" corresponds to Lev. 17.8–9, blood is prohibited in Lev. 17.10,12, things strangled are prohibited in Lev. 17.13, and sexual immorality is prohibited in Lev. 18.6–23. On first blush, Bauckham's case seems strong, and many scholars have followed his argument, or instead have suggested that the

---

[5] Arnold, *Genesis*, 111.

[6] For a helpful and lengthy discussion on covenant signs, see Michael V. Fox, "The Sign of the Covenant: Circumcision in the Light of the Priestly *'ot* Etiologies," *RB* 81 (1974): 557–96.

[7] See his detailed discussion in "James and the Gentiles (Acts 15.13–21)," in *History, Literature and Society in the Book of Acts* (ed. Ben Witherington; Cambridge: Cambridge University Press, 1996), 154–84, here 154.

Noahic covenant lies in the background to the decree, or perhaps some combination of both texts.

The first problem with this sort of reasoning, in regard to Lev. 17–18 specifically, is that James is not writing to or about "the stranger or alien in the land" and Gentiles were not expected to keep a modicum of Jewish food laws outside the context of the Holy Land and outside of a context of a Jewish majority community. James is quite specifically writing to Gentiles living in the Diaspora, many of whom have not had and did not have direct contact with the Jewish congregation or synagogue in various places such as Galatia. Secondly, James quite specifically says that his motive for wanting the Gentiles to avoid these four things is that "Moses is read in the Diaspora synagogue" week after week. In other words, James is concerned that the Gentile behavior in these new church plants will be a bad witness to Jews, and James wants Jews in whatever locale to hear the Gospel (from Paul and Peter and presumably others too).

Thirdly, as I have argued extensively elsewhere, the word εἰδωλοθύτων in v. 29 must be compared to the phrase τῶν ἀλισγημάτων τῶν εἰδώλων in v. 20, and in both cases what is being referred to is *not* eating non-kosher meat but rather to not eating meat in the presence of idols, the very thing that Paul himself is busily prohibiting in 1 Cor. 8–10. The issue is not primarily menu but venue. The term εἰδωλοθύτων is a Jewish-Christian polemical term which is basically not found in literature prior to the time of Paul and Luke and is certainly not found in Leviticus (LXX). The issue is the spiritual pollution of coming into contact with idols, in idol temples. James is prohibiting Gentiles from continuing to eat at pagan dinner feasts in pagan temples, where (Jews assumed) you would find all four of these things together – the pollutions of idols and meat sacrificed and eaten in the presence of idols, blood (in the meat), things strangled (not a Jewish practice), and sexual immorality.[8] So in fact we find Paul implementing James' decree in 1 Cor. 8–10.

Does this have anything to do with Gen. 9? On the surface of things, it might, since in that chapter we not only have a permission to eat meat but without the blood, but also a sad tale of sexual misbehavior, apparently. But that story is about Noah and his descendants, who *already have a covenant relationship with God*. It is not at all clear that this could be said to be behind James' ruling for Gentiles who are now coming to God not through the Noahic covenant but through the preaching of the Good News about Jesus and the New Covenant involving Jews and Gentiles together. In other words, they were coming to faith not through the vehicle of a pre-existing covenant with God's people such as the one with Noah, although one can argue Noah was a Gentile, certainly not an Israelite, since Israel and the Mosaic covenant did not exist as yet. Much more logical is the assumption that what James has in mind in talking about synagogue preaching of Moses week to week is idolatry and immorality, the two things at the very heart of the Ten Commandments. Gentiles who want to avoid being a bad witness to Jews need to stay away from pagan temples, the very heart of idolatry and immorality, in the Jewish view of things. The New Covenant is not a renewal of the Noahic one.

[8] See the detailed discussion in Ben Witherington III, *What's in the Word: Rethinking the Socio-Rhetorical Character of the New Testament* (Waco, TX: Baylor University Press, 2009), 89–101.

The Covenant with Abraham

The language of covenant certainly comes up again in Gen. 12–21, and there are some rather clear echoes of the Noahic covenant in the story of Abraham and his relationship and covenant with God. The narrative in Gen. 15 is pivotal in many ways in the Abram cycle of stories because it brings to light covenantal theology in a way we have not seen before, except with Noah. Here as in the Noah narratives, it is God who initiates, stipulates, and confirms the covenant and its sanctions. Abram is the passive recipient of its benefits. He was in need of more assurance than just a promise, and thus God performed a sacred rite that sealed the promises and made clear that Yahweh was determined to make them come true.

We've had occasion, while discussing the narrative thought world of the OT, to spend some time on the Abraham narratives, but here we need to consider the issue of the presentation of the covenanting between God and Abraham in more detail.[9] Gen. 15, as it turns out, has been a major focus of OT scholarship, particularly in regard to critical studies of Genesis in particular and the Pentateuch in general. In fact, one study has even suggested that Gen. 15 is a theological compendium drawing together in one place many of the major themes of the Pentateuch.[10] To some extent, these sorts of arguments are chicken and egg arguments. This chapter could just as well be the source of later Pentateuchal and Prophetic reflections on the Exodus, Sinai, wilderness traditions, as the residue of such later texts being edited into a summary here.[11] Our focus must be on Gen. 15.7–21, where we have an extremely important description of a covenant ratification ceremony. A second dialogue between God and Abraham is initiated by God to provide some assurance to Abraham about the promise of "land" and "seed." Rather than just making promises, as before, here God makes covenant with Abraham to make clear that these promises will come true.

The dialogue begins with God's self-revelation to Abraham, "I am Yahweh" (v. 7, cf. 17.1 – "I am God Almighty"). The greater the revelation, one would presume, the greater the understanding and assurance of God's commitment to his promises. Notice that the way God makes clear his identity, is not only by self-naming, but also by reminding Abraham that he was the one who brought Abraham from Ur in the Chaldees to this land that his line will one day possess. As Arnold says, the similarity to Exod. 20.2 (cf. Lev. 25.38 and Deut. 5.6) can hardly be accidental. Abraham is the paradigm for future close encounters with Yahweh by Moses and others. The covenanting here foreshadows the later covenanting with Moses. Yet there is a big difference. This covenant is with Abraham *himself*, who does not yet have a legal heir, or a people. The Mosaic covenant, by contrast is quite specifically the inauguration of a relationship with a people, and not accidentally it is there that the language of holiness, of a people set apart by God, crops up for the first time, first with Moses at Sinai, then later with Moses and his people at Sinai, having escaped Egypt.

But how was Abraham to know God's promises would come to fruition? Moses already had a people, and was simply heading for the land. Abraham, by contrast, is in the land

---

[9] See pp. 127–35 above.
[10] J. Ha, *Genesis 15: A Theological Compendium of Pentateuchal History* (Berlin: De Gruyter, 1989).
[11] See Arnold, *Genesis*, 152.

but has no people. Verse 9 seems at first not to help Abraham's conundrum. He is charged with bringing animals, apparently sacrificial animals. While we may puzzle over this, Abraham in vv. 10–11 seems to understand quite well. Notice how he divides and arranges the animals, getting them ready, apparently, for some sort of ritual. Notice that this whole sequence of events is called in v. 18 "a covenant."

What is going on here is a solemn ritualistic covenant oath. When one passes between the pieces of the sacrifice, one is invoking the oath curse on oneself if one does not keep the promise made. But the shocking thing here is that it is Yahweh who is passing between the corpses, not Abraham, invoking a curse upon his divine self! "Such a conditional self-curse has here been transferred to Yahweh in the form of the smoking fire pot and flaming torch (vs. 17), by which Yahweh enacts his own death should he fail to fulfill his promises to Abram."[12] One wonders if yet another reason Paul finds so many resonances in the Abraham covenant with the New Covenant is that in both stories, "the death of God" comes into play, as here Yahweh, and there his Son, inaugurate a covenant by means of invoking the oath curse on themselves! The cup of God's wrath which Jesus submitted to drink, here God invokes on his own head!

This act of covenanting assures Abraham of four things (the Hebrew being emphatic here "know this for certain," or as we would say "you can take this to the bank"): (1) Abraham will have offspring, though they must dwell in a foreign land for a while (v. 13). Notice the collective use of the term "seed" here, which Paul will draw on in Galatians; (2) in due course Yahweh will judge the foreign land, liberate God's people, and they will leave that land with "great possessions" (v. 14); (3) Abraham will live a long and peaceful life, and will not have to endure the bondage of his descendants in that foreign land; (4) Abraham's seed will "come back here" in the fourth generation from his time, which is to say after the Amorites iniquity comes to full flower, justifying their ouster from the land (Deut. 9.4–5).

Now the most important observation about this act of covenanting is that *it is not a unilateral promissory covenant*. Some scholars have viewed it this way (as they have the Davidic covenant, too).[13] Arnold, however, is correct that all such ANE covenants were binary, not unilateral, in character. They involved both promises and obligations, and indeed notice that even at the outset, Abraham had to bring the animals, provide the sacrifice, in this case. "Implicitly, the passive partner had some obligation or promise to uphold, otherwise we have only a promise and no covenant at all."[14] This is exactly correct. The covenant is not a parity agreement, it is asymmetrical, *but mere promises do not a covenant make*. God had already made promises, but it was not until he made covenant with Abraham here that Abraham was assured the promises would come to fruition.

Arnold helpfully sums up both this covenanting and the one with Noah:

The first covenant in the Bible was God's commitment to save Noah and his family from death in the floodwaters. The second covenant is God's commitment to Abram to provide land to his descendants ... Covenant-living was not only the means [I would say the reason] of salvation from the flood,

---

[12] Arnold, *Genesis*, 159, and on the ritual itself, which is known in the ANE, see B. J. Collins, "The Ritual between the Pieces," in *The Context of Scripture* (ed. W. W. Hallo and K. Lawson Younger; Leiden: Brill, 1997–2002), vol. 1, 160–61.

[13] See e.g. Wenham, *Genesis 1–15*, 333.

[14] Arnold, *Genesis*, 160.

but the Bible's solution to the sin problem defined earlier in the Primeval History (Gen. 2.4–4.16; 6.5,11–12). Noah's covenantal righteousness resulted in salvation, and it therefore anticipates and previews Yahweh's covenant with Abram. The great patriarch's righteousness (vs. 6) has resulted in salvation from a life of barrenness, and therefore hopelessness.[15]

All this is germane to the later discussions of the Abrahamic covenant in the NT, in particular in Paul.

It may seem strange, to those who know of the preoccupations of early Jews with Moses, including its great thinkers such as Philo, that Paul, the former Pharisee, devotes considerable time and space to Abraham and his story (Rom. 4; 9.6–15; 11.1; Gal. 3.6–18; 4.21–31) but gives Moses far less ink. For Paul, Abraham is the critical example of faith prior to the time of Christ. Gal. 3.8 emphasizes: "And the Scripture, foreseeing that God would set right the Gentiles by faith, declared the Gospel beforehand to Abraham." Abraham is both prototype and exemplar of Christian faith, or at least of the process which came to be called justification by grace through faith. He heard the first preaching about trusting God and it being reckoned to him as righteousness or at least right-standing with God and he responded appropriately. Abraham is in effect seen by Paul as the ancestor and model for both Jew and Gentile. Even Gentiles share in the faith of Abraham (Rom. 4.16) and with Jewish Christians become his heirs and beneficiaries of the promises given to him through Christ (Gal. 3.14).

Paul looks at the Abraham story, as he does all such stories, through Christological, and to a lesser degree ecclesiological, glasses. Thus, the story elements which come to the fore are those that are most germane to his Christian audiences. What he omits from the story of Abraham (the sacrifice of Isaac, the Sodom and Gomorrah story, the entertainment of the angels, the Melchizedek incident) is as revealing as what he includes.[16] Paul's urgency is to show that Abraham is a paradigm of faith and that the promises to him are fulfilled in Christ, and in Christ's people, who become Abraham's heir.

The linear reading of the story of Abraham from Gen. 12–17 and beyond leads to the conclusion we find in Rom. 4.11–12 that circumcision is only the seal or sign of the righteousness or right-standing that Abraham had already obtained through faith in God, as we have noted when we discussed the role of Abraham in Chapter 5. Paul also concludes from this sequence of events that Abraham can be the father of Gentile as well as Jewish believers, for like them he believed without having been circumcised and was accepted on that basis (Rom. 4.1).

In Rom. 4.23–24, Abraham is depicted as Exhibit A of relating to God on the proper basis of eschatological faith: "Now the words 'it was reckoned to him' were not written for his sake alone, but for ours also. It will be reckoned to us who believe in him who raised Jesus our Lord from the dead." Since this story is a scriptural story it is not seen as merely analogous to the story of Christians but in fact the model or paradigm for the Christian story in regard to the issue of faith.

I must stress again that of absolutely crucial importance for mapping out the lines of Paul's narrative thought world is the connection Paul makes between the Abrahamic and

---

[15] Arnold, *Genesis*, 160–61.

[16] And this omission of Melchizedek from the Abraham story Paul tells is a very clear clue that he is not the author of Hebrews, for that writer's imaginative use of the Melchizedek story generates a whole new approach to Christology, with Melchizedek seen as a type of Christ the High Priest.

the New Covenant, particularly in Gal. 3–4. The Abrahamic covenant is seen as being fulfilled in Christ, and so the New Covenant is the consummation of the Abrahamic one. Both of these covenants involved both the circumcised and the uncircumcised, and thus circumcision ceases to be seen as the crucial thing. Gen. 15 precedes Gen. 17 and so faith takes precedent over circumcision in Paul's thought world. Both the Abrahamic and the New Covenant involve children given by the grace of God, both involve an "everlasting" covenant, both promise that all the nations of the earth will be blessed (see Gen. 17.6). But the price Paul pays for seeing the Abrahamic covenant as fulfilled in the New Covenant, as he does in Gal. 4, for example, is that the Mosaic covenant is viewed as an interim arrangement. He does not advocate the notion of covenantal continuity between the Abrahamic and Mosaic covenant and the new one. To the contrary he contrasts the Mosaic covenant with the new one in terms of their permanence and also some aspects of their character.

The Covenant with Moses

Many scholars over many decades have certainly seen the concept of covenant as one of the keys not only to understanding OT theology, but a key to grasping the relationship between the OT and the NT, a bridge concept binding the two "testaments" together. After all, the phrase "Old Testament" simply means "old Covenant" and this implies there is a "New Covenant or Testament" as well. But in the history of scholarship, particularly OT scholarship during the twentieth century, there have been many who have noted: (1) that the language of covenant is frankly not all that common in the OT. There are large sections of the OT where it is neither mentioned nor seems to be implied; (2) the terminology of *berit* is overwhelmingly found in Deuteronomy, of the books of the Pentateuch, and so the suspicion has arisen that the concept is a late one and reflects the exilic or more likely post-exilic editing of the corpus of materials by "the Deuteronomistic historian." In other words, the lack of such language in the pre-exilic prophets suggests that in its earliest stages, Israel did not have a "covenant" relationship with God. The Deuteronomic understanding of the pre-exilic history was projected back into the earlier period, "particularly in terms of a covenant with the Fathers at Sinai, whereas in actual fact the covenant theology first arose as an attempt to combat the threat to the religious identity of the nation in crisis in the seventh century."[17] We may thank Julius Wellhausen for the initial push in this direction in terms of the analysis of covenantal theology in and of the OT, and in fact the pendulum has swung back and forth on this issue in the last hundred years.

On the one hand, it is undeniable that there is editing in the Pentateuch that reflects a time well after the time of Moses (e.g. "the X were *then* in the land" or "until the time of the sin of the Amorites had reached its zenith" and so on). The question becomes how heavy-handed the editor was with his source material. As Childs points out, we have evidence in Gen. 50.25; Exod. 13.5.11; 32.13; and Num. 11.12; 14.23 of the notion of a promise of land sealed with a divine oath, and these texts are not suspected of being Deuteronomistic anachronisms. *In other words, there is early evidence of covenantal language in the Pentateuch, a language that the Deuteronomistic editor seems to have amplified.*

---

[17] Childs, *Biblical Theology*, 413–20, here 416.

Secondly, the way the relationship of God's people to God is described is not that of "natural kinship," either early or late in the traditioning process.[18] Thirdly, much of the history of tradition discussion has too quickly dismissed the evidence about covenants from the ANE, including the famous Hittite suzerainty treaties. It is ironic that a history of tradition discussion would leave out of the discussion actual historical examples of covenanting from well before the period of Israel's exiles, north and south! Fourthly, too much of the discussion has focused too narrowly just on the term *berit* when in fact one needs to look at a cluster of terms and ideas, such as election, promise, oaths, curses and blessings, as well as covenant, to understand when "covenanting" is actually being discussed. The fact that some texts, for instance Exod. 24.3–8, describe a covenanting event or ceremony and even refer to a "book of the covenant" but without the later notion of a covenant being sealed by a pledged word rather than a ceremony, which is typical of what we find in Deuteronomy, shows that the Deuteronomistic editor is not the inventor of the notion that the ancients celebrated covenant ceremonies, and that includes Moses. In other words, early, middle and late, covenants are in play in the OT, and the Deuteronomistic editor is just highlighting and amplifying things that were already there in the most primitive material in the Pentateuch. Here Child's summary can be commended, showing just how important "covenant" is to OT theology and indeed biblical theology:

Israel's primeval history is construed as a series of covenants, starting with Noah (Gen. 9.8ff.) and continuing with the promise of land and posterity sealed in a covenant to Abraham and his descendants (Gen. 15.1ff; 26.1ff; 50.24). The covenant with Moses at Sinai, which is both introduced and concluded with Deuteronomic formulation (Ex. 19.3–8; 24.3–8) interprets the whole event as a covenant with Israel, repeated in chapters 32–34 of Exodus, and given a unified covenantal interpretation of both Israel's past and future in the Book of Deuteronomy (5.2ff; 7.6ff; 26.16; 29.1ff.). The Deuteronomistic historian pursues Israel's tragic history of covenantal disobedience through the destruction of the nation (Josh. 24.19ff.; 2 Kings 17.7ff.). Israel incurred the righteous wrath of God because of the disobedience of God's covenantal law. Finally, Israel's prophets speak of a restoration of the nation in covenantal terms. For Hosea, it will be a covenant with the creation and a betrothal in steadfast love (Hos. 2.16ff., ET) for Jeremiah a new covenant (31.31ff.) and for Ezekiel a "covenant of peace" (34.25) for blessing and security (cf. Isa. 42.6; 49.8; Mal. 3.1). Daniel is confident that in spite of those who violate God's covenant, there remain those who stand firm in faith awaiting their promised deliverance (11.32; 12.1–3). In sum, regardless of the age and the circumstances lying behind the Deuteronomic covenant formulation, its theology became the normative expression of God's relation to Israel and served as a major theological category for unifying the entire collection comprising the Hebrew scriptures.[19]

We've already had occasion to analyze in depth the "Ten Words"[20] but here it is important to remove some of the Christian stereotypes about "the Law" and more specifically about the Mosaic Law and covenant. In the first place, as E. P. Sanders has rightly stressed

---

[18] Childs, *Biblical Theology*, 417–18.

[19] Childs, *Biblical Theology*, 419. This rather conservative conclusion can be contrasted strongly with that of Feldmeier and Spieckermann, *God of the Living*, 447–58, who are still following Wellhausen and company in minimizing or denying covenantal language and praxis as a reflection of actual pre-exilic relationships between God and his people. This is of a piece with the denial of there even being an Exodus and a covenanting at Mt. Sinai brokered by Moses. They are, however, right to criticize Reformed Federal theology and what it has done with the discussions of covenant in the Bible, for example the notion of unilateral promises or unilateral covenant is read into the biblical text (see the discussion above, about the Abrahamic covenant).

[20] See pp. 146–54, above.

for many decades, starting with his classic study *Paul and Palestinian Judaism* (1977), the Mosaic covenant is not a "law" covenant, in the sense that "law" is the means of getting into the chosen people.[21] The Mosaic covenant reflects the gracious act of God in redeeming his people out of Egypt and bringing them to Sinai and covenanting with them there. "Law," or better said, commandments and obligation, are not about "getting in" but rather about "staying in" or responding to God's gracious initiative. A strong contrast between law and grace is a caricature of the Old Covenant vis-à-vis the New Covenant, and especially of the Mosaic covenant. Both the Mosaic and the New Covenants are founded and grounded in God's grace, to which God's people are beckoned to respond by entering into a binding relationship with God. Proper biblical theology, like *all* the biblical covenants, reflects the grace of God from start to finish.

The second caricature that needs to be eliminated from the discussion of the Mosaic covenant is that commandments and laws are inherently legalistic and should be contrasted with grace, the Spirit, and the like. Legalism is a particular approach to law or commandments, it is not something inherent in commandments. The human problem is not "legalism" and God's grace is not about enabling people to ignore "the law" and avoid being "legalistic."

The third caricature that needs to be eliminated from the discussion of the Mosaic covenant is the notion that there was something inherently defective about the covenant and in particular about its "law" or commandments. No, says Paul, in Rom. 7, the Mosaic Law is "holy, just and good" and is a gift of God. The problem with the Law, is not the Law itself – it is fallen and sinful human beings and the way they respond to the Law. The Law is a gift of God's grace to his people. True, the Law is not the Gospel about redemption in Christ. True, the Law in itself can tell a person what they ought to do but cannot enable them to do it (only God's Spirit can do that in the life of a fallen person). But the Law should not be faulted for something it was never intended to be – either the Gospel or the Holy Spirit! The Law should be appreciated for being a revelation of God's will for his people, and, as Ps. 119 suggests, a light unto our path to prevent us from stumbling in the ever-present dark.

The fourth caricature that needs to be eliminated from the discussion of the Mosaic covenant is the idea that "keeping the Law" is a horrible, onerous thing that is a burden no Jew could manage to fully bear. They could not perfectly keep the Law.[22] This is not how Jews then or now view things. They see the Law, and the keeping of the Mosaic Law, as a delight, not drudgery, as a blessing, not a burden. And, as Paul himself indicates in Phil. 3, when he evaluates his own pre-Christian performance, "in regard to a righteousness that comes from the Mosaic Law I was blameless." By this he does not mean he was perfect, he simply means he did not break any of the laws. Blameless before the Law is one thing, faultless and perfect is another, but he is attesting to the fact that a zealous Jew could keep the Law in the sense of not violating its prohibitions, and if there was an accidental violation, well, there were sacrifices to deal with that, and forgiveness to be had.

---

21 E. P. Sanders, *Paul and Palestinian Judaism: A Comparison of Patterns of Religion* (Philadelphia: Fortress Press, 1977).
22 This of course was one of the classic arguments of the Continental Reformers. See S. J. Chester, *Reading Paul with the Reformers* (Downers Grove, IL: InterVarsity Press, 2017).

In terms of biblical theology, however, this is not all there is to say about the matter. While Jews then and now see the Mosaic covenant as a "forever covenant" between God and his people (and they believe that whatever Jer. 31 means, it must have something to do with the renewal of the Mosaic covenant and the writing of it on human hearts), *this is not how that early Jew Paul sees the matter after he became a follower of Christ.* Further, I don't think Jesus saw it that way, either, since he speaks of a New Covenant inaugurated in his death, as a ransom for the many. Paul tells us in perhaps his earliest letter, Galatians, that the Mosaic covenant and its Law were *pro tempore*, for a specific period of time in the salvation history of God's people, "until the time had fully come, and God sent forth his Son born of woman, born under the Law to redeem those under the Law out from under the Mosaic Law" (Gal. 4).

Paul compares the Law's role ever since Sinai as being like a παιδαγωγός. This word should never have been translated teacher, though clearly the Mosaic Law has some peda-gogical functions. The word in Paul's context means "a childminder." In a socially elite home, the παιδαγωγός was the slave who looked after a child, walked him to and from school, rehearsed his *alpha betas* with him, and in general was a guardian of the child until he ceased to be a minor. Gal. 3–4 should be read carefully in the original context, while studiously ignoring the later anachronistic reading by Luther of this material. The παιδαγωγός has a positive, not a negative role to play in the life of a growing child, but that role is only *pro tempore*. As Paul stresses in the beginning of Gal. 4, the Mosaic Law and covenant were until the time of the coming of the Christ, who inaugurates a New Covenant.

Because Paul takes this view of salvation history, he does not think that obedience to the Mosaic Law is incumbent on any follower of Jesus – be they Jew or Gentile. Paul may choose from time to time to be "the Jew to the Jew" and be Torah-true (see 1 Cor. 9), but his oddness of language there must be stressed. What does it mean for a former zealous Pharisee to say I can be the Jew to the Jew? It means he now sees himself predominantly in a different category, namely a follower of Christ, belonging to Christ, and as such, keeping some aspects of the Mosaic Law is a blessed option (see e.g. the story in Acts 18.18 about his Nazaritic vow), but *not an obligation, even for a Jew like himself*. Why not? Because, as Paul makes clear in 2 Cor. 3–4, the New Covenant eclipsed the glory of the Mosaic cov-enant, and it has become obsolete or annulled. It was not, after all, a "forever covenant," in Paul's view. I hasten to add that various early Jewish Christians disagreed with Paul's view on this, perhaps even James, who may have thought Jewish Christians should remain Torah-true.

Finally, the New Covenant is not without obligation or "law," indeed even Paul talks about "the *law* of Christ" (see Gal. 6 and 1 Cor. 9). Both the Mosaic covenant and the New Covenant involve grace and obligation, both contain mercy and demand, and there is overlap in the commandments in the two covenants. For example, the prohibition against adultery and against killing is not merely reaffirmed, it is intensified in both Mt. 5–7 and in Rom. 12–13. There is overlap. Christians should ask themselves, why you would suspect that God would require less in the New Covenant and with the general dispensation of the eschatological Holy Spirit, than in the case of the Mosaic situation? To whom more is given by God, more is required by God. The demand for holiness and righteousness and acts of compassion and mercy is not lessened in the New Covenant.

To this point we have been engaging in a deck-clearing exercise, so that the Mosaic covenant could be appreciated without loading a lot of Christian baggage into the examination of that covenant. In the next chapter, we will spend considerable time unpacking the situation Jesus addresses. Here a number of more key points need to be stressed: *(1) covenants are bilateral, and as they involve individuals are conditional. The covenant must be kept, or at least the covenant provisions for remedying law-breaking must be followed so there can be forgiveness and the bond between God and the believer is not severed. (2) Election, as it is described in both the OT and NT is a corporate concept. There is a chosen people, an elect group. This does not guarantee the salvation of all individuals within the group. They can be elect, and yet not "saved" ultimately, in the Christian sense of the term.*[23] *(3) The difference between election, which is for specific historical purposes, and salvation needs to be kept steadily in view. The OT, when it speaks about salvation, is referring to: (a) rescue from danger; (b) healing; (c) vindication of the righteous in human history (e.g. Noah). What it is not about is "salvation by grace through faith in Jesus the Messiah." And herein lies a major difference between the Mosaic covenant and its era, and the New Covenant. There is no Christological focus or redeemer figure in the Mosaic covenant. And finally (4) the obvious proof that election is one thing and salvation in the Christian era is another is that Christ, in various places (see e.g. Eph. 1) is portrayed as "the Elect One," "the Righteous One" of God, and he is in no need of "salvation"! As Hebrews will stress, while he was tempted like all humans, he did not sin. Salvation in the Christian sense has to do with saving fallen, sinful human beings, not mere rescue from danger, not mere giving of health, though it can involve both of those things. Christian believers are only elect if they are "in Christ," just as Jewish believers in the era of Moses were elect if they were within the Mosaic covenant and a participant in the chosen people. Election and the Christian sense of salvation from sin are two different, though related concepts, and how one views these concepts will affect how one views covenants. In my view, the notion of unilateral covenants is not a biblical concept.*

And herein lies the problem of Reformed Federal theology that Feldmeier and Spieckermann rightly warn against. In both the OT and in the NT, apostasy is certainly possible by individual "chosen ones" and frankly a person is not eternally secure, until they are securely in eternity. Short of eternity, they must live by grace and with faith, trusting and obeying God. We will say much more about this in the next chapter.

Here a summary from John Goldingay is in order. He stresses that covenantal theology is characteristic not just of the OT but of Paul's (and I would say Jesus') world view.

The Torah and Paul hold together as an integral whole what God has done and what we must do. The prophets and Jesus hold together as an integral whole what God is about to do and what we must do. "Jesus' eschatological message and his ethical message constitute a unity"; he is "both the prophet who proclaims the irruption of God's Reign and the rabbi who expounds God's Law." Like the Sermon on the Mount, then, the Torah was never designed as a means of getting into a relationship with God. It was designed to shape the life of people who have already been granted life. While the contents of the Torah, issued from a wide range of historical and social contexts linking the material in Exodus and Leviticus with Sinai, declares that all of it works out the implications of the Exodus

---

[23] On which see the discussion on pp. 349–81, below, about Chad Thornhill's treatment of election on this subject.

and the covenant making at Sinai. Conversely, placing Deuteronomy on the other side of the period during which the Exodus generation died affirms the legitimacy and necessity of adapting the original revelation to later contexts.[24]

This is exactly right. What it does not say is that while the Mosaic covenant went on, and still in some sense goes on, the coming of the Son is a game changer, and a covenant changer, and we will examine that in the next chapter.

The Covenant with David

Our last port of call in this chapter must be a closer look at the covenant discussion in 2 Sam. 7 compared and contrasted to what is said in Dan. 7. Here is the text:

The LORD declares to you that the LORD himself will establish a house for you: [12] "When your days are over and you rest with your ancestors, I will raise up your offspring to succeed you, your own flesh and blood, and I will establish his kingdom. [13] He is the one who will build a house for my Name, and I will establish the throne of his kingdom forever. [14] I will be his father, and he will be my son. When he does wrong, I will punish him with a rod wielded by men, with floggings inflicted by human hands. [15] But my love will never be taken away from him, as I took it away from Saul, whom I removed from before you. [16] Your house and your kingdom will endure forever before me; your throne will be established forever."

David is denied the privilege of building God a house, and instead is promised dynastic succession, focusing in the first instance on Solomon, who will build God's "house." He will treat Solomon like a son, and he will discipline him when he gets out of line, even severely discipline him, but he will not stop loving him, unlike the case with Saul. The promise involves the Davidic house and kingdom being established *olam*, which, we have suggested, means on an ongoing basis.

To this we must compare Dan. 7.9–14 and here the context is just as important as in 2 Sam. 7. It reads:

As I looked,

thrones were set in place,
   and the Ancient of Days took his seat.

His clothing was as white as snow;
   the hair of his head was white like wool.

His throne was
   flaming with fire,
   and its wheels were
   all ablaze.

[10] A river of fire was
   flowing, coming out
   from before him.

Thousands upon thousands attended him;
   ten thousand times ten thousand stood before him.

The court was seated,
   and the books were opened.

[24] Goldingay, *Biblical Theology*, 118.

[11] Then I continued to watch because of the boastful words the horn was speaking. I kept looking until the beast was slain and its body destroyed and thrown into the blazing fire. [12] (The other beasts had been stripped of their authority, but were allowed to live for a period of time.)

[13] In my vision at night I looked, and there before me was one like a son of man,[a] coming with the clouds of heaven. He approached the Ancient of Days and was led into his presence. [14] He was given authority, glory and sovereign power; all nations and peoples of every language worshiped him. His dominion is an everlasting dominion that will not pass away, and his kingdom is one that will never be destroyed.

This is of course a part of an apocalyptic vision but notice that in the case of 2 Sam. 7 there is also a strong connection with direct revelation from God. In Dan. 7, Daniel has been describing four beastly or inhuman empires, and he is being reassured by God that ultimately, they will be replaced by a humane empire ruled by a human figure, "one like a son of man." Here we do not have a promise of dynastic succession, but rather the rule of a single person, the son of man "forever and ever." Not only so, he is depicted as judging the earth on behalf of the Ancient of Days, who has bequeathed him this authority and task, and finally, we are told that the nations will worship him. 2 Sam. 7 is about Jewish dynastic succession of the Davidic line, but this is absolutely not the case with Dan. 7. The kingdom or dominion of the Son of Man, unlike the beastly empires, will never be destroyed. It is the final frontier, the last empire, the one that will not strike out.

The empire of the Son of Man will be universal in scope and involve universal worship of the Son of Man. This is so much more than a promise of a future to a particular people called Israel, and to a particular monarchial line, the Davidic one. In particular, the Son of Man doesn't need to become God's "adopted son" like Solomon, to use the language used at the coronation of kings in the ANE. No, he comes from heaven on the clouds, and like the Ancient of Days, is to be worshipped by all peoples and tribes and tongues and nations. Now it is appropriate to ask – who could this be? It cannot be a mere human descendant of David. Jews do not worship human beings, however much they may revere some of their leaders. And Jewish kings do not demand universal worship either, nor do they descend to earth trailing clouds of glory, nor will they be the judge of all the earth, when the final Judgment Day happens and "the books are opened." As we turn now to the NT, and its covenantal discussions, this comparison and contrast has to be kept ever before us, if we are to understand either the New Covenant or Jesus, the one who called himself the Son of Man, but who does not call himself "son of David," though others did.

And So?

We have reviewed all the enacted OT covenants in this chapter, and have urged that the concept of covenanting does indeed go back to the patriarchal era, and is not a later Israelite idea, retrojected back into the earlier period. What is true is that the Deuteronomic editor has amplified this covenant theme in various ways and places. We have also stressed that like other ANE covenants, the covenants between Yahweh and Noah, and then Abraham, and then Moses, and then David were not "forever" covenants. Each covenant lasted until God decided to start afresh with his people, after they had violated and broken the previous covenant. They had no inherent expiration date, but they also did not have an "in perpetuity" clause. Furthermore, like other bilateral ancient covenants the agreements all had conditions, which is why there were both curses as well as blessings connected to a covenant. They were neither unilateral nor unconditional. They were, however, a reflection of God's gracious and yet demanding character. These were in no sense parity agreements – God laid down the law, set up the sanctions, made the promises, and so on. The human covenant partner was to voluntarily hear and heed the covenant agreement. They had no negotiation rights. We also pointed out that God made promises outside as well as inside covenants, and one must be able to distinguish between God's promises which simply reflect God's character, and the promissory clauses in some covenants. Finally, at the end of the chapter we began to note the difference between 2 Sam. 7 and Dan. 7 – one speaking of possible dynastic succession on an ongoing basis (but not unconditionally) and the other speaking of a single individual judging and ruling the nations in perpetuity and being worshipped by them. The next chapter will elaborate on why this comparison and contrast is so critical to understanding biblical theology.

9

Covenanting and Theologizing after the
Incarnation and before Pentecost

All Scripture is divided into two testaments. What preceded the advent and passion of Christ –
that is the law and the prophets – is called the Old; but what was written after his resurrection
is named the New Testament. The Jews make use of the Old, we of the New. Yet they are not
dissonant. The New Testament is the fulfilling of the Old, and in both there is the same testator, even Christ who suffered death for us and made us heirs of his everlasting kingdom ...
When, therefore, we who in times past were blind, and as it were shut up in the prison of folly,
were sitting in darkness, ignorant of God and of the truth, we have been enlightened by him,
who adopted us by his testament; and having freed us from our cruel chains, and brought us
out to the light of wisdom, he admitted us to the inheritance of his heavenly kingdom.

Lactantius, *Divine Institutes* 4.20

We indeed who are of the church rightly receive Moses and read his writings, believing that
he is a prophet who wrote down the future mysteries which God revealed to him in symbols,
figures, and allegorical forms, which we teach were fulfilled in their own time ... Therefore,
the law and all things that are in the law are, according to the opinion of the apostle, "imposed
until the time of the reformation." ... Those whose craft is to make tokens from copper and
to pour statutes, before they produce a true work of copper or of silver or of gold, must first
form figures from clay to the likeness of the figure image. The model is necessary only until
the work that is principal is completed, for when that work for which that image was made of
clay is completed, its use is no longer sought ... For the artist and creator of all himself came
and transformed "the law which has but a shadow of the good things to come" to "the true
form of these realities."

Origen, *Homilies of Leviticus* 10.1.1–4

For as in a painting, so long as one only draws the outlines, it is a sort of "shadow," but when
one has added the bright paints and laid in the colors, then it becomes "an image." Something
of this kind also was the law.

Chrysostom, *Homily on Hebrews* 17.5

What Hath Jeremiah Wrought

Undoubtedly one of the most misused texts in the OT is the passage in Jer. 31 where the
prophet speaks about the New Covenant. The context is very clearly a poetic and prophetic
discussion about the restoration of Israel and Judah after the exile, and as such it is much
like similar discussions in Third Isaiah (Isa. 56–66). But there are some things in this passage

that could and should lead one to think that Jeremiah is not merely talking about "covenant renewal" here. Because that is the case, and because this text is so important to several of the writers of the NT and to Jesus himself, to judge from the Last Supper pericope, we are placing this discussion here as a bridge to discussing Jesus' own teaching during his ministry. Further, since, other than Paul, the author of Hebrews gives us the most detailed discussion of Jeremiah's prophecy, and he is discussing it with fellow Jews who follow Jesus, we will attend to that discussion before dealing with Jesus' interaction with fellow Jews, and his special teaching of his own disciples. It must be noted from the outset that this prophecy was seen as crucial to two very different early Jewish groups. "The sectarians of Qumran understood themselves to be the men of the New Covenant. But the New Covenant for them was nothing more than the Mosaic covenant with strong legalistic tendencies."[1] The other group was of course the Jesus movement. Here then is the translation.

"The days are coming,"
    declares the LORD, "when I
    will make a new covenant
with the people of Israel
    and with the people of Judah.
[32] It will not be like
    the covenant I
    made with their
    ancestors
when I took them
    by the hand to
    lead them out of
    Egypt,
because they broke my covenant,
    though I was a
husband/lord to them,"
declares the LORD.
[33] "This is the covenant I will make with the
    people of Israel after that time," declares the
    LORD.
"I will put my instruction in
    their minds and write it
    on their hearts.
I will be their God,
    and they will be my people.
[34] No longer will they teach
    their neighbor, or say to one
    another, 'Know the LORD,'
because they will all know me,
    from the least of them to the
greatest," declares the LORD.
"For I will forgive their wickedness
    and will remember their sins no more."

---

[1] J. A. Thompson, *The Book of Jeremiah* (Grand Rapids, MI: William B. Eerdmans, 1980), 580.

First of all, notice that Jeremiah is talking about the future. He is not suggesting this covenant is being inaugurated in his own day, indeed it is not to be inaugurated until after the return from exile, and if one reads the context generously, it means not merely the return from Babylonian exile, but the return in general of Jews in the Diaspora (much as Zechariah also spoke of). Secondly, v. 32 is emphatic – this covenant, this new one, will *not* be like the one or ones made with the ancestors long ago. In other words, it will *not* be like the Mosaic covenant, and perhaps it is also implied not like the Abrahamic or Noahic or Davidic ones, either. God is willing to "re-covenant" with his people because of his own merciful nature, and in spite of the fact that they broke those Old Covenants. Notice too, the language of God as husband (or "Lord," the sentence here has *ba'alti*, which can mean "I was lord," which might better suit the covenant language here cf. Jer. 3.14).[2] The violation of the covenant by Israel was so severe, it was like a wife betraying her husband, like adultery, like a violation of one of the Ten Words. This is similar to the discussion in Hos. 11.[3]

You will notice as well that Yahweh says nothing about "fixing" the Old Covenant. No, he is talking about trying again with his people, with a new covenant.[4] This is not surprising. It is right to emphasize that Jeremiah is not talking about Yahweh starting with a new and different group of people. The naming of Israel and Judah as the focus of the New Covenant rules out such supersessionist ideas. The Old Covenant is the Mosaic one with God's people, and the New Covenant is also with God's people.[5] What makes possible this New Covenant is not a covenant renewal ceremony, but rather forgiveness by God and a starting over with his people. "All the newness is possible *because* Yahweh has forgiven. Indeed, beginning again in and after exile depends upon Yahweh's willingness to break out of a system of rewards and punishments, for the affront of Israel and Judah could never be satisfied by punishment."[6]

In the ANE, when a covenant was broken the maker of the covenant had a choice of either just imposing the curse sanctions and ending the relationship or starting afresh with a new treaty. God did indeed invoke the curse sanctions of the Mosaic covenant, and his people went off into exile. By rights, this should have been the end of the story. It is not the end, *not because* God promised to keep up his end of the previous bargain no matter what, come what may, however unfaithful Israel would be. No, God's love for his people has to do with his *character*, not with his having bound himself to a broken covenant. It is right to note as well that the Deuteronomistic editor emphasizes again and again, as here, that Israel kept breaking the "old" covenant. W. Brueggemann rightly stresses: "The Old

---

[2] *Ibid.*, 581 n. 2.

[3] See Feldmeier and Spieckermann, *God of the Living*, 458 n. 25.

[4] Contra the first half of the remark of Goldingay, *Biblical Theology*, 447, who says: "He did not speak of giving a new Torah; there was nothing wrong with the Torah itself." Surprisingly, Goldingay says precious little about the notion of a "new covenant" and its implications and fails to come adequately to grips with what Paul says in 2 Cor. 3 about the "old covenant." The same complaint can be made about Childs, *Biblical Theology*, 355, who says "the new covenant reiterated the initial commitment and promised a new form of its actualization (Jer. 31.31ff.)." This fails to do justice to the contrast that stands right within the text of Jer. 31 itself, never mind how the NT writers read this text.

[5] Rightly emphasized by various of the commentators. It is perhaps this prophecy that Paul has in mind in Rom. 11.25ff. when he thinks of "all Israel being saved," which presumably would mean both Judah and Israel.

[6] W. Brueggemann, *A Commentary on Jeremiah: Exile and Homecoming* (Grand Rapids, MI: William B. Eerdmans, 1998), 294.

Covenant from Sinai was resisted until it was broken and abrogated. The new covenant will not be resisted because the Torah ... will be written on their hearts."[7] "The passage must have been shocking in Jeremiah's day and thereafter; after all, the passage implies that Yahweh will draw up a fresh contract without the defects of the old, implying in turn that he could improve on the old one, that he had learned something from the failure of the old."[8]

This New Covenant will be genuinely different in that it will deal with the very root of the problem, the root that is producing bad fruit in Israel's life, namely that God's people are fallen human beings, and unless God changes them from the inside out, the same old pattern or cycle of sometime obedience to God followed by breaking the covenant will still go on endlessly. Again, the problem is not with God's Law or God's revelation, the problem is with God's fallen people. And perhaps it is well to stress here that the word *Torah* can certainly be rightly translated as "instruction" and this suits what also comes in these verses, namely a statement about knowing the Lord from the heart, not about obeying a Law. Holladay rightly points out that the imperative "know Yahweh" as an exhortation and summary of covenant obligation is unique in the OT.[9] I would say this is because the New Covenant is not simply identical with a renewal of the old one. The New Covenant is about knowing God from the heart and knowing his instruction by heart as well. This also comports with the emphasis on the least to the greatest "knowing Yahweh." This is about intimate and relational knowledge.

The emphasis on the "instruction" being written on the heart here suggests in part that even God's people are somewhat alienated from God. They do not adequately know God. "In the new covenant, there will be no Moses and no tablets, instead YHWH will write the Torah on the heart of the Israelites, human beings' access to God, and thereby enable knowledge of God without mediation. The fact that the Israelites will receive direct knowledge of Torah within is the consequence of the forgiveness of sins (31.34)."[10] This is why the prophet says that when God writes his instruction on their minds/hearts, only then will they truly know God from the inside out, and not merely the outside in. Then, in that day it will be unnecessary to exhort "know the Lord" because all of them, yes, all of them, will know God. Notice as well that this New Covenant involves the forgiveness of sins, indeed even of wickedness.

Again, this has to do with the loving and compassionate and merciful nature of Yahweh, not with pre-existing, much less eternal covenant obligations, obligations God is bound to, even if his people break the covenant. *HESED* means mercy, not covenant faithfulness. The translators of the LXX got this right, again and again. All this must be kept in mind when we consider the state of God's covenant relationship with his people between the coming of Jesus and Pentecost. Finally, I would suggest that Paul is wrestling with the implications of this text in Rom. 10–11. He believes that there has ever always been only one people of God, so if some Jews reject their Messiah Jesus, they are for the time being broken off from the people of God, but they can be grafted back in again, when Jesus returns (Rom. 11.25ff.) by grace through faith in Jesus, through God's mercy and

---

[7] *Ibid.*, 293.
[8] W. L. Holladay, *Jeremiah* 2 (Minneapolis, MN: Fortress Press, 1989), 197.
[9] *Ibid.*, 198.
[10] Feldmeier and Spieckermann, *God of the Living*, 457.

forgiveness as stipulated here in the New Covenant. The New Covenant is still with God's people. But its basis is in the merciful and gracious character of God, his willingness to forgive sins. Its basis is not: (1) covenant renewal of the Mosaic Law and covenant; (2) God keeping Old Covenant promises despite the covenant being broken and annulled.

There is something else of interest as well in regard to how the LXX treats the New Covenant passage. Feldmeier and Spieckermann put it this way:

> In the Septuagint version of Jeremiah, in contrast to the Hebrew version, the promise of the new covenant occupies a position farther towards the end of the book. Jeremiah 38 LXX (31 MT) belongs to the block of text (37–42 LXX; 30–35 MT) that precedes the passion of Jeremiah, which constitutes the conclusion of the Greek Book of Jeremiah, with the sequence of great promise and prophetic suffering. More than in the Hebrew version, the question arises as to whether the promise of the new covenant will ever have its hour. No wonder the *berit hadasa* (Jer. 31.31) ... cited in the New Testament as the διαθήκη καινή (Jer. 38.31 LXX) also gave its name to the whole collection of Scriptures written in the certainty that the act of God once promised has occurred. From this perspective, Paul called the highly regarded and necessary witness, although his compatriots did not understand it, παλαιὰ διαθήκη "the Old Covenant" (2 Cor. 3.14). Following this tradition, the two Testaments have given each other their names in Christian tradition.[11]

Here it will be in order to consider how Jeremiah's "new covenant" promise is interpreted and applied in various NT texts, especially in Hebrews. A little further exploration of the use of the term "covenant" in the later context of the NT era will not go amiss here, either.

Covenant in the LXX and in the NT

The word *diathēkē* is in the LXX the translation of the Hebrew word *berit*. We are accustomed to translating it "covenant," or possibly "testament" (as in the OT) but both words have a wider range of meaning than that.[12] As we have already mentioned, there were various sorts of ancient treaties, and the ones we are talking about in the Bible are rather like lord–vassal treaties, and thus in their stipulations they are essentially examples of the lord dictating terms to the vassal. However, this doesn't make them unilateral, it makes them asymmetrical, unlike parity agreements.[13] They are not the result of a mutual agreement between two parties. This likely explains why it is that *berit* is always translated with the word *diathēkē*, rather than *synthēkē*, for the latter would convey the idea of a mutual agreement between two equal parties. The biblical covenants are in fact more a declaration of the divine will for God's people, and therefore the terms in question mean something more like a decree, *except* that the people bind themselves to actively obey and keep it, hence the word covenant/treaty. It is this latter activity that makes the covenant bilateral, though asymmetrical.[14]

It is likely the unique relationship of God and his people which dictates how this word should be translated, for in fact we do not find the late classical meaning in the Bible of "compact" or "contract," with rare exceptions. It is also true that, with two possible

---

[11] Feldmeier and Spieckermann, *God of the Living*, 458.
[12] See K. M. Campbell, "Covenant or Testament? Heb. 9.15,17 Reconsidered," *EvQ* 44 (1972): 107–11.
[13] See above.
[14] See the previous discussion on the covenant with Abraham, pp. 295–8, above.

exceptions, we do not have the meaning "testament," as in last will and testament, where we are talking about the dispensation of property as required by the testator at the point of his death. The two exceptions are in fact important. As we shall see, it is probable that the meaning "will" or "testament" is found in Heb. 9.16–17 and in Gal. 3.15–17. There the death of the testator is referred to and so we should likely translate "will" or "testament" in these two places.

It is not, however, characteristic of a normal covenant, unlike a will, that the testator must die for it to be in force, indeed quite the opposite. When a lord makes a treaty with a vassal it is understood to be in force so long as the lord shall live, and sometimes unto the time of his descendants but not necessarily. In this regard, of course, we may think of a marriage "covenant." All of this becomes of particular importance since the author of Hebrews does use the term *diathēkē* some 17 times, and it is only found 13 times elsewhere in all the NT (nine in Paul), which is perhaps surprising, for one might have expected more to be said about the "new covenant."

One interesting factor is that the testator, or the one who draws up the covenant, can in fact abrogate it if he so chooses. This was as true of ancient lord–vassal treaties as it was of contracts and wills in the first century AD. For example. P. Oxy. 492.9 includes the warning of the will-maker that: "So long as I live I am to have power over my own property, to make any further provisions or new dispositions I choose and to abrogate this will, and any such provisions shall be valid." *Athetesis* (abrogation) is technical legal language and our author chooses to use it at Heb. 7.18 to make clear where things stand with the "first" or Old Covenant.[15] In this case, only God can annul a covenant he has made with his people and Heb. 7.12 says God was prepared to do that (so also 7.18). This of course goes flatly against the dominant strain of Jewish thinking about this, which suggests that the Law does not pass away, perish, nor is it abrogated but rather survives in all its glory (see 4 Ez. 9.36–37; 2 Bar. 77.15; Philo, *Moses* 2.14–15; Josephus, *Apion* 2.272). This was based on a particular understanding of texts such as Ps. 19.7, which says that the Law was perfect, reviving the inner self (cf. Ps. 119). Here as elsewhere in his discussion of covenants, the author of Hebrews resorts to using technical and legal language (cf. e.g. *aparabaton* in 7.24, which means inviolate and so remaining valid).

Perhaps what most essentially characterizes a *berit/diathēkē* is the absolute confirmation of the agreement (by strong oath, even an enactment of a maledictory oath, e.g. by circumcision) and its binding character. Now there is a good deal of technical or juridical language that goes along with the idea of a *diathēkē*, such as when the treaty or disposition is ratified, sworn to, annulled, confirmed, made valid, legal, enacted as law (cf. 8.6). This sort of language one will also find in the discussion in Heb. 8–10, mixed in with a good deal of cultic language (draw near to God, cleansing of sins, etc.).

Another two key terms dealing with this matter are *egguous* – surety, guarantor – and *mesitēs* – mediator (the latter of which can mean a mediator between two hostile parties, or a person with whom the warring parties deposit an object in dispute, or a witness in a lawsuit, or the person who guarantees the accomplishment of an agreement or promise,

---

[15] See rightly H. Attridge, *A Commentary on the Epistle to the Hebrews* (Minneapolis, MN: Fortress Press, 1989), 203 n. 71 and examples cited there.

a guarantor). We are now prepared to look in more detail at how the author of Hebrews both translates and interprets "the new covenant" passage in Jer. 31.[16]

In the section in Heb. 8 we are about to examine we find *the longest single quotation from the OT found in the NT* – a quotation from Jer. 31.31–34, which in fact is the only prophecy in the OT where a "new covenant" is specifically mentioned, though it may be alluded to in some of the remarks of Isaiah and Ezekiel.[17] A portion of this same OT prophecy will also be found again at Heb. 10.15ff. It is thus of fundamental importance to our author in order to establish his arguments about the obsolescence of the Old Covenant, and the necessity and efficacy of the new one, and, ironically, he must do it by quoting from the very source that he says speaks of an obsolescent covenant. Rhetorically, this is a tricky business, and so he must carefully choose the portions of the OT which can be said to be self-critical or suggest a moving on from the Mosaic Covenant. One of the key rhetorical markers that we should see the sub-section Heb. 8.7–10.18 as a unit is that it begins and ends with a quotation of Jer. 31, the longer one coming at the outset of the section. It is no accident that this is the longest OT quotation in this or any other NT book. Our author is trying to convince Jewish Christians that the "first" covenant is outmoded, and so he must do it using the very source of religious authority they most revere – the OT. The length of the quotation here reflects our author's need to make his point about the New Covenant with Jewish Christians in Rome in an emphatic and decisive manner. Notice that he alters the text very little, lest the audience complain that the idea was in his handling of the text rather than in the text itself. The central or core thesis of this discourse must be established on the basis of the best authorities and arguments one can muster, those most likely to persuade Jewish Christians, who are seriously considering fading back into the woodwork of the Jewish community in Rome.[18]

Perhaps here also is the place to note that our author keeps in balance two fundamental perspectives throughout 8.1–10.18, the vertical one and the horizontal one, but it is historical consciousness that is the controlling factor. The vertical comparison of the earthly and heavenly sanctuary is found in 8.1–5, 9.1–14, 9.23–10.18, but these are intermingled with and seen in light of the discussion of the two covenants at 8.6–13, 9.15–22, and 10.15–18 (note both themes in 10.15–18 as the section is being wrapped up). The proof that our author's fundamental perspective is ultimately horizontal, looking to the future, is not only found in chapter 11, but comes from the very fact that he believes that what is now true in heaven will one day come down and be true on earth. Thus, current heavenly realities represent and anticipate horizontal things to come. It is interesting that the priesthood will be dealt with on the heavenly side of things, due no doubt to Christ being the believer's high priest in heaven, and covenant is dealt with on the historical level, on the earthly side of things.

The vertical highlights what is going on in the horizontal – thus Aaron's priesthood was there to work in terms of the Old Covenant (and it becomes clear that for our author,

---

[16] Here Childs' remark may be correct when he says (*Biblical Theology*, 439): "it would seem most likely that the author was consciously exploiting the double meaning of *diatheke* as both covenant and testament to illustrate his point that Christ died to ensure the validity of the promised eternal inheritance."

[17] As Hagner, *Encountering Hebrews*, 113, says, it is stunning that Jer. 31 is not cited elsewhere in the NT, though we find allusions at Rom. 11.5; 11.27 and in Jn. 6.45.

[18] On all of this in greater detail see my *Letters and Homilies for Jewish Christians*.

when he speaks of the first covenant he always means the Mosaic one, as opposed to the New Covenant), even though his service was vertical – lifting up offerings to fix the relationship between God in heaven and his people on earth. Likewise, Christ, though he is now in heaven, has put into operation the New Covenant, and continues to do so from heaven, with its effects on earth. Of course, the association of New Covenant with Christ in heaven lends to it the eternality and finality and perfection of heaven itself. It is thus impossible to interpret these chapters from a purely Platonic or Philonic perspective. As 8.13 will make clear, the main point is a historical one – we now have the fulfillment of the promises and institutions of the old order, thus the New Covenant annuls and makes obsolescent the Old Covenant.

It comes as something of a surprise that besides the fact that Jer. 31 is seldom cited in the NT (nor for that matter are other relevant prophetic texts about a coming everlasting covenant – see Ezek. 11.19–20; 16.60–63; 36.26–29; 37.26–28), there is in general only a little discussion about a "New Covenant/Testament" in the NT! We may look to texts like Lk. 22.20 or 1 Cor. 11.25 or 2 Cor. 3.6 and Gal. 4.24 for some reference to this idea, but it is our author who most explains and discourses on this subject, though it often seems to be just below the surface in other NT texts. My explanation for this is that in all those other texts just alluded to the audience is largely Gentile and hardly needed much convincing to talk about a new agreement between God and humankind. This discourse, however, is directed to Jewish Christians considering going back to Judaism, hence the stress here.

One thing is important rhetorically. If one is going to introduce an idea that is difficult to accept, one needs an unimpeachable witness. Thus, our author quotes at length from Jer. 31 at the beginning and end of this section to prove his point that there is a New Covenant that makes previous ones obsolete. "Rhetorically, the persuasiveness of a speech depends not only on its logic but also on the listener's conviction that the one speaking is reliable" (Quintilian, *Inst. Or.* 4.1.7).[19] Thus, especially with his central argument, our author puts forth his star witness, God, who vouches for the truth of what our author is saying by means of these Scripture quotations, nicely edited to make his point crystal clear. As it turns out, the New Covenant has a better warranty, a lifetime guarantee, and it is backed up by a better guarantor, not Moses but the Messiah and God himself.

Translation[20]

For if that first [covenant] was faultless, there would not have been a place for a second. For finding fault with them he says "Behold days are coming, says the Lord, when I will bring to an end/accomplish upon the house of Israel and upon the house of Judah a new covenant. Not according to the covenant which I made with their fathers in the day I took hold of their hands to lead them out from Egypt, because they did not remain in my covenant and I overlooked them," says the Lord. "This was the covenant which I will make with the house of Israel after those days," says the Lord. "I will put my law in their mind/understanding, and upon their hearts I will write it.[21] And I will

---

[19] C. Koester, *Hebrews* (New York: Doubleday, 2001), 389.

[20] What follows is my own translation of Heb. 7.7–10.18, including my own rendering of the author's rendering of the LXX of Jeremiah.

[21] NB: these two clauses are likely parallel, saying the same thing in two different ways, since the heart is also the center of cognition in Hebrew anthropology, the point of which is that God will not only make them understand but he will change them so they will receive and live by his word.

be to them for a God, and they will be unto me for a people. And no more will they teach each his fellow citizen and each his brother, saying 'know the Lord,' because all will know me from the least unto the greatest of them because I will be merciful to their wrongdoing and I will remember their sins no more forever." In saying 'new' he treats as old the first but being worn out and growing old it is near to disappearing.[22]

9.1 Now on the one hand the first [covenant][23] had a regulation of worship for the earthly holy place/sanctuary. For the first tent was constructed a tent in which was a lampstand and a table and the laying of the shewbread; this was called the Holy Place. But behind the second curtain on the other hand a tent called the Holy of Holies, having a gold censer/incense altar and the Ark of the Covenant which was covered all over with gold, in which there is a gold jar having the manna and the rod of Aaron which sprouted and the tablets of the covenant, but above which was cherubim of glory overshadowing the place of propitiation/mercy seat concerning which it is not now [time] to speak in detail.

But when this was constructed thusly, into the first tent continually the priests are going performing acts of worship, but into the second [tent] only once a year the high priest goes, not without blood, who offers for himself and the people for sins of ignorance.

Showing this the Holy Spirit had not yet revealed the way of the holy/way into the Holy Place, while the first tent is standing which is a parable for the present time in conformity with which gifts and sacrifices being offered are not able to make perfect the conscience of the worshipper. Only upon food and drink and different washings having imposed fleshly regulations until the reformation/putting right/new order.

But Christ appeared, the high priest of the good things that came with him, through the better and more perfect tent which is not hand-made, this is not a part of creation, nor through the blood of goats and calves but through his own blood he entered once for all into the Holy Place and found by himself eternal redemption. For if the blood of goats and bulls and the ashes of the red heifer when sprinkling the common/impure consecrate (them) so that they have the purity of the flesh, how much more will the blood of Christ who through eternal spirit offered himself unblemished to God purify our consciences from dead works unto the worship of the living God.

And for this reason, he is mediator of the new covenant in order that death having happened for the redemption of the transgressors on the basis of the first covenant, that those called might receive the promise of the eternal inheritance. For where a testament is involved it is necessary that the death of the testator be involved, for a testament is operative upon death since it is never valid while the testator lives. Hence, not even the first [covenant] has been inaugurated without blood. For when he proclaimed each commandment according to the law of Moses to all the people, taking the blood of calves [and of goats] with water and crimson wool and hyssop, and sprinkled the book itself and all the people, saying "This is the blood of the covenant which God enjoined for you." But also, the tent and all the vessels of worship were likewise sprinkled with blood. And nearly everything is cleansed in/by blood according to the law, and without shedding of blood there is no forgiveness.

It is necessary then for the figure/emblem of that which is in heaven be cleansed by this means, but the heavenly [sanctuary/things] by better sacrifices than these. For Christ did not enter into a hand-made Holy Place, the ante-type/representation of the true Holy Place but into heaven itself now revealed to the face of God for us. Not in order to offer himself frequently, like the high priest entering into the Holy Place yearly in the blood of another, since it would have been necessary for him to suffer often from the foundation of creation. But now once for all at the consummation of the ages he is revealed for the annulment/destruction of sins through his sacrifice. And just as it is in store for human beings to die once, and after that judgment, thus also Christ has been offered once for many to bear upon himself sin, a second time without sin he will appear to those awaiting eagerly for salvation.

---

[22] NB: the midrashic technique of taking up a key word into the following argument.

[23] While a few scribes took the word "first" here to refer to the "first tent" (cf. mss. 81, 104, 376), in Heb. 8.13 it clearly refers to the covenant, and so we should see the feminine form of "first" to have the same referent here. See Koester, *Hebrews*, 393.

10.1 For the law was a shadow of the good things to come, not the image of the thing itself. Yearly its sacrifices, which are offered continually, are never able to perfect those drawing near. For would they not have stopped offering them, seeing that those worshipping, once cleansed no longer have consciousness of sins? But by them [i.e. the sacrifices] remembrance of sins happens yearly, for it is impossible for the blood of bulls and goats to take away sins.

So it is that He says entering into the cosmos "sacrifice and offering you did not wish, but a body you prepared for me. Burnt offering and sin offering you did not approve." Then he said "Behold I have come, in the scroll of the book it is written concerning me, to do, God, your will." Earlier it was saying that "sacrifice and offering" and "burnt offering and sin offering you did not wish nor approve of" such as those offered according to the law. Then he said "Behold I have come to do your will." He does away with/abolishes the first in order to establish/confirm the second. By which will we have been made holy through the offering of the body of Jesus Christ once for all.

And on the one hand every priest stands daily offering worship and offering the same sacrifice often, such as are never able to remove sins. But on the other hand, when this One offered one sacrifice for sins continually/forever, he sat down at the right hand of God, henceforth waiting until his enemies are made a footstool for his feet. For one offering perfected continually those being sanctified.

But the Holy Spirit also testifies to us for after saying "This is the covenant which was drawn up for them after those days," says the Lord, "I will put my law in their hearts and in their minds I will write it and their sins and wickedness I will remember no more forever." But where there is forgiveness of these, there is no longer an offering for sin.[24]

In this lengthy quotation, our author in fact follows the LXX very closely, which in turn follows the Hebrew very closely. The only noticeable change of significance our author makes is in Heb. 8.8, where he uses the verb *synteleō* (accomplish or fulfill) instead of the verb establish (*diathesomai*) found in the LXX. It may be that this change was suggested to our author by a text like Jer. 34.8,15 (Jer. 41 in LXX) where the phrase *syntelein diathēkēn* is found in reference to a covenant made under Zedekiah. But the change is significant in terms of our author's hermeneutics. It is only with the New Covenant that God's purposes are actually completely fulfilled or accomplished by God himself through Christ. Only in it are things brought to completion and perfection. And it is after all God who fulfills his own prophecy not merely to establish a New Covenant, but through Christ to fulfill both its obligations and promises. Thus, this change is significant.

The two changes by the LXX of the Hebrew is that the LXX omits from v. 32 the phrase "although I was like a husband to them" and in v. 33 "within them" becomes "in their minds" in the LXX. Neither in this quotation, nor in the exposition that follows on the Tabernacle in Heb. 9, does our author give way to allegorizing. He understands these matters fundamentally from a historical perspective. Thus, it must be stressed that he does not try to alter the original meaning of this text insofar as its fundamental substance is concerned. He still sees it as addressed to the house of Judah and Israel, not to the church, but that would include Jewish Christians. However, though this message was offered to

---

[24] This is my own translation. There are several interesting textual variants in these 18 verses: in 10.1 our earlier mss. P[46] has "shadow and image" rather than having "shadow not the image." The latter reading is probably correct since it is so widely supported but also because *eikon* normally means something more than a mere copy, rather it normally means an exact representation, and the way the sentence is worded we would expect a contrast here, for our author is going to go on and speak of contrast using *men ... de*. See H. Attridge, "The Uses of Antitheses in Hebrews 8–10," *HTR* 79 (1986): 1–9. Also in 10.1 some very good mss. have the plural "they are not able," including Aleph, A, C, P. This may well be original but the singular is also well supported by P[46], H, K, etc., and is perhaps preferable. In v. 11 various mss. have high priest instead of priest. This is likely a later correction in light of 5.1 or 8.3.

Israel by Jesus and his immediate successors, they by and large rejected the idea of its fulfillment through Christ, hence it takes on a wider audience. It is a striking fact that of all
the early Jewish sects and their offshoots, *only Christians* saw Jer. 31.31–34 as a crucial
text that indicated a real replacement of the Old Covenant. The only other group to give
significant attention to this text, the Qumran community, took it to mean the perfecting of
the Old Covenant – by means of following the Teacher of Righteousness' reading of Torah
the Qumranites would be able to perfectly observe the Law.[25]

We will not attempt to give a detailed exposition of the lengthy quotation from
Jeremiah, but a few points are worth stressing. The stress is on the "new" covenant, which
will accomplish three new things: (1) God will put his "Torah" into their very minds/con-
sciences/hearts. The inwardness, or perhaps better said the inward effect of this new sort
of instruction, is stressed; (2) "all shall know me" in an intimate and free way, unknown
previously; (3) "their sins I will remember no more," forgiveness will be involved not only
for sins committed out of ignorance, but even deliberate ones, which was not true under
the Mosaic covenant. Notice that the statement in Jeremiah is comprehensive – remember
sins no more; (4) in v. 8 what is said to be blameworthy is not "it" but "them." The fault
primarily lies with the people, only secondarily with the first covenant.[26] Notice that v. 9
laments "they did not remain faithful to my covenant."[27] Finally v. 13 is important as it
provides our author's concluding remark on the Jeremiah quotation.

As Hagner says "The words 'will soon disappear' may well be an allusion to Jesus'
prophecy concerning the destruction of the temple, known to the author and readers
from oral tradition underlying the Synoptic Gospels (see Mk. 13.1–2 and parallels). The
word 'soon' clearly seems to indicate that Hebrews was written before the destruction of
the temple in AD 70. Was the Roman invasion of Jerusalem already on the horizon?"[28]
D. deSilva is helpful in translating the key phrase in v. 13 "God rendered it out of date …
The Old Covenant is likened to a law that is outdated and practically out of use. All that
remains is to erase it from the books."[29] This of course was not the view other Jews held
of the Mosaic covenant, which was seen as eternal (cf. Sir. 17.12; 4 Ez. 9.36–37; 2 Bar.
77.15; Josephus, *Apion* 2.272).

It is also important to bear in mind that in the larger argument of this homily, G. B.
Caird has argued that Jer. 31 is the last of the four key OT texts (Pss. 8, 95, 110 and
Jer. 31) that control the drift of the argument, all other allusions being ancillary. "His
argument falls into four sections, each having as its core an OT passage which declares
the ineffectiveness and symbolic or provisional nature of the OT religious institutions."[30]
There is, however, more to it than that. Our author has been moving progressively from a

---

[25] See S. Lehne, *The New Covenant in Hebrews* (Sheffield: JSOT Press, 1990), 32–61.

[26] See Hagner, *Encountering Hebrews*, 113.

[27] There is a good body of literature on this subject. See D. G. Peterson, "The Prophecy of the New Covenant in
the Argument of Hebrews," *Reformed Theological Review* 38 (1979): 74–81; W. C. Kaiser, "The Old Promise
and the New Covenant: Jeremiah 31.31–34," *JETS* 15 (1972): 11–23; Lehne, *The New Covenant in Hebrews*;
R. L. Omanson, "A Superior Covenant: Hebrews 8.1–10.18," *Review and Expositor* 82 (1985): 361–73.

[28] Hagner, *Encountering Hebrews*, 115.

[29] David deSilva, *Perseverance in Gratitude: A Socio-Rhetorical Commentary on the Epistle "to the Hebrews"*
(Grand Rapids, MI: William B. Eerdmans, 2000), 287.

[30] G. B. Caird, "The Exegetical Method of the Epistle to the Hebrews," *Canadian Journal of Theology* 5
(1959): 44–51.

comparison of Christ and angels, to Christ and Moses to Christ as high priest vs. Aaronic/ Levitical priesthood, to heavenly vs. earthly sanctuary, all in the service of indicating what we find stated in 8.13 clearly – "In saying new, he makes old the first [covenant] being worn out and growing old, it is near disappearing." This is the essence of our author's case – the Old Covenant has had its day and is now ceasing to be.

THE FIRST COVENANT	THE NEW COVENANT
Called "first" – 8.7; 9.1,15,18	Called "new" – 8.8,13; 9.15; 12.24
First covenant as good but weak – 8.7–13	"New" covenant as "better" – 7.22; 8.6
First covenant temporary and now obsolete – 8.6,7,13	"New" covenant as eternal – 13.20[31]

Not surprisingly the same contrast between the first and the new covenant in regard to obsolescence and permanence is also applied to the priesthoods enunciated or mandated in each of those covenants. Again, the author of Hebrews is not saying that the first covenant was a bad thing, to the contrary he sees it as a good thing foreshadowing a better thing. But he does indeed believe that since the better covenant has come, the first has been eclipsed and made obsolete. In fact, he things there was a built-in obsolescence to the Old Covenant because it could not "perfect" anything, it could only point to such perfection, and one of the chief reasons it was "weak and ineffectual" is that it was providing rules for fallen human beings. In other words, the problem lay not only in the lack of power in the Law but the lack of capacity in the covenant-keepers. The author will also stress that there is even atonement for sins not covered under the Mosaic covenant, "sins with a high hand" (cf. Acts 13.39).

Aristotle stresses that when two contracts or covenants or laws exist on the same topic, one must determine whether the former nullifies the latter or vice versa (*Rhet.* 1.15.25). He also stresses that the reliability of the covenant depends on the reliability of the guarantor (*Rhet.* 1.15.21). It is interesting that in Roman law, which presumably our audience was familiar with, there was no question but that the later edict or treaty superseded the earlier one. For example, Claudius' banishment of Jewish Christians from Rome in AD 49 was annulled by the coming of the new Emperor, which set all such arrangements in the obsolete category. Thus, our author could assume both on the basis of scriptural and cultural logic that the audience would likely find his argument here persuasive.

Chrysostom, as usual, sums things up aptly: "In calling it new, Paul [sic] says, 'he treats the first as obsolete, and what is becoming obsolete and growing old is ready to vanish away' ... Paul here uses a familiar [rhetorical] figure of speech, as if one should say the house is not faultless; that is, it has some defect, it is decayed. The garment is not faultless, that is, it is coming to pieces. He does not, therefore, here speak of the Old Covenant as evil, but only as having some fault and deficiency" (*Homily on the Epistle to the Hebrews* 14.6–7).

Jesus and His Discussions with Disciples and Other Jews

The first thing to note is that the coming of Jesus meant the coming of God's divine saving activity, otherwise known as the Dominion of God, *but it did not mean an instant inauguration of a new covenant.* That in fact will not happen prior to the sacrifice of Jesus

---

[31] Hagner, *Encountering Hebrews*, 104.

the Passover lamb, a sacrifice which does indeed inaugurate the New Covenant. In the meanwhile, the situation during Jesus' ministry is a "betwixt and between" situation in which Jesus has numerous discussions and debates with other Jews about the import and implementation of the Mosaic covenant. The Mosaic covenant is still in force, and still under debate.

What Jesus *does do*, however, is provide new teaching to his disciples that often goes beyond, and occasionally goes against, the Mosaic strictures and requirements. He not merely intensifies the Law, he sets up some new laws, like "no divorce," "no anger," "no physical harm to others," and more. Jesus' teaching is a preview of coming attractions of what will or should be the case once the New Covenant is properly inaugurated after the death, resurrection, and Spirit-sending of Jesus. The Gospel writers understood this, which is why they include so much of Jesus' teaching in their Gospels written for later Christian audiences. Jesus' teaching for his disciples, unlike Moses', was not an "interim" ethic, it did not have a shelf life, or a label saying "not valid after this date." Jesus' teaching was for the whole eschatological age, until he returns. With this framework, we can look at some of the discussions by Jesus of the Mosaic Law, and some of his own new teaching as the Kingdom dawns, and the New Covenant is promised and beckons, but is not yet begun.

About Marriage and Divorce and Singleness

Our earliest reference to Jesus' teaching about divorce comes from the 50s, and is found in 1 Cor. 7.10–11: "to the married I give this command (actually, not I, but the Lord): 'A wife must not separate from her husband. But if she does, she must remain unmarried or be reconciled to her husband. And a husband must not divorce his wife." Paul knows nothing of the famous exception clauses in Mt. 5.32 and 19.9. The tradition he knows is surely the earliest one, since it is so radical, and it can also be found in Mk. 10, to which we turn. The material has to be handled carefully, because not merely the First Evangelist, but also Mark, has clearly edited his source material, perhaps especially with an eye on his largely Gentile audience in Rome.[32] Here is what the text says:

Some Pharisees came and tested him by asking, "Is it lawful for a man to divorce his wife?"
3 "What did Moses command you?" he replied.
4 They said, "Moses permitted a man to write a certificate of divorce and send her away."
5 "It was because your hearts were hard that Moses wrote you this law," Jesus replied. 6 "But at the beginning of creation God 'made them male and female.' 7 'For this reason a man will leave his father and mother and be united to his wife, 8 and the two will become one flesh.' So they are no longer two, but one flesh. 9 Therefore what God has joined together, let no one separate."
10 When they were in the house again, the disciples asked Jesus about this. 11 He answered, "Anyone who divorces his wife and marries another woman commits adultery against her. 12 And if she divorces her husband and marries another man, she commits adultery."

From a historical point of view, it is possible that the Matthean version of this story is in some ways closer to bedrock, with the interlocutors asking Jesus about the grounds for divorce, since Mosaic law clearly enough allows for divorce. Deut. 24 has a key phrase about *erwat dabar*, literally "some unseemly thing," as the grounds for divorce, a phrase

---

32 On the background and context see Witherington, *The Gospel of Mark*.

ambiguous enough to be interpreted in various ways. Many seem to have understood the phrase to mean if the wife committed adultery, and Jesus clearly enough does speak about adultery, but some in fact, at least in the later rabbinic discussions, took the phrase to give permission for divorce if the wife did something non-sexual that was not pleasing – like burn the food. In any case, in Jesus' context, ordinary women could not divorce, only husbands could divorce (a distinction Paul knows about in his phrasing of the matter in 1 Cor. 7). Jesus, however, will have none of this. His teaching is simply "no divorce" and he is quite clear – the Mosaic teaching which permitted divorce was given because of the hardness of human hearts. This was not God's original intention at all and divorce should not happen now that the Kingdom is coming!

Jesus, in other words, is appealing to God's original creation design as outlined at the beginning of Genesis. He takes Genesis to be talking about the marriage of Adam and Eve, and he believes that once a couple has coupled, and there is a "one-flesh union" between them, there should be no divorce! Period. One must remember that Jesus believes the final divine saving activity of God is breaking into history through his ministry, and as such, there would be no more concessions to sin and human fallenness. By implication, Jesus is suggesting that Moses' teaching, at least on this subject, was *pro tempore*, for a period of time until the Kingdom broke into human history. New eschatological occasions teach new duties.

When Jesus is asked about his radical teaching "in house" by the disciples he says that a man who divorces his wife and marries another commits adultery against her (i.e. the first wife), because, in Jesus' view, the one-flesh union from the first marriage still is ongoing. It has not been dissolved by a writ of divorce. Notice that the last saying of Jesus speaks about a woman divorcing her husband and marrying another thereby committing adultery (with the new husband presumably, since this is patriarchal-style marriage he is referring to, with husbands and wives playing slightly different roles). Some scholars have pointed out that this last verse may be a Markan expansion of the prohibition since Gentile women could divorce their husbands, but non-elite Jewish women in the setting of Israel could not. This may be correct, but in any case, Jesus' teaching is "no divorce." He overrules, or annuls, Moses' permission of divorce. He is not naïve about the fact that people do divorce, or that third parties can put a marriage "asunder." Perhaps equally importantly, Jesus' view is that God brings two people together and joins them to each other. This is why he says "let those whom God has joined together ..." He does not say let those whom a rabbi has joined together, or the State has joined together. In his view, marriage is of God, going all the way back to Adam and Eve, and Moses' permissions or commands reflect an attempt to deal with human fallenness and sin. But Jesus had come to change that situation.

Another part of his teaching, which in the Matthean parallel in Mt. 19 is attached to this discussion, is a dictum about remaining single, which many have seen as Jesus providing a rationale for why he himself never married. Perhaps this is partially correct, but notice that in Mt. 19.10–12, the disciples go ballistic when Jesus says, in essence, no divorce, and they reply "then it is better not to marry" and Jesus replies "Not everyone can accept this teaching, but only those to whom it is given." This saying is probably the origin of Paul's theology of *charisma*, that is, that one must have a grace gift from God and a calling to remain single for the sake of the kingdom. Then Jesus goes on to talk about three classes of eunuchs – those who are born that way, those who have been made eunuchs by others, and those who have made themselves eunuchs. Since so much of Jesus' teaching involve sapiential language and dramatic metaphors, Jesus is probably not advocating a male cutting off his own genitals, though folk like Origen later thought so. Probably he is talking about remaining single for the sake of Kingdom ministry, which seems to be how Paul understands his teaching as well.

It cannot be emphasized enough, however, that providing a theological rationale for remaining single in the light of the coming kingdom is just as radical a teaching as no divorce, since it appears the vast majority of early Jews took the commandment "be fruitful and multiply" to apply to all able-bodied Jews. The notion of deliberately abstaining when you could be marrying and bringing more Jews into the world would have been seen as a violation of yet another commandment in the Pentateuch. But again, Jesus, like Paul after him, is speaking in the light of the dawning eschatological age, which affects everything.

Paul caught the drift of such teaching when he also says in 1 Cor. 7.29–31: "What I mean, brothers and sisters, is that the time has been shortened. From now on those who have wives should live as if they do not; those who mourn, as if they did not; those who are happy, as if they were not; those who buy something, as if it were not theirs to keep; those who use the things of the world, as if not engrossed in them. For this world in its present form is passing away."

Notice that Paul doesn't say, "the time is short" (a really bad translation of ὁ καιρὸς συνεσταλμένος ἐστίν·). The word συνεσταλμένος means "shortened," not "short." It is a maritime term applied to the contracting or bunching together of sails, limiting their exposure to the wind. Paul is referring to the Christ event in the past which has already changed the σχῆμα, the form of this world, and made contingent all its institutions, including the institution of marriage. There are no major eschatological events preventing Jesus from coming back sooner, rather than later, so one must always be prepared. He will come like a thief in the night, at an unknown and unexpected time. The theology of "possible (but not certain) imminence" is also in play in texts like this one.

The implications of Jesus' teaching about marriage, divorce, and singleness were understood quite well by Paul. For one thing, it meant women no longer were *required* to play the roles of literal wives and mothers as the Kingdom dawned. They had permission as did male disciples to remain single for the sake of the Kingdom, if in fact that was their calling and gifting. This meant new roles for women in the Jesus movement, both during his lifetime and thereafter, as can be seen by the roles women such as Priscilla, Phoebe the deacon, and Junia the apostle played as co-workers of Paul. In Jesus' case, and because he was ministering just to Jews in a Jewish ethos and setting, there were some limitations to just how radical he was prepared to be. The witness about the Kingdom to "the twelve tribes of Israel" could best be accomplished by choosing 12 male disciples to lead the way and sending them out two by two to bear witness that the Kingdom was at hand, dawning. This did not prevent women from being his followers and disciples, but the situation prior to the inauguration of the New Covenant and Pentecost was such, that there had to be miracles and "ocular proof" for women to assume all their new roles in the Jesus movement.

Ocular proof, at least to the inner circle of disciples, came when Jesus appeared first to the female disciples at his tomb on Easter and commissioned them to go proclaim the

Easter message to the male disciples. Further ocular proof happened when the Spirit fell on all the men and women in the upper room in Jerusalem at Pentecost, and Peter correctly interpreted the event as a fulfillment of the prophecy of Joel about just such an event. After these sorts of culture-shattering events, the roles of both men and women changed in the service of Jesus, as Acts and Paul's letters attest. It is thus appropriate to recognize that the period between the birth of Jesus and his death is an interim period, and during that period, Jesus engaged in debates about Mosaic Law with his fellow Jews on its own terms and as if it was still an active covenant, which it was. Let us consider now some of this material.

Corban, Food Laws, Purity Laws, and Sabbath Keeping

When Jesus had dialogues or debates with other fellow Jews about the Mosaic Law, he would on occasion give instructions to those inquisitors within the Mosaic system, assuming they would continue in that covenant rather than become his disciple. Becoming his disciples required a more radical commitment than just being a good follower of the Mosaic Law. This is quite apparent from the story of the so-called "rich young ruler." At no point did the Mosaic Law demand that devout Jews who indeed might become disciples of this or that Jewish teacher or prophet or sage "sell everything, give to the poor, and come and follow me." Even Elijah allowed Elisha to go and do something for his family before he became a prophetic understudy of Elijah (see 1 Kgs. 19.19–21). The point I am stressing is that *it is a mistake to assume that what Jesus says to non-disciples in the context of early Judaism is what he also wanted all his disciples to do. The difference between his advice to, for instance the ten lepers, and his advice to his own disciples is important.*

Let's take the issue of corban first, a discussion in what may be in the most controversial of all Markan chapters – Mk. 7, here vv. 5–13. The discussion comes in the context of Jesus accusing the Pharisees and the teachers of the Law of being "play-actors" which is what the word ὑποκριτής actually means, though perhaps in Jesus' context the translation "hypocrite" is most apt. It is referring to the difference between how a person appears, and appears to act, and how they really are, and this is actually the only time the word appears in Mark, but it occurs much more frequently in Matthew. Jesus cites Isa. 29.13 as a basis for the accusation. Isaiah was referring to God's people in general who give lip service but not life service to God. The nub of the quotation comes at the end with the reference to "merely human rules." Here Jesus is accusing them of compromising the actual Mosaic commandments by their "traditions," the way they nuance and interpret the Law in the light of their traditions.

Jesus then gives an illustration of what he means. The commandment to honor parents was being compromised, Jesus even says "annulled," by the invoking of the principle of corban, a word which means "given" or in this case "dedicated/set aside/pledged to God." The term "honor" in the phrase "honor your father and mother" was apparently often taken to mean provide financial assistance to when needed (see Prov. 28.24).[33] It was indeed possible for a person in Jesus' era to declare by means of a vow using either the term "corban" or *konam* that one's parents were prohibited from benefiting from some

[33] See Witherington, *The Gospel of Mark*, 226.

piece of property or material asset because it had been set aside already for other purposes, for example dedicated to God or the temple treasury. Unfortunately, by Jesus' day this practice had come to be used, not because one was especially pious necessarily, but in order to put a material possession *out of the reach* of parental use.[34]

Jesus takes this to be an absolute violation of one of the Ten Commandments and he says that his interlocutors do "many things like that." They were not putting a hedge of protection around the Mosaic Law by such oral traditions, they were compromising it. Sometimes Jesus sounded like a strict interpreter, even an intensifier of the Mosaic laws, and sometimes he sounded like someone who was setting aside some of the Mosaic laws. It was confusing even to his disciples. What one notices about such things is Jesus' sovereign freedom. He feels free to handle the Law in various ways, and in accord with his larger belief that God's final saving activity is already happening.

Since we are already there it will be good to go on and deal with the *cause célèbre* from this chapter – Mk. 7.14–19. Did Jesus really say that there was no unclean food? Many scholars have doubted he said such a thing, not least because his earliest disciples didn't seem to get the memo. Consider for example the story about Peter having to have a vision in Acts 10 before he comes to realize that there is no unclean food, it's all a gift from God. The actual saying of Jesus in question is "Nothing outside a person can defile them by going into them. Rather it is what comes out of a person that defiles them." This saying could be subject to a variety of interpretations. For example, the second half of the saying could be referring to excretion from the body, which was certainly seen as defiling. This is not, however, how the saying is interpreted in what follows.

The Matthean form of the saying in Mt. 15.11 reads "what goes into someone's mouth does not defile a person, but rather what comes out of their mouth, that is what defiles them." This is more specific than the Markan form of the saying, making clear that the orifice in question in both cases is the mouth, and indeed Mk. 7.20–21 suggests that Mark would certainly agree with this interpretation of the puzzling saying. James Dunn, after going back and forth on what the original form of Jesus' saying might be, admits that "the radical character of a saying which set inward purity antithetically against ritual purity is fully of a piece with Jesus' teaching as a whole. Jesus is generally remembered as one whose teaching on the Law and on human relations as governed by the Law was characteristically searching and radical in one degree or another."[35] I agree with this conclusion. I would also stress that *many of Jesus' followers did not fully understand some of the more radical parts of his teaching until well after Easter and Pentecost, including inner-circle disciples like Peter.*

A major difference between the holiness movement known as Pharisaism and the Jesus holiness movement was not so much the goal (both wanted God's people to be holy unto the Lord) but the means by which this was to be achieved. One followed a program of Levitical reform, applying various of those laws to all Jews in a priesthood-of-all-believers sort of move. The other taught that God himself was intervening through Jesus and

---

[34] See the discussion by J. A. Fitzmyer, "The Aramaic Qorban Inscription from Jebel Hallet et Turi and Mark 7.11/Matt. 15.5," *JBL* 78 (1959): 60–65. See also Mish. Ned. 5.6, Babba Kamma 9.10, Philo, *Spec. Leg.* 2.16; Josephus, *Ant.* 4.73.

[35] J. D. G. Dunn, *Jesus, Paul, and the Law: Studies in Mark and Galatians* (Louisville, KY: Westminster, 1990), 52, but see the whole discussion, 37–60.

changing people from the inside out, and thus the message which could be called "the Gospel according to Leviticus" was no longer appropriate to the eschatological times inaugurated by John the Baptizer and Jesus. Let me be clear that Jesus is not saying here that he is unconcerned with all things ritual. If that was his view, he would never have told the lepers to go wash themselves and present themselves to the priest so that they could be certified clean. This was important for those who would continue to be part of early Jewish communities not involved in following Jesus. *Jesus' advice to those folks is one thing, and his teaching to his own disciples and the ethic he offers them is another.*

Thus in Mk. 7.20–23 Jesus emphasizes what is after all at the heart of the Mosaic Ten Commandments – heart purity, for unfortunately all sorts of bad things can come forth from a sinful heart – thoughts and then deeds involving sexual immorality, theft, murder, adultery, greed, malice, lewdness, envy, slander, arrogance, and much more. Jesus, it will be seen, both here and in Mt. 5–7 is not just about policing deeds, he is challenging one's very thoughts and feelings toward one's fellow human beings. The rather consistent tendency of some NT scholars to underestimate the radical edge of some of Jesus' teaching is unfortunate, and fails to take into account not only the clear eschatological context and flavor of his teaching, but also where Paul got the idea that a mixed congregation of Jews and Gentiles needed to realize that all food is from God, and so long as one is not participating in idol feasts (1 Cor. 8–10), one can eat whatever one is served with no pangs of conscience (cf. 1 Cor. 8–10 to Rom. 14), but if one does have such scruples about food Paul does not say, "well that's what the Mosaic Law said in the first place" but rather "let each be persuaded in their own minds" and "whatever you cannot do in good conscience, you should not do, when it comes to 'things indifferent' " (adiaphora).

This is an astounding set of statements from a former Pharisee, and one has to ask, where did he get such ideas? The answer lies there in Mk. 7, if we will but listen closely. Jesus was a radical Jew when it came to some parts of the Mosaic Law. In some case, he wanted to ratchet up and intensify the volume on the commandments, in some case he wanted to set them aside. It's the freedom with which he handled these matters that speaks volumes about his self-understanding, and his understanding of the eschatological moment he lived in.

What about the Sabbath controversies, which we find again and again in both the Synoptics and John?[36] It is a fact that there were various debates in early Judaism about "what constitutes work prohibited on the Sabbath." One rule that seems to have been prevalent, and leaned in the direction of compassion, was that anything that was a matter of life and death could be done on the Sabbath without violating the Law, but Jesus complains that some of those who were sticklers for strict interpretation of what counted as work, were also those who, when their animal fell into a ditch on the Sabbath, and was not in danger of dying, nonetheless would be rescued by that same person. Jesus' approach to the Sabbath seems to have been as follows: (1) Sabbath is a day of *shalom*, of focusing

---

[36] You will notice that while in the early church there were some circumcision controversies, when it came to Gentiles joining the Jesus movement (see e.g. Galatians), there are none in the Gospels themselves. All male Jews were already circumcised in Jesus' context and there was no debate about the matter, any more than in eighteenth-century England, where everyone Anglican got baptized as an infant, there was any debate in that church about whether the practice was appropriate or not. In fact, John Wesley constantly ran into folk who said they had been baptized and so "christened" = "christianed," then, and did not need to be born again. A similar problem seems to have confronted Jesus, if Jn. 3 is to be believed.

on those things which promote health and healing, including of course rest from arduous tasks; (2) therefore, alleviating someone from some disability or disease was a perfectly appropriate activity on the Sabbath since it promoted the "shalom" or well-being of that person; (3) Jesus intimates that God is always working, including on the Sabbath, and so this suggests that his reading of Gen. 2.2 is that the phrase "and God וַיִּשְׁבֹּת" meant not that God *stopped all activities and rested from all work, but rather he ceased from* his creating activities and saw his work was very good. In other words, God Almighty hardly needed a rest break, but he did "cease" from his creating activities. Jesus then would suggest that this did not mean a ceasing from any and all kinds of activities and work. There may also be one more implication of Jesus' argument there, namely that he sees himself as part of the divine identity, and so in the category of God, and so, like God he can work on the Sabbath whatever may be the rules for mere mortals. Let's look at some of the Sabbath controversy texts briefly.

Let us provide some context by looking at the very first miracle tale in Mark (Mk. 1.21–28), which just happens to deal with a healing not only on the Sabbath but in the synagogue. The important thing to note from the outset is v. 22 – "the people were amazed at his teaching because he taught them as one who had [inherent] authority, not as the teachers of the Mosaic Law." The conclusion, in v. 27, indicates, the reaction of the attendees at the service in Capernaum is "What is this? A new teaching, and with [inherent] authority."

The passage emphasizes both the newness of Jesus' teaching and his independent authority in teaching and healing. Jesus, does not use footnotes ("Gamaliel says …"), unlike other teachers, nor does he say "Yahweh says …" He speaks on his own authority, with his own voice, and if we were to look elsewhere, he also certifies the truthfulness of his own sayings, bearing witness to his own veracity by starting various of his saying with "Amen I say to you …" though we do not see this in this particular passage. "Amen" would normally be an after-the-fact affirmation by a second party of what someone else has just said that they affirm as true, or as something that should happen.

First of all, notice that we are not given a summary of what Jesus taught on this occasion. It is not the *matter* but rather the *manner* of teaching that is remarked on. Jesus' teaching does not seem to be based on his learning, unlike the scribes or Pharisees. Notice how the scribes are regularly connected with the theme of authority and with the discussion of Jesus' authority in various places in the pre-Passion narratives in Mark (Mk. 1.22; 2.6,10; 3.15,22; 11.27–29,33). It would seem that Jesus' exercise of his innate authority and teaching caused no little stir among the scribes, who maybe even saw what he was doing as a threat to their own authority over the people.

The action Jesus performs in the synagogue is an exorcism, something that Mark especially highlights as part of Jesus' ministry, and about which the Fourth Evangelist is quite silent. Verse 27b is difficult to punctuate. It could read "what is this new teaching with authority?" or it could read "What is this? A new teaching, with authority he even commanded the unclean spirits." Most scholars take the word ἐξουσία with what precedes it and so modifying the term teaching, particularly because a powerful teaching had already been referred to in v. 22. The word ἐξουσία can of course mean either power or authority, or in some cases both, and surely it is both here – Jesus teaches with authority and power, and he exorcizes demons with authority and power as well.

Now you will look high and low and you will not find any stories of prophets performing exorcisms in the OT, or for that matter priests, sages, kings, or scribes either. Jesus' confrontation with the dark powers is part of the large apocalyptic and eschatological character of Jesus' ministry. The dominion of God cannot come on earth as long as Satan rules the lives of various of God's people, and indeed Gentiles as well (see the story of the Gerasene demoniac). Things are so bad that even demons are speaking out in the synagogue service, according to Mk. 1 and Jesus has come to "bind the strong man and set free his captives" (Mk. 3). The portrayal of Jesus in Mark is often stark and dark, and even radical at points, and the portrayal of what Jesus was prepared to say and do on the Sabbath is of a piece with this larger portrayal.

Mk. 1.43–45 has sometimes been seen as part of the so-called "messianic secret" motif in Mark, first popularized by W. Wrede, but it is doubtful that that is a very helpful way of reading this particular text. In the first place, neither Jesus nor the healed man say anything about Jesus' messianic identity. Remember, the northern prophets Elijah and Elisha were also famous for healing, and so a healing in itself did not need to carry messianic freight. So, when Jesus tells the healed man not to make a public announcement about Jesus having healed him, one suspects that Jesus is more concerned about the man himself, and his ability to return to normal Jewish village life.

To that end, he tells the man that instead of trumpeting his healing in public, he should go to the priest, offer the appropriate sacrifices that Moses commanded "for your cleansing" as a testimony to the fact. Unfortunately, the man did just exactly what Jesus told him *not* to do, which made things difficult for Jesus himself. He began to be thronged by people needing or wanting some sort of healing or physical help. This outcome is not what Jesus intended, for as he says earlier in the chapter, "let us go somewhere else where I can preach there also, for *this is why I have come*" (Mk. 1.36). Jesus came to proclaim the good news. He did not set out to this or that destination to heal people unless he was bidden to come there for that purpose. His healings were acts of compassion but were not his main purpose. Why not? Because, physical help and healing is a temporary solution to a human problem. But Jesus was offering everlasting life through the reception of his preaching with repentance and change of life. The preaching and teaching was his main purpose and the reason he traveled here and there. He stayed to heal upon request.

Our next text to consider is Mk. 2.23–28. Here Jesus and his disciples are traveling on the Sabbath and it is noticed that the disciples are hungry and doing a little gleaning of wheat at the edge of a field in order to have something to eat. While gleaning on the edge of a field in itself was permitted normally (see Deut. 23.25), and not considered theft, doing it on the Sabbath could be said to constitute work, and so when some Pharisees heard about this, they objected to the behavior of Jesus' disciples, on the grounds that he should be keeping them in line. In fact, Exod. 34.21 seems quite clearly to prohibit gleaning on the Sabbath, as do later Jewish sources like the Mishnah. As various commentators have pointed out, the only plausible context for a dispute about the plucking of grain is during the ministry of Jesus in the context of disputes with other Jews. It is not a matter early Christians, and especially not early largely Gentile Christian congregations, would be debating.[37]

---

[37] See rightly, M. Casey, *Aramaic Sources of Mark's Gospel* (Cambridge: Cambridge University Press, 1998), 141–50.

Jesus' response to the critique of the disciples' behavior appeals to the earlier example of King David satisfying his hunger in an unorthodox manner (hence there was biblical precedent) and also he issues a dictum – "the Sabbath was made for the benefit of humankind, humankind was not created in order to keep the Sabbath."[38] The notion of the Sabbath being a gift from God to human beings is common both in the OT and in early Jewish literature (cf. Exod. 16.29; Jub. 2.17; Mekilta 109B on Exod. 31.24). We may also point to the interesting saying in 2 Bar. 14.18: "And you said that you would make for your world a son of man as the manager of your works, to make it clear that he was not made for the world, but rather the world was made for him." The action of the disciples, then, in taking nourishment on the Sabbath, is appropriate according to Jesus, for "the earth and the fullness thereof" belongs to humankind. It is possible, and various scholars would say probable, that Mk. 2.28 is another Markan parenthetical remark (as for instance 7.15 may be). It asserts that Jesus, as the apocalyptic Son of Man of Dan. 7, is lord even over the Sabbath and its regulations. The action of the disciples is just what should happen on the Sabbath – restoration and nourishment, making for *shalom*, wholeness and well-being.

There are good reasons not to see Mk. 2.28 as a general maxim true of all human beings: (1) the Sabbath was not given to all human beings, only to Israel for its particular *shalom*; (2) the available evidence from early Judaism agrees that the Sabbath was given for God's people by God but that same evidence does not speak of Jews ruling the Sabbath or overruling some Sabbath ordinance; (3) it was certainly not believed that all and sundry persons are lords over the Sabbath; (4) here as elsewhere where we have a ὥστε clause in Mark, it introduces a conclusion. Note Mk. 15.5, where a final result clause is the comment of the narrator, as it is here. Here again, Mark is emphasizing that Jesus, the Danielic Son of Man, is the only person who has authority over all humankind and human kingdoms and human rules.[39]

The Sabbath is assumed to be still "in force" because the Mosaic commandment about keeping the Sabbath is still applicable during Jesus' ministry. Jesus does not dispute this, but what he does insist on is that he has the authority to interpret the rules according to their larger divine intent. The New Covenant does not have Sabbath regulations and even warns against globalizing Sabbath regulations in Rom. 14 and Col. 2.16, but the New Covenant has not yet been inaugurated during the ministry of Jesus, and Jesus here is responding to outside critics who continue in the praxis of early Judaism.

If we move on to Mk. 3.1–6, it is in order to cite M. Yoma 8.6 at the outset: "Whenever there is doubt whether life is in danger this takes precedent over the Sabbath." But is a man with a withered hand an example of a person whose life is in danger? No, that does not seem to be the case. But Jesus broadens the discussion by asking "Is it legally permitted (on the Sabbath) to do good or to do evil, to save life or to kill?" The first half of the question suggests situations that are not restricted to life-threatening ones, which actually is grounded in what Deut. 30.15ff. suggests. Perhaps, from Jesus' viewpoint, the real issue is that this man, in the synagogue according to Lev. 21.16ff., was not permitted to fully participate in the worship of God in the temple, indeed he could not even enter it. But the

[38] See Witherington, *Jesus the Sage*, 167–69.
[39] See Witherington, *The Gospel of Mark*, 131–32.

further issue here is again, what constitutes work? After all, Jesus heals by simply speaking a word of healing.

What we actually see here is Jesus as an agent provocateur. He controls the scene in the synagogue. He tells the man to stand in the middle of the congregation. He raises the questions his interlocutors studiously refuse to respond to. He speaks in binary opposites, not giving the option that it would be fine to do nothing at all in this case on the Sabbath since it is not a life-threatening situation. Mark seems to present this story as a turning point in the early ministry of Jesus, according to the response in Mk. 3.6. The man with the withered hand might not be in a life-threatening situation, but Jesus seems to have created one by his actions for himself.

The issue here is not merely that Jesus' *halakah* is more compassionate than some others, but that he has the authority and freedom to interpret things in novel and even radical ways that many will see as a violation of Sabbath rules and Sabbath rest. He even dares to tell his audiences what the real intent of God was in giving the Sabbath, as if the audience had wrongly interpreted the intent and purpose of that well-known and long-standing Mosaic commandment. This is a new teaching, and with authority, but it is not yet the inauguration of a new covenant. The teaching is directed to the general Jewish public, not to his disciples. That sort of teaching we find in Mt. 5–7, to which we turn now.

Teaching for the Disciples

There was obviously some "in-house" teaching that Jesus gave to his own disciples, and which was not intended for the general Jewish public. Sayings like "take up your cross and follow me" remind us that what Jesus was prepared to say to his own followers was not the same thing as he was saying to the general Jewish public. It is thus no accident that when the First Evangelist collected various sayings of Jesus and put them into the form we know as the Sermon on the Mount in Mt. 5–7, a collection of what some have humorously called Jesus' Greatest Hits, the sayings are said to have been offered in the presence of the crowd but *directed* toward the disciples. The character of the teaching needs to be remarked on as well.

This is wisdom teaching that includes beatitudes, aphorisms, parables, and the like. And "laws" or commandments are talked about as a sort of wisdom teaching. To be sure it is prophetic or eschatological wisdom teaching, signaled by the mention of Jesus having come to fulfill "the Law and the Prophets" not to abolish them. What Law means in that phrase is not entirely clear – perhaps the whole Pentateuch but clearly not the whole OT since "the Prophets" are mentioned as well. More importantly to "fulfill" is not the same as "to reaffirm" or simply "obey." To fulfill may mean to complete the purpose of something. If one fulfills a prophecy, then the prophecy is no longer outstanding, or waiting for fulfillment. Of course, the record of the Law must stand as a witness until it all comes to fruition or is fulfilled for and within God's people, but it should be remembered that Jesus called his disciples to a higher standard of righteousness, higher even than that of pious Pharisees. Moses is not simply being reaffirmed *in toto* here for Jesus' disciples.

Notice that in the actual teaching in Mt. 5–7, Jesus: (1) intensifies some Mosaic teaching; (2) abolishes some Mosaic teaching (on oaths and permission for divorce); (3) changes some teaching so that there can be no rationale for violence at all for Jesus' disciples, and

(4) adds totally new teaching unheard of before.[40] Again, this is not simply an affirmation of the Mosaic covenant and its strictures, it is a treatment of Moses with considerable freedom, and modification of his teaching. Jesus sits to teach, and hands no stone tablets to his disciples. Sometimes he intensifies the OT demands, sometimes he set those demands aside, sometimes he offers new teaching which can either supplement or supplant a previous Mosaic teaching. Jesus on the Mount is not Moses on the Mount *redivivus* or revisited. He is depicted as a great sage, teacher, commandment-giver.

Instead of starting with imperatives, Jesus starts with blessings, eschatological blessings. Those who currently are "poor" (or "poor in spirit"), mourning, meek, hungering and thirsting for righteousness, merciful and pure in heart are told about what will be the case for them in the Kingdom. The only exception is the poor in spirit, about whom it is said theirs is already the Kingdom. When you believe that the divine saving activity of God is breaking into human history already, that is a game changer. This is why scholars talk about the already and not yet eschatological flavor of Jesus' teaching. The ethic he is enunciating assumes an already changed situation from the Mosaic era, but it does not assume that the Kingdom, God's saving reign, has come fully upon earth, hence the prayer "thy Kingdom come."

The nature of discipleship is defined in terms of "salt" and "light" in Mt. 5.13–16. We have two metaphors followed by explanatory parables. Salt was used as a metaphor for the sowing of wisdom into a situation in early Judaism. A disciple who loses his wisdom grows foolish/useless = salt which loses its savor becomes foolish/insipid/useless. There is a play on words here in the Aramaic with salt = *tabel* and foolish = *tapel*. The metaphor of light is also about being a witness to the world. The point is, if the disciple ceases to function in the one capacity in which he or she is valuable, bearing witness, then that disciple is worthless, fit only to be cast out.

A disciple did not become one to hide his light under a lampstand, for the dark world needs the witness, it needs illumination and revelation to see itself as it is. Notice the word "world" here. Jesus is already thinking about the witness of his disciples not merely to Israel, but to the world. There is a universalistic bent to this saying.

Mt. 5.17–20 must be seen as a qualifier to the antitheses that follow these verses, lest one think Jesus was some kind of renegade Jew who was anti-Torah. Verse 17 is meant to make clear that Jesus did not come to abolish the Torah or the Prophets. Note that the discussion is about both, not just about the Law. Presumably this is a reference to the whole OT, which Jesus did not come to annul, but rather to fulfill. Again, this is eschatological language indicating that something is coming to its completion. Jesus reassures that not a jot or tittle, even the smallest mark on a Hebrew letter, will pass away before it's all fulfilled, but the word fulfilled must be given its eschatological due here. The end or goal or purpose is being reached. Jesus is bringing forth the reality to which the Law and the Prophets pointed. Jesus is not declaring anything untrue, he is saying that some of it has been fulfilled and has served its purpose and is not applicable to his disciples. The Law is not lost or invalidated, it is just that some of it no longer applies, having been fulfilled now that the Dominion is at hand. It was applicable to the era when the Mosaic Law was part of a covenant which is about to be eclipsed with the New Covenant. Discipleship to Jesus

---

[40] For a detailed discussion of this important material see Witherington, *Matthew*, 113–73.

and his teaching involves more rigorous obedience, not less than before, as what follows makes clear.

Mt. 5.21–48 sets up a series of famous antitheses. The formula "you have heard it said, but I say to you" is found sprinkled throughout this section of the "sermon" (vv. 21, 27, 31, 33, 38, and 43) so the contrast is not just involved with one sort of tradition, but several. On the one hand, one can say that the central Torah teaching about loving God and neighbor wholeheartedly is reaffirmed here. And one can also rightly say that to go beyond the Law by way of intensifying it, is not to go against it. Matthew in his presentation of Jesus has already suggested that Jesus is God incarnate, God's Wisdom come in person ("Immanuel") and so the issue here is not merely hermeneutics, not merely that Jesus eschatologically interprets the Law, though there is some truth in that idea.[41] Precisely because Jesus believes he has set the eschatological drama in motion, it is not merely time for new interpretations or enforcements of old laws, but a time for a new wisdom as well, which incorporates, but also redirects the old wisdom/Torah.

For example, there would be no more concessions due to the hardness of heart (see above on Jesus' marriage teaching) and in fact there are plenty of Mosaic laws meant to contain sin and evil which assume fallen human nature. The original intentions of God in creation is what Jesus is affirming in his "Endzeit als Urzeit," the end-as-the-beginning sort of teaching. Jesus not only prohibits what Moses allows (e.g. oaths, divorce, murder) but Jesus also allows what Moses prohibits ("work" on the Sabbath, eating "unclean" food, or better said, eating all food as a clean gift from God).

It is Jesus' sovereign and lordly freedom in the way he handles Torah, adding to it and subtracting, and intensifying in light of the new eschatological situation, which this passage epitomizes. Jesus assumes that a new eschatological situation has already dawned, and a new covenant is coming, and he has the divine authority not merely to announce these things but to inaugurate them. If asked, perhaps he would have said as well, "you can't violate a law that is fulfilled and no longer binding on God's people." Jesus is not a law-breaker, rather he is a new covenant maker. Admittedly, it was going to be confusing since the New Covenant was to incorporate some of the old Mosaic commandments in some form.

In this passage, six different topics are addressed – anger, lust, divorce, oaths, revenge taking, and love. Jesus is trying to get at the heart of the matter, the root causes of various serious sins and deal with the problem at the source. The heart of the problem is a problem of the heart, just as Mk. 7.21 so eloquently puts it: "For it is from within, out of a person's heart, that evil thoughts come – sexual immorality, theft, murder, adultery, greed, malice, deceit, lewdness, envy, slander, arrogance, and folly. All these evils come from inside and defile a person." Whether that is an instance of *ipsissima verba Jesu* or a Markan summary of the gist of Jesus' ethical teaching, it is accurate, and it is what this and other portions of the Sermon on the Mount are driving at. And as a text like Jn. 3 shows, Jesus knows that there has to be a change within the heart, a new birth, a new creation of the fallen person and their self-centered heart and life if there is indeed going to be new behavior and praxis.

---

[41] On which see D. C. Allison, *The Sermon on the Mount: Inspiring the Moral Imagination* (New York: Crossroad, 1999), 59–61.

Whereas Moses' central Ten Commandments only deal with one "internal issue," covetousness, Jesus deals with them extensively. It is not sufficient to contain evil, God wants changed persons who leave behind their inclination to do evil. Avoiding murder is not good enough now that the eschatological age is at hand; Jesus will hold his disciples to a higher standard of righteousness involving anger, which often prompts sinful behavior such as killing. Notice that in Mt. 5.21–26 the term "brother" keeps coming up. This is teaching for his disciples, not for the crowds in general. *Jesus' ethics of the Kingdom were never intended to be imposed on the general society who are not disciples of Jesus. This is insider or particular community ethics.*

A certain escalation can be seen as anger boils over – first there is reference to the beginning of the problem – someone gets mad. Then, they vent, using epithets like the Aramaic word *raka*, a term of contempt, and this can escalate further to "you fool." But as the sin gets worse, note the escalation of its punishment – "subject to judgment" then "answerable to the council" and then finally "in danger of hell fire." This is typical hyperbolic wisdom language, but it should be taken seriously. Jesus means there are moral consequences, potentially even afterlife consequences to a disciple's behavior in this life. It should be added that Jesus is talking about behavior toward fellow disciples here, involving verbal abuse. He is not talking about so-called righteous anger at sin or serious wrongdoing, something Jesus himself displayed in the temple (Mt. 21.12–17). There is such a thing as righteous anger ("be angry but sin not") and there is such a thing as sinful anger. It is possible that there is a deliberate echo of the story of Cain and Abel here, the deadly anger of one brother against another (see 5.23–24).

Why no oaths? Jesus is of course not talking about what we would call "swear words" but about invoking God's name to vouch for the truth of something one has said. Jesus thinks this is unnecessary if one is simply transparent and truthful. Jesus is calling for a higher standard of integrity so that one never needs to use oaths, one's word is one's bond, one's yes means yes, and one's no means no. No exaggeration, no equivocation, no oaths needed. Unlike Philo (*Deca.* 92) Jesus is not concerned with mere excessive swearing, he is concerned with the heart of the matter, what motivates such swearing or oath-taking in the first place.

Mt. 5.38–42 indicates that in light of the new eschatological situation, disciples must be proactive, acting on what they know they ought to do, not reacting to some wrong done to them. Disciples do not return evil for evil, they do not retaliate, they do not later take revenge. The Matthean form of the "turn the other cheek" saying perhaps refers to the slapping of someone with the back of one's hand, as an insult which would normally set in motion a reciprocity cycle of reprisals which usually escalated. It is possible that the focus here is on a refusal to take legal action in a secular court against someone who is a brother, something Paul himself prohibits in 1 Cor. 5. Verse 40 then deals with the opposite situation where the believer is taken to court. The advice of Jesus here amounts to suggesting that if someone wants to sue you and take your shirt, give them your cloak as well. This advice should be contrasted with Exod. 22.25–26/Deut. 24.12–13, where the cloak at least is said to belong permanently to the original owner.

Verses 41–42 then illustrate the single principle of doing good to the neighbor, even to the enemy, *regardless of how they treat you*. This ethic not merely goes beyond the "eye for an eye" Mosaic teaching, it sets it aside and starts over from scratch in a radically different direction.

The disciple is to take action always on the basis of one's already extant commitment to follow Jesus' teaching. And then there is the matter of giving with no thought of return, following the gracious character of God. This goes beyond earlier commands about almsgiving. Self-sacrifice and love replace self-interest and self-protection as the ethics of the dawning Kingdom. It assumes that Jesus has already inaugurated this new eschatological age.

Mt. 5.43–48 closes and sums up the antitheses section of the Sermon on the Mount. Verse 43 begins with a partial quotation of Lev. 19.18 (see the fuller version at Mt. 19.19), which only leaves out the "as yourself" part of the quotation and is followed by an imperative nowhere found in the OT – "hate your enemies." There is something of a parallel from Qumran (1 QS 3–4, 9–10; 19.21–22). Whether this is something Jesus had heard someone say is not clear. In any case, we should resist the tendency to whittle off the hard edges of his teaching, including these dramatic contrasts. Our focus must be on the positive command to love your enemies and even to pray for those that persecute you. Jesus is urging counterintuitive behavior, conduct not conditioned by kinship (ethnic, social, or religious) or reciprocity. Showing hospitality to an enemy is one thing (Prov. 25.21), loving them is taking things to another and higher level. Notice that the illustration in v. 45b is of God's indiscriminate love shown through sun and rain benefiting both the righteous and the wicked. Jesus is insisting that his disciples' love must go beyond in-group love.

It is important to avoid taking v. 48 out of context. Jesus has just explained that the disciples are to love indiscriminately, as God loves. The key word in this verse is *teleioi*. But should we see this as referring to character, or conduct, or even wholeness in relationships? Probably, this verse has nothing to do with a state or condition of sinless perfection. It is rather talking about a conduct or activity of loving indiscriminately like the Father loves. Possibly Deut. 18.13 stands in the background here or Lev. 19.2. D. Hill gets the gist of this in saying: "The emphasis is not on flawless moral character, but on whole-hearted devotion to the imitation of God, not in perfection of his being but of his ways … In their acts of love, reconciliation, and faithfulness, the disciples are to show God's attitude to men, that perfection in love which seeks the good of all."[42]

Note that this advice is not for some elite group within the disciples, but for disciples in general. It may presuppose that the disciples will receive the Spirit in due course, which will enable them to live by and live into such striking and demanding imperatives. Certainly, these imperatives are eschatologically and Christologically grounded, and eventually Pneumatically enabled and empowered. The Kingdom at this juncture is a work in progress, and so is the response to its mandates between the Incarnation and Pentecost.

The paradigmatic "Lord's prayer" which is actually the disciple's prayer in Mt. 6.5–15 comes in the midst of Jesus' discussion in Mt. 6 of the three pillars of early Jewish piety – almsgiving, fasting, and prayer. This prayer is found in a somewhat different form in Lk. 11, and there this teaching is in response to the disciples asking Jesus to teach them a signature or characteristic prayer for them specifically. In Luke, it is explicit that this is a prayer for disciples, but then it is probably implicit in Mt. 6 as well. Notice that the phrase

---

[42] D. H. Hill, *The Gospel of Matthew* (Grand Rapids, MI: William B. Eerdmans, 1972), 56.

"pray in this manner" suggests an outline of how to pray and what to pray for, rather than an itemized or complete list of the things one must pray for. In Mt. 6 the disciples are first given examples of how not to pray, before being told how to do so and what its general content should look like. Notice that we have a contrast here between public and private praying, and also between praying to show off one's piety, and prayer as a form of sincere devotion to God. One should not see this as a critique of all forms of public or corporate prayer or formulaic prayer, either. Indeed, the Lord's prayer is a formulaic prayer. Jesus is concerned about hypocrisy. To avoid the temptation to show off, Jesus says, go into a small room in the house, perhaps a closet, close the door and pray as follows ...

Throughout this discussion it is clear that Jesus sees prayer as conversation with God, not as a means of informing an ignorant God, or motivating an uninterested deity, or getting the attention of a neglectful God. Notice that Mt. 6.6c says pray in private and God will "restore it to you." This suggests a situation where the disciple has been wronged or defrauded of something. Jesus urges reliance on God to redress the balance. The language of restoration could, however, be taken to mean that God will make it worth your while if one prays in a self-effacing and honest manner.

From the outset, a filial relationship is appealed to. We have seen much earlier in this study that Jesus, who himself addressed God as Abba, teaches his disciples to do so as well, suggesting that they can have the same intimacy with God that he has. This is something distinctive of Jesus' teaching, as we have seen.[43] Verse 7 contrasts the mindless repeating of names and phrases of the Gentiles, which certainly does not connote a personal relationship with a deity, but rather an attempt to manipulate or get something from a deity by correct "name" calling, so to speak. Jesus says that sort of prayer is pointless and ineffective. Jesus may also be contrasting the compact Lord's prayer with the verbosity of the Gentile praying. The reference to "our" throughout the prayer (our Father, our sins, our bread) makes clear that in Matthew this is a corporate prayer, not a purely private one. Notice as well the reassurance at v. 8 that the Father already knows what his child needs.

In light of the eschatological context and flavor of the prayer, what is being asked is that a day will come on earth, as in heaven, that God's name is properly hallowed, that his Kingdom and will fully come on earth. In this regard, this is much like the ending of the Christ hymn in Phil. 2.5–11, which speaks of a day when every knee will bow and every tongue confess Jesus is Lord, and the kingdoms of this world will become the Kingdom of God. The prayer, of course, makes evident that the situation is "not yet." These things have not yet been fully realized on earth, else they would hardly need to be prayed for. Verse 10 indicates that God's will is already perfectly done in heaven, where God dwells.

Verse 11, whatever else one wants to say about it (does it suggest a person living day to day, hand to mouth?), indicates that one needs to depend on God even for the most basic necessities of life – bread, the staple of the ancient diet. Here there may be an echo of the early Jewish Kiddush prayer, which speaks of God as the one who brings forth bread from the earth.

The second "we" petition speaks of debts and forgiveness, so we must think not just of material indebtedness, though that is involved, but also other forms of indebtedness. Note

[43] See pp. 59–62, above.

the strong emphasis that a person who refuses to forgive will not be forgiven when the Kingdom comes on earth (noting vv. 14–15, pointing to an eschatological or final forgiving at the day of judgment). There is a connection between being forgiven by God and forgiving others, just as there is a connection between loving God and neighbor, which notably Jesus says is the great commandment (singular). The real gist of the petition here is "forgive us, just as we on a lesser scale forgive others." An unforgiving disciple of Jesus is an oxymoron.

The noun πειρασμός in v. 13, can mean either "test" or "tempt" and the context has to determine which it is in a given case. Possibly Jesus is drawing on an old Jewish prayer, "do not bring me into the power of a sin, a temptation, a shame" (BT Ber. 60b). The Aramaic original would be something like "cause us not to enter" or better "do not allow us to enter." In any case, God is not viewed here as the source of temptation. Rather the Evil One is, and probably the last petition then reads "and deliver us from the Evil One." It should be stressed that the idea of evil as an abstract concept doesn't really exist in the OT or the NT. Only evil deeds or an Evil One show up. Turning evil into a mere force, or power, or even just a malignant idea is a modern preoccupation which should be resisted. Early Jews certainly believed in a personal Evil One and in his minions, demons.

This prayer suggests that if we have our priorities right, we will pray first and foremost that God's plan and his glory be manifested on earth before we ask for personal favors or help. Praise and thanksgiving precede petition and pleading. The prayer also suggests that it is both appropriate and wise to pray for the basic necessities of life – daily food, daily deliverance from temptation and sin and the Evil One, daily asking for forgiveness with a willingness to forgive others, in short daily praying about the physical and spiritual necessities of life. Before we pray for something, it is always wise to ask, does our prayer measure up to this model prayer, and am I prepared to sign Jesus' name to it ("in Jesus' name, Amen")? That is, is this something Jesus would pray for?

We have now seen more than enough in our selective discussion of the famous Sermon on the Mount to demonstrate that Jesus is not simply applying OT teachings to his disciples or using a new hermeneutical approach to the OT. The ethics of Jesus are grounded in the new eschatological situation, and in particular in his own coming and the coming of the divine saving activity we call Kingdom/Dominion. While the ethics of Jesus for his disciples involves some reiteration of some OT teaching, it also involves new teaching which *replaces* some of the Mosaic teaching, making it obsolescent. The upping of the level of ethical demand, dealing with issues of the heart (the source of all things good and bad in a person's behavior), bespeaks the eschatological situation where Jesus takes for granted that God is doing a new thing, writing his teaching on the human heart as Jer. 31 promised, inaugurating a new covenant, fulfilling various long outstanding prophecies such as the one in Joel 2 about the gift of the Spirit, and more.

It is important, then, to be able to distinguish the teaching of Jesus specifically directed to his own disciples, which the Evangelists later correctly saw as applicable to Christians anywhere and everywhere, and the dialogues and teaching Jesus gave during his ministry to non-disciples, and even adversaries, where he operated on the basis of the shared Mosaic covenant context. What Jesus says to persons who do not become his disciples, or who wish to debate the import of Mosaic legislation, is one thing. What he says to his disciples is another.

While there is some overlap between the two sorts of teaching (e.g. both for Jesus' disciples and for the general public, Jesus' advice is to render taxes to those to whom taxes are owed, including the temple tax, but render unto God what only God deserves and is owed), the emphasis must lie on the differences. Jesus is proleptically giving teaching that will be an essential part of the New Covenant once it is inaugurated through his death. In the meanwhile, we should not be too hard on the disciples during Jesus' ministry, as they do not yet have the Spirit, and much of Jesus' teaching they did not grasp until after Jesus' death and resurrection, as, for example, Jn. 2.22 indicates. A retrospective reflection on Jesus' teaching in the light of Easter was a game changer. Then, the light began to fully dawn on the disciples in regard to their new expected behavior (see e.g. Acts 2.42–47; 4.32–37). Even so, as Acts 10 suggests, it took a while for these pious Jews to work out all the implications of Jesus' sometimes enigmatic sapiential teaching, so full of metaphors and parabolic images.

The Last Supper, the Last Cup, the New Covenant

The last week of Jesus' life is critical to understanding Jesus' own views about the New Covenant. We have already seen how his teaching for his disciples, and his behavior in regard to things like the Sabbath and food laws, betoken the dawning of the new eschatological age. His behavior was frequently controversial, deliberately so at times. This is very clearly the case when Jesus "cleanses" the temple and then predicts, according to Mk. 13, that the temple is going down for the count within a generation. Temple-centered religion, an essential focus of early Judaism with its festivals and sacrifices, would be no more. This would not be the end of *the* world writ large, but it would be the end of the world of early Judaism. A change was going to come, and before it all happened, Jesus gave teaching to his disciples to prepare them for a new and eschatological stage in the life of God's people, a stage announced by Jeremiah, who was clear that this would not involve a mere renewal of the Mosaic covenant, but rather a new covenant. Without the temple, Leviticus and the various roles of priests and Levites and sacrifices could no longer literally or fully be lived into or fulfilled. Judaism would have to change to carry on. Jesus prepared his disciples for that change by prophetically speaking about it and foreshadowing the coming disaster through his action in the temple, and most of all by what he did at the very end of his life, beginning with the Last Supper, and carrying on through his death and resurrection.

The Lasting Supper: The Supper That Finally Satisfies

In their discussion of the tradition history that leads to the various accounts of the Last Supper, Feldmeier and Spieckermann note that both the Synoptic tradition and Paul agree that "Jesus himself interpreted his imminent death with the aid of the covenant idea."[44] This is absolutely correct. They go on to suggest, however, a radical difference between the Matthew/Mark version of the tradition and the Luke/Paul version of the tradition, and about this point, they are wrong. They argue that "the version offered by Mark and Matthew follows Exod. 24.8 in speaking of the blood of the covenant, that is, they

---

[44] Feldmeier and Spieckermann, *God of the Living*, 459.

recognize in Jesus' representative sacrifice of his life (Mk. 14.24 par. Matt. 26.28, 'poured out for you') the confirmation and renewal of the Sinai covenant. In contrast, the tradition received by Paul, which Luke also follows (see Luke 22.20) appeals to the promise of the new covenant from Jeremiah 31.31 in which God writes his law directly in the human heart."[45]

The major problem with this analysis is that *all* covenants were inaugurated or confirmed through a sacrifice involving, of course, the shedding of blood. The reference to the blood of the covenant in Matthew and Mark does not need to be seen as a reference to the Mosaic covenant at all, much less the renewal of that covenant. Even the Abrahamic covenant involved a sacrifice and thus the shedding of blood. No, in all of our sources, both the Synoptics and Paul, the Last Supper is associated with an act of covenanting which foreshadows the full inauguration of the New Covenant through the death of Jesus. The death of Jesus has nothing to do with a renewal of the Mosaic covenant. That is to completely ignore the Kingdom and eschatological context of Jesus' teaching, including his teaching at the Last Supper, to which we now turn.

In a recent discussion I had with my friend Professor A.-J. Levine, I was probing whether she knew of any evidence whatsoever in early Judaism outside the NT that the Passover lamb and sacrifice ideas were combined with the notion of "the taking away of sins" through the scapegoat ritual. Her answer was – she knows of none.

And neither do I.[46] This combination is of course found on the lips of John the Baptizer in Jn. 1.29 (cf. v. 36). I would suggest it is also found in Paul, if one compares 1 Cor. 5.7–8 to what Paul says in 1 Cor. 11 about the Lord's Supper and its proper celebration. But could it be at least implied in the Last Supper account as well? Even if not, the idea is present in the NT, and it suggests that the death of Jesus averts God's judgment on Jesus' disciples and takes away their sins as well.

Probably the earliest account we have of the Last Supper comes from about 51–52 AD and is found in 1 Cor. 11, though of course this is not merely a historical recitation, but rather a telling of the story of the Last Supper as a part of the current Lord's Supper practice in Corinth. Paul says "I received from the Lord [I assume he means through one or more of his original disciples – Peter, perhaps] what I also passed on to you: The Lord Jesus, on the night he was betrayed, took bread, and when he had given thanks broke it and said 'This is my body which is for you; do this in remembrance of me.' In the same way, after supper he took the cup, saying: 'This cup is the new covenant in my blood; do this, whenever you drink it, in remembrance of me.' For whenever you eat this bread and drink this cup, you proclaim the Lord's death until he comes." This account needs to be compared to our most primitive Gospel account in Mk. 14, which reads as follows:

[12] On the first day of the Festival of Unleavened Bread, when it was customary to sacrifice the Passover lamb, Jesus' disciples asked him, "Where do you want us to go and make preparations for you to eat the Passover?"

[13] So he sent two of his disciples, telling them, "Go into the city, and a man carrying a jar of water will meet you. Follow him. [14] Say to the owner of the house he enters, 'The Teacher asks: Where is my guest room, where I may eat the Passover with my disciples?' [15] He will show you a large room upstairs, furnished and ready. Make preparations for us there."

---

[45] *Ibid.*, 459–60.
[46] Email conversation, September 17, 2017.

[16] The disciples left, went into the city and found things just as Jesus had told them. So they prepared the Passover.

[17] When evening came, Jesus arrived with the Twelve. [18] While they were reclining at the table eating, he said, "Truly I tell you, one of you will betray me – one who is eating with me."

[19] They were saddened, and one by one they said to him, "Surely you don't mean me?"

[20] "It is one of the Twelve," he replied, "one who dips bread into the bowl with me. [21] The Son of Man will go just as it is written about him. But woe to that man who betrays the Son of Man! It would be better for him if he had not been born."

[22] While they were eating, Jesus took bread, and when he had given thanks, he broke it and gave it to his disciples, saying, "Take it; this is my body."

[23] Then he took a cup, and when he had given thanks, he gave it to them, and they all drank from it.

[24] "This is my blood of the covenant, which is poured out for many," he said to them. [25] "Truly I tell you, I will not drink again from the fruit of the vine until that day when I drink it new in the kingdom of God."

[26] When they had sung a hymn, they went out to the Mount of Olives.

There has been endless debate among scholars as to whether this depicts a Passover meal or not. The eating of the lamb and the traditional words of interpretation of the Passover meal are not found in this account, or the other Gospel accounts. On the one hand, Mark says the meal took place on the first day of the feast of Unleavened Bread, but he also says on the day the Passover lamb was slaughtered. The Johannine account suggests that Jesus himself was killed on the day of the sacrifice of the lambs. They actually could both be right, since by the Jewish way of reckoning things, days run from sundown to sundown, so if the Passover meal was celebrated by Jesus on Thursday evening, as it appears to be, then this would already be the beginning of the day on which the lambs were sacrificed, normally the next morning or afternoon. Complicating matters further is the fact that Mark may be following the Roman means of reckoning time, rather than the Jewish one, and one can debate the same about the Fourth Gospel. In the end, I have concluded that Jesus did celebrate, but reinterpreted, a Passover meal, held earlier than normal, on the Thursday evening of that week.[47]

The crucial part of this is that rather than simply reciting the interpretation of the bitter herbs or the bread of haste, Jesus feels free to take the bread at the outset of the meal, give thanks, break it, and interpret it as a symbol of his soon to be broken body. In the Markan form of the tradition, it only really becomes clear that he is talking about death, his coming death, when there is a reference to blood, his blood of the covenant shed or poured out for many. The word "covenant" is clearly part of the original Markan text. Many scholars have thought that the word "new," which occurs in *many* Markan manuscripts (A, E, Delta, 18 minuscules), and in the Byzantine texts (F, H, Sigma, in addition to E, as well as in Italian and Slavonic and Coptic and Syriac translations and in Italian in lectionaries) is a later carry-over from the Lukan parallel or from 1 Cor. 11.[48] This is far from certain, since the geographical and linguistic diversity of those manuscripts which

---

[47] See the still helpful discussions of J. Jeremias in *The Eucharistic Words of Jesus* (3rd edn.; London: SCM Press, 1974) and also Ben Witherington III, *Making a Meal of It: Rethinking the Theology of the Lord's Supper* (Waco, TX: Baylor University Press, 2008).

[48] See Metzger, *Textual Commentary*, 95.

include the word "new" is considerable. The reading was known widely. Notice the close connection between bloodshed and covenant made in Mark and Paul.

In any case, Jesus' actions and interpretations are new, and suggest that the inauguration of a new covenant is about to happen by means of his death. What is especially remarkable about what is happening at this meal is that Jesus is so certain that his death is going to benefit his disciples that he symbolically hands out tokens and pledges of that benefit *before he even dies.* It should also be added that the interpretation of the elements at Passover was of course known to be symbolic in character, the bitter herbs were not literally the bitterness of bondage, or the bitterness the Hebrews experienced in Egypt, they merely represented it. Had Jesus been literally saying "this becomes my body" or "this becomes my blood," the disciples would not have partaken in the ritual, indeed they might well have run out of the room screaming, for cannibalism was no part of early Judaism, and in any case, as Jeremias showed long ago, what Jesus said in Aramaic would not have involved a stative verb like "to be" or "to become." It would have simply been "this, my body," "this, my blood." The whole notion of transubstantiation or even consubstantiation is a later imposition on these early, thoroughly Jewish, texts.

The implication of what Jesus says is twofold: (1) Jesus himself is the Passover lamb, and his coming death inaugurates the New Covenant. All three Synoptic accounts, plus the Pauline account in 1 Cor. 11, suggest both implications. At what point was this associated with the forgiveness of sins? After all, early Jews didn't think in terms of ritual human sacrifice as a way to atone for sins, so far as we can tell. My suggestion would be that because there was a tradition that Jesus from the cross forgave sins, even of his executioners (Lk. 23.34), and since already Jesus had associated his death with the Passover sacrifice, it was but a short step to what we find in Jn. 1 – "Behold the Lamb of God that takes away the sins of the world." Jesus is both the Passover lamb of Exodus, and also the scapegoat of Lev. 16. This is part and parcel of the attempt in John to show that Jesus is the fulfillment not just of the prophecies of the OT but also of the institutions of the OT – he is the temple or tabernacle where God's presence dwells, he is the fulfillment of the feast of Unleavened Bread being the Bread of Life, he is the fulfillment of the Passover feast, he is the fulfillment of the Festival of Lights being the Light of the World. Jesus is not only the means to sustain life (bread, living water), he is the resurrection and the life.[49]

A couple of further points are worth noting. In Mark, Jesus indicates that he will partake of "the fruit of the vine" again in the Kingdom, which not only suggests that Jesus foresees something positive beyond his coming death, but one wonders if the followers of Jesus took this to be a reference to Christ's spiritual presence at the celebration of the Lord's Supper, which, while by no means identical with the Last Supper, is partially derived from it.

The phrase "the blood of the covenant poured out for many" is crucial, and the phrase "for many" in particular suggests a substitutionary sacrifice. It is on behalf of many, and in their stead. This saying should be exegeted in light of Mk. 10.45, where Jesus already said he came to give his life as a ransom on behalf of (and in place of) the many. The contrast here is between the one who is providing the ransom, and the many who get the benefit, not between "many" and "all" as if Jesus was saying his death was not intended for the

---

[49] See the brilliant exposition in J. B. Lightfoot, *The Gospel of St. John* (Downers Grove, IL: InterVarsity Press, 2015).

sake of "all." Clearly, the interpretation of Mk. 10.45 in 1 Tim. 2.6 rules out the latter interpretation of the Markan saying.

And So?

We have considered in this chapter the approach to the New Covenant, and the New Covenant teaching during the period of Jesus' earthly ministry. *We noted the important distinction between what Jesus was teaching his disciples and how he interacted with non-disciples who lived in an ethos where the Mosaic Law and covenant was seen as ongoing.* Yet the teaching given to the disciples foreshadowed a changed covenant situation was coming. It may also be significant that we have: (1) no teaching by Jesus of his disciples as to whether or how they should keep the Sabbath; (2) no evidence at all that Jesus ever used or recommended ritual washing in a *mikveh* for his disciples, and yet this was a very prevalent practice in both Galilee and Judaea. By contrast, he does recommend in Jn. 9 the blind man go wash in the pool of Siloam, but that is perhaps not quite the same thing. It is not a mere ritual; it's part of the process of his healing; (3) nor does Jesus teach his disciples to tithe, rather he recommends the example of the sacrificial giving of the widow with her two *minas*. We may contrast this with Mt. 23.23, where he urges the Pharisees, who are certainly not among his disciples, to be consistent and not only tithe their condiments but practice the weightier elements of the law – deeds of justice and mercy. Again, this is not advice to Jesus' own disciples, but to those continuing under the yoke of the Mosaic Law.

When one examines closely all the evidence, it becomes clear that Jesus is preparing his disciples for the coming change of situation caused by the inauguration of a new covenant, through his coming death, resurrection and Spirit-giving, while continuing to give advice about the Mosaic Law to those who will continue under that covenant. Jesus is not suggesting a renewal of that covenant either in his teaching of or in his praxis with his disciples. The in-breaking of the divine saving activity or reign leads to the coming of a new covenant situation which would properly only begin after Jesus completed his earthly ministry and sent the promised Spirit from on high. We must turn now to a consideration of what is said about the New Covenant by Paul, our earliest post-Easter witness to Christian reflection on the matter, noting that, unlike the author of Hebrews, Paul is overwhelmingly addressing Gentiles, and thinking entirely of the new creation and situation in the body of Christ. *As it turns out, one needs to have a firm grasp not only of historical progression from the OT to the NT but even the progression within the NT, with a further recognition that there is progressive revelation accompanying this historical progression. What Jesus said to his contemporaries who were still busy keeping and interpreting the Mosaic covenant is one thing. What he said to his disciples about the theology of the coming New Covenant is another.*

10

New Covenanting in the Eschatological Age of the Spirit

> It is one of the distinguishing features of the New Perspective on Paul to set Paul's Theology – justification in particular – in a decidedly covenantal framework … in Wright's work … we find a repeated emphasis on covenant theology as basic to virtually all of Paul's thought, indeed as the unifying center to all Paul's theological reckoning.
>
> Garwood Anderson[1]

> The life of believers is lived between what Jesus has done and what Jesus will do, and the Lord's Meal brings home both past and future. We bring home the memory of Jesus dying, until he comes. The motif of bringing home the memory links the Lord's Meal and the celebration of the Passover, which was the context of the meal that the ongoing Lord's Meal continues … In continuation of that dynamic, the congregation's celebration of the Lord's Meal involves people reliving the dying of Jesus as if they were there. Its effect is to bring home the reality of that event and involve people in it once again, so that its effect on their lives is reinforced.
>
> John Goldingay[2]

A different sort of bridge between the testaments (other than a text like Jer. 31.31), old and new, is the study of intertextuality, the use of the OT in the NT, and one of the most insightful efforts in this direction is that of Richard Hays. In his important work, *Echoes of Scripture in the Letters of Paul*,[3] Hays spends considerable time unpacking his reading of 2 Cor. 3.1–3, with its reference or allusion to Jer. 31.31 and its context. He begins by pointing out the apparent parallel between Jeremiah talking about a law written on the hearts of God's people, and Paul's reference to the Corinthians being "our letter inscribed on our hearts known and read by all people."

Paul is referring to a letter of reference or recommendation, not to a law or set of laws, but in both texts something is written on the heart. The textual question is whether the letter is written on "our hearts" or "your hearts" (the latter reading supported by the important manuscript Aleph, and various lesser witnesses including 33, 88, 436, 1881) and clearly in 2 Cor. 7.2 the phrase is "your hearts," where Paul asks the Corinthians to make

---

[1] G. Anderson, *Paul's New Perspective: Charting a Soteriological Journey* (Downers Grove, IL: InterVarsity Press, 2016), 28–29.

[2] Goldingay, *Biblical Theology*, 367.

[3] Hays, *Echoes of Scripture in the Letters of Paul*, 125–31.

room for him in "your hearts." On the whole, the metaphor works better if Paul is talking about the new creation that has happened in the Corinthians' lives, and the fact that they are his letters of recommendation, the proof of his apostleship. God, so to speak, has recommended Paul's ministry by inscribing his love and presence in their hearts.

Paul will develop, in 2 Cor. 3.7–18, a contrast between his own ministry and that of Moses, involving a contrast between the Old Covenant and the new one that Jeremiah spoke of. Hays is probably correct that Paul's reference in v. 3 to that which is "inscribed not with ink but by the Spirit of the living God" may allude to Exod. 31.18 (cf. Deut. 9.10–11), where we hear about the stone tablets inscribed by the "finger of God." If so, it is a contrasting comparison, because when Paul speaks about the New Covenant, he says in 2 Cor. 3.3, "not on stone tablets but on the tablets of fleshy hearts." Again, Hays may be right that Paul is thinking of yet another passage as well, this time Ezek. 36.26 (LXX), where we have the phrase "fleshy hearts" there contrasted with hearts of stone. In the view of Paul, something written on the heart eclipses the Ten Words written on stone tablets.[4]

Hays thinks that therefore the contrast here means "texts will no longer be needful. Scripture will have become a 'self-consuming artifact'; the power of the word will have subsumed itself into the life of the community, embodied itself without remainder."[5] Despite the eloquence of this, this is clearly not quite assessing the situation properly. Paul is not contrasting a ministry that focuses on OT scriptural texts as opposed to a ministry that focuses on the Spirit's work in the human heart. Jeremiah would have been shocked by such a conclusion because it is precisely "the Law," the "written Law," which he says is to be written on human hearts. There is no written Law/Spirit contrast in Jeremiah, nor for that matter in Exodus or Ezekiel. It is rather a both/and situation. The problem with the Old Covenant is not that it involves written texts. So does the New Covenant, indeed it involves various texts from the Old Covenant! The problem is that without the Holy Spirit to inscribe things on the heart, the situation with God's fallen people will never significantly change.

What Hays especially misses is that Paul is talking about the effects of the two covenants on fallen human beings. The Old Covenant came attended with glory and was a good and holy revelation of God (cf. Rom. 7.1–5 and 9.4). The *effect*, however, of the Old Covenant on fallen people was not merely to reveal their sin, but, as Paul will put it, to turn sin into trespass – a willful violation of a known law. The Law was purposed to be life-giving, but its effect without the work of God's Spirit is death-dealing on people trapped in sin.

Paul has an additional point, however. The ministry of Moses, and the "Old Covenant" (here referred to as such for the first time), has had its day. The eschatological hour has arrived and the New Covenant of Jeremiah is the covenant for the eschatological age. Just as the glory on Moses' face was annulled or eclipsed by the greater glory from the face of Christ, so the Old Covenant of Moses has been annulled in the light of the coming of the New Covenant prophesied by Jeremiah. In v. 9, Paul contrasts the "administration of condemnation" (the effect of the Law, not its intent) with that of righteousness.

Note that the neuter participle τὸ καταργούμενον agrees with "that which was glorified" in v. 10, and so applies to the whole Old Covenant, symbolized or even embodied by

---

4 *Ibid.*, 128–29.
5 *Ibid.*, 129.

Moses. This means that what is said to be annulled in v. 14 is not merely the veil over the minds of God's people, but the obsolete Old Covenant. When Paul says "the letter kills, but the Spirit gives life" he is not contrasting two different hermeneutical approaches or ways of interpreting the OT, he is talking about the difference between the effect of the Old Covenant without the Spirit, as opposed to the salvific effect of the New Covenant applied by the Spirit. It is a tale of two covenants he is telling, not a tale of two ways of reading the OT. Literal interpretation vs. spiritual interpretation is not even on the horizon in this discussion by Paul.

As in Gal. 3–4, Paul is arguing on the basis of his covenantal theology, and what he says quite plainly in Gal. 4 is that the Mosaic covenant was good but *pro tempore*, for a certain period of time or age that is now passing away, in the light of the eschatological age and the New Covenant. The OT remained Holy Writ, and Paul will continue to use it as such, again and again, even with audiences largely Gentile. The issue is not that the OT is passing away. Rather the issue is that God's people are no longer under the old Mosaic covenant, but rather under the New Covenant, which has its own commandments, its own obligations, and, in due course, its own written texts, the text of the NT.[6] The age of the Spirit changes the ability of God's people to respond to the demands of God's Word, even inscribing that Word on their hearts.

To further reflect on Paul's covenant theology, we must turn to Gal. 4. In Gal. 4.21–31, Paul is countering the possible arguments not of non-Christian Jews, but of some fellow Jewish Christians whom he sees as bewitching his converts in Galatia. This passage contrasts considerably with 1 Thess. 2.14–16, where Paul is quite clearly talking about some non-Christian Jews. Paul viewed the Mosaic covenant as an interim solution for God's people, a sort of guardian of them, until Messiah came.[7]

It is not surprising, then, that he saw Jewish Christian advocates of the Mosaic Law being imposed on Gentile Christians *after* the coming of Christ as being almost as misguided as Hagar when it came to the issue of who was going to inherit the Abrahamic blessings and promises and how they would do so.

In short, though the Mosaic Law had an important function in its day and time, its day and time had come and gone, and had been superseded by what Christ brought to God's people. In this argument, then, it is not an accident that Paul tells us that Sarah and Hagar represent *two different covenants*. The story of two women becomes a tale of two covenants in Paul's creative hands. To go back to observing the Mosaic Law was tantamount to submitting again to bondage and a renouncing of the Gospel of Christ and the New Covenant he instituted. Christians no longer have Jerusalem, or the Mosaic covenant and Law, as their mother. Rather "the Jerusalem which is above is free and she is our mother" (Gal. 4.26). I must stress at this juncture that we are dealing with an intramural debate between Paul and other Jewish Christians in regard to how Christians, including Gentile Christians, should live. There is no contrast here between Judaism and Christianity. It needs to be said, however, that the view that Paul is *simply* offering teaching that applies *only to Gentiles* does not work here or elsewhere, either.[8]

---

[6] See my discussion in *Conflict and Community in Corinth: A Socio-Rhetorical Commentary on 1 and Corinthians* (Grand Rapids, MI: William B. Eerdmans, 1995), 377–82.

[7] The fuller form of this argument can be found in Witherington, *Grace in Galatia*, pp. 321–57.

[8] But see the recent book by P. Fredriksen, *Paul: The Pagans' Apostle* (New Haven, CT: Yale University Press, 2017).

While it is certainly true that Paul sees the New Covenant as the fulfillment of the Abrahamic covenant and the replacement for the Mosaic covenant, he certainly does not see Christianity as replacing Judaism. Indeed, for Paul, being in Christ, the Jewish messiah, is simply the proper development of the one people of God. The people of God has become Jew and Gentile united in the Jewish messiah.

W. D. Davies was right when he said long ago that "in accepting the Jew, Jesus, as the Messiah, Paul did not think in terms of moving into a new religion but of having found the final expression and intent of the Jewish tradition within which he himself had been born. For him, the Gospel was according to the Scriptures [see e.g. 1 Cor. 15.3–5]; it was not an alien importation into Judaism, but the true development of it, its highest point, although in its judgment on the centrality which some Jews had given to a particular interpretation of the Law it showed a radicalism, which amounted to a new creation."[9] Exactly so.

Nor is Paul defending Gentile Christianity at the expense of Jewish Christianity. Rather, as Gal. 3.28 indicates, he is announcing a true people of God which has come forth as the true development of early Judaism and which places all persons on equal footing at the foot of the cross and in the presence of God. Ethnic distinctions and previous religious customs and rituals are not given any particular soteriological significance in this people of God united in Christ.

When circumcision, Sabbath keeping, food laws, and other boundary-defining aspects of Judaism are assigned some sort of salvific status or essential status, Paul opposes such a notion. Paul has no problems with being the Jew to the Jew in order to win some, or being the Gentile to the Gentile to win some; what he is rejecting is the necessity of keeping the Mosaic Law if one is a Christian. To the contrary, Christians are called to fulfill a rather different Law, "the Law of Christ" (Gal. 6.2), which has several components: (1) imitating the life pattern of Christ; (2) obeying various of the imperatives of Christ, which Paul reiterates; (3) keeping those OT commandments which have been reiterated by Christ and/or his apostles; and perhaps (4) obeying the imperatives of the apostles, including his own, which are viewed as extensions of Christ's teachings. Does Paul then call the church, Israel? Some have thought so on the basis of Gal. 6.16. Some have contrasted the phrase here ("the Israel *of God*") with the phrase in 1 Cor. 10.18 which speaks of Israel after the flesh. But context is important in coming to a conclusion at this point. Clearly enough, in at least some places in Rom. 9–11 Paul does use the term Israel to refer to non-Christian Jews. In other words, he is capable of using it in its ethnic sense. When he says "and in like manner all Israel will be saved" in Rom. 11.25 he distinguishes this group of saved persons from the full number of the Gentiles who have been grafted into the true people of God. Gal. 6.16, however, is connected to Gal. 6.15 and the entire phrase in question reads "neither circumcision nor uncircumcision matters; what counts is a new creation. Peace and mercy on all who follow this rule *and* on the Israel of God." This seems to echo the nineteenth benediction of the Shemoneh Esreh, which reads: "Bestow peace, happiness, and blessing, grace, and loving-kindness, and mercy upon us, and upon all Israel, your people." Here as in Galatians there is a distinction of two groups, "us" and "all Israel" in the latter case, and "those who keep the rule" and "all Israel" in the former case. *But*, the

---

[9] W. D. Davies, "Paul and the Gentiles: A Suggestion Concerning Romans 11.13–24," in *Jewish and Pauline Studies* (Philadelphia: Fortress Press, 1984), 153–63, here 160.

"us" in the benediction is a subset of all Jews! And we may suspect that since Paul still views himself and other Jewish Christians as Jews, the "all those who follow this rule" would of course include himself, whom he is perhaps distinguishing from the as of yet not saved "Israel of God." If that is correct, then even in Gal. 6.16 "the Israel of God" is not a reference to the church.[10]

As Rom. 9–11 makes so abundantly clear, Paul agonizes over the fate of Jews who have not, or not yet, accepted their messiah. He says at the outset of Rom. 9 that he would even be prepared to be cut off from Christ if they could be saved, and in the end, at Rom. 11.25, he foresees an eschatological miracle of conversion of Jews to Christ. It is hard to imagine Paul using the term Israel to refer either solely or mainly to Gentiles who have never yet been a part of Israel. One must bear in mind that it is a largely a Gentile audience Paul is addressing in Romans, including in Rom. 9–11 (see 11.13). All things considered, then, we may think that Paul uses the term Israel in Gal. 6.16 as he uses it in Romans to refer to non-Christian Jews. In any case, the future peace and mercy Paul sees for "the Israel of God" is going to come from Christ and it is going to come on the same basis as it does for Gentiles – through the mercy of God and by means of faith in Jesus Christ.

1 Thess. 2.14–16 reflects a trenchant critique of acts of violence committed against Christ and Christians by some Jews. This echoes the prophetic critique by Jesus of some in Israel found in Mk. 12.7–9. First, we should notice that though Paul himself had been guilty of persecuting Christians in his former pre-Christian life, here Paul distinguishes himself from "the Jews" in question. We may compare Rom. 9.24, 1 Cor. 9.20, and 2 Cor. 11.24. Taken together the phrase seems to mean for Paul something primarily religious rather than something ethnic – in other words, it refers to non-Christian Jews, just as the word "Israel" seems to do so for Paul. What angers Paul is not merely persecution of Christians by some Jews, but the role of some Jewish officials in the death of Jesus.

This is perhaps why Paul in Rom. 11.17–21 will go on to argue that such Jews have been temporarily broken off from the people of God, due to their unbelief. Another aspect of this passage which calls for comment is the reference to heaping up their sins, which likely echoes Mt. 23.32 (and before that Gen. 15.16; Dan. 8.23; 2 Macc. 6.14). That Paul seems to rely strongly on the Jesus tradition here suggests that he sees himself as simply continuing the sort of prophetic critique of Israel that Jesus had engaged in. Paul seems to be referring to some sort of judgment falling on those responsible "at last" or "until the end," though whether that means until the end of history, until the end of their lives, or until it reaches the full extent of judgment is hard to say.

The intramural debate between Jesus and Jews, and Paul and Jews is indeed something of an in-house debate. Jesus, it will be remembered, not only foresaw divine judgment coming on the Jerusalem temple, he foresaw judgment coming quite specifically on the Jewish officials presiding over his own demise (Mk. 14.62). And yet at the same time such polemics did not forestall Jesus from talking about a future for Jews as well, and Paul follows the same sort of line, as we shall see.

As we have already dealt with 2 Cor. 3 in this chapter, here we need to simply reiterate that while Paul foresaw the demise or obsolescence of the Mosaic covenant and its Law, he nonetheless was utterly convinced that God had not forsaken his first chosen people or

---

[10] A second but less likely option is that Paul is referring to the Judaizers.

reneged on his promises to them. Rom. 1 announces that the Good News is still for the Jew first, and also Gentiles, and Rom. 9–11 explicates how God might work all this out despite the fact that the majority of Jews had rejected Jesus at the point he was writing in the late 50s AD. What 2 Cor. 3 reminds his mostly Gentile converts in Corinth is that Moses and his ministry and Law were glorious and not to be disparaged, even if they had had their day, and were part of the fading glory of an earlier ministry and non-eschatological era.

But what about the eschatological hope of Israel? What would the future hold? It seems clear enough that Paul believes that God had revealed to him a remarkable, even apocalyptic secret truth about his fellow Jews. The truth he will insist on to his largely Gentile audience in Rome is that God was not finished with non-Christian Jews yet. He would insist that those who had rejected Christ were in the first place not all Jews (he himself was Exhibit A that even a very strong opponent of Christ and his followers could become a strong proponent of the same). He would insist that they had been temporarily and temporally hardened and broken off from the people of God until the full number of Gentiles had been saved. Then, and in like manner, by grace through faith in a merciful God, "all Israel would be saved" (Rom. 11.25). Of course, this apocalyptic mystery involved exactly the reverse of the way most early Jews viewed how salvation would work. They thought it would involve the bringing back to the fold of all Jews first, including Diaspora Jews, and thereby the Gentiles would wake up and see Jews streaming to Zion, would grab their coattails and ask to go with them. After all, this would be a reasonable interpretation of many texts such as Ps. 22.27; Isa. 2.2–3; 56.6–8; Micah 4.2; Zech. 2.11; 14.6 (cf. Tobit 13.11; 14.6–7; Ps. Sol. 17.34; Test. Zeb. 9.8; Test. Ben. 9.2). Paul then reverses the order of things.

In a very real way, what Paul is trying to deal with in Rom. 9–11 is the question of theodicy, attempting to justify the ways of God, both to Jews and Gentiles. He is trying to answer the question "Has the Word of God failed?" Apocalyptic teaching had always been concerned with the justice question. When would justice come for God's people? When would his promises be realized? Using the reassuring language of election, foreknowledge, and the like (Rom. 9.11,23; 11.2–7,32), Paul makes clear that all will turn out right for Jews, and therefore Gentiles have no reason to think, much less to boast, that God has replaced his former people with a new Gentile one. In short Rom. 9–11 is a boaster-buster of an argument, and a *tour de force* at that, in which God's saving righteousness in relationship to Israel is vindicated. Paul has a dialogue with an imaginary interlocutor and out-argues him on the matter. You will notice that in the midst of this argument Paul does not cease being the radical about the Mosaic Law. Rom. 10.4 is succinct and clear: "Christ is the fulfillment and so the end of the Mosaic Law as a way either of obtaining or maintaining right-standing with God." Righteousness and right-standing now come through faith – for everyone who confesses Jesus is Lord (10.5–8).

There is then a future for Israel in Christ, but no future for the Mosaic covenant and its Law. The eschatological age requires another covenant, the new one, with a new law called the Law of Christ. The point here is much the same as in 2 Cor. 3 – the end of the Mosaic covenant has been brought about by the coming, the death, and the resurrection of the messiah. *That* Law is at an end and Christ brought it to its end and goal and fulfillment. Christ concludes both the process of election and the Mosaic Law covenant in himself. The election goes from Abraham to his seed, to his ultimate seed Christ, to those who are in Christ, both Jew and Gentile alike, and so God is at no point ever without a people, and furthermore he has not rejected his former people in order to include Gentiles. The unbelieving Jews are only at present temporarily broken off from God's people.[11] In fact, one can say that the real consummation of salvation history cannot come until Israel is amongst the saved in some significant way. While the phrase "all Israel" as it occurs in the OT and elsewhere *never* refers to every single Israelite (cf. 1 Sam. 7.5; 25.1; 1 Kgs. 12.1; 2 Chron. 12.1; Dan. 9.11; Jub. 50.9; Test. Lev. 17.5), it does refer to a large number of them. But when will this happen? There are two clues in Rom. 11.

Firstly, Rom. 11.15 and its phrase "life from the dead" suggest that at the resurrection is when "all Israel" will be saved. This is also suggested even more strongly by Rom. 11.26b, which speaks of the Redeemer coming forth from heavenly Zion and turning back the impiety of Jacob. This is a partial quotation of Isa. 59.20–21 with some modifications (on heavenly Jerusalem see Gal. 4.26) and it is hard to doubt Paul has Jesus in mind as that Redeemer who is coming back from heaven. This means that God alone in the person of his Son will save Jacob, not the church's mission to Jews. Paul seems to expect only a few converted Jews along the way prior to the return of Christ and to see a place for such a witness (see Gal. 2.7–8), though the "big bang" results are not expected before the return of Christ.

Eph. 2.11–22 is one final text we should consider at this juncture. This text, like what we have already seen, suggests that Gentiles only have fellowship with God through the Jewish messiah and his faithful followers, Jewish Christians. Here Paul suggests that it is the death of Christ which has made possible one people of God, both Jew and Gentile united in him. Gentiles who were once excluded from fellowship with Jewish saints are now included because Christ has broken down the middle wall or partition between them. This again is not about the replacement of Israel with the church, but rather the inclusion of Gentiles into the ongoing people of God who are now located "in Christ," seen as the proper and natural development of God's people.

The straightforward way of translating Eph. 2.15 is: "the law of commandments in regulations has been abolished." This might be taken to mean only certain Mosaic laws which separated Jews and Gentiles, but against this is the fact that what had created the separation in the first place was the Torah *as a whole*, the observance of which made the Hebrews God's set-apart people. In light of Rom. 10.4 this seems a likely reading of this text. These two texts then agree that it is Christ who has abolished or terminated that Mosaic covenant with its regulations. Eph. 2 concludes with the picture of Jew and Gentile being built into a new temple or house of God in which Gentiles are viewed as fellow citizens with God's people (i.e. Jewish Christians), called saints here in v. 19 and elsewhere in Ephesians.[12] Like an arch with a keystone, which alludes to Christ who rules his people from above, Jews and Gentiles, the two columns of the arch, have now been united in Christ. The question we must ask at this juncture is whether Jesus himself said anything remotely like all of this.

Clearly enough, when Jesus was ministering there was as of yet no "church" like the one Paul had to deal with, nor did Jesus ever distinguish himself from "the Jews" in the

---

[11] See the argument in Witherington, *Jesus, Paul, and the End of the World*, 118–21.

[12] On which see Ben Witherington III, *The Letters to Philemon, the Colossians, and the Ephesians: A Socio-Rhetorical Commentary on the Captivity Epistles* (Grand Rapids, MI: William B. Eerdmans, 2007).

way Paul did, though both of them were highly critical of Jewish religious officials on various occasions. There was, then, no question for Jesus about the relationship between Israel and the church, as there was for Paul. After all, the church did not exist before Pentecost. Yet it is of more than of passing interest that Jesus, like Paul, seems to have seen many of his Jewish contemporaries as "lost" and in need of repentance and redemption.

The parable in Mk. 12.1–9 ominously warns of judgment if the tenders of the vineyard reject the coming of the Son to the vineyard. And we should not underestimate the importance of the fact that Jesus gathered a community centered on 12 disciples whom he saw as his agents sent out to free or redeem lost Israel, rather than "be" Israel. By design, Jesus confined his ministry and that of his immediate followers to Galilee and Judea and Samaria, it would appear. They were to focus on the lost sheep of Israel and go nowhere amongst the Gentiles. This implies that Jesus thought that Jews were in need of the sort of new birth Jn. 3 tells us Jesus spoke to Nicodemus about, and this included the most religious of them, including pious religious teachers like Nicodemus.

Was there to be a future for Israel if they did not respond positively to the overtures of Jesus and his inner circle? Mt. 19.28/Lk. 22.30 suggests that the answer to this question was yes, but notice that Jesus speaks of the Twelve judging the 12 tribes of Israel when the Dominion was fully realized on earth. What is perhaps most interesting about this saying is that Jesus did not simply identify his inner circle as the new Israel. Rather, Jesus foresaw that they would have a relationship of authority in relationship to Israel.

It would appear that Jesus defined holiness in mostly or purely moral terms, unlike the Pharisees and other early Jews, seeing as obsolete for his own disciples the laws about clean and unclean (see on Mk. 7, above). This allowed him to spend time with sinners, tax collectors and other outcasts without ever once being depicted as having gone through the *mikveh* thereafter for the sake of ritual purification. We should not think of Jesus making repeated trips to the Jordan for cleansing. The water ritual he went through at John's hands was a one-time rite of passage, and so a once and once only event. And he, like John, believed that all Israel needed to repent and go through the cleansing that that ritual depicted. God could, as John had warned, raise up children of Abraham from stones if need be. Neither heredity nor ritual purity would be any guarantee of blessing when the Dominion came fully on earth. It is no accident that we do not find Jesus anywhere affirming things like circumcision, offering animal sacrifices in the temple, or claims that heredity determined whether one was a Jew or not. The crucial question, then, for Jesus seems to have been, as for Paul, who counts as a true Jew or on the macro-scale who counts as Israel?

On the whole it would appear that Mt. 19.28/Lk. 22.30 does not seem to be referring to participating in the final judgment being pronounced on Israel, but rather to ruling over them, like judges did earlier in the history of Israel. But of course, for this to happen one must assume that it will happen in the Holy Land. Did Jesus speak about that?

As it turns out, Mt. 5.5 is probably about just such an eschatological outcome: "Blessed are the meek, for they shall inherit the earth." This is surely an echo of Ps. 37.11, which promises that the meek will inherit the earth (or the land) and experience peace. This saying in Mt. 5.5 may be an echo of Isa. 61.7: "Instead of their shame my people will receive a double portion, and instead of disgrace they will rejoice in their inheritance; and so they will inherit a double portion *in their land*, and everlasting joy will be theirs."

In my view, several of Jesus' beatitudes seem to be drawn from Isa. 61, which, not incidentally, Jesus also draws from, according to Lk. 4, in his inaugural sermon. It is worth noting that Jesus sees moral prerequisites for inheriting. It is the meek, not all Israel, who are said to inherit here, which reminds us of some of Paul's future Dominion sayings. Does Jesus say any more about Israel and the eschatological future? Mt. 8.11–12/Lk. 13.28–29 immediately comes to mind. The concept of a messianic banquet of some sort was widespread in early Judaism and was based in the OT itself (Isa. 25.6–7; 65.13–14; Ezek. 39.17–20; 1 En. 62.14; 2 Bar. 29.4; 4 Ez. 6.49ff.; 2 En. 42.5), and in fact multiple texts in the Jesus tradition seem to refer to it besides the one we have just mentioned (Mk. 14.25: "drink it anew in the Dominion"; Lk. 14.15 2: "blessed is the one who will eat at the feast in the Dominion"; Mt. 22.2–14: the parable of the royal banquet). Mt. 8.11/Lk. 13.28–29 says "many will come from the east and the west and sit at table with Abraham, Isaac, and Jacob in the Dominion of God, but you will be thrown into outer darkness. There people will weep and gnash their teeth" (see 2 Esd. 1.38–40).

What do we deduce from this saying? First of all, of course, Jesus expects the actual patriarchs to be present, presumably after the resurrection of the righteous, at this messianic banquet. This shows that Jesus had no interest in replacing the Israelite religion with some non-Jewish form of religion. It was Jews who had been promised a place in the Dominion, and Jesus foresaw at least some being present then and there. Secondly, this saying in all likelihood refers to the inclusion not just of Diaspora Jews, but also of some Gentiles at this meal (on the Gentiles streaming to Zion see above and cf. Test. Ben. 9.2; Ps. Sol. 17.31). The shocking aspect of this saying is the displacement motif – some Jews will be displaced by some Gentiles at the banquet, if the Jews do not repent and respond more appropriately to Jesus' ministry.

Now it must be said that envisioning table fellowship of Jews and Gentiles at all in this fashion probably shows something about how radical Jesus' views were about the issue of food and dining regulations (see Mk. 7.15 and the Markan commentary in v. 19). We might want to consider the parable of the wild mustard bush (Mk. 7.24–30), which with its reference to birds nesting once the bush was fully grown probably alludes to Gentiles getting in on the party.

While Jesus did not initiate a mission to Gentiles during his ministry, he does foresee their participation in the Dominion and so we may assume that Mk. 13.10; 14.9 and Mt. 28.19a tell us something about what he wanted his community to do after the time of his ministry when it came to "the nations." Was Jesus implying something important when he staged his important temple action in the court of the Gentiles itself, for example suggesting that they belonged there with God's Jewish people? Probably so.

And So?

If we sum up what we have learned, it appears that both Jesus and Paul foresaw a future for Israel and believed Gentiles would be included in the final salvation God had in mind for his people. Neither proclaimed a complete replacement of Judaism by some other and non-Jewish form of religion. Gentiles were to be grafted into the Jewish people of God. Notice how Paul in Rom. 15.8 affirms that Christ (like Peter later) became a servant of the circumcised to confirm the promises of God to the patriarchs. The historical Jesus did indeed direct his ministry to Israel, whom he called the lost sheep of Israel, which might refer to all Israel, or perhaps the least, last, and lost amongst Israel.

Both Jesus and Paul agonized over the negative response of their fellow Jews to the good news Jesus and his followers proclaimed, and both affirmed Israel's first claim on the promises God had made to Israel. While Paul does not really refer directly to God fulfilling a territorial promise, Jesus probably does. Of course, Paul spent his ministry mostly focusing on Gentiles, whereas Jesus almost never left the Holy Land and focused on his fellow Jews. But it is notable that both Jesus and Paul seem to have defined true Israel on the basis of a family of faith and a doing the will of God concept. Bearing in mind their critiques of Torah and temple, nevertheless neither one of them ever spoke of Israel being replaced by a church, or about God ever having more than one people of God at any point in human history. The true Israel was simply the continuation of the previous true Israel of God, based on some sort of righteous remnant concept. Presumably, Paul saw Jewish Christians as that remnant.

But both Jesus and Paul had a radical vision of how that true Israel should believe and behave. Neither saw the continuation of the Mosaic covenant as the way things should go. Rather, God's eschatological saving activity was breaking into human history, and it was time for a new covenantal relationship between God and his people. This would involve a fresh vision of how things would look like going forward, and one could say that perhaps Paul, better than others, caught the radical character of Jesus' vision of the eschatological family of faith and its implications, especially for Gentiles. But of course, Paul picks up the ball and runs with it in directions Jesus never mentioned or alluded to. Nevertheless, there is a compatibility in their visions of the New Covenant, especially when one takes into account the difference between Jesus' and Paul's *Sitz im Leben* (one entirely Jewish, the other apparently mostly Gentile), and if one also takes into account the difference between what Jesus says to his own disciples, and what he says in public discourse with others. Both of them also have a theology of election or chosenness when it comes to God's people and we need to come to grips with that in the next chapter.

11

The Election Results[*]

God is sovereign and has destined all things from before the foundations of the universe.
He does not sit around in heaven awaiting the election results.
Meredith Kline[1]

If there is indeed a God who covenants with a particular group of human beings, this inherently raises the question of the nature of the "chosenness" of those people, and why they are chosen – to what ends? As we have already noted, certainly one of the consistent themes of the Bible is that the God of the Bible is an Almighty God. When the discussion turns to the issue of "election" or God's chosen people, the issue is not whether God is powerful enough to determine the outcome of all things great and small, from the motion of an atom to the largest decision a human will make, or from the way the universe evolves to the way that human history writ large progresses. *Of course*, the only living God who is Almighty could determine or predetermine everything in various ways.

The question is not what is *possible* for the biblical God but rather, "Does the Bible say or imply that God *exercises* his sovereignty or almighty power in such a way that the power of contrary choice, or freedom of choice is ruled out for every human or other supernatural being in the universe? Is whatever happens, God's will? And how exactly does God's will come into play, when it comes to the salvation of fallen human beings?"

These questions become especially pressing when it is recognized that all is not right with the world, that sin and evil exist, indeed there is even such a thing as the Evil One, if one takes seriously what various NT writers say about Satan. The recognition, present throughout the Bible already from Gen. 2–3 right through to the Book of Revelation, of the existence of violations of God's will, called sin, and malevolency even of a cosmic sort, the old problem of *theodicy*, leads to question about the nature of God's sovereignty. Even

---

[*] This chapter began life as a dialogue with Chad Thornhill about his fine book *The Chosen People* which appeared in another form on my Patheos blog from December 14 to December 29, 2015. Some of that material is used here with the kind permission of Chad.

[1] This is the gist of a dictum I heard over and over again in Kline's fascinating lectures on the OT at Gordon-Conwell Theological Seminary between 1974 and 1977. I owe him a great debt, as should be obvious from all the discussions about covenant and the nature of covenants in this study. We simply disagreed on how God exercises his sovereignty and what election amounts to.

creation itself seems to be suffering from a curse, or as Paul was to put it in Rom. 8, it has been subjected to futility, yearning for the day of its own liberation.

These dilemmas of course are not really a problem for polytheists, because they can predicate good coming from one deity and evil from another. That distinction will not work in a monotheistic system of thought. But if God is almighty and also all good, how and why is there even evil or sin in the world? This question is especially pressing in an Augustinian or Calvinistic or Lutheran system of thought where absolute divine predetermination is a major feature of the theological worldview. Amazingly, some have even suggested we just revise our views of the biblical God and accept that God is the author of both good and evil. After all, doesn't Isa. 45.7 say: "I form the light and create darkness, I bring prosperity and create disaster; I, the LORD, do all these things"?

These sorts of questions need to be properly framed if we are talking about biblical theology, and not later Augustinian theology, or Lutheran theology, or Calvinistic theology and so on. Too often, the later theologies of Catholic, Orthodox, Reformed, and even Wesleyan theologians have been read back into the Bible and biblical theology in unhelpful ways. The sin of anachronism is with us always in such discussions, sadly. And what can further bedevil these discussions is the failure to read the biblical texts in a way congenial to their original contexts.

In this case, I am thinking of the problem of reading the Bible with late Western individualistic eyes, when in fact corporate or group identity was the primary thing in antiquity and individual identity was secondary. There could be, for instance, a group of people chosen by God for particular tasks in human history, without there being any implications whatsoever about the salvation of particular individuals within the group. Indeed, there could even be individuals anointed and chosen by God for specific purposes, without any implications that *that* person is a "saved" individual, or even that that person is a monotheist! Consider what Isaiah tells us God said about "Cyrus my anointed one" (Isa. 45.1)! Clearly, chosenness, election, anointing in the Bible are more complex ideas than we might think on first glance.

Take for instance the fact that in the OT what the term *salvation* even means is not really fully identical with what it means in the NT (i.e. "believe on the Lord Jesus Christ and you will be saved"). The temptation to over-read the OT ideas about election, chosenness, salvation in the light of similar NT ideas, as if they were simply identical with the NT ideas about such things, has too often been a temptation succumbed to, rather than resisted. Doing this, however, ignores not only the progressive nature of biblical revelation and salvation history, it also ignores the considerable distance and difference between worldviews now and then. So, it will be appropriate for us to proceed with caution in discussing these controversial matters.

As a final preliminary remark, I want to warn against two tendencies too often present in these sorts of discussions – the over-spiritualizing of the NT discussions of "salvation" and the over-materializing of the OT discussions of the same topic. What I mean by this, for example, is that the OT does indeed use the language of redemption and salvation to talk about God rescuing his people from literal bondage in Egypt, but we must beware of thinking that *that* language has no spiritual dimensions to it. The rescue, after all, is in order to further the spiritual relationship God has with his chosen people.

There is plenty of grace and spirituality in the OT relationship between God and his people. And at the other end of the canon, the language of salvation in the NT, and especially in the Gospels, can often refer to literal rescue, or healing, or ordinary help, or redemption from literal slavery, as well as what Christians call the new birth or the new creation or being born again. But there is this difference. While the OT does talk about God's people having remarkable religious experiences from time to time (see e.g. Isa. 6 or Ezek. 1, or the story of Jacob wrestling with the angel), what it does *not* really discuss in the NT sense of the term is *conversion*, from one religion to another by a Hebrew or Jew. Perhaps we could talk about Ruth *converting to Yahwism*, but by and large conversion is not a topic in the OT – change and improvement, yes; conversion to the worship and service of a new deity, no.[2]

To some degree one can attribute this difference to the fact that the NT has a strong focus on the evangelism of Gentiles, who indeed would have to dramatically change their religious orientation to join Jews in the worship of the biblical God. But then what does one do with Jesus' demand that pious old Nicodemus be "born again," or with St. Paul's testimony that he was flattened on Damascus Road and thereafter became a Jesus worshipper?

Conversion for a Gentile seems easier to understand, but what does it mean for a Jew to say "if anyone is in Christ Jesus he or she already is a new creature ..."? These sorts of questions, and the related issues of election and chosenness, must be explored in this chapter. I will be working backwards through these ideas, starting with the NT, where the more complex issues are raised, and then assessing what we may say about the OT material.

Election, Second Temple Judaism, and Paul

In my view one of the more important studies in recent years on the whole subject of election and the chosen people of God is Thornhill's in his monograph *The Chosen People*. What follows here is an edited version of some of the essential parts of the discussion he and I had on my Pantheos blog.

BEN: In a detailed study of salvation language in the OT, followed by salvation language in Luke-Acts (see the Appendix to my Acts commentary), I pointed out that salvation in those contexts largely refers to rescue, or healing, or ransoming out of bondage, and does not refer to the later Christian notion of salvation from all sins and the gift of everlasting life. Indeed, the OT says precious little about going to heaven, or a positive afterlife beyond Sheol or "being gathered to one's ancestors." Only in very late material, such as Dan. 12.1–3, do we begin to hear about actual bodily resurrection as a future for the believers. This led to my conclusion that while we hear a good deal about God electing a chosen people in the OT, and even picking non-chosen ones like Pharaoh or Cyrus for a special role in human history, that this seems to have very little to do with the salvation of particular individuals as understood in Christian sources including the NT. How would you assess this suggestion?

CHAD: Yes, I think that makes good sense of the OT data. The soteriological language used in the NT in a broader, more spiritual sense, tends to be used in a more narrow, almost strictly physical, sense in the OT. The exception would be the developments you note in the later prophetic literature,

---

[2] Even in the case of Namaan it appears he wants to add Yahweh to his buffet of deities, although his asking the prophet for permission to continue to go to a pagan temple with his ruler may suggest otherwise.

which I think begins to take shape with more clarity in Isaiah, Jeremiah, and Ezekiel, and is certainly most clearly developed in Daniel. The rescue envisioned throughout the OT is typically either the rescue of an individual from their oppressors (e.g. David), the rescue of Israel from its captors, or some other form of physical delivery, such as healing.

Passages which are often read as anticipating spiritual salvation or eternal life in other places in the OT seem to me to be drawn more from Christian assumptions than from the OT contexts themselves. What I think is interesting about how the NT develops this, is that Christian interpreters have historically focused almost exclusively on the spiritual aspect, while neglecting the physical dimension of salvation. This does not mean, of course, that God always delivers Christians from harm (nor did he always deliver Israelites), but I think it does mean a more complete view of salvation in the NT also takes into account the restorative dimensions of salvation, where the restoration and transformation of the whole person is in various ways in view.

BEN:　Have you had the occasion to read John Barclay's landmark book *Paul and the Gift*? It would seem that in various ways it supports some of your major theses.[3]

CHAD:　I think his suggestion that grace carries with it expectations of behavior or obedience is correct, and it seems to me this flows out of both what he argues concerning the nature of gifts in the ancient world as well as how *pistis* language is used in various places throughout the NT, though particularly in Paul. My book will focus more on the latter than on Paul's understanding of divine grace, but I am of course encouraged that Barclay's work develops something complementary.

BEN:　On p. 20 n. 21 you suggest that we should see that God's commitment to the covenant is unconditional, but from the human side of the equation it is conditional depending on how Israel relates to the covenant. The condition is Israel's willingness to abide within the covenant's demands. The question this raises for me is not the conditional nature of the Israel side of things, but whether we ought to be talking about covenant singular, or rather covenants plural, as Paul does in Gal. 4 and Rom. 9, and whether there are differences between the various covenants between God and his people. Are you assuming the "one covenant being renewed again and again in various administrations" model of covenant theology?

CHAD:　I would say there are distinctions between the various covenants, and of course different biblical scholars count the number of covenants differently. I was quite impressed a few years back by a presentation from Dan Block entitled "Covenance" at an annual ETS session. Block's argument, if I recall correctly, was that the Abrahamic, Mosaic, and new covenants should be viewed as a single line of covenants which clarify and/or renew, but do not necessarily replace or override the earlier versions. The Noahic and Davidic covenants (and possibly others which might be counted separately) are distinct from these. Paul's discussions typically focus upon the Abrahamic/Mosaic/new covenant(s), and though there are differences between them, I think Block's suggestion that they stand in a single linear path makes good sense. So in a sense, yes, I would see these as one covenant being renewed over time (so not including Noahic, Davidic, etc.), though there is both a sense of continuity, and discontinuity, as to how the new covenant develops out of these. In terms of the conditional nature of the covenant on Israel's part and the unconditional divine commitment to it, works like Jubilees and Pseudo-Philo, and even the sectarian literature at Qumran, develop this in some pretty compelling ways and I think subsequently reveal how Jews during the period largely would have understood the covenantal arrangement(s).

BEN:　I must say, I don't agree with Dan Block and the notion of one covenant in various administrations, but more on that in a minute. You adopt the method called speech-act theory. Explain briefly the assumptions and approach of this method, and how it can help the discussion of election.

CHAD:　I would first want to clarify that speech-act theory is an aspect of my method which I integrate in ways similar to how Mark Adam Elliott, in his *Survivors of Israel*, implements it.[4] Speech-act

---

[3] For a detailed discussion of *Paul and the Gift*, see below.

[4] M. A. Elliott, *The Survivors of Israel: A Reconsideration of the Theology of Pre-Christian Judaism* (Grand Rapids, MI: William B. Eerdmans, 2000).

theory goes back to J. L. Austin and recognizes that utterances operate on several levels. It typically recognizes three levels to an utterance: the locution (the utterance itself), the illocution (the intended significance of the utterance), and the perlocution (the effect or intended effect produced by the utterance). In terms of how this relates to interpretation, it recognizes that texts don't just say something (i.e. convey information), but they also *do* something (i.e. create intended responses for their readers). So, when accounting for the socio-historical context of a text, I think a part of our interpretive considerations should be what the text was intended to do, not just what we think it meant.

Election language, for example, in both Pauline and Jewish literature, at times is utilized in order to encourage or assure the hearers of their position with God's people (e.g. Rom. 8.28ff.), especially when the hearers are currently facing persecution. At other times, it is used to serve as a warning against succumbing to certain societal pressures (e.g. 2 Thess. 2). How we understand the language then, in my view, should seek to understand the intended effects of the communication in addition to the other contextual factors (social, historical, cultural, lexical, grammatical, etc.) involved in interpretation.

BEN: While I recognize the need to study early Jewish documents from just prior to the time of Paul's writings, and the dangers of focusing on later post-70 Jewish works, I am a little puzzled there isn't a chapter in this book summarizing what the OT says about election and salvation, especially since it is the OT that Paul cites again and again in Rom. 9–11 when he focuses on this subject. Is there a reason for this lacuna?

CHAD: Yes, the reason is primarily that I didn't have a long enough word count! The OT background to the NT is, of course, immensely important. There has been quite a bit of good work developing what the OT says about election. Most scholarly treatments of that material end up viewing divine election in the OT as a primarily collective/national idea. What I found in my research was that a focused discussion of how this develops and/or shifts in the Second Temple period was largely lacking. There were, of course, those who had examined it in relation to other aspects of Second Temple thought, but none that had done so specifically with the intent of seeing how the Second Temple framework relates to the NT, or Paul's writings. There has also been some very good work lately on Paul's use of the OT, particularly in Rom. 9–11 (Brian Abasciano, for example, has been developing this in great detail), so I didn't see any particularly unique contributions I could bring in that area. Both of those areas (OT theology and use of OT in the NT) are essential to understanding the NT but were not the "gap" in Pauline discussions I was seeking to fill.

BEN: One of the things that surprised me about your response about the covenants is that it does not reflect the work of various OT scholars, such as Meredith Kline, who made quite clear how similar the OT covenants, in particular the Mosaic one, were to ANE king–subject or lord–vassal treaties. By this I mean that when a covenant was broken, and especially when it was flagrantly broken, and repeatedly broken, then the lord, in this case Yahweh, simply enacts the curse sanctions that are part of the covenant, and *that covenant is over*. The ruler may or may not choose to have a new covenant with the subjects, but if he does it is emphatically not a renewal of the previous covenant. Rather, it is a new covenant entirely, a new contract, in which the ruler may choose to have some of the same stipulations in it as in the previous one. So, I am dubious about the notion of "one covenant in several administrations" even if applied just to the Abrahamic, Mosaic, and new covenants. There is little doubt in my mind that the Israelites broke the Mosaic covenant to pieces, and repeatedly, and God sent them off to exile, both the northern and southern tribes, which was the implementation of the curse sanctions. Thus, while I agree with your point about God's unconditional commitment to a people, this does not imply a commitment that involves relating to them on the basis of one covenant in various administrations. Indeed, it shows the graciousness of God's character that he is willing to start over with a new contract in Jesus. I thus find the suggestion of Block unappealing as it ignores the ANE analogies. How would you respond?

CHAD: I suppose I would begin by recognizing that we find throughout the OT a remnant, however small, of those who are faithful to the covenant. Even if the prophets themselves are the only faithful ones remaining, there still remains a portion of the people who continue in the covenant. It is still possible, of course, to view the covenant with the nation as broken based upon the majority having utterly disobeyed the stipulations. The covenant curses also certainly play a part in how we understand what is going on with Israel at various points in the OT, and N. T. Wright, in particular, has taken up consideration of this and placed it in his larger interpretive narrative for what the NT authors think is going on with Jesus' ministry and death and resurrection.

The new covenant, even in Jer. 31, is envisioned as a "new" thing and it is clear in the context that the prophet understands that Israel has broken the covenant. There is, however, and I think this was part of Block's point and where I would push back, still continuity in that the Law of God will be put in the people's hearts. This is not, in Jeremiah, anticipated as a new Law with new stipulations, so in that sense, though there is a qualitative difference between the Mosaic covenant and the new covenant in Jeremiah, there remains continuity with Israel being God's people and following God's Law. The question, of course, then becomes how the NT writers appropriate that material. It seems to me that the discontinuity tends to be overemphasized, so I would be inclined to say that the NT writers understood the new covenant as still bearing a good deal of continuity with what Jeremiah envisioned, though obviously with some new angles as well. So, while I would recognize the discontinuity (i.e. there is something "new" about it), and certainly the failure of Israel to faithfully follow God on the whole, I think we should also recognize the way in which the new covenant is framed as being in some sense a continuation of God's previous relationship with Israel which has been now expanded to the Gentiles.

BEN: And I would say that what you are seeing in the OT and NT is not an ongoing covenant, but the consistent character of God being revealed through several covenants and through thick and thin. God is faithful and consistent to his own just and merciful, righteous and compassionate character. In your second chapter, you say that in early Jewish literature, *elect status is linked to the character and quality of the individual and their faithfulness, rather than to some soteriological status (i.e. of being saved).* Could you unpack this notion a bit more for us?

CHAD: In the second chapter I focus primarily upon examining the various ways in which individuals, usually named and usually prominent figures in Israel's history, are described in some of these election-focused passages. What I find remarkable is that *never* is there an indication that what the Jewish authors *mean* by "elect" when talking about these individuals is "chosen by God for eschatological salvation." Rather, the clear emphasis is either upon God's choice of an individual for a particular task or role (e.g. Aaron as priest or David as king) or upon the character of the individual, or sometimes both. In the case of the latter, election language seems to primarily take on the meaning of "excellent" (which is in the range of meaning for the word group) and is used in some cases as largely synonymous with terms like "holy" or "faithful" as a means of piling on the character description.

BEN: You begin your discussion with Sirach, and show that when the author in fact comments on the basis of election for Moses, it is described as happening in connection with his character – his meekness and faithfulness. This seems quite similar to what we hear elsewhere in Jewish literature about Abraham being credited with righteousness because he faithfully was prepared to sacrifice his son Isaac (reading the Abraham story backwards from the Akedah to his call). You cite S. Grindheim (on p. 30) approvingly when he says "divine election [is] based on the ethical and religious quality of the elect." I would see this as exceedingly important because I've presented in *Jesus the Sage* considerable data to show the influence of Sirach not only on Jesus but also on James, his brother, as well. What is even more important is that Jesus ben Sira, while reflecting clearly a theology of election, reveals no noticeable theology of the afterlife! In other words, he does not connect election with individual salvation in the hereafter, whether by life in heaven or resurrection. Say more about your reading of this data, and the relevance you see it having in helping us interpret the NT data.

CHAD: Sirach has always been one of my favorite Second Temple texts for so many of the interesting developments which it creates as well as for ways it appears to influence the NT writers and, as you suggest, possibly Jesus himself. There are a few passages from ben Sira relevant to the topic, but the highlight is probably 44–50 and the hymn of the fathers. Here God's choosing of Moses, for example, is preceded by the author's description of Moses' character. The movement then is from character to choice, rather than vice versa. This pattern is reflected in numerous other places as well. Again, it seems the key significance lies in the fact that there is no soteriological linking with this terminology and the character traits precede God's "choice." For these individuals, to be "elect" is to be of excellent character and/or selected for a particular role. In terms of the NT, I think it is important that first we resist the temptation to see this as some sort of Pelagian arrangement in the minds of these Jewish authors, since service, not soteriology, is what is in view. Likewise, when we find this kind of language applied to individuals in contexts similar to what we find here, we must also resist the temptation to read some sort of predetermined soteriological arrangement into the terminology when that is clearly *not* what these Jewish authors meant in their writings as it related to God choosing particular individuals.

BEN:　In your discussion of the non-canonical "Davidic" psalms you point out how the phrase "chosen one" parallels the phrase "holy one" and this status becomes the basis for a plea for salvation, or in this case rescue. This suggests to me that the author or authors saw election as one thing, and salvation as another. Am I right? And indeed, as you say, it appears that one sees oneself as chosen on the basis that one is upright or holy. It is because David is pious and pure of heart that he is viewed as "a man after my own heart." Yes? David is chosen not because of some inscrutable predetermined will of God, but because God viewed him as the right man for the job? Right?

CHAD:　In the "Additional Psalms of David," I think the psalmist is largely following the pattern we find in the OT, where salvation is primarily from physical danger rather than from sin or eschatological judgment. David's plea in these psalms for deliverance seems to rest on the office which he held, and thus if God did not deliver his "elect one," that is, his chosen ruler over Israel, the success of the Davidic kingdom will be hindered or derailed. Since David's role is divinely sanctioned, for David to be destroyed means for God's purposes to be thwarted. It seems clear, as you note, in these psalms that David is the "right man" based upon his character, which is the impetus for God's choice of him for the job. Again, the election language applied to David here individually is clearly character- and role-oriented.

BEN:　The material in 1 Enoch seems to further associate being chosen with being righteous, and obeying God's law. It involves corporate election, and the term "chosen," as G. Nickelsburg stresses, is particularly applied to the righteous remnant who keep the covenant. In other words, E. P. Sanders, at points, in straining to show that "being chosen" is purely a matter of God's gracious favor, and not a matter of God knowing something about the chosen, has "over-egged" the pudding, as the British would say. In fact, texts like 1 Enoch say both things. God's choice is gracious, but the chosen are the righteous, the obedient, in the end. Comment?

CHAD:　In 1 Enoch, we move into a slightly different situation since there is eschatological salvation envisioned in the book. There is a sense, then, in which we could say the "elect" are the "saved," if we want to use those terms, but there is no indication in the book that election means a pre-temporal choice by God for these individuals to be delivered. The combination of the election terminology in the book with terms like "righteous" and "holy" seems to again, as Nickelsburg notes, emphasize the quality of the community. Sanders tilts the equation too far in the divine agency side of the equation for most of the Jewish literature he interacts with, ignoring, I think, often the counter-indications in those texts which suggest that obedience and some conditional situation is in view. I focus more on the specifics of that in later chapters, but I do find there to be quite a bit of odd and unnecessary tension between the divine–human situation in terms of how Sanders understands what is going on in these texts.

BEN:　As you point out, both in the OT and in early Jewish sources the focus of the election language is on being chosen for a particular task or function, like "my servant Cyrus," which has nothing to do with that particular individual's salvation (in the Christian sense of the term). With this sort of Jewish precedent, why do you think it is that Christian readers of Paul have often simply assumed that election necessarily has to do with salvation, rather than function, purpose, or task?

CHAD:　As I discuss later, I think there is a sense in which election *is* connected to soteriology, but it cannot be reduced to it and should not be seen as operating on the individual level as a soteriological activity. *There are simply no examples of language used in Second Temple sources which understand God to be choosing individuals for eschatological salvation.* [And I would add, there are no texts in the OT either about God choosing particular individuals for eschatological salvation, if by that one means a choice not grounded in something about the chosen one. So, for instance, in Dan. 12.1–3 it is the righteous who get the good resurrection.] There are lots of examples of individuals being chosen for particular roles or tasks. So I think part of the interpretive confusion is that the terminology itself has been filled with concepts which arise in later interpretation and the historical context and original implications of the language have been largely overlooked. There are, of course, passages which lend themselves to being read as reinforcing that kind of interpretation (e.g. Rom. 8–11), and I deal with those in later chapters. *Where election language and eschatological salvation intersect, the text always has the collective in view.*[5]

BEN: I would imagine that one sort of pushback against your presentation in this book would be to say, rather dismissively, "Well, that may well be true of the use of election language in those early Jewish sources, but Paul is different." I like to say a text without a context is just a pretext for whatever you want it to mean. It appears to me that if one ignores the bearing of the early Jewish context of Paul's discourse, then one is very likely to read the text anachronistically, reading into Paul later Christian (and in this case Reformation) ideas. How do you respond to that kind of pushback and problematic reading of Paul?

CHAD: I have this conversation from time to time with my students when I suggest the necessity of approaching interpretation in conversation with the ancient thought world(s), and in particular with Jewish sources. I think this partly results from accepting too hard of a break between Judaism and Christianity within the pages of the NT. While that break certainly came more definitively later, within at least most of the NT period, and certainly for Paul, I think the evidence indicates that Christianity was understood as a Jewish sect rather than as a separate religion. The history of interpretation certainly also has something to do with this bent toward reading Paul's election language anachronistically. The greater distancing between Christians and Jews which followed in the centuries after the NT and the controversy between Augustine and Pelagius both significantly shifted how Christian interpreters approached these questions. Augustine, of course, was greatly influential on the Reformers as well, and with Protestantism taking its theological cues primarily from the Reformers, we have thus distanced ourselves both theologically as well as culturally and historically from the NT.

I think my response would be simply that if we are not situating Paul's thought in the first century as a first-century Jewish follower of Jesus, then where are we situating his thought? As you suggest, to fail to contextualize his theology in the first century matrix means that we contextualize Paul wherever we want, whether with the Reformers or within postmodern thought, etc. In my view, the only way to truly anchor the NT's teaching and avoid eisegetical understandings is to read it within the thought world of its point of origin.

BEN: Jubilees is a very interesting early Jewish text. Explain if you will the difference between what you call corporate *representation* (sometimes called federal headship – e.g. "as in Adam all die …") as opposed to the notion of corporate or group election. It would appear you have both such concepts in Jubilees, and election involves the grace of God and final salvation involves necessary obedience to the covenant (God will save the faithful). Expand on these concepts for us.

CHAD: Corporate representation is when a particular figure (such as Abraham, Jacob, Isaac, etc.) stands as a representative of a certain group to the extent that the activities or characteristics of that individual are expected of and/or projected upon the group. In the Book of Jubilees, it is most prominently Jacob who functions in this manner as a sort of microcosm of the group which the author identifies as the people of God. Jacob is thus portrayed as a paradigmatic law-keeper in that he is properly circumcised, honors his parents, does not intermarry with Gentiles, etc. Jacob's covenant status is contrasted with that of Esau, who likely represents for the author either Gentiles or apostate Jews. God's choice of Jacob and "some of his descendants" (i.e. it is not progeny alone which places one among the elect) is based upon his foreknowledge of Esau's covenant-breaking behavior.

---

[5] Unless otherwise indicated, a sentence like this in this chapter involves emphasis added by me.

The message of the book is thus that those who identify with Jacob (i.e. properly observe the Law as outlined by the author, particularly obeying commands which were Jewish distinctives) are God's people, and all others, or perhaps primarily apostate Jews, stand in the line of Esau as those under God's judgment. The other implicit message in the book is for the faithful to remain so and for the apostates to change their ways, and thus be reconciled to God and his people. This indicates that the author does not view this as a predetermined arrangement which cannot be affected by the behavior of the individual. So in a sense, this is a collective view of election, though it focuses on the collective by means of the representative. There are other ways that Jubilees indicates a corporate election scenario, such as the remark that only "some of the sons" of Jacob will be included in God's elect. Salvation in Jubilees is not simply a matter of God's grace through election, though the covenantal arrangement is indeed graciously given. Faithful obedience (though not perfection, since atonement is possible for a majority of sins) is required for God's people.

BEN: Certainly, one of the major agendas of E. P. Sanders in his landmark books, including *Paul and Palestinian Judaism*, was to make clear that early Judaism was not a religion of works righteousness, as opposed to Christianity which was a religion of grace. He seeks to demonstrate that grace is the basis of salvation in Jewish literature, to which God's people respond with covenantal nomism. It seems to me that, again and again, Sanders reads Judaism in light of the later Christian theology of salvation by grace through faith, often neglecting the evidence that while Judaism was certainly not a graceless religion, nevertheless, there are numerous texts which suggests that God chooses and rewards the righteous, by which is meant those who keep the covenant, whereas the damned are the wicked like Esau, or those who keep breaking the covenant. Say more about where you see Sanders getting the variety of views in early Judaism wrong. For example, in Jubilees election seems to be: (1) corporate (happening within Jacob/Israel) and (2) it is tied not to physical descent as the deciding factor but is contingent on righteousness or religious purity.

CHAD: Yes, Judaism certainly does sound very Protestant in many of Sanders' descriptions. I think it is clear that Jubilees views election as corporate and conditional. I argue in the book that I think this is by and large the way most Jews, as represented in the extant literature, understood election. The few exceptions do not move away from this framework, but rather are ambiguous in their descriptions. With Jubilees in particular, Sanders puts quite a bit of weight upon 1.17–29, which he sees as envisioning a national future restoration of Israel, and thus the salvation of all (or at least nearly all) Jews. In my view, this ignores or misconstrues the major thrust of the book, which warns the Jewish people against the judgment which will result from their disobedience.

I think the more likely scenario, as Mark Adam Elliott has argued, is that most Jewish writers, and here in particular the author of Jubilees, understood the faithful to be in the minority of Jews, and thus judgment to be in the present upon most of the Jewish people. Thus, all the warnings and exhortations to obedience which occur throughout the literature are seeking to point the unfaithful back toward obedience to the covenant stipulations. This does not mean we should view Judaism as a works-salvation religion, any more than we should view Christianity as a works-salvation religion. In both cases, the offer of salvation is graciously extended by God alone, not earned meritoriously through "good works," but committing oneself to the salvific arrangement (i.e. the covenant) entails obligations on the part of God's people. Christianity has its own "do's and don'ts," and to ignore how that is framed in the NT, just as to ignore the situation in Judaism, is to import a theology foreign to it.

BEN: It has always surprised me how NT scholars have frequently neglected the insights one can gain from a work like the Parables of Enoch, where we see the messianic figure called the Righteous One = the Elect One = the Son of Man, and his people likewise are the elect ones precisely because they are the righteous ones. Talk to us about the insights for understanding the NT theology of election, and equally importantly NT Christology, from a work such as this or even a work like the Testament of the Twelve Patriarchs. How is this material relevant to understanding both Jesus and Paul in the NT?

CHAD: 1 Enoch is another fascinating piece of Jewish literature. In particular, the Son of Man figure, which occurs in a portion of the work most scholars date prior to the NT, has some interesting parallels with Jesus' Son of Man language in the Gospels. This is due in part, of course, to both of these traditions drawing upon the Dan. 7 Son of Man material. The Son of Man figure in Dan. 7 is given authority to rule and is served by the nations, and thus is presented as somewhat of an exalted figure. In 1 Enoch, there is a very close identification between this "Son of Man" figure (who is also called "the Righteous One," "the Elect One," and the "Before Time") and the elect (i.e. the people of God). The judgment in this portion of 1 Enoch is focused upon the unrighteous rulers who are oppressing the people. The "Son of Man" secures the victory of God for his people and vindicates them before these rulers and the world. The Son of Man also acts as a light to the nations and is somehow a catalyst for repentance for the unrighteous before the final judgment, when the wicked are destroyed. The conditional nature is thus reinforced in Enoch's vision, and the fate of the elect ones is closely associated with this Son of Man figure.

The Testaments also provide some important insights into Jewish Messianic scenarios. As is sometimes thought of the Qumran materials, the Testaments at times seem to indicate the presence of two Messianic figures, Levi and Judah (i.e. a priestly messiah and a ruler messiah). Sometimes the priestly messiah is prominent in the Testaments, and at other times it is the ruler messiah who takes center stage. As it relates to election, there is a possibility that Levi and Judah also act as sort of corporate representatives of the elect people in the Testaments who are to be emulated, though this is not as clear as what we find in Jubilees. The emphasis on the righteous character of the elect, though not reinforcing specific legal requirements as Jubilees does, also points to the conditional nature of election for the author of the Testaments.

BEN: You see Gal. 1.15–16 as being about God's choosing Paul for a specific task, namely being the apostle to the Gentiles, noting the echoes of the calling of prophets (Jer. 1.4–5; Isa. 49.1,5–6) in earlier Jewish literature. The language, in other words, is not, or at least not primarily, about a soteriological matter. You then stress that Rom. 16.13 connects being *chosen* with the character of the one chosen, in this case Rufus (perhaps the son of Simon of Cyrene), not as Tom Schreiner suggests, namely that election here is connected with the eternal salvation of Rufus. How you see the relationship between election and salvation if salvation is a gratuitous gift of God's grace?

CHAD: In both of these instances, election language is applied to individuals and is *not* in a context which is soteriologically charged. The only way we would end up interpreting these texts as indicating individual predestination to salvation is if we preload that into the terminology. On the collective level, speaking broadly, I would say that God has chosen to form a people who reflect the image of his Son to the world. This people are "the saved," but election and salvation should not be equated. I wouldn't see election as a part of an *ordo* as much as it is a facet of soteriology which has soteriology in broad terms (eschatological salvation but also transformation and mission) in view.

BEN: Would it be fair to say that Paul, in commenting in 1 Cor. 15 about both Christ and Adam being representative heads of a group of people, may be suggesting that if one is in Adam, one is bequeathed his legacy of sin and death, but if one is in Christ, that one derives salvation and everlasting life? My point would be that election can refer to either of these federal heads, and salvation is to be found only in connection with Christ – those who are in him are the latter fruits, who will rise to a good resurrection when he returns. In other words, there is no salvation if one is not in Christ, the Elect One, but we can certainly distinguish these two concepts. For example, Christ is the Elect One, but he is not "the saved one." He has no need of salvation in the Christian sense.

CHAD: Yes, I think it is safe to say that Paul sees Christ, however we view the Adamic condition, as the only place in which that plight can be resolved. It seems to me there is not a case to be made, or at least no plausible one, from the NT that any other arrangement was in mind. I've tried to read the "Radical New Perspective" with openness to their position, and while I think they can help clarify aspects of Paul's identity and thought, to suggest some sort of a two-ways scenario, where Jews continue keeping Torah and Christ is for Gentiles exclusively, runs roughshod over Paul's theological framework, and especially Rom. 9–11. On the other side of the equation, a universalistic understanding of Paul likewise doesn't work, based on how he understands salvation as conditioned (it is only "in Christ") and in light of his Jewish backgrounds, which always anticipates some sort of final judgment of the wicked. Christ as the "Elect One" certainly could not have the implication of Jesus as one God has predetermined to save, and this again would confirm what we see in the OT and Jewish literature as it relates to election language applied to individuals always being character- or role-oriented.

BEN: Share briefly your understanding of 2 Cor. 5.14–21 and its relevance for your thesis about election in Paul.

CHAD: I would see 2 Cor. 5.14–21 as another example of how Paul piggybacks upon the corporate representation framework found in Jewish literature and applies it to Christ. There is representation in the death of Christ in which it both affects believers on a soteriological level while also leading them to their own death. This death to self which Paul sees as a part of the Christian soteriological process I think also reflects Jesus' own understanding of discipleship as presented in Mk. 8–9. There is both, then, as J. D. G. Dunn suggests, a representative and a participatory sense to Christ's death in which he both takes on and dies the death of humanity while also calling humans to participate in his death for their salvation/transformation. As the end of the passage indicates, this reconciliation to God which they experience then becomes a part of their identity as the reconciled who bring reconciliation.

While we often make distinctions between salvation, transformation, and mission, I think the case can be made that Paul sees these as one thing. To be saved is to be transformed. To be transformed is to bring transformation to others. These are not categories which should be wedged apart but which must be seen as mutually informing. Thus, in light of this, Wright suggests that we find the essence of election theology here in this passage, since through the faithfulness of Israel's Messiah, the people of God are transformed to be agents of the kingdom and representatives of the work of God in Christ. In a sense, then, to not see election in this passage is to think of it only as a part of a soteriological *ordo* and not how it functions in its OT and Jewish context, which, though having soteriological implications, is primarily about the kind of people God's people should be.

BEN: One of the greatest difficulties to overcome in trying to get people to see the Bible with ancient rather than modern assumptions, is the problem of modern radical individualism warping the way we read the text. I remember the day I first realized that the you in Philippians was "ya'll" when Paul says "work out ya'lls salvation with fear and trembling for God is working in the midst of ya'll to will and to do." That totally changed the meaning of the text in my mind. What had been viewed as an individual quest, turned into a group project when I finally grasped what Paul was saying. To what degree would you say our individualistic and even narcissistic culture has led to repeated misreading of what early Jewish literature and the NT says about election, salvation, and even God's choosing of a people?

CHAD: I think another passage which has a strong indication of that mentality is 1 Cor. 3.16, which could be rightly translated as "Don't you all know that you all are God's people and the Spirit of God dwells among you all?" In other words, "God's Spirit lives among you as the people of God," not "God's Spirit lives in the heart of you, the individual Christian." I also like to point to what I refer to as the "communal imperatives," which are the majority of the commands, found in Paul's letters where he instructs believers to carry out spiritual directives which can only be fulfilled through relationships with others.

There are many other places, of course, from which this point could be brought out, such as the honor/shame dynamics of the ancient world, the nature of the ancient Mediterranean family dynamic, etc. Joe Hellerman's work has been helpful to me in seeing the importance of the collectivistic mindset of the ancient Mediterranean world and its implications for how we read and apply Scripture. I'm not sure in terms of history of thought when the individualistic mindset became dominant in the West, but the Enlightenment certainly I think was a factor.

I think an unintended consequence of the Reformation was also the individualization of Christianity, whereby ecclesial authority was diminished, the individual interpretation of Scripture was elevated, and the importance of the individual conscience became central. These ideas certainly are ingrained into the very essence of the American construction of society as seen in the Declaration of Independence and other early American documents. Since we swim in the waters of our culture, I think it is a natural result that we end up reading these texts in this highly individualistic way, and it is not until we understand the dramatically different way in which the ancient world was organized that we can appreciate the radically different way the early church operated in contrast to how most churches understand themselves today.

BEN:　In your third chapter, you deal at some length with the Qumran material. It seems to me always a risk to use highly sectarian literature as a litmus test of what "the average Jew" in the first century believed. This would be rather like claiming that the Branch Davidians near Waco were characteristic of what Christians in Waco believed at that time. What seems clear to me is that the Qumranites are sectarian Jews, who think "they" are the true Israel, the righteous remnant, and other Jews are not. Clearly enough election is not ethnically defined for them, at least in a broad sense, as including just any kind of Jew. Coupled with this is their theology of apostasy to explain why "not all Israel is true Israel." *You point out of course that election is a term used of a group, and the evidence of election of an individual unto personal salvation is lacking.* This is very interesting since some readers of this corpus of literature have emphasized the focus of the Qumran community being on predestination of certain persons for salvation. You also point out that there is a strong emphasis even to those within the sect that they must keep the Law to "stay in" the elect group. Right? Explain this interesting combination of ideas. In most ways, the material in 1 Enoch seems to share these sorts of perspectives as well. Yes?

CHAD:　I'm not sure I would see the Qumran community quite as far on the fringes as the Branch Davidians, but I understand the analogy. I would agree that they certainly weren't viewed as in the mainline of Jews, but I think that in many ways their beliefs reflect much of what is found in other Jewish texts of the period, which is the main thing I try to bring out. To that extent, I would argue that Jubilees, 1 Enoch, Psalms of Solomon, etc. also view their communities as the true Israel. It is not just a Qumranian phenomenon. In their soteriological structure, I think they roughly parallel most of the Jewish writers, though they seemed to have understood the size of the people of God as much smaller. So, all of these communities were in some sense exclusivistic, but they vary in how broadly that is defined. The overwhelming majority of Qumran scholars interpret the sect as deterministic in their orientation, and thus reflecting some form of soteriological predestination. Even so, I think the focus is still upon the collective, not individuals. But I also argue that the determinism of the sect has been overstated, and there are indications throughout the Qumran literature which seem to me to suggest that this is the case. I wonder at times how far Josephus' descriptions of the Jewish sects have influenced scholarly opinion on this.

I was happy to find a small handful of Qumran scholars who share in my assessment, but it certainly is not the majority. As far as the conditional elements, they were certainly present at Qumran, and probably far more strictly so than any other Jewish sect, and those who were once in the community can be expelled from it, and thus expelled from the hope of eschatological salvation if they break the covenant stipulations. To me, a corporate framework makes better sense of this than saying, as some scholars do, that this means the sect would have viewed apostates as never actually belonging to the community. That is certainly a possibility, but never one that the texts themselves spell out.

BEN:　One of the more interesting phrases to study which crops up in early Jewish literature, in the OT, in the Mishnah, and in Paul is the phrase "all Israel." I can't find a single case where it means "every last Israelite," but clearly it is a sizable group that is being referred to. And salvation, when it is mentioned (e.g. both in Paul and the Mishnah) in connection to "all Israel" refers to the salvation of the group with a list of exceptions given in the Mishnah. Corporate election or even salvation doesn't seem to rule out apostasy or an exclusion list in this literature. And yet, there is not a denial that the apostate *were* once a part of "all Israel" or "God's Chosen." Would you agree? This means that election is not unconditional and requires the appropriate response.

CHAD:　Yes, there is never an explicit denial of this in the literature, at least not that I've seen in my readings. The closest we come to it in the NT is in 1 John, where we are told "they went from us but they were not of us." [But this same document warns the whole audience strongly against committing apostasy in 1 Jn. 5.] That is certainly not consistently stated in the NT, where cases of apostasy are described. Thus, B. J. Oropeza, in his excellent three-volume study on apostasy in the NT, qualifies his approach by saying he is looking at the textual phenomenon of apostasy, not the theological framework we apply to understand it. The question of whether these individuals "were never really saved" is largely a theological question, not one which the texts directly address themselves, and so we should recognize that how we answer that question largely depends not on our exegesis (though it of course must be rooted in it), but on larger theological questions which arise from the texts.

BEN: On p. 82 you summarize some of your findings from the exploration of various selections from early Judaism as "while God preserves the chosen people as a whole, each individual's fate is determined by their keeping or forsaking the covenant." This suggests that election or salvation when it comes to the individual is conditional in nature. It not merely expects a positive response, it requires it. Yes?

CHAD: Yes. I think it is important to point out that the consequent statement which often rebuts this is that it makes salvation dependent upon humans and not upon God. I would suggest that this is a bit of a *non sequitur*. This shouldn't be equated to humans meriting salvation in some Pelagian or semi-Pelagian construal. Rather, this is the arrangement which God himself has instituted and it requires an initial human response and (for Paul, Spirit-enabled) ongoing faithfulness in the life of the believer to the covenant stipulations. There is no divide between salvation and obedience for Paul. Rather, the two must go hand in hand. Just as in Judaism, there are none in the covenant who repeatedly break the covenant stipulations and do not repent, so it is in Paul. The Western evangelical idea that the "saved" can pray a prayer and not follow God obediently is completely foreign to Judaism and NT Christianity.

BEN: Your exegesis of 2 Thess. 2.13–15 I find much more compelling than that of Greg Beale's. One of the things that I found surprising again and again when I was writing my 1–2 Thessalonians commentary and reading right through Beale was the assumption that regeneration precedes faith, and indeed causes it, rather than the new birth and faith coinciding as the sinner repents. Beale's view causes all sorts of misreading of texts like 2 Thess. 2.13–15. Unpack for the readers how your reading of that Pauline text differs from Beale's exposition. Is the basic reason you disagree with him because your reading makes better sense when Paul is compared to his Jewish contemporaries on these sorts of subjects?

CHAD: There are a number of complications about 2 Thess. 2 that make it a difficult passage, particularly in the beginning of the chapter. Concerning specifically 2.13–15, there is a text-critical issue in v. 13 (actually one of several in that verse) which raises the question as to whether the text reads the Thessalonian believers were chosen "as first-fruits for salvation" or "from the beginning for salvation." This obviously significantly changes the meaning of the text. The text-critical information seems to, from a number of directions, favor the "as first-fruits" reading, which would thus mean Paul is making more of a salvation-historical point than a point about the temporal sequence of God's choosing. There are also several indications in the text that Paul recognizes the place of the human response.

First, in the verses which precede 2.13–15, Paul seems to indicate that God's deluding of the wicked comes *after* their rejection of him (again, this is something Oropeza has done some very helpful work on). Second, I think there is sufficient ambiguity in the two genitive constructions (ἁγιασμῷ πνεύματος and πίστει ἀληθείας) to hesitate about reading this as a description of an order of salvation. Furthermore, the combination of ἁγιασμῷ and πνεύματος could be taken in several ways, such as "spiritual sanctification." Beyond the hesitations from the grammatical features, Paul seems to draw a contrast here between those who do not love the truth in 2.10 and those who trust the truth in 2.13. If that is the case, and Paul indicates in 2.10–11 that God's rejection of the wicked is because of their initial rejection of him, this makes it all the more unlikely Paul is working within a predestinarian soteriological framework here.

When this is coupled with Paul's exhortation in 2.15 for the Thessalonian believers to hold fast to the traditions which they were taught (i.e. an exhortation to perseverance with an implicit warning against apostasy, which would be unnecessary in a double predestination scenario), and the collective and conditional nature of Paul's Jewish background, it seems to me that a deterministic reading does not work well in the context. To put it in other terms, if Paul is departing significantly from Jewish election theology, it seems to me he would do so in a much clearer way which distinguishes his thought from his contemporaries. There are not in my estimation sufficiently compelling reasons which suggest that this is what Paul has done.

BEN: One of the real problems for the double predestinarian reading of texts like 2 Thess. 2.13–15 is that it then becomes difficult to understand why Paul insists that the audience must continue to hold fast to the traditions they have received or behave in particular ways lest they "fall from grace" (a Pauline phrase found in Galatians). It seems especially odd "if they could not have done other-wise." It does not appear, on the surface of things, that ethics amounts to merely the response of a grateful heart for a predetermined final salvation. It looks more to me like Paul sees the response to the Gospel, and the faithful living he exhorts the audience to, as part of the sanctification process, to which the believers themselves must contribute as they work out their salvation with fear and trembling, as God works in their midst to will and to do. Obviously, they cannot do this without God's grace working within them, but they do indeed have a choice about how they respond to and live out of that grace. In other words, Paul is not an affirmer of the P in the Calvinistic TULIP configuration, and if that is right, then the other four points also have to be reconfigured. Would you agree?

CHAD: Indeed. Some commentators will argue that Paul's warnings, implicit and explicit, against apostasy are hypothetical warnings. This has always struck me as a bit strange. Would I warn, for example, my children against something which I did not think could actually happen (e.g. be careful playing outside in case aliens try to abduct you!)? The way I discuss this with my students is that regardless of what theological framework you are using to approach Paul (i.e. "once saved always saved" or "salvation can be forfeited"), we need to hear and teach and preach Paul's warnings with the same urgency he delivers them. There are obviously major pastoral implications with this subject, and we ought not to deal haphazardly with it and engender unnecessary doubt in the life of the Christian, but neither should we in good conscience allow the Christian to continue in a mentality which does not take seriously the warnings of Scripture along with its assurances. And yes, I would fully agree, as I discuss in my sections on Romans, that the animating factor in the life of the believer which engenders faithful obedience is God's grace and the gift of the Spirit. This isn't simply, as Wright says so well, an encouragement to pull up your moral bootstraps and work your way to heaven. But neither can apathy, complacency, or indifference to the teachings of Scripture be allowed to settle in the Christian life.

BEN: I was struck by your summary in this chapter. The question that should be asked when discussing these interrelated matters of election, calling, persevering, obedience is, who are God's people, not how may an individual be saved? This is why the answer to the question is sometimes "the righteous," sometimes "those who are keeping the covenant," sometimes "those who persevere in faith despite trials," and so on. The answer has to do with the human response to the divine call, and in Christian terms, to the Gospel. You quote D. Capes *et al.*, p. 89 n. 111, effectively: "Paul always uses the term "elect" to refer to those *who are already members of God's people*. He never uses it to prescribe who is going to be saved. Instead he employs it to remind those who have answered God's call that they are members of God's covenant people." In other words, elect or chosen, etc. is after-the-fact language, language used to reassure those who have responded to the Gospel that they are truly God's people. Our modern individualism has led us to focus on the question of how can an individual be saved. Paul's election language focuses on who are God's people and how can you tell? Right?

CHAD: Exactly. The election debate for Paul and his Jewish contemporaries was not "how are God's people saved" in terms of teasing out the order of salvation, but rather "who are God's people" or "what markers or conditions identify them?" In some sense, the debate about election was a debate, as the New Perspective on Paul would put it, about the boundary-markers of God's people in Judaism. I think one of the difficulties with some NPP approaches (which I generally consider my approach to embrace when the New Perspective is defined as some form of a non-works righteousness understanding of Judaism) is they see a largely agreed-upon definition of what constituted the boundaries in Judaism. I attempt to argue that this was an inner Jewish dispute with some inherently conflicting definitions, and Paul enters into that discussion with some surprising, and some less surprising, qualifications. If election in the OT is collectively oriented (which I think many if not most would agree it is), to jump to individual predestination in the NT without some clear historical, cultural, or social contextual indications, is misguided. Once we recognize what elements constituted the inner Jewish debate, I think it becomes much clearer to see how Paul enters that discussion and does not go off on some other trajectory completely unrelated to it.

BEN: Chad in a further chapter you talk about the "limited non-nationalistic understanding of election" (p. 135) as permeating early Jewish literature. By this I take you to mean that Jews did view themselves as God's chosen people, but while their ethnic identity was a *primary* marker of who was chosen, it was not a *sufficient* one or even always an *exclusive* one (i.e. even non-Jews, if they became Torah-observant and got circumcised, could be considered part of the chosen people). By this I mean that the chosen are said to be those who are the righteous, those who obey Torah, those who keep the commandments, those who are faithful to God, and so on. In short, the election is conditional on the character of the response. Unpack your phrase "limited non-nationalistic election" a bit more.

CHAD: Yes, by this I would mean that Jews viewed themselves as God's chosen people, but being Jewish (i.e. a part of the nation or ethnic group) was not sufficient for being in God's people. This looks different for different authors or groups in terms of what conditions or markers they emphasize, but ultimately it was faithfulness to the covenant, variously defined, which marked them as God's people. The Sibylline Oracles gets closest to a more nationalistic perspective where a majority of Jews are recognized as God's people, though there are some implicit indications even there which suggest that this may be narrowed to the righteous alone. The Torah, and adherence to its instructions as variously interpreted, was what marked out God's people, not simply ethnicity or belonging to the nation. This is in contradistinction to the perspective I encountered in many NT scholars who assume that the Jewish view of election was simply nationalistic or ethnic. I don't think this sufficiently accounts for either what we see in the OT or in Second Temple literature.

BEN: You make the salient point that in texts like Gal. 2.15–3.14 Paul is focused on the locus in which salvation happens, namely "in Christ," and so the issue of identity is primary and modality is a secondary issue. So, for example "those from the circumcision" means those who belong to the circumcision party. And "those in Christ" refers to the sphere in which one's identity is found and shaped. Justification doesn't come from participation in the works of the Law, but rather through the faithfulness of Jesus. Help us to understand this concept of spheres of influence that establish one's identity and relationship with God. Explain the difference between Paul's use of *ek* (from) with Jews, and *dia* (through) with Gentiles when it comes to the issue of being part of the chosen people.

CHAD: I think Paul's prepositions in Galatians are particularly interesting and seem to follow along the lines of what K. Snodgrass (though he acknowledges the idea precedes him) terms as "spheres of influence." Paul's prepositions (in particular *ek*, *en*, *dia*, and *hypo*) in Galatians are heavily spatial in their orientation. On this view, the question Paul is answering is not "how is a person justified?" that is, "by what means?" but rather, "*where* is a person justified?" or "in what realm or sphere is the locus of justification?" S. Stowers takes the distinction Paul seems to make between *ek* and *dia* as indicating that the Jews' soteriological arrangement was already in place and Christ died to bring in the Gentiles (i.e. a "two-ways" approach). Wright suggests, and I think is more likely correct, that the distinction between the prepositions is a spatial one in the sense that the Jews were already "*in*" or "*near*," having been partakers of God's covenant promises already (though in a partial sense of course), while the Gentiles were "far off" and had to be brought "in" or "near." It seems to me that sort of explanation can make sense of why Paul uses these two prepositions here and in Romans in several places without assuming that they are just stylistic accidents. Paul thus turns the partisan language, as D. Garlington terms it, of those "from the circumcision" on its head in order to determine where their own, and more importantly where the Galatians', principle source of identity actually lies.

BEN: At a recent SBL session on Paul and Israel, one of the repeated proposals was that Paul's whole argument in Romans and Galatians is all about how Gentiles alone have come to be saved, or a part of God's people, or both. Some of the presenters went whole hog for the two peoples of God view, some for the two ways of salvation but in the end one people of God. What is wrong with these kinds of readings of Paul?

My friend Larry Hurtado critiques such approaches as follows, and I'd be curious about what you think of his rebuttal. "John Marshall (University of Toronto) contended that Paul's promotion of faith-in-Jesus was solely intended for non-Jews ('Gentiles'). So he took Romans 10.9–13, where Paul urges confession of Jesus as 'Lord' and faith that God has raised him from death, as having to do with Gentiles making these steps. Noting that Romans seems to have Gentile Jesus-followers ('Christians') as the addressees (or at least the primary/main addressees), Marshall contended that this should dispose us to read such passages as really about Gentile believers. In Marshall's view, Paul's anxiety about Israel in Romans 9–11 was over their failure to endorse and take part in a mission to Gentiles."

I don't find Marshall's case persuasive, largely because I think that the context, for example the immediate context of Rom. 10.9–13, makes it fairly clear that Paul wanted both Gentiles and Jews to join him in his faith-stance toward Jesus as Messiah and Lord. Paul's expressions of considerable anguish in Romans about the religious stance of his ancestral people (e.g., 9.1–5; 10.1–4), together with a similar view of things in 2 Cor. 3.12–4.6 (where Paul also refers to "hardened" minds and veiled eyes of "the sons of Israel"), seem to me to require us to see Paul as holding that a positive stance toward Jesus was required, the alternative being disobedience to God. That is, as I read Paul, the problem with "Israel" wasn't that they didn't join in the Gentile mission, but that they didn't recognize and confess Jesus as Messiah and Lord."

CHAD: I think Hurtado is certainly right. It is hard to read Rom. 9–11 as not addressing as a part of Paul's argument the Jewish rejection of Jesus and its consequences. For starters, the stumbling stone in Rom. 9.32, their ignoring of the "righteousness of God" (whom I take as a personification of Christ in 10.3), there being "one Lord for all" in 10.12–13, specifically of both Jews and Gentiles, and the crescendo in Rom. 11 where Paul states that they have been cut off and that they will be grafted back in if they do not persist in their *apistia*, all seem to be indications that Paul views Jesus as God's definitive self-revelation and "way," to borrow from John's terminology. Too much exegetical gymnastics is required around these issues in the text which are so clearly pointed at Jewish rejection of Jesus in order to make a two-covenants or two-peoples view work. Part of our limitation with Paul is he primarily addresses Gentile audiences in his letters, so we don't have him fully spelling out what he thinks the relationship between the Law, Jesus, and the Jewish people is. I think we have enough indications, however, in Rom. 9–11 in particular, about his concern for his people and his desire to be cut off from Christ for their sake (indicating that he himself, as a Jew, was "in Christ") to take it with confidence that Paul viewed Jesus as the universal means by which God is reconstituting humanity, both Jews and Gentiles.

BEN: If you had to characterize Paul's view of the relation of the Mosaic and the new covenant, what would you say? Is it different from his view of the relationship between the Abrahamic covenant and the new covenant, and if so, in what way? What does Paul mean by saying he died to the Law?

CHAD: To use a Facebook phrase, "it's complicated!" I'll admit this is an issue I'm still working through, though I have some basic bearings which I've found helpful in navigating some of the more difficult texts. I think understanding continuity in the structure and generally in the prescriptions of the covenants helps to ease some tensions that otherwise might come about. As I mentioned earlier, in Jeremiah's new covenant passages, no indication is given that a new Law would replace the Mosaic Law when the new covenant would come, but rather the Law would be written on their hearts.[6] It seems to me that Paul understands this to happen with the giving of the Spirit and so, Rom. 8, for example (which I examine in later chapters), joins up together the Law with the "Spirit of life." I think Paul, and Jewish Christians in general, continued to be Torah-observant, and there was some expectation for Gentile Christians to understand and fulfill the Law to some

---

[6] Here, I would disagree. There was already law or commandments or instruction (Torah) before there ever was a Mosaic covenant. And when Jeremiah talks of an "instruction" written on the heart, he need not be specifically alluding to Mosaic Law. He would be alluding to God's ethical demand that he always makes on people he has a relationship with – starting with Adam!

extent, though there were obviously specific commands from which they were exempt. For example, we don't see evidence in the NT that Jewish Christians ceased circumcising their male children, but clearly this was not required or even advisable for Gentiles. The purity regulations, festivals, Sabbath, and other aspects of Israel's Law were not understood to be "in force" for Gentiles, and we see that it is around these issues the conflicts often exist.

On the other hand, Gentiles were expected to adhere to other aspects of the Law, particularly as it relates to its sexual ethic and the love command. It seems to me it is often underplayed that Paul expects Gentiles to fulfill the Law by obeying one of its commands (love your neighbor) which he views as encapsulating the essence of all of the others. Paul binds Gentiles to other specific commands here and there in his letters, but I think what I already mentioned largely summarizes the essence of what was expected of Gentiles, which were largely commands unrelated to specific aspects of Jewish ethnic identity. The Abrahamic covenant is different in the sense that its scope is much broader and is what Paul seems to understand as the area of the OT covenants by which Gentiles are brought into God's people. This doesn't mean that the Law is unrelated to Gentiles, since the new covenant has its Law, but Gentiles are not entering into the Sinai covenant as Israel did in the OT.

Concerning Paul and dying to the Law, it is awfully hard to resist the temptation to read some of Rom. 7 into what he says here in Gal. 2. If I'm right that Paul is primarily focused on identity rather than modality in his works–Law/faith(fulness)–Christ contrast, and if table fellowship is the catalyst for what launches Paul's discussion in 2.15, it seems that he is saying in 2.17–20 something along the lines of (if I might paraphrase) "if while seeking to be justified in Christ, we share table fellowship with Gentile sinners, does being in Christ make us sinners? If I re-erect these boundaries between Jews and Gentiles which I myself have already taken part in breaking down, am I a Law-breaker? For through the Law (which could not impart life to humans) I died to the Law (its natural result apart from the Spirit) so that I might live to God through my identification with and participation in the work of Christ." I wouldn't see Paul necessarily saying here that as a result, the Law has no consequence for him or anyone. Rather, I think he is recognizing the Law's limitations and the futility of attempting to go to that realm of existence "under the Law" when the gift of the Spirit has come through being "in Christ" (cf. 3.1ff.).

BEN:　What does it mean to say that Jesus is the Elect One of God, and those are elect who belong to him?

CHAD:　Going back to the representative head notion, Jesus is the representative head of the people of God (and obviously much more than that as well). Those who are "in Christ" are being transformed into his image, so they share in his identity by being identified with him. The Christian life means a life of conformity; being conformed to the image of Jesus. Jesus is the "Chosen One" since he is God's chosen agent of redemption. This does not mean he is the "Redeemed One" or that God elected Jesus for salvation. Rather, as I argued in chapter 2, this fits into the "missional" (and "ethical") understanding of election, which is what is typically applied to individuals. The "elect" then who are "in Christ" take on that mission (and ethic) by nature of their identification with and belonging to him.

BEN:　What is the significance of translating Gal. 3.2 as "from the works of the Law" as opposed to "from the hearing of faith"? Is faith contrasted here with works, or is it rather hearing that is contrasted with works?

CHAD:　I think Paul's *ek* uses continue in the line of the "spheres of influence" I mentioned above, so what he is distinguishing is still whether the primary identity marker is the Law or [Christ's] faith(fulness). Grammatically here, the parallels are between works/hearing and Law/faith. Many translations make the fundamental contrast here between believing and doing. That seems to me mistaken for a few reasons. First, hearing and faith both carry with them behavioral implications (Louw-Nida gives a possible gloss on the word for hearing here as "believing and responding to" something). I think it is clear here that Paul does not just have audible receipt of information in mind. I also think it is fair to read this in light of the earlier contrasts in Gal. 2, where the "works of the Law" contrast was with the "faith(fulness) of Christ." I think it is reasonable to assume that Paul expected his hearers to continue to carry that conceptual framework with them here just a few sentences later. I take the force of Paul's questioning here, then, as "if you received the Spirit by being 'in Christ' (i.e. upon your response to his faithfulness), will you now try to live in the realm of the Law apart from Christ and the Spirit?" In other words, if they received the Spirit, which allows them to fulfill the Law (cf. Rom. 8) apart from minding Jewish purity regulations and being circumcised, why did they think that doing these things now would add something to their status? Abraham then becomes the paramount example because he received the promises prior to being circumcised and he belonged to the right party (i.e. "the from fathers" not the "from the circumcisioners"). So Paul is essentially asking them – Why would you want to go the wrong way and put yourself at a disadvantage now?

BEN: One of the problems with the New Perspective or at least some of its advocates is trying to limit the discussion of works of the Law to boundary-markers – circumcision, Sabbath, and kosher keeping. It seems to me this is too narrow a definition of the phrase works of the Law, even if in some cases the focus is on those things "because the Judaizers are trying to get Gentiles to cross the boundary into Judaism." So, to contrast that with the notion that "the Messiah and his death and resurrection" provide the boundary for God's people now, is not quite grasping the nettle that Paul is contrasting two entire covenants, and the boundaries of the new one include far more than a Christological affirmation. How do you view these things?

CHAD: Yes, I think the limited view of works of the Law as referring only or primarily to circumcision, Sabbath, and purity regulations does not do justice to the variations within Judaism at this time. Certainly, circumcision and purity regulations are at least a part of the problem, or perhaps the majority of the problem even, in Galatians, but in Romans, Paul, while including circumcision in his discussion, seems to have a broader range of meaning in mind. This doesn't also mean Galatians doesn't necessarily, but I think it is very difficult to make the case that this is Paul's concern in Romans as well from the content of that letter alone. I take Paul's fundamental problem in Galatians to be with Gentile Christians trying to operate in the sphere of the Law (by which I mean that sphere of existence which is marked by Torah and ignores or lacks the coming of the Messiah and the gift of the Spirit) as if circumcision was somehow a prerequisite for belonging to God's people. Clearly their receipt of the Spirit is confirmation for Paul that they are already in the people of God, and so to identify themselves with the realm of the Law which is not marked by the Messiah and the Spirit is basically deadly for them. To put it another way, to act as if nothing changed with the coming of Christ and the gift of the Spirit in terms of how Gentiles become a part of God's people is to underestimate and misunderstand the magnitude of the new reality which has been inaugurated with the coming of Christ.

BEN: Our friend Scot McKnight defines faith as "the initial and continual response of trust in and obedience to Christ by a person for the purpose of acceptance with God" (p. 141 n. 164 in your book). This seems to be loading an awful lot into the word "faith." Wouldn't it be better to say that obedience flows from faith?

CHAD: I like McKnight's definition because I think it combines three elements that are loaded within the *pistis* word group itself. Now obviously in a post-James Barr world, we can't equate words with concepts, but "faith" is most clearly connected to this word group, so I think pulling our understanding from its possible range of meanings is helpful. BDAG gives three main glosses for *pistis*, which are basically: (1) faithfulness/fidelity, (2) trust, and (3) belief. Louw-Nida offers similar glosses. *I like to say these roughly equate to a behavioral dimension ("faithfulness/fidelity"), a relational dimension ("trust"), and a cognitive dimension ("belief").*

I think many evangelicals tend to emphasize the cognitive dimension and may also include the relational dimension, but the behavioral dimension ("the obedience of faith") is usually missing. McKnight, Murray Harris, Scott Hafemann, Don Garlington, and others in various ways have suggested that the full image of faith in the NT includes all three. This does not mean, of course, that every time we see *pistis*, all three glosses are present, but I think in various places we get a flavor for each as a part of what Paul understands "faith" to be. By including "obedience" or "fidelity" in the definition, this is not to say that we somehow earn our salvation, but instead it recognizes that the transformation of the believer, their "faithfulness," is not an add-on or an option, it is the essence of what salvation is about, not just getting us off the hook for our sins, but conforming us to the image of Christ.

BEN: I agree with your point on p. 173 that "works of the law" probably is not meant by Paul to refer just to the boundary-markers of Judaism (circumcision, Sabbath keeping, kosher), but is used more broadly by Paul to refer to any and all works of the Mosaic Law. I also agree that he is not talking in Rom. 3 about the inability to keep the Law perfectly. He is talking about the basis of right-standing with God under the new covenant as opposed to that basis in the Old Covenant. Right-standing is obtained by grace through faith in the faithfulness of Jesus. Yes?

CHAD: Yes, going back to the "spheres" notion in Gal. 2–3 again I think is helpful. As Paul will come to inquire in Romans, and argues in Galatians, if the Law in and of itself was sufficient to bring eschatological life, then why did Christ need to come? The Law's purpose was to both mark out God's people as distinct from their neighbors and to provide a framework for ethical living fitting of the people of God. But it was limited in what it could affect. If the "works of the Law" (variously understood by different Jewish groups in terms of what has prominence) are the realm of justification or the primary marker of God's people, then Gentiles must, in essence, become Jews to be in God's people. This is what I take Paul to mean when he says "for we reason a person to be justified by faith apart from works of the Law. Or is God for the Jews only? Or is he also for the Gentiles? Yes, also for the Gentiles!" If the Law is the defining marker, in that "sphere," so to speak, Gentiles either must become like Jews or be left out. For Paul, Jesus' faithfulness, and the initial and ongoing response of the believer to it, is the only means of identifying who the people of God actually are.

BEN: Unpack the idea on p. 174 that the reason Paul uses two different prepositions *ek pistis* for Jews, *dia pistis* for Gentiles, is that for Jews who were already in a covenant relationship with God, what has happened is covenant renewal, but for Gentiles it's a genuinely new covenant, since they enter the chosen people from outside. This seems to require you taking *ek* to mean "from within." But is there really a basis for that reading of the preposition?

CHAD: As we also see in Gal. 2, Paul's prepositions seem to be making some sort of distinction between Jews and Gentiles. If we take these prepositions spatially, there is a "nearness" which I think is indicated by *ek*, and a "farness" indicated by *dia*. This is not to say there are two different ways of salvation for Jews and Gentiles, but rather, I think somewhat in a salvation-historical sense, it recognizes they come from two different starting points. As Paul began the chapter (and also brings up in Rom. 9), the Jews had certain advantages, but those advantages in and of themselves do not constitute them being right with God (which I think most Jews, again, would have agreed with to some extent). The other option to take would be that there is no distinction intended between the prepositions, which many commentators accept. Their presence seems to be more than accidental or a mere stylistic flare to me.

BEN: What does it mean to say that Abraham is in a sense the first Gentile convert, not the first Jew, in the sense that he was declared in right-standing with God on the basis of his trust in God, and not on the basis of keeping the (later)Mosaic covenant and doing its works of the Law? Abraham was "justified" before he was circumcised and so before he kept any such Law. You interestingly suggest that perhaps Abraham becomes the parade example of how God justifies the ungodly (which ironically is also why he can be called the father of many nations, not just the forefather of Jews), and therefore there is no basis in the Abraham story for Jewish exclusivity when it comes to who counts as the people of God – right?

CHAD: There is an interesting development in some of the Second Temple literature where Abraham is portrayed as a paradigmatic Law-keeper. We see this as anachronistic since the Law wasn't yet given, but the presence of this theme in various places (e.g., Pseudo-Philo, Ben Sira, Jubilees, etc.) demonstrates the vision of many Jews of the period that Torah observance was what defined God's people, and Abraham, being the father of Israel that he was, would then necessarily need to likewise be Torah-observant. Paul turns that argument around in Rom. 4, demonstrating "from the Law" (i.e. the Pentateuch) that Abraham was considered right with God prior to his circumcision. Abraham then becomes Paul's paradigm for Gentile inclusion in the people of God apart from full Torah observance (again, circumcision is his primary focus here, but it need not necessarily be limited to that).

Paul asks in Rom. 4.9 if the divine blessings come only on the circumcised, or also on the uncircumcised. The conundrum he raises is that if the answer is on the circumcised only, then Abraham himself would have been exempt since the covenant was initiated before he was circumcised! To put it another way, if only those in the sphere of the Law are right with God, Abraham himself would be left out. As both uncircumcised and circumcised, Abraham is capable of being the father of both Jews and Gentiles.

BEN: One of the interesting dances back and forth in Ephesians is the distinction between Jews and Gentiles, with the reminder that Gentiles came into the people of God as the Johnny-come-latelys, and at the same time the stress that in Christ whatever the person's background, all are equal. Would you take Ephesians as a sort of object lesson to Gentiles to appreciate their fellow Jewish Christians and the heritage they have shared with them, while at the same time maintaining their equality in Christ, with the "middle wall of partition" that has been torn down being the Mosaic law covenant?

CHAD: Yes, I think Eph. 1–3 is largely about calling the Gentiles to remember their dependence upon Israel for the inheritance which they have received. Paul does not lay out explicitly what the issue was with this church (or churches), but I think that is a fair conclusion to draw from what he explains in those chapters. So Gentiles need to recognize the historical primacy of Israel for their own salvation, while also recognizing that now they are joint heirs and not just second-class citizens in the people of God. There would be no inclusion of the Gentiles in God's people if there first was not a covenant people.

As he demonstrates in Romans and Galatians, Paul (who I take to be the "mind" behind the letter to the Ephesians even if it is not penned from his hand) does not expect Gentiles to become Jewish. Those markers which separated Jews and Gentiles in the realm of the Law (Paul mentions only circumcision in the immediate context, but certainly there were other barriers created by the Law as well) no longer separate them in Christ. Gentiles stay Gentiles, and Jews stay Jews, just as males stay males and females stay females, but both are formed into one, unified, cooperating, equal people through the reconciliation accomplished in Christ's death.

BEN: One of the least convincing parts of Wright's argument in *Paul and the Faithfulness of God* is the attempt to say that Jesus = Israel = the church of Jew and Gentile incorporated into Jesus. Ephesians certainly does not support such a notion of Israel, where "Israelites" are clearly distinguished from Gentiles. Gentiles are indeed incorporated into the body of Christ and so into Christ, and thereby are heirs to the promises and connected to the Abrahamic covenant as in Gal. 4, but they are not integrated into the Mosaic covenant and that covenant community of non-Christian Jews. Say a bit about your vision of both the problems and the promise of Wright's aforementioned big book.

CHAD: I don't think it's easy to tie the Israel and church language together in Paul's letters to be referring to the same thing. There is a sense in which the national identity takes a back burner and the church identity comes to the fore. The way I describe it is that there is one people of God who, in the new covenant, is made up of Jews and Gentiles together in Christ. Gentiles do not become Israelites. Israel does not become the church or vice versa. Paul never makes statements which give us indications that all of these identities are completely collapsed. In terms of Wright's big Paul book, I certainly overall agree with his starting point and approach in terms of framing Paul's thought in communication with the Jewish and Greco-Roman world.

The biggest problem with Wright's big book is how big it is! I do appreciate Wright's attempt to draw together a cohesive narrative from the OT to the NT as a means of making sense of Paul and some of the larger contours of what he develops I think are helpful. Wright also focuses on Jesus as the locus of election and works with something of a participationist soteriological model, which I find overall helpful. I think in some way the symbolic representation of Jesus = Israel makes sense in certain places, but in some, if not perhaps most, places I think he tries to make the narrative a bit too smooth where it isn't obviously present at all. It seems that in some places he denies a replacement perspective in what he is articulating, while in others (such as p. 831), it seems as if that is precisely what he is articulating. This happens also with his narrative approach overall, which, again, I think is helpful in some places and feels strained in others. I found, for instance, his description of sin being located and isolated in Israel as God's purpose of the Torah in order to deal with sin through Israel's Messiah confusing (pp. 895ff.). Where Wright also sees the Torah as having a majorly negative role (cf. p. 862), I would articulate things a bit differently. I also felt his discussion of the role of the Spirit in regeneration was a bit unclear (pp. 952ff.). In some places, he uses stronger causal language to describe the Spirit's role in creating faith, and in others "inspirational" language. The lack of precision felt a little bit as if he was hedging his bets on the matter.

BEN: You finish this lengthy chapter by saying that God's people are defined around the crucified and risen Jesus and faith in him is the only boundary one has to cross to get into the people of God. You suggest that God's promise to Abraham to be a blessing to the nations could not be fulfilled any other way, in Paul's view. Say more about this Christological redefining of the boundaries between insiders and outsiders, between God's people and even other non-Christian Jews.

CHAD: I think that in a sense Paul came to understand that this redefinition of the boundaries of God's people was essential in order for a meaningful ingathering of the Gentiles to occur. The corollary of it was also, as he discusses in Rom. 9–11, a temporary Jewish rejection, which I think Paul views to ultimately be eschatologically resolved. So, as it relates to the Jew–Gentile relationship, the redefinition of boundaries ("in Christ" vs. "works of the Law") was fundamentally necessary. Beyond this, Jesus' death and resurrection accomplishes what the Law could not, in that the Law did not have a mechanism to overcome the problem of sin and death. It could not impart eschatological life even if it could lead God's people into "the good life," in the sense of their personal flourishing for the remnant who were faithful. So, Jesus' death unbinds the powers of sin and death and his resurrection and the subsequent impartation of the Spirit results in the giving of eschatological life to his people as well as their empowering to walk faithfully in covenantal relationship with God.

BEN: In chapter 5 it becomes clear that early Jews mostly thought that election was conditional, and the condition was faithfulness to the Mosaic covenant and its Law. You quote D. deSilva approvingly as follows: "fidelity to the covenant ensures peace, sin against the covenant brings punishment, and repentance and renewal of obedience leads to restoration" (p. 150). So only faithful Israelites remain in the covenant relationship and they do so by obedience, by being Torah-true, and in that sense righteous. Outside the Pauline corpus is there any evidence that "all Israel" will be saved regardless of their behavior, which is to say, is there any evidence of unconditional election of Israel with the outcome entirely determined by the Almighty, not affected by the human response? It seems clear that some of these texts even suggest that the majority of Jews will be lost.

CHAD: It seems to me there is *not* as it relates to the literature which I reviewed. My focus was specifically on materials from the Second Temple period which were primarily in and around the Judean area (with some exceptions) which pre-date Paul or roughly date to his time period. So, I can't speak definitively outside of that group of texts in terms of, say Philo or post-100 CE Jewish literature. But within that group of texts, which in my mind is the best representation we have of the nature of Jewish beliefs around the period of the NT, it seems to me the answer is a resounding no.

BEN: At one juncture in this chapter you suggest that the Jewish Sibylline Oracles may be an exception to the rule that election is conditional on a certain response. But this seems to me to be an argument from silence, namely that just because the Oracles are silent about the judging of wicked Jews does not necessarily imply that the author or authors think "all Israel will be saved." What do you think about this suggestion?

CHAD: Yes, I would say it is an exception to the extent that it is ambiguous. I don't think there are any clear indications in the Sibylline Oracles of the unconditional election of all Israel and there are some implicit indications of a conditional view of election. So, it is not an exception in that it contradicts that model but rather that it just doesn't make explicit statements one way or the other.

BEN: Was the Testament of Moses the only example of a text which seemed to clearly exclude Gentiles from God's salvation of human beings, and limit it only to some Jews?

CHAD: In my research, it was the only one which so forcefully seemed to reject any possibility for Gentile salvation. In most texts, it is clear that the Gentiles are predominantly viewed as outsiders, but we do not find other explicit statements that they are destined for damnation. In many texts, we find positive remarks about Gentiles (e.g. 2 Macc.) which I think very much leave open the possibility. In others, like the Animal Apocalypse of 1 En., we find wholesale Gentile inclusion at the eschaton. I think the OT prophetic literature itself, with its expectations of the gathering of the nations around Zion, likely influenced most Jews from being too adamant about the damnation of all Gentiles, but the Testament of Moses seems an exception to that larger pattern.

BEN: Some readers of your book, having already read Sanders' classic study *Paul and Palestinian Judaism* will be very surprised to hear there are early Jewish texts which reject the notion of unconditional election of "all Israel" and quite to the contrary affirm that a majority of God's people appear to be under his judgment, with only a righteous remnant being saved (see Psalms of Solomon, Dead Sea Scrolls, pseudo-Philo, Testament of Moses). Unless you want to call *all* of these documents sectarian in character and a-typical, it would seem that many if not most of Paul's Jewish contemporaries operated with a righteous remnant concept. And some will surely ask you – Is this different from the view or views we find in the OT itself? And why is it, do you think, that some of these apparently minimalist texts are prepared to entertain the salvation of some Gentiles, at least at the eschaton, while others are not?

CHAD: Yes, it is interesting to me that Sanders came to the conclusion he did concerning the Apocryphal and Pseudepigraphal texts. He primarily examines Ben Sira, 1 Enoch, Jubilees, Psalms of Solomon, and 4 Ezra. In my reading, each of these texts strongly evidences a more conditional understanding of the covenant, with Ben Sira perhaps being the least obvious. I think this raises some problems for Sanders' interpretation in places. It seems to me by starting with the Rabbinic material, which I would view, following J. Neusner, as less reliable depictions of Second Temple thought, that Sanders may have then taken that framework and the famous statement in M. Sanh. 10.1 that "all Israel has a share in the world to come" and applied it as the lens through which he read Second Temple Judaism. I think Sanders' critique against older views of Judaism as "works-righteousness" based rather than grace based is overall very helpful. But this is one area where I think his study does not adequately account for the data.

It is interesting as well that in M. Sanh. 10.1–3, it is said that those who deny the resurrection, those who read from heretical books, those who pronounce the tetragrammaton, Jeroboam, Ahab, and Manasseh, the spies, the wilderness generation, and idolaters, all groups which include or are predominantly Jews, do not have a share in the world to come. So even the Mishnah here portrays covenant belonging as conditional. I do think this largely meshes with how the covenant is portrayed in the OT as well, though what distinguishes it, at least in part, is the emphasis in some of these texts on certain aspects of keeping the Law as primary over and against others. Concerning the salvation of the Gentiles, many of the texts which entertain either a possible hope or a clear hope for the salvation of some or many Gentiles (though not all, since those who oppress God's people in particular are excluded) seem to me to follow the prophetic tradition of the nations being gathered to God to worship and serve him (e.g. Pss. 2.8; 22.27; 82.8; 98.2; Isa. 2.2–4; 11.10–12; 52.10; 61.11; 62.2; 66.19–20; Jer. 3.17; 16.19–21; 33.9; Ezek. 36.22–23; 37.28; Dan. 7.14; Zeph. 3.9,20; Zech. 9.10). This is met, however, within that same literature with proclamations of judgment and destruction against the nations as well. So, part of what is displayed in the Second Temple literature is either maintaining that tension between judgment and salvation as the prophetic literature does, or favoring one aspect of it, as the Testament of Moses does, by declaring the condemnation of the Gentiles.

BEN: On p. 172 you say "God displayed his 'rightness' through the faithful obedience of Jesus, even to the point of death [on a cross]." In what sense was it right for God to send his Son to a death on a cross? Do you mean this was a demonstration of God's righteous character and his judgment of sin, or do you take *dikaiosune*, as Wright tends to do, as meaning something like God's covenant faithfulness?

CHAD: I think Paul is wrestling here, similar to and as a sort of preview of Rom. 9–11, with how to understand God as still being faithful to his promises to Israel if there is large-scale Jewish rejection of the Messiah and if Gentiles are brought in, seemingly dissolving any special relationship God had with Israel. So, God's "right" action (his acting "above the bar" in a sense or acting in "redemptive charity" and "uprightness") for both Jews and Gentiles has been made manifest in the faithful life and death of the Son. I don't think construing the *dikai*-language primarily as "justice" here completely fits in the scheme Paul has set up. Being revealed "apart from the Law" I take to indicate, as a segue of sorts, that Paul is beginning to dismantle the notion that Gentile converts must be fully Torah compliant, as he begins to make more clear in 3.27ff. So, I think in a sense it could be construed as faithfulness to the covenant promises, meaning most likely the promises to Abraham, though Paul does not explicitly establish that here. If used in a non-covenantal sense, I think it would simply refer to God's upright, charitable, "above the bar" character in his dealings with fallen humanity. I would thus take the relational element in the passage as probably more at the forefront of Paul's mind based upon how he sets up this section in 3.1–8.

BEN: I must say I find Dunn's discussion of *hilasterion* unsatisfying, and at some points wrong. That word absolutely is used in wider Greek literature to refer to the assuaging of some deity's wrath, and so to propitiation. It appears to me that Dunn wants to reduce the term to mean expiation of sin, and this does not work, because one has to ask why for example in the OT the blood is applied to the contact point with God within the tabernacle, to the very horns of the altar? Sin is only expiated if a righteous God is propitiated. Say more as to why you seem to agree with Dunn (p. 172 n. 89).

CHAD: Part of the difficulty with *hilasterion* here is its limited usage in the NT (only here and in Heb. 9.5) and in the OT (only a handful of times, primarily in Exodus and Leviticus). In the OT, it is usually translated as "mercy seat" and identified with the Ark of the Covenant. The mercy seat is associated primarily with God's presence in these texts (cf. Exod. 25.21; Lev. 16.2; Num. 7.89) with the exception of the day of atonement ritual described in Lev. 16.13ff. In Lev. 16.16, it states that blood is placed on the *hilasterion* to purify the holy place because of the sins of the people. The atonement for the people appears to take place on the altar outside of the tent, not at the mercy seat, which is described in 16.17ff. So the "mercy seat" as the place of the atonement for the sins of the people doesn't seem to me to be what is described in Leviticus. Rather what happens at the mercy seat is purification, or removal of the effects of sin on the sacred space, and various OT commentators affirm that to be so.

I wouldn't deny that there are frameworks of propitiation elsewhere within the word group, but it seems to me that the *hilasterion* language from the LXX as it relates to the day of atonement is more closely related to purification than appeasement. Dunn's point, which is of course debated, is that atonement in the OT acts on sin (i.e. atonement is "for a person" or "for sin") rather than on God and suggests that is the background from which Paul is drawing. I think the closest linguistic parallel to what we find in the NT usage probably actually comes from 4 Macc. 17.22, where the seven martyrs are a *hilasterion* which prompts God to rescue Israel, which Dunn goes on to address in the section which follows. There are certainly in a sense more questions (at least for me!) than answers in this section of Romans, where Paul is mixing various metaphors together, using some unclarified language, drawing on a variety of OT themes, and bringing them all together in a very dense formulation, particularly in 3.24–26.

BEN: The discussion in chapter six about the heavenly tablets in Jubilees and their relationship to the book of life and the book of destruction is especially interesting in light of the discussion in Revelation where we have a warning that some people's names can be blotted out of the Lamb's book of [everlasting] life, contingent on behavior. It appears that we are being told that while some things seem to be foreordained, one's eternal destiny is not one of them or at least one's destiny is in part conditional based on one's behavior after one is in the book of life – would you agree?

CHAD: The majority of references in Jubilees to the heavenly tablets refer to laws which are eternally ordained along with their consequences. Beyond these occurrences, though, certain events are also said to be recorded in the heavenly tablets. Some take this to mean the author is working within an absolutely deterministic framework. In some of these instances, the text seems to indicate that it still has the legal function of the tablets in mind. In others, they act as a register of the righteous and the wicked, recording the deeds of each individual, apparently for use at the final judgment. There are also indications that these records have some fluidity, since names can be blotted out, for example, of the book of life. In other words, they do not record a pre-programmed fate for every individual, but rather are a record of the fate of each individual, which can change should their relationship to God change (e.g. should the wicked repent). So, yes, there are some events which are foreordained, but it seems to overstep the data to suggest that all of human history is thereby foreordained, including the destiny of each individual person. Beyond this, since part of the purpose of Jubilees, just as many books of the period, is to reinforce the faithful and call the wicked to repentance through warnings of judgment, this purpose seems to be defeated by an overarching, meticulous form of determinism.

BEN: I've always found it puzzling when hardline Calvinists insist on God's will being the real bottom line of the divine existence. By this I mean a lot of them seem to say that "God knows things in advance, only because he wills them in advance," otherwise his knowledge would be contingent on various external factors. What furthermore puzzles me is the notion that God's sovereignty means God can do anything that is logically possible to do, even including doing evil. I would have thought it would be better to say that: (1) God can only act in accordance with his nature or character, so by definition God cannot sin, nor can he be tempted or inclined to do so; or (2) even if it is theoretically possible that God could do evil or sin, since God has the power of contrary choice like humans do, he would never choose to do it because he has a perfect and perfectly holy nature. What I take the almightiness of God to mean in the Scriptures is that he is almighty to save, almighty to do any good thing in accord with his nature, since his will is not separate from his nature or knowledge. There are ever so many things that happen in this fallen world that God cannot be held responsible for, including, ironically, what insurers call "acts of God."

Of course, we can talk about God's permissive will, things God allows to happen, but does not necessarily condone, but at some juncture one has to have a concept of whether or not God gave beings other than himself the power of contrary choice, or whether he determined all things from before the foundations of the universe. If in fact God made space in his universe for beings other than himself to have some modicum of freedom of choice between one outcome or another, then God is not the only actor in the universe who should be held responsible for his behavior. The question then becomes – are fallen human beings *non posse non peccare*, not able not to sin, and so in the bondage to sin? I would say there are texts in the OT and NT which suggest this is so, but at the same time there are texts which suggest that by God's grace one can recover the power of contrary choice, whether by prevenient or saving grace. I wonder what your reflections are on these sorts of complex matters?

CHAD: I tend to view sovereignty through the lens of reigning since the terminology is connected. To say God is sovereign is to say that he is the ruler of the cosmos. This does not, by definition, require a meticulous form of determinism. Those who say it does are simply loading determinism into the meaning of "sovereign," where I don't think the biblical accounts require that. One of the interesting passages for me which connects to this sovereignty language is the Lord's prayer. To pray, "May your kingdom come, may your will be done, on earth as it is in the heavens," seems to recognize that not everything which is happening on earth, then or now, is God's will. In other words, it is not God's will when people disobey God's will!

I think saying that God is not the only actor is right. Humans have significant creaturely freedom (which of course does not mean that they are free to do anything they want or can think of). God is the supreme actor, but this does not mean humans have no role to play. We cannot take this, as you suggest, to mean that humans then can pull themselves from their depraved state and save themselves, or even that they have an uninfluenced path to salvation. This is part of what I found unsatisfying about Wright's language of the Spirit's role in salvation in that it seems to want to create both an influencing role and a causal role. In my view, humans do not receive the divine gift of salvation apart from the work of the Holy Spirit, which occurs through receiving the good news about Jesus. The Spirit's work does not, however, guarantee an outcome, it does not have a causative force, since the human, being drawn and prompted by the Spirit and upon hearing the truth, must ultimately respond to it. So, the work of God, both in what Christ accomplished and in the ongoing work of the Spirit through the people of God in the world, precedes any "decision" a person might make.

Salvation is truly gracious, it is generously and freely offered by God to the world, on the basis of the work of the Son, through the moving of the Spirit, but ultimately must be received and appropriated.

BEN: One of the things this chapter suggests is that the deterministic language that we find for example even in the Qumran texts has to do with the fact that God set up a moral structure to the universe such that "whatsoever one sows, that he shall [eventually] reap" if one does not repent. Put another way, sinful actions have negative consequences, and the reverse with good deeds. The idea that God has predetermined that actions have moral consequences seems to be what even some of the most deterministic texts at Qumran are really arguing for. Would you agree?

CHAD: Most scholars who study the Qumran materials have taken it as a foregone conclusion that the sect operated under an exhaustive form of determinism. The Hodayot, or "Thanksgiving Hymns," evidence this perhaps most dramatically. In 1 QH 7, for example, we read "the wicked you have created for [the time] of your wrath, from the womb you have predestined them for the day of slaughter." This seems pretty clearly a form of double predestination. The hymnist goes on, however, to write, "For they walk on a path that is not good, they reject your covenant, their soul loathes you." 1 QH 12 states that the wicked "have not chosen the path of your [heart] nor have they listened to your word." This seems to indicate that the sectarian who wrote this hymn understood there to be some place for human volition. So even in these more deterministic texts there are indications that there may be more of an interplay at work. There are petitions, for example, for God to intervene and prevent the sectarian from sin.

In the Damascus Document, we seem to find a sort of foreknowledge understanding in which God does not choose those whose evil deeds he knows ahead of time. The author also admonishes his hearers to "choose what he is pleased with and repudiate what he hates." So viewing this not as an exhaustive form of determinism, but rather as some combination of God ordaining what is good and what is evil (i.e. some pre-existing divine law or order) and knowing ahead of time the actions of the wicked or righteous, seems, at least to me, to make sense of some of the tensions we find in the Qumran literature between the more deterministic language and the presence of petitions, admonishments to choose the righteous path, and mechanisms in place to deal with apostasy from within the chosen community itself.

BEN: In the back and forth between divine action and human response, or divine determinism and human responsibility you seem to want to stress that insofar as we are talking about Paul, while he refers to both these things, we should not take him to mean "that God acts in such a unilateral manner so as to make the presence of human responsibility either illusory or meaningless" (p. 212). You add that Paul does not see God and human beings as equivalent actors in the human drama, so that their actions have the same force or efficacy. *You simply want to leave room for viable non-coerced human choice for which they can be held morally responsible – right?*

CHAD: Yes, that is exactly right. And that is the interplay which I think we also see across the spectrum of Jewish literature. While some texts (Jubilees, Qumran, 1 Enoch, etc.) emphasize the divine prerogative, they do not eliminate, at least in my view, the presence of human volition. Likewise, texts which emphasize human volition (Ben Sira, Psalms of Solomon, etc.) do not indicate that human agency is somehow independent of the working of God (i.e. there is no works-based salvation in view). There does not seem to be any truly deterministic framework present in the Second Temple literature. Rather there is an interplay between divine agency and human agency which exists in the Jewish framework. I think Paul is working within this framework as well. The initiative and prerogative of the work of salvation lies with God. Humans do not bring something to the table which can bring about their own salvation. This does not mean, however, that there is no place for human agency at all. Rather, Paul sees the presence of both, though not of equal measure or efficacy, at work in the divine plan.

BEN: On page 213 you say that the Law is not the problem, but rather sin, the Law being the hireling of the tyrant sin. The problem with this assessment is that even if human beings were not fallen, the Law is still not the Holy Spirit. The Law can tell a person what they ought to do, but it cannot enable them to do it. Furthermore, Paul says that the Law, in effect, turns sin into trespassing, a willful violation of a now known law, so if we are talking about fallen human beings, the Law certainly makes things worse. This is not to say that the Law is the bad guy, it's just that in Paul's view the Law is impotent. It cannot change human nature. Talk a bit more about your view of Paul's view of the Law. Why do you think that "law" in Rom. 8.2 must refer to the Mosaic Law? This is not at all clear to me, especially when Paul talks about "another law" at the end of Rom. 7 which is clearly not the Mosaic Law, and in fact Paul uses the term *nomos* in a variety of ways. For example, "the law of Christ" does not refer to Christ's take on the Mosaic Law *in toto*. It also includes the teaching of Jesus, the teaching of the apostles, as well as those portions of the Old Covenant that are reaffirmed.

CHAD: This is where I take some cues again from Snodgrass and his "spheres of influence." Snodgrass takes the genitives here as spherical where Paul contrasts "the Law of the Spirit of life" with "the Law of sin and death." These are not two Laws or simply "principles," but rather the Law in the realm of the Spirit where it can properly function because the human actor is empowered, or the Law in the realm of sin and death where human flesh lacks the empowering influence of the Spirit. The problem, as I see it, which Paul discusses in Rom. 7 is that sin and death, taking advantage of the impotency of human flesh, co-opted the Law and used it for their own purposes (i.e. to bring death and increase sin). So, it was not the Law which was the problem, but humans. The Law, Paul says, is holy, righteous, and good (7.12).

The two Laws which Paul contrasts in 7.22–23 seem to me to preview what he says in 8.2. The Law of God is at war with the Law of his mind and makes him captive to the Law of sin. These are not different Laws or simply principles, but rather the same Law under different operating forces. The "ego's" mind (whoever Paul is describing here with "I," which is, of course, debated), his will, so to speak, is aligned with the Law of God, but his flesh, weakened and lacking empowerment from the Spirit, is enslaved to the Law of sin. Since the focus on chapter 7 has been on the Mosaic Law in particular, and Paul continues with the *nomos* language, it seems to me that discussion spills over also into chapter 8.

BEN: Talk about your reading of Eph. 1. It sounds rather like Markus Barth's view that Christ is the elect one and we are only elect insofar as we are in him. This would make good sense of the statement that God chose us "in Christ" because at least Christ existed, according to Paul, before the foundations of the universe, whereas we did not. It's not just about choosing before the foundations of the world, it's about choosing *someone* back then. I agree with your point about *pro-orisas* simply meaning deciding in advance, without any necessary deterministic component being implied. Do you take the reference to "saints chosen in Christ" to refer to Israel being chosen in Christ the Elect One, or perhaps to Jewish Christians like Paul being chosen in advance to be the light to the nations? Regardless of how one parses this, it seems clear that election is one thing and salvation is another. Jesus is the Elect One and yet he doesn't need to be saved! Israel's election was to a particular historical purpose, and some of Israel is clearly "not saved" along the paths of history. In fact, I would say that the OT does not talk about salvation in the Christian sense, of being saved in Christ meaning being given everlasting life.

CHAD: Election ultimately occurs "in Christ" (I would say as does also salvation, sanctification, etc.), so Paul I think is framing his discussion here in a participationistic model. Those who are "in Christ" are the "chosen people." So, God's choice occurs before the foundation of the world because Christ has always been God's chosen sphere of salvation. To put it another way, I think God's plan all along was for humans to be conformed to the image of Jesus. In the incarnation, of course, that becomes clear. Humanity as it has always been intended to be is what Jesus himself is, and those "in Him" are, are becoming, and will become, just that: like Jesus. I think that the "saints" language in Ephesians, particularly through chapter 3, makes good sense contextually to be seen as referring to Israel, or more specifically to Jewish Christians. So, what Paul is actually doing in Eph. 1.3–13 is developing something of a salvation history of the people of Israel.

This section is packed with language straight out of the OT about the people of God. They are "chosen," "holy," "in love," "adopted," "redeemed," "forgiven," full of "wisdom," have the revealed "will" of God, "hoped beforehand in Christ," etc. It would take a dissertation (maybe one has already been done?) to tease out all of the OT allusions which are packed into those verses. So, they are the people of God, but the divine plan was a single plan all along. Jewish Christians stand not just in the line of promises made in the OT, they also stand within the fulfillment of those promises through the work of Christ. If Paul is working toward addressing the problem of the need for Gentiles to appreciate their dependency upon God's promises to Israel, to establish the history behind those promises first seems to me a necessity, and thus a satisfying interpretation of what is going here at the beginning of the letter.

BEN: Eph. 1.13 seems particularly crucial for your argument that up to then Paul is talking about the Jewish believers, and the priority of their being addressed first by the Gospel, but in 1.13 the "also you" refers to the turn to the Gentiles. Help the readers understand this exposition by Paul.

CHAD: It seems more than coincidental to me that Paul consistently uses first person plural pronouns in Eph. 1.3–12. There is a lot of "we" and "us" going on. When he gets to 1.13, he states, "in whom also you ('ya'll'), when you ('ya'll') heard the word of truth ..." There is then some interchange between the "we" and the "you" throughout Eph. 1–3. Some have suggested this is just stylistic variation, which I don't think sufficiently explains the data. Others have said that Paul is probably just referring to his companions with the "we" language, but his companions barely figure at all in the letter. What does figure prominently in the letter, and especially in the first three chapters, is the relationship between Jews and Gentiles in the people of God. So, in light of that, I think Paul's "we's" clearly refer to Jews or Jewish Christians, and his "you's" refer to Gentile Christians, in particular those who are the intended audience(s) of the letter. [This point could be furthered by the suggestion that Eph. 1.1 refers to two groups – the saints (i.e. the Jewish Christians) *and* those (Gentiles) who are faithful in Christ.]

BEN: You deny Paul is talking about double predestination in Eph. 1. What then are we to make of statements about being dead in sin, or being children of wrath? Is Paul talking about their condition before conversion, or at the eschaton?

CHAD: In the context of this statement in Eph. 2.1–2, Paul has just mentioned the resurrection of Jesus in 1.20. So I think the connection here with death is not describing a predetermined state but rather is working within the conceptual framework of the resurrection life. Those who are not "in Christ" have not shared in his resurrection and thus are dead in sin. I don't see any need contextually to read any more into it than that. If Paul's pronouns are indicative of his audience here, which I think they are, Paul is specifically speaking to these Gentile converts who were formerly under the rule of the "powers," the powers which are still operating over those who are not in Christ. That Paul does not intend "children of wrath" or "sons of disobedience" as descriptions of those predestined by God for judgment seems clear since he is talking about the former state of his own audience who are now believers. In other words, their position changed from "out" to "in" when they trusted in Christ, which would not be possible if Paul were referring to a previously determined and fixed state.

BEN: What does it mean to say that God prepared beforehand good works for the saved to walk in, rather than saying God prepared the people before hand for good works? What's the difference?

CHAD: I take this to mean something similar to what we saw at Qumran and in other Second Temple texts where God has determined right and wrong, good and evil, and their boundaries. The kind of works which God's people, those conformed and being conformed to the image of Christ, are to be doing have been determined ahead of time. From a theological perspective, though this is not explicit in the text, I would say that the good activities which God has for his people to do flow from God's nature rather than being something which God arbitrarily determined. In other words, because God is good and God is love, the good works which are predetermined for his people are those which flow from God's very essence as good and love. The intended result of God's preparations are that his people will walk in the works he has prepared, indicating again, it seems, a serious volitional component to the whole schema. Paul develops the theological framework for that case here and lays out its ethical implications beginning in chapter 4 of the letter.

BEN: In terms of the *modus operandi* of this book, one of the basic approaches you take is to argue that if an idea is not found elsewhere in early Jewish literature, then it is wise to query whether we can be so sure that this idea is found in Paul's letter. And this applies especially to the notion of individual predestination unto salvation. Of course, it can always be objected that "Paul is the exception to many rules" but I think this sort of approach to the evidence places the burden of proof on those who would want to insist that Paul is eccentric in his beliefs about such important matters. Would you agree?

CHAD: Yes. The way I like to put it is that if we think Paul is departing significantly from his Jewish context, we should expect to see significant clarification to explain the departure. We see this with how he speaks about his view of Jesus, for example, where, though sharing in some of the contours of Jewish Messianic thought, there are some fairly startling departures (e.g. applying OT texts about YHWH to Jesus or placing him within a reframed Shema). Those things stand out significantly. When Paul takes up discussion of election, he does so without any significant revision to the framework. Instead, he basically takes the language "as is." Paul's startling departure is not with how election is framed, but rather that it is oriented completely around Jesus as the defining marker of God's people and that the chosen people now include Gentiles as full members apart from full adherence to the Torah. Christianity was birthed out of Judaism, and indeed in its first few decades was in all likelihood viewed as a Jewish sect. We thus should not expect to find too severe a contrast present between them.

BEN: You could conclude that even in Rom. 8.28ff. Paul has said nothing that would contradict the earlier conclusion that Paul takes a corporate and conditional view of election. One of the planks on which you build this conclusion is the fact that Paul uses the language of foreknowing, not only in Rom. 8, but in Rom. 9–11 as applied to non-Christian Israel, so foreknowing surely cannot mean "fore-loving" or "fore-choosing" of particular individuals to be saved from before the foundation of the universe. Unpack your thoughts about these matters for us.

CHAD: Some commentators suggest we should take Paul's comment about foreknowledge as God's fore-loving of individuals as covenant members. The problem here is that Paul uses the same verb in Rom. 11.2 as he is discussing God's choice of Israel. Paul's argument there is operating clearly around a corporate framework since only a remnant of Israel has accepted God's Messiah. It simply cannot be said that foreknowledge here is fore-loving, unless one holds that God's covenant love with Israel meant all Israelites were "saved," when clearly in the context Paul is suggesting otherwise. If we view Paul's language in both Rom. 8.28ff. and Rom. 11 as focusing on the collective and not individuals predetermined for particular soteriological states, we can make better sense of the verb in both places. Further, we might also recognize that Paul is borrowing again extensively from OT vocabulary without giving it necessarily new import beyond its reorientation "in Christ" and Gentile inclusion. So, when we read a Jewish Paul speaking of "the saints," "sonship," "calling," etc., we must hear these first as concepts which spring from the OT, traverse through Second Temple Judaism, and have a sense of content already as Paul adopts them. Paul is using these terms in a slightly different sense in that this is all oriented now around Christ, but he is not upending the import of those terms and what they stood for in Jewish theology. The language is the language of Israel, applied to the one people of God in Christ, who are heirs of God's promises.

BEN: You quote my colleague Craig Keener to good effect, namely "a sovereign God could sovereignly allow much choice and still accomplish his purposes." This is so on the macro-scale, but if we scale it down to the individual this would seem to mean that individual human beings have the ability to frustrate or reject God's purposes for their individual lives. Yes? Or would you say that God does not have specific salvific purposes for individuals, but rather only for the group known as God's people?

CHAD: I think that humans can reject God's intentions for them must be clear, given what Paul lays out in Rom. 9–11. In a sense Israel, or we might say a majority of the Jewish people, has done just that. They have stumbled over the stumbling stone (i.e. rejected God's Messiah). They are cut off from Christ. They are more Esau than Jacob. They are playing the part of Pharaoh by opposing God's promises. They are vessels of wrath. They have not pursued God's righteousness. All of these things are written by Paul as indictments against Jews who have rejected Jesus.

In terms of God's purposes, I take Paul and others in the NT to indicate that God's salvific intention is that all of humanity come to the knowledge of his Son, be freed from sin, be given resurrection life, and be transformed to the image of his Son. Because God has granted humans to have significant freedom, this is not the case, because not all have committed themselves to God's offer. God's promises are sure because he is faithful, and his people are secure because they are in Christ. As Oropeza argues, Rom. 8.28–39 is written to ensure and encourage the collective because they are going to experience collective persecution. They are promises to the people as a community of faith. They should not be taken as an *ordo* describing how God's eternal decrees have been arranged. That, I think, is clearly beyond the intentions Paul has in this section of the letter.

BEN: It is very telling and interesting that in Paul's little list in Rom. 9.1ff. of the things that are Israel's divine privileges and which set Israel apart what he does *not* mention is circumcision, Sabbath, and kosher food laws. What do you make of this? It would seem that Paul does not see Israel as mainly defined by the boundary-markers so often debated by the New Perspective folks.

CHAD: You could perhaps smuggle them in, in the covenants or the Law, but they are clearly not his focus here. I think in places those come to the fore of the discussion in Paul, particularly in Romans and Galatians, because they were particular issues which had arisen in those communities. Circumcision in particular seems to have become a major issue among early Christians. I think a couple of elements exist which give us some pause from categorizing that completely as Paul's focus. First, as I have argued, different Jewish authors of the period do not necessarily place the same degree of emphasis upon those elements. They show up with some prevalence across the literature, but they are more important for the author of Jubilees, for example, than they are for the author of 2 Maccabees or the Testaments. So, to flatten those issues out as framing the entire discussion I think may be a bit unwarranted. This doesn't mean those issues weren't at the fore of what Paul was dealing with, but there seems to be more to the story as well.

I think faithful Law observance in general is part of Paul's target here because he is arguing that Jews must submit to God's Messiah. Ethnicity and Torah aren't sufficient in this new age which has broken into history in Christ. If they were, Gentiles would be exempt and Jesus would be irrelevant. Going back to the spherical approach, operating within the Law as the primary means of identity for God's people leaves out Gentiles and the Messiah. The Messiah himself is the primary means of identity, which means Jews who assume ethnic identity and/or Torah observance are sufficient are left outside of the blessings which Jesus secures.

BEN: One of the rabbit trails that Protestantism has run down since its inception is the notion that Paul is contrasting faith with "good works" as though "good works" were somehow problematic for a *sola fidei* view of salvation. You've rightly pointed out that Paul has no problem with good works, he even says in Ephesians that believers were created in Christ to do them, and instead what he takes exception to is the insistence that his Gentile converts must do "works of the Mosaic Law" in order to complete their salvation or better said to be truly part of God's people. To a large extent, we owe this false dichotomy to Luther, rather than Calvin or Wesley, and it still haunts us. If you were asked what the relationship is in the Christian life between faith and good works, what would you say? What does Paul mean by "work out ya'lls [you plural] salvation with fear and trembling"?

CHAD: I think, in part, the Pelagian controversy pushed the church toward that sort of interpretation of Paul's letters, which Luther then picks up as well. The desire became to remove any inkling of human activity (any "work") from the process of salvation so as to avoid any Pelagian slips. Because many have divorced the two from one another, we see a great divide in much of popular evangelicalism where we have those who hold to some form of "faith alone" salvation in which good works are optional. In large measure, however, I think we should view salvation as transformative. There are a couple of ways we see this in the NT.

The "salvation" word group (*soter-*) has within it the "healing" or "restoration" aspect of meaning, so salvation can be not just rescue or forgiveness, but also restoration. Justification itself, as many theologians have recently developed, has an ethical orientation. Election, as I have argued in places in my book, has an ethical orientation. I've also mentioned this with the "faith" word group as well (*pist-*), where these words can take on the dimension of "faithfulness" or "fidelity" in addition to "trust" or "belief." So, God's salvific purposes are not just redemptive in the sense of forgiving someone of their sins and then letting them go about their business, God's salvific purposes are ultimately about the complete transformation of the individual into the image of Christ, something which begins in the here and now but ultimately is completed in the eschaton. *So as long as we view "good works" as something which comes after salvation as an option or simply as evidence of salvation rather than as its outflow and a part of what salvation itself is, I think we will continue to misunderstand the dramatic sense in which the Christian life is "in the now" reoriented.*

In terms of Phil. 2.12 (chapter 2 being one of my favorite Pauline texts), it comes in the context of 2.1–11, where Paul is instructing the community to live in unity by putting the needs of others above their own just as Christ himself did as our example. In 2.12, Paul tells the community (ya'll, plural) to work out their salvation since God is at work among them. So, the whole thrust of the passage beginning in 2.1 is communally oriented, and Paul picks up that emphasis again here after grounding their behavior in Christ's model of self-sacrifice. I would say working out their salvation here is not working to earn their salvation, but rather collectively cultivating their unity as God's people as the outworking of their identity as the people of God.

BEN: One of the confusions of Tom Schreiner and other committed Calvinists is the assumption that when Paul talks about individuals like Jacob and Esau in Rom. 9, he is referring to them *not* as representative heads of a people, but as isolated individuals, and so Paul must be talking about the double predestination of particular individuals. As you point out, even when Paul uses the singular pronoun it can refer to the representative head of a group of people. I find this whole Calvinistic line of argument: (1) far too modern, considering the dyadic personality of ancient peoples and how they viewed themselves as primarily parts of collectives; and (2) more to the point, it completely ignores for example Gal. 4, where Hagar and Sarah very clearly represent two groups of people – namely they are the prefigurements of the Judaizers and of Paul and those who agree with him. Paul lines up those who represent Arabia, Sinai, and the "now" Jerusalem and slavery in one camp, and those who represent the Jerusalem which is from above and those who are free in another.

In some ways, I find this just as individualistic and wrong as Rick Warren's whole discussion of God having a "will" for your individual "purpose-driven life" which is somehow custom tailored to the individual and much more particular than what the NT says about the will of God for believers in general – namely their sanctification, their exercising of God's gifts in their lives, etc. We seem to insist on reading the Bible through highly individualistic late Western eyes, and the reading of Paul especially suffers from this malady. Would you agree?

CHAD: As I developed in earlier chapters, the concept of corporate representation was alive and well in Jewish literature, and at times was specifically connected with the concept of election and the language surrounding it. Jacob and Esau themselves in Jubilees serve as representatives of two groups. Jacob serves such a function throughout the OT as well. Paul is working with this existing framework of Jacob and Esau as representatives, but he reorients what this entails. There is a sense here too that God's choosings are counterintuitive. It is not the older, but the younger. I think this is significant, because Paul completes his argument by stating explicitly that God's people are not just made up of Jews, but also Gentiles. This would have been counterintuitive to many Jews, so Jacob and Esau both serve as corporate representatives and as illustrations of the fact that God is the one who gets to make the rules.

I think the bigger problem with the individualistic interpretation is that Paul is not answering the question here of how God decides who to save. He is rather answering the question of why we should think Gentiles can be included as full members in God's people without submitting fully to Torah, and why many Jews are being left out. This is not, then, about God's "fairness," as some translate *adikia* in 9.14, but about his rightness, or faithfulness, if you will. Paul gives the explicit download of the argument from 9.1–23 in 9.24: Jews and Gentiles are both in God's people, and this is not based on ethnicity or Torah observance, but their identification with and commitment to God's Messiah.

BEN: Another "Durham man," B. J. Oropeza, has written a very fine book on apostasy in the NT.[7] One of the things he stresses is that Paul's discussion of "the vessels of wrath" is a discussion of

---

7 B. J. Oropeza, *Apostacy in the New Testament Communities*, vol. 1: *In the Footsteps of Judas and other Defectors* (Eugene, OR: Wipf and Stock, 2011).

Israel currently cut off from the people of God, but they are capable of being reunited with God's people by grace and through faith in Jesus, and indeed in Eph. 2.3 these vessels of wrath can and have in some cases already become followers of Christ. In other words, Paul is not talking about the final predetermined destiny of particular individuals, but rather their current state of affairs, which Paul goes out of his way in Rom. 10–11 to make clear can be a temporary state of affairs, not a predetermined destiny. In our own age, it seems that one of the reasons for the resurgence of the appeal of hardline Calvinism with its dictums about "eternal security" and a radical reading of God's sovereignty which must rule out any other viable actors having the power of contrary choice is the uncertainties in our changing and progressively less Christian culture. Believers are looking for a kind of absolute theological comfort food when it comes to salvation, rather than having to live by faith and faithfulness, as we are called to do. What is your perspective on these things and our cultural malaise?

CHAD: If we view the vessels of wrath in 9.22 as referring to, at least primarily, Jews who have rejected Jesus, as seems clear from 9.23–24, then to view this as a fixed state, just as in Eph. 2, does not appreciate the full scope of Paul's argument, since Paul states in 11.23 that they will be regrafted if they do not continue in their *apistia*, their "un-faith" in Jesus. So yes, it seems this is very much about the current state of affairs, and again answers the question of why we should think Gentiles can be included as full members in God's people without submitting fully to Torah while many Jews are being left out.

I suppose part of the issue is that we tend to read the Bible first and foremost as speaking to us in our context. When we step back and try to understand what it meant in its original context first, sometimes we end up seeing things differently. When we approach Romans not as Paul's timeless articulation of his soteriology, but rather a letter written in real time and space to real people struggling with real issues related to the different ethnic identities which were a part of the early church, I think Paul's argument makes more sense. With that in view, it becomes apparent that the first 11 chapters of Romans are basically about Jews and Gentiles in the people of God. Perhaps some of the motivation for that interpretation lies in a quest for certainty. Perhaps it resonates with some as the church's "true heritage" since some of the interpretive impetus comes from the Reformers. I'm not sure as to the motivations. I do think, however, it lacks explanatory power and scope for what is actually going on this passage and in the letter as a whole.

BEN: At one point in your discussion you object to two familiar lines of argument assumed to be Pauline: (1) that perfect observance of the Mosaic Law was impossible for fallen people (this despite Paul saying in Philippians that he was blameless when it came to the observances of the Mosaic law) and (2) the assumption that asserting that one had obeyed the Law = asserting moral perfection. Even when one broke a law, there were provisions in the Law to make amends, to make atonement. I find this especially puzzling. I have lived in the city of Lexington, Kentucky for 23 years without violating its laws, but this by no means should suggest that I am a morally perfect person. Moral or spiritual perfection goes well beyond law-keeping, just as Christian ethics involves lots of positive things "against which [and for which] there is no law." I don't think Paul is suggesting the Law couldn't be kept by devout Jews. To be blameless before the law is not the same as to be faultless. Why do you think this becomes such an issue for Protestant interpretation of Paul?

CHAD: I think that interpretation raises problems on a number of levels.
First, it makes the entire OT basically about God teaching humans a lesson about how they cannot be perfectly obedient and thus be saved. It also, as Sanders of course argued to get the NPP ball rolling, ignores that Jews in the Second Temple period weren't trying to earn their salvation through perfect obedience. They were concerned with faithfulness to the covenant, which is a different matter altogether. The other problem is that Paul never says any of this. It is read as an implicit premise, but it is not a necessary one, and one which I think confuses things more than it clarifies them. This was, of course, a large part of K. Stendahl's critique in his famous essay.

Paul is established as a paradigm for the existential journey to salvation where denunciation of the Law is the sinner's recognition that they cannot save themselves. Paul is thus decontextualized in order to make his journey relatable. But this also flattens out what he actually says. Paul was not experiencing an existential crisis about how he could be saved, knowing that his works were not good enough, when he encountered Jesus. Augustine's crisis, which became Luther's crisis, in the history of interpretation became Paul's crisis. But Paul never speaks of such a crisis when he gives his own narrative. This is why our starting point in interpretation should begin with the original context, its historical, cultural, and literary setting, and then proceed forward through the history of interpretation. Too often, however, we start with our starting place and end their as well. This reflects our narcissistic culture as well, since it attempts to make our story one and the same with Paul's.

BEN: On p. 245, you take "the righteousness of God" throughout Romans as referring to Jesus himself, the righteous one, so that when Paul contrasts the righteousness which comes from doing works of the Law, with the righteousness of God, the latter would seem to refer to the righteousness which comes from accepting Christ. Thus, you disagree with the view, it would seem, which equates "righteousness of God" with the covenant faithfulness of the Father to his prior agreements with Israel. Have I understood you correctly? And where do you stand on the "imputed righteousness" concept? Does Christ's righteousness substitute for the need of believers to be actually righteous?

CHAD: I think there is a pretty clear connection between Rom. 10.3 and 3.21–22. There Paul very closely associates the righteousness of God with the faithfulness of Christ. This is similar as well, I think, to Rom. 1.17, though different verbs are used, where the righteousness of God is revealed in the good news. If the good news is the message about Jesus, and God's righteousness is revealed in it, then God's righteousness is revealed in Jesus' faithfulness.

Circling back to Rom. 10.3, when Paul says that they have ignored the righteousness of God and were seeking to stand in their own righteousness, I think he is saying they have ignored Jesus and are continuing on in Torah. The problem is that Torah, Paul says in 10.4, was supposed to lead them to Jesus (I take *telos* as "goal" rather than "end" here for a variety of reasons).[8] This doesn't necessarily clearly tie into Rom. 3.5, which is the other mention of the phrase "righteousness of God" in Romans, though Paul could be anticipating his further description in 3.21–22. This is less, then, about Jews trying to earn salvation by keeping the Law or doing "good works" and not being able to measure up, than that they have rejected God's Messiah, who the Torah should have helped them to recognize and to whom they should submit. So I wouldn't see Paul's discussion about righteousness in these passages as primarily about imputation. That doesn't mean that Paul might not develop that elsewhere, but I don't think that is his focus here.

BEN: On p. 250 you say election does not stand on ancestry or keeping of the Mosaic Law, but rather, in Paul's view, on whether or not a Jew or Gentile embraces the Messiah and obeys the Gospel call to faith as the means of right-standing with God. The problem, then, for Israel is not merit-based theology or even legalism, but rather the simple failure to embrace Jesus their Messiah. Unpack this for readers a bit.

CHAD: I think there are a number of indications through Rom. 9–11 that this is what Paul is after. I previously mentioned Paul's Isaac/Ishmael (ethnicity) and Jacob/Esau (Torah observance) contrasts in the beginning of Rom. 9. If election is not based on these factors, the question is raised in 9.14 as to whether or not God is righteous. Paul's response is to invoke the Moses/Pharaoh contrast, indicating that those who are hardened now are the Jews who have rejected Jesus (which is confirmed in chapter 11, I think further indicating that this is what Paul was talking about in chapter 9).
Paul then asks why God still finds fault and who resists his will? He answers by invoking the potter metaphor, which illustrates that God is free to form his people however he chooses, even if that means a people made of both Jews and Gentiles. The Jews who have rejected the Messiah are now vessels of wrath, not the Gentiles who have trusted him. The Gentiles attained the "from faith" righteousness but the Jews did not because they stumbled over the stumbling stone, that is, Jesus

[8] I would disagree with his point here. *Telos* here surely means end. Christ is the end of the Mosaic Law, not in the sense that the Law pointed to him or pointed him out, because – it doesn't! Jesus doesn't show up as the great Lawgiver like Moses. No, Paul surely means that Christ is the end of the previously assumed means of maintaining right-standing with God.

(cf. 9.32–33). Paul then remarks at the beginning of chapter 10 that they missed the goal of the Law, which was Jesus (i.e. the righteousness of God). The righteousness which they lacked was Jesus himself, not because they were chasing an unobtainable form of righteousness which could come through obedience to the Law. They must confess Jesus as Lord and embrace his resurrection (10.9). Their rejection is not for the lack of hearing, since they heard the good news but have not heeded it (10.16–18). So, though there is a remnant who have trusted Christ, in which Paul is included, the rejection of God's Messiah means most Jews are outside of the people of God. Paul states, however, that this will be reversed if they do not continue in their lack of faith in Jesus (11.23).

BEN: Admitting that the matter is complex, I am wondering whether you've considered the evidence for *houtos* meaning "in the same manner" in Rom. 11.25–26, which would suggest that Paul envisions the final salvation of "all Israel" on the very same basis, by grace through faith in Jesus, as for Gentiles. I would also suggest that when Paul associates the miracle of Jacob's repentance and turning with "life from the dead" and "the Redeemer coming from heavenly Zion/Jerusalem" to accomplish this task (noting the way he paraphrases Isaiah, largely following the LXX) he must be talking about an event at the *parousia* which follows the full number of Gentiles coming in. The mystery Paul refers to is the reversal or the order of salvation – Gentiles first, Jews later. Comment a bit.

CHAD: I do think that Paul envisions the Jewish regrafting as occurring through faith in Christ. I think seeing the "Deliverer" of 11.26 as Christ makes sense contextually. I'm not sure if *houtos* is carrying all of that freight in terms of conveying that Jews will be regathered through the same means as Gentiles, but I think the reading in the context is clear that Jesus is the resolution. I also think that understanding the mystery here as the reversal of the order of salvation makes sense. My understanding of "mystery" language in Paul (which is a transliteration rather than a translation) is that Paul uses it to talk about some secret which was previously unknown which has now been disclosed. So, Paul is explaining the mystery, not alluding to some hidden or obscure knowledge which he doesn't make known. Since he immediately speaks about the fullness of Gentiles and the partial hardening of Israel following that comment, it seems the likely referent. I think it is certainly possible to read the *parousia* as the time of the occurrence from the coming from Zion language, but Paul doesn't seem to be concerned here with primarily describing the time frame as much as assuring that this will come about.

Chad's Summary

I hope to have demonstrated the value and necessity of placing Paul's election language back in its original context, which was a decidedly Jewish one. As we reviewed the Jewish literature, we discovered a view of election that was grounded in God's promises to the patriarchs. This overwhelmingly emphasized the collective nature of election as a concept that applied to a bounded community. When individuals were in view, their role, their character or their representation of a group was emphasized, never their being chosen for a particular soteriological standing. Likewise, the Jewish literature was decidedly conditional, with the various authors defining who was "in" and who was "out" by different means and markers. This typically meant that Gentiles were excluded, along with many or most Jews, from the people of God. We can thus express these tendencies as described below:

(1) At times, the description of individuals or a group as "elect" emphasizes primarily their character or piety rather than a particular, predetermined, soteriological standing (Ben Sira, Testaments, Additional Psalms of David, 1 Enoch).

(2) When individuals are mentioned as "elect," the identification either (a) recognizes them as such because they represent or mediate for a corporate group (Jubilees,

Testaments, Dead Sea Scrolls, 1 Enoch), or (b) describes a vocational calling (e.g., king, priest, etc.; see Ben Sira, Psalms of Solomon).

The picture of election is primarily conditional, either implicitly (Tobit, Ben Sira, Baruch, Wisdom of Solomon, Sibylline Oracles, pseudo-Philo) or explicitly (Jubilees, Testaments, 1 Maccabees, 2 Maccabees, Psalms of Solomon, Dead Sea Scrolls), in that a number of Jews, whether a majority (Jubilees, Testaments, 1 Maccabees, Psalms of Solomon, Dead Sea Scrolls, 1 Enoch, Testament of Moses) or an undefined number (Tobit, Ben Sira, Baruch, 2 Maccabees, Wisdom of Solomon, Sibylline Oracles, pseudo-Philo), were presently apostate and outside of the covenant. The concept was thus not nationalistic or ethnic, but primarily remnant-oriented.

(3) The conditions of the covenant emphasized vary throughout the literature, and included circumcision, general piety, Sabbath observance, ritual purity, abstinence from sexual immorality, avoidance of intermarriage with Gentiles, proper calendrical and festival observances, resistance of Hellenization and idolatry, support for the Hasmoneans, rejection of the Hasmoneans, honesty, humility, proper interpretation and application of the law, rejection of the corrupt leadership in Jerusalem (e.g. the priests, Pharisees, Sadducees, Sanhedrin, Maccabees, or Hasmoneans), and association with/allegiance to a particular community and its understanding of the law or its specially received revelation.

(4) In spite of the conditional nature, God's election of Israel was still primarily presented as a corporate, not an individual, concept. This is clear from the many uses of corporate or national terminology and imagery, such as use of the moniker "Israel" or "Judah" when referring only to the pious, vine and plant imagery, association with a righteous person (e.g. Enoch or Noah) or an explicit invocation of the remnant motif.

Some texts make an allowance for the possible inclusion of Gentiles in the eschatological people of God (Sibylline Oracles, 1 Enoch, pseudo-Philo), though largely Gentiles are considered to be wicked and sinful by nature. God's mercy and human obedience do not exist in mutually exclusive terms. The recognition of Israel's sin is widespread throughout the literature. At times, God's mercy means his decision not to reject Israel completely, though they are deserving of such a fate. This does not create, however, *carte blanche* for Israel to be licentious, as they needed to remain faithful to the covenant (as variously defined) in order to receive the covenant blessings.

(5) God's sovereignty and human freedom do *not* exist as mutually exclusive terms. While certain things, such as the declaration of what is good and what is evil, the final judgment and its rewards or punishments, and the election of Israel/the remnant are described as being predetermined, in no text does this negate human freedom and the responsibility to be faithful to the covenant with God. That God has an overarching plan is clear, but that every nuance within that plan, including the individual actions of humans, is preordained, is not.

(6) There is a real possibility, except once the final judgment comes, for the apostates to repent and commit themselves to keeping the covenant as well as for those in the "true Israel" to commit apostasy and reject the covenant and its blessings.

As we looked at Paul's letters, we did not find a drastically different picture. Paul similarly worked within a collective and conditional framework. Like his contemporaries, he viewed the elect as a restricted group. In his most explicit election texts, Paul never concerns himself with God choosing specific individuals to receive eschatological salvation. Rather, in his most explicit election texts (in particular Gal. 2–3; Rom. 3; 8–11; and Eph. 1–2), Paul always concerns himself with what it means for Gentiles to be a part of God's people. Recognizing this aspect alone should cause us to step back and ask what exactly Paul is doing. When we see these sociological divisions and Paul's attempt to bring a theological resolution to the problem of Gentile inclusion and majority Jewish exclusion, we recognize that Paul does not explore an abstract theological doctrine of God determining each individual's eschatological fate, but rather wrestles with how to make sense of God's actions in light of the covenant with the patriarchs. Paul deals in detail with how to resolve this dilemma, adamant that God has freedom to work how he chooses, has indeed fulfilled his promises to bless the nations through Israel and has renewed the covenant through his faithful and loving act in the Messiah. This public display of Jesus and miraculous vindication through the resurrection act as the sign that God himself has truly intervened. And through this act, the law took its proper place in the realm of the risen Jesus and the Spirit, where God's people, those who identify with his Messiah and submit to his Spirit, receive the enablement to fulfill this law and thus receive the promised eschatological life. For Paul, as for his contemporaries, election controversies were more about who God's people were than how they were God's people.

Among Jews of the period, the concept of election came to signify the "true Israel" or "remnant," meaning those Israelites who remained faithful to the covenant. For Paul, the terminology takes on quite the same meaning. In referring to those who have trusted in Jesus as "elect" or "chosen" or "called," Paul claims that it is those who have been united with God's Messiah who are actually in right-standing with God. Torah-faithfulness apart from obedience to the good news of God expressed through Jesus has become useless. For Paul, obedience to God comes only through identification with Jesus. Thus, Jesus' own faithfulness both grounds the faithfulness of the believer and brings God's declaration of "rightness" to them.

And So?

Occasionally I am asked something to the effect of "What difference does it make how we think about election?" or "What does this view 'do' that others don't?" It seems to me that this view better fits within the thought world of Second Temple Judaism. The more we immerse ourselves in that world, the better we will make sense of Paul, a Jewish follower of a Jewish Messiah, and his letters. Several very practical implications also arise from this view. Space does not permit me to articulate these more fully, though we have touched briefly on each at various points in our discussion.

Much of the early Jewish discussion of the "elect" concerned their piety more than whether or not they were, or would be, "saved." They shared a deep concern, though expressed in different and competing ways, with living faithfully to God's commands as expressed in his covenant with them. Paul expresses a similar concern in his articulation of the faithfulness required of God's people in Christ. For Paul, this faithfulness is enabled through the gift of God's Spirit, but not at the expense of elimination of the responsibility and commitment of the individual. Paul still calls God's people to obedience to his law, though he expresses this in a more condensed formula based on the emulation of the Savior and the love of God and others.

Paul's Jewish contemporaries also shared a common concern to distinguish God's people from the rest of the world. This sometimes resulted in extremes, as we saw at Qumran or in the Maccabees. Each group, however, wrestled with how to remain faithful to God and resist the attractions and temptations of the world. This came, after all, from God's own declaration for his people to be set apart for service to him. When Paul declares believers, including Gentiles (!), elect, holy, righteous and called, he calls on this rich history of God's covenantal people. Those in God's Messiah would likewise need to live in a way that distinguished them from the world, for this was their calling. And again, the Messiah himself emulated this lifestyle, and God's Spirit will enable those who belong to him to reflect Jesus. As it was for Israel, this meant living in ways counterintuitive to the larger culture, dying to their own desires that they might live for God, and subsequently, and perhaps ironically from a human perspective, in doing so actually live life as God had intended all along.

The various Jewish sects of the period represented in our literature had deep convictions about how to define the boundaries of God's people. This likewise fostered an important sense of unity in those communities. Paul too, perhaps more adamantly even, held a deep concern for the unity of God's people, especially in light of the reconciliation of Gentiles to God. When competing identity markers, such as circumcision or collective cultural wisdom, challenged the centrality of the Messiah and his cross and resurrection, Paul felt compelled to strip those things of their significance. In doing so, he both continued to elevate the primacy of obedient commitment to Jesus as the central marker of identity and sought to promote the unity of God's people around the primary marker. This unity required people from differing racial and socioeconomic backgrounds to learn to function together as a united, reformed, renewed people of God. In the case of Jews and Gentiles, long-held religious beliefs and animosities created tensions and hostilities among God's people. Paul would not allow these problems to continue to fester but rather dismantled any notion, whether an idea, a practice or a person, that might be exalted to the status which Jesus alone held. Paul would allow God's people in Christ to be defined by no other means than the Messiah's life, death, and resurrection.

Finally, election from its inception in the biblical text through much of the Second Temple literature, and certainly in Paul, held a central position in the mission of God's people. God chose Israel for his special possession in order to bring the Abrahamic blessing to the nations. This missional aspect of Israel's calling is echoed through the prophetic literature of the OT and through many Second Temple texts. For Paul, this blessing in one sense had been accomplished since God had brought the Gentiles into his people as full members through Christ. In another sense, both as it pertains to unbelieving Gentiles and paradoxically to unbelieving Jews, this missional call of God's people to bless the nations still endured and had not yet found its final fulfillment since there still existed those "outside the camp."

What Else?

We have been able only to scratch the surface of this topic in our examinations of and reflections on these texts. I hope through this discussion that we might increase our awareness of the Jewish context of the NT and the ways in which we can better understand its message within that context. I have attempted to offer an account of the relationship between Paul's thought and his Jewish background, which is both contextually sensitive and recognizes the connecting points and the divergences between them. In doing so, I have developed a view that attempts to deeply appreciate the continuity between Paul's thought, the covenantal theology of the OT, and his background as a first-century Jew. I have aimed at providing a "thick description" of Paul's theology of election, accounting for these various contexts as important influences on his theological articulations.

These contexts act as spotlights that, when thrown on their subject, allow us to appreciate the details of what we view. My study has also aimed at a rich theological description of these beliefs set within the ancient thought world rather than our own. Such a view also, as I have summarized briefly, creates important practical implications for how we understand human responsibility, Christian unity, faithful obedience to God, and the core identity of God's people. Though we face challenges in how we apply these ideas in our own context, which is in some ways very different from Paul's and in others quite similar, by seeing Paul's convictions in their historical and cultural contexts we can better allow them to shape our own.

All of the above final conclusions reflect Chad's view, but it will be seen that except for the places indicated in the previous dialogue I strongly agree with his understanding of Paul's views on election and his attempt to situate it in the context of other early Jewish discussions. I also agree with his take on the New Perspective on Paul, which rightly interprets *pistis Christou* (at least in the case of most of its advocates, though not James Dunn) to mean the faithfulness of Jesus Christ, and also rightly agrees with Sanders that early Jews, by and large, were not trying to earn their salvation by "works righteousness." This is a later caricature of early Judaism. Further, I think the New Perspective critique that stresses that Paul is not opposing "legalism" nor is he asserting that the Mosaic Law could not be kept due to human fallenness (there is a difference between being blameless before the law, and moral perfection) is helpful. In our next chapter, we must look more closely at where exactly the "later" followers of the Reformers and Reformed theology went off the rails, especially in their interpretations of the Pauline Gospel. Here a quotation from C. K. Barrett will not go amiss:

You cannot ever become so good a Christian as to be secure, beyond all fear of falling … This means you must watch your step when you talk about Christian certainty. Karl Barth once wrote, "God lends people certitude, but he denies them security." That hits it off precisely. God be thanked for the precious loan of certitude, the joyful assurance in which we rejoice, confident that when Christ took away the sins of the world, he took away mine, and there is therefore no condemnation for those that are in Christ Jesus. But beware. The moment you see any Christian, and especially yourself, turning this kind of living assurance into security, you may know that there and then he has lost the truth. There is no security but Christ, none in our learning (even in our theological learning), none in our Church and ministry, none in our virtue or religious experience. We have at once the assurance and the insecurity of faith.[9]

---

[9] From a sermon on 1 John, in *Luminescence*, vol. 2: *The Sermons of Charles Kingsley and Fred Barrett* (Eugene, OR: Cascade, 2017), 325.

12

Where the Reformation Went Wrong

God encounters people in justification only outside of themselves and the righteousness received remains an alien righteousness.

Stephen Chester[1]

The Reformer is always right about what's wrong. However, he's often wrong about what is right.

G. K. Chesterton

Issues of Imputed Righteousness and Election

The previous dialogue with Chad Thornhill is helpful in clarifying a whole variety of issues in regard to election, God's chosen people, covenants, predestination, and God's sovereignty, thus some of the problems with Luther's, Melanchthon's, and Calvin's readings of Paul have already been dealt with in the previous chapter. Since Paul is the flashpoint for such discussions, especially in Protestant circles, it has been important to show at some length how this issue plays out when we evaluate Paul properly in the light of both the OT and his early Jewish context.

To refresh our memories the following are some of the most important takeaways from such a discussion: (1) the language of chosen people, and so the concept of election, is primarily a corporate concept in the biblical literature and in early Judaism as well. One is "elect"" if one is in Israel in the OT and early Judaism, and one is "elect" if one is "in Christ" in Paul and elsewhere in the NT. The boundary that must be crossed since the Christ event in order to be among God's people is Christ himself, faith in Christ; (2) when individuals are spoken of as "elect" in the OT and in early Jewish literature, this is often a statement about their character and behavior being Torah-true, they are the righteous. It is not a soteriological statement *per se*.

Even when the discussion is about future resurrection in Dan. 12.1–3, it is the righteous who get the "good resurrection" and shine like the sun. At other points, individuals are treated as representatives (Jacob and Esau) of groups, and comments about them, for

[1] Stephen Chester *Reading Paul with the Reformers: Reconciling Old and New Perspectives* (Grand Rapids, MI: William B. Eerdmans, 2017), 175.

instance in Rom. 9–10, are not comments about their individual salvation. Indeed, even comments about someone being God's anointed and chosen leader, like Cyrus in Isaiah, is not a comment about that person's individual salvation. Election is one thing, salvation is another, though these two categories are related to one another in some of the literature; (3) the language of predetermination is meant to make clear that God has a plan, a blueprint that he is working out for his people, and it makes clear that he is the most powerful actor in the drama, and there is no close second; (4) both God's great power and the human power of contrary choice are affirmed in the early Jewish literature, which in the same breath affirms the possibility of faithfulness and of apostasy. Paul fits quite well into that discussion, holding those things in tension. The predetermination of particular individuals for eternal salvation without regard to their own choices or character or behavior is not really found in this literature. Even the Qumran texts, sometimes pointed to as an exception, are probably not, as Thornhill discusses above. But a good deal more can and should be said about the linchpin concept of "the alien righteousness of Christ."

Let us first turn to the idea of Christ's righteousness being imputed to the believer, based on a certain reading of Rom. 4 and other texts in Romans.[2] Rom. 4 speaks of Abraham trusting God, and it being credited to him as righteousness. That is, *Abraham's faith/trust was credited as Abraham's righteousness.* Paul simply takes this discussion from Gen. 12–15 at face value and does not amend the text of Gen. 15.6 LXX in any real way. Where, then, did the idea of Christ's righteousness being imputed to the believer actually come from?

It comes to some degree from the unhelpful rendering by Erasmus of the Latin Vulgate's presentation of the key text. The Vulgate has "Abraham believed God, and it was reputed (*reputatum*) unto him unto justice (*iustitiam*)." Erasmus was not satisfied with this rendering and drawing on the context of the legal language of his day rendered it "Abraham believed God and it was imputed (*imputatum*) to him for justice." This is found in Erasmus' first edition of his Greek NT (1516), and it might have been a minor footnote in the history of the Reformation except that Melanchthon and Luther both used Erasmus' NT and later Lutheran orthodoxy followed both Erasmus' translation and his understanding of *dikaiosune*, to the point that "imputed righteousness" or "imputed justification" became a received and popular idea in that Protestant tradition. Luther himself did not usually use the language of imputation, but in later Lutheran orthodoxy it became common.[3]

Here is where we note that Erasmus was wrong in his assumption about the provenance of the language about "reckoning." This is not an example of a judicial or juridical term, it is business language, bookkeeping language – the language of credits and debits. We see this very sort of use of that language in Ps. 106.31 and 1 Macc. 2.52 and also in Philem. v. 18. This goes along with the early Jewish idea of the good and evil deeds of a person being recorded in a ledger (Esth. 6.1; Dan. 7.10; Test. Benj. 11.4; Jub. 30.17). Yes, there are probably some legal overtones when Paul couples Gen. 15 with a passage about

---

[2] For considerably more detail along these lines see the relevant discussions in Witherington, *Paul's Letter to the Romans.*

[3] Stephen Chester makes this point clear in his fine study *Reading Paul with the Reformers.* Later Lutheran and Reformed readings of the key Pauline texts should not necessarily be laid at the feet of the original Reformers. One of the real virtues of that book is that Chester shows that Protestants, and he specifically focuses on the contributors to the so-called New Perspective on Paul, are still reading Luther and Calvin in light of their later followers, and so are mistaking what the Reformers said on various of these matters.

sins being covered and forgiven or even pardoned (ideas he borrows from the psalmist once in Romans, which Paul hardly ever uses otherwise) and so *not credited*, but nothing is said about Christ's righteousness being credited *instead*. And again, if Abraham and his faith is standing as the prototype or model for Paul's audience, it is Abraham's own faith which is credited as Abraham's righteousness.

Paul would have been appalled at the notion that Christians after conversion do not need to go on and be righteous and holy, and lead righteous lives, just as he would be appalled, as an early Jew, with the idea that Christ is righteous in the believer's place such that the believer's righteousness is just a legal fiction – he is counted as righteous, but not counted on to be righteous. Even worse would be the notion that when God looks at believers, he is deceived about their actual moral state, seeing only "the righteousness of Christ" or, even more erroneous, the idea that God is prepared to look the other way and will not hold believers accountable for post-conversion sins because of Jesus' atoning death. Paul would have concluded that various of these notions turn God into an unrighteous deity. Luther, however, got around some of these problems by combining his notion of alien righteousness with the notion of the union of the believer with Christ. Some of the things he says makes it sound as if Christ is the Siamese twin of the believer, joined at the hip, with all the righteousness being in Christ, and not in the believer himself.[4]

Rom. 5.12 became a very important text for discussion of these matters vis-à-vis the notion of original sin. The text reads "So it is that through one human being sin entered the world, and through sin, death, and thus death spread to all human beings, because all sinned." Augustine famously based his interpretation of this text on the Latin Vulgate *in quo* (in whom), which was a mistranslation of the Greek ἐφ' ᾧ, which means "in that" and the further problem is that in Augustine's Latin translation the second reference to death is "omitted" with the result that "sin" *rather than* "death" becomes the subject of the verb spread – i.e. "sin spread from Adam to all humanity by generation not by imitation by all humanity."

It should be remembered that Augustine is critiquing and trying to avoid the perceived errors of Pelagius in his later discussions of Romans. The upshot of this mistranslation and misreading of Rom. 5.12, coupled with Augustine's later conclusions that Rom. 7 (in light of the mistranslation of Rom. 5.12) must be referring to the plight even of Christians, is that "righteousness" of any sort is impossible for the fallen human being, since original sin has been seminally transmitted to the whole human race. Ergo, only imputed righteousness could remedy this problem. Augustine, as it turns out, was more nearly right in his earlier reading of Rom. 7 as referring to those outside of Christ. Luther, the former Augustinian monk, is in fact heavily indebted to Augustine's later reading of Rom. 7 and basically reiterates it.

This of course makes no sense at all of Paul the Christian's claim, late in life, that in regard to a righteousness that comes from keeping the Mosaic Law, he was *blameless* during his pre-Christian days (Phil. 3.6)! Apparently, in Paul's view, human fallenness did not create a situation of "total depravity" but rather a situation where a person was inclined to sin and suffered from "the heart turned in upon itself" (self-centeredness), but by the help of God and his Word and grace could avoid breaking Mosaic Laws, for this is what

---

[4] See Chester, *Reading Paul*, 175–217.

blameless means in that sentence.[5] It does not mean pure as the driven snow, it does not mean morally perfect, it does not mean fulfilling all the positive love commands to the degree God desires. It means avoiding committing the "thou shalt nots."[6] And this brings up another problem with the Reformers' exegesis of Paul, then and in their descendants – they assumed that the Law could not be kept, that it was *impossible* to do so. Among other things, this has never been the view of devout Jews, and is not today. Paul would not be an advocate that one cannot *avoid* breaking the Law. But one must remember that the Mosaic Law does not cover all the things that the Law of Christ does. It does not cover anger, for example, or adultery of the heart. It allows various things due to hardness of heart, as we have already seen earlier in this study, things which are no longer allowed now that Jesus was bringing in God's saving reign and realm.

The interpretation of "imputed righteousness" was bolstered by a certain kind of rendering of 1 Cor. 1.30 as follows: "It is because of him that you are in Christ Jesus, who has become for us wisdom from God – that is, our righteousness, holiness and redemption." The sentence in the Greek is convoluted. What is clear is that Paul says that Christ has become the believer's wisdom from God. The phrase about Christ is, however, parenthetical and there is no word "our" connected to any of the three attributes at the end of the sentence. Furthermore, the Reformers had to insert the word *kai* (and) before the last clause to make it say that Jesus is our Wisdom *and* righteousness, etc. But the Greek sentence reads literally "But from him, *you are* (in Christ Jesus, who has become our wisdom from God) righteousness, and holiness and redemption." Nothing is said here about Christ being righteous or holy or redeemed *for us*. The object of the verb "you are" is righteousness, holiness, redemption. Yes, these qualities come to the believer "from him" but Paul is describing qualities of the believer, *not qualities Christ has in the place of or on behalf of the believer*. This latter correct interpretation of the matter is confirmed when one looks at 2 Cor. 5.21: "God made him who had no sin to be sin for us, so that in him we might become the righteousness of God."

[5] If by "total depravity" one means only that sin affects every aspect of who we are, that is, it is extensive or total in the scope of what it taints in the person, then the term is fine. If, however, by that one means that sin is intensive in the individual, that he is bad to the bone, that there is nothing good to say about the person, that the image of God in the person has been erased, not merely defaced, then no, that's apparently not Paul's view. Sin, however, can be an addictive form of behavior such that one can talk about a person being in bondage to sin, as we see described in Rom. 7.14–25. The person knows better but cannot do better. Clearly, in light of Phil. 3.6, Paul doesn't see that as describing himself and his own past. What I take this to mean is that obviously the grace of God was at work before the coming of Christ, in the lives of some individuals more than others. Some were given the grace to obey the Law, some were given the gift of wisdom, and so on. What was not yet given was the grace of salvation in Christ.

[6] It is telling how poor the Reformers' exegesis is of this text in Philippians. While the Reformers did use Phil. 3.6 to refute the notion that Paul struggled with a guilty conscience before his conversion, what they failed to deal with is that this is Paul's "Christian" assessment of his pre-Christian life. Calvin, in an artful dodge, suggests that what Paul is really saying is that Paul is admitting he was blind enough back then to consider himself justified in God's sight since no one could reproach him for law-breaking. Paul says nothing here of that sort. His Christian assessment is that he was blameless under the Mosaic Law requirements. He will go on to say that he exchanged all the pluses of his own previous life for something greater, and he was prepared to consider the former good things as *skubala* in comparison to receiving Christ. He is using a *synkrisis* here and he is not contrasting a bad thing with a good thing, but rather a good thing of temporary value with a much better thing of lasting value. He makes the same sort of argument in 2 Cor. 3, where he contrasts the New and Old Covenants, both attended with glory. See Chester, *Reading Paul*, 122–25, on the Reformers' artful dodges in dealing with Phil. 3.6.

Paul is not talking about Christ himself (who does not need to "become" righteousness, and no, he is not talking about alien righteousness). God actually wants the believer to become holy, through the internal working of the Holy Spirit of course. To a very considerable extent, Lutheran and Reformed theologians, and even various of the current exponents of such theologies, have not corrected the mistakes Augustine made, but in fact have reinforced them in various ways, and this in turn has skewed the interpretation of election and related concepts as well. The verb "become" in the final clause makes very clear that Paul is talking about something that happens *to and in the believer*, not something that happens for them in someone else, namely Jesus.[7] Yes, it only happens to them because they are in Christ. No, it is not referring to something wholly alien that exists only in Christ himself, who is somehow thought to be in some sort of union with the believer that doesn't actually make the believer righteous!

We've already had occasion to talk briefly about Eph. 1.4–14 but a few further comments are in order here. Close attention has to be paid to the phrase "in Him," which Paul keeps ringing the changes on in this passage. Believers are chosen "in Christ," who is the Elect One of God, for it is he who existed before the foundation of the universe and was picked by God to be the Savior. Even Calvin recognized that is what Eph. 1 is talking about, and of course Karl Barth followed Calvin, and his son Markus produced a magisterial commentary on Ephesians, with this being the right reading of the text. Chrysostom had long ago said that "God's choosing us in Christ means God chose us through faith in Christ." There is nothing at all in any of these texts against the notion that an unconditionally and eternally loving God might limit his own absolute freedom in order to allow humans to respond to him freely with the aid of divine grace or the work of the Spirit.[8]

God treats human beings as persons responsible for their own life choices, especially the most important ones. For any behavior to be genuinely loving or virtuous, it must involve the power of contrary choice. So, the concept of election here is incorporative, "in Christ." This idea of corporate election in Christ of both Jew and Gentile was intended as comfort for those who already believe, comfort that they can make the final eschatological goal because God will be working in them and be with them to the very end. Here Christ is the Elect One who does not need to be saved, but as the Elect One he does the saving, and salvation later in the opening long Greek sentence in Ephesians is said to happen by grace and through faith in Jesus the Elect One.[9]

---

[7] And one may wish to ask, as well, what in the world does it mean that Christ *became sin for us*? It does not mean he was turned into a sinner. At most it could only mean that he became the sin-bearer, the scapegoat for us, which actually just means that he bore the punishment for our sin, since sin is not a literal burden laid on Christ while on the cross. The one other live possibility is that it means he bore the guilt and punishment of sin for us. So "he became sin" simply cannot mean what Luther, taking the text hyperliterally, said it meant – namely he became a sinner for us! Were that the case, he could not be the sin-bearer who takes away the sin. Interestingly, in all of early Judaism the only place we hear the combination of "behold the lamb of God, who takes away the sins of the world," which seems to combine the scapegoat notion with the Passover lamb idea ("Christ our Passover was sacrificed," says Paul in 1 Cor. 5.7), is in Jn. 1.

[8] On Karl Barth's reading of such texts see now M. Galli, *Karl Barth: An Introductory Biography* (Grand Rapids, MI: William B. Eerdmans, 2017).

[9] For a detailed discussion of this passage see Witherington, *Letters to Philemon, the Colossians, and the Ephesians*, 227–37.

We turn now to a proper reading of the *crux interpretum* – Rom. 8.28–30. First of all, the context is that of a discussion of the work of the Holy Spirit in the believer who has "set us free from the law/ruling principle of sin and death" and helps us in our weakness, even when we have trouble praying. The Christian is not a person in the bondage to sin any more, whatever degree of degradation he or she may have experienced previously. Then the text reads: "But we know that for those who love God, all things work together [or if we follow P⁴⁶, A, B, and a few other mss., 'God works all things together …'] for good for those called according to choice/purpose [the word 'his' is not present in the Greek manuscripts]. For those whom he knew before hand, he also destined beforehand to share the likeness of the form of his Son, so that he might be the first born of many brothers and sisters. Those he destined beforehand, he also called, and those he called he also set right, and those he set right, he also glorified."

In v. 28 Paul makes a statement that he considers is or should be common knowledge. The statement is about "those who love God." Normally, Paul talks about God loving us, but not here. Here he is talking about the Spirit-empowered believer who loves God. The passage all the way through to the end of Rom. 8 is intended as a reassurance to Christians that God's power and providence is working for their good, and working on and in them, and indeed is in charge of "all things" such that the Christian doesn't need to worry about Satan, or circumstances, or illness, or other persons separating one from God and his plan in due course to make the believer fully conformed to the image of Christ finally by means of resurrection, but already now internally and progressively by means of sanctification (so 2 Cor. 4.16).

The discussion here is not about how one *becomes* a person who loves God, how a person becomes saved, how a person becomes a believer. It is about the destiny and destination of those who are *already* in Christ. This is especially clear because the relative pronoun οὕς, which occurs in both v. 29 and v. 30, has as its sole antecedent "those who love God," not "those who are one day destined to love God," not "those who were chosen before the foundation of the universe." The text quite plainly tells us that God foreknew "those who love God" and destined them in advance for a glorious conformity to the image of his Son. This text then has nothing to do with the notion that God arbitrarily plucked some persons out of the mass of unredeemed humanity to be justified or saved in the first place.

Since the language of destining is in play here, it is in order to point out that Paul is also not ruling out the possibility of "making shipwreck of one's faith" here, something he speaks about as early as in Gal. 5.19–20 and as late as in the Pastoral Epistles (1 Tim. 1.19–20).[10] Apostasy is a willful rejection of the work of God in the believer, a willful rebelling against God's presence in one's life, which grieves the Spirit and can lead to spiritual disaster. Apostasy is not about "losing" one's salvation, as if it could be misplaced. It is about what Heb. 6 says it is about – crucifying Christ afresh in one's life by rejecting the saving work of God already done in one's life.

---

[10] Notice the language about Paul turning them over to Satan, the very same thing we hear about the Christian guilty of incest who is a member of the Corinthian church in 1 Cor. 5. Church discipline, of course, is only administered to those who are believers.

And so, it is to be noticed that in the listing of the things that cannot separate a believer from the love of God, there is only one thing Paul quite studiously doesn't list – *the believer himself!* In short, this passage is neither about: (1) being destined to become a Christian, nor is it about (2) the eternal security of the Christian. God, when it comes to salvation, does not exercise his sovereignty in that way. What the passage is about is reassuring Christians in Rome that no Emperor, or governor, nor any celestial power, nor any human circumstance or disease can snatch a saved person out of the hands of an Almighty God. Herein is a great assurance, but what it is not is an affirmation of eternal security.

Why not? There are a variety of reasons, but the most important one is this – the heart of any relationship with God is love. It is the great commandment – "you shall love the Lord your God with all your being!" But love, unlike some things in life, cannot be pre-determined, coerced, or manipulated. It must be freely given and freely received or else it is not love.

God, as a text like Hos. 11 has already shown us, is a great lover, a great wooer of human beings to be his people. And that love must be freely received, and freely requited. In short, God gives humans and angelic beings a modicum of grace and freedom to freely return his love. Call it prevenient grace, call it the work of the Spirit enabling a person to respond to God's wooing, but here's the crucial bit – *God's grace does not work like a magnet does on iron filings. God is courting persons, not doing a science experiment as he calls and chooses people. God's grace enables our response, but it is not irresistible. Like other gifts of God, the recipient must freely exercise the gift that is given for it to be beneficial.*

Finally, it should have been abundantly clear from a close look at the language of "fore-knowing," which is found not only in Rom. 8 but also in Rom. 9–11, that God's knowing of something in advance does not mean that God has caused that something to happen in advance. That God works all things together for good for those that love God *does not mean all those things are good in themselves*, or that God has willed them all. God is not the author of sin and evil in the OT or in the NT. He is the Holy One who neither tempts nor can be tempted by anyone (see James 1).

God's knowledge is based on not only his own willing and actions but his absolutely omniscient knowing of the willing and actions of all other beings in the universe. God knew in advance who would love him before they did and planned a wonderful redemptive future for them, including final conformity to the image of his Son by means of resurrection. And that indeed will be glorious.

God reveals enough about our future to give us hope and great expectations, but not so much that we do not have to live by faith every day. But God has assured believers who trust God day after day that no outside person or force or circumstance or tragedy or disease can separate them from his love. We have absolute assurance that for those who remain "in Christ" the future is as bright as the promises of God.

We do not need, and we have no right to demand, that God guarantee our eternal security come what may, and do what we will. That would be to demand that we should not have to live by faith, seeing through a glass darkly, each day. That would be to demand "knowing as we are already known" and already "seeing face to face." But that is not the condition of the believer in this life. He is called a believer, and a truster, for a reason. "For faith is the *assurance* of things hoped for, and a conviction about things not yet seen" or known (Heb. 11.1). Assurance is one thing, certainty and eternal security is another.

What Does "the Righteousness of God" Refer To?

I take it as axiomatic that we should read Paul in light of his own Jewish and Greco-Roman contexts, and the previous discussion with Chad Thornhill in the last chapter shows the importance of this. While we may read Paul alongside the Reformers, they were not, any more than we are, infallible interpreters of Paul. So, we need to bear in mind from the outset that to question what the Reformers said about "wholly alien righteousness" or "the righteousness of Christ" or even "imputed righteousness" is not the same thing as questioning Paul himself. So, let's start with a few facts, if we may.

Firstly, the noun phrase "the righteousness of Christ" *does not show up anywhere in Paul*. Not once. Secondly, the term *theos* overwhelmingly refers to God the Father in Paul. The exceptions to this rule are exceedingly rare. In Phil. 2.6 it is stated that the Son has equality with God, but even in that sentence the word God refers to the Father. Rom. 9.5, however, seems to be a genuine exception to the rule, in a doxological remark, and Titus 2.13 may also be a reference to Christ as God, although the phrase "God our Savior" elsewhere in Titus refers to the Father, and the sentence in question can be read as "while we await the blessed hope and the manifestation of the glory of our great God and Savior Jesus Christ" or the last clause can be "of the great God *and* our Savior Jesus Christ," in other words, both of them. Now I have no problems with the idea that Paul thought of Christ as God, or as part of the divine identity, to use Richard Bauckham's language. But it is a fact that of the myriad uses of the term *theos* in Paul's letters, I have just mentioned *all* the likely cases where it does *not* refer to the Father. The default must surely be that when we find a use of the term in Paul, unless there are good contextual reasons to think otherwise, the term very likely refers to God the Father. And that brings us first to Rom. 1.16–17, the thesis statement of Paul's magnum opus:

For in the gospel the righteousness of God is revealed – a righteousness that is from the Faithful One unto faith, just as it is written: "The righteous will live by faith."

What does the phrase "the righteousness of God" mean in that thesis statement? I am on record already in my Romans commentary as saying it definitely doesn't refer to God's covenant faithfulness. Why would God feel *obligated* to keep his Mosaic covenant promises when the covenant had been broken over and over again by his people? When the covenant is broken, since it is absolutely *not* a unilateral and unconditional covenant, and since Paul says in Gal. 4 and 2 Cor. 3 that it was a temporary covenant until Christ should come, and is also an obsolete covenant that Christ brought to an end as a way of righteousness (Rom. 10.4), there is no reason at all to read the phrase "the righteousness of God" to refer to his loyalty to a pre-existing covenant. No, the righteousness of God is a reference to God's character and action, and the clear proof of this is what follows in Rom. 1.18–32, where we hear about the wrath of God against present idolatry and immorality. E. Käsemann was right – the righteousness of God is a statement about God's action, and what we can be sure of is that God will be faithful to his own character. He will be consistent, the same yesterday, today, and forever. He is not quixotic when it comes to his character. But as for broken covenants, he has no obligation to them, and the New Covenant is not simply a renewal of the Mosaic one. According to Paul it is the fulfillment of the Abrahamic one (again Gal. 4).

In Rom. 1.16–17, then, we have a reference to the righteousness of God the Father, not Christ's righteousness, and here it is apposite to point out that *God the Father did not die on the cross for us, so this phrase does not likely have to do with Christ's atoning death* on the cross or imputed righteousness from Christ to us, etc. Since we have been unable to be righteous (which is far more than being merely blameless and avoiding breaking the law) through keeping the Mosaic Law, God gives his righteousness to those who believe, in some, as of yet, undefined sense. The first-time listeners in Rome to Rom. 1, most of whom were not Paul's own converts, would never guess that Rom. 1.16–17 refers either to Christ's righteousness or to "God's covenant faithfulness."

Rom. 3.22 should also be considered, since it is the recapitulation and amplification on the thesis statement in Rom. 1.16–17. Here Paul says "but the righteousness of God comes through the faithfulness of Christ [or, if you insist, through faith in Christ] unto all those believing." I personally don't think Paul is being redundant here, so clearly the better translation is "through the faithfulness of Christ." In other words, we get the righteousness of God the Father objectively through the work of Christ on the cross, and this only comes "unto" all those believing subjectively because of the finished work of Christ on the cross. Again, Christ is the mediator of our getting this righteousness which comes from God the Father. He is the means, but it is not Christ's righteousness that we are getting!

What then of Phil. 3.9? There are several ways to translate this but to my mind the one that makes most sense involves an allusion to the death of Christ, by using the phrase "the faithfulness of Christ," which refers to his faithfulness even unto death on the cross. Thus, the verse reads, "so I might be found in Him not having a righteousness of my own that comes from the Mosaic Law, but rather one that comes *through* the faithfulness of Christ, the righteousness that comes *from God himself* based on faith." In the Greek, the distinction here is clear that righteousness comes to us through (*dia*) Christ the mediator, but it comes from (*ek*) God the Father. In other words, it's God the Father's righteousness we are talking about which we received because of the finished work of Christ on the cross.

So let's put the pieces together now: (1) the basis of the believer's right-standing with God the Father is the atoning death of Jesus; (2) Christ faithfully became the sin-bearer and took the punishment for our sins, so that we could be reconciled to God the Father; (3) but the goal was not merely to re-establish our relationship with God, but to change our fallen character, so that we can begin to emulate the character of Christ, with the eventual goal of full conformity to the image of Christ; (4) this is not about a "wholly alien righteousness," or Christ being righteous in our stead, or a legal fiction where God counts us as righteous when we are actually not. It is about becoming new creatures in Christ and being inwardly renewed day after day.

In short, the Reformers were so worried about "works righteousness" and "meriting salvation" that they over-read these texts in a way that referred to the righteousness of Christ himself, when in fact they refer to the righteousness of God the Father, the one who said in the first place, "be ye holy, as I am holy." This makes far better sense of the sequence from Rom. 1.16–17 to Rom. 1.18–32, where it is the wrath of God which is depicted as one sort of expression of the righteousness of God, and few would dispute that Rom. 1.18–32, with its echoes of Genesis, is about God the Father. *For biblical theology, all of this leads to a very significant conclusion indeed. It means that we need to learn everything we can from the OT and the NT about "the righteousness of God the Father" because that is the righteousness available to us through our Lord Jesus Christ.*

Let me be clear – salvation is by grace through faith. Sanctification is by grace through faith and results in our working out our salvation as God works in us to will and to do. None of this has anything to do with meritorious good works, or works being the basis of salvation. What it has to do with is correctly interpreting Paul in his original Jewish context.

On that score, the Reformers dropped the ball in various ways and as Stephen Chester has shown, various of their descendants keep making those mistakes. And here perhaps is the place to revisit the whole "grace" question, particularly in the Pauline corpus, and I can think of no one who can help us more with that subject that John Barclay, so as we draw this chapter to its close a reflection on Barclay's recent magisterial work *Paul and the Gift* is in order.

Reconfigured Grace

Barclay's *Paul and the Gift*[11] has reconfigured the discussion of "grace" in Paul's letters (and elsewhere) in important ways. Here it will be useful to summarize some of the key thrusts of this study and its implications for a biblical theology of grace going forward. It needs to be understood from the outset that this particular study is the first of two, and what is yet to be studied is what could be called the horizontal use of "gift"/grace language in Paul, for instance when he talks about the gift of his congregations for famine relief for the "saints" in Jerusalem.

This first study concentrates on the more "vertical" and "theological" (in the proper sense of the term) use of the *charis* language. Barclay in his detailed taxonomy of "gift" comes up with what he calls six perfections of the term: (1) superabundance (the size or character of the gift); (2) singularity (God's character as giver and nothing-but-giver); (3) priority (the timing of the gift before any initiative from the other side); (4) incongruity (the mismatch between the gift and the worth of the recipient; (5) efficacy (the ability of the gift to achieve the giver's intentions); and (6) non-circularity (gifts that escape any system of exchange or reciprocity). Barclay takes off on the observation of E. P. Sanders that Judaism is a religion of grace and covenantal nomism. True, says Barclay, *while grace is everywhere in Second Temple Judaism, it is not everywhere the same.* Thus, Paul may agree with all his fellow Jews that God is gracious, but which of these perfections did they adopt, and which did he?

One of the things that seems clear enough to me is that some NT scholars want to unnecessarily limit the meaning of the term *charis* and its OT counterparts because of the enormous theological implications of the word in various contexts. Part of the problem is the misreading of OT terms like HESED which we have already dealt with in this study,[12] and Barclay himself emphasizes "*the recent mistaken opinion that 'God's righteousness' means 'God's covenant faithfulness':* it *does* have that reference in certain textual contexts, but the lexeme 'God's righteousness' does not mean 'God's covenant faithfulness'"

---

[11] John M. G. Barclay, *Paul and the Gift* (Grand Rapids, MI: William B. Eerdmans, 2015).
[12] See pp. 288–91, above.

everywhere or outside of those contexts."[13] Exactly right. Words only have meanings in particular contexts and the spectrum of meaning is considerable when it comes to the term *charis*.

Further, Barclay is right to emphasize that *charis* in the larger corpus of Greek literature has three interrelated meanings: the quality of charm/agreeableness; benevolence or the gift/favor given; and gratitude. All of these meanings can be found in the NT as well as in wider Greek. He stresses: "The word *charis* itself does not have the specific sense of an undeserved or incongruous gift. It takes on that nuance in Paul but only because it there refers to God's gift given in the Christ-event. From that basis, and through translation into Latin (*gratia*) and its interpretation by Augustine, 'grace' has taken on the connotations of an unmerited gift, but we should not import that sense into every NT use of the word *charis*. The word relates to the domain of gifts, and gifts are normally given (for good reason) to fitting or worthy recipients. There is no reason to think that *charis* = undeserved gift. Only the context can indicate if that is the (unusual) sense required in particular cases."[14]

Barclay defines "gift" more particularly as follows: "Gift denotes the sphere of voluntary, personal relations, characterized by goodwill in the giving of benefit or favor, and eliciting some form of reciprocal return that is both voluntary and necessary for the continuation of the relationship."[15] There are several key points about this: (1) *the modern notion of "giving with no thought of return" is absolutely not part of the ancient concept of "gift" or grace. On the contrary, the gift is intended to set up a relationship. Nor is the notion of anonymous giving to be imported into the discussion of grace in the NT*; (2) the idea of predetermination of outcome (not merely predetermination of divine giving of grace), is also not to be imported into Paul's discussion of grace. Here's the way Barclay puts the matter:

> [I]t would be problematic for Paul, as for us, if our response to grace could not be considered in any sense "voluntary" (i.e. truly willed). Note how much he emphasizes in 2 Corinthians 8–9 that the Corinthians' gift (*charis*) to Jerusalem should be voluntary and not an extraction (2 Corinthians 9.5); otherwise in his eyes it would *not be a gift*. Now, "voluntary" in Paul's eyes does not mean "free of any external influence" (see how much effort he puts into persuading them to make this voluntary gift!): he does not labor under our illusion that we can and should act as completely autonomous individuals. But he does expect that God's work in us generates our own willing (Phil 2.12–13), as freed agents who could do otherwise (it is possible, in Paul's eyes, to fall out of grace).
>
> There is the tendency, in a line of interpretation from Augustine, through Calvin, to Jonathan Edwards, to "perfect" (radicalize or absolutize) the efficacy of grace, to the point where it causes, constrains, or compels our own wills. This is to turn God's agency/will and our agency/will into a zero-sum game: the more of one, the less of the other. But God's will is not on the same level as ours, working in the same causal nexus.[16]

---

[13] See my blog at Patheos, *The Bible and Culture*, discussion with Barclay about the book in the Fall of 2015, www.patheos.com/blogs/bibleandculture/2015.

[14] Barclay, *Paul and the Gift*, 562–74.

[15] *Ibid.*, 575.

[16] This from the email exchange in September 2015 which led to the blog posts in October 2015, used by kind permission of John.

He goes on to help clarify in what ways the Arminian rather than Calvinist view of the efficacy of grace seems closer to what Paul means as follows:

As far as I understand Arminianism (and I am not an expert), it represents a refusal to perfect the efficacy of grace as that had been developed in the later Augustine and in Calvinism. That is to say, while Arminians say much about the superabundance, the incongruity and the priority of grace (in the form of prevenience), they resist the strong notions of determinism or causation that became central in Calvinist understanding of the efficacy of grace. Hence, in Arminianism, the Spirit enables and helps us to respond to God's grace, and frees our will to do so, but God does not determine our response: we are freed by grace genuinely to accept or reject salvation. Hence the Arminian resistance to predestination if that is understood as predetermination, to limited atonement (a doctrine that only makes sense if God has from the beginning already predetermined who will respond to the saving work of Christ), and to the perseverance of the saints (Arminians insist that apostasy is genuinely possible).

Of course, notions of the efficacy of grace are bound up with how you understand the relation between divine and human (believer) agency, and zero-sum calculations (the more God is at work, the less we are) are perhaps not the best way to figure this. Thus, I hope my analysis will help those in the Wesleyan tradition to say: we believe fully in God's grace, and maximize (like Paul) its incongruity, but we just won't follow Calvinists in perfecting its efficacy in the way they do – but it is not clear that one has to do so in order to have a theologically adequate view of grace.[17]

What then are the implications of Barclay's study of gift for the concept of imputed righteousness? Here he says the following:

The notion of Christ's righteousness "imputed" to us is an attempt to spell out the "imputed" ("reckoned") language of Rom. 4.5, etc. as combined with verses like 1 Cor. 1.30 ("Christ became our righteousness," etc.) and 2 Cor. 5.20 ("so that in him we become the righteousness of God"). Theologically, it represents an insistence that whatever is said about our righteousness can be said only on the basis of our union with Christ: it is not (or not just) that grace is infused to aid us in our path of righteousness, but that everything "righteous" about the believer is founded on Christ. *Personally, I don't find the language of Christ's righteousness being imputed to us the most helpful (or an exegetically necessary) way of spelling that out, but the theological concern is real, and we certainly need to find ways of talking about the believer's righteousness that continually refers back to the gift of their new self and new agency by grace.* Luther's *simul justus et peccator* scheme is one way to do that, though ... I prefer something like *simul mortuus et vivens* (because I do not read Romans 7 as about Christian experience). Calvin puts more stress on our righteousness, but then insists that that is always imperfect and stained with sin, and its imperfections constantly require to be covered by Christ's righteousness. As I say, perhaps the language itself is less important than the anxiety not to let the Christian faith become another kind of moralism, and to keep insisting that who we are as well as what we do is always dependent on the unmerited grace of God.[18]

Barclay is helpful in other ways too, in regard to constructing a biblical theology. As can be seen in the following excerpt from our conversation, he thinks one big problem is taking a particular idea, or even a particular take on the idea of grace and perfecting that idea in a way that leads to contradicting various texts, for example texts that speak of Christ dying for the sins of the world, and those reflecting the divine intent in the first place. This is one reason why in this study I've stressed doing theology out of various parts of the canon, not just on the basis of Paul's main letters, and have stressed paying attention to the whole witness of the Bible on things like *HESED* and grace and God's salvation.

---

[17] *Ibid.*
[18] *Ibid.*

Barclay puts the matter this way:

One of the tasks of theology is to draw out the coherence of the various voices in the Bible, and that will mean a certain amount of systematization (or, alternatively, selection). I don't think that the effort to show connections or logical coherence is the problem so much as *the inclination to draw out a theme more and more along a certain trajectory (in my terms, perfecting it to the nth degree).* Where that perfection ends up contradicting the biblical texts (as in the examples one could cite with regard to "limited atonement") one has to ask whether that perfection (in this case the efficacy of grace) is really necessary or helpful theologically, or whether it is following a problematic form of logic. As you hint, one of the problems is that we tend to place God's agency and ours into a competitive relationship (the more of one, the less of the other). In my view, *the transcendence of God's freedom does not require that our freedom is constrained in the way that is often supposed ("if God willed this to happen, I can't have had real freedom to choose").*[19]

Obviously, in some forms of Protestant theology the *bête noire* is "works religion" or earning one's salvation, and so there has been a tendency to try and explain away the language of rewards in the Kingdom for good works, assuming that would amount to "earning" one's salvation. Here again, Barclay's discussion lays bare the fallacy in this whole line of thinking. I agree with him that Calvin does better justice to the reward language than Luther did. Barclay puts it this way:

Calvin was trying to take account of the fact that the biblical texts, OT and NT, speak of God's reward, such as the "crown of righteousness" for Paul and for those who long for Christ's appearing (2 Tim. 4.7–8). But Luther and Calvin also wanted to give decisive weight to the truth that Christ died for the ungodly (Rom. 5.6), so that salvation is by no means simply a reward for the righteous who merit it. They therefore wanted to draw a distinction between what, following Paul, we may call the foundation (which is Jesus Christ, the unmerited gift, 1 Cor. 3.11) and the various things that believers build up on that foundation, which might be hay and stubble, or silver and gold (1 Cor. 3.12–15). The important thing is that even the silver and gold would be worth nothing at all without the foundation on which they stand. But inasmuch as they are the sorts of things (actions and characters) that delight God, one can imagine God's delight in welcoming them (for which one might use the metaphor of reward). I have tried to explore this in the chapter on Romans 1–4 (chapter 15 of *Paul and the Gift*), where I argue that the incongruous gift of grace is designed to produce, at the last, *a kind of congruity between the holiness of the believer and the holiness of God.* So I think Luther and Calvin absolutely got what Paul was talking about with regard to the incongruity of the Christ-gift, and that is important to maintain. *But in my view Calvin gave a better account than Luther of the reward language of the New Testament, which is not, however, about salvation as reward, but about God's welcome of the alignment of our lives to his character and will, inasmuch as it arises from the new self, whose very being is gifted by grace.*[20]

It will be useful at this point, because John Barclay and I had an extended conversation about all sorts of critical matters involving Paul's theology of gift and grace, to give a small sample of the discussion as it impacts this particular study. Consider the following:[21]

BEN: One of the themes that arises multiple times in the *New Perspective* discussions (or the Radical Perspective end of that spectrum) is the notion not only that Paul is addressing specific situations in Galatians and Romans, but that in fact his theology of grace and God's righteousness

---

[19] Again, this is from our exchange in September 2015, but in addition Barclay consistently points to his own further discussion of these kinds of matters in the "Introduction" to John M. G. Barclay and Simon Gathercole, eds., *Divine and Human Agency in Paul and his Cultural Environment* (London: Continuum, 2006), 1–8.

[20] From the email exchange in September 2015.

[21] All part of the email exchange and later blog posts from September and October 2015.

is quite specifically tailored to his dominant audience – namely *Gentiles*. To me, this insight can be overplayed, because Paul is not just saying that "justification by grace through faith" is how Gentiles get into the body of Christ. He is saying that that is how *everyone* gets in, including himself, surely. For example, in Rom. 1 he stresses that the Good News about righteousness and faith in Christ is for "the Jew first" and also for the Gentile.

My point is that *I don't think a two-track model of salvation works as an analysis of Paul's thought*, especially when Rom. 11.25ff. seems to make clear that "all Israel will be saved in the future" "when the Redeemer comes forth from heavenly Zion and turns away the impiety of Jacob." You don't talk about the impiety of Jacob if you think they are already saved by some other means than Christ, and you don't talk about Jewish branches temporarily broken off from the people of God, so they can be reintegrated into that group by grace through faith in Jesus, if you are touting a two-track model of salvation. In short, it seems to me that very few of the *New Perspective* folks, going all the way back to Stendahl, really grasp the nettle when it comes to the radical nature of Paul's thought when it comes to how exactly non-Christian Israel is and will be saved. Do you agree with this line of thinking, or does it have some flaws in it?

JOHN: You are right that Stendahl, in consort with Gager and Gaston in his day, and followed now by the "radical new perspective" (Stowers, Zetterholm, etc.) were/are very unwilling to find in Paul anything that suggested that Paul expected Jews to change in practice or belief, and one way to argue that is to say that his negative comments about the authority of the law are only as it relates to Gentiles (his only audience).

Basically, I agree with you that Paul does expect Jews like himself to be challenged, and reconstituted, by the Gospel, even if he finds a deep connection between what God has done in Abraham etc. and what he has done in Christ. In my reading of Rom. 9–11 (chapter 17 of Paul and the Gift) *I agree with you that Paul expects ethnic Israel to be saved by faith in Christ – though this will be not an addition to, and certainly not a denial of, their Jewish scriptural heritage, but rather its fulfillment, since God has constituted Israel all along by an incongruous grace (which I take to be the root of the olive tree in Rom. 11).*

BEN: Let's talk a bit about the phrase "works of the Law," which is so prominent in the discussions by the *New Perspective* folks. Dunn, among others, wants to argue that the phrase refers to the boundary-defining rituals which separate Jews from Gentiles – namely circumcision, kosher laws, and Sabbath keeping. Paul is combatting nationalistic chest-thumping and hubris. The assumption behind this assumption seems to be that Paul couldn't possibly be suggesting that "all possible works of the Mosaic Law" are passé, or no longer binding on any of God's people. And behind that is the assumption of Reformed theology that Paul held to a "one covenant in various administrations" view of covenant theology.

Yet Paul quite clearly in Gal. 4, 2 Cor. 3–4, Rom. 9.1–5, and Rom. 10.1–5 in fact tells us that Christ is the end or fulfillment of that Mosaic law covenant, and that the new covenant is connected through Christ with the Abrahamic covenant, not the Mosaic one which was a *paidagogos*, a temporary childminder until Christ came. Paul affirms multiple covenants given by God to his people, not one covenant in many administrations. In short, what is at stake is not a Lutheran reading of the Mosaic Law, but a Calvinistic and Reformed one. Why do you think this part of the discussion has become so heated, so often? Why does it seem, at least to me, that Dunn and Tom Wright "protesteth too much" on these sorts of issues? What is your take on all this?

JOHN: I have a discussion on "works of the law" in chapter 12 of *Paul and the Gift* (when we get to Gal 2.15–16) and think on exegetical grounds that it means just "the practice of the Mosaic Law" and does not single out, or prioritize, any particular works like circumcision, etc. In that respect I disagree with Dunn, who, influenced by his Reformed training (he refers to the Westminster Confession), is not inclined to allow any general critique of the Mosaic law, or any sense that its era may have come to an end. Of course, how to read *telos* in Rom. 10.4 (as "end" in the sense of cessation or "end" in the sense of fulfillment) is at the exegetical heart of this whole debate, which has divided Lutherans and Calvinists from the very start. As you say, in Gal. 3 Paul makes clear that the Mosaic Law had an authority for a limited time (starting 430 years after Abraham and until

Christ): he does not think it is wrong as such, but it is no longer the final authority for those in Christ (even if they fulfill its core intention by walking in the Spirit). Romans brings out more this sense of the core intention of the law ("the work of the law," Rom. 2.15; or "the just requirement of the law," Rom. 8.4), which indicates that believers do what the Law, at heart, was looking for. But that its final authority is broken even for Jews is clear in that, even in Romans, Paul can say that he is persuaded in the Lord Jesus that nothing is unclean in itself (Rom. 14.14) and that "the Kingdom of God is not food and drink, but righteousness and peace and joy in the Holy Spirit" (Rom. 14.17). The Torah's rules remain an honorable cultural tradition, which Paul wants the weak to be allowed to continue (Rom. 14–15); but they also have to recognize that one can live to the Lord (God/Christ) in ignoring kosher rules, as well as in honoring them.

BEN: Don Carson and others of those who wrote in the volume entitled *Variegated Nomism* seem to be engaging in what I would call a rearguard action to protect the old Calvinistic analysis of early Judaism, in particular that there were numerous advocates in early Judaism of "works right-eousness" which Paul is critiquing. They totally want to avoid the notion that Paul is in fact saying that the Mosaic covenant, and not either legalism or works righteousness, is the real issue here. As you suggest, one of the main reasons for this whole approach is not just allegiance to a traditional Reformed analysis of Paul, but an attempt to perfect a variety of concepts conjured up by the word *grace*, all at once, or to mush them up together. Why do you think that people as different as Carson and Doug Campbell want to push this button?

JOHN: It is always tempting to push a concept to its logical extreme, and Christian theologians have for centuries enjoyed claiming that others have a defective understanding of grace because those others don't perfect it in the way they think it should be. I read Carson as pushing all the Calvinist buttons (even in the language he uses), and Campbell as a natural-born radical who is influenced most by Barth but wants to push even Barthian perfections of grace to their nth degree. There is an attraction in being a "purist" in these matters (others are then compromisers who don't properly see the truth), and I guess Paul's own polemics on this topic encourage people to think that the more they are polemical the more they are like Paul ... But we sometimes apply Pauline polemics to topics he did not get hot under the collar about.

BEN: Two of the biggest contributions of your book, in my judgment, are: (1) demonstrating at some length the various ways *charis* terminology was used in Paul's world, and how differently it was used in a benefaction culture from how it is often used in the modern context when we talk about "giving with no thought of return" and the like. What shocked me is how little the discussions of grace in Paul in the last century have even reflected a knowledge of this important contextual information for understanding Paul. And, somehow, the *New Perspective* folks have to some degree pushed "grace" to the margins of Paul's discussion in Romans and elsewhere – amazing! (2) I espe-cially think your sixfold taxonomy is very helpful for sorting out which aspects of grace Paul is indeed perfecting (e.g. its priority) and which he is probably not perfecting. What happens if and when Protestant scholars, especially, realize that they have been evaluating Paul far too much in light of their own historical theological traditions, and not enough in light of Paul's own cultural context, both Greco-Roman and Jewish?

JOHN: The older books on grace (Moffatt) did show some knowledge of the ancient world, and Harrison's recent book on grace in the Greco-Roman world is a recovery and development of that tradition. But there was always the tendency to take Paul as the exception: others thought gifts required a return, but Paul believed in the unilateral or unconditional gift (in the sense of requiring no return), etc. I have tried to feed in important resources from the anthropology of gift, to expose and critique modern notions of gift, and to question how much these modern notions apply to Paul, and thus to approach Paul with a more open mind: which of the possible ways of perfecting divine grace did he employ and which did he not? As you will see from the second half of my book, I think the key perfection for Paul is *incongruity* (God gives in Christ without regard to worth), but this does not mean that the gift is also given with no thought of return. The disaggregation of the dif-ferent perfections of gift is, for me, the key methodological work of *Paul and the Gift*, and I have had systematic theologians tell me that it would have saved an awful lot of controversy in Christian history if these distinctions had been made clear earlier!

And So?

In a real sense, one of the keys to understanding this particular study of biblical theology with its subtitle of *The Convergence of the Canon* is that I am trying to read the whole biblical witness while taking into account Barclay's helpful taxonomy of grace and how it helps us allow the varying different nuances of the term shed light on notions of election, atonement, salvation, reward, and other related ideas in a holistic discussion of biblical theology. This study would not have been possible without John Barclay's detailed work on this matter. At the end of the day, it is important to stress that many key theological concepts such as grace, righteousness, election, salvation, covenant do not stand alone. They are closely related to one another, and how you interpret the meaning of one of these key terms affects, necessarily, how one interprets the others. If you get one of them basically wrong, you are likely to get the others at least partially wrong. And then there is the further problem that when you treat these terms not as a part of efforts at theologizing into particular contexts, not as a part of God's ongoing progressive revelation of his will and ways and of the knowledge of God in history but rather as some sort of set of abstract ideas which one must move around the Scrabble board until all the pieces are used and connected to one another, you are bound to misunderstand biblical theology. And especially if one undertakes such an exercise without paying close attention to the *telos*, the goal that the revelation is pressing toward, the goal that eschatological history is pressing toward, one has not done justice to the subject. Accordingly, in the next chapter we must consider the endgame, the endtimes, the final future theologically conceived.

13

Faith in the Final Future: The New Creation

The future is as bright as the promises of God.
Attributed to both William Carey and Adoniram Judson

The rapture will not be secret but open and manifest. Its purpose will not be to whisk the elect away from the earth for a while until Christ returns for a "second" Second Coming. The purpose of the rapture is to allow the saints to meet Jesus in the air as He returns and be included in His entourage during His triumphal descent from Heaven. His coming in this manner will be attended by the general resurrection, the final judgment, and the end of the world.
R. C. Sproul[1]

The Story Thus Far ...

By way of synopsis, we have established that God is the most essential item in the symbolic universe which configures and reconfigures everything else that could even be called fundamental assumptions. The one, unique, living God is the colossus that blots out any other possible suns, with all light, all revelation coming from this one deity. God is not argued for, he is assumed, presupposed, depended upon. What is especially remarkable about this, whether we think of the OT context or the NT context is the environment that Jews inhabited was polytheistic from start to finish, and there are many indications just how tempting it was to commit idolatry and go after foreign gods.

Yet even the writers of the OT kept insisting Yahweh was unique, he was the only true, the only living, the only creating and redeeming deity to be encountered. The other spiritual beings out there did not deserve to be called God with a capital "G." Yes, they existed, and had some influence, but Yahweh was so different, so "almighty," so great and glorious that there was constant resistance to simply adding Yahweh to someone else's pantheon of deities. Others might start there, perhaps calling Yahweh "the Most High God" but at the end of the day, Yahweh was incomparable. The further one gets in the OT, the more emphatic, not the less emphatic, the cry becomes in the language of exilic Isaiah – "no

---

[1] Long ago, I took R. C. Sproul's apologetics course at Gordon-Conwell Theological Seminary in about 1976. This was one of things he stressed when talking about the future and the erroneous Dispensational views about the rapture.

one is like the Holy One of Israel." No one, but no one. The monotheizing tendencies of the OT writers becomes more emphatic the further one works through the OT chronologically. The Bible begins with the revelation of the Father, which is the main revelation throughout the OT, it continues to the revelation of the Son in the Gospels, and then in Acts and elsewhere we have the revelation not only of the person of the Holy Spirit, but of the work of Father, Son, and Spirit together, and we learn, for instance in Hebrews, that all along, the Father, the Son, and the Spirit were speaking in and by God's Word.

We also saw that the way that the divine identity was conceived was complex. It could include the notion that this one God could express the divine identity in more than one personal form. And while some might expect that the Jewish conception of God might get simplified over time, in fact progressive revelation went in quite the other direction. Yet, this process was not about elevating "exalted angels" like Michael or Gabriel to the throne of God. No, it was about unveiling a "one like a Son of Man" who descends from heaven, is given all authority, all the kingdoms by the Ancient of Days (Yahweh in person) and is to be worshipped by all and is to be the judge of all. It is, to use an inadequate analogy, a bit like a matryoshka doll, which appears to be just one doll, but on closer inspection there is another doll inside, and yet another one inside that doll as well.

That we are well on the way to a theology of the Trinity in the NT is clear enough from the fact that the Father is seen as a person, the Son is seen as a person, and the Spirit as well is seen as a person, a *parakletos* or agent of the Son, just as the Son is seen as a personal agent or advocate of the Father. And yet with all this, the writers of the NT are not prepared at all to turn in their monotheistic credentials. No, they will instead modify the Shema to *include these other persons in the one God* (1 Cor. 8.6). You may call this a strange sort of monotheism, but monotheism nonetheless it is.

We then spent no little time dealing with the narrative thought world of both the OT and the NT and saw that the stories the Bible tells are overwhelmingly the stories of God's people, not the story of "everyone." This is even true in Genesis, where the writers are unconcerned that Cain and Abel find wives from "elsewhere" or that Cain is sent off to a land where other human beings live but are not children of Adam. And the same can be said about Noah and his kin. The story of salvation history has to do with the origins, journeys, and destinies of God's people, and others come into the story only insofar as they get on (and stay on) the chosen people's train or interact negatively with God's people. This is true from Genesis to Revelation.

The big difference in the NT is of course is that there is a massive evangelistic effort to recruit "the others," "the nations," "the pagans" to get them on board the glory train of Father, Son, and Holy Spirit. But where exactly is this train headed? Where is the final frontier? Where can one find the new creation so long longed for? We intend to deal with that question in this chapter, but a few more preliminary remarks are in order first.

The manner in which God relates to his people is through covenants, and we have spent considerable time examining the nature of biblical covenants, their similarities and differences with other ancient treaties, the differences between the various OT covenants with Noah, Abraham, Moses, David, and of course the promised New Covenant of Jeremiah. We dealt with the relationship of sacrifice to the inauguration of these covenants, and in Appendix B the reader will find a detailed discussion of how the death of Jesus was viewed as an atoning and New Covenant inaugurating sacrifice, bringing salvation in the form of both forgiveness of sins and personal transformation. The New Covenant is the last covenant, for it comes as part of the inauguration of the "end times," the eschatological final saving intervention of God in this world in the person of his Son, Jesus.

We also examined the relationship between the concept of covenant and the concepts of chosenness and election, and noted several key points: (1) election is a corporate concept in both the OT and the NT – it involves a chosen people Israel in the OT and it involves all those who are in Christ in the NT. Christ is the Elect One, the Righteous One, in the NT and we stressed that his being elect does not involve him needing to be "saved." He is the Elect One who saves others. In other words, election is one thing, salvation is another. (2) Election in the OT does not guarantee the salvation of particular Israelites, to be sure we hear of many of them defecting, falling by the wayside along the way. Indeed, the ones called "the elect" frequently are those who are the righteous, and it is no accident that in Dan. 12.1–3 as well as in Jn. 5 we hear that there will be a positive resurrection of the righteous. Their behavior has something to do with this outcome. There is no idea in the OT of certain persons being chosen before the foundation of the universe to receive eternal salvation, indeed the Christian idea of salvation by grace through faith in the crucified and risen Jesus is absent from the OT. This is not to say that there isn't plenty of grace and rescue and intimate relationship between God and his people in the OT. There certainly is. (3) Further, we noted that it is a misreading of covenant theology to think in terms of one covenant between God and his people in many administrations. God keeps loving and redeeming his people because of his *character*, because that is the kind of person God is, not because of his unilateral faithfulness to a broken covenant, for instance a broken Mosaic covenant. Indeed, covenants were not in antiquity unilateral, they were always bilateral, even when there was a suzerain and a vassal involved. And finally, covenants all had promises and stipulations. There were not promise covenants vs. law covenants. (4) The concept of election focuses on the Elect One who inaugurates the New Covenant by means of his death. Persons enter the saved people by grace through faith in Jesus. For those who love God, God has planned a wonderful future of sanctification and glorification and finally full conformity to the image of the Son at the resurrection of those in Christ. Finally, we become what we admire. (5) God is all about his character being replicated in his people, and to that end he is about our "becoming the righteousness of God," which has to do with imparted righteousness, not imputed righteousness. The noun phrase "the righteousness of Christ," interestingly enough, does not exist in the Pauline literature. Salvation indeed involves grace from start to finish, but there is need for a full and free and faithful response to that grace every step along the way. God did not predestine some "to love God," rather God knew in advance, as Rom. 8 says, who would do so, and those he destined for a glorious future. For freedom, Christ has set us not only free from sin, but free for a loving response to God with our whole hearts, and for loving our neighbor as self. (6) Freedom, the power of contrary choice, on the other hand, means that however unlikely, apostasy is not impossible for a follower of God, and of Christ, hence the numerous warnings to Jews and Gentiles, both in the OT and in the NT against apostasy (see e.g. Heb. 6). Yes, there is an assurance of salvation and a gift of the Spirit, but assurance is not eternal security, it is rather a stimulus to faith and faithful living. The Spirit can indeed be grieved, and Paul even warns against quenching the Spirit. (7) All of this has to do with how God actually exercises his sovereignty, and the Bible is consistent in saying that God makes room for angels and human beings to have a modicum of freedom of choice so their response to God may be in love, and not by coercion, or predetermination.[2] Love, in any case, if it is real love cannot be manipulated, coerced, or predetermined, and the freedom the Bible refers to is not merely the absence of feeling compelled, it involves the actual power of contrary choice through the aid of God's grace. Virtue would be impossible if our behavior could not be otherwise, whether in a good or bad direction. And lastly, (8) this empowering of sentient beings who are less than God explains the origins of sin and evil. Angels and humans are responsible for such things, not the almighty God, who cannot even be tempted, and tempts no one (James 1). Bearing these things in mind, we turn to the final future.

The Beginning of the New Creation

There is a reason Paul speaks of Christ as the last Adam. In his view, he is the beginning of the new creation, God starting over again with the human race from the beginning. Before there could be "if anyone is in Christ there is a new creation" there had to be a new creation involving Jesus himself. Whether one speaks of the incarnation, of the Word taking on flesh and dwelling among us (Jn. 1), or one speaks of a virginal conception, which is seen as the means by which the incarnation happens (Lk. 1 and Mt. 1), either way we are talking about a new creation that involves Jesus himself and we must examine both of these ways of theologizing about the significance of the coming of the Son of God. Before there could be a new announcement of the Good News about God's divine saving activity breaking into history, and before there could be a new covenant, there had to be a new person, a new Son of Man, born of woman, born under the Law, to redeem those under the Law and those outside the Law once and for all. Let us consider the virginal conception first and its theological significance.

The Virginal Conception

Our concern here is with the theological significance of the virginal conception, having dealt with the historical and exegetical issues in Lukan and Matthean commentaries.[3] The most important point to make about the relationship between Isa. 7.14 and these accounts in the Gospels is that it is highly unlikely that the OT text generated these stories. The Hebrew text of Isa. 7.14 says simply that a nubile young woman (whose virginity is implied) will conceive and give birth to a child, and while the LXX uses the word *parthenos* the text doesn't state *by what means* a virgin will conceive, and the normal assumption in early Judaism was that it would be in the normal way, though the text could be read otherwise. My point is this – it is the event in the life of Mary that led to a rereading of Isa. 7.14, on the assumption that somewhere in the prophecies of the OT this significant

---

[2] It is one of the more interesting artful dodges of Reformed theology that we owe primarily to the greatest early American theologian, Jonathan Edwards, who suggested in his landmark work *The Freedom of the Will* that what that freedom amounted to was our not feeling coerced or manipulated, even though we did not have the power of contrary choice and the outcome of our choice was predetermined!

[3] See Witherington, *Matthew*, and Levine and Witherington, *The Gospel of Luke*.

event must have been mentioned. The event led to the reinterpretation of the text; the text did not generate this story.

The story of the virginal conception is not a *theologoumenon*, a non-historically based theological story. Another very good reason to come to this conclusion is that early Judaism was an honor and shame culture. Knowing that there was no precedent for a virginal conception, this story would read as a story about a woman pregnant out of wedlock, and so a story about a major sin. An early Jew would not make up a story like this, because it could always be understood to allude to Jesus being illegitimate. And, of course, this was precisely what was suggested by a pagan named Celsus in the second century (Origen, *Contra Celsum* 1.32), namely that Mary committed adultery with a Roman soldier named Panthera, and a few note the first-century epitaph, found in Germany, of a fellow conveniently named Tiberius Julius Abdes Pantera. The potential for this story to suggest something scandalous makes it highly unlikely the story was made up. And just to make things ultra-clear, in Mt. 1.25 we hear "and he [Joseph] was not knowing her until she gave birth to a son."

So, what are the theological implications of this story? Firstly, that the miracle transpires at the point of conception, not at the point of birth, so we should not call this a story about a virgin birth. Secondly, the miracle involves the Holy Spirit "overshadowing" Mary, which might suggest protection. In any case, the point is that the child is a gift from God. Does the story also suggest that this means of the Son of God entering the world was necessary so that Jesus could be like pre-fallen Adam, with no taint of sin, no fallen nature? This certainly makes theological sense, not least because in Luke's account we are told that Mary's child will be holy from conception due to the power and influence of the Holy Spirit being involved (1.35) but also because in Luke's genealogy (Lk. 3.38) the comparison with Adam is made – Jesus is son of Adam, son of God. Like the first Adam, he would not be a human being on earth at all without a miraculous creation by God, directly. Also like Adam, he did not come into this world a sinner or with a sin nature. The implication is that sin is not a natural limitation of human nature. The natural limitations of time, space, knowledge, power, and mortality Jesus *does* partake in, being truly human, but he does not partake in sin, nor succumb to temptation. The human race was starting over again in basically the same way it started in the first place – with this difference. This time God the Son was coming in person as Jesus, and because both these things were true, about his divinity and his humanity, this made the virginal conception all the more necessary, for God could not be conjoined with a fallen human nature. And lastly, this brings up one further point. The virginal conception rules out the notion of adoptionist Christology, the idea that Jesus got a promotion to divinity by means of the resurrection. So what is going on in Jn. 1?

The Word Takes on Flesh

It is not a surprise that Jn. 1 profoundly informed the way the discussion went about the two natures of Christ at the Council of Chalcedon in the mid-fifth century AD. Then, too, the parallels between Gen. 1 and Jn. 1 have been noted so many times that it hardly needs to be belabored and we've already discussed these things when we talked about the Christological hymns.[4] But what is not often noted is that one of the implications of those parallels is that

---

[4] See above.

God is starting his creation over with the pre-existent Word of God taking on flesh in the person of Jesus. Not only was the Word present and involved with the original creation, the Word becomes the first eschatological event of the new creation. Like the first Adam, this one also must face temptations and difficulties, but unlike the first one he will pass the test, becoming "the first born of many brothers and sisters," many new creations.

There are some seven places in the NT where Christ is called God, or to put it another way where there is a unique Christological use of the term θεός. In all other instances in the NT, the term θεός refers to the one Christians called the Father, and Jews knew as Yahweh. Jn. 1.1 is of course the most famous of these Christological uses of the term, but one can also cite the following diverse uses of this newly applied God language: Rom. 9.5 (probably the earliest such reference appears in a doxological remark), Titus 2.13; 2 Pet. 1.1; Heb. 1.8; Jn. 1.18, 20.28. Several of these use the modifier "my" or "our" which could be said to make a personal rather than exclusive claim, on a parallel with 1 Cor. 8.4–6 – where Paul says there are gods many and lords many, but for us there is one God, the Father, and one Lord, Jesus Christ. The personal modifier "my" or "our" means that this is the Christian community's deity, but it does not, in itself, rule out that there might be others. Jn. 1.1 and Rom. 9.5 especially are of a different ilk.

Sometimes it has been queried, for instance by the Jehovah's Witnesses responsible for the New World Translation, why the definite article is not used in Jn. 1.1 for "the Word" and so they suggested the translation "a god" (or divine being). The problem with this is that they don't adequately know Greek grammar! When you have a stative verb "to be" and a post-positive subject, in this case "God" (so the text literally reads with proper word order "and God was the Word") a post-positive subject in Greek does not take the indefinite article.

And, of course, there is a very good reason why the writer would not want to call the "Word" "*the* God," because he does not believe that the Word exhausts the Godhead. Indeed, in the same sentence he has already also called the Father God! The term God here is used of both the Father and the Son in the same way. This is truly remarkable. *This means that the term God here has a generic meaning, not referring to just one person, Yahweh, but to all those who share the divine identity. This sort of use of the term God is distinctive, especially since it includes someone who took on flesh and became a real historical person – Jesus of Nazareth. There is no precedent for this precise sort of use of God language in the OT or early Judaism.*

New Testament scholars have often been apt to suggest that what is going on here is the transfer of "God" language to the Son, just like the transfer of Lord language from the Father to the Son (see 1 Cor. 8.4–6). While this may be correct, if Richard Bauckham is right, what the author may be intending is to simply signal that the term θεός refers to the divine identity in general, which in this case is said to involve both the Father and the "Logos," two distinguishable persons, both part of the one divine identity, the only true and living God. If that is the case, then the author is not an early advocate of binitarian-ism, indeed what he says about the Spirit in Jn. 14–17 rules that out anyway, but rather an early adopter of a redefinition of the term God to mean something like "the divine identity" (in multiple persons). In any event, this passage, the so-called Christological hymn in Jn. 1, is deeply indebted to earlier discussions about the role of Wisdom in crea-tion and redemption in Prov. 3, 8–9, Wisdom of Solomon, Sirach, 1 En. 42. Wisdom is a personification in the OT, is identified with Torah in Sirach, taking on the character of something tangible, God's written word, and is then identified with a person in Jn. 1. The term λόγος, rather than σοφία, is likely used because it is a reference to a Son, God's only begotten Son, since the word for wisdom in both Hebrew and Greek involves a noun of the female gender. But the description here and in Col. 1 and in Heb. 1 is clearly very indebted to the description of Wisdom in the aforementioned Jewish texts. It should be noted, then, that Wisdom is a personification of a quality or attribute of the biblical God in the OT, part of the divine identity itself. It is not seen as a separate deity or the promotion of an angelic being to a second deity, but rather simply part of the divine identity. This, I would suggest is exactly how the author of Jn. 1 sees the matter as well. The Son is the only begotten or "natural" Son, all other sons and daughters of God are such by adoption, or as it is described in John – reborn of God, born again.

So, to sum up, in the Fourth Gospel we are hearing how the pre-existent Son of God, who is also appropriately called God, became Jesus of Nazareth, taking on flesh and being truly human, whereas in Luke and Matthew we are hearing how the last Adam who is also the Son of David came to be a human with an unfallen, untainted human nature, and started the race all over again. The former is more about the divine identity side of the equation, the latter is more about the truly human side of the equation, but both are emphasizing that being part of the divine identity and being a genuine human being as God intended are not in competition with one another but can be two sides to the identity of one and the same person. It is important to emphasize this because nothing is said about Jesus of Nazareth having two natures in any of Gospels. Actions and words are simply predicated of the one person, Jesus, the Son of God, the last Adam, the Son of Man, the Christ. Some of these predications are not appropriate before the incarnation.

For example, there was no *Jesus* before he was conceived in the womb of Mary the Virgin. There was no last Adam until that happened, either. What there was, was God's Wisdom, and God the Word, and the pre-existent only begotten or unique Son of God before all worlds. But we have not yet broached the crucial topic of divine condescension, which we must now do. How is it possible for the Word to take on flesh, the Son of God to become the Son of Man, the First before all creation and all creatures, to become the last Adam, the one who restarts the human race? The first thing to say is that the old *kenotic* theory doesn't work. The Word did not cease to be the Word in order to become Jesus. The Son of God did not cease to be the divine Son when he became Jesus. But clearly, the Incarnation involves a change, a taking on of true humanity, a human identity, yes, a human nature.

Here Phil. 2 helps us with understanding the divine condescension. The Christ hymn there exhorts us to have the same mindset as Christ:

Who, being in very nature God,
did not consider equality with God something to be used to his own advantage;
⁷ rather, he made himself nothing
by taking the very nature of a
servant, being made in
human likeness.
⁸ And being found in
appearance as a man,

he humbled himself
by becoming
obedient to
death – even death
on a cross!
⁹ Therefore God exalted him to the
highest place and gave him the
name that is above every name,
¹⁰ that at the name of Jesus every knee
should bow, in heaven and on earth
and under the earth,
¹¹ and every tongue acknowledge that Jesus
Christ is Lord, to the glory of God the
Father.

There is much we have already said about this,[5] but what I want to emphasize here is the following. (1) We are talking about divine self-limitation through the free choice of God the Son. (2) He accepts the natural limitations of being human – limitations of time, space, knowledge, power, and mortality. He does not take on the limitations of sin, which is not a God-given or "natural" human limitation. It would appear from Gen. 2 that the tree of life in the Garden was not there by accident, or for no good purpose. Perhaps Adam and Eve are envisioned as vulnerable to being harmed even killed, hence the positive and protective environment. Their nature may not be inherently fallen, subject to natural decay and death, but as humans they are fragile, vulnerable, mortal. Had they chosen to eat of the tree life, presumably they would have been "immortal" in the sense that going forward they had everlasting life, and would not be subject to disease, decay, and death.[6] Jesus' mortality, that he could be killed, places him in the same category of the original couple before the Fall. And perhaps the exclusion of the couple from the Garden was so they would not eat of the tree of life after their sin, and so become everlastingly fallen creatures. No, God knew that after the Fall, they needed to have their very natures transformed, not merely made permanent. (3) In order to be truly human, Jesus does not draw on his divine power and identity to perform miracles, though he could do so. Rather he performs them by the power of the Holy Spirit that anointed him at the baptism. Thus, he can command his disciples to do the same works, by the power of the Spirit later, and even suggests they will do even greater "works" than he did. (4) Jesus truly knows what he knows, and he has a clear channel reception to what the Father tells him, yet he must still listen to the Father, he must learn things along the way (Lk. 2.41–52), and indeed he needs to be informed of things like "who touched him." Christ's life is not a charade in which he pretends not to know things, pretends to be tired, pretends to not be able to do some things, pretends to be tempted by Satan. Finally, there are things the Father knows that he has not revealed to the Son in his early days (Mk. 13.32). As I said, he partakes of the limitations of time,

---

[5] See above.
[6] Here the famous story by Jonathan Swift, Dean of St. Patrick's Cathedral, Dublin and author of *Gulliver's Travels*, about the man who asked for everlasting life but not everlasting youth comes to mind and so he gets older and older, and more and more decrepit, but is unable to die.

space, knowledge, power, and mortality we all share. Jesus is truly human. The trick is to understand how he can be both 100 percent true, genuine unfallen human, last Adam, and at the same time a 100 percent participant in the divine identity. My answer is, by divine self-limitation, which is what Phil. 2 tells us.

In addition, Phil. 2 also tells us that not only was there a change for Jesus at the incarnation, but there was a change for Jesus at the resurrection. He assumed a new role – risen Lord and took on a new stage in his career. He was an appropriate object of worship, before whom all should bow and confess him to be the risen Lord, and this did not take anything away from God's glory, it added to it. As a true human, Jesus is obedient to God the Father, even unto his death on the cross. He is Adam gone right, rather than Adam gone wrong. In the process of describing this, Paul tells us that true humility is the quality of a strong person who steps down and serves others, taking the form not merely of a human but of a servant. Humility is not an attitude about self (such as feelings of low self-worth), but rather a self-reflexive action – "he humbled himself," which is probably the main thing Paul has in mind when he says "have this mind in yourself that was also in Christ Jesus." He probably also means that true humility means letting God do the exalting, not exalting oneself. Our role, like Christ's, is to serve others and be obedient and faithful even unto death, even if it involves martyrdom. All this provides us with the appropriate background for grasping the temptation scenes in Mt. 4 and Lk. 4.

The Temptations of the Son of God

Mt. 4.1–11
Then Jesus was led by the Spirit into the wilderness to be tempted by the devil. ² After fasting forty days and forty nights, he was hungry. ³ The tempter came to him and said, "If you are the Son of God, tell these stones to become bread."

⁴ Jesus answered, "It is written: 'Man shall not live on bread alone, but on every word that comes from the mouth of God.'"

⁵ Then the devil took him to the holy city and had him stand on the highest point of the temple. ⁶ "If you are the Son of God," he said, "throw yourself down. For it is written:

"'He will command his angels
concerning you, and they will lift
you up in their hands,
so that you will not strike your foot against a stone.'"

⁷ Jesus answered him, "It is also written: 'Do not put the Lord your God to the test.'"

⁸ Again, the devil took him to a very high mountain and showed him all the kingdoms of the world and their splendor. ⁹ "All this I will give you," he said, "if you will bow down and worship me."

¹⁰ Jesus said to him, "Away from me, Satan! For it is written: 'Worship the Lord your God, and serve him only.'"

¹¹ Then the devil left him, and angels came and attended him.

James 1 of course tells us that God, in his divine being, cannot be tempted and tempts no one. But that does not settle the question for a person who is at one and the same time both truly human and truly divine. And I would suggest that Jesus is being tempted in a very unique, one could even say odd, way in this passage, for these are not ordinary temptations he is facing, and Satan does not say: "If you are a genuine human being, then …" No, he says "if you are the divine Son of God I know you to be … then …" In other words, these are the temptations not merely of Jesus as last Adam, though they are that, but temptations someone who participates in the divine identity would and could face.

To put things bluntly – Satan is tempting Jesus to push the God button which he genuinely has, tempting him to do things mere mortals cannot do. But if Jesus does that, he will be violating the commitment to divine condescension, violating his true humanity, and acting in ways not available to the rest of the human race. Think about it. You may have known someone who can turn bread into stones, I've known a few bad cooks in my day who worked in my coffee shop years ago, but I've never met any sane person who had the ability or even thought he had the ability to turn stones into bread. Nor have I met any sane person who thought they could throw themselves off the heights of a tall building and would experience no harm, because their angel entourage would come to their rescue. Nor have I met any human who thought a Faustian bargain with the devil, in which one worships the devil would result in a person becoming the ruler of the whole world, even *pro tempore.*

In short these are not normal temptations at all. They are temptations faced by the truly human and yet truly divine Son of God, the temptation to draw on his divine identity, and thereby obliterate his genuine humanity, his divine self-limitation. And indeed, we could turn to that other major temptation at the other end of Jesus' ministry, the temptation in the garden to avoid "the cup" of God's wrath, avoid the cross. Again, no normal or sane person thinks that they can be the savior of the world, even by martyrdom. But the one who in Mk. 14.32–42 prayed to Abba in the garden knew that he was called to be the human, yet more than human savior of the race, by submitting to an atoning death on the cross, allowing the curse sanctions of the Mosaic covenant to be exhausted on himself, and at the same time inaugurating a new covenant in his blood through his death on Golgotha. Whether in the wilderness that Adam and Eve experienced after the expulsion from Eden, but that Jesus experienced before he went into the world to minister, or in the garden where Jesus passed the test, unlike the first Adam, Jesus resisted very unique temptations that only the divine Son of God could or would face. And it was all because he was both part of the divine identity, and at the same time because of divine self-limitation, fully human. As the author of Hebrews would stress, "tempted like us in all respects, save without sin" (Heb. 4.15). He can identify with us as truly human, but, interestingly, the portrayal in the Synoptics focuses on his unique temptations as the Son of God who took on a human nature.

The Last Adam According to Paul

In two places Paul reflects on the first and last Adams, 1 Cor. 15 and Rom. 5.12–21, and in a further place he allows the first Adam to speak for himself about the experience in the garden, in Rom. 7. 7–13. Let us look at each of these texts in turn. Both of the first two references involve a type of rhetorical comparison called a *synkrisis* in which a comparison is made, and the emphasis is on the contrast more than on the similarity. So, for example, in 1 Cor. 15.45–49, while the first Adam was a living being, the last Adam was a life-giving Spirit, or perhaps better said, a giver of the life-giving Spirit. Notice that Paul also contrast the origins of these two persons – the first was out of the dust of the earth, while the last Adam was out of heaven. This is a comment on dramatically different origins.

On the other hand, in view of v. 49, what Paul may mean is that the first Adam was earthy and earthly in nature, whereas the last Adam was heavenly in nature, and so Paul envisions believers bearing the resurrection nature like Christ at the eschaton. But the word image is important here. We were created in the image of the first Adam, but we will be conformed to the image of Christ by means of resurrection (cf. Rom. 8.29).

The comparison in Rom. 5.12–21 also stresses contrast and uses a "how much more" form of argument as well. The concept of headship clearly enough comes into play in this text. Adam, being the first head of the human, race sinned, and death (perhaps spiritual death, perhaps both spiritual and physical death is meant) entered the world as a result. But despite this influence of Adam on all, death came to all because they imitated Adam, and themselves sinned. The many died because of the trespass of the one person, though Paul wishes to have it both ways – they also died because they too sinned. Death is said to have reigned from the time of Adam to Moses even before sin was turned into trespass for many by the coming of the Mosaic Law that defined what counted as a trespass.

A new sort of grace also came by one person, and with it the gift of salvation. And the one person in question is Jesus Christ. Notice the "how much more" form of the argument in both v. 15 and v. 17. Many were made sinners by the disobedience of the first Adam, and many were made righteous (not just counted righteous) by the obedience of the last Adam, Christ. The emphasis on the obedience of Christ is present both here and in Phil. 2.5–11 as well. The point is that unlike the first Adam, Christ was obedient to God from start to finish and never gave in to the temptations he faced, indeed he was obedient to God's will in regard even to his death, death on the cross.

Finally, there is the remarkable rhetorical "impersonation" in Rom. 7.7–13 in which Adam retells his own story. There he reminds us that he was alive before the Law existed, indeed before there was any commandment at all. Indeed, he was the only one about whom that was true, other than his wife, Eve. He explains that when the commandment came not to eat of the tree of the knowledge of good and evil, then the possibility for sin appeared on the horizon. Sin in these verses is personified as well, and one can substitute the "the snake" and make very good sense of the argument. Apart from *the* commandment, the snake had nothing to tempt Adam with, no act of rebellion and disobedience to suggest. But when the commandment came, the snake sprang into action.

Notice that the commandment mentioned is "thou shalt not covet," one of the Ten Commandments. Early Jews speculated about which of the Ten Commandments Adam was originally given, and the conclusion was that it was the prohibition of coveting, in this case coveting the forbidden fruit. Adam then complains that the snake used the commandment (asking "Did God really say …?") to tempt him and deceived him into thinking death would not result from disobedience. Adam was the only one given a single commandment, and throughout this passage, it is a single commandment alone that the "I" refers to. The commandment was good in itself, but the snake used it to tempt and deceive Adam, and to spiritually kill him, through the act of disobedience to God. And so the sorry tale of Adamic sin is retold in expansive form in Rom. 7, having already been outlined in Rom. 5.12–21. Emphasis is placed on the contrast between the obedience of the last Adam and the disobedience of the first. Christ is seen as Adam gone right, for he not only comes to save people from their sins, he himself accepts the consequences of human sin and saves us from judgment for those sins as well. But Jesus is not the only one for whom the new creation has taken place. To some degree this is also the story of those who are in Christ.

New Creation in Christ

Paul does not use the term *christianoi*, or partisans of Christ. Instead, his regular terminology is to say that Christ followers are "in Christ." This suggests not only that Christ is an "incorporative" personality, which points toward his divine identity, but it says something about the human followers of Christ as well. Unlike Christ, they do not yet have resurrection bodies, but, nonetheless, there has been a real change in them, through union with Christ. Paul puts the matter this way: εἴ τις ἐν Χριστῷ, καινὴ κτίσις τὰ ἀρχαῖα παρῆλθεν, ἰδοὺ γέγονεν καινά.

This could be translated several ways. Literally it reads "If one is in Christ, new creation/creature; the old has passed away, behold the new is here." κτίσις can be either creation or creature, and to judge from Rom. 8.20 the translation probably should be creation. Paul enunciates a theology of a fallen world in Rom. 8.19–20, a world enmeshed with and by humankind's problems, and looking forward to the "liberation from bondage" of the sons and daughters of God, because along with that comes the future liberation of creation itself from its "futility." Thus, all of creation is in a state of groaning, longing for the coming of the new creation, but in part, this has already happened for the believer, not externally, for the body is wasting away, but rather internally – affecting a person's mind, spirit, emotions, will.

Paul puts it this way in 2 Cor. 4.16: "Though outwardly we are wasting away, yet inwardly we are being renewed day by day." Paul's anthropology rules out the notion that one is both the old person and the new person simultaneously. No, clearly one is a new creation a new creature in Christ, but in an old body which is wasting away. The change, the new creation, has happened inwardly, and is actually not just a one-time event (to put it in Johannine terms – the new birth), but an ongoing "renewal." The believer, then, is in a state which is better than the state of the world in general, the *schema* of which is passing away. The believer is in an already-and-not-yet state, which is to say, in an eschatological condition. Unlike the last Adam, Christ (whether before or after his resurrection), *we* live in fallen bodies, are subject to the frailties and temptations of fallen flesh. And yet inwardly the new has already come and keeps coming, working, changing.

Thus, the tension in the Christian life is an inner–outer tension, not an old person–new person tension. Put another way, as Gal. 5 suggests, the Spirit is pulling the believer from the inside in one direction, but the flesh, "the sinful inclinations," are pulling him in another direction. As Rom. 8 makes clear, however, the internal work of the Spirit in the present is but a foretaste of glory divine. Paul, the businessman, calls the gift of the Spirit the "downpayment" or "earnest money" (ἀρραβών, 2 Cor. 1.22), by which is meant the Spirit is a sort of reassurance or guarantee that much more is to come later. Despite all Paul says about spiritual gifts in 1 Cor. 12–14 and elsewhere, he sees all this as but a preview of coming attractions.

Thus, in a sense, Christ is the new creation, the new Adam, when he comes, and his death, resurrection, Spirit-giving triggers the beginning of the new creation in the lives of

Christ's followers. But neither the material creation, nor other creatures, nor the physical bodies of believers themselves have yet been renewed, restored, resurrected. That all awaits the return of the Son of Man from heaven, which will trigger the resurrection of believers, and a whole series of eschatological events, climaxing in the new heaven and the new earth. It is interesting how the new creation comes on the installment plan, so to speak, some now, more when Christ returns, much more after death is finally defeated once and for all. It can also be said that salvation has three tenses – I have been saved (the new creation), I am being saved (sanctification), and I shall be saved (resurrection and full conformity to the image of Christ). Until one is through all three tenses of salvation the situation is still tense – already and not yet.

The Dead in Christ

Our earliest glimpse of the future of "the new creation" comes in 1 Cor. 15.22–26, where Paul says:

For as in Adam all die, so in Christ all will be made alive. [23] But each in turn: Christ, the first-fruits; then, when he comes, those who belong to him. [24] Then the end will come, when he hands over the kingdom to God the Father after he has destroyed all dominion, authority and power. [25] For he must reign until he has put all his enemies under his feet. [26] The last enemy to be destroyed is death.

Notice that it is not everyone who is "made alive" when Christ returns, but only those who belong to him. 1 Thess. 4 implies the same thing – Christ will return and the dead in Christ will be raised, and the living Christians will be transformed into Christ's resurrection likeness. This distinction of the resurrection of believers from the resurrection of anyone else is hardly surprising in light of discussions like Dan. 12.1–3, where the resurrection of the righteous is separated from the "other" resurrection, and we may compare Jesus' words in Jn. 5.28–29, where he speaks of dual outcomes from the resurrection, and clearly Rev. 20 speaks of two resurrections, the good one at the beginning of the millennium and the other way at the end of that period.

In the case of Paul, his theology of new creation is that believers are being conformed to the image of Christ, and only believers get that kind of resurrection renovation, not everyone. So, in fact, he only really focuses on the resurrection of believers at the beginning of the time when Christ returns. The implications of 1 Cor. 15.24–26 are that there is a period of time when Christ is putting things under his feet, extending the divine reign throughout the earth. Death is personified as the last enemy to be overcome, and perhaps what that means is that the rest of those in the land of the dead will be raised at the end of this period, and "death will be no more" (i.e. there will be no one left in the land of the dead = Sheol = Hades). This whole scenario seems to be expanded in Rev. 20, as we shall see, but first a few more points are needed about the way Paul envisions the future.

All the details of the series of eschatological events Paul envisions as happening are not clear, but in 2 Cor. 5 Paul gives us a series of clues when he says:

For we know that if the earthly tent we live in is destroyed, we have a building from God, an eternal house in heaven, not built by human hands. [2] Meanwhile we groan, longing to be clothed instead with our heavenly dwelling, [3] because when we are clothed, we will not be found naked. [4] For while we are in this tent, we groan and are burdened, because we do not wish to be unclothed but to be clothed instead with our heavenly dwelling, so that what is mortal may be swallowed up by life.

⁵ Now the one who has fashioned us for this very purpose is God, who has given us the Spirit as a deposit, guaranteeing what is to come. ⁶ Therefore we are always confident and know that as long as we are at home in the body we are away from the Lord. ⁷ For we live by faith, not by sight. ⁸ We are confident, I say, and would prefer to be away from the body and at home with the Lord. ⁹ So we make it our goal to please him, whether we are at home in the body or away from it. ¹⁰ For we must all appear before the judgment seat of Christ, so that each of us may receive what is due us for the things done while in the body, whether good or bad.

Let us start with the last point first. There is accountability for the Christian for their behavior in this life, involving rewards and punishments. Note that salvation is not viewed as a reward, but as E. P. Sanders has rightly recently stressed,[7] early Jews had no problems with combining the notion of God's gracious salvation or redemption as a gift, with the notion of rewards and punishments in the end times or afterlife. They held these ideas in tension. And in fact, we see Paul in 1 Cor. 3 stressing that ministers in particular will be held accountable for either building with gold, silver, and precious stones, or building their ministries with hay, stubble, and straw, which work will not pass the final fire test, though the minister will escape "as through fire." Paul does not tell us whether this review of deeds happens at death or at the eschaton, at the final judgment after the resurrection. It could be either.

What is clearer is that Paul sees three states of being: (1) life in this world in a "tent," a temporary and mobile dwelling, used as a metaphor for the body, and a very apt metaphor too, for someone who made tents; (2) being naked, which is what Paul calls being absent from the body and present in spirit with the Lord, at home with the Lord; and (3) being further clothed (presumably with the resurrection body), which Paul much prefers over option (2), nakedness being seen as not a preferable state by an early Jew, especially not while in the presence of God. One wonders if Paul is thinking of that embarrassing scenario in Gen. 2. In any case Paul sees being present with the Lord in heaven or Paradise (he uses a variety of language, see e.g. 2 Cor. 12.4) as an interim or temporary condition on the way to being "further clothed" with the resurrection body, and personally he would have preferred to live until Christ returns and simply have the further clothing put on top of his current "tent." While we dwell in the tent, we groan, like creation groans, awaiting our liberation from "this body of flesh." Notice that the resurrection body is also called an eternal building, to be contrasted with the temporary tent.

Another event Paul envisions happening before the return of Christ, but definitely as a part of the eschatological "program," is described in 2 Thess. 2:

Concerning the coming of our Lord Jesus Christ and our being gathered to him, we ask you, brothers and sisters, ² not to become easily unsettled or alarmed by the teaching allegedly from us – whether by a prophecy or by word of mouth or by letter – asserting that the day of the Lord has already come. ³ Don't let anyone deceive you in any way, for that day will not come until the rebellion occurs and the man of lawlessness is revealed, the man doomed to destruction. ⁴ He will oppose and will exalt himself over everything that is called God or is worshiped, so that he sets himself up in God's temple, proclaiming himself to be God.

⁵ Don't you remember that when I was with you I used to tell you these things? ⁶ And now you know what is holding him back, so that he may be revealed at the proper time. ⁷ For the secret power of lawlessness is already at work; but the one who now holds it back will continue to do so till he is taken out of the way. ⁸ And then the lawless one will be revealed, whom the Lord Jesus will

---

[7] In his capstone book, *Paul the Apostle: His Life, Letters, and Thought* (Minneapolis, MN: Fortress Press, 2015).

overthrow with the breath of his mouth and destroy by the splendor of his coming. [9] The coming of the lawless one will be in accordance with how Satan works. He will use all sorts of displays of power through signs and wonders that serve the lie, [10] and all the ways that wickedness deceives those who are perishing. They perish because they refused to love the truth and so be saved. [11] For this reason God sends them a powerful delusion so that they will believe the lie [12] and so that all will be condemned who have not believed the truth but have delighted in wickedness.

Again, the return of Christ is the trigger event for more eschatological events, including not only the resurrection of the righteous, but also judgment upon some anti-god world ruler who is lawless. Here there could very well be a reference to the Emperor cult, and the demand for worshipping the Emperor. Notice that Paul does not envision some sort of Armageddon or battle between human armies. Christ simply shows up and judges the ruler directly. This is very much the same scenario that plays out in Rev. 20.7–9, where instead of a battle, there is just fire from heaven and an execution. In neither Revelation nor in Paul is there a final battle between Middle Eastern foes. There is simply the appearance of the judge and the execution of judgment.

While John of Patmos is in no way reluctant to say things about "the lake of fire," the judgment of those who are part of the second resurrection at the end of the millennium, the fate of the lost, Paul in fact says next to nothing about hell or the fate of the lost. Indeed, Jesus himself, at least in Matthew, says far more about Gehenna and the negative afterlife than Paul does. And John also has a vivid description of a threefold fall of Satan from heaven to earth (see Rev. 12 and compare Lk. 10.18), from earth to the pit (Rev. 20) and from the pit to the lake of fire (Rev. 20.10). The driving focus of NT eschatology, even in Revelation, is on the final state of affairs *on earth*, not in heaven. This is why the disciples were instructed to pray "thy kingdom come, thy will be done *on earth*, as it is in heaven," and why the saints in heaven are not satisfied (Rev. 6).

The New Heavens and the New Earth

What good would it be for there to be new creatures in a worn-out old earth, still groaning and long for liberation? The answer of the NT writers is, "no good at all." Resurrection after all is about embodied existence in a material realm, and both need to be redeemed, restored, renewed. In Heb. 12, the writer presents us with the magnificent tale of two mountains – Sinai and Zion – and the indestructible Kingdom comes finally to the latter. The author is providing us with a tale of two theophanies, just as the author of Revelation presents us with the contrastive tale of two cities – Babylon the harlot and new Jerusalem the bride. Here is what the author of Hebrews says:

But you have come to Mount Zion, to the city of the living God, the heavenly Jerusalem. You have come to thousands upon thousands of angels in joyful assembly, [23] to the church of the firstborn, whose names are written in heaven. You have come to God, the Judge of all, to the spirits of the righteous made perfect, [24] to Jesus the mediator of a new covenant, and to the sprinkled blood that speaks a better word than the blood of Abel.

As John will stress in Rev. 21–22, the heavenly city comes down, and there is a corporate merger of sorts between heaven and earth, with the former being the change agent and the latter being changed. The vision is deeply indebted, of course, to Isaiah and his vision of final things, but John himself makes clear that God is not abandoning his first creation, or his creatures. He is coming to dwell in their midst forever, in a holy environment that will be an appropriate dwelling place for a holy God and his saints. There, there will be no suffering, sin, or sorrow. There, there will be no disease, decay, and death. There all things will be made new, whether this involves a drastic makeover of our home, or a whole new earth (Heb. 12 suggests the former, and 2 Pet. 3 may suggest the latter). The focus in any case is on the final product, not the process, but again Christ is the change agent who not merely announces but makes all things new.

Finally, there is also John's vision in Rev. 20 that there will indeed *not* be universal salvation. There will be those who participate in the second resurrection who will be judged and sent to the fiery place. Jesus suggests the same in the parable of the rich man and Lazarus in Lk. 18. This is hardly surprising, for all eschatological scenarios in the Bible envision moral consequences for how one relates in this life to God and the godly life he calls us all to. Indeed, the NT envisions eternal consequences for persistent and perpetual wickedness. This theme comports with the strong emphasis, especially in apocalyptic literature, that God in the end will see that justice is done, not without mercy, but nonetheless, it will be done.

John's scenario in Rev. 21–22 does not involve the clichéd "pie in the sky by and by" but rather a feast on earth for all its worth. The final destiny of believers is not somewhere out there, but down here on *terra firma*, in the new earth. God is depicted as Immanuel, God with us, and finally faith will become sight, knowledge will become complete, hope will be realized, and love eternal will reign forever, both between God and his people and between one person and another. But what about Israel? John has little to say about Israel's future, but Paul and Jesus both envision Israel having a future.

The Future of Israel: The First Chosen People

In Rom. 9–11, Paul lays out a scenario which he says was revealed to him "in a mystery" (i.e. a vision, presumably). The normal Jewish final state of affairs was assumed to be rightly described at the end of Isaiah, or in Zechariah, as the return of Jews to Zion. Jesus speaks of his own Twelve sitting on thrones judging the 12 tribes of Israel at the eschaton along with the Son of Man (Mt. 19.28), as well as speaking of a messianic banquet involving everyone from Abraham to the last disciple ever reborn coming from the east and the west (Mt. 8.11). Paul says that the vision he had of the future involved first the full number of Gentiles being saved, and brought into the people of God, joined with the Jewish believers in Jesus, but then Paul foresees the return of the Redeemer from heavenly Zion to earth, at which point "all Israel will be saved," presumably meaning a large number of Israelites who as of yet are not believers in Jesus. They will be saved "in like manner" to the Gentiles, by grace through faith in Jesus, not by some other means and not because of some previous obligation to a now defunct covenant, but because God will be true to his loving character, and the things he wants to do for his people – for God is not like a human being. He is not fickle, he is faithful and true to his word. In this way, salvation is not out of obligation or covenant duty toward anyone, but entirely due to the pure mercy of God.

The return of Christ, the resurrection of those in Christ, the reigning upon the earth until all enemies have been subdued, including death, the last judgment, the recognition of her messiah by Israel, the messianic banquet, the dwelling with God eternally on earth, a new earth, a renewed earth, these are the things yet to come. This of course is a breath-taking scenario, to say the least, but it is what one would expect from a God who is both the Creator of all things great and small, and the redeemer of all as well. Salvation will be universally available, and indeed when Christ returns, Paul is prepared to talk about every knee bowing and every tongue confessing in heaven, on earth, under the earth, that Jesus is Lord. But some will confess this not as a heart belief, presumably, but simply because they cannot deny the ocular proof that Christ has returned and reigns. For others, they will confess this with their whole hearts, as believers in Christ who are confessing their faith. When God, Father, Son, and Spirit comes to reign on earth, no creature will be able to ignore or avoid the truth that God is, God reigns, and we all belong to God – Creator, Sustainer, Redeemer. God desires that none should perish, but all have everlasting life, but, sadly, there are those who prefer the familiarity of their own hell to someone else's offered but alien heaven.

And So?

I get asked quite frequently when the end times will begin, and what the sign of its coming will be. I regularly answer that the end times began almost 2,000 years ago, in the womb of a teenager named Mary. That pregnancy was not merely a harbinger of things to come, it was the beginning of the end of the old world, and the beginning of the new creation – God starting the human story over again with the last Adam. As for the end of the endtimes, of that day or hour no one knows, even Jesus didn't know while he lived on earth (Mk. 13.32). So there is no point in theological weather forecasting, despite pious curiosity which knows no bounds. What we can say for sure, however, is that as a result of the death and resurrection of Jesus, which Oscar Cullmann famously called D-Day against the evil powers, we know for sure that VE Day is coming, for Christ was only the first fruits of the resurrection. Someday, we shall be made like him and see him face to face. And considering the present state of the world, it can't come soon enough. But remember the warning of C. S. Lewis: when the author of the play steps out on the stage, the play is over. No time to change your mind, no time for amendment of life. Only time for truth, and consequences, only time for every knee to bow before the King of Kings. Only time to remember the benediction the brother of Jesus gave us long ago:

To him who is able to keep you from stumbling and to present you before his glorious presence without fault and with great joy – to the only God our Savior be glory, majesty, power and authority, through Jesus Christ our Lord, before all ages, now and forevermore! Amen.

14

The Threefold Cord: Theology, Ethics, and Praxis

A threefold cord is not easily broken.

Eccles. 4.12

Unlike in my large study of NT theology and ethics, *The Indelible Image*, I have not tried in this work to deal in detail with the intertwined nature of theology and ethics in the Bible. I have rather focused on a way of looking at biblical *theology* that is faithful to its symbolic universe, its narrative thought world, and its theologizing proper. But I would be remiss if I did not give some attention to how this theologizing intersects with the ethics and praxis urged in the Bible. This is especially important since the real thrust of the OT is to create a holy people for a holy God, a people who both practice their faith and live it out. "Be holy, as I am holy" is not God's pipedream for fallen humanity, it's God plan of redemption for his people. Salvation is not just about belief, it is about behavior, or put another way, it's about trust and obey, or "the obedience of faith and faithfulness."

Clearly, how one envisions the importance of biblical ethics will depend on how one envisions God's means of salvation. By this I mean that if one thinks salvation is something unilaterally predetermined by God before the foundation of the universe, then ethics is nothing more than a programmed response of gratitude for singular grace. On the other hand, if human behavior in response to God's initiatives in love and grace has something to do with salvation, if in fact we must work out our salvation while God works in us to will and to do, and that working out involves our free response to grace, then that makes ethics not an afterthought, but rather the outworking of salvation in response to God and to our fellow human beings.

But what about praxis? As we have observed various times, Judaism is far more about orthopraxy than orthodoxy. How important is orthopraxy – prayer, fasting, sacrificial giving, worship, the Lord's Supper, baptism, and more, in Christianity? Where does work fit into discipleship, and when does it become ministry for the Lord? We will try to address some of these issues in this chapter. But we must begin by dealing with the theological intersection between theology and ethics in the Bible, namely the image of God in human beings.

Intersection in the Image: "Be Holy as I Am Holy"

God, as it turns out, is not just interested in what we believe. Nor is he just interested in having a relationship with us. He is interested in replicating his moral character in us, or as it is put in the NT, he is interested in replicating the character of Christ in us. In *The Indelible Image*, I argued this way:

[T]he relationship of theology to ethics, at least in the New Testament, is not an abstract thing but rather something very organic. To sum up succinctly, God wants his moral and spiritual character (and behavior) replicated in his people. As God is holy, just, righteous, loving, compassionate, merciful … so also, he expects his people to be. The way this transformation happens is through the new birth, progressive sanctification … and finally glorification. In other words, this transformation and conformation has everything to do with one's final salvation. The way this transformation happens involves the initiative of God's grace, but also it involves the human response, the imitation of Christ, the doing of works of piety and charity. Eph. 2.10 puts it this way: "For we are God's handiwork, created in Christ Jesus to do good works, which God prepared in advance for us to do." It appears that the Christian life, from the dawning moments of divine intent, was not only about belief and trust in God, however correct, but also about behavior as something necessary for final salvation where there was time and opportunity for it, behavior being the working out of belief in living practice.[1]

Students of early Jewish literature would hardly be surprised with this conclusion, since it is replete with emphases on how behavior, obedience to God, is absolutely necessary to remain in good standing with God. Ethics and praxis, much more than orthodoxy, were the hallmark of the way early Jews looked at their religion. But is the giving of imperatives to believers, an urging of human beings to strive toward an impossible ideal, to embrace a utopian ethic? Here the answer is, perhaps surprisingly, NO!

The reason God can give his people imperatives is: (1) because he is working on us and in us to will and to do; (2) because we are his witnesses, when people look at us they should see the divine character, what God is like; (3) because having been created in the image of God, we have a unique capacity for relationship with God, and for the imitation of God in Christ, not of course without a lot of grace involved all the time; and (4) because salvation is not just about the gift of everlasting life, it's about being conformed to the image of Christ, reflecting his qualities and character traits. As it turns out, merely being in the image of God is not enough, especially when the image is warped by human fallenness. No, we must be sanctified and become like the One we admire – just, merciful, righteous, compassionate, holy, loving. The writers of the NT, rather like the writers of the OT, were not advocates of *simul justus et peccator*, a person simultaneously in right-standing with God and in bondage to sin. And the reason they did not advocate such a theology is that they had such a high view of God's gracious work in his people.

The Spirit's work in the believer does not supplant or merely supplement human efforts, but rather enables the imitation of Christ. Humans of course could never even approximate the imitation of Christ's character without incessant empowerment by God's gracious Spirit. That grace is constantly being given by a God who loves us relentlessly, and whose desire is that none should perish, but all have everlasting life. What would the point

---

[1]　Witherington, *The Indelible Image*, vol. 1, 19.

be of Christ dying on the cross as a ransom for all (see 1 Tim. 2) if God didn't intend to empower all those who respond to the gift of the new creation with ongoing power and grace to live out the Christian life?

2 Pet. 1.3–4 is rather emphatic about the empowerment. It says: "God's divine power has given us *everything we need for a godly life*, through our knowledge of Him who called us by his own glory and goodness. Through these things, he has given us his very great and precious promises, so that through them we may be partakers of the divine nature, having escaped the corruption in the world caused by evil desires." It is perfectly clear from the larger context of this dictum that the author is not talking about the later notion of *theosis* or the divinizing of merely mortal persons. He is not talking about believers becoming omnipotent, omniscient, and so on. What he *is* talking about is the actual transformation of the inner being of a person, just as Paul did in 2 Cor. 4, such that the inner life of that person mirrors the moral character of God in Christ. When Paul talks about the fruit of the Spirit being love, joy, peace, patience, kindness, goodness, self-control, and so on in Gal. 5 he is talking about genuine character formation by God's living presence in the believer's life.

There is of course some mystery to all this. The believer must not quench or grieve the Spirit. A process is involved as more and more of the inner life is sanctified by the Spirit. And if we ask about the role that knowledge plays in this whole process, our author says clearly that all the moral equipping comes from knowing him, embracing what and whom we know. In other words, both faith/trust in God and a certain knowledge of God are prerequisites to and an ongoing component of progressive sanctification, progressive conformity to the character of Christ.

All this is necessary for the possibility of virtue, good ethical conduct, in the believer's life. The image of God was effaced but not erased by the Fall, and it is being restored and renovated by God's salvation project. That reclamation project enables the believer to agree with Paul in 1 Cor. 10, when he says "no temptation has overcome you that is not common to humankind, such that with the temptation, God provides an adequate means of escape." The Christian has been set free from the bondage to sin, and set free for virtuous behavior, implementing the fruit of the Spirit in one's life through good works.

This is not just about good intentions, but also about good efforts, good works, though of course external factors and forces can intervene and interrupt our actions and prevent them from becoming perfectly carried out. The issue here, however, is that the Spirit enables not just good intentions but good actions, often with good outcomes, but not always, since many things can prevent a good and godly outcome. "The best-laid plans of mice and men oft go astray …" But in the case of the Christian, they should not go astray for some "internal" reason in the believer, for the believer has both sufficient power to resist temptation, being no longer bound to sin, and sufficient power to do good.

The Conduct and Praxis of a Believer

Rom. 12.1–2 speaks directly to the interface between theology, ethics, and praxis. Belief in God leads to worship of God, which in turn involves presenting oneself to God, to become God's property, his living sacrifice. From this flows not merely the practice of worship but the practice of a worshipful and godly life. In the New Covenant, worship changes, and when worship changes it should be clear that this is not an instance of covenant renewal. Jesus in Jn. 4 says "the day is coming, and now is when true worshippers will worship the Father in Spirit and in truth for they are the kind the Father seeks." He says that the true worship will be focused neither on Mt. Gerizim nor on Mt. Zion in Jerusalem. The old form of worship involving priests, temples, and literal sacrifices is at an end. And the reason the coming of the Kingdom inaugurates a change in worship, is severalfold: (1) because God is spirit, and worship should comport with the character of the one worshipped; (2) because literal sacrifices are no longer needed since Christ our Passover lamb has given himself to atone for the sins of the world, past, present and future, because he is our heavenly high priest – accept no substitutes – and because he is the locus of God's presence, which is to say the temple; and (3) because we are being changed, being conformed to the image of Christ, the nature of our worship should change as our own nature more nearly conforms to God's nature.

Henceforth worship is about presenting oneself as a living sacrifice to God; this is one's logical worship or reasonable service or both. Heb. 13.15–16 will also suggest God accepts a sacrifice of praise as well as of self, putting it this way: "Through Jesus, therefore, let us continually offer to God a sacrifice of praise – the fruit of lips that openly profess his name. And do not forget to do good and to share with others, for with such sacrifices God is pleased." So, sacrifice of self means not only presenting oneself totally to God, as belonging to God, but also to self-sacrificially aid and share with others, as well as praising God. Again, a dramatic change in the character and focus of worship reflects a dramatic change in covenants. The Levitical code in general, apart from love of God and neighbor wholeheartedly, is not reaffirmed in the New Covenant.

New Covenant worship is to involve not just verbal praise of an ordinary sort, but also the following: "speaking to one another with psalms, hymns, and songs from the Spirit. Sing and make music from your heart to the Lord, always giving thanks to God the Father for everything, in the name of our Lord Jesus Christ" (Eph. 5.19–20). Notice that in addition to singing the old favorites, namely the psalms, there is also mentioned "spiritual songs," perhaps songs prompted by the Holy Spirit for Christian worship, and also hymns, possibly Christological hymns like the one in Phil. 2.5–11 or Jn. 1.

What is also missing is an instituting of new festivals – gone are the feasts of Unleavened Bread, Booths, Hanukkah, and so on. Paul warns in Col. 2.16–17: "Therefore do not let anyone judge you by what you eat or drink, or with regard to a religious festival, a New Moon celebration or a Sabbath day. These are a shadow of the things that were to come; the reality, however, is found in Christ." Yes, it's OK to attend such things from time to time, but it is not mandatory, because it is not an obligatory part of Christian worship, not even for Jews, never mind for Gentiles. It is adiaphora, things one can either participate in or not, but not a requirement for being a follower of Christ. And the reason these things are mere options, not obligations, is because the New Covenant inaugurated by Christ's death leaves the Mosaic covenant largely obsolete. More needs to be said, however, about the new celebration of the Lord's Supper grounded in the Last Supper, and with an echo of the Passover Seder.

The Lord's Supper

As sociologists of religion have reminded us, an entrance ritual is one thing, a confirmation ritual another. The former is a ritual of union, of entering the community for the first time (and so a ritual a person should go through only once), the latter is a ritual of communion, of ongoing affirmation of one's allegiance to the community and its values. Baptism is an entrance rite, and we will deal with it below, but the Lord's Supper is a confirmation rite. The former is passively received. The person in question does not baptize him or herself, and because it is a passive ritual it can be performed on anyone, young or old. They do not have to actively engage in the ritual. This is why in the early church it was practiced on whole households, including small children, even infants. The Lord's Supper, however, has as part of its liturgy "take ... eat" and, furthermore, recognize the significance of the symbols. That requires conscious choices and decided action. One can partake in the Lord's Supper in an unworthy manner because it requires active participation by everyone partaking of it. The earliest church did not practice infant communion.

Sociologists also tell us that such regular rituals encode in their language and symbols the core theology or values of the community. What would we deduce they are from the Lord's Supper and baptism? In both cases at the heart of the faith in question is the death and resurrection of Jesus. Thus, for example, Rom. 6 suggests that water baptism is like being buried with Christ. It has to do with the death of the old self, and encodes the promise that real change can happen, that one can become a new creature, and the old can pass away. The Lord's Supper has to do with receiving the benefits of Jesus' sacrificial death, by partaking of the symbols of the staff of ancient life – bread and wine. One needs to partake of the everlasting life Christ is offering again and again in this life. But one needs to die to one's old self only once. One crosses the boundary into the community of the saved for the first time only once, and baptism symbolizes that act. At the boundary of the community stands the death and resurrection of Jesus, and at the heart of the community stands the death and resurrection of Jesus also, but the believer must first participate in the death and burial of his or her old self, before participating in the benefits of the crucified and risen Lord.[2]

If one were to ask Paul which of these rituals is more crucial to church life, his answer I think would be unequivocally the Lord's Supper, since it is a repeated sacrament that the body of Christ is regularly, as a whole, meant to partake in. You get the sense of this not only from the discussion in 1 Cor. 10–11 about the Lord's Supper but also from two other facts:

(1) Paul in 1 Cor. 1, troubled perhaps by the Corinthians' misunderstanding of baptism's significance, as they seem to have seen it as having some sort of magical power that could even benefit the dead through proxy baptism (see 1 Cor. 15.29), is prepared to say "I thank God I didn't baptize more of you." One cannot imagine him saying, "I thank God I didn't save more of you," so clearly the ritual of baptism is not seen as essential for salvation (though it is essential for obeying Christ's Great Commission).

---

[2] Detailed discussions of these two sacraments and their social and theological significance can be found in Ben Witherington III, *Troubled Waters: Rethinking the Theology of Baptism* (Waco, TX: Baylor University Press, 2007); Witherington, *Making a Meal of It*.

(2) There is not a single place in the NT where we are told how baptism should or shouldn't be practiced by Christians, which of course is why there has been an eternal debate about baptism, its recipients, the amount of water, who should be allowed to perform baptism and so on, in all of church history. The *Didache* is perhaps the first place where some rules for the ritual are actually laid down. Very different is the treatment of the Lord's Supper in 1 Cor. 8–11, where we are told what is and isn't appropriate when this repeated sacrament is practiced. The Lord himself instructed his disciples how to participate in the sacred meal, and he partook of it himself. As for baptism, Jesus baptized no one (Jn. 4.1–3) and he only instructed his followers to do it as part of disciple-making, not giving them detailed instructions, which is to say, without telling them how, and on whom to practice it.

The discussion of the Lord's Supper in 1 Cor. 11 comes in the context of a larger discussion of what sort of religious meals one ought and ought not to participate in. In particular, 1 Cor. 8–10 is warning Corinthian Christians, presumably mostly Gentiles, not to go to feasts at pagan temples, where pagan deities were worshipped, and indeed where it was believed pagan deities dined with the feasters. The issue was one of venue rather than menu for Paul is fine with buying meat in the meat market that had been previously sacrificed to idols and eating it in someone's home. But it was not just a matter of venue, it was a matter of spiritual pollution in Paul's view. Eating at a pagan temple feast was a matter of dabbling with demons, as Paul calls them. The point is, while there are "no gods but one" there are other spiritual beings out there, connected with pagan worship that can influence the feaster in negative ways.

Notice that when the word εἰδωλόθυτον comes up in texts like Acts 15.29 or 1 Cor. 10.25–27 or Rev. 2.14, 20 it is always associated with sexual immorality in the critique, and not accidentally Paul compares what's going on in pagan temples to the golden calf episode in Exod. 32. The combination idols, meat sacrificed to an idol, and sexual immorality is what Paul is concerned about, because such celebrations were not by any means purely secular in nature, indeed, religion in the ancient world was intertwined with everything. Plutarch puts it this way: "It is not the abundance of wine, or the roasting of the meat that makes the joy of festivals, but the good hope and belief that the god is present in his kindness, and graciously accepts what is offered" (*Moralia* 1102A). Spiritual harm or pollution is the concern of the Apostle to the Gentiles, not food laws.

There are clues, allusions in 1 Cor. 10, as to how Paul views the Lord's Supper. Notice for example at 1 Cor. 10.16 that he refers to "the cup of blessing," a technical term for the wine cup drunk at the end of a Jewish meal over which a grace is said: "Blessed are thou O Lord who gives us this fruit of the vine." This is probably the cup Jesus identified toward the end of the Last Supper meal as the cup of the covenant in his blood. Again, the point is that the New Covenant is enacted by Christ's death.

Notice as well the term *koinonia*, which refers to a sharing in common of something with someone, it could be with God, it could be with fellow worshippers, it could be both. The point is that the term refers to a group activity, or more to the point a group bonding activity. It should not be translated "fellowship," which is one possible result of *koinonia*. This is why Paul gets so irate over some eating their meals without waiting for all to be present. But what does it mean to "share/participate in common in the blood of Christ"? It seems clear that Paul does not take a purely symbolic view of this repeated ritual. He seems to think that a real spiritual communion with Christ and others is involved. Possibly he is thinking of a sharing in the benefits of Christ's death – cleansing, forgiveness, salvation – but certainly he is thinking of drawing close to and being in the presence of Christ.

Gordon Fee has suggested, quite plausibly, that Paul sees the sharing in the cup as a vertical sharing with/in Christ, while the sharing in the bread is a horizontal sharing with fellow believers as the body of Christ. Thus, the phrase "a sharing in the body of Christ" would not refer to either Jesus' own physical or transcendent body or some spiritual participation in Christ's own body, but rather a sharing with one another *as* the body of Christ. If one compares 1 Cor. 10.16–17 this makes perfect sense, because Paul goes on to say "because there is one bread, we who are many are one body."[3] Paul is talking about spiritual communion with Christ and also with one another, and so it is no surprise that he sees partaking of the ritual in an unworthy manner as a sacrilege, leading to direct spiritual harm. The other side of this is that this means that Paul sees the ritual itself as a sacrament, not merely a symbolic replay of the Last Supper. That we are on the right track here can be shown by reflecting on what Paul's near-contemporary Philo says: "he to whom sacrifice has been offered makes the group of worshippers partners in the altar and of one table" (using the term *koinonia*; *De spec. leg.* 1.221).

It is likely that Paul does not view things the way his Gentile converts might have done, in terms of the notion of actually consuming the deity in the meal. Certainly, in early Judaism sacrificial food was never viewed that way, and again if the disciples at the Last Supper thought Jesus meant that, they would have taken it to be cannibalism and would have run out of the room screaming. Thus, Paul probably means the following: (1) spiritual communion with Christ and one another; (2) sharing in the spiritual benefits of Christ's sacrifice, not sharing in Christ's metaphysical being or in his glorified flesh. Paul, it would appear, does not see the Lord's Supper as the means of "partaking in the divine nature" (2 Pet. 1.4; see above). According to 1 Cor. 10.19, Paul believes that demons use pagan temple feasts to entrap people in a spiritual web that is harmful.

Turning now to 1 Cor. 11.17–34 itself, the only full exposition on the Lord's Supper in the NT, we must remind ourselves, as 1 Cor. 11.2 indicates, that Paul is correcting problems, he is dealing with abuses in Christian worship. He is not telling us everything we ought to know about the sacrament. Indeed, this corrective activity of what goes on in Christian worship runs from the outset of 1 Cor. 11 through the end of 1 Cor. 14. There are lots of problems. Nevertheless, if we read the text carefully we can learn a good deal about how the Lord's Supper was viewed and practiced in the mid-first century AD.

First of all, the social setting for the Lord's Supper is in someone's home, presumably a home large enough to accommodate quite a few people. Secondly, the Lord's Supper is part of a proper meal, possibly a Christian love feast. The problem was that presumably the host had set up the meal, like most ancient meals, in a stratified way, so that the more elite diners got better food, and the less elite diners, some of whom came later, after they finished work, did not get the good seats or the good food. Paul's sees this as a travesty, indeed a violation of the very meaning of the Lord's Supper and of Christian *koinonia*, for the Lord's Supper was meant to bind the group together as one, not reinforce pre-existing pecking orders in society.

---

[3] G. D. Fee, *The First Epistle to the Corinthians* (Grand Rapids, MI: William B. Eerdmans, 1987), 469–70.

Paul then is concerned with two aspects of what is going wrong – the disorderliness of the affair, and the inequality of the proceedings. Both of these things were common at Greco-Roman dinner parties, but one senses that what especially incenses Paul is that his converts do not understand the spiritual danger they are in, or the spiritual benefit they could have – on the one hand turning the sacrament into a sacrilege, or on the other hand, treating it properly and deriving the benefit of genuine communion with Christ and one another.

Further, there is supposed to be equality in the body of Christ and in its rituals and worship. Here we have a clear indication that Paul is not simply applying the protocols of a patriarchal and stratified structure of the household to the Christian meeting. Even though the meeting happens in the house of one of the more well-off Christians, Paul insists that they carry on in a way that comports with the equality that should exist in the body of Christ, *without regard to social distinctions and social status.* The meeting involves sacred time and events, not sacred space or buildings. Presumably, the venue had suggested otherwise to the host. These occasions are to be regulated by sacred traditions Paul learned and passed on to his converts.

If we try to figure out the exact protocol here, it would seem that the Lord's Supper transpires after the main meal, and perhaps during what would normally be the *symposium*, the after-dinner drinking party with the after-dinner speaker. I say this because Paul accuses some Corinthians of being drunk at the Lord's meal. It would appear that at this point in time, the Lord's Supper was not yet transformed into a separate ritualistic part of worship distinguishable from a fellowship meal. Rather meals and the Lord's Supper were all part of one event. And the problem is that the "haves" were not only not showing respect for the "have-nots," even worse they were not showing respect for the Lord and his meal. The meal itself is being violated, not just general fellowship.

1 Cor. 11.23 indicates that Paul has previously passed on the sacred tradition about the Lord's Supper to the Corinthians, a tradition he received "from the Lord," which presumably means from the Jerusalem church. You will notice that he says no such thing about having passed on a tradition about baptism, and indeed the ever-creative Corinthians have generated their own practice of proxy baptism for the dead. Clearly, the Lord's Supper ritual was a higher priority initially than baptism (see again 1 Cor. 1). This same verse makes clear that the Lord's Supper involves a historical memory of an actual event. In other words, it is unlike pagan rituals, which were connected with mythological stories. Possibly, the Corinthians saw the Lord's Supper as like a funerary meal, a memorial meal for a deceased friend. But the Lord's Supper does not merely celebrate the deceased Jesus, one actually communes with the living Christ, and one proclaims his death until he returns by such celebrations. The Lord's Supper, then, differed from such funerary memorial meals, but it also differs from the Passover, in that Passover celebrates what Yahweh did for his people, whereas the Lord's Supper celebrates what a historical person, Jesus, did on the cross.

The reference to Jesus' betrayal or "handing-over" (since *paredideto* can mean either) certainly distinguishes this meal from all pagan celebrations that focused on myths. This beginning of the ceremony reminds us of the tragic betrayal of Jesus by one of his own disciples. A few details of what Paul says are crucial: (1) Paul does not associate the breaking of the bread with the breaking of Jesus' body, despite later textual variants slanting things in that direction; (2) we note the double reference to "in remembrance of me" after both the word about the bread and about the cup. Only Luke and Paul have the memory clauses, and Luke is likely dependent on Paul; (3) Paul alone says that as often as they drink the wine cup they should celebrate the Lord's Supper. Not all ancient meals, especially those for the poor, involved wine; (4) at the Last Supper, Jesus' language was clearly symbolic, like that of the Passover, because he was not yet dead, indeed he was physically, tangibly present with his disciples then, and modifying elements in the Passover ritual to refer to himself; (5) the phrase "for you" (only in 1 Cor. 11.24/Lk. 22.19–20) likely alludes to Isa. 53.12. Jesus gave his body on the believers' behalf, or in place of them. Breaking the bread recalls that self-giving; (6) the word "new," as in New Covenant/Testament, here is fatal to the notion that this was seen as a last will and testament meal or funerary rite. It refers to the founding of a new relationship between God and his people through the death of Jesus. The ceremony of the Lord's Supper is a visible word proclaiming the dead but risen Jesus until he returns; (7) notice that Paul does not specifically link the cup to Jesus' blood. Rather the cup is "in my blood," i.e., instituted by his shed blood. Paul says nothing about the wine being or representing Christ's blood. That is found in Mark's account. The reference in 1 Cor. 11.27 is to Christ's actual body, which was crucified.

It should be stressed that 1 Cor. 11.27 is not referring to "unworthy" participants, but to participants partaking of the ritual *in an unworthy manner*. No one, in any case, is worthy of the death of Jesus, or of partaking in the sacrament. That is not the issue here. Paul says that those who partake in an unworthy manner are guilty, in some sense, of the body and blood of Jesus. And they are partaking without "discerning" the body, which probably means without realizing that they are part of the body of Christ. In any case, Paul is accusing some of sacrilege and even goes so far as to suggest that this abuse is why some have gotten sick and died! Notice that when Paul refers in v. 29 to discerning the body, he doesn't say "body and blood" or even "discerning the Lord." The issue here is disunity in the body of believers, and not being cognizant that the meal is to be shared with others equally, and at the same time. It is meant to be a group-building ceremony. Probably he is not referring to the later notion of not recognizing the sacramental presence of Christ in the elements of the ritual. No, they are to recognize the presence of their brothers and sisters in Christ at the meal, that they are all one in the body of Christ (see 1 Cor. 12).

What Paul says in 1 Cor. 5.7–8 is telling: "Christ our Passover is sacrificed for us, so let us celebrate the festival, not by eating the old bread of wickedness and evil, but by eating the new bread of purity and truth." The death of Christ is meant to supersede the old Passover. Notice the "our" in the phrase. But it is also meant to change the pattern of the behavior of the participants. Paul alludes to the Christian meal as a matter of eating the bread together, something Acts 2 suggests as well. The meal reinforces, again and again, the centrality of the death of Jesus for this new religious movement and reinforces the benefits of that death for all believers. They are all equal at the foot of the cross, all equally in Christ's debt for salvation and new life.

Baptism

It is in no way surprising that when the Christian movement began to emerge from early Judaism, with its many water rituals ranging from John the Baptizer to ordinary cleansing in a *mikveh*, that a water ritual was thought important as a sign or symbol of the new movement, in particular, as a symbol of entrance into the New Covenant community. As we have already noted, there are no instructions about how to perform a Christian baptism in the NT, but clearly enough it is distinguished from John's praxis in both Acts 18 and 19. And then of course there is the debate about whether baptism in the name of Jesus, found in the early chapters of Acts, meant one thing and baptism in the name of the threefold deity (Mt. 28) meant another. Perhaps the most important thing that can be said at the outset is that unlike the Lord's Supper, which is an extreme makeover of the Passover meal, probably, due to the changes Jesus made, Christian baptism was not a do-over of any previous Jewish ritual. For one thing, it was a boundary-defining ritual, performed only once, when someone converted or joined the household of faith. For another thing, it is not associated with repentance in preparation for and to avoid the coming wrath of God, in the way John's ritual was. But what was this ritual all about, theologically speaking? Rom. 6, in some ways, gives us our best clues.

First of all, we have to admit that we have no evidence that Paul got his theology of water baptism (not to be confused with Spirit reception) from Jesus or even the early church. There is this similarity between what we find in Acts and in Paul – the latter speaks of being baptized into Christ, the former of being baptized in the name of Jesus (see Acts 2). In regard to the latter, I would suggest that the reason for that formula is that it is Jews being baptized, and they already believed in the first person of the Trinity. They were not changing religions from a pagan one to a biblical one, unlike Gentiles (see e.g. 1 Thess. 1 – turning from idols to the living God). What they were doing was adding faith in Jesus to their already extant faith in Yahweh.

Perhaps Paul knew of the practice of John the Baptizer, who connected a ritual of repentance for those who were already card-carrying Jews, in the face of the coming judgment of Yahweh which John foresaw. Jesus of course, as Mk. 13 suggests, foresaw it as well, and spoke of it taking the form of destruction of the center of Jewish worship – the temple – within a generation. We need to look closely at the language of Rom. 6, where Paul talks about being buried with Christ in baptism, with a side glance at Gal. 2, where Paul says of himself "I have been crucified with Christ. It is no longer I who live but Christ who lives in me."

Perhaps the first question we need to ask is, does Paul envision the sign of the New Covenant, baptism, rather than circumcision, as in some way like the covenant sign for the Mosaic covenant? A pertinent question would be, does it symbolize what is left behind (with an implicit promise not to return to it), or rather what is yet to come? Put another way, is baptism, like circumcision, a sign of the oath curse, the sanction applied to a person if they violate the covenant? Circumcision clearly is such a sign – "you and your descendants will be 'cut off' if you do not keep the covenant." What better way to symbolize this, than the cutting off of the foreskin from the organ of generation? We will need to take into account the possible connection between what Paul says in Colossians about Christ's death being a circumcision of sorts (while Christ himself calls it a baptism to be baptized with). First, Rom. 6.1–14.

Rom. 6.1–14 is not, in the first place, a discussion about baptism, but rather about sin, death, the Law, grace, and life, a whole constellation of theological ideas.

Paul says nothing here about humans who administer this rite, any more than he does in Gal. 3 or 1 Cor. 12. He indicates in 1 Cor. 1 he himself administered the rite on some, but not all, of the converts in Corinth, and he is glad he did not baptize more, considering what the Corinthians made of it. Paul's main concern in Rom. 6 is the spiritual experience that was symbolized or depicted in the ritual. As Doug Moo rightly says, since water baptism comes up in only two verses in Romans, but faith is the subject of nearly every chapter, "genuine faith, even if it has not been 'sealed' in baptism, is sufficient for salvation."[4] This is certainly what one would have deduced from Paul's comments in 1 Cor. 1 as well.

Paul in succinct fashion explains that being baptized into Christ means being baptized into his death. "We were buried with him in baptism." In the immediately preceding sentence Paul spoke of "having died to sin." Thus, baptism is associated with death and burial, and in particular with death to sin. In some unexplained way, this is connected to Jesus' death and burial. Somehow, being baptized into his death entails the death of our old self. And perhaps this is what Paul is alluding to when he says that he has been crucified with Christ, and his old self no longer lives, but rather Christ lives in him. *Note that at no point does Paul associate baptism with or depict it as a form of resurrection to life.* Resurrection is what follows death and burial. It is not the same event, and indeed, resurrection may occur considerably later. Resurrection is paired in Rom. 6 with the subsequent "walking in newness of life." But as for baptism itself, it is all about death to sin, and burial of the old self.

As we have already noted in our discussion of 2 Cor. 5.17,[5] Paul actually believes that the old self, the old control center of a human personality, has died, has passed away. He believes that a real spiritual change has happened to the new believer. In Rom. 8.1–3 he puts it this way: "the believer has been set free from the ruling principle of sin and death"; in the contrasting statement at the beginning of Rom. 7.5–6 he puts it this way: "For when we were in the realm of the flesh, the sinful passions aroused by the Law were at work in us, so that we bore fruit for death. But now, by dying to what once bound us, we have been released from the Law so that we serve in the new way of the Spirit, and not in the old way of the written code." It could hardly be clearer that Paul sees even Jewish Christians as no longer bound to the Mosaic Law covenant and its demands, but he is equally clear that the believer has died to what once bound him or her. Baptism then, rather like drowning, is seen as depicting the death of the old person. And this brings us to Col. 2.11–12: "In him you were also circumcised with a circumcision not performed by human hands. Your whole self, ruled by the flesh was put off when you were circumcised by Christ, having been buried with him in baptism, in which you were also raised with him through your faith in the working of God, who raised him from the dead."[6] The closeness of this phrasing to Rom. 6.6 is unavoidable, except that here Christ's death is directly called the circumcision of Christ. Putting the pieces together in terms of covenantal theology we get Christ's death is the enactment of the oath curse of the Mosaic covenant on Jesus himself, who was "cut off from the land of the living." In regard to believers, at conversion a real

---

4 D. Moo, *The Epistle to the Romans* (Grand Rapids, MI: William B. Eerdmans, 1996), 366.

5 See above.

6 NB: this translation (the NIV) has a mistake in it. It should read "in whom *also* you were raised ..." In other words, this is not resurrection through baptism.

spiritual change happens, the person has their old nature put to death, which in effect is circumcision in us. Paul, however, makes clear that he is not talking about some *ex opere operato* effect of the ritual of baptism itself for he says this "circumcision" done to the believer's old self is not done by human hands, in other words, it is the work of the Spirit. What seems obvious from comparing Rom. 6 to Col. 2 is that Paul is comparing circumcision in some respects with baptism, both involving a cutting off, a death, even a burial.

What baptism is talking about is what we sometimes call regeneration. It depicts the negative side of the work of Christ, such that the old sinful nature dies. Baptism is not a confirmation ritual depicting our faith response to the work of God, but rather it depicts the initial work of God in the life of someone becoming a believer. It is rather a one-time initiation rite, unlike the Lord's Supper, which is a confirmation rite, to be done repeatedly. Notice, however, that there is a big difference between circumcision and baptism – the latter is a gender-inclusive ritual, which is a rather clear sign that no patriarchal covenant of the past is being renewed in the New Covenant. It will be from the very outset, shown by its sign, baptism, a more egalitarian and gender-inclusive religion.

For Paul, baptism provides a valid picture, a visible Word, depicting Christ's death and the death of the old nature of the believer. It depicts God's judgment on sin, a sign of the enactment of the oath curse. But Jesus' own baptism on the cross means that he endured the sanctions of the Mosaic covenant for the believer, making possible a new covenant and new spiritual relationship with God in Christ, as Rom. 8 says at the outset: "There is now no condemnation for those who are in Christ Jesus" and why? Because the ruling principle of Life, the work of the Spirit, has set us free from the law or ruling principle of sin and death.

Can more be said? Baptism by immersion could be said to foreshadow Spirit baptism of the sort Paul describes in 1 Cor. 12. It is the latter which actually produces union with Christ through his body, the community of believers ("by one Spirit we have all been baptized into one body and given one Spirit from which we drink"). The Spirit is not the human administrator of the act of water baptism, but the Spirit is indeed the one who joins us to the body of Christ, whether before or after the act of water baptism. And as Peter suggested in Acts 10, if one has already been immersed in the Spirit and manifesting spiritual gifts, there is no reason at all why that person shouldn't immediately receive water baptism (cf. Acts 8). It is perhaps good to add that since Paul doesn't really associate water baptism with resurrection (Col. 2 says "in whom also you were raised," not "in which you were also raised") but rather with death and burial, both the death and burial of Christ and the death and burial of the believer's old self, he is not drawing on Hellenistic mystery ideas about dying and rising through some ritual. Baptism is a rite of passage, but in itself, it does not produce the transition, it depicts the work of the Spirit in "crucifying the old self," as Paul so vividly says about his own spiritual experience.

Baptism, according to Eph. 4.5, is one of the "ones" – one Lord, one faith, one baptism. It is placed in this category because unlike ritual washings in early Judaism, it was to be performed only once, or put sociologically, a rite of passage or a boundary-crossing ritual is to be performed only once because the reality it depicts happens only once to an individual person.

Water baptism is a plea or pledge unto God for a good conscience, for a cleansing and renewing: "create in me a clean heart, O God, and renew a right spirit within me." Notice the order of the events described in 1 Cor. 6.11: "you were washed" precedes "you were set apart." It does not follow it. Again, if baptism is a symbol of God's initiative of grace with a lost person, then it is not a symbol of our response to that grace. And since no one baptizes themselves, it is a passive ritual like circumcision; anyone entering the covenant community at whatever age can receive this rite. Baptism by the Spirit into the one body is what makes it possible to say what Gal. 3.28 says: "in Christ there is neither Jew nor Gentile, slave nor free, no male and female." No water ritual could produce that sort of outcome, only spiritual transformation can.

Some comments on Jn. 3.5–6 and 1 Jn. 5.5–8 are in order here. Neither of these texts, which are highly metaphorical in character, is actually talking about water baptism. In the former, "birth out of water" (paralleling birth "out of the Spirit"), refers to physical birth, as the very next verse makes quite clear – flesh gives birth to flesh. The waters break, and a new physical life comes forth from the woman. One must be physically born before one can be spiritually reborn or experience birth from above. The second text, 1 Jn. 5.5–8, speaks of the three witnesses, and they have sometimes been assumed to included baptism and the Lord's Supper because of references to water and the blood (the third witness being the Spirit). This is incorrect, however. Water refers to the birth of Jesus just as water refers to physical birth in Jn. 3, and blood, which never ever is a term used alone for the Lord's Supper, refers to the death of Jesus. The three witnesses then are the incarnation, the death, and the Spirit. There is no commentary here or in Jn. 3 on water baptism.

Both Heb. 10.22–23 and 1 Pet. 3.21 do in fact refer to water baptism. The Hebrews passage refers to both water baptism and internal spiritual cleaning. The author is concerned with the cleansing of the guilty conscience, but he does not say that the water ritual could effect such a change, rather he distinguishes the two things by the conjunction "and." We need to bear in mind, however, that for adult converts coming into the New Covenant community from outside, the water ritual may indeed come close on the heels of the cleansing of the heart, and in any case the latter is aptly symbolized by the former. Conversion is one thing, however, ritual initiation is another, as is shown in Acts, where we find both the pattern water then Spirit reception (Acts 8), and Spirit reception then water (Acts 10), then distinction between John's and Christian baptism in Acts 18–19. Baptism most obviously symbolizes spiritual cleansing (Heb. 10.23; Acts 22.16; and see the language in Eph. 5.26–27). But it is a striking fact that the most dominant image that comes to the minds of the NT writers when they think about baptism is death, and not just any sort of death, but death as a judgment of God, and that brings us to 1 Pet. 3.21.

In some ways, 1 Pet. 3 is the appropriate place to conclude our discussion of the praxis of water baptism. Here baptism is the antitype of the Noahic flood – through which some few were saved, but most were judged and lost. Thus, water symbolizes a redemptive judgment in that passage, as it does in Rom. 6, where the old person is judged but the new person is saved. What is unique about this passage is that we are told something about how baptism saves: "not the removal of dirt from the flesh, but the appeal unto God for a good conscience (or possibly a Christian life)." The grammar is complex here but the word "baptism" comes right before these two clauses explain what baptism is, *not how it saves*, which only comes at the end of the verse in the "through" clause.

The phrase "not the removal of dirt from the flesh" probably alludes to what circumcision does, and so an analogy is being drawn between one initiation rite and another, and a contrast between the two signs of redemptive judgment in the Bible. The parallel natures of the two rites, as in Col. 2.11, are likely being recognized here. Baptism is, however, not merely like circumcision, which removes "dirt" from the flesh. Rather, baptism is an inquiry or appeal or pledge of, or for, a good conscience. Again, the Greek here is difficult. Mt. 16.12 uses the same verb to refer to a request. Is baptism a request or appeal for a cleansed conscience, a new self? Note Acts 22.16, where Paul is told to be baptized while calling on the Lord. Water baptism could be seen as an appeal for Spirit baptism, or for the ability to live with a clean conscience. We must bear in mind that we are talking about what baptism actually *is* here, not what accompanies it. Perhaps the best way to sum things up is "baptism is not circumcision, but rather an appeal or pledge unto God for a Christian life, or clean conscience." Baptism is the covenanting with God and is the first step in the undertaking of a Christian life. Baptism saves only in that it symbolizes that God alone can save through the resurrection of Christ, and God alone answers the prayer for grace to live the Christian life. What is very clear, as J. D. G. Dunn made evident in his excellent early study, is that the popular notion that conversion necessarily precedes baptism and baptism should be seen as a seal or testimony or confession to conversion and commitment previously made is nowhere clearly stated in the NT. Nowhere.[7]

To a very real degree, what is depicted in the NT is missionary baptisms, by which I mean the baptizing of those who enter the community from outside the community. The question of what to do about the children of believers raised within the church is neither raised nor answered in the Bible, that being a second-generation kind of question when there were Christian parents wondering what to do with their children in terms of the faith. This absence of discussion about children is not surprising, since the NT is a testimony to earliest Christianity when it was primarily a missionary movement, not a discipleship operation.

But I would be remiss if I didn't point out that the Great Commission says that Jesus' last command was to make disciples, and the way to accomplish that was to: (1) baptize them, and (2) teach them. If there is a reason to the ordering of those two activities, it suggests that water baptism in the name of the threefold God is indeed an initiation rite, not a confirmation ritual. Certainly, when the church emerges from its "underground" or "unrecognized" period, baptizing of even infants was already a regular practice, in both the West and the East. Some of this of course has to do with the way corporate personality worked in antiquity. Families, households, joined religions, usually following the head of the household.

It was not about "making an individual decision for Christ" as it is in a highly individualistic modern or late-Western age. When Paul says he baptized the household of Stephanas in 1 Cor. 1, we should not imagine that he neglected the slaves and the small children. The whole family needed to be united in Christ, and the picture is the same in Acts 16.15, where Paul converts Lydia and we hear "When she and the members of her household were baptized, she invited us to her home."

Baptism and the Lord's Supper both have symbolic reference to the death of Christ, and the spiritual benefit of that death for those who follow Christ. While the Lord's Supper is clearly treated as a sacrament in 1 Cor. 10–11, we may debate whether that is the case for water baptism or not. Clearly, to judge from 1 Cor. 1 or Acts 18 and other texts, it was not

---

[7] J. D. G. Dunn, *Baptism in the Spirit* (London: SCM Press, 1970).

necessary for salvation, but it was important in symbolizing the transition from the old person to the new person, and the death of the old self. Water could symbolize cleansing, but the cleansing or washing away of the old self involved a judgment on the old fallen self. But what about walking in newness of life? What sort of theologizing is done about that in the NT?

Theologizing about the New Life in Christ

Perhaps the most important thing that can be said on this front is that in a Greco-Roman world where few people believed that a person could really change their personality or even their behavior patterns, followers of Christ believed that by God's grace this could and did happen. If we may put it this way, if the God of the Bible could harden Pharaoh's heart (and the hearts of others), he could also soften them, or give a person a new heart. And the heart was viewed as the control center of human personality. It was the thing which directed thoughts, feelings, the will. A heart of stone could be replaced with a new heart, a heart for God. It is especially the case that the followers of Jesus believed in such a transformation, though there are instances in the OT as well (e.g. Naaman in 2 Kgs. 5). But what did this transformation amount to? Was it just a reorientation of belief? Someone comes to have sincere belief in and trust in God, who had none before?

Actually, no. None of the evidence we have suggests that it was just a matter of establishing or reestablishing a relationship with God. None of the evidence suggests that it was just a matter of being given "right-standing" with God, though that is part of the starting point. Whether through the language of new birth, birth again, or new creation or new creatures, there was the belief that the control center of human personality could be transformed such that temptation could be resisted and good works could be performed, or at least attempted, since performance can be interrupted or inhibited by intervening persons, events, circumstances.

Partly, this was believed because it was believed that a real dying to old self, and living to God, a death and resurrection of a spiritual or internal sort, could really happen. The notion that one could simultaneously be the person described in Rom. 7.14–25 and the person described in Rom. 8 never occurred to them. That idea we may thank Augustine and then Luther for. But there was also realism in this belief. Change in a human person's lifestyle and behavior patterns would often be gradual, a product of progressive sanctification, the progressive inner work of God's Spirit, renovating the thoughts, the emotions, the will. As Paul says at one juncture in 1 Thess. 4:

It is God's will that you should be sanctified: that you should avoid sexual immorality; [4] that each of you should learn to control your own body in a way that is holy and honorable, [5] not in passionate lust like the pagans, who do not know God; [6] and that in this matter no one should wrong or take advantage of a brother or sister. The Lord will punish all those who commit such sins, as we told you and warned you before. [7] For God did not call us to be impure, but to live a holy life. [8] Therefore, anyone who rejects this instruction does not reject a human being but God, the very God who gives you his Holy Spirit.

In other words, old behavior patterns could and should be left behind. Holiness of heart and life was God's will for every believer. And when a believer did not behave that way, a stern corrective was coming, as any reading of 1 Cor. should make apparent. The ethics is grounded in the assumptions that: (1) God has already begun the inner transformation of the person, and (2) by God's grace, one can do the will of God, can live a holy life. One has a choice about one's behavior. The ethical seriousness of the NT is founded and grounded in these basic assumptions, and so the NT exhortations are never of a sort like this: "Well, we know you can't really behave much differently, but it's the thought that counts, your good intentions are good enough." No. When Paul says for instance that if a Christian pursues a pattern of behavior that involves murder, or adultery, or theft, or a hundred other serious sins (see Gal. 5), that person will not be entering the Kingdom of God, he's not kidding! Good works cannot get one saved (though there are rewards for good works), but a pattern of immoral behavior amounts to moral apostasy and can prevent the Christian from entering God's kingdom in the end.

In short, the ethical seriousness of the NT involves the assumption not only that Christians should be held responsible for their behavior, but that if their behavior persistently is of an immoral sort, they can sin their way right out of a place in the Kingdom of God. These warnings, such as we find in Gal. 5, are given to all Christians, because none are eternally secure until they are securely in eternity. None. There is a reason why John of Patmos warns all the members of the church at Sardis in Rev. 3.5 that God can blot someone's name out of the book of everlasting life if they don't behave as well as believe. But at the same time, there are equal reassurances that: (1) God can and does give the aid, support, grace necessary for a believer to stand and withstand any and all temptations (see Eph. 6.10–20); and (2) apostasy, whether intellectual or moral, does not happen by accident. One cannot accidentally "lose" one's salvation, like losing a pair of glasses. Apostasy by definition is a deliberate and willful rebellion against the very presence of God in one's life, a grieving of the Holy Spirit. It requires conscious and repeated repudiation of God's presence, power, work in a person's life. This is what the author of Heb. 6 calls a deliberate crucifying of Christ afresh. It is why Paul in Gal. 5 speaks of a person whose pattern of behavior earns the label of thief, adulterer, and the like. Paul is not talking about a single or singular serious sin, like say that of King David, which is regretted, repented of, and one is restored from. The writers of the NT firmly believe that a person can change, that their behavior can improve with the aid of the Spirit and God's grace, that giving into temptation is not inevitable, and that God holds Christians responsible for their behavior, indeed they all must appear before the *bema* seat judgment of Christ to give an account of the deeds they have done in the body (2 Cor. 5) and this applies especially to ministers (1 Cor. 3).

As Chaucer once said about the clergy, "if gold rusts, what then will iron do?" The ethical seriousness of the NT reflects the profound belief that God's amazing grace really can change sinners into saints.

Most of all, what needs to be stressed is the Christological shape or pattern the Christian life is supposed to take. One is called to the imitation of Christ, the replication of Christ's character and also his chosen behavior in the life of the believer. And here is where we note that the ethics of the New Covenant in various ways go beyond, and in some case against the ethics of the Mosaic covenant. Moses wants no murdering, Jesus wants no unrighteous anger that leads to killing of any sort. Moses wants only sincere and serious oaths, Jesus wants no oaths at all.

Moses wants limited grounds for divorce, Jesus wants no divorce at all. Moses wants tithing of God's people. Jesus wants sacrificial giving, which can go well beyond tithing. And so on. The reason Jesus and Paul and other followers of Christ can make such "extreme" ethical demands is that they believe that the Kingdom is indeed coming, that God's salvation is already at work, that the believer already has the ongoing, powerful presence of the Spirit continually in their life, and that God's grace is sufficient to enable a believer to do what God asks them to do, or at least to attempt it, and if there is failure, it will not be because of lack of effort on the part of the believer. It will be because of intervening circumstances or persons or events. The writers of the NT are convinced that "to whom more (grace) is given, more should be expected," both in terms of belief and behavior.

To be sure, the Christian is not expected to become Christ or even have a messiah complex. The imitation has to do with following the moral pattern of Christ's life, living self-sacrificially, living into and out of teaching such as we find in Mt. 5–7 or Rom. 12–15. It means, in that memorable passage in 1 Cor. 13, loving in like fashion to which Christ loved. Without wholehearted love of God and neighbor, and even love for the enemy, all the rest achieves nothing for the individual in question. The fruit of the Spirit described in Gal. 5 speak of a person being molded by the Spirit into the likeness of Christ, and the fruit of the Spirit matures the person so that when they exercise the gifts of the Spirit, they do so in an other-conscious, self-sacrificial way. Love builds up the body, pride and arrogance puff up the individual.

What also gives urgency to the ethics of the Bible in general and the NT in particular is the belief that there is a living God, and he could intervene at any given moment and call the world to account, including the household of faith, where judgment quite properly begins. The form this sanction takes in the NT is of course the eschatological uncertainty about the timing of Christ's return. He will come like a thief in the night, so the believer must be found about the Master's business, living a Christ-like life, sharing the Good News of the Gospel as if tomorrow could be the day Christ returns. The ethics of the NT is grounded in the eschatological things Christ has already done – died, rose, and sent the Spirit – which leads to the death of the old person and the new creation in the believer here and now, with the Spirit joining the person to the body of Christ, and the Spirit becoming an ongoing source of life, light, power, presence. But the ethics of the NT has the further sanction of "not yet." The Kingdom has not yet come fully on earth. Christ has not yet sat on the *bema* seat and judged the behavior of believers. Christ has not yet returned, so the believer must live prepared for the conclusion of human history. The believer must be prepared to live betwixt and between the already and the not yet, living out of the already (we are already new creatures in Christ), and earnestly longing for the not yet (we are not yet fully conformed to his image).

It is interesting as well that the new life in Christ, when it comes to ethics, involves a good deal of freedom of choice. Food choices, clothing choices, spouse choices, job choices, and many other things become matters of adiaphora as the Kingdom comes. Partly this is because all human choices other than responding to the Gospel have become relativized, as have all human institutions, including marriage. The form and institutions of this world are passing away. The Christian life thus involves some ethical improvisation, and contextualization in regard to matters adiaphora. We do not need to all dress, or think, or work, or eat alike.

Whatever the believer does, they are to do to the glory of God, and in good faith, and if there is something one cannot do in good faith, then it is sin for that person (see 1 Cor. 8–10). But it is not a hollow cry when Paul says "for freedom Christ has set us free."

Paradoxically, while Jesus upped the ethical cost of discipleship, at the same time he reduced the number of required commandments to follow. Taking up one's cross and following Jesus turned out to be both more and less demanding in different ways than taking up the yoke of the Mosaic Law. And one of the new tasks had to do with spreading the Good News. Israel was expected to be a light to the world, but the expectation involved the notion that the light would attract the non-Jews, and they would come seeking the light, and join the Jewish people. Jesus on the other hand commissioned a great evangelistic effort. *Christianity became the sole evangelistic religion of any consequence in the Greco-Roman world, in a way that the OT neither anticipates nor foreshadows. It is one thing to let one's light shine. It is another thing completely to take lights to everyone everywhere, looking for the people who dwell in deep darkness, and give them the lighted lamp you hold. In a polytheistic world, real evangelism, based on a belief that there is only one savior for all the world, did and does seem obnoxious to a world committed to a multi-religious approach to salvation. That was as true in the Greco-Roman world as today in ours.*

Preaching for a Verdict

One of the mysteries that is seldom explored is that on the surface, the Bible says very little about what we call preaching – the exposition of a pre-existing biblical text, usually in a religious venue, except when one may be involved in evangelistic or mission preaching, which could be anywhere. Ironically the one example of preaching we find in the Gospels is Jesus expounding Isaiah in his home synagogue in Nazareth (cf. Mk. 6 and Lk. 4). Sometimes, the mistake is made of confusing prophecy with preaching. Of course, both can involve an oral proclamation, but prophecy is not, for the most part, an exposition of pre-existing biblical texts. To the contrary, prophecy is sharing a late or fresh word from God that the prophets has just been inspired to speak. The assumption that preaching = prophesying has various problems with it.

And then there is the further issue that "preacher" or "proclaimer" is nowhere to be found in the gift lists in the NT – apostles yes, prophets yes, teachers yes, healers yes, "evangelists" yes (once, in Ephesians!), but "local church preachers" you will look for in vain. Sometimes scholars have suggested that the "herald" is something of a model for the preacher. After all, the word κῆρυξ, which we translate as "herald," is the basis of the word "kerygma," the preached Word. But the role of the "herald" was to announce the coming of the king, or governor, or the like. He was not a preacher of a pre-existing sacred text of any kind. Now, occasionally, a "herald" would read out an official proclamation of a king, but this was simply a matter of reading the words, not a matter of expounding the meaning of the words, or the like. The herald would be closer to the lector in a church who reads out the Scripture lesson but does not do the preaching.

This in no way is to deny that there is plenty of proclamation mentioned in the NT. We see in Acts Paul regularly proclaiming the Good News and using OT texts as either a taking-off point, or as a source of illustrations of the Good News. But Paul, of course, is both an apostle of Jesus Christ and a prophet, not to mention a Pharisaically trained teacher. And as I have been emphasizing for a long time, if you want to see what Paul's proclamations were like, besides studying the speech summaries in Acts, simply read his letters. They are basically speeches with an epistolary prescript and postscript. Apart from those two parts of the document, this is what Paul likely would have said, had he been there.

So, what do we learn about the earliest Christian "preaching" from Paul's letters? We learn that Paul, and the author of Hebrews, and presumably others, conformed their speeches to various of the rhetorical conventions of their day.[8] Rhetoric was the art of persuasion in the Greco-Roman world, and various proclaimers and evangelists used it as a tool of persuasion, including Paul. A good deal can be learned about ancient "homilet-ics" so to speak by reading Aristotle's treatise on *Rhetoric*, or better still the compilation volume by Quintilian entitled *Institutions of Orations*. Of course, it is true, that the heavy lifting was believed to be done, and rightly so, by God the Spirit, when it came to convict-ing, convincing and converting people. But that did not in any way deter well-educated Christian leaders from using the oratorical skills and techniques of the day to help per-suade people.

Was there a difference between evangelistic proclamation and proclamation to those already disciples? Perhaps. It seems clear from Acts that proclamation in the synagogues or with Jewish Christians (see Hebrews and perhaps 1 Peter) involved both OT texts, and the Good News kerygma. In some ways, Paul's letters can be something of a test case because it appears that he is mostly writing to a mixed audience, largely composed of Gentiles, but with some Jews as well. And yes, he does use OT texts, quoting and alluding to them, even in a letter like Romans, where he says at one juncture that he is addressing Gentiles. But on closer inspection, Paul is not so much spending time expounding pre-existing scriptural texts, as using them to illustrate or confirm other points he wants to make, points dealing with specific situations and problems his congregations are facing.

As I have said at length elsewhere, the basic way the OT is used in the NT does not so much amount to exegesis of those texts, though that may be presupposed, as using those texts homiletically to make other points.[9] The writers of the NT think the OT foreshadows and sometimes foretells or provides types of things happening in the eschatological age, but they do not act like later Christian preachers trying to read the OT *as if it was* the NT, or as if Christ could be found under every rock in the OT. It is not necessary to go into detail here about the use of the OT in the NT, since we have dealt with that in great detail in three other studies. What we can say is that there is no question that the writers of the NT see the OT as Holy Writ, and equally they see the teaching of Jesus and the apostles as the living Word of God as well (see e.g. 1 Thess. 2.13). In 1 Thess. 2.13 it is quite clear that the proclamation of the Good News is viewed as more than mere human words, but

---

[8] On which see my textbook, Ben Witherington III, *New Testament Rhetoric: An Introductory Guide to the Art of Persuasion in and of the New Testament* (Eugene, OR: Wipf and Stock, 2009) and more broadly Witherington, *Invitation to the New Testament*.

[9] On which, see Witherington, *Isaiah Old and New*; *Psalms Old and New*; *Torah Old and New*.

indeed as the living Word of God which changes lives, even the lives of pagans who were turning from idols to the true God and had no previous knowledge of God's Word.

What we see in the NT are perhaps the first attempts at a biblical theology intertwined with a biblical ethic by Jewish followers of Jesus using both the OT and the kerygma to proclaim or explain the Good News. But in both cases, it is a New Covenant theology and ethic. It is not about a mere renewal or extension of previous biblical theology and ethics. Rather, some of the old is incorporated into a new framework with much new teaching added.

I say Jewish followers of Jesus because, apart from perhaps Luke, who nonetheless seems to know the LXX and may have been a God-fearer, and perhaps whoever was the compiler of that composite document called 2 Peter, the NT was written by Jews who indeed knew the Hebrew Scriptures in some form and to some degree, and believed it was Holy Writ.

What we have been discussing in this chapter is the intertwining of theology, ethics, and praxis, and all of this has a Christological flavor to it, even the praxis of the Lord's Supper and Baptism, as well as the proclamation. If we ask the question why there is not any exposition of the many parables or aphorisms of Jesus in the rest of the NT, a partial answer would that a movement so focused on evangelism, public proclamation, and first teachings must focus on the soteriologically crucial portions of the story of Jesus, about his coming, born of woman, born under the Law (Gal. 4), about his death, and about his resurrection. In the early stages of the movement, it's all about making converts, and discipleship, while important, is a secondary concern. Paul's letters reflect the earlier preaching, but are basically examples of disciplining those who are already at least partially formed disciples, however immature. It is quite unnecessary to assume that, for instance Paul, bless his heart, simply didn't know much of the teaching of Jesus. Texts like 1 Cor. 7 and 11 and Rom. 12–14 make clear that such a view is false. The issue has to do with focus and audience, not knowledge, in all likelihood. Whatever the handicaps of the writers of the NT may have been when it comes to knowing the teachings of Jesus and the earliest kerygma, we do not have such excuses. We have the whole canon to work with. But the *way* we use it makes all the difference.

We have suggested that the following ways of using the material are inadequate for constructing a proper *biblical* theology: (1) If we are following the lead of the writers of the NT, then it will never be adequate to suggest that the New Covenant is simply a renewal and extension of the Mosaic covenant. That's just bad covenant theology from a Christian point of view. (2) Equally inadequate, though it may not be inaccurate, is the thematic approach which picks a theme like "the living God" and works through the canon on the basis of the theme, or perhaps picks many themes and slots various texts, in proof-text fashion, into separate "theme" piles. (3) Even more inadequate is the practice of anachronism, of reading back into the NT later Protestant or Catholic or Orthodox theology. In regard to things like Christ being part of the divine identity, or the beginnings of Trinitarian discussion, those things *can already be found in the canon*, though the implications, amplifications, and applications quite appropriately were worked out later, from the fourth century on. (4) Reading the canon without attention to progressive revelation and salvation history in general is not adequate. This becomes obvious when one starts comparing what Jesus says about the theology and ethics of marriage and divorce and comparing it to what is said in Deuteronomy. (5) Reading the NT back into the OT does not respect the givenness of a word on target to extant specific audiences of the OT. Equally, looking for previews of coming attractions about almost everything in the NT in the OT reflects an over-reading of the OT into the NT.

The relationship between the two testaments, as we have seen in this study, is more complex than either of those two hermeneutical moves suggests. For one thing, one has to take into account the new, even at times radically new, aspect of the New Covenant. The eschatological flavor of the NT from start to finish at times emphatically emphasizes the newness, whether we are talking about a reversal of the order of who gets saved when (full number of Gentiles first, then Jews – Rom. 11) or about the turning of requirements in the OT into adiaphora or a matter of personal choice in the NT, or the very significant change of the ritual symbols of the movement, with baptism being a more egalitarian sign of the covenant than circumcision (see Gal. 3.28). God was doing a new thing, not just continuing an old thing, all the while being faithful to his own character, which was both just and merciful, both righteous and compassionate. It is not covenant faithfulness that characterizes the God of the Bible, but *HESED*, reflecting his consistent character, which emphasizes mercy, love, and compassion for his world of human beings while not neglecting justice, righteousness, and holiness. It is no accident that in the NT the nouns applied to God are love, light, life, whereas the adjectives are holy, righteous, just.

What I hope we have shown in this study is that an additive model with some finesse in dealing with the progressive nature of revelation works better than the approaches mentioned in the previous paragraph. By additive I mean you build from the presuppositions or givens of the symbolic universe up. Out of the symbolic universe and based on that bedrock comes the narrative way of thinking about theology, the narrative thought world. And the narrative thought world of the OT and that of the NT are different enough that we have treated them in two chapters, though clearly the NT thought world grows out of the OT one in various ways. For example, what Paul says about the Abraham story, that the Gospel of trust reckoned as righteousness was pre-preached to him, is not exactly what is going on in Gen. 12–15 but it is sufficiently based in the OT narrative to be coherent with its thrust. A development of the story has happened in the light of the Christ event, but it is recognizably the same Abraham with some of the same elements in Gal. 3 and Rom. 4. Then once the story board is laid out, out of that one can examine the theologizing that comes out of those narratives and is spoken into the various contexts of the early church.

This model is organic enough, interlocking enough, to make sense of the layered nature of biblical theology. Like excavating an archaeological tel, unless one digs down to bedrock, one doesn't know where the starting point really is of such thinking and self-expression. But the presupposition, the symbolic universe, is not necessarily evident. One has to ask what the unspoken theological givens are. The stories are on the surface in the accounts of salvation history, but in the NT, when you are dealing with Paul's discourses for instance, they show up only occasionally but are often just below the surface of the texts. And furthermore, they are assumed as a basis for the arguments Paul and others make, and the theologizing the writers of the NT do.

If we ask about the unity or coherence of biblical theology, the short answer is that a variety of voices, in a variety of ways, are speaking and reflecting on the very same living

God, the one God of the Bible, and the stories of his relationship with the chosen people. These stories are going somewhere, heading for the new creation and a permanent relationship with God. They presuppose the lostness, alienation, of even God's people from their own God. Thus, after the initial tales of creation, the Bible settles down into an oft-repeated tale of repentance, redemption, reconciliation, rescue, and the like. But that requires a lot of salvation history, and a lot of persons in many generations to be saved. The constant factor is the one true God, whose character is the same yesterday, today, and forever.

However, no one knew that the divine identity included three persons, Father, Son, and Spirit, before the incarnation of the Son and before he began speaking of the Spirit as a person distinguishable from the Father and the Son. Without progressive revelation, the complexity of our God could not even begin to be known. The people of God during the Mosaic covenant truly saw through a glass darkly, or as Paul put it, with a veil over their hearts. As the author of Hebrews puts it in Heb. 1, partial and piecemeal was the revelation of God and his salvation plan and his relationship with his people, until the coming of the Son. Much more could be said along these lines, but this is enough to prompt further reflection. In our final chapter, we will reflect on some of the implications of this study. For now, I am content to say – *no biblical theology is adequate that does not do justice to the Trinitarian nature of God revealed in the Christian canon.* Christian theology cannot afford to be Christomonistic. Too often in Protestant theology, Christ is the overwhelming focus in some traditions, and the Spirit in others, but we neglect the theology of God the Father. In this study, we have attempted to avoid that error.

15

And So? A Cautionary Conclusion

There is a very good reason this volume is entitled "*a*" biblical theology. Obviously, there are a variety of ways one could write such a volume, and a variety of approaches one can take, not least because the matter is quite complex, and no two persons are going to read all the relevant texts in the same way. Simply *trying* to undertake this task has been a humbling experience. No wonder there have been whole generations of scholars who have avoided it like the plague! Who is sufficient for such things? And that question is all the more appropriate in an age of over-specialization and too few general practitioners of the reading and interpreting of the whole Bible. I am tempted to suggest that unless one has actually (1) taught both the OT and the NT, and (2) done scholarly work on both Testaments, and (3) plumbed some of the depths of the issues of intertextuality, and (4) unless one has actually taken on the arduous task of actually writing some commentaries on biblical books, working through them from start to finish, one should abandon hope of doing even an adequate biblical theology.

It is in some ways easier to say how *not* to undertake the task than how to do so, and clearly the big problem will always be anachronism – reading later concerns, later theologies, our own agendas, our own cherished theologies, or modern world views, and the like back into the biblical text. Further, we must be constantly warned of the dangers of only cherry-picking those portions of the text that suit our predilections. I have tried hard to avoid these sins in writing this book. The reader will have to decide if I have at least partially succeeded.

What I am confident of is that the methodology of looking at the symbolic universe, the narrative thought worlds, and then the theologizing does bear good fruit in our considering what a many-layered and progressively revealed biblical theology might look like. As I said at the outset, even opening one's mouth and saying "biblical theology" rather than biblical theologies, implies that one believes there is some coherency and consistency to the symbolic universe, the narrative thought worlds, and the theologizing we find in the Bible. I am happy to admit I believe this is true, and hopefully this volume has partially justified this belief.

What I am also confident of is that theology should never be done in an abstract way, as if it were an exercise in assembling a history of developing ideas. No, the theology is embedded in certain historical, social, rhetorical contexts and a failure to carefully do contextual exegesis on the way to understanding the theology is a recipe for misinterpretation and even disaster. Further, the study must involve reading the biblical texts *in their own languages*. We could have avoided a lot of the Augustinian mistakes if Augustine himself hadn't relied on interpreting the NT in Latin, *a language it was not originally written in*, and then become such an influential and towering theologian of the church at a critical juncture in its development. To be fair, Augustine helped us in many ways, especially with his *Confessions*, but we could have done without some of his influence on that Augustinian monk turned reformer, Martin Luther.

In the election chapter I went out of my way to engage in dialogue about the Jewish context of Paul's theology because inevitably it is Paul's theology, in a Protestant context especially, that gets turned into theological McNuggets, and interpreted quite apart from the setting of early Judaism in which Paul's thinking and theology came to fruition. Pauline theology has suffered *more* than most other sorts of biblical theologies from decontextualization at the hands of Protestant preachers, teachers, and even scholars. Perhaps the election chapter shows a way forward that doesn't involve ignoring or stripping the ideas out of their original Jewish contexts.

What are some of the positive major insights or conclusions of this study? We may list the following: (1) without a deep concern for careful contextual interpretation and the historical givenness of the text, much can go wrong when one attempts to do biblical theology. In particular, the OT must be allowed to have its own say, its own contribution to biblical theology, which is chiefly to provide us with a portrait of Yahweh, the creator God, and how he called and formed a people which came to be called Israel. (2) Biblical theology also requires a commitment to a theology of progressive revelation. Really, proto-Trinitarian and then Trinitarian thinking does not begin before the Christ event, and then only gradually does it become clear that even Binitarian thinking (a Godhead involving the Father and the Son) will not be adequate. The NT canon is progressively more Trinitarian the further one goes in the canon. This is not simply an evolutionary or chronological development, because some of the highest Christology is some of the earliest – for instance in Paul's letters and perhaps in Hebrews as well. (3) While covenantal theology is a very important part of biblical theology, it is critical to realize that with the exception of the New Covenant, none of those covenants were everlasting or permanent covenants, and it is incorrect to say that there has just been one covenant between God and his people, in many administrations. Furthermore, there are no unilateral or unconditional covenants in the Bible, either. Furthermore, *HESED* means mercy, not God's tenacious loyalty to a particular covenant, say the Mosaic covenant. God is faithful to his character, and to his promises based on his character, but covenants come and go, are fulfilled or become obsolete until the new Christ-inaugurated and Christ-centered covenant appears. (4) God's grace, like God's love, is *not* given with no thought of return. On the contrary it is intended to start an ongoing relationship and the recipient is expected to love God with his or her whole heart. Nor is grace, even in the NT, "perfected" in such a way that it becomes totally irresistible, such that we can deny there actually are apostasy texts in the Bible. This is not even true of Pauline or Johannine theology, never mind biblical theology. (5) Election and salvation, though interrelated matters, are not identical matters. For example, Christ is God's chosen one, his anointed Elect One, but he does not need to be saved. Furthermore, in both the OT and the NT one can be among or a part of the elect people, and in the end not be saved. Furthermore, as we noted repeatedly, salvation in the OT does not refer to "salvation by grace through faith in Jesus Christ." Indeed, it often refers simply to God rescuing, redeeming from bondage, or healing some OT figure or group. One has to have an understanding of how the concept of salvation grew and developed as time went on and the canon grew larger. (6) While covenantal nomism is an adequate way to speak about the Mosaic covenant, which was indeed inaugurated and sustained by God's grace, the New Covenant does not lack commandments or law, called the Law of Christ, so the old Protestant contrast between a law covenant and a grace covenant, or worse a God of law and judgment in the OT pitted over against a God of grace and redemption in the New Covenant, does no justice to either the OT or the NT, to either the Mosaic or the New Covenant. (7) Finally, we used the word "convergence" in the subtitle precisely because all the pieces of a necessary full-fledged biblical theology do not emerge until all the lines of development about the Father, Son, and Spirit and redemption converge in the NT, and in particular from about the Gospel of John on in the NT, reading progressively through the canonical witness rather than just chronologically.

I do not wish to end on a strident note. I am quite glad that there has been a renaissance in the last twenty or so years of attempts to do and write volumes on biblical theology. This certainly beats the despairing of such attempts and tasks in the latter half of the twentieth century. But it is clear to me that there is much to still be done before we will truly, adequately understand biblical theology. As a famous New England poet once said of another but not unrelated subject:

> Whose woods these are I think I know.
> His house is in the village though;
> He will not see me stopping here
> To watch his woods fill up with snow.
>
> My little horse must think it queer
> To stop without a farmhouse near
> Between the woods and frozen lake
> The darkest evening of the year.
>
> ...
>
> The woods are lovely, dark and deep,
> But I have promises to keep,
> And miles to go before I sleep,
> And miles to go before I sleep.[1]

Like Frost's tale of the doctor making house calls, I feel that I know the woods of biblical theology, but having spent so much time in them, I have to admit, I am not yet out of them, not yet *out of the woods*, and that actually is a good thing. God's house of course is in heaven, and someday I will do better than see through a glass darkly, or only know in part while gazing on it from afar. But as I have stopped and taken time to ponder my subject in detail and carefully, I feel I also have a right to say that these biblical woods are also lovely, dark, and deep, and as for understanding them, I also have promises to keep (of which the production of this volume is one fulfillment) and likewise hopefully miles to go before I can sleep the sleep of one who knows as he is known, miles to go before I am truly "out of the woods."

---

[1] From Robert Frost, "Stopping by Woods on a Snowy Evening," *New Hampshire* (New York: Henry Holt, 1923).

Appendix A

Biblical Theology and NT Theology: A Dialogue with Francis Watson

It is one of the fundamental assumptions of this entire study that what is historically false cannot possibly be theologically true. As applied to this particular part of our study what I mean, for instance, is that books written by Jews for Jews, and not for Christians in the first instance, who did not yet exist, cannot lead to the conclusion that the OT is simply a Christian book and its truth can only be properly understood or interpreted by faithful Christians. This whole approach to the matter seems to me to entail a fundamental denial of the very nature of God's revelation and its progressive character, and furthermore a denial that the biblical message is not merely for the found but also for the lost. A theology of revelation or canon or of the Spirit that involves ignoring the historical facts, or worse, denying them, is not a proper biblical theology at all.

To take one example, Francis Watson in his stimulating study *Text and Truth: Redefining Biblical Theology* insists that the "Spirit of truth bears witness to the grace and truth that are to be found in the enfleshed Word not directly but *in and through the Christian community – in and through its preaching and worship, its sacraments and canonical texts. These texts are foundational to the life of the church, not on the legalistic and biblicistic grounds that they possess an inherent, absolute authority to which we are bound to submit, but on the grounds that in them we encounter the particular life upon which the communal life of the church is founded: the life that is the light not only of the church but of the world.*"[1] On this showing the Spirit did not show up on planet earth prior to or outside the context of the church. There was no direct encounter between God and his chosen people, the Jews, prior to the coming of Christ and the Spirit to the followers of Jesus. I would not want to deny that the church is one place where God reveals his truth through his Word, but it is surely not the only place, otherwise evangelistic preaching in a place where there is no church would be nothing more than words full of sound and fury but accomplishing nothing. There is a further problem with this salvo as well – as I have pointed out at some length in my study *The Living Word of God*.[2] The Bible does indeed have an inherent authority precisely because it tells the truth about the matters it

---

[1] Francis Watson, *Text and Truth: Redefining Biblical Theology* (Grand Rapids, MI: William B. Eerdmans, 1997), 1, emphasis added.
[2] Witherington, *The Living Word of God*.

discourses on. It does not merely have an authority because in it we encounter the Life, the Lord about which it speaks, though of course that is true as well.

Yet another problem with this whole approach has to do with making "texts" prior to almost all else. Listen to what Watson says: "The Word made flesh is never encountered [never?] without textual mediation, for Jesus is only recognized as such on the basis of a prior textuality. Jesus is initially acknowledged as Christ and Lord because that which takes place in him is said to take place 'according to the scriptures'."[3] While I quite agree that "the life of Jesus did not take place in a text-free vacuum"[4] it did take place *in what was largely an oral culture, not a culture of texts*. Furthermore, prior understanding of at least some of the Bible doesn't seem to have been a prerequisite for grasping at least some of the meaning of the Christ event, or having an encounter with God in Christ, otherwise, the pagans in Thessalonike, who turned from idols to the one true God, would never have been converted to Christ.

There were undoubtedly some who encountered Jesus without prior knowledge of the Hebrew Scriptures, and some of them indeed became his supporters, his partisans, his followers. One cannot well imagine the Gadarene demoniac as a student of the Hebrew Scriptures who understood Jesus on the basis of prior textual knowledge. To the contrary it was the encounter with Jesus that will have led various people into a proper relationship with the text of the Scriptures. There were both mediated and unmediated encounters with Jesus, just as there have always been both mediated and textually unmediated encounters with the Holy Spirit and God the Father as well. It is one thing to say that Jesus, God, the Spirit could not be fully understood without an understanding of the Scriptures. It is quite another to suggest that the church has a monopoly on the truth, or on the encounter with and grace of God, or that it can only happen in the context of Christian community, worship, and the sharing of Christian texts. One can only wonder what the Muslim "followers of Issah" who have never read the Bible nor been part of a church would think about such assertions. I am confident they would find something terribly wrong with such notions.

On the other hand, Watson is right that the text of both testaments, Old and New, are needful if one is to understand the full scope and meaning of the revelation of God in Jesus Christ. On this basis, Watson goes on to insist that "all Christian theology must be biblical theology."[5] I would agree with this assertion if by it one means that NT theology is founded and grounded in the Hebrew Scriptures and is dependent on them as a revelatory source in various ways. NT theology cannot stand alone, nor should Christian interpreters become the followers of Marcion.

This fact, however, does not make the Hebrew Scriptures in the first instance "the church's book," nor does it mean that we may expect to find full-blown Christian theology in the OT – for instance a doctrine of the Trinity, or a doctrine of salvation by grace through faith in Jesus. It is precisely the historical realities reflected in the OT which rule out such a theological approach. Christian theology which draws on the OT cannot be done in some sort of ahistorical or flat way that does not take into account the progressive revelation of God and the fundamentally pre-Christian character of the OT.

---

[3] Watson, *Text and Truth*, 1.
[4] *Ibid.*, 2.
[5] *Ibid.*

The attempt to turn the OT into a Christian allegory involves a failure to grasp the historical nettle, and at the end of the day is a bad example of historical anachronism. The OT is primarily about the revelation of Yahweh, the one Christians call God the Father, and only in a secondary sense, and by way of promise and prophecy, a revelation of the Son and the Spirit. If the actual theological substance of the OT is taken into account, and not merely its contemporizing hermeneutical use by later Christians, then in fact it is possible to say that what we have in the OT is truths that could equally well be affirmed by Jews, Christians, and Muslims *and are affirmed by them, though the uses they make of these texts varies.*

The fact that these truths may not be sufficient in themselves unto Christian conversion or salvation is another matter. Truth is no less true simply because it is, as the author of Heb. 1.1 suggested, "partial and piecemeal." *It is crucial to keep steadily in view both the historical givenness of the biblical texts and their theological character. They always and everywhere speak about a God who reveals himself in space and time in various ways to various persons, both saved and lost, both Jew and Gentile, both literate and illiterate, both textually aware and oblivious to biblical texts. Abraham did not encounter and follow God's directives on the basis of a prior understanding of Holy Writ mediated to him through a community of faithful interpreters of the Genesis sagas.*

I quite agree with Watson, however, that the Bible is irremediably theological in character. It is all about God, and God's relationship with various human individuals and groups. The Bible's history cannot be readily abstracted from its theologizing or vice versa. There is of course a good reason for this – God is committed to involvement in the messiness and contingencies of human history and always has been. Indeed, it should be said that God, as the creator of all things including all human beings, is the one who made history possible, viable, having purpose and a goal, and so on. Further, I quite agree with Watson that the segregation of biblical studies from theological studies has led to the impoverishment of both fields. Exegetes are working on inherently theological texts! Biblical theologians require exegetical study to come to grips with the subjects of their own fields of interest and inquiry. Watson is right to complain about the rigid divisions of these fields in the guild.

Watson urges a "dialectical" interdependence between the OT and the NT, decrying the tendency to see the OT as merely background for the NT. He urges "the notion of a dialectical unity between the two bodies of writing, constituted as 'old' and 'new' by their relationship to the foundational event that they together enclose and attest, only makes sense from a theological standpoint."[6] I would agree with this assertion in principle, but I would add that such an assertion only makes sense from a historical viewpoint as well. After all, the terms "old" and "new" refer to time and space, and events that happen in time and space and objects that are created in time and space, such as the various parts of the Bible. Here is where I must insist, however, that unless one does justice to both the historical and theological character of these texts, *one will not be doing theology properly, nor doing history justice.*

What do I mean by this? Well for one thing I mean that the OT does not cease to be Christian Scripture simply because it mostly tells us about God the Father and his

---

6 *Ibid.*, 5.

relationship with the universe, the world, a people. Patrology in the more antique and theologically loaded sense is just as much a part of Christian theology as Christology is. The fact that with benefit of hindsight and further revelation Christians came to view the Father through the lens of the Son and the Spirit does not mean that we cannot appreciate what is going on in the OT on its own terms, and furthermore recognize that the Christian doctrine of God would be severely and seriously impoverished without what the OT has to say about the matter. For example, the holiness, justice, mercy and indeed the love of God would be far less clear if we did not have the Hebrew Scriptures.

Watson is calling scholars to practice "biblical theology." He defines it as follows: "Biblical theology is *biblical* that is, concerned with the whole Christian Bible; it is more than the sum of OT theology and New Testament theology, understood as separate disciplines. Biblical theology is *theology*. Where attempts are made to limit it to a purely descriptive capacity, it quickly becomes redundant and the expression passes out of use."[7] While I am in sympathy with the thrust of both of these sentences some qualifications are needed. Firstly, while biblical theology may be more than the sum of OT and NT theology, if it is truly "Biblical" Theology it cannot be *other* than OT and NT theology lest it cease to be biblical in the proper sense.

By this I mean that biblical theology can only be constructed out of OT and NT theological material. It has no other resource. And when it goes beyond what is said in the OT and/or NT it has to be ever so careful not to go *against* what is said in those sources. I do not think that biblical theology can or should be attempted without reliance on both OT and NT theology, and the work of those scholars who labored long in the vineyard of OT or NT theology. This includes reliance on the work of various non-Christian scholars, and means indeed that the attempt to build or frame a biblical theology cannot be seen as a task which involves only reliance on or dialogue with Christian interpreters. In other words, *a hermeneutical ecclesiological apriori is a mistake when one is attempting to do a biblical theology worth its salt, and open to all insights from whatever sources and scholars.* Watson later rightly stresses that the biblical texts are both theologically motivated and also genuinely historiographical in intent and character.[8]

Secondly, I must insist that the proper order of things is that discovering and discerning the character of OT theology and NT theology on its own merits must be seen as a necessarily prior enterprise to the constructing of a biblical theology, not least because we have all seen what happens when the Bible is read through the grid of later Calvinist or Arminian or Lutheran, or Orthodox or Catholic systematic theology – namely, the biblical text is read anachronistically and is gerrymandered for various later theological purposes and battles about which the biblical writers were innocent and were not interested in.

From a hermeneutical point of view, since Christians are not under the Old Covenant in any of its manifestations, how exactly the OT is the basis of Christian theologizing is a delicate question in various regards, and it is not sufficient to say that the OT must simply be read Christologically, though that is one of the tasks the NT writers themselves undertake and encourage us to undertake.

---

[7] *Ibid.*, 8.

[8] *Ibid.*, 10. He is referring here to the Gospels but the same point could be made about any and all biblical narratives that are historical in substance.

More helpful are Watson's trenchant criticisms of postmodern and reader-response approaches to the biblical text. He throws down the gauntlet at the beginning of his essay on this subject, stressing:

A Christian faith concerned to retain its own coherence cannot for a moment accept that the biblical texts (individually and as a whole) lack a single determinant meaning, that their meanings are created by their readers, or that theological interpretations [*sic* – surely he means interpreters] must see themselves as non-privileged participants in an open-ended, pluralistic conversation. Such a hermeneutic assumes that these texts are like any other "classic" texts: self-contained artifacts, handed down to us through the somewhat haphazard processes of tradition, bearing with them a cultural authority that has now lost much of its normative force, yet challenging the interpreter to help ensure that they will at least remain readable, and continue to be read.[9]

Watson is right to assert that an author's meaning is encoded into the words by which he conveys it and we can know something of the author's intention in saying such things by studying his words in their original contexts. Writings, perhaps particularly inspired writings, have the intention of communicating something of importance to one or more recipients. Watson puts it this way: "When A speaks to B about x, what B receives is not a communication about x that might have come from anywhere ... but a communication that is distinctively A's communication. To understand and to respond to the communication is therefore not only to understand and respond to what is said about x but to understand and respond to A. Communication is an irreducibly *interpersonal* event."[10]

This is right on target. If one properly understands a text then one has understood what the author intended to say and does say. The text cannot be severed from its original author, since it is an expression of the mind of that author, nor can or should it be assumed that the meaning of the text is to be generated by the receiver of the communication. "Verbal meaning is not so ephemeral ... Readers can only receive meaning, they cannot *create* it."[11] Can there be a secondary significance to a text not originally intended by the author? Well yes, that is possible, but as Watson goes on to stress "true 'significance' is to be found *in the single, verbal meaning itself*, that is in its enduring ... force. The notion of a secondary, ephemeral 'contextual significance' is therefore subordinate to the primary universal significance this text claims by virtue of its role as 'gospel'."[12] I would prefer to substitute the phrase "Word of God" here for the term "gospel."

Equally helpful is Watson's stress that the biblical author is concerned not merely that the audience understand, but that they act. There is of course a distinction between understanding a communication and choosing to respond appropriately to it. "An adequate interpretation of the literal sense of a text will seek to explain not only what the author is *saying* but also what he or she is *doing*." Watson reminds us that even with lack of clear understanding of what an author or speaker is saying, we may still know what he wants, precisely because of the context. He gives the example of encountering a border guard speaking in a foreign language one does not know. One correctly surmises that the guard

---

[9] *Ibid.*, 97. No doubt Watson would strongly object to Dale Martin's attempts to say the opposite of this in his *Biblical Truths: The Meaning of Scripture in the Twenty-First Century* (New Haven, CT: Yale University Press, 2017).

[10] Watson, *Text and Truth*, 102.

[11] *Ibid.*, 104. Or at least, they ought not to be trying to re-create the meaning.

[12] *Ibid.*, 106.

is performing a speech-act wanting the listener to produce his passport. The speech-act is successful even though one has failed to understand the meaning of most or all of the words, because the context made clear what the speaker wanted.[13]

Watson goes on to stress that normally speech-acts require a certain context if they are to achieve their intended effect: "to make a promise or issue a command presupposes a complex set of prior conditions and relationships."[14] This is true, but only up to a point, or else a speech-act could never communicate successfully with a stranger or a foreigner unaware of the author's context and not sharing the author's community. Evangelism would be impossible if one takes too narrow a view of what preconditions are required for genuine communication.

Watson is quite right, however, that the intention of the author should not be divided from the text of the author, as if intent lies only in the mind of the speaker or writer, and the words are something else. He rightly warns that "It misunderstands authorial intention as a purely psychological event that precedes and constrains the words, exerting a continuing influence on the text from the outside. Against this view, authorial intention is to be seen as primarily embodied in the words the author wrote."[15] "Authorial intention is the principle of a text's intelligibility, and cannot be detached from the text itself. The capacity of writing to extend the scope of a speech-act in space and time precludes an understanding of authorial intention purely in terms of the author's immediate historical context."[16]

But it is not just the capacity of writing that does this, for we are dealing with the living Word of God, not just any kind of communication. We are dealing with words that God uses repeatedly to convey not merely his meaning but his presence, his salvation, and many other things. Watson's work is extremely valuable in helping us understand and appreciate that biblical texts are not ink blots into which one can read what one wants to find there. To the contrary these texts have meaning, a meaning God himself has inspired the biblical writer to write or record (if the message was first delivered orally). Even more, what we have in these texts is not merely encoded information and meaning, what we have is revelation from God.

---

[13] *Ibid.*, 116. I appreciate this example, having had this very experience on the border between Estonia and Russia once, where the speaker spoke in Russian, and I did not know what she said, but did know what she wanted, and the intent or purpose of the speech-act was clear in regard to how I ought to respond. But then she handed me an arrival card printed in Cyrillic script that I was expected to fill out. At that juncture, I had to guess what was wanted in various slots. The card was a less clear communicator than the speaker.

[14] *Ibid.*, 117.

[15] *Ibid.*, 118.

[16] *Ibid.*, 123.

Appendix B

The Death of Sin in the Death of Jesus: Atonement Theology[*]

Setting up the Context of the Discussion Properly

The language of atonement in Greek is difficult to translate into proper English, as a glance at recent translations will show where we find: atonement, atoning sacrifice, propitiation, expiation, sacrifice for sin, and even remedy for defilement (which makes the matter seem as if ritual defilement were the main problem). And sometimes the writers of the NT do not do the expected thing. For example, in 1 John the author is talking about a person, Jesus Christ, but he does not use the noun *hilaster*, which means one who offers or makes atonement. He chooses the more abstract noun *hilasmos*, perhaps to indicate that Jesus is paradoxically enough both the sacrifice and the priest who does the offering. A brief review of this language and its cognates may help a bit here.

There are two verbs used in the LXX to denote atoning action, *hilaskesthai* and *exilaskesthai*. While the latter term is never found in the NT, it is found in the LXX over 100 times, and it is also found in the earliest church fathers (cf. 1 Clem. 7.7; Hermas, *Vis.* 1.2.1), where it clearly refers to propitiation. *Hilaskesthai* is a much rarer word, found only 11 times in the LXX and twice in the NT, Lk. 18.13 (where it seems to be a plea for mercy) and more relevantly Heb. 2.17, where it seems to refer to Jesus' propitiating of sins of the people as the High Priest in heaven. In Zech. 7.2 and Mal. 1.9 the meaning is clearly propitiation.

The lack of use of *hilaskesthai* in the LXX is more than compensated for by the use of the cognate *hilasterion*, found 27 times in the LXX, 22 instances of which are referring to the mercy seat cover, or more broadly to the Ark of the Covenant. That cover is where the blood was sprinkled for the propitiation of sin, being the spot nearest to God that was possible. The mercy seat did not need cleansing, the people needed cleansing from the effects of their sin but that was only possible if God's righteous anger against sin was dealt with. We find this same noun used in Heb. 9.5, where it certainly refers to the mercy seat itself and the atoning that went on at that spot. The only other use in the NT is found at Rom. 3.24–25, where the stress is on the fact that God put forward Jesus as a *hilasterion* by his blood.

---

[*] Part of what follows was originally given as a plenary lecture at the 2014 meeting of the IBR, adapted and adopted for this volume.

As J. D. G. Dunn has said about this verse, the logic here is that God's wrath, previously discussed at some length in Rom. 1, is somehow averted by Jesus' death (cf. 2 Macc. 7.38), and averted amazingly enough according to this text by God offering to himself his own Son as atoning sacrifice.[1]

A few misconceptions need to be pointed out at this juncture. It is not true that *hilaskesthai* in the LXX is not associated with God's wrath. It certainly is in Exod. 32.12–14 and Dan. 9.16–19, so the translation "propitiation" cannot be ruled out by saying there is no precedent in the LXX for such a rendering. Furthermore, since 1 John, where we find the language, is written to a dominantly Greco-Roman context (that is, it is not written to Christians living in Jerusalem or Galilee) it is in order to point out that *hilasterion* normally refers in Greek literature to propitiation of wrath. We may consider one example, a Greek inscription found at Kos: "The people, for the Emperor Caesar, son of God, Augustus, for salvation to the gods [offer this] propitiatory sacrifice [*hilasterion*]."[2] It seems likely, then, that propitiation is in view in Rom. 3.24–25, and C. K. Barrett concludes in his commentary on that text: "This amounts to the paradoxical claim that God propitiates God ... The paradox is rooted in the nature of God. It is the nature of God to be irreconcilably opposed to sin; it is the nature of God to love sinners and to seek reconciliation with them. No one but God could resolve the problem; and God himself could be faithful to both aspects of his being only at the cost of the Cross."[3]

Returning now to the review of key terms, we note that *hilasmos* is a noun found ten times in the LXX, at 1 Jn. 2.2 and also at 1 Jn. 4.10 (the only two occurrences in the NT). Notice that the latter text is much like Rom. 3.24–25 in that it is stated plainly that God is the one putting forward Jesus as *hilasmos*. One gets the distinct impression that what we are dealing with in the use of this terminology involves an exchange or action that transpires between the Father and the Son, not an action that is primarily focusing on what goes one within the believer as a result. When the author of 1 John wants to talk about the cleansing effect of atonement he does so directly by using that language (i.e. *katharise* in 1.9).

It would appear that both the Beloved Disciple and Paul believed that unless God's wrath is propitiated by Christ's death, the effects of our sins are not expiated and so we do not receive either cleansing or, equally importantly, reconciliation and communion with God after the alienation caused by sin.[4] The issue, then, being dealt with in this terminology involves guilt and cleansing, but it also involves far more than that and tells us something profound about the righteous character of God which cannot be compromised just because God loves his creatures. Fortunately for the sinner, the propitiating merit of Christ's death is continual. 1 John says he *is* the atoning sacrifice, not "he was the propitiation."

There is one more related term of consequence, *hileos*, found some 35 times in the LXX, and it refers quite specifically to God as God turns the divine anger away from his people, and we have this same sense of the term in Mt. 16.22 and Heb. 8.12 quoting

---

[1] J. D. G. Dunn, *Romans 1–8* (Waco, TX: Word, 1988), 151.
[2] W. R. Paton and E. L. Hicks, *The Inscriptions of Kos* (Oxford: Clarendon Press, 1891), no. 81, cf. also no. 347.
[3] C. K. Barrett, *The Epistle to the Romans* (2nd edn.; Peabody, MA: Hendrickson, 1991), 74.
[4] See Westcott, *Epistles of St. John*, 44–45.

Jer. 31.34, where it is usually translated "be merciful," which is the same thing as to turn away wrath. It is true of course that the Hebrew root *KPR* lies in the background which has as its basic meaning to cover or cover over, and there can be little doubt that in various places in the LXX propitiation is in view (see Ps. 106.30 LXX and Sir. 45.23). Zech. 8.22 could hardly be more direct. It refers to many coming to Jerusalem "to propitiate the face of the Lord." In the context of various of the LXX uses of the relevant terminology, the wrath of God is referred to directly. For example, in Micah 7.18–19 we hear that "God does not retain his wrath forever because he delights in mercy." The Beloved Disciple as well is perfectly familiar with the connection of disobedience, sin, and divine wrath as a consequence, as Jn. 3.36 shows.

One of the major problems one sees in the great debates about the meaning, significance, and effects of the death of Jesus is the problem of anachronism. Already in the classic discussions, which begin at least as early as Anselm, significant terms, ideas, concepts are being read into NT texts, resulting in skewed interpretations of some of the more crucial and explicit NT texts which deal with atonement for sins. This trend, unfortunately, did not end with the patristic period but continued on into the Reformation period, and indeed into the modern period. Juridical ideas and theories which did not even exist in the first century AD, or did not have the bearing they were later to have, have been imported into the discussion *ad libitum*, with telling effect. For example, the theory that Jesus' death provides a ransom *to Satan* so that the sinner may be freed from bondage to the Diabolical One is not only absent from the NT, it is a theory that goes against the grain of much of what is said about the matter in the NT. Bondage in sin is not the same thing as demon possession, nor does the NT suggest that *God owes* or pays Satan anything.

Unfortunately, the discussion has become rancorous at times, to no good end, with one Christian group or another anathematizing another (e.g. is the atonement limited or unlimited, and if limited who limited it?), despite the fact *that no ecumenical council in Christian history ever established what an orthodox belief about the atonement should and must include or exclude.*[5] As a historian, a NT scholar, and an exegete I am sometimes tempted to throw up my hands when some of these sorts of discussions are used as a sort of Ockham's razor to exclude one or another person from: (1) one's denomination, or (2) one's academic or theological society, or (3) even from the category of biblical orthodoxy. It follows from this introduction that the discussion of the atonement must be set up in careful terms, not taking theological terms in the NT in isolation from their original historical, rhetorical, social, and religious contexts. It is to those contexts that I now turn.

Getting the Context Right

Most religions in the Greco-Roman world, like most religions in the ANE, had three things in common – temples, priests, and sacrifices. One of the real problems Christianity must have had in the first three-plus centuries of its existence was establishing that it

---

5 Robert W. Jenson, *Systematic Theology*, vol. 1: *The Triune God* (Oxford: Oxford University Press, 2001; first pub. 1997), 187: "It is one of the more remarkable and remarked on aspects of theological history that no theory of the atonement has ever been universally accepted. By now this phenomenon is itself among the things that a proposed theory of atonement must explain."

was indeed a *religio* and should be taken seriously as such, despite the fact that it had no temples, no priests, and offered no literal sacrifices. True, some pagans feared that those Lord's Supper meals were clandestine acts of cannibalism, but those fears were based on rumor, not reality. Anyone who has read the works of scholars like Ramsay MacMullen or R. L. Wilken or A. D. Knox, to mention but three, will realize that Christianity will have appeared to most outsiders as some sort of philosophy of life, and all the more so as it became detached from and disassociated from early Judaism and its praxis. But if a non-Christian probed a bit deeper, he or she would discover a lot of discussion in early Christianity about non-philosophical matters like atonement for sin. And since early Christianity was the only genuinely evangelistic religion in the Greco-Roman world at the time, eventually such comparisons were likely to be made by outsiders as well as insiders.

If one probes Greco-Roman religion, and indeed early Jewish religion when it comes to atonement thought, it becomes very clear indeed that offering sacrifices and making atonement was seen as a way to deal with one or another god's anger with some action or attitude of the suppliant. It is hardly possible to remove the notion of anger or wrath and the notion of appeasement or satisfaction from these discussions and have anything significant left to say about the atonement thought in play. And if a non-Christian Jew or Gentile in the middle of the first century had read the following words in Romans, "for the wrath of God is revealed from heaven against all ungodliness" (Rom. 1.18), and then went on to peruse the discussion of the *hilasterion* in Rom. 3, it can hardly be doubted that they would conclude that the Christian God as well was a God who was angry about sin and demanding atonement, or justice, or satisfaction, or some such thing as a result. And when such a demand is stated or implied, we are most definitely in the territory of the term "propitiation," which might also include the notion of "expiation," though not necessarily. It was not Jonathan Edwards who invented the notion of a Christianity that included the concept of sinners in the hands of an angry God. My point is simply this – it takes a lot of ignoring of the larger religious context and conceptualities about God or the gods to be able to exclude ideas like appeasement, propitiation, divine wrath, and the like from the discussion of the atonement in the NT *whatever other sorts of concepts we might want to include in the discussion.*

The second important contextual matter that needs to be attended to at this juncture is the *interrelatedness* of so many of the crucial ideas. By this I mean that one's conception of the atonement will be affected by one's conceptions of both sin and God, to mention but two crucial correlates. One of the merits of Gary Anderson's book *Sin: A History* is not merely to emphasize that ideas have a history, they develop and change over time, but also to make clear that ideas are interrelated things and they have consequences, often devastating consequences.[6] To this I would add that when you are dealing with something as complex as atonement for sin, *you are not simply dealing with ideas or the history of ideas and a* religionsgeschichtliche *approach to the matter will hardly be adequate, not least because it is the praxis of making atonement which also affects if not determines how one views ideas about atonement.* Herein lies one of the great problems for theologians – the danger is that history and praxis will be ignored, and one will try to settle

---

[6] Gary Anderson, *Sin: A History* (New Haven, CT: Yale University Press, 2009).

theological controversies simply on the basis of debating ideas, or rearranging ideas, or logically thinking through and connecting ideas.

But alas for such approaches, before ever there were Christian ideas about the death of Jesus, there was the *event* of the death of Jesus, and it might be useful to ask if Jesus had any crucial religious or theological thoughts about the meaning and consequences of his coming death. Too often the discussion of atonement has begun and ended with some squabbles about whether St. Paul believed in propitiation as well as expiation when it came to atonement theory. Indeed, sometimes there has been the sneaking suspicion that Paul invented Christian thought about the atonement, and that we should blame him for the negative consequences. I am not one of those cynics, and I do not think we can get at a NT theology of atonement through an appeal that amounts to "back to Jesus" with the implied agenda "away with and away from Paul, the first great corrupter of pristine Jesus religion."

No, as I have argued in detail (perhaps too much detail) in my two-volume work *The Indelible Image* a NT theology of anything needs to involve *everything* the NT has to say on the matter, and this includes the atonement. What I intend to do in what follows therefore is to look at a variety of the things Jesus and the NT writers seem to think and say about atonement, whether it is congenial to our modern discussions or even my denomination's Wesleyan discussions of the matter or not. There is of course not time or space to include everything in this discussion, but we can make inroads in the right direction. Let's start with Jesus.

Jesus the Ransom in Place of the Many

Of the various Synoptic texts we could focus on, I want to mention and discuss just three: (1) Mk. 10.45; (2) Mk. 14.36; and (3) Mk. 14.23–24. In some ways, Mk. 10.45 is the most crucial of these, but as we shall see, the other two are also very important, not least because we have a form of the so-called "Words of Institution" also in 1 Cor. 11, which makes evident that the tradition about what Jesus said at his last meal with his disciples was handed down at an early juncture by those who were present at that meal to persons like Paul.

I have argued at length for the authenticity of the logion in Mk. 10.45 elsewhere and do not need to repeat that argument here.[7] I will also not repeat my discussion of whether the Servant songs may be alluded to in this saying. In my judgment, they surely are. Most tellingly, the contrast in both Isa. 53 and in Mk. 10.45 is between the one who does the suffering and the many for whom he suffers, not between the many as opposed to all. In other words, we have the classic contrast between the one and the many here, and this text does not favor the view that Jesus died for some rather than all. The "many" here is the "all" minus the sufferer himself, in this case Jesus. The one person for whom Jesus did not need to die was Jesus himself. In other words, the variant of this saying found in 1 Tim. 2.6, which speaks of Christ as a ransom for *all*, got it right. Jesus' death had potentially universal benefits.

---

7 Witherington, *The Gospel of Mark*, *ad loc.*

The second crucial thing to be said about Mk. 10.45 is that the noun *lytron* and its cognates entail in the LXX of Exod. 13.13–16 the concept of a substitutionary sacrifice. Indeed, Yahweh's work for Israel is described as a *lytron* throughout Second and Third Isaiah (35.9; 41.14; 43.1,14; 44.22–24; 52.3; 62.12; 63.9). It is of course also true that we find the notion of a ransom paid by one party for the sins of another in the Maccabean corpus (2 Macc. 7.37–38; 4 Macc. 6.27–29; 17.21–22) as well as at Qumran (1QS 5.6; 8.3–10; 9.4). In short, there is no reason why Jesus could not have spoken of his death as a ransom, indeed as a substitutionary sacrifice for others.

The third thing to mention about Mk. 10.45, as my old mentor, C. K. Barrett once pointed out to me, is that the *basic notion* is the substitution of something *of equivalent value*. One has to ask how the death of one man could be of equivalent value to all the sins of the many? This would have to be a very unique death indeed and not just the death of an ordinary person, like say a Judas Maccabee. There is an exalted Christology implied in this saying, and I would suggest as well that what is implied is that Jesus was not a sinner and did not need ransoming himself. Therefore, he was free to provide the ransom for all the others, who indeed did need it, for they were in thrall to sin.

Fourthly, this saying explains the purpose of the Son of Man – why he came into the world as a human being in the first place, as 1 Tim. 2.6 makes even more clear. There was a sin problem, and God could not pass over sin forever. He could not simply forgive it without the provision of an adequate atoning sacrifice. This tells us something profound about the holy and righteous character of God. Just because God is love does not mean that God ceases to be holy, or ignores the issue of justice and righteousness in order to be forgiving. The death of Jesus was meant to put to death once and for all the sin problem in this sense – that a sufficient once for all time and all persons atoning sacrifice would never be needed again.

Lastly, Jesus the servant came to set people free, ransom them from the wrong sort of servitude so that they could commit themselves to following the Son of Man and take up the right form of servitude. Ransom in this context refers to the deliverance of a slave or prisoner from some sort of bondage, in this case sin, and it also tells us something profound – God was prepared to go to great lengths to accomplish this redemption. God wanted his possession, his people back (see Lev. 25.47–55).

The exposition suggested above comports nicely with what we find in Mk. 14.36. Jesus asks that "this cup" might pass from him, if it be possible and in accord with God's will. Is Jesus simply having a failure of nerve in the face of death by execution? This would not be Mark's view. Mark's view is that the cup in question is the cup of God's wrath or judgment on sin, and texts like Isa. 51.17 (cf. Zech. 12.2) make this quite clear. Jesus realizes in the garden that his death will be no ordinary death. It will be the judgment of God on sin, including the sins of God's people as the Isaianic reference suggests.

This brings us to the words of institution in Mk. 14.22–24. I have always found it remarkable that Jesus could be talking about some sort of benefit of his coming death *in advance of his dying*. More to the point, Jesus is talking about a positive benefit of his coming death for his disciples, so sure is he that there will be such an outcome. The reference to "my body" when coupled with the reference to the blood poured out for many, is surely a reference to the breaking and piercing of that body, leading to death. This dying inaugurates a new covenant which otherwise could not begin.

Put another way, covenants like suzerainty treaties were inaugurated by a sacrifice, and in the case of the New Covenant it was Jesus' death that "cut" and inaugurated the covenant. Here the old discussions of Meredith Kline are still valid and valuable.[8] It is worth adding of course that Jesus' audience were Jews, and had they thought he was literally talking about drinking his blood and eating his flesh, they would have run out of the room screaming. Rather, in the context of a Passover meal it was clear enough that he was reinterpreting some of the elements of the meal that had previously had other symbolic significance. Now the meal shared by the disciples would be focusing not on an Exodus or Passover from long ago, but rather one inaugurated on a cross in Judea in AD 30.[9]

Paul and the Mercy Seat

A long time ago (1974), James Dunn wrote a telling, and typically provocative, essay on Paul's theology of atonement.[10] At one juncture in the essay Dunn suggests the following while discussing Rom. 3.25: "the way in which Christ's death cancels out man's sin is by destroying it – the death of the representative sacrifice is the destruction of the sin of those represented, because it is the destruction of man's sinful flesh, of man as sinner ... 'God designed him to be the means of expiating sin by his sacrificial death'."[11]

Now the problems with this reading of the *locus classicus* in Rom. 3 are severalfold. (1) Paul did not believe that Jesus had sinful flesh, indeed he goes out of his way to say that Christ appeared *in the likeness of sinful flesh*, which is a different matter. Jesus is not merely Adam gone right in Paul's theology, though clearly enough he is portrayed as the eschatological Adam who does not sin, and is the founder of a new race of persons who are neither Jews nor Gentiles but a third thing. Jesus, in Paul's theology, was neither a sinner in the active sense of the term, nor did he bear a sin nature. The author of Hebrews is equally clear on this point. (2) *Hilasterion* has a semantic range which includes mercy seat, expiation, and propitiatory sacrifice, with the former of these renderings being the literal one. The term is most certainly associated with God's wrath in Exod. 32.14–14 and Dan. 9.16–19 in the LXX. In fact, propitiation of wrath is *the normal meaning* of this term and its cognates in Greek literature, and it is surely how a largely Gentile audience would have heard the term.

Consider for example an inscription found on the island of Kos that reads, "The people, for the Emperor Caesar, son of God, Augustus, for salvation to the gods [offer this] propitiatory sacrifice [*hilasterion*]."[12] God, in Paul's view, is both the offerer and the recipient of this sacrifice that Christ makes. God, in other words, averts his own wrath through offering his Son as a sin offering. God propitiates himself, and in the process expiates (cleanses us from) sin.

---

[8] Kline, *By Oath Consigned.*
[9] Witherington, *Making a Meal of It*, pp. 20–35.
[10] J. D. G. Dunn, "Paul's Understanding of the Death of Jesus," in *Reconciliation and Hope* (ed. R. Banks; Grand Rapids, MI: William B. Eerdmans, 1974), 125–41.
[11] Dunn, "Paul's Understanding of the Death of Jesus," 130–31.
[12] Witherington, *Paul's Letter to the Romans*, 108.

This is quite similar to what we find in the famous story of Yahweh passing through the pieces of the sacrifice with Abraham observing, and in effect invoking the oath curse penalty on himself if the covenant promises are not upheld.[13]

C. K. Barrett gets at the very heart of the matter: "The paradox is rooted in the nature of God. It is the nature of God to be irreconcilably opposed to sin; it is the nature of God to love sinners and to seek reconciliation with them. No one but God could resolve the problem; and God himself could be faithful to both aspects of his being only at the cost of the Cross."[14] We should also note the emphatic position of the word "all" in Rom. 3.23 at the beginning of the sentence. It was God's plan that Christ die for the sins of *all*. But equally clearly, while Christ's death is *sufficient* to atone for the sins of all, it is only *efficient* for those who have faith in Christ and in his blood sacrifice. And this death of Jesus reveals the righteous judgment of God on sin, while at the same time providing a propitiation for that sin that allows God to forgive sins without ignoring or passing over their sin.

Rom. 3.26 says that God previously showed tolerance, not fully judging sin, but that that forbearance could not go on forever. Pardon without atonement would not have been just or right for a God in whom there is no darkness or shadow of turning. Rom. 3.21–26 makes clear that Christ's death is the definitive revelation of God's paradoxical saving righteousness, which not merely gives us right-standing with God and pardon, but which liberates the sinner from the bondage to and of sin, and in this sense frees them up to begin to be actually righteous in thought, word, and deed. This is why Paul does not stop at the forensic sense of righteousness here but adds (offering here a literal rendering):

for all have sinned and lack the glory of God, being *righteoused* [no accounting language about being reckoned righteous here] freely by his grace through the ransom which was in Christ Jesus, whom God set forth as a means of propitiation through the faith in his blood as a proof of his righteousness, through the overlooking of previously committed sins, in the tolerance of God, for the proof of his righteousness in the present time, unto his being righteous and setting right those through faith in Jesus.

The Hapax Sacrifice

Perhaps no text in the NT so clearly makes evident the obvious connections in the ancient mind between priests, temples, and sacrifices as Hebrews does. Jesus has to be shoehorned into the Melchizedekian priesthood in order for him to be able to offer the proper sacrifice, and indeed be the proper sacrifice. And no NT book makes clearer that the sacrifice of Jesus makes obsolete all previous sacrifices and otiose any future ones. It was *once for all*, says the author. Furthermore, no author makes clearer the connection between covenants, priests, temples, and sacrifices. And for this author what is very clear is that the New Covenant, grounded in the prophecy in Jer. 31 which is a major text for this author, is no mere renewal of any older covenants. It is, as the author says, "ad infinitum" – better, greater, more adequate, perfect, and frankly final. Whether one calls this supersessionism run riot, or "completionism," to coin a term, our author is clear that we don't need any more human priests, sacrifices, or temples. Jesus fulfilled and completed all of that, and the heavenly sanctuary was the blueprint and prototype for any earthly ones in any case.

---

[13] See above, pp. 288–305.
[14] Barrett, *Romans*, 74.

Our author is nothing if not ambitious and comprehensive in the way he views Christ's atonement. Several aspects of this need to be highlighted.

Firstly, note that our author does not think that the death of Jesus merely provides right-standing with God. To the contrary, Jesus the perfect sacrifice without blemish offered himself to God and as a result the blood of Jesus purifies our conscience from dead works so that we can worship the living God (Heb. 9.14). And this brings up another crucial point. Atonement theology is or implies worship theology, and when the situations with priests, temples, and sacrifices changes, so should worship. Jesus foresaw this when he said the day was coming when neither on Mt. Zion nor on Mt. Gerizim, but anywhere and everywhere one worships in Spirit and in truth it will happen (Jn. 4). In other words, one doesn't need a sacred zone, a priest, a literal sacrifice any more to offer the living God true worship – Jesus paid it all, and changed the patterns of worship into an eschatological mode. All now have free and direct access to God because all believers have free and direct access to Jesus who is their intercessor in the Heavenly Holy of Holies.[15] Secondly, our author is adamant that God could not forgive sin without a blood sacrifice. He puts it this way: "without the shedding of blood there is no forgiveness of sins" (Heb. 9.22).

So much for the modern notion that Jesus' death was not absolutely necessary in order for God to forgive our sins. To those who like to make such statements these days, our author would rebut, "if Jesus' death was not both the absolutely necessary and sufficient sacrifice to procure for us the forgiveness of sins, if God could do it just because God is a nice God who likes to forgive sin, then strangely enough that God is not a good God, not a good Father, for what Father would put his only and beloved Son through that agony if it was not the one means necessary to save the world?"

Thirdly, as Heb. 9.26 puts it, Jesus didn't just come to *pay* for sins, he came to *remove* them. At the heart of the Book of Hebrews is a theology of sanctification that tells us that we are indeed intended to go on to perfection, intended to be purified from sin, beginning now, and continuing on in our lives. A theology of atonement that does not realize that both what we call justification and what we call sanctification are involved and implied, in that atonement is not a NT theology of atonement. Heb. 10.10 says "it is by God's will that we have been sanctified through the offering of the body of Jesus Christ once for all." Our hearts have been sprinkled clean from an evil conscience, and we should live accordingly (10.22). I must say it is a mystery to me how some theologians can talk about the sovereignty of God's grace and yet refuse to come to grips with the implications of texts like Heb. 10 or Rom. 8 which tell us that as a result of Jesus' death and by God's Spirit and grace we have been actually set free from the bondage to sin and death, not just in principle but in reality. A theology of the power of God's grace should entail a robust theology of sanctification, which theology, by the way, John Calvin certainly exhibits in his *Institutes*.

Lastly, the author of Hebrews works out the Christological implications of Christ being our perfect high priest, namely, that unlike all previous priests, this one was without sin. He was temptable but not contemptible (Heb. 4.15). And the point the author makes is that the Son was virtuous in resisting sin, for he could have done otherwise. Therefore, he

---

[15] See Ben Witherington III, *We Have Seen his Glory: A Vision of Kingdom Worship* (Grand Rapids, MI: William B. Eerdmans 2010).

becomes the paradigm of faithfulness, as well as the paragon of virtue, and the trailblazer and finisher of faith, whose example Heb. 12 says we must follow until he returns in a blaze of glory.

The Atoning Sacrifice for the Whole World

1 John is an epideictic homily that uses the good preacherly practice of repeating key ideas and themes over and over again, but with variations. One of those themes is laid out in 1 Jn. 1.7 and 2.1–2, where we hear about Jesus Christ the Righteous One and what he did and does for us and in us. 1 Jn. 1.7–9 speaks not only of our sins being forgiven but of our being cleansed from sin, cleansed from all unrighteousness. And we are told quite specifically that it is the blood of Jesus that does this cleansing, this sanctifying.

1 Jn. 2.1–2 becomes even more specific and in some ways echoes Hebrews – when we sin we have an Advocate with the Father, Jesus the Righteous One. Though Christ is not called a High Priest here, the job description fits. These verses give us an opportunity to talk more fully about the implications of the *hilas-* root and its various meanings.

The question still remains as to where the focus lies in 1 John when this terminology comes up, and I agree with the lengthy and careful discussion of R. Brown that there seems to be more focus on cleansing, not surprisingly since our author is writing pastorally and he is not giving an abstract discourse on the nature of Jesus' atoning death, but on its benefits for the audience namely forgiveness and cleansing. I also agree that the echoes here of the Day of Atonement ceremony as described in Lev. 16 where the priest sprinkles blood of the mercy seat seem clear, especially 16.16: "thus he shall 'cleanse' the Holy Place from the impurities of the Israelites and from their wicked acts in respect to all their sins." We find this text in Leviticus directly applied to the work of Christ the high priest in Heb. 9–10. Nevertheless, the idea of propitiation is clearly implied.[16]

Sins do not need atoning for, if God does not need to be propitiated. They could simply be forgiven and cleansing could come through forgiveness rather than through an atoning sacrifice. But clearly enough our author does think that Christ's atoning sacrifice was necessary for the forgiveness of sins, as does Paul. It is thus right to use the translation atonement or atoning sacrifice, recognizing that while propitiation is clearly implied in 1 Jn. 2 and 4 the focus is on the benefits of the sacrifice for the sinner, namely cleansing and forgiveness. It is not in the end an either/or matter, for both propitiation and expiation are necessary to take care of the sin problem and reconcile God and humankind. And the marvel is that the Advocate is propitiator, expiator, and propitiation all in one. Lastly, it will be well to remember that the earliest commentators on 1 John were not squeamish when it came to saying that God's righteous wrath against sin must be propitiated. For example, Bede puts it this way: "In his humanity Christ pleads for our sins before the Father, but in his divinity, he has propitiated them for us with the Father" (*On 1 John*, PL 93.90). Notice once again the strong stress in 1 Jn. 2.2 that Christ is the atonement not just for the believer's sins, but for the sins of the whole world.

---

[16] See the following articles: C. H. Dodd, "HILASKESTHAI, Its Cognates, Derivatives, and Synonyms in the Septuagint," *JTS* 32 (1931): 82–95; H. Clavier, "Notes sur un mot-clef du johannisme et de la sotériologie biblique: *hilasmos*," *NT* 10 (1968): 287–304; R. R. Nicole, "C. H. Dodd and the Doctrine of Propitiation," *Westminster Theological Journal* 17 (1954–55): 117–57.

The Suffering Servant and His Precious Blood

No document in the NT more alludes to Christ as the fulfillment of the Servant Songs in Isaiah than 1 Peter. Our task here must be to focus on 1 Pet. 1.18–19 and 2.24. Verses 18–19 need to be read together and reveal what Christians know or ought to know about their redemption. The key term we must examine first is the verb *elutrōthēte*, which here means either redeem or ransom. The idea of ransoming of course implies a form of redeeming, but the converse is not necessarily true. So, we must examine how to translate this term. In favor of the translation 'ransom' is: (1) the "not … but" structure we have here which contrasts two means by which one can be ransomed; (2) the reference to money – which was so often used to ransom various sort of captives or slaves; (3) "ransom" must be the meaning in Mk 10.45 and it is quite possible and likely that Mark was dependent upon Peter for his gospel, which would thus suggest a similar translation here (cf. Titus 2.14); and (4) the use of the term in pagan and Gentile contexts would normally conjure up the idea of being bought out of slavery or buying oneself out of slavery (cf. 1 Cor. 7.22ff.; Gal. 5.1; Rom. 6.14–23).

If we ask to whom this ransom was paid, the text does not say; however, it surely cannot be Satan, since neither Christ nor God owed Satan anything. Later patristic theology went in the wrong direction here. Most assuredly it is the price paid to God himself and the Judge who will indeed condemn us and cast us out if our sin is not dealt with, covered, paid for. A just God requires a just payment for sin – no more, but definitely no less. This implies that forgiveness for God is *very costly indeed* – nothing but Christ's death was a sufficient price for ransoming believers from sure destruction and slavery to sin. God's love, then, is a holy love: holy in that sin must be dealt with, paid for before forgiveness can be offered or a declaration of no condemnation pronounced, loving in that Christ paid that price with his blood *in our stead*. Not all the money in the world could have paid for our multitude of sins and bought us salvation.

Such things, though valuable, are perishable and could not purchase something of eternal worth. Notice here that Peter's emphasis is on being ransomed from previous useless (or futile) and sinful behavior. There is probably a play on words here for the word *timē* refers to the price, in this case the price of manumission paid in the temple to the deity, and in turn the deity then pays the slave owner back, less a commission. But it is not a *timē* of silver or gold that ransomed the believer but rather the *timiō*, the precious or valuable blood of Jesus that did the ransoming and paid the price. We may hear in this verse an echo of Isa. 53.7 in preparation for the fuller Christological statement in 2.22–25, where Christ is more extensively portrayed as the Suffering Servant of Isaiah, but already here Peter begins to paint that portrait. Jesus is seen as the flawless and faultless lamb.

Christ also did not die so that believers might sin all the more, now having a sure means of forgiveness. As Paul, Rom. 6.1–2, says, "shall we go on sinning, so grace may increase? God forbid!" Rather, Christ spilled his precious blood so believers might be purified and holy. Christ's death, if we are to receive its benefits, implies our death to our previous sinful ways.

The reference to Christ's blood as like that of a pure and spotless lamb (on the sinlessness of Christ see 1 Pet. 2.22; 2 Cor. 5.21; Heb. 4.15; 7.26; 1 Jn. 3.5) of course conjures up the idea of a sacrificial lamb. The Passover lamb in OT times was apparently not seen as an animal which if sacrificed made atonement (see Exod. 12.5). However, it had begun to have this significance in Jesus' day in contemporary Judaism (cf. Jn. 1.29,31; 1 Cor. 5.7). Since Isa. 53.7 seems to be in the background here, the atoning significance is surely implied. Of course, a lamb, if it was to be offered, had to be perfect (Exod. 12.5; 29.1). On blood as a means of redemption or as a price see Eph. 1.7; Heb. 9.12, 22; Rev. 1.5; 1 Clem. 12.7; Rev. 5.9. Let us turn now to 1 Pet. 2.24.

1 Pet. 2.24 gives Peter's view of the atonement in some depth. Christ took up the cross or bore on the cross in his own body our sins, which is to say the punishment for our sins. That it is "in his body" stresses Christ's humanity. He was truly human and redemption came through a real historical person. He suffered too, he suffered unjustly, he suffered for those who deserved to suffer as sinners. Sins here may be seen as a burden that Christ lifts from human beings (against Anderson, who over-schematizes things, suggesting the burden notion was replaced by the debt notion of sin by NT times). Since Isa. 53 is likely in the background here, it is likely also that the implied idea is that Christ bore the punishment for human sins *in their stead*. Thus, we have here substitutionary atonement by the suffering servant. It is also implied that Jesus takes away human sins, i.e., heals us. To what end? Not just so that humans may experience redemption, but so that they may die to sin and live to righteousness, as Christ himself died for sin and lived to righteousness. Christ's death, if one accepts it, requires of us a willingness to go and sin no more, lest one crucify Christ afresh by one's further sins. Thus, theology leads to ethics necessarily in 1 Peter. To accept Christ means to agree to follow in his righteous footsteps, and not to crucify him afresh by sinning again.

"By his wounds (welts, weals) we are healed of our sin sickness": *mōlōpi* means weal, that is, it refers to the marks on the body of one who has been whipped, such as a slave (cf. Isa. 53.5). We must remember that in Phil. 2, Jesus is said to be a suffering slave and he received a slave's final punishment – crucifixion. What better way to encourage Christian slaves here in 1 Peter than to say in fact that Jesus voluntarily became a slave for your sake? He knows what you go through. He's been there, too. Sin is also seen here as a disease that affects the whole person, not just his behavior, but his desires, his thought patterns, etc. It is a deadly cancer of which one must be healed lest one be lost. And atonement, then, must mean and offer more than forgiveness or right-standing, it must go "as far as the curse is found."

And So?

We have roamed far and wide in the NT for the purpose of exploring in some depth its atonement theology. What we have discovered is a repeated pattern. The authors of the NT, or at least the ones we have examined here, agree that Jesus' death should be seen as a propitiatory sacrifice, dealing with the problem of sin and sinners in the hands of a righteous God who cannot pass over sin forever, but does wish to love his creatures forever. We have noted the uses of the language of ransom and cleansing and forgiveness that were all intertwined with the language of propitiation and expiation. We also noticed that there is an emphasis on the comprehensive scope of Christ's death – sufficient to atone for the sins of all and efficient for those who believe. The scope of the atonement's benefits is limited by the response to the atoning death of Jesus, not by God. We also saw an emphasis on the substitutionary nature of Christ's sacrifice. It should have been us on the cross. If there was one person who did not deserve to pay for sin, who did not deserve to die on the cross, it was Jesus himself, the Righteous One who paid the price for the Many. We talked about the notion of ransom, which clearly implied bondage, in this case bondage to sin, but not debt to Satan, much less possession by demons. 1 Peter goes further and talks about being in bondage to false and fruitless ideas about God and life as well.

It is important to add at this juncture what I did not say. I did not say that a penal substitutionary propitiatory sacrifice is the *only* image of Christ's death that exists in the NT, nor is it the only language used to describe the atonement. What I would say is that it is the *dominant* model in the NT, and however squeamish this truth may make some folks because of its implications about God's character, at the end of the day one should not pit the love of God against his justice, or the righteousness of God against his mercy and forgiveness.

Indeed, an adequately biblical theology of the atonement will show how all of these attributes of God are seen to be in play in the death of Jesus on the cross. Who wants to live in a world where justice is not finally done, as well as a world where love conquers all? It is worth saying, however, that it is probably not an accident that when it comes to predicating nouns of God he is called light and life and love, but the adjectives appended to these terms include holy, righteous, just, and many more. God's love is a holy and just love, not love without holiness, and not holiness without love – thank God.

Finally, I have stressed that the effects of the death of Jesus amount not just to gaining us right-standing with God, but also freeing us from the bondage of sin, cleansing us from sin, cleansing our consciences from guilt, and enabling us to live sanctified and holy lives that glorify God and edify our fellow human beings. In the end, atonement is just another way of talking about salvation, and as Titus 2.11 says "the grace of God *has appeared*, bringing *salvation to all*, training us to renounce impiety and worldly passions and in the present age to live lives that are self-controlled, upright, and godly while we await the blessed hope" who indeed will come and eliminate suffering sin and sorrow, disease, decay and death once and for all. Amen and Amen.

Annotated Bibliography

This material is used by kind permission of Zondervan Publishing House.

In addition to the resources found in the footnotes, as further reading we reproduce a part of a bibliography, "101 Books on Biblical Theology: An Annotated Bibliography," with kind permission of Zondervan. The bibliography was compiled by Brittany D. Kim, Darian R. Lockett, and Charlie Trimm. For the fuller version including resources on OT and NT theology see https://info.zondervan .com/p/biblical-theology/bibliography/.

(1) Biblical Theology: What It Is and How to Do it

Turn to First

Grindheim, Sigurd. *Introducing Biblical Theology.* New York: Bloomsbury T&T Clark, 2013. (280 pp.)
Grindheim aims to introduce the biblical storyline, while also highlighting several key themes and concepts more recognizable from systematic theology. In fifteen concise chapters, the book moves from Genesis to Revelation, highlighting themes such as "The God Who Interacts," "Made for Fellowship: Human Beings as Created," "God Came to Us: The New Testament Picture of Jesus," and "A Life Transformed: The New Life of the Believer." Each chapter concludes with a list of further reading and discussion questions.

Hamilton, James M. Jr. *What Is Biblical Theology? A Guide to the Bible's Story, Symbolism, and Patterns.* Wheaton, IL: Crossway, 2014. (128 pp.)
Defining biblical theology as discerning the interpretive perspective of the original authors, in Part 1 of this book Hamilton offers concise chapters considering the narrative and plot of the Bible's big story. In Part 2 he describes the Bible's symbolic universe (imagery, typology, and patterns), and finally Part 3 outlines the Bible as a "love story." A helpful introductory text strong on tracing the broad contours of the Bible's storyline.

Lawrence, Michael. *Biblical Theology in the Life of the Church: A Guide for Ministry.* IXMarks. Wheaton, IL: Crossway, 2010. (240 pp.)
Lawrence aims to help pastors respond to the questions and challenges they face in ministry by developing a strong theological foundation. In his first section, he lays out some tools for interpreting biblical texts and for doing biblical and systematic theology. His second section tells the story of the Bible using five overlapping biblical-theological storylines (creation, fall, love, sacrifice, and promise). In his final section, he offers case studies, applying his method to a few biblical texts, and suggests various ways biblical theology can be used within the church.

Next Steps

Goldsworthy, Graeme. *Christ-Centered Biblical Theology: Hermeneutical Foundations and Principles*. Downers Grove, IL: InterVarsity Press, 2012. (240 pp.)

Goldsworthy's contribution to the study of biblical theology has been enormous. Here he offers methodological reflections on what biblical theology is and how to do it well. In particular, he stresses the importance of typology for reading the diverse sections of the Bible as a unified narrative (exemplified in his work below, *According to Plan*).

Hasel, Gerhard. *New Testament Theology: Basic Issues in the Current Debate*. Grand Rapids, MI: Eerdmans, 1978. (258 pp.)

Though written 40 years ago, Hasel's introduction is still a helpful guide to the history, theory, and methods of NT theology. After an opening chapter on the history and development of the discipline, Hasel discusses various methodologies for doing NT theology (his discussion of a Salvation History approach at the end is particularly helpful). Then in the final three chapters he considers various centers of NT theology (anthropology, Salvation History, and Covenant, to name a few), discusses the relationship between the OT and the NT, and finally shares his own "multiplex" approach. His work is helpful for understanding the history of NT theology and some of the issues involved; however, his particular approach has not been influential in subsequent discussion.

Hasel, Gerhard. *Old Testament Theology: Basic Issues in the Current Debate*. 4th edn. Grand Rapids, MI: Eerdmans, 1991. (272 pp.)

For many years Hasel's book was the standard introduction to OT theology. Although there have now been significant developments in the field since the book's last revision, it still offers a helpful discussion of many of the key issues an OT theology must address. After summarizing the history of the discipline, Hasel describes various approaches to OT theology and considers the questions of its relationship to history, whether the OT has a center, and how the Testaments are related. Finally, he outlines his own multiplex approach, which traces the development of particular themes.

Klink, Edward W. III, and Darian R. Lockett. *Understanding Biblical Theology: A Comparison of Theory and Practice*. Grand Rapids, MI: Zondervan, 2012. (192 pp.)

Proceeding with the conviction that there is not only one way to practice biblical theology, Klink and Lockett briefly consider the key criteria included in any biblical theology and then offer a spectrum of five types of biblical theology along with examples of particular scholars representative of each type: BT1: Historical Description; BT2: History of Redemption; BT3: Worldview-story; BT4: Canonical Approach; and BT5: Theological Construction. The book does not argue for any one of the types, letting readers decide for themselves.

Sailhamer, John H. *Introduction to Old Testament Theology: A Canonical Approach*. Grand Rapids, MI: Zondervan, 1995. (332 pp.)

Sailhamer characterizes different approaches to OT theology as a series of choices about four key issues: (1) Is the theology based on the biblical text itself or on the historical events the OT describes? (2) Does it use a historical-critical approach to the OT or does it focus on the final canonical form? (3) Does it read the OT like any other book or as the inspired word of God? (4) Does it present the theology of the OT as a (historical or thematic) progression or as centered around key theme(s)? Sailhamer then outlines his own approach, which is based on the biblical text in its canonical form, read as the word of God, and is organized as a progression following the threefold structure of the Jewish canon: Law, Prophets, and Writings.

Advanced Studies

Barr, James. *The Concept of Biblical Theology: An Old Testament Perspective*. Minneapolis, MN: Augsburg Fortress, 1999. (736 pp.)

While this large and somewhat unstructured book's main point is to critique virtually every aspect of biblical theology, it looks at the discipline from a wide variety of perspectives and helpfully seeks to find as many flaws in the endeavor as possible that serious students of biblical theology will need to grapple with. In particular, Barr advocates for granting more importance to a history-of-religions approach (coupled with historical criticism) that accounts for changes in Israelite religion over time rather than seeking a synchronic and never-changing OT theology.

Bartholomew, Craig, Mary Healy, Karl Möller, and Robin Parry, eds. *Out of Egypt: Biblical Theology and Biblical Interpretation.* Scripture and Hermeneutics Series 5. Grand Rapids, MI: Zondervan, 2004. (528 pp.)
Part of the larger Scripture and Hermeneutics Series, this volume is a collection of 17 essays grouped around the themes "Approaches to Biblical Theology," "Great Themes of the Bible," "Parts of the Bible and Biblical Theology," and "Theological Interpretation and Biblical Theology." A strength of the volume is the range of contributors – both biblical scholars and theologians offer essays on, for example, the connection between biblical theology and the clarity of Scripture, theological exegesis, and preaching, as well as methodological reflections and particular case studies in Zechariah, Romans, and Hebrews.

Hafemann, Scott J., ed. *Biblical Theology: Retrospect and Prospect.* Downers Grove, IL: InterVarsity Press, 2002. (300 pp.)
This collection of 19 essays from a theology conference at Wheaton College examines biblical theology's past and looks toward its future. Key issues that are addressed include the significance of the canon's shape (particularly the OT in its Jewish order of Torah, Prophets, and Writings), the role of creation in biblical theology and its relationship to redemptive-history, the relationship between the Testaments, and the degree of unity in the canon. Although a variety of perspectives are represented, there is general agreement that biblical theology should focus on the biblical text in its final canonical form and that it should be normative for the life of the church.

Mead, James K. *Biblical Theology: Issues, Methods, and Themes.* Louisville, KY: Westminster John Knox, 2007. (336 pp.)
This volume offers a technical discussion about biblical theology, including its history, issues, methods, and themes. Mead demonstrates well how biblical theology stands at the crossroads of several related disciplines: exegesis, history, systematic theology, etc. After an opening chapter canvassing the history of biblical theology, the next three chapters discuss the various issues, methodologies, and themes arising from the discipline, and a final chapter describes the prospects for the future of biblical theology.

Ollenburger, Ben C., ed. *Old Testament Theology: Flowering and Future.* 2nd edn. Sources for Biblical and Theological Study 1. Winona Lake, IN: Eisenbrauns, 2004. (560 pp.)
This volume introduces the variety of approaches to OT theology by offering excerpts from key thinkers in the field from 1930 to the time of publication. After a few introductory essays in Part 1, Parts 2–4 proceed roughly chronologically, covering the changing landscape of OT theology in the twentieth century, while Part 5 contains more recent writings that have significantly reshaped the conversation. Some of the excerpts outline the author's method, while others present a sample of how their method is applied.

Perdue, Leo G., Robert Morgan, and Benjamin D. Sommer, eds. *Biblical Theology: Introducing the Conversation.* Library of Biblical Theology. Nashville, TN: Abingdon, 2009. (337 pp.)
Though an "introduction," this edited volume is not for the beginner. Rather than defining or promoting a particular approach to biblical theology, in four chapters the authors introduce the scholars who have shaped the conversation about biblical theology. Sommer asks whether there can be a "Jewish biblical theology" and Perdue surveys OT theologies since Barth's commentary on Romans, while Morgan surveys NT theologies. The collection concludes with Perdue's final essay reflecting on the numerous hermeneutical approaches on offer.

Watson, Francis. *Text and Truth: Redefining Biblical Theology.* Grand Rapids, MI: Eerdmans, 1997. (352 pp.)
Watson offers a collection of discrete essays that nonetheless cohere together around an understanding of biblical theology as "an interdisciplinary approach to biblical interpretation which seeks to dismantle the barriers that ... separate biblical scholarship from Christian theology" (p. vii). The essays are divided into two parts: "Studies in Theological Hermeneutics" and "The Old

Testament in Christological Perspective." The first three essays in Part 1 criticize various ways historical and literary tools are applied to the NT, and the final essay critiques the "neo-Marcionism" of Schleiermacher, Harnack, and Bultmann. Part 2 explores Christian ways of interpreting the OT. Nuanced and sophisticated, Watson's work reads like a manifesto on theological interpretation.

(2)   Whole-Bible Biblical Theologies

Turn to First

Alexander, T. Desmond. *From Eden to the New Jerusalem: An Introduction to Biblical Theology.* Nottingham: InterVarsity Press, 2008. (208 pp.)

Alexander tells the meta-story of the Bible by beginning with the story's end in Rev. 20–22 and showing how it fulfills God's purpose for the world and humanity at creation. Each chapter approaches the meta-story from a different angle by tracing a major theme through the Bible: God's presence in the temple, God's rule as king, the defeat of Satan, redemption through sacrifice, the holiness and wholeness of God's people, and the contrast between the corrupt kingdoms of this earth and the coming kingdom of God in the new heavens and new earth.

Bartholomew, Craig G., and Michael W. Goheen. *The Drama of Scripture: Finding Our Place in the Biblical Story.* 2nd edn. Grand Rapids, MI: Baker Academic, 2014. (272 pp.)

Bartholomew and Goheen focus on the Bible as a unified story about the kingdom of God, which they recount as a drama in six acts: (1) creation, (2) fall, (3) redemption begun in Israel, (4) redemption realized through Christ, (5) the church's mission as witness, and (6) redemption consummated with the renewal of all creation at Christ's future return. The book encourages readers to make the biblical story their story and consider the part they are called to play in that drama. This is a great read for those who are trying to make sense of how the Bible fits together or how it is relevant for our lives today.

Hafemann, Scott J. *The God of Promise and the Life of Faith: Understanding the Heart of the Bible.* Wheaton, IL: Crossway, 2001. (256 pp.)

Hafemann's work, written for the serious reader in the church, is a biblical theology of the triune God that stresses the implications of God's character, as seen through the story of the Bible, on Christian character – summarized by faith, hope, and love. Each chapter focuses on a particular question ("Why do we exist?"; "What does it mean to know God?"; "Why do people suffer?"); while focusing on the overall message of the Bible itself – moving in linear fashion from creation, to the fall, to God's covenant relationship with Israel, and finally to the climax in Christ.

Roberts, Vaughan. *God's Big Picture: Tracing the Storyline of the Bible.* Downers Grove, IL: InterVarsity Press, 2003. (160 pp.)

Influenced by the storyline of Scripture as outlined in Goldsworthy's *According to Plan* (see below), Roberts offers a simplified version of the biblical narrative summarized in eight epochs all focusing on the theme of the kingdom of God: patterned kingdom, perished kingdom, promised kingdom, partial kingdom, prophesied kingdom, present kingdom, proclaimed kingdom, and perfected kingdom. Along with a concise and very helpful opening discussion of kingdom as a central theme in the Bible, each chapter concludes with a helpful set of study questions, making the book ideal for a small group study.

Next Steps

Gladd, Benjamin L., and Matthew S. Harmon. *Making All Things New: Inaugurated Eschatology for the Life of the Church.* Grand Rapids, MI: Baker Academic, 2016. (224 pp.)

According to Gladd and Harmon, the Bible defines the church as the end-time people of God in the inaugurated new creation, and further, Christians are to live in light of this biblical identity. The first chapter, written by G. K. Beale, sets out a biblical theology of inaugurated eschatology (the "already–not yet"), and the rest of the book views the church and all its practical ministry through this wide-angle lens.

Goldingay, John. *Biblical Theology: The God of the Christian Scriptures*. Downers Grove, IL: InterVarsity Press, 2016. (608 pp.)
Goldingay follows up his immense *Old Testament Theology* (Downers Grove, IL: InterVarsity Press, 2003–9) with a *Biblical Theology* that reflects his considerable theological insight and characteristically accessible style. The volume is organized around key themes – for example, God, revelation, creation, God's people and how they should live – but it also shows some narrative progression from creation to God's final victory. Although Goldingay sees the fundamental unity of the Scriptures as a single story, he also acknowledges tensions in the biblical text and is reticent to harmonize them.

Goldsworthy, Graeme. *According to Plan: The Unfolding Revelation of God in the Bible*. Downers Grove, IL: InterVarsity Press, 1991. (251 pp.)
Goldsworthy traces the theme of the gospel of the kingdom, showing how it unifies the narrative of the OT and the NT. The work begins with a short discussion of method and how to do biblical theology, which is followed by a presentation of the theme of kingdom traced through the narrative of Scripture. He has also written a more focused book on method and defining biblical theology as a discipline, called *Christ-Centered Biblical Theology* (see above).

Kaiser, Walter C. Jr. *The Promise-Plan of God: A Biblical Theology of the Old and New Testaments*. Grand Rapids, MI: Zondervan, 2008. (432 pp.)
In this volume Kaiser develops his earlier work in *Toward an Old Testament Theology* (Grand Rapids, MI: Zondervan, 1978) into a whole-Bible theology. As a center, he focuses on the single, unified promise-plan of God, which he sees as beginning with God's declaration that Eve's offspring will crush the serpent in Gen. 3.16 and continuing through God's covenants with Abraham, Israel, and David, before culminating in the work of Jesus. Kaiser traces this promise-plan through both Testaments, following a chronological rather than a canonical order and giving significant attention to resolving interpretive difficulties.

Pate, C. Marvin, J. Scott Duvall, J. Daniel Hays, E. Randolph Richards, W. Dennis Tucker Jr., and Preben Vang, *The Story of Israel: A Biblical Theology*. Downers Grove, IL: InterVarsity Press, 2004. (320 pp.)
A collaborative effort by six scholars from the Pruett School of Christian Studies at Ouachita Baptist University, this book takes Israel's story as its central theme. Grounding that story in Deuteronomistic theology, the authors summarize it as a recurring narrative of sin–exile–restoration. They then trace that story through each major section of the biblical canon, giving greater emphasis to the NT and also showing how Second Temple Jewish literature forms a bridge between the Testaments.

Scobie, Charles H. H. *The Ways of Our God: An Approach to Biblical Theology*. Grand Rapids, MI: Eerdmans, 2003. (1038 pp.)
Scobie aims to make the academic study of the Bible useful for the church. Taking a thematic approach to biblical theology, he surveys 20 topics organized under four primary headings: "God's Order," "God's Servant," "God's People," and "God's Way." Within each chapter, he traces the development of a theme from its initial proclamation and (prophetic) promise in the OT to its fulfillment and ultimate consummation in the NT. Although the book's length may be intimidating for some, its clear structure and subject index make it useful as a reference work. It also goes beyond many biblical theologies in offering brief but thoughtful reflections on how the Bible might address contemporary ethical issues, such as abortion and euthanasia.

VanGemeren, Willem. *The Progress of Redemption: The Story of Salvation from Creation to the New Jerusalem*. Grand Rapids, MI: Zondervan, 1988. (544 pp.)
Focusing on the story of redemption, VanGemeren states that the center of the "Bible is the incarnate and glorified Christ, by whom all things will be renewed" (p. 27). Taking this point of departure, the book traces the progress of God's revelation through Scripture, from Genesis to Revelation, in the tradition of Vos' *Biblical Theology* (see below). The guiding focus of the work is to show how God, through Christ, works out the restoration of all things from the Fall to the New Jerusalem. It provides a good example of connecting grammatical-historical analysis of individual passages to understanding passages and books within the context of Scripture as a whole.

Williams, Michael D. *Far as the Curse Is Found: The Covenant Story of Redemption*. Phillipsburg,
    NJ: P&R, 2005. (336 pp.)
Rather than starting his account of the progression of the covenants with creation, Williams begins
with the resurrection, moves to the exodus, and then considers creation. This helps him emphasize how the resurrection, specifically God's ultimate plan of redemption, makes sense of creation.
Beyond his interesting way of beginning, the rest of the book moves through a typical sequence of
God's unfolding covenants ending in new creation. This represents a view of biblical theology from
a Reformed theological perspective.

More Detailed

Childs, Brevard S. *Biblical Theology of the Old and New Testaments: Theological Reflection on the
    Christian Bible*. Minneapolis, MN: Fortress Press, 1992. (770 pp.)
Following his *Old Testament Theology in a Canonical Context* (Minneapolis, MN: Fortress, 1985),
Childs here applies his canonical approach to the whole Bible. Some of the introductory material
summarizing the history of biblical theology and outlining his own approach has been republished
as *Biblical Theology: A Proposal* (Facets; Minneapolis, MN: Augsburg Fortress, 2002). The bulk of
the work surveys the OT (following the sequence of Israel's witness to its history) and the NT (following the historical development of tradition about Jesus) and then presents a biblical-theological
synthesis of major themes, such as God's nature, the people of God, Christ, reconciliation, law and
gospel, and the kingdom of God.

Gentry, Peter J., and Stephen J. Wellum. *Kingdom through Covenant: A Biblical-Theological
    Understanding of the Covenants*. Wheaton, IL: Crossway, 2012. (848 pp.)
Rather than systematically accounting for every biblical-theological theme running through
Scripture, Gentry and Wellum attempt to erect the scaffolding needed to guide the reader through
the storyline of the Bible. That scaffolding is made up of six successive biblical covenants – with
Adam/creation, Noah, Abraham, the Israelites, David, and the church. Through the succession of the
covenants, God works to establish his kingdom, his glorious reign over all of creation. Because the
Bible itself is structured by these successive covenants, Gentry and Wellum argue that one's biblical
theology should be governed by the theme of covenant as well.

Hamilton, James M. Jr. *God's Glory in Salvation through Judgment: A Biblical Theology*. Wheaton,
    IL: Crossway, 2010. (640 pp.)
Hamilton argues that the center of the Bible is "salvation through judgment to the glory of God"
(p. 56), as a way to include both God's mercy and his hatred of sin as well as the frequent connection between the two (for example, God rescued Israel by judging Egypt). In the heart of the book
Hamilton works his way through the Bible canonically (following the Hebrew canon in the OT)
before ending by addressing various critiques of his view and showing how it affects contemporary
ministry.

Schreiner, Thomas R. *The King in His Beauty: A Biblical Theology of the Old and New Testaments*.
    Grand Rapids, MI: Baker Academic, 2013. (736 pp.)
Schreiner has demonstrated his biblical-theological range in writing a Pauline theology, an NT theology, and here a whole-Bible biblical theology, which systematically works through each book of
the Bible, describing its main theological themes. Each book is taken in its canonical order with
some notable exceptions in the NT: Acts is considered along with Luke, while the Gospel of John is
grouped with John's Letters. Giving the entire work an overarching structure, Schreiner organizes
his biblical theology into nine parts.

Vos, Geerhardus. *Biblical Theology: Old and New Testaments*. Grand Rapids, MI: Eerdmans, 1948.
    (440 pp.)
A classic in biblical theology from a Reformed perspective, Vos' work highlights the organic development of God's self-revelation throughout the Scriptures, giving significant attention to the idea of
covenant. His divides the OT into two parts: "the Mosaic Epoch," covering God's revelation from
creation through Moses, and "the Prophetic Epoch," surveying prophetic revelation from Samuel
through the writing prophets. His treatment of the NT focuses on the birth and ministry of Jesus.

Wright, Christopher J. H. *The Mission of God: Unlocking the Bible's Grand Narrative*. Downers
   Grove, IL: InterVarsity Press, 2006. (582 pp.)
Wright presents a missional hermeneutic as a foundation for holistic missions today, arguing that
the mission of God is the center of the Bible. The heart of the book has three main sections: "The
God of Mission" (who is known through Israel and Jesus and who confronts idolatry), "The People
of Mission" (primarily focused on the OT and Israel's role as those chosen to bless the world), and
"The Arena of Mission" (the role of creation, the image of God, and the nations). Wright moves
beyond the texts usually associated with missions by examining such themes as the exodus, the
jubilee, and ethics. Wright's shorter book *The Mission of God's People: A Biblical Theology of the
Church's Mission* (Biblical Theology for Life; Grand Rapids, MI: Zondervan, 2010) addresses similar issues.

Author Index

Ancient Source and Scripture Index